The History of the
MERCHANT TAYLORS' COMPANY

The earlier of two pre-Reformation hearse-cloths belonging to the Merchant Taylors' Company. It dates from *c.* 1480–1500.
Merchant Taylors' Company

The History of the MERCHANT TAYLORS' COMPANY

Matthew Davies
and
Ann Saunders

MANEY

2004

All rights reserved. No part of this publication may be reproduced, stored in a retrieval system, or transmitted in any form or by any means, electronic, mechanical, photocopying or otherwise, without the written consent of the copyright holder. Requests for such permission should be addressed to Maney Publishing.

© The Merchant Taylors' Company, 2004

The right of Matthew Davies and Ann Saunders to be identified as authors of this Work has been asserted by them in accordance with the Copyright, Designs and Patents Act 1988.

Statements in *The History of the Merchant Taylors' Company* reflect the views of the authors and the Merchant Taylors' Company, and not those of the publisher.

ISBN 1 902653 99 8

Published by Maney Publishing, Hudson Road, Leeds LS9 7DL, UK
www.maney.co.uk

Maney Publishing is the trading name of W. S. Maney & Son Ltd

Typeset, printed and bound in the UK by
The Charlesworth Group

CONTENTS

	PAGE
Foreword	vii
Authors' Preface and Acknowledgements	xi
Abbreviations	xiv

PART ONE THE MEDIEVAL COMPANY

CHAPTER ONE	Origins: Tailors and Linen-Armourers	3
CHAPTER TWO	'Ghostly Treasure': The Fraternity of St John the Baptist 1350–1530	19
CHAPTER THREE	The Government of the Medieval Company	35
CHAPTER FOUR	The Company and the Craft	49
CHAPTER FIVE	Company, City and Crown 1350–1500	71

PART TWO REFORMATION TO RESTORATION

CHAPTER SIX	The Company and the Reformation	93
CHAPTER SEVEN	The Company and Education in the Sixteenth Century	109
CHAPTER EIGHT	Daily Life in Elizabethan London	127
CHAPTER NINE	The Clothworkers, the City and the Crown	141
CHAPTER TEN	The Turn of the Century	151
CHAPTER ELEVEN	Prelude to the Civil War	165
CHAPTER TWELVE	The Company in the Civil War	181
CHAPTER THIRTEEN	Restoration, Fire and Rebuilding	199
CHAPTER FOURTEEN	Troubled Times	211

PART THREE THE COMPANY IN THE MODERN WORLD

CHAPTER FIFTEEN	The Long Eighteenth Century	225
CHAPTER SIXTEEN	The Nineteenth Century	237
CHAPTER SEVENTEEN	The Twentieth Century	249
Epilogue		265
Appendix One	List of Masters, 1300–2003	269
Appendix Two	List of Clerks, 1398–2003	275
Appendix Three	The Value of Money, 1300–2002	277
Select Bibliography		279
List of Subscribers		283

Index 285

Colour Plates I–VIII *following p.* 34
IX–XVI *following p.* 114
XVII–XXIV *following p.* 210

FOREWORD

In the year 2003 the Merchant Taylors' Company celebrated the 500th anniversary of the grant of its Charter from Henry VII in 1503. The letters patent recognized the guild in the name of 'Merchant Taylors'. There had been six earlier charters, all referring to the 'Fraternity of St John the Baptist of Tailors and Linen-Armourers', the first of which was granted by Edward III in 1327. The significance of being described as 'Merchant Taylors' was that it recognized the growing numbers of members of the Company who traded in cloth and other goods, rather than in finished garments. The charter was strongly resisted by other 'mercantile' companies, but in achieving it the Company confirmed its rise to a position among the 'Great Twelve' companies of the City of London.

If the Fraternity of St John the Baptist proved to be unique in the incorporation of the term 'Merchant' into its title (although only after the Haberdashers had been forced to abandon a similar title in 1510), it was also unusual in other respects amongst the craft guilds of medieval London. Even before the end of the fifteenth century it was actively recruiting fraternity members from outside the ranks of its craft, and had established close links with both the Church and the Crown. One of its key functions was the provision of charity; the earliest Wardens of the 'Tailors and Linen-Armourers' were known as 'alms collectors'. With the changes that came as the result of the Reformation its activities were greatly expanded by the foundation of schools by its Masters, and other prominent members, many of which survive to this day.

With a large membership, the Company had been enabled to construct its Hall and chapel on the present site. By the mid-sixteenth century many funerals had become very grand affairs at Threadneedle Street, or Broad Street, as it was then known, or at the Company's other chapel in St Paul's Cathedral. Such events raised large sums for charitable funds, and two of the Company's greatest treasures, the magnificent hearse-cloths, originate from this time. The celebrated 'Billesden Award' of 1484, between the Merchant Taylors' and Skinners' Companies, had established the unique annual alternation of precedence of the two guilds, ranking sixth or seventh in the City of London, which has been faithfully honoured ever since.

By the start of the seventeenth century, when the Company had already been in existence for three hundred years, its basic form, and activities, were thus firmly established. In the middle of the century, however, it was not immune from the huge shocks which so greatly changed the City of London; the Civil War seriously depleted the Company's wealth, while the destruction of the Hall and of most of the Company's rented estate in the Great Fire was a financial disaster as well as curtailing its social activities. Gradually the Company's fortunes were restored, and the Hall was rebuilt on the same site. Had Sir Christopher Wren had his way,

London would have been rebuilt as an imposing city of brick and stone, with wide, straight streets, and new churches with towers, domes and spires, all of this crowned by St Paul's, built to the design of the Great Model, still to be seen at the Cathedral. The ceremonial archway that became Temple Bar, which returns to London between St Paul's and the new Paternoster Square in 2004, was intended to be located at the north end of a rebuilt London Bridge, with elegant terraced houses to the full width of the river on either side of the roadway. A monumental column as the focal point where the straight streets were to radiate into the 'new' City from the north end of the bridge would celebrate the magnificence of the 'Carolingian Era'. Merchant Taylors' Hall would probably have been relocated nearby, close to where the 'Monument' now stands.

Wren, incidentally, had a close connection with the Company as his father and his uncle had attended the Company's school in Suffolk Lane. His uncle became a bishop, and both men were Registrars to the Order of the Garter. Much of what Wren intended eventually happened, of course, but he underestimated the power of property and political interests, and the conservatism of the City and Church authorities. The City was indeed rebuilt in brick and stone, but largely on the pre-Fire street plan. There were many 'new' churches, with towers, domes and spires, but sited as in medieval London. St Paul's was rebuilt, but not to the Great Model design.

The Company's own buildings have, perhaps inevitably, been a source of both joy and anguish. If the medieval Hall was destroyed in the Great Fire, its successor, much altered over 250 years, was again destroyed at the start of World War II; the present Hall is thus the third design, only just fifty years old, but still in the same shell, on the same site. In 1851, however, no national disaster was needed to generate destruction. On the day before a full livery dinner the entire, huge ceiling of the Hall collapsed spontaneously, narrowly avoiding wiping out the Master, Wardens, Court, and a large number of the livery at a stroke!

In spite of such alarms the Company has continued to build, and to manage property. Christopher Boone was not a Merchant Taylor, but he identified the Company as a suitable steward of his legacy. His large estate in Lewisham, or the parish of Lee as it then was, became our responsibility at the end of the seventeenth century and has enabled us to provide almshouses, social housing and two nursing homes for the benefit of the population of south-east London. We also became responsible for Christopher Boone's Chapel, Lewisham's only Grade I 'Listed Building', and attributed to Wren; its conservation remains an anxiety to us! We have continued to be involved in property development in the City including, most recently, establishing its first five-star hotel, which opened in 2002. But perhaps the boldest development of all was to move the school from the Charterhouse to Sandy Lodge in 1933. It was a courageous step by the Court, and to appoint a brilliant young architect, William Godfrey Newton, to carry out the commission, which has continued to influence the design of educational buildings to this day, was nothing less than inspired.

The Company's charitable giving continues very actively, and is now directed to both organizations and individuals, targeted to where it will make the greatest impact, and can encourage further support from elsewhere. Many individual beneficiaries are former pupils of our 'family' of schools. The Company continues to recruit nearly sixty per cent of its membership through apprenticeship, demonstrating our fundamental belief in the potential of young people. The Company's tradition of hospitality also continues, and up to 40,000 people a year greatly enjoy events of every kind at the Hall.

If all of this indicates a strong sense of continuity, it should also be said that at the beginning of the twenty-first century there is a sense of vigour and purpose in the Company. The membership — apprentices, freemen and the livery — are all increasingly engaged in its affairs. The right to the freedom has always passed through the male or female line in the Company, and 2003/4 is the first year in which women members of the livery become eligible to apply for election to the Court and thus to become Master.

With so active a future in prospect, what better time could there be to review the last seven centuries of the Company's history as the platform on which to build the next? We should therefore be particularly grateful to Sir Edward Studd for taking the initiative in 1996 to persuade the Court to commission the preparation and publication of this *History of the Merchant Taylors' Company*. We should also express our gratitude to the authors, Matthew Davies and Ann Saunders, for the depth of their researches and their tenacity in having achieved this splendid outcome, and to Stephen Freeth, one of our livery and Keeper of Manuscripts at Guildhall Library, for his assistance on many fronts. We should also record our appreciation to Maney Publishing, for producing such a splendid volume. I commend this fascinating story of the Company's history to its members, to those outwith who are interested in this unique Fraternity, and to successive generations.

John Howard Penton
Master 2003/2004

AUTHORS' PREFACE AND ACKNOWLEDGEMENTS

THE WRITING of this new History of the Merchant Taylors' Company has been split between the authors along chronological lines, reflecting their particular areas of interest and expertise. Matthew Davies was responsible for researching and writing about the earlier history of the Company, up to and including the Reformation and the sixteenth-century educational foundations (Chapters One to Seven). To these Ann Saunders contributed material on the reign of Queen Mary and the foundation of Merchant Taylors' School. Ann is the sole author of the remaining chapters, covering the Company from the accession of Elizabeth I to the rebuilding of the Hall after World War II.

The authors wish to thank all those who have helped them to research and write this book. They are most grateful to the Merchant Taylors' Company for having entrusted the task to them, and in particular to the History Committee: Sir Edward Studd (Chairman), Sir Geoffrey Holland, Mark Barty-King and Stephen Freeth. At the Hall, the Clerk, David Peck, and the Beadle, Robert Henry, gave steadfast support, as did John Bayford (Assistant Clerk), Anne Scott and Lorraine Phillips. Stephen Freeth deserves a double measure of gratitude, both as a Committee member, and as Keeper of Manuscripts at Guildhall Library. During the five years that it has taken to research and write the book, he has catalogued the volumes and loose papers which fill a furlong of shelving in the strongrooms below Guildhall where the Company's archives now safely rest. The knowledge he has acquired during this process has been invaluable, together with his painstaking checking of original references. He also contributed substantially to the Bibliography. He, and Sir Geoffrey Holland, have read and commented on the final draft with particular care. We both owe them much for their precision. Whilst every effort has been made to ensure consistency in the spelling of names, it should be noted that surnames, in particular, were not standardized until the eighteenth century.

The staffs of Guildhall Library's Manuscripts Section, Printed Books, and Prints and Maps have supported us cheerfully. Dr Pamela Taylor listed over a hundred boxes of loose papers. John Fisher, Jeremy Smith, Lynne MacNab, and Michael Melia helped tirelessly over the illustrations; all the photography, save where otherwise accredited, was taken by Robert Pullen with exemplary skill. Annie Hunter and her team have laboured to ensure smooth delivery of documents and heavy tomes. James Sewell, OBE, and his staff in the Corporation of London Records Office were equally supportive, as were the staffs of the British Library, the Public Record Office (now part of The National Archives), London Metropolitan Archives, Lambeth Palace Library, the London Library, and the National Monuments Record, now part of English Heritage.

The archivists of other City companies lent their aid. We thank especially David Beasley (Goldsmiths), David Wickham, FSA, and Alexandrina Buchanan (Clothworkers), Ursula Carlyle (Mercers), Raya McGeorge (Fishmongers), and Robin Myers, FSA (Stationers). At St John's College, Oxford, Sir Howard Colvin and Dr Malcolm Vale made us welcome and helped our research. The staffs of the schools associated with the Company have given full support: we thank particularly Mr Gabitass, headmaster, and Geoffrey Brown, archivist, at Merchant Taylors' School, Sandy Lodge; Mr Dawkins, and Mrs Mills and her staff, at Great Crosby; Mr Trafford, who also took photographs, and Helen O'Donnell at Wolverhampton Grammar School; Mr Magill and Mr McNee at Foyle & Londonderry College; and Mrs Judith Dewey, school governor at Wallingford. Liverymen and former pupils have offered us memories and suggested corrections. Reginald Adams, the late Hume Boggis-Rolfe, Donald Bompas, Walter Clode, James Corden, the late John Gibson, John Owens, John Penton and Michael Skinner have all contributed. Charles Hind generously lent Ann his uncle's collection of books about the school.

The authors are especially grateful to fellow historians who have contributed references, ideas and enthusiasm to this project. In particular, they would like to thank Caroline Barron, Anne Sutton, Vanessa Harding, John Schofield, and other members of the seminar on Medieval and Tudor London at the Institute of Historical Research, where early versions of some of the chapters were read. Ian Archer read and commented, most helpfully, on Ann's early chapters. Fiona Kisby, Eva Griffiths, and Simon Bradley gave advice. Nigel Sleigh-Johnson permitted us to draw on his unpublished PhD thesis, while Claude Blair allowed us to see a draft of parts of his forthcoming history of the Armourers' and Brasiers' Company. Matthew Davies wishes in addition to thank his present and former colleagues, especially Linda Clark and Hannes Kleineke at the History of Parliament Trust, and Derek Keene, Heather Creaton, and Olwen Myhill at the Centre for Metropolitan History, for their support and encouragement.

Ann Saunders thanks Mrs Joorun of the Company's almshouses at Lewisham, and David Short and Mrs ten Hove of Ashwell, Hertfordshire, who all made her welcome. Help has been offered by, and accepted gratefully from, Peter Barber, FSA (British Library); Stephen Croad, MBE, FSA (National Monuments Record); Robin Harcourt-Williams, FSA (Hatfield House Archives); Sam Holland, FRIBA, the third member of the team who restored the Hall, and Simon Houfe, Sir Albert Richardson's grandson; Hazel Forsyth (Museum of London); Raymond Lowe, churchwarden, St Jude-on-the-Hill; Dr Noel Mander, MBE, FSA, organ builder; Susan North (Victoria and Albert Museum); Dr Thom Richardson (Royal Armouries, Leeds); Dr Francis Sheppard, formerly Director of the Survey of London; Kay Staniland, FSA, scholar; Alan Swannell; Jean Tsushima, FSA, Hon. Archivist to the Honourable Artillery Company; and David Webb, FSA, formerly Librarian, Bishopsgate Institute. Ann's chapters would not have been written without Roger Cline's help; he willingly lent scores of books from his inexhaustible library devoted to the history of London. Anne Buck, OBE, formerly Keeper of the Gallery of English Costume at Platt Hall, Manchester, and Veronica Stokes, FSA, formerly Archivist to Coutts Bank, have shouted encouragement from the wings.

The team at Maney Publishing — Michael Gallico, Liz Rosindale, and Linda Fisher — have laboured heroically to make this volume handsome and to speed it through the press. Ann, electronically illiterate, remembers gratefully her cousin and god-daughter, the late Anthea Lecky, who typed the first draft; Linda Fisher completed the work expertly. The authors also thank Ann Hudson for compiling the index.

Finally, both authors owe a great debt to their respective spouses, Jane Sherwood and Bruce Saunders. Their warmest thanks go to them for their support, patience and good humour during the researching and writing of this book.

Matthew Davies
Ann Saunders

ABBREVIATIONS

BL	British Library
Cal. Letter Bk A, B, C, etc.	*Calendar of the Letter Books Preserved among the Archives of the Corporation of the City of London*, ed. by R. R. Sharpe, 11 vols (A–L) (1899–1912)
Clode, *Memorials*	C. M. Clode, *Memorials of the Guild of Merchant Taylors of the Fraternity of St John the Baptist in the City of London* (1875)
Clode, *Early History*	C. M. Clode, *The Early History of the Guild of Merchant Taylors of the Fraternity of St John the Baptist, London, with Notices of the Lives of Some of its Eminent Members*, 2 vols (1888)
CLRO	Corporation of London Records Office
Court Minutes, ed. by Davies	*The Merchant Taylors' Company of London: Court Minutes, 1486–1493*, ed. by Matthew Davies (Stamford, 2000)
CPMR	*Calendar of Plea and Memoranda Rolls of the City of London, 1323–1482*, 6 vols, ed. by A. H. Thomas (I–IV) and P. E. Jones (V–VI) (Cambridge, 1926–61)
CPR	*Calendar of Patent Rolls* (1901–)
CWCH	*Calendar of Wills Proved and Enrolled in the Court of Husting, London, 1258–1688*, ed. by R. R. Sharpe, 2 vols (1889–90)
GL	Guildhall Library
PRO	Public Record Office (now part of The National Archives)
Riley, *Memorials*	*Memorials of London and London Life in the XIIIth, XIVth and XVth Centuries*, ed. by H. T. Riley (1868)
Stow, *Survey*, ed. Kingsford	John Stow, *A Survey of London, Reprinted from the Text of 1603*, ed. by C. L. Kingsford, 2 vols (Oxford, 1908)

PART ONE
THE MEDIEVAL COMPANY

CHAPTER ONE

ORIGINS: TAILORS AND LINEN-ARMOURERS

At this time many of the people of the trades of London were arrayed in livery, and a good time was about to begin.

(*Croniques de London*, early fourteenth century)[1]

LONDON'S LIVERY COMPANIES have retained the ability to fascinate those who have sought to explain their origins, and their longevity. As more and more records have become accessible it has been possible for writers to delve more deeply than ever before into the history of these institutions, which came to play so prominent a part in the social, political and economic life of the capital.[2] Despite this, much about the early years of the City companies remains hidden from modern eyes. Few company records survive from before 1400, and so today those looking to discover more about the livery companies often have to rely upon chance references for clues as to their beginnings and early activities. Nevertheless, investigation of the 'silent years of London guild history' has persisted, and made good progress. Of particular interest for modern writers has been the development within many of the City's diverse trades, in the thirteenth and early fourteenth centuries, of 'guilds' or 'fraternities' (the words are used interchangeably): among them was the Fraternity of St John the Baptist founded by the City's tailors, which in 1503 was granted a seventh royal charter, by Henry VII, that conferred on it the title of 'Merchant Taylors' Company'.[3]

THE CITY OF LONDON AND ITS GOVERNMENT

Between 1000 and 1300 London grew dramatically, to become one of Europe's largest metropolises (see Col. Pl. I). By the early fourteenth century it may have contained within its walls, and ever-expanding suburbs, as many as eighty thousand people. Yet only some twenty-five per cent of the City's adult male population were enfranchised, that is, admitted to the freedom of the City as 'freemen', and so able to claim the various privileges which had been granted by successive royal charters to those who were citizens. Freemen were the only residents of London entitled to participate in the political life of the capital, buy goods with the intention of re-selling them, and keep shops for retailing goods. In return, citizens swore loyalty to the City government, and undertook to pay taxes levied on them and to carry out public duties when required. Access to the freedom of the City was closely regulated and jealously guarded: it could be obtained either through apprenticeship to a citizen, by redemption (through the payment of a sum of money to the City Chamberlain), or by patrimony. By the early fourteenth century a young immigrant to London would typically have sought to become an apprentice, for with the growth of London's economy apprenticeship within one of London's many and diverse trades was the most popular means of obtaining the freedom. After completing a training of at least seven years, the newly qualified craftsman could seek to join the exclusive ranks of the City's freemen.[4]

Those who obtained the freedom were able to take their place in a City which had changed dramatically over the preceding two hundred years, a period when an expanding economy and population went hand-in-hand with the City's gradual independence from royal control. The government of the City was now largely in the hands of its citizens. Until the granting of a charter by Richard I in 1190 two Sheriffs, royal officials appointed by the King, had ruled the City. Now the Mayor was London's chief

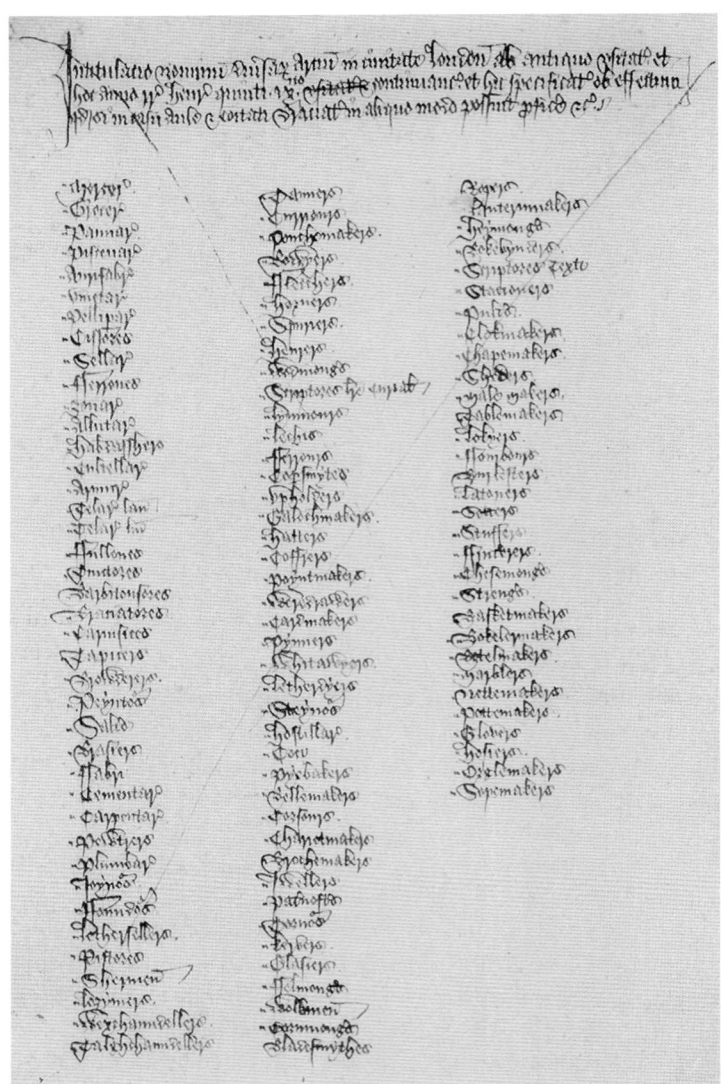

FIGURE 1. A list of 112 crafts of the City of London in 1422, drawn up by the Clerk of the Brewers' Company. The Tailors (*Cissores*) are listed in eighth place.
Guildhall Library, MS 5440, fol. 11ᵛ. Reproduced by kind permission of the Brewers' Company

magistrate and leader of the government of the City, with the two Sheriffs, though still the King's representatives, increasingly subordinate to him. Beneath the Mayor were the Aldermen, prominent citizens who exercised jurisdiction over the City's twenty-four wards, administrative units formed out of much older private estates and jurisdictions. The structure of London's government was rooted in the wards, where assemblies of citizens met, under the eye of their alderman and ward officers, to resolve local problems. It was the wards that, by the 1280s, were responsible for selecting freemen to attend meetings of what became known as the Common Council, which, like the Court of Aldermen, met in Guildhall. This framework of government was largely in place by 1300, and was accompanied by the consolidation of the roles of the City's own law courts and by the creation of new administrative offices. The posts of Common Clerk, Common Serjeant and Recorder, for instance, all date from the reign of Edward I (1272–1307), and it is no coincidence that this period also saw the beginning of important series of civic records, such as the 'Letter Books' and the rolls of the Mayor's Court, which provide us with much of what we know of the City, its government and its people at this time.[5]

The diverse trades and occupations practised by London's citizens figure prominently in these records, for by 1300 it had become common for freemen to identify themselves by their craft. More than 180 trades can be found, testifying to the range of goods produced and sold in the capital. The individuals named include both wealthy merchants, such as vintners, grocers and mercers, many of whom imported and exported a wide variety of commodities, and also poorer, more specialized tradesmen, such as quilt-makers, cheesemongers and bowyers. In 1422 the Clerk of the Brewers' Company drew up a list of 112 of the City's 'ancient' crafts, arranged in rough order of size and prominence: heading them were the Mercers, Grocers and Drapers, with the tailors (*Cissores*) in eighth place, while further down the list were crafts such as the 'galochemakers', 'pyebakers', 'glasiers' and 'sopemakers' (see Fig. 1).[6] The identification of individuals according to craft reflected not only the growth of London's economy and the importance of its industries, but also the way in which citizens, as well as being residents of particular wards and parishes, were also linked, through shared skills and products, with fellow artisans and merchants throughout London. These common interests were responsible for the development of organizations within the crafts, and for the increasingly prominent role which the trades were to play in the government of the City.

MISTERIES AND FRATERNITIES

Contemporaries used specific terms to describe the crafts and craft organizations of the thirteenth and early fourteenth centuries. Particularly prominent was the term 'mistery' (Latin *misterium*, medieval French *mestier*, *métier*), the collective noun applied to all those who professed to follow a particular trade, as in, for example, the 'mistery of fishmongers'. Also widely used was *officium*, normally translated as 'craft', which was also used to denote those of one trade. Neither term implied anything about the level of organization within a craft. As London's population and economy grew during the thirteenth century, however, the City government increasingly came to rely upon representatives of the misteries, often known as Wardens, who would be permitted to enforce regulations relevant to their particular crafts. Little else can be inferred by the use of the term 'mistery', however, and certainly not the existence of an association of any kind. Where they have been discovered, these associations were known by a variety of interchangeable terms, of which the most commonly used were the Latin *fraternitas*, *gilda*, and *congregatio* and the French *confrerie*.

These terms were widely used to describe the religious fraternities which were founded with increasing frequency by lay people throughout Europe from the thirteenth century onwards. Many were established within parish churches, while others were attached to religious houses or hospitals. At the heart of this movement was the medieval notion of the community of the living and the dead, a notion expressed most vividly in the belief that Masses, prayers and good works could expedite the soul's passage through Purgatory. Fraternities drew strength from these beliefs through their focus upon collective worship and charitable activity: alms were given to members in financial difficulty, and it was normal for the fraternity to bear the costs of funeral arrangements. They were founded by groups of men, and sometimes by groups of women, who were not blood relatives, but who nevertheless wished to use the analogy of brotherhood in order to achieve these aims. This led to the use of robes or 'liveries' to emphasize these bonds, as well as to the popularity of feasts and other ceremonial occasions.[7]

In London and many other towns and cities, fraternities also became popular among those who practised a particular trade. In these cases the fraternity acted not just as a means to express religious and charitable aspirations, but also as a focus for commercial and political interests. In some towns membership of the relevant fraternity was compulsory for all those who wished to make, or trade in, particular commodities, but in other urban centres, including London, they were chiefly exclusive organizations for the wealthiest and most prominent artisans. As well as having religious and charitable functions, they normally exercised a wider economic jurisdiction over particular crafts.[8] In London there is no doubting the role of these institutions as the forerunners of what would later be known as the 'livery companies', named after the robes which members came to wear on ceremonial occasions. Yet the historical relationship between the two is not a simple one, not least because in the thirteenth and fourteenth centuries it was by no means inevitable that the crafts would become organized in this way. While some, such as the Skinners, Tailors and Goldsmiths, formed well-supported and successful fraternities dedicated to the feasts of Corpus Christi, St John the Baptist and St Dunstan respectively, others, notably the Vintners and Ironmongers, never founded proper fraternities and, initially at least, developed few structures beyond what were needed for the administration of their own crafts. Certain crafts were also concentrated in certain parts of the City, and this may have meant that a formal craft organization was, for many years, superfluous, the crafts being supervised at a local level by more informal networks.[9] Conversely, it is clear that some crafts became organized earlier than others as a result of external pressures: the Grocers, for instance, may have founded their guild of St Antholin partly because of a growing need to protect their commercial interests.[10] By the fifteenth century, these differences of emphasis had largely been eroded: most of the crafts had by this time adopted the visible trappings of guild life, whether it was the wearing of liveries, the celebration of services for members living and dead, or the distribution of alms to those who had fallen upon hard times. These apparent similarities in structure and function should not, however, disguise their diverse origins.[11]

The dedications of these fraternities to particular saints and feast days should be noted at this point. Guilds and fraternities throughout Europe commonly adopted patron saints that had some connection, even if often rather tangential, to the craft in question. Guilds of tailors were frequently dedicated to St John the Baptist, almost certainly because of the references in Matthew 3:4 and Mark 1:6 to the clothing worn, and perhaps made, by the saint in the desert: 'John's clothes were made of camel's hair, and he had a leather belt around his waist. His food was locusts and wild honey.' John the Baptist's role as the harbinger of the Lamb of God was also important, and representations of the saint in paintings and illuminated manuscripts frequently show him with the Holy Lamb. Indeed an example, shown in Colour Plate IIA, can be found in the illuminated lectionary owned by Stephen Jenyns, the second Merchant Taylor to be chosen as Lord Mayor (1508). This was also the reason why the Lamb was subsequently incorporated into the Arms of the London tailors. The dedication to the saint was shared by tailors' guilds in other towns and cities in England, including Bristol, Exeter, Oxford, Salisbury and York. The Nativity of the saint (24 June) was commonly chosen as the date of the annual feast, although the Decollation (29 August) was also used. It is worth remarking, however, that some of the London craft fraternities were not dedicated to saints or feasts with obvious connections to their occupations. In the case of the Skinners, for example, their dedication to the feast of Corpus Christi may perhaps reflect origins in a parish fraternity that was subsequently 'taken over' by skinners.[12]

THE CITY AND THE CRAFTS 1250–1300

What all the crafts of thirteenth-century London had in common, however, was an increasingly well-developed sense of identity, which naturally encouraged them to seek to regulate their own affairs. A fraternity was one way in which such ambitions could be expressed, but by no means the only one. The expectations of the leaders of the crafts were rising in the mid-thirteenth century, as the economy of the City began to grow and diversify: some misteries, such as the Goldsmiths and Vintners, had already been accorded a limited role in regulating their own affairs. By the 1250s the ambitions of the crafts had set them upon a collision course with conservatives among the City's aldermen, who asserted the traditional role of the wards in governing the City and who regarded the misteries, which were not constrained by ward boundaries, as a threat to their positions. The rise of the crafts in London was thus part of a fundamental constitutional debate. At the heart of the matter was the role which the increasingly vocal misteries should have in the government of the City. In the 1260s these struggles became closely bound up with the divisions in London caused by the civil war between the King, Henry III, and the barons led by Earl Simon de Montfort. Prominent among the conservatives was Alderman Arnold FitzThedmar, author of an important contemporary chronicle in which he bitterly attacked a fellow alderman, the populist Thomas FitzThomas, during whose time as Mayor (1261–65) the City had committed to the baronial cause. FitzThomas was said to have 'pampered' the City populace by giving a voice to the 'commons of the City' and, in addition, had encouraged the crafts to draw up regulations for themselves.[13] Another target of his polemic was Walter Hervy (Mayor 1272–73), who was said to have granted charters to various (unnamed) crafts. These were revoked during the mayoralty of his successor, Henry le Waleys, who had Hervy arrested for good measure, a move which seemingly heralded a defeat for the crafts.[14]

In the event, the last two decades of the thirteenth century were far from being disastrous for the crafts. The very dominance of conservative elements in London created a stable atmosphere conducive to gradual reform. This was particularly so from 1285 to 1298 when Edward I took the government of London into his own hands and appointed royal Wardens in place of the Mayor.[15] There was a growing recognition that the misteries had become indispensable to the government of the City, and could be used to buttress the traditional authority of the wards rather than undermine it. In particular, the City authorities increasingly looked to the crafts as the best means of regulating access to the all-important freedom of the City. As we have seen, the freedom could be obtained through apprenticeship, by redemption or by patrimony, and apprenticeship in particular gave the misteries an ever more powerful voice in a period which saw increasing immigration into London. In 1274–75, according to one source, a new register of apprentices and redemptioners was begun, with enrolment of the names of apprentices and freemen made compulsory.[16] Two further measures are noted in the City records over the next twenty years: in 1282 Mayor Henry le Waleys ordered all the misteries to present the names of their freemen and apprentices to the Court of Aldermen, and a similar order issued by the royal warden in 1294 required the 'better and more discreet' men of the misteries to compile a record of their members on the grounds that 'misdoers and disturbers of the King's peace' had come to be hidden among the 'good men' of the City.[17] These difficulties were still in evidence in December 1312 when a petition from the 'good men of the commonalty of every mistery' sought reassurance that a newcomer to the City would not be allowed to take up his freedom until his 'condition and trustworthiness' had been certified to the Mayor and Aldermen by the merchants and craftsmen of the trade he wished to practise.[18] These concerns were addressed in the important charter granted to the City by Edward II in 1319, in which for the first time it was laid down that admission to the freedom could only be obtained through one of the recognized misteries. Moreover, strangers in the City had to find six men from their chosen craft to act as guarantors of their standing and future conduct before they could be admitted. From this date onwards it was usual for freemen to describe themselves as 'citizen and tailor', 'citizen and mercer' and so on in all legal and quasi-legal documents. This charter thus marked a watershed in the history of the crafts. It set the seal upon many of the changes which had taken place in London over the previous fifty years, and provided a further stimulus to the development of organizations within the misteries.[19]

THE TAILORS' FRATERNITY: EARLY EVIDENCE

We can now attempt to trace the beginnings of organization among the tailors of London. It is perhaps not surprising that little is recorded of them in this period: though clearly a large craft, the City's tailors were not as prominent in City affairs as the mercantile crafts such as the Grocers, or those such as the Vintners and Goldsmiths which had strong links with the Crown. Tailoring was an artisan occupation which was based around the manufacture of different types of clothing and other related items such as bed-hangings: profits were generally smaller than those which could be achieved through trade in commodities such as wool, cloth, wine or spices. Wealth and political status went hand in hand, and because the tailors were not among the great merchants of the capital they did not provide any aldermen, let alone a mayor, until the fifteenth century. Nor do

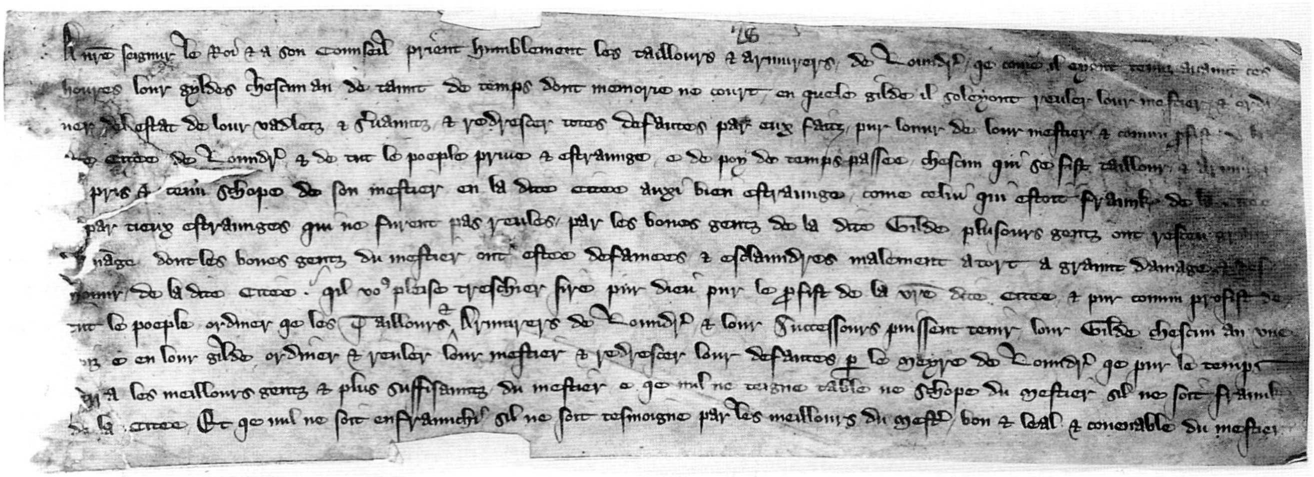

FIGURE 2. Petition of the Tailors and Linen-Armourers, 1327.
Public Record Office, SC8/260/12978

the tailors of London appear to have been concentrated in any particular area of the City, unlike the pepperers of Soper Lane, the driving force behind the Grocers' fraternity, or the Skinners, many of whom lived and worked in the Peltry which ran southwards from the church of St John Walbrook. The establishment of Tailors' Hall in Broad Street (now Threadneedle Street) from the mid-fourteenth century might suggest that leading tailors were concentrated in that part of London, but there is no evidence of this in the returns made for taxes raised in 1292 or 1309.[20]

Anecdotal evidence must be used with caution. In an entry in his chronicle for late November 1267, for instance, FitzThedmar described serious rioting in the City of London between 'certain of the craft of goldsmiths and certain of the craft of tailors (*quosdam de officio cissorum*)'. They were joined by men of the parmenters (robe-trimmers or furriers) and tawyers (leather-workers) and the ensuing disorder lasted for three days before being brought under control. More than thirty rioters were arrested by the Sheriffs and thrown into Newgate prison; they were later tried for various offences, including the murders of men whose bodies had been thrown in the Thames, and a number of men were hanged. In the absence of other information it might be tempting to regard such evidence as indicating some sort of organization among the tailors at that date. However, this would be premature. The disorder noted by the chronicler probably had as much to do with the tense political climate in London at a time of continuing strife between the King and his barons, as with craft identities and rivalries. Whilst not doubting the spirit of these tailors, their riotous behaviour only goes a certain way towards our goal of finding the origins of the Company.[21]

Less dramatic, but probably more significant, is the will of a citizen of London named Robert de Mounpeillers among the deeds and wills formally approved and enrolled in the City's Husting Court in 1278. Among the bequests Mounpeillers made to his sons was a rent charge on a shop and solar (upper room) which were said to belong to the Tailors. This might indicate that senior tailors, perhaps officials such as a master and wardens, were holding property on behalf of the rest of the craft. If so, this is our first evidence of organization within the mistery.[22] Slight though this evidence is, there is every likelihood that the Tailors and their associated craft, the Linen-Armourers (for which see below) had indeed developed structures for self-regulation by the close of the thirteenth century. John Stow, the unrivalled sixteenth-century chronicler of London's history and everyday life, was himself a freeman of the Merchant Taylors' Company. As such he had unique access to the already extensive archives of his company when he wrote his *Survey of London* in 1598. His account of the 'origins' of the company is of more than usual interest:

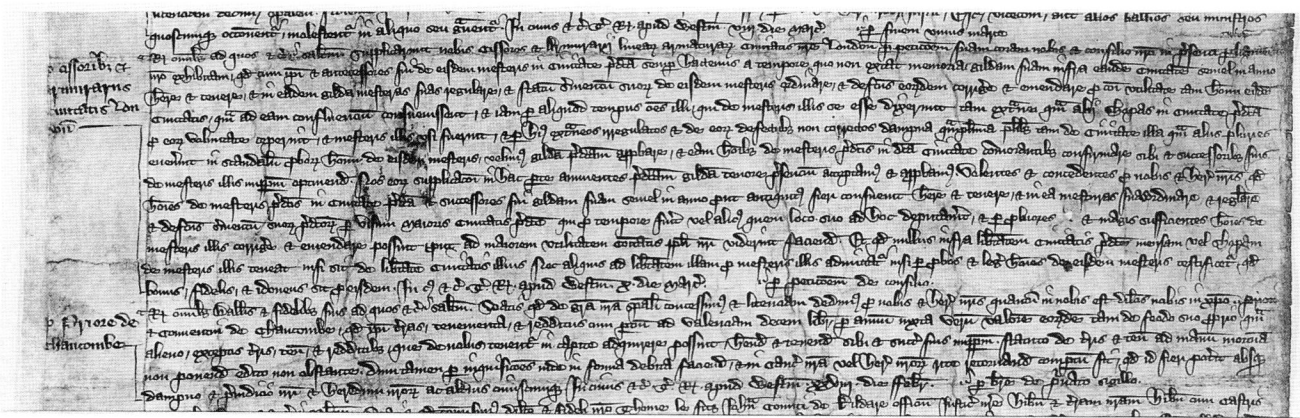

FIGURE 3. Enrolled Letters Patent of Edward III, 10 March 1327.
Public Record Office, C66/166, m. 22

I find that King *Edward* the first... confirmed this Guild by the name of Taylors and Linnen armourers, and also gaue to the brethren thereof authority euery yeare at mid-sommer to hold a feast, and to choose vnto them a gouernour, or Mayster with wardens: whereupon the same yeare 1300, on the feast day of the natiuitie of saint *Iohn Baptist*, they chose *Henry de Ryall* to be their pilgrim, for the maister of this misterie (as one that trauelled for the whole companie) was then so called... and the foure wardens were then called Purueyors of almes.[23]

How reliable is this? It is impossible to reconstruct the actual sources used by Stow in this instance, but the surviving records of the Company do contain clues. Inventories of the Company's books taken in 1609 and 1689 show that the Company had in its possession a series of nine manuscript books, labelled 'A' to 'I', of which the earliest was said to begin in the year 1299. Book 'I' still survives as the earliest complete book of minutes of the Company's Court (1562–75), but the others, with the exception of parts of two fifteenth-century books, disappeared in the eighteenth century. It is likely that the early books were similar to the surviving fourteenth-century books of the Mercers' and Grocers' Companies, which contain a mixture of accounts, minutes and ordinances (craft regulations); if so they would undoubtedly have provided Stow with much of what he included in his *Survey*.[24] He might have gleaned further information from another manuscript listed in one of the inventories as 'one other auntient book in paper contaynyng the names of all the M[aste]rs and the Wardens of this company sithence the yere Anno Domini 1300 being the xxviiith yere of the raigne of King Edward the First'. According to Charles Clode, Master in 1873–74, this 'invaluable book' was produced by the Clerk in 1865 but had vanished from the archives ten years later when Clode compiled his *Memorials* of the Company.[25]

Stow's evidence suggests that the Fraternity of St John the Baptist received some sort of royal confirmation from Edward I in 1300 which ratified its jurisdiction over the City's tailors and linen-armourers. Unfortunately there is no evidence that 'letters patent' were obtained by the Tailors from Edward I: normally a copy of such letters would have been enrolled in the royal Chancery, but nothing relevant survives in the chancery rolls for that period. Nonetheless, Stow's claim emphasizes the important position of the fraternity within the craft as a whole.[26] Stow clearly regarded the Master and Wardens of the Fraternity of St John the Baptist as responsible for regulating the affairs of the mistery generally. Like the members of other fraternities, it is probable that the Tailors by this time wore livery robes and hoods on ceremonial occasions, particularly their annual feast on 24 June, the feast day of their patron saint, St John the Baptist. The Master named by Stow, Henry de Ryall, was certainly a suitable individual to be chosen for that office: also known as Henry le Taylor, he was a prominent common councilman who makes several appearances in the City records between 1300 and 1305.[27]

Further clues are revealed by Stow's claim that the terms 'pilgrim' and 'purveyors of alms' were

FIGURE 4. A linen-armour 'jack', c. 1560.
Royal Armouries Collection, Leeds

originally used for the Master and Wardens. Confirmation of the use of these terms can be found among some of the earliest documents surviving in the Company's archive. In 1351 John de Totenham, a prominent carpenter, granted a small rent charge to five tailors, John Pecche, William de Derby, Robert de Gyldeford, Giles de Westmill and Roger de Cologne. Pecche, already prominent in the craft, was described as *peregrinus* (pilgrim) while the other four were referred to as the *collectores elemosinarum* (alms collectors). The use of these titles is unique among the London livery companies, and suggests that the Fraternity of St John the Baptist was especially conscious of its role as a provider of charity to members who had fallen on hard times.

The term 'pilgrim' is particularly evocative of the contemporary enthusiasm for crusading and pilgrimage. A number of English fraternities in the medieval period, including that founded by the tailors of Lincoln, even provided funds for pilgrims to travel to the Holy Land or to the popular shrine of St James at Compostela in northern Spain. It is uncertain, however, whether the Master of the London tailors was actually required to undertake such journeys on behalf of his brethren, as Stow implies.[28]

It is clear from these references that by 1300 the Tailors had laid the foundations for what would eventually become one of the most successful of the fraternities founded within the crafts of London.[29]

However, further early evidence is hard to come by. This is partly a consequence of the apparent loss of important records belonging to the Company from that period: much more can be said about the fraternity after 1398, when the surviving accounts begin. Even records which might be expected to reveal something about corporate life within the craft are not especially helpful. On 10 March 1327, following a petition submitted to the King and his council, the 'Tailors and Armourers' of London obtained their first charter, more correctly referred to as 'letters patent', a document which confirmed their right to hold an annual assembly and to 'rule their mistery and order the state of their workmen and servants and redress all faults by them committed' (see Figs 2 and 3).[30] Unlike subsequent charters obtained by the Tailors there is no mention of a fraternity or even of a Master and Wardens. This does not mean that Stow was wrong. The crafts which obtained charters at this time, a group that also included the Goldsmiths and Skinners, may have felt no need to obtain royal confirmation of the status of their fraternities. This was to change later in the century, particularly when guilds came to acquire property in their own right. For now, however, other priorities loomed larger, notably the need to define and expand the regulatory functions of the crafts in the decades which followed the granting of the 1319 charter to the City of London. By obtaining royal letters patent the Tailors and the other misteries demonstrated their self-confidence, and their willingness to look outside the City to the Crown for confirmation of their rights and privileges.

City records likewise do not reveal much about craft fraternities, probably because the government was mainly concerned with economic regulation. This can be seen in an entry in one of the City's 'Letter Books' from November 1328, when lists were drawn up of men who were to be responsible for governing twenty-four of the City's numerous crafts. Each mistery had a group of governors in proportion to its size: the tailors, already among the largest of the crafts, were to have twenty, a number exceeded only by the twenty-one for the fishmongers and the twenty-four for the butchers.

At the other end of the scale, the cappers, girdlers and painters were to have four each. This, and a subsequent list compiled in 1340, suggest that the principle of drawing upon senior craftsmen to help in the regulation of the misteries was becoming well established, and that we should look in these groups for the origins of the 'Courts of Assistants' which later came to act as the governing bodies of the livery companies. The list of 1340 was among the early 'constitutional' documents copied into an early-sixteenth-century illuminated book which is still owned by the Company. The men named in these lists were certainly prominent within the craft: John Pecche, one of the governors of 1328, went on to become the 'pilgrim' of 1351, while two of the 'alms collectors' noted in that year, Roger de Cologne and Giles de Westmelle, or Westmill, were listed among the leading tailors of 1340.[31] A further step towards the effective regulation of the craft was taken in 1364, this time at the request of the Tailors themselves. After reciting the terms of their charter, they asked the City to confirm a new ordinance which would allow access to the freedom only after six out of a named group of leading tailors had certified the 'condition' of each candidate. Once again, the list contains several men whose prominence within the fraternity is attested by later documents.[32]

TAILORS AND LINEN-ARMOURERS

Stow's evidence, together with the charter of 1327, confirms that as early as 1300 the London tailors were closely identified with another, allied trade, the linen-armourers. The nature of this specialist occupation is discussed more fully in a subsequent chapter, but in essence practitioners of this craft made soft armour, one of the four basic types of armour in common use in the Middle Ages, the others being mail, scale and plate armour. These garments could be worn either alone, or above or underneath metal armour. Surviving English examples include the Black Prince's 'jupon', now in Canterbury Cathedral, and others now in the Royal Armouries Collection (see Fig. 4).[33] Ordinances for the regulation of all types of armour were issued by the Mayor in 1322 to deal with abuses in the

FIGURE 5. Foundation arch, late fourteenth century, under the south-east wall of the Great Hall. Discovered during the excavation of the Muniment Room in 1919.
Guildhall Library, MS 34353/1

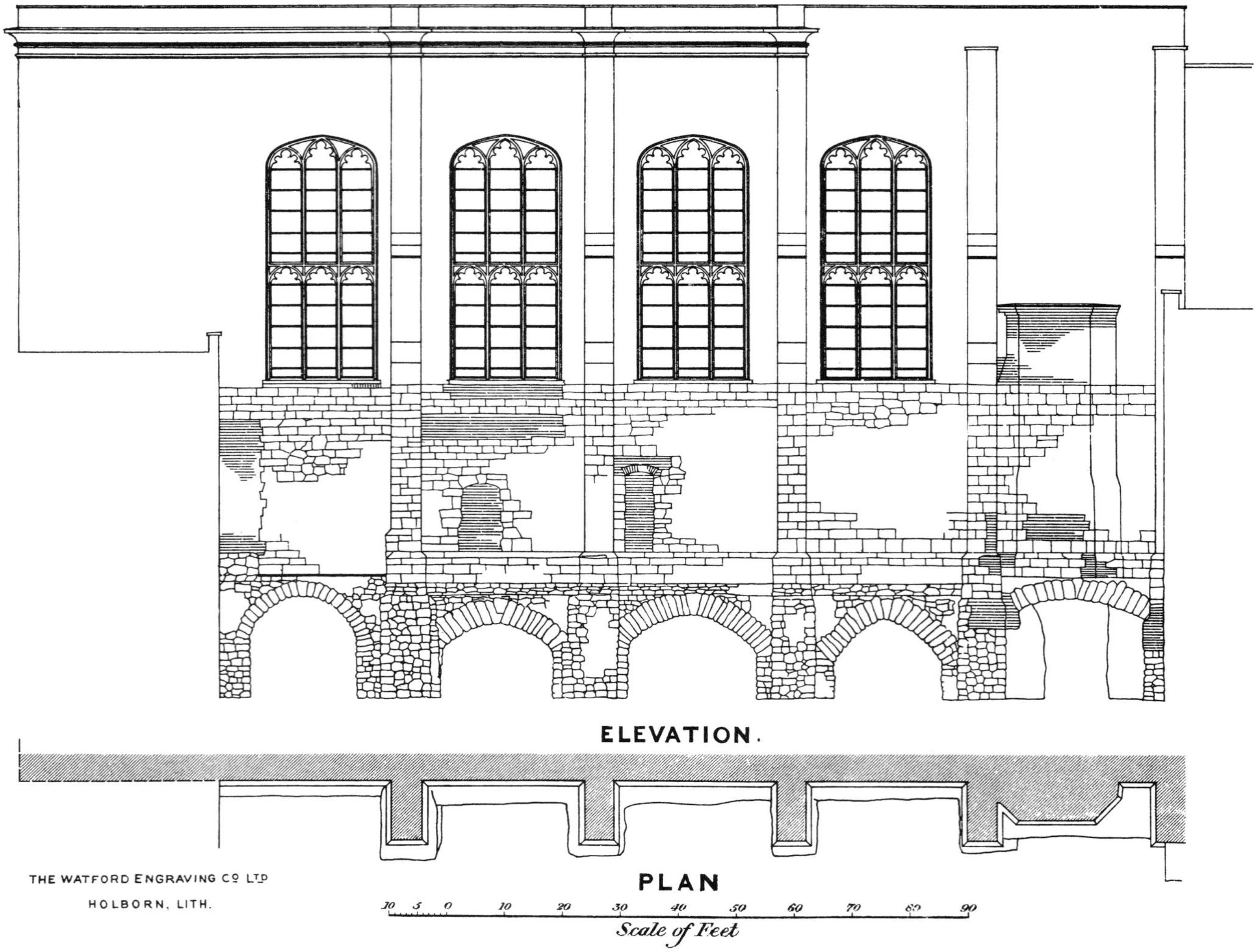

FIGURE 6. Elevation of the north wall of Merchant Taylors' Hall, showing foundation arches, as exposed by demolitions along Threadneedle Street, in 1910.
Guildhall Library

manufacturing processes, but by this date the linen-armourers were already closely associated with the tailors. Four linen-armourers were among the twenty men who were chosen by the Mayor in November 1328 to govern the mistery of Tailors and Linen-Armourers.[34]

The coming together of the two crafts was a natural development, for the linen-armourers had as much, if not more, in common with tailors as they did with armourers who worked mostly with mail or plate. Yet this in itself does not explain why the linen-armourers were singled out for such a formal alliance, or indeed why any large, diverse mistery would wish to link itself in such an explicit manner with a small, specialized occupation. Close examination of the records of the Company and the Crown in this period can shed some light upon these questions. The answer appears to lie in the growing importance of linen-armourers and other associated craftsmen in the Great Wardrobe, the institution responsible for supplying goods ranging from robes to military hardware to the King and the royal household. Once the Wardrobe became permanently established in London (from 1311), it became an important centre for the production of goods in the capital, and something akin to a 'factory' environment in a world dominated by the small workshop. Separate departments dealt with the manufacture of the various types of goods needed by the King, his family and household: by the close of the thirteenth century, the King's tailor headed a large department, while smaller, specialist sections had been created for the King's paviliner or tent-maker and also for his armourer. While the King's tailor had always been a key employee, the importance of the other two offices increased significantly with the onset of the wars with Scotland and France under Edward I and his successors.[35]

During the reign of Edward III there is evidence of connections between the London Tailors and these important royal servants. First, in May 1332 Edward's paviliner, John de Yakesley, acquired from Edmund Crepin a 'great and principal messuage [dwelling-house]' in the parishes of St Peter Cornhill, St Benet Fink and St Martin Outwich, together with a great gateway towards Cornhill and another gateway onto 'Bradestrete' (Threadneedle Street). In November 1345 Yakesley granted the property to a London merchant, John de Aystwick, and in July 1347 Aystwick conveyed it to twenty-six tailors. It was on this estate that the Tailors built their Hall, which the Company has occupied continuously ever since. At about the same time the Tailors were connected with Edward III's armourer, John de Coloigne, a linen-armourer who served the King in this capacity until his death in 1357.[36] Coloigne's involvement in the craft in the City had been apparent as early as 1334, when he was commissioned to provide clothing for 100 foot soldiers to campaign against the Scots. He was to be paid £11 15s. 8d., and an additional 14s. 2d. was allocated for wine for the tailors working under his direction.[37] He was a relative of Roger de Coloigne, one of the 'alms collectors' noted in 1351, and in 1340 both men had been named among the governors of the Tailors and Linen-Armourers in London. Seven years later John was named as one of the first trustees of the site of Tailors' Hall, and there is also evidence to connect him with Edmund Crepin, whose conveyance to Yakesley had started the whole process.[38]

These links continued into the later fourteenth century through such men as Thomas Carleton, an embroiderer who was one of Coloigne's successors as royal armourer. He too became an influential member of the Fraternity of St John the Baptist, and on his death in 1389 left substantial property in Wood Street to the fraternity on condition that a priest was found to sing for his soul daily in St Paul's Cathedral.[39] The adoption of the name 'Tailors and Linen-Armourers' was therefore a direct recognition of the importance of men such as Coloigne and Carleton within the craft, and of the status they had attained within the Great Wardrobe of the King by virtue of their specialist skills. The Company retained this name until 1503 when a charter granted by Henry VII reincorporated it as the Merchant Taylors' Company. Symbolism also ensured that John de Yakesley's place in the Company's early history was not forgotten: in 1481 the Tailors' first grant of arms incorporated a pavilion into the design, and in one of the Company's two pre-Reformation hearse-cloths the image of a pavilion is set between the blades of a pair of scissors (see Frontispiece and Fig. 15).[40]

FIGURE 7. Line drawing of the fourteenth-century undercroft, by Robert Randoll, *c.* 1910.
Guildhall Library

THE TAILORS AND THEIR HALL IN THE
FOURTEENTH CENTURY

Like most associations of its kind, the Fraternity of St John the Baptist needed a physical space for its activities, such as the collection of quarterly alms payments or the celebration of the annual feast day. Premises were especially important as a forum for resolving disputes between craftsmen and for drawing up and enforcing regulations. Many of the craft fraternities founded in the thirteenth and fourteenth centuries were initially located in religious houses or parish churches: the Saddlers were attached to the college of St Martin le Grand, the Skinners to the church of St John Walbrook, and the Grocers to St Antholin's, while the Drapers became established first at St Mary of Bethlehem (by 1361) and later at St Mary le Bow.[41] Gradually each of these crafts acquired premises of its own, normally after a group of senior craftsmen or merchants had agreed to act as trustees for this purpose. Predictably, those crafts which later made up the 'Great Twelve' companies were at the forefront of this movement, and of these the Tailors were among the earliest to establish a permanent home.[42] Unlike the halls of the Skinners or Goldsmiths, however, Tailors' Hall does not seem to have been in a part of London closely associated with their trade. Indeed the choice of site in what was then known as Broad Street may have been purely accidental, based upon little more than John de Yakesley's own connections with that part of London.

The history of the site has been well documented, and only the essentials need be repeated here. In the late thirteenth century a 'principal mansion' in Cornhill, with the houses adjoining it, was acquired by a prominent alderman, Ralph Crepin, who conveyed it to his son Walter in 1299. The property then passed to Walter's own son, Edmund, who held it until May 1332 when, as we have seen, it was sold to John de Yakesley. The Company's own archive contains copies of all these deeds, and of the subsequent transactions in which the property was conveyed to John de Aystwick who then, in July 1347, settled it upon a group of twenty-six tailors.[43] Unfortunately, whatever their value for details of ownership, such documents do not reveal much about how the buildings were used. Did the Tailors and Linen-Armourers start meeting there soon after Yakesley's purchase in 1332, or only in 1347 when the site was settled on the fraternity's trustees? No definitive answer is possible: all that can be said is that the estate passed through the hands of a number of trustees, until in June 1392 the Master and Wardens of the Fraternity of St John the Baptist purchased from the Crown a licence allowing property to be granted to the fraternity 'in mortmain'. This was necessary to fulfil the provisions of a statute passed the previous year which had attempted yet again to restrict the granting of property into the 'dead hand' of the Church, and of other institutions with religious functions such as guilds and fraternities. By the late fourteenth century many fraternities were seeking to acquire property in their own right, but the statute of 1391 required them to obtain a licence, or alternatively a charter, for this purpose.[44] The licence, obtained on 23 June, enabled Simon Winchecombe, citizen and armourer, and his three fellow trustees to grant to the Fraternity of St John the Baptist

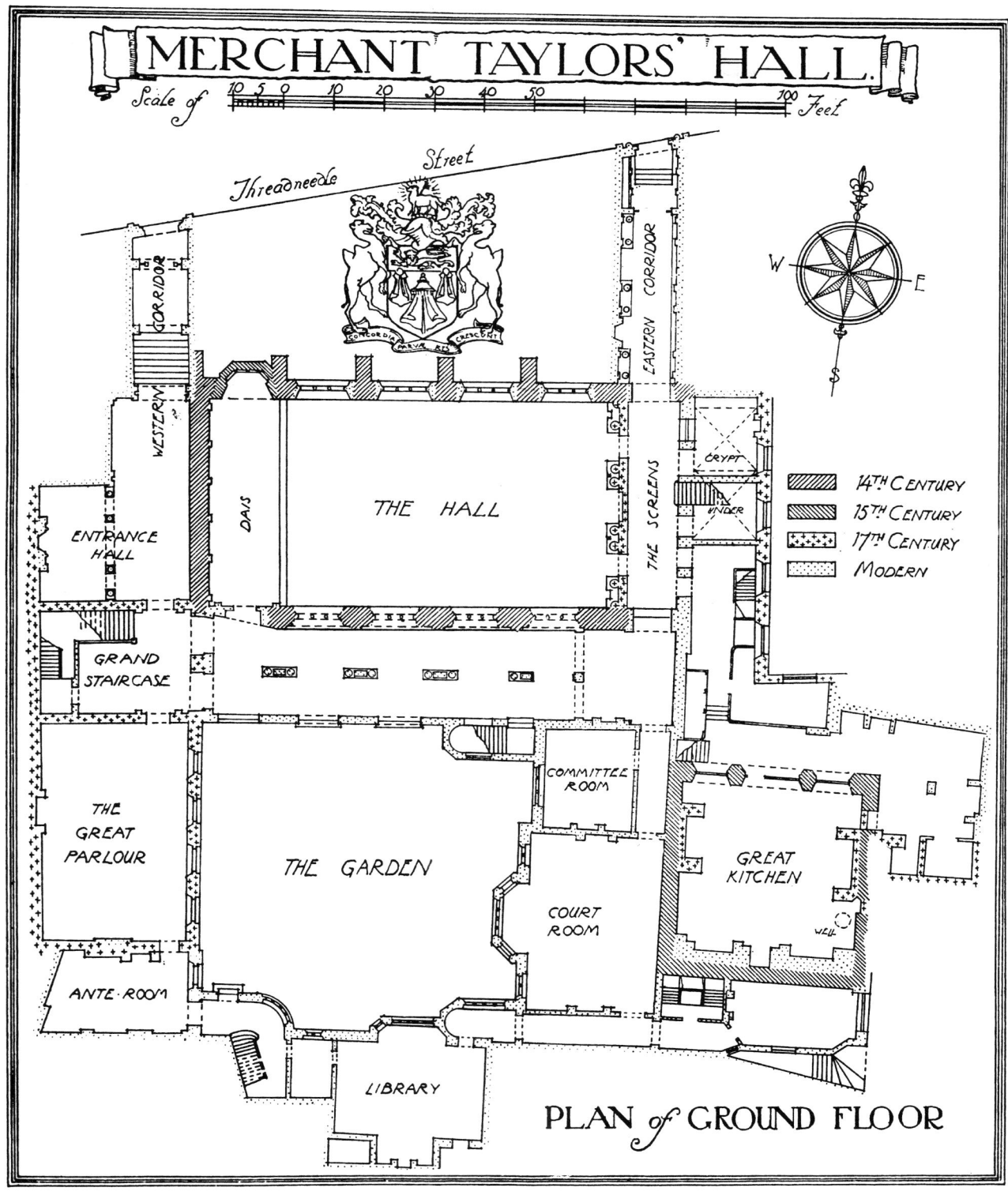

FIGURE 8. Plan of the pre-war Hall buildings showing the phases of building.
Royal Commission on Historical Monuments, 1929

all those two messuages and eleven shops of which one messuage called 'Taillourshalle' and the aforesaid eleven shops are on the south side of Brade Street [Threadneedle Street] in the parishes of St. Benet Fink and St. Martin Outwich, and the other messuage is on the north side of Cornhill in the parish of St. Peter Cornhill.

The conveyance itself was dated 24 June, the feast of the Nativity of St John the Baptist, the day of the fraternity's annual feast and elections.[45]

This marked the final stage in the acquisition of the site by the Tailors, a process which had begun almost exactly sixty years before. The messuage in the parish of St Peter Cornhill is probably to be identified with the 'principal mansion' owned by Crepin, and which stood on the site of what is now No. 2 White Lion Court. In the early fifteenth century it was rented out, first to the Earl of Devon and later to a succession of schoolmasters, for £6 13s. 4d. per annum and was described as 'le viell' hostiell' ('the old hall'). The phrase suggests that it was the Tailors' first meeting place, and was superseded by 1392 by the other messuage on the site, now known as 'Taillourshalle', which lay slightly further north in the parish of St Martin Outwich.[46] This is where the common hall has stood ever since. Its medieval foundations were uncovered during excavations in 1910 and 1919 (see Figs 5 and 6), and investigation of these suggests a building date in the latter half of the fourteenth century, after the site as a whole was settled on the twenty-six tailor trustees. With the incorporation of other buildings, 'Tailors' Hall' came to include associated rooms such as the kitchens (known to exist in 1388), a parlour, chapel and court room; to the east of the common hall are two surviving bays of an undercroft, which also date from the fourteenth century (see Fig. 7). As we will see, further building works took place in the fifteenth century and survivals of these include an enlarged kitchen and an oriel window, incorporated into the north-west corner of the common hall (see Fig. 8).[47]

By 1400, therefore, the Tailors and Linen-Armourers had become established in what has been the Company's home for the last six hundred years. The speed with which it did so, compared with some of the other greater companies, was testimony to the important connections established in the early fourteenth century by members of the fraternity with individuals such as Yakesley, whose patronage and assistance were invaluable. This achievement was all the more remarkable because the craft, though large and diverse, did not yet possess wealthy and influential figures such as headed the mercantile crafts of the Drapers, Mercers and Grocers. As the next chapter will show, the rising fortunes of the Fraternity of St John the Baptist were closely linked with the ambitions of members of the craft to achieve greater prominence in business and among the City's ruling élite.

NOTES

1. *Chronicles of the Mayors and Sheriffs of London AD 1188–1274, and the French Chronicle of London, AD 1259–1343*, ed. by H. T. Riley (1863), p. 253.
2. Among the classic works on this subject are: W. Herbert, *The History of the Twelve Great Livery Companies of London*, 2 vols (1834–37); G. Unwin, *The Gilds and Companies of London* (1908, 4th edn 1963); and S. L. Thrupp, *The Merchant Class of Medieval London* (Chicago, 1948, repr. Ann Arbor, 1962). For recent contributions on particular companies, see E. M. Veale, *The English Fur Trade in the Later Middle Ages* (Oxford, 1966), on the Skinners; T. F. Reddaway and L. E. M. Walker, *The Early History of the Goldsmiths' Company, 1327–1509* (1975); I. W. Archer, *The History of the Haberdashers' Company* (Chichester, 1991); and P. Nightingale, *A Medieval Mercantile Community: The Grocers of London, 1000–1485* (New Haven, 1995).
3. A. F. Sutton, 'The Silent Years of London Guild History before 1300: The Case of the Mercers', *Historical Research*, 71, no. 175 (1998), pp. 121–41; E. M. Veale, 'The "Great Twelve": Mistery and Fraternity in Thirteenth-Century London', *Historical Research*, 64 (1991), pp. 237–63; M. Davies, 'The Tailors of London: Corporate Charity in the Late Medieval Town', in *Crown, Government and People in the Fifteenth Century*, ed. by R. E. Archer (Stroud, 1995), pp. 161–90; M. Davies, 'The Tailors of London and their Guild, c. 1300–1500' (unpublished D.Phil. thesis, University of Oxford, 1994), ch. 1.
4. Thrupp, *Merchant Class*, pp. 2–3; C. M. Barron, 'London 1300–1540', in *The Cambridge Urban History of Britain. Volume I: 600–1540*, ed. by D. M. Palliser (Cambridge, 2000), p. 400.
5. C. M. Barron, 'The Later Middle Ages: 1270–1520', in *The British Atlas of Historic Towns, III: The City of London from Prehistoric Times to c. 1520*, ed. by M. D. Lobel (Oxford, 1989), pp. 43–44; Barron, 'London 1300–1540', pp. 403–04.
6. E. M. Veale, 'Craftsmen and the Economy of London in the Fourteenth Century', in *The Medieval Town 1200–1500: A Reader in English Urban History*, ed. by R. Holt and G. Rosser (1990), pp. 127–28.
7. C. R. Burgess, '"A Fond Thing Vainly Invented": An Essay on Purgatory and Pious Motive in Later Medieval England', in *Parish, Church and People*, ed. by S. Wright (1988),

pp. 56–84; S. Reynolds, *Kingdoms and Communities in Western Europe 900–1300* (Oxford, 1984), ch. 3, esp. pp. 67–75; Davies, 'Charity', pp. 161–90; B. McRee, 'Charity and Gild Solidarity in Late Medieval England', *Journal of British Studies*, 32 (1993), pp. 195–225; G. Rosser, 'Going to the Fraternity Feast: Commensality and Social Relations in Late Medieval England', *Journal of British Studies*, 33 (1994), pp. 430–46.

8. On this subject see, for example, Reynolds, *Kingdoms and Communities*; D. Palliser, 'The Trade Guilds of Tudor York', in *Crisis and Order in English Towns 1500–1700*, ed. by P. Clark and P. A. Slack (1972), pp. 86–116; R. Mackenney, *Tradesmen and Traders: The World of the Guilds in Venice and Europe, c. 1250–c. 1650* (1987); R. F. E. Weissman, *Ritual Brotherhood in Renaissance Florence* (1982); S. L. Thrupp, 'The Gilds', in *The Cambridge Economic History of Europe*, III, ed. by M. M. Postan, E. E. Rich and E. Miller (Cambridge, 1963), pp. 230–80.

9. Veale, '"Great Twelve"', pp. 240–52.

10. Nightingale, *Grocers*, pp. 43–49. The pepperers (later the Grocers) were among eighteen unlicensed guilds fined as early as 1180: *Pipe Roll 26 Hen. II*, p. 153.

11. Veale, '"Great Twelve"', pp. 249–50, 256–57; M. Davies, 'Artisans, Guilds and Government in London', in *Daily Life in the Late Middle Ages*, ed. by R. H. Britnell (Stroud, 1998), pp. 125–28.

12. Veale, '"Great Twelve"', pp. 237–63.

13. *De Antiquis Legibus Liber*, ed. by T. Stapleton, Camden Society, 34 (1846), pp. 55–57.

14. Sutton, 'Silent Years', pp. 134–37.

15. Nightingale, *Grocers*, p. 81; Sutton, 'Silent Years', pp. 135–37.

16. *Chronicles of Edward I and Edward II*, ed. by W. Stubbs, 2 vols, Rolls Series (1882–83), I, *Annales Londonienses*, pp. 85–86; *CPMR*, 1364–81, p. xxvii.

17. *Cal. Letter Bk B*, p. 241; *C*, p. 84.

18. *Cal. Letter Bk E*, pp. 12–14.

19. For discussion of the significance of this charter, see G. A. Williams, *Medieval London: From Commune to Capital* (1963), p. 282; Thrupp, *Merchant Class*, pp. 3–4; Nightingale, *Grocers*, pp. 144–45.

20. Veale, '"Great Twelve"', pp. 253–54; Veale, *Fur Trade*, pp. 44–47; *Two Early London Subsidy Rolls*, ed. by E. Ekwall (Lund, 1951), pp. 85–86.

21. *De Antiquis Legibus Liber*, ed. by Stapleton, p. 99.

22. Sutton, 'Silent Years', p. 121; *CWCH*, I, p. 38.

23. J. Stow, *A Survey of London*, ed. by C. L. Kingsford, 2 vols (Oxford, 1908), I, p. 181. The italics are Stow's.

24. The inventories are now GL, MSS 34360; 34361, p. 3. Book 'I' is now GL, MS 34010/1. See also H. L. Hopkinson, *Report on the Ancient Records in the Possession of the Guild of Merchant Taylors of the Fraternity of St. John the Baptist in the City of London* (1915), pp. 99–101. For the remnants of these earlier books, see *The Merchant Taylors' Company of London: Court Minutes, 1486–1493*, ed. by M. Davies (Stamford, 2000), pp. 6–8.

25. Hopkinson, *Ancient Records*, pp. 3, 105; Clode, *Memorials*, p. 2n.

26. The Skinners' Fraternity of Corpus Christi did not come to have full control of the mistery until the 1340s, while at least one other mistery contained rival associations: the fraternity founded by the drapers of Cornhill came to govern that craft, not the equally prominent guild of the associated craft of 'burellers' in St Mary Abchurch: Unwin, *Gilds and Companies*, p. 106; Veale, *Fur Trade*, p. 107.

27. *Cal. Letter Bk B*, p. 185; *C*, pp. 67–68; *Cal. Early Mayor's Court Rolls*, ed. by A. H. Thomas (Cambridge, 1924), p. 180.

28. GL, MS 34127 (the Company's 'Wills Book'), p. 12; Davies, 'Charity', pp. 161–90. See also C. Tyerman, *England and the Crusades 1095–1588* (Chicago, 1988), ch. 10; T. Smith, *English Gilds*, Early English Text Society, 40 (1870), pp. 157, 177, 180, 182, 231. There also existed at Ludlow a guild of 'palmers', i.e. of pilgrims who had returned from the Holy Land with a palm branch, ibid., pp. 193–99.

29. The subsequent development of the fraternity is explored below, Chapter Two.

30. *The Charters of the Merchant Taylors' Company*, ed. by F. M. Fry and R. T. D. Sayle (1937), pp. 12–13.

31. *Cal. Letter Bk E*, pp. 231–34; *F*, pp. 52–53; GL, MS 34004, fols 23^v–24. For the origins of the Court of Assistants, see Davies, *Court Minutes*, pp. 3–6.

32. *Cal. Letter Bk G*, pp. 161–62.

33. C. Blair, *A History of the Armourers' and Brasiers' Company* (forthcoming), Ch. 1.

34. *Cal. Letter Bk E*, pp. 231–34.

35. T. F. Tout, *Chapters in Administrative History*, 6 vols (Manchester, 1927–33), IV, pp. 389–91; Veale, 'Craftsmen and the Economy of London', p. 132.

36. GL, MS 34127, pp. 2–6.

37. R. R. Sharpe, *London and the Kingdom*, 3 vols (1894–95), I, pp. 179–80; CLRO, Letter Book E, fol. 1. The full list of items to be supplied was not included in the printed calendar.

38. *Cal. Letter Bk F*, pp. 52–53; GL, MS 34130 (the Company's 'Evidence Book'), pp. 6–8; CLRO, Husting Rolls (HR), 71/23.

39. *CWCH*, II, pp. 272–73; GL, MS 34127, pp. 5–6; Davies, thesis, p. 57. See also H. Kleineke, 'Carleton's Book: William FitzStephen's "Description of London" in a Late 14th-Century Common-place Book', *Historical Research*, 74 (2001), pp. 117–26.

40. See Chapter Four.

41. Unwin, *Gilds and Companies*, pp. 95–107; Veale, '"Great Twelve"', pp. 258–59.

42. For the early company halls in general, see J. Schofield, *The Building of London from the Conquest to the Great Fire* (1984), pp. 116–17. For the use of trustees, see below, n. 44.

43. The transactions are recorded in detail in H. L. Hopkinson, *The History of Merchant Taylors' Hall* (Cambridge, 1931), pp. 5–11; GL, MS 34130, pp. 2–12.

44. In 1272 the Statute of Mortmain was passed to slow the rate at which property was being granted permanently away from the Crown and into the 'dead hand' (*mortmain*) of the Church. Guilds and fraternities of all kinds, because of their religious functions, were covered by this legislation. To circumvent the law it became common for property to be held by trustees, usually members of the fraternity concerned, who would then 'allow' the fraternity to use the premises, and ensure compliance with the law. See H. M. Chew, 'Mortmain in Medieval London', *English Historical Review*, 60 (1945), pp. 8–15.

45. *CPR*, 1391–96, p. 139. An inquisition held in that year, prior to the alienation, valued the properties at £10, which was almost certainly an underestimate: PRO, Chancery Inquisitions *Ad Quod Damnum*, C143/413/13; GL, MS 34130, pp. 2–12.

46. This distinction was noted by Hopkinson, *Merchant Taylors' Hall*, p. 10.

47. J. Schofield, *Medieval London Houses* (1994), pp. 44, 69–70; Schofield, *The Building of London*, p. 117; Hopkinson, *Merchant Taylors' Hall*, pp. 17–18, 41–47, 53–54; GL, MS 34130, p. 10.

CHAPTER TWO

'GHOSTLY TREASURE': THE FRATERNITY OF ST JOHN THE BAPTIST 1350–1530

BY THE END of the fourteenth century most of London's major crafts had established organizations for their most important members, usually in the form of 'guilds' or 'fraternities'. The Fraternity of St John the Baptist, founded by the City's tailors and linen-armourers, was at the forefront of this movement, and the aim of this chapter is to trace its development over the ensuing two centuries. During this period the Fraternity of St John the Baptist grew into the largest and most extraordinary of those founded by the London crafts, and might with some justification be viewed as one of the most remarkable of the craft fraternities founded in late medieval England. This chapter will focus on a number of key themes in the fraternity's history, such as its active recruitment of 'honorary' members, the employment of priests in its own chapels and elsewhere in London, the growing importance of charitable provision, and the significance of the annual feast.

The Tailors were well aware of the significance of their fraternity, and were keen to advertise its qualities. In 1464–65 a payment of 10s. 1d. was noted in the Master's accounts for 'the composition, writing, illuminating and painting of a table of indulgences and remissions of this fraternity granted by divers Popes, archbishops, bishops and other prelates ... which hangs in the church of St. Paul's'.[1] The 'table' — probably painted on a wooden board — was intended to be displayed in a chapel by the north door of the cathedral church, dedicated to St John the Baptist, which the fraternity had used for many years as a place of worship. While the original table no longer survives, its contents were incorporated, along with a full set of the Company's ordinances, into a fine early-sixteenth-century illuminated manuscript book. The earlier material was originally put together in 1456, and includes a list of indulgences and other religious privileges granted to the fraternity which must have formed the basis of the illuminated table in St Paul's in 1464–65. It placed great emphasis upon the 'goostly tresoure' built up by the fraternity over many years, and went on to list these spiritual 'assets' in great detail. They included the fraternity's charitable activities, its chapels at the Hall and in St Paul's, and its 'confraternal' links with no fewer than eight religious houses in and around London.[2] No comparable series of documents survives for any other London livery company, and this unique statement of the fraternity's spiritual heritage is testimony to the way in which London's tailors created an organization which went far beyond what was usual for a craft fraternity, even in a city as large and diverse as London (see Col. Pls IIIA and VIB).

MEMBERSHIP

The most striking feature of the Fraternity of St John the Baptist was its recruitment of members from outside the ranks of the craft. These men and women normally paid the same admission fee (20s.) as tailor members and were required to contribute to the alms box of the fraternity on a quarterly basis just like everyone else. At the same time, it was made clear that these non-tailor members would have no say in the running of the fraternity or the wider craft, could hold no office within it, and could not benefit themselves from the alms payments they made. The difference between the two categories of members was reflected in the fact that the so-called 'oute broders' had to swear a different oath on admission to that of their tailor counterparts. Tailor brothers had to swear to obey the rules and ordinances of the craft, to attend quarter-days and other meetings when summoned, and not to 'refuse nor forsake the crafte of tayllours for noon other'. Their non-tailor counterparts, on the other hand, promised merely not to take legal proceedings against their fellows, nor to give their livery robes to a disgraced brother, and to pay all their membership dues. These oaths were recorded in a book compiled by the Clerk in 1491 and which survives in the archive of the Company. The establishment of a distinct category of membership for those from outside the craft was an important step in enabling the fraternity to recruit widely, without jeopardizing its identity as the Fraternity of St John the Baptist of Tailors and Linen-Armourers. This recruitment was dramatic, with more than a thousand non-tailors admitted in the first half of the fifteenth century (see Table 1).

So who were these non-tailor members? Admissions were recorded in the Master's accounts, alongside those of tailor liverymen, and so it is possible to construct a more or less complete list of those who were admitted from 1398 until the early 1470s, when the Company's accounts for the next decade or so become too damaged to be useful. There is also evidence that the practice of admitting prominent individuals from outside the craft was already well established by the late fourteenth century. During what was to become a celebrated banquet held for James I at the Hall in 1607 (see below, Chapter 10), a 'roll in vellum' was presented to the King by the Clerk of the Company on which were inscribed the names of 167 illustrious members who had been admitted from the 1350s until the reign of Henry VIII. The roll appears now to be lost, but the contents were copied into the Court minutes before this occurred. In the reign of Edward III (1327–77) admissions included Roger, Lord Mortimer, Humphrey de Bohun, Earl of Hereford, and Simon Sudbury, the Bishop of London murdered by Wat Tyler's rebels in 1381.[3] From 1398 onwards the names read more and more like a *Who Was Who* of late-medieval English society. At the top were reigning monarchs such as the victor of Agincourt, described in glowing terms as 'nostre tres excellent seigneur le roi henri quinte' (admitted in 1413–14). Henry's two brothers, John, Duke of Bedford (1406–07) and Humfrey, Duke of Gloucester (1413–14) were also admitted, as were two brothers of Edward IV, Richard, Duke of Gloucester (later Richard III), and the equally ill-fated George, Duke of Clarence. Both were admitted in 1462–63. Noble families, such as the Percies, Nevilles, Staffords and Beauchamps, were also well represented. The admissions lists, particularly those of the first half of the fifteenth century, are practically a roll-call of the English nobility in the turbulent period which saw the outbreak of civil war during the 'Wars of the Roses'.

Yet the roll presented to James I merely listed the most important of these so-called 'honorary' members, those whose names would impress a visiting monarch. The 167 prominent noblemen and clergy admitted between 1351 and 1510 were far outnumbered by more than a thousand other men and women whose admission fees are also recorded in the fifteenth-century accounts. Slightly lower down the social scale, for example, the Tailors admitted important knights, esquires and gentlemen, including famous soldiers such as Sir John Fastolf and Sir Andrew Ogard who had been at the forefront of the English campaigns in France during the latter stages of the Hundred Years' War, as well as royal officials such as Thomas Chaucer, Speaker of the House of Commons and son of the poet. Members of the royal households of the period were also prominent — Henry VI's apothecary, Richard Hakeday, was admitted in 1444–45. The clergy of England were also heavily represented, accounting for more than 150 admissions. As well as the rectors of various churches with which the Tailors were associated — particularly St Martin Outwich — clergymen and members of religious orders from many parts of the country were admitted as brothers of the fraternity. These included five bishops of London, three bishops of St Davids, and Henry Beaufort, the powerful Cardinal Bishop of Winchester and financial backer

TABLE 1
Admissions to the Fraternity of St John the Baptist, 1398–1473

Years	Tailors	Non-tailors	Total
1398–1445	487 (10.36 *per annum*)	1031 (21.93)	1518 (32.29)
1453–1473	168 (8.4)	197 (9.85)	365 (18.25)
Total	655 (9.78)	1228 (18.33)	1883 (28.10)

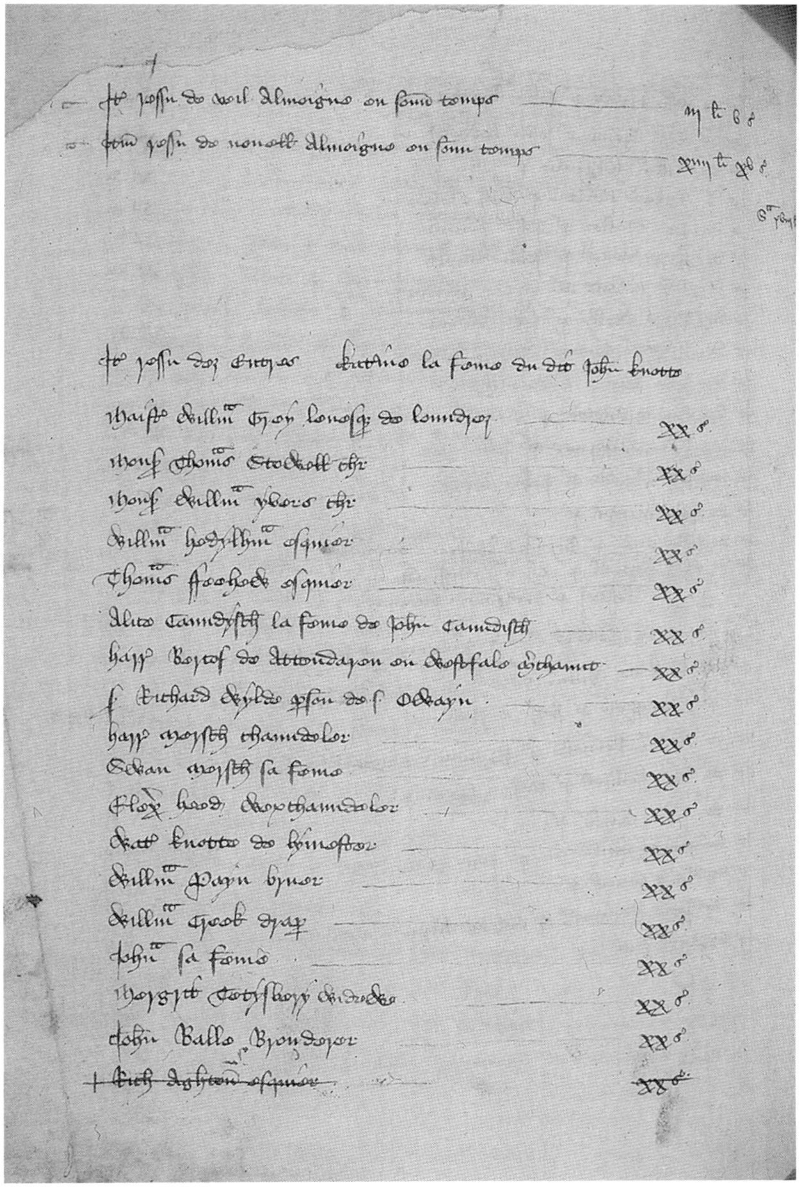

FIGURE 9. Admissions to the Fraternity of St John the Baptist, 1427–28. The list is headed by 'Maistre William Grey levesque de Loundrez', i.e. William Grey, Bishop of London.
Guildhall Library, MS 34048/1, fol. 183

of the Lancastrian kings. Abbots and monks were admitted from twelve religious houses, including Westminster Abbey (see Fig. 9).

The largest group (448) was made up of London artisans and merchants, men who were members of other companies but who nevertheless wished to share in the spiritual and social benefits of membership of the Fraternity of St John the Baptist. Among these were prominent mercers such as Richard Whittington and Geoffrey Boleyn (great-grandfather of the ill-fated Queen Anne), while the forty-two grocers included John Young and his apprentice, another future Mayor, (Sir) John Crosby. Despite the increasing rivalry between the Tailors and the Drapers (see below, Chapter Five), several prominent members of the latter company also joined the fraternity, including John Gedney, Mayor in 1427–28 and 1447–48, and John Norman, Mayor in 1453–54, who was said to have been the originator of the processions which took place on the Thames after the elections of the Mayor and Sheriffs. Lesser occupations were also represented, including the painters and stainers, some of whom were employed to decorate the Company's chapels, and a solitary individual described as a 'mattress-maker'. Parallels for this remarkable membership are few and far between in late medieval England. The nearest equivalents in London were the Skinners' Fraternity of Corpus Christi, which also recruited prominent individuals from other crafts, and the Fraternity of the Parish Clerks.[4] Outside the City, the closest parallels are with guilds which did not represent particular crafts, but instead acted as associations for the most prominent citizens of towns, regardless of occupation. An example is the important Holy Trinity Guild in Coventry, which recruited from the élite of the town, but also admitted gentry and merchants from other cities including London and Bristol.[5]

Despite its extraordinary recruitment, the Fraternity of St John the Baptist remained clearly identified with the Tailors and Linen-Armourers of London. This had obvious advantages: to secure economic and political objectives it was necessary to have friends in high places, all the more so in the case of both the Tailors and the Skinners, whose members were not as wealthy or as well connected as those of the Mercers, Grocers and Drapers in this period. We saw earlier how the Tailors and Linen-Armourers may well have owed their early prominence in London to connections with the Crown, and it is probable that they began admitting high-profile 'non-tailor' members partly as a way of continuing and extending these links. There were several occasions when these connections proved vital. One of these was the acquisition of a new charter by the Tailors in 1440. This proved highly controversial in the City, and particularly among the Drapers, who claimed that their rights to 'search' the shops of their workers for defective goods and illegal practices had been infringed. The charter itself was obtained with the help of Henry VI's uncle, Humfrey, Duke of Gloucester. The Duke had been admitted as a brother in 1413–14, and the Tailors had been careful ever since to cultivate him and his household: over the next two decades three tailors obtained the freedom of the City by redemption 'al request del duic de Gloucestre', while several members of the Duke's household, including his secretary Walter Sheryngton, were admitted as brothers of the fraternity. The link was strengthened still further by the admission of Eleanor Cobham, Duchess of Gloucester, in 1433–34, followed by her own secretary in 1438–39. While negotiations with the Crown for the charter were under way in 1439, the Tailors paid Gloucester £30, with another £8 6s. 8d. given to Adam Moleyns, Clerk of the royal Council, who had himself been admitted as a brother in 1437–38.[6]

Of even greater significance were the Company's links with Henry VII, who, in January 1503, conferred on it the title of Merchant Taylors' Company. The loss of the Master's accounts from 1484 to 1545 means that we cannot tell exactly when Henry was admitted as a member, although his name occurs on the roll presented to James I in 1607. From other sources it is apparent that the Company quickly established strong links with the first Tudor king. John Percyvale was elected as Master of the Company in the summer of 1485, and soon afterwards was the first member of the Company to be knighted. Several other prominent members supplied large quantities of cloth for Henry's coronation.[7] As we shall see, the charter of 1503 caused much controversy in the City — evidence, for many, of the Tailors' ambition. The grant to the Company formed part of a wider agreement with the King: in December 1503 the Master, Edmund Flower (founder of Cuckfield Grammar School), and the Wardens, entered into a formal agreement with Henry in which they undertook to celebrate an anniversary service in the church of St Martin Outwich, to be attended by all liverymen, to pray for his 'prosperous and happy estate' during his lifetime, and for his soul in perpetuity after his death. The agreement made mention of the 'special privileges and favours' bestowed on the Company by King Henry.[8] These events go some way towards explaining the Tailors' desire to admit prominent and influential people into their fraternity. So, too, does the chronology of these admissions: most took place during the first six decades of the fifteenth century, a crucial period which saw the Tailors acquire three charters, achieve representation for the first time on the City's Court of Aldermen, and build up substantial wealth through property endowments.

However, membership of the fraternity was not restricted to those who could be of practical use. It was extended far more widely, to include individuals from all walks of life and from many different parts of the country. One explanation is simply that a large membership was in itself beneficial to the public image of the fraternity. For those from 'lesser' crafts, membership of a more high-profile fraternity would have had a status value, and was perhaps a way of establishing vital social and business contacts. It should be remembered, however, that in the medieval period such 'worldly' concerns were often bound up with religious motivations. Fraternity membership was a popular means for laymen and women to express their piety through collective devotion and mutual support, and to benefit from the prayers of their fellow brothers and sisters.[9] In London, as we have seen, the Tailors' fraternity stood out in the way in which it recruited members from beyond the ranks of the craft of tailoring. The surviving wills of the period contain many bequests to guilds and fraternities in the City, and from these it is clear that the Fraternity of St John the Baptist was a popular target for men and women wishing to make provision for their souls. As early as 1369, for instance, William Passeware, a draper, asked his executors to divide half his goods between certain churches, hospitals, monasteries and the Fraternity of St John the Baptist. The number of bequests from non-tailor members increased in the fifteenth century: in July 1400 a draper named Robert Somerset left the sum of 5 marks (£3 6s. 8d.) to the Tailors, more than three times the amount he left to his own company. Six years later John Mapylton, citizen and marbler, left 13s. 4d. to the alms box of the Fraternity of St John the Baptist 'of which I am a brother'.[10] Naturally, such bequests were far outnumbered by those from London tailors, the most important of which involved bequests of property. Yet even by the 1460s, when bequests from outside the craft were less common, the Tailors could still count on legacies from men such as John Bracy (d. 1470), a tallow-chandler.[11] The admission of men and women from outside the craft was not solely an exercise in public relations or in political advancement, therefore, but reflected the importance of the fraternity's religious and charitable functions and its place in the religious culture of pre-Reformation London.

CHAPELS AND CHAPLAINS

Religious observance lay at the heart of the activities of lay fraternities, including those founded within crafts. Masses were said and sung for the souls of deceased members, and the act of praying for the soul of a brother or sister, or taking part in charitable giving, could in turn help to speed one's own soul through Purgatory. To fulfil this function the Tailors employed two full-time chaplains, who by the early fifteenth century celebrated Mass in the fraternity's two chapels, one at the Hall and the other in St Paul's Cathedral (Figs 10 and 11). It is not clear which of these chapels came into use first. While other craft fraternities — such as the Skinners' Corpus Christi fraternity — appear to have begun life attached to a parish church, there is no evidence that the Tailors were initially based in St Paul's before moving into their Hall. If, as suggested in Chapter One, the Tailors and Linen-Armourers were established in their Hall by the mid-fourteenth century, it is likely that the connection with St Paul's came later. Evidence for this can be found in the early-sixteenth-century description of the fraternity's 'goostly tresoure', which states that use of the chapel in St Paul's, 'halowed in thonoure of St. John Baptiste', was granted to the Tailors by Simon Sudbury, Bishop of London between 1361 and 1375. Initially the Tailors probably employed just one priest, but in 1389 the King's armourer and embroiderer, Thomas Carleton, left a substantial portfolio of property in the parish of St Alban Wood Street to the fraternity in order to fund the salary of a priest to sing Mass for his soul in the chapel in St Paul's in perpetuity, an arrangement known as a 'chantry'. From this point onwards, therefore, the Tailors were able to use this priest as a second chaplain to the Company as a whole.[12]

The chapel in St Paul's gave the fraternity a prominence that it exploited to the full. Between 1375 and 1381, for instance, the Archbishop of Canterbury and sixteen bishops were said to have granted an 'indulgence' of forty days' remission of sins to those 'that put theire helpyng handes to the laude of God in this chapell'; and in 1399 the fraternity obtained a

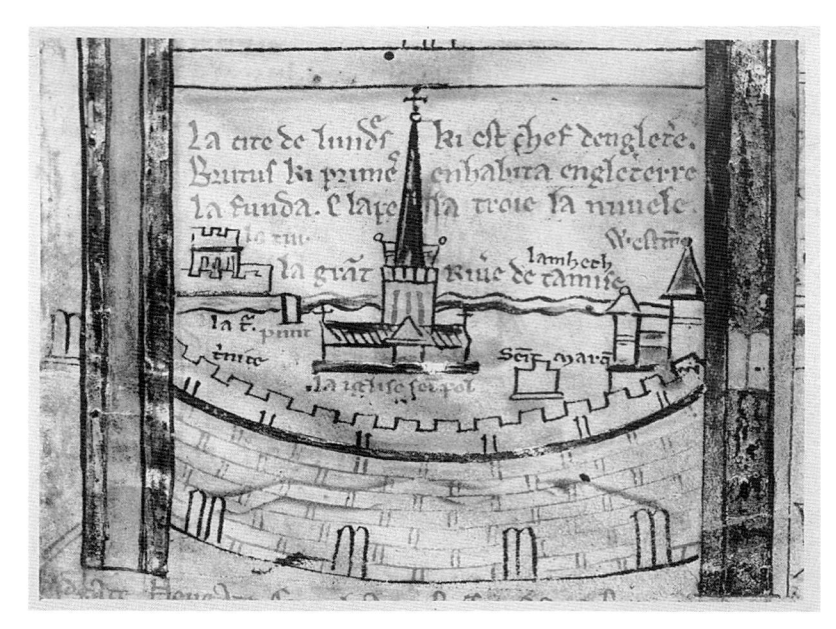

FIGURE 10. View of London, c. 1250, showing St Paul's Cathedral. From the late fourteenth century the Company held services in a chapel in the Cathedral, dedicated to St John the Baptist. This scene is part of an illustrated itinerary depicting a journey from London to Jerusalem, in Matthew Paris, *Historia Anglorum*.
British Library, Royal MS 14. C. VII, fol. 2

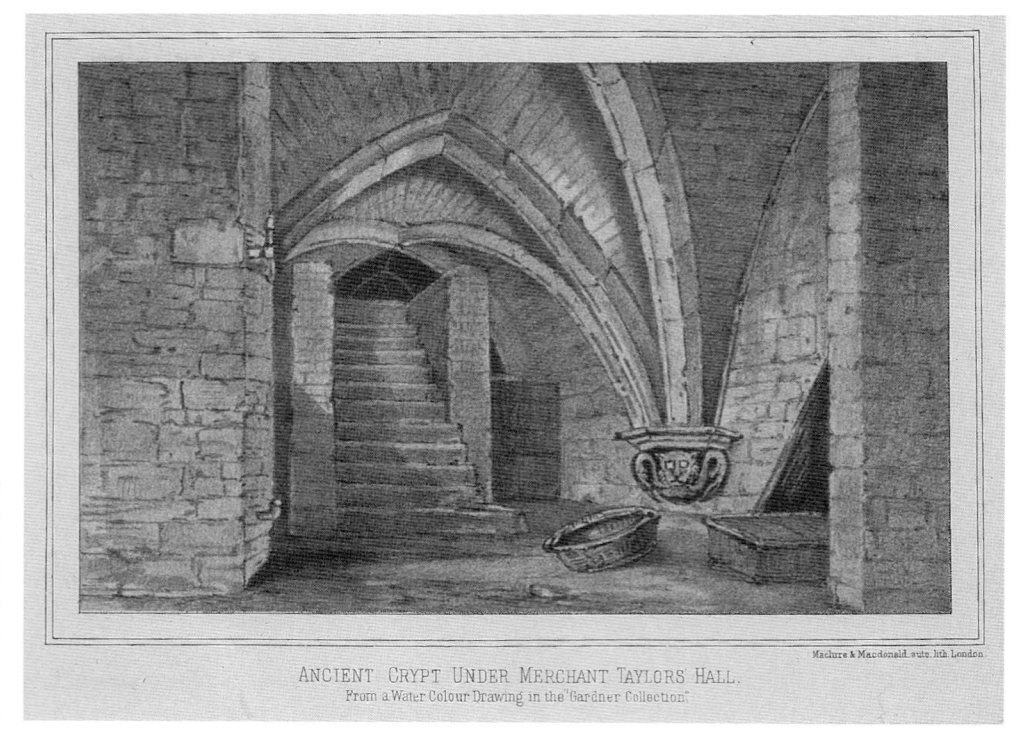

FIGURE 11. The fourteenth-century undercroft at Merchant Taylors' Hall, as engraved c. 1880. It is thought that the chapel may have stood above this, at the east end of the common hall.
Guildhall Library

grant from Pope Boniface IX of 100 days' remission 'to all cristen people that wyll putte to theire helpyng handes to the makyng of the said chapell or to the mayntenaunce of Goddes servyce in the said place', and to all those who visited the chapel on certain days and gave alms.[13] In the summer of 1454 the Bishop of London — himself a member of the fraternity — celebrated Mass in the chapel in St Paul's on the feast of the Nativity of St John the Baptist (24 June). By 1464, when new pews were installed at the fraternity's expense, there was no more appropriate place in which to display their table of grants and privileges to an admiring public.[14] In the meantime the Company's connection with St Paul's had been strengthened by the foundation of another chantry there, this time by Lady Beatrice de Roos, widow of Maurice, Earl of Desmond (d. 1358), Thomas, Lord Roos (d. 1384) and Sir Richard de Burley (d. 1387). By an agreement dated 12 April 1409, the Tailors agreed to pay a chaplain a salary of £8 out of property in Lime Street which she conveyed to the fraternity. In 1408–09 William Whaddon, the first 'chapeleyn de madame de Roos', was admitted to the fraternity, and the following year he received his first salary of £8.[15]

Despite these developments at St Paul's, the chapel in the Hall remained an important focus for the fraternity's worship. The exact location of this chapel remains unclear, but it is probable that it was located over the undercroft on the east side of the common hall (see Fig. 11).[16] Like the chapel in St Paul's, it was in frequent use: regular payments for the washing of vestments and altar-cloths in both chapels, and for the purchasing of candles, appear in the Master's accounts. In 1438 the chapel was refurbished, and a large quantity of Flemish cloth was bought and made into an altar-cloth, two side cloths and a 'frontell', which were then decorated by Roger Aleyn, the fraternity's resident painter-stainer. A further 26s. 8d. was paid for 30 feet of 'whitglas for the wyndow' — a luxury few companies could yet afford. A joiner was paid 20s. for 'le crest en le chapel' — perhaps containing elements of the Company's arms of 1481 — and a painter completed the job by painting and gilding the 'crest' and painting the chapel ceiling with gold stars. Four years later the finishing touches were put to the chapel when Aleyn was employed 'for makyng of the crucifixe'.[17] In 1455 the Tailors obtained formal permission from Pope Calixtus III to celebrate Mass and other divine services in the chapel at the Hall, although they had already been doing so for decades.[18] This was a clear demonstration of their commitment to maintain a fully functioning chapel and chaplains within their own premises, perhaps as a way of ensuring that the rituals of the fraternity could be kept private. One such ritual surrounded the election and installation of the new Master and Wardens, an early description of which occurs in the earliest Court minutes of the Company:

The same daye [5 July 1493] the forenamed maister and the iiij wardeyns sworen in the daye of Nativitee of Seint John Baptist last passed and his next predecessour Maister Povey and the iiij wardeyns late with the same M. Povey within the chapell perteignyng to this present place herd their Masse of tholy goste and after Masse don and seyde the new M. and the iiij wardeyns to hym electe came into this parlour and were sette in their romes and places by their said next predecessours . . .[19]

In the meantime the Tailors also acquired the advowson of the parish church of St Martin Outwich (Fig. 12). Until its demolition in 1874 this church lay close to the Hall, on the corner of Broad Street (now Threadneedle Street) and Bishopsgate Street. The advowson was granted to the Company by John Churchman, a London grocer and alderman who had long been connected with the Fraternity of St John the Baptist. In his grant, dated 20 July 1405, Churchman also conveyed to the Tailors four messuages and seventeen shops in the parish, some of which lay between Tailors' Hall and St Martin's and were, as part of the arrangement between the two parties, subsequently demolished to make way for an almshouse (see below).[20] Of all the benefactions made to the Company before the Reformation, this was undoubtedly one of the most important. From 1405 onwards St Martin's became another focus for the Tailors' religious observances, being larger than both of the chapels they were already maintaining. The close ties with the church were emphasized not just by the Tailors' right to choose and present the rector, but also by the decision taken by a number of prominent liverymen to be buried there and to make arrangements for the celebration in the church of Masses for their souls after their deaths. Indeed, by the time of the Chantries Acts of 1545 and 1547, which abolished such practices, St Martin's was the location for three chantries (with priests saying Mass daily) and ten annual services, known as 'anniversaries' or 'obits', celebrated for the souls of benefactors. These were all administered by what had by then become the Merchant Taylors' Company. Appropriately enough, the first of the chantries to be established in St Martin's was that of

FIGURE 12. North-east view of the church of St Martin Outwich by Robert West (d. 1770) and William Toms (d. c. 1750). The advowson of the church was granted to the Company in 1405. It was demolished in 1874, and its monuments moved to St Helen Bishopsgate.
Guildhall Library

Churchman himself, and his anniversary service was held on 25 January. The Company also paid half the salary of another chantry priest in the church, who celebrated Masses for the souls of John and William de Oteswich, who had substantially enlarged the church in the fourteenth century. The fine alabaster tomb of John de Oteswich and his wife is now in St Helen Bishopsgate (see Fig. 13). Also now in St Helen's is the tomb of Hugh Pemberton (d. 1500), who was Master of the Company in 1482–83 and an alderman from 1494 onwards. One of the wealthiest members of the Company at that time, he supplied cloth worth more than £75 for the coronation of Henry VII, and was a regular exporter of cloth to the Continent. He was buried in the chancel of St Martin's, and a chantry was established there by the Company out of a bequest made by Katherine, his widow, on her death in 1508.[21]

The foundation of chantries and anniversary services was the single most important reason for the dramatic expansion of the Company's income in the fifteenth century (see Table 2).

FIGURE 13. The tomb of John de Oteswich and his wife, formerly in St Martin Outwich and now in St Helen Bishopsgate. Their garments are elaborate and are the sort that would have involved skilled tailoring.

National Monuments Record, English Heritage

TABLE 2
Income and expenditure of the Fraternity of St John the Baptist, 1399–1465

Year	Total Income	Income from Property	Expenditure
1399–1400	£133 2s. 8d	£12 1s. 9d	£119 17s. 10d.
1424–25	£173 7s. 11d	£97 2s. 10d	£143 12s. 4d.
1444–45	£189 18s. 0d.	£105 3s. 10d.	£189 9s. 7d.
1464–65	£233 14s. 8d.	£155 4s. 8d.	£206 15s. 4d.

The usual means of establishing such arrangements was through a testamentary bequest, frequently of property. By the time of the Reformation the Company was paying the salaries of no fewer than nine priests out of the revenues of property left to the Company for that purpose. As well as those in St Martin's, a number were employed in other parish churches in London. Peter Mason, for instance, Master of the Company in 1407–08, was a well-respected parishioner of St Peter Cornhill and one of the founder members of a fraternity established there in 1403. When he came to make his will nine years later, he bequeathed extensive holdings to the Tailors, asking the Master and Wardens to pay a chaplain to celebrate Mass daily for his soul in St Peter's. The first of these chaplains, Thomas Bradenham, took up his duties in 1412–13 and received his annual stipend of £7 until his death in 1461, making him the fraternity's longest-serving fifteenth-century chaplain.[22] In common with much of the property acquired by the Company in this period, the income generated by Mason's tenements near the Great Conduit was more than enough to pay a chaplain. The Tailors received £12 13s. 4d. from tenants there in 1412–14, and in 1546 Mason's three substantial houses yielded £13 6s. 8d. per annum.[23] These arrangements were typical, and their successful management brought the Company further bequests of property.

The Company also administered a large number of anniversary services. Most were permanent foundations, and hence were also supported by bequests of property; others were temporary and could be paid for out of bequests of cash. The number of anniversary services grew rapidly during the fifteenth century, so that by 1545 no fewer than twenty services were held throughout the year in a dozen parish churches, a figure which does not include the numerous temporary anniversaries that had 'expired' by that date. The accounts and earliest Court minutes of the Company provide some details of what occurred on these days, a typical example being the anniversary of Hugh Cavendish (d. 1460):

Item thobite of Hugh Caundishe holden at Seint Martyns Oteswych the xij daye of Juyn and than spent in potacion, prestes, clerke, to the maister of the company, iiij wardeyns, the clerk, the bedell, chaundeler [waxchandler providing candles] and offeryng and for xxxvj quarters of coles distributed to thalmesmen accordyng to the last will of the said Hugh xviijs. vjd. ob.[24]

The 'potacion' referred to the food and drink that were consumed after Mass, normally comprising relatively simple fare such as bread, cheese, wine, and ale. In Cavendish's case, and in the case of several other benefactors, coals were distributed to residents of the Company's almshouse, or else to poor residents of the parish. This accounts for the relatively large sum of 18s. 6½d. which was spent on Cavendish's anniversary — the usual amount being between 5s. and 10s.

CHARITY

Charitable concerns were part and parcel of the functions of fraternities in the Middle Ages. Most expected their members to make regular payments to a 'common box', a source of income which could be used to help poor and sick brothers and sisters, and to provide those who died with a decent funeral. It is worth recalling here that the earliest Wardens of the Tailors and Linen-Armourers were known as 'alms collectors', and as the Company grew in size and wealth, charity remained a central function. Its activities were to be greatly expanded in the sixteenth century with school foundations, and, following the changes brought by the Reformation, with the reapplication of monies that would once have been spent on Masses and prayers to payments for the poor and sick. In the fifteenth century, assistance was directed exclusively at tailors who were members of the fraternity — liverymen — and their families.[25]

Each liveryman was expected to pay 1s. to the alms box every year, and this went some way towards meeting their obligations towards their less fortunate fellows. This income was swelled by the alms payments made by the so-called 'honorary' members of the fraternity, who were obliged to pay on the same basis. Inevitably, members who rarely came to Tailors' Hall were less reliable when it came to paying their dues: Robert Fitzhugh, Bishop of London from 1431 to 1436, failed to pay any alms at all during his time as a brother. His executors were more forthcoming and handed over 19s. 'for his alms, in arrears by 19 years' in 1436.[26] Alms income generally amounted to between £14 and £17 a year between 1400 and 1460, the years for which the most accurate figures can be calculated. By contrast, payments to almsmen and their families regularly exceeded £30 per annum, indicating that the Company was drawing substantially upon its other income streams, such as bequests, entry fees and income from property, in order to meet its obligations. The payments varied according to need, but by the 1450s the most needy almsmen received a total of 17d. a week. This was one of the highest stipends paid by any of the London companies: the Goldsmiths provided 14d. a week to nine poor goldsmiths, and the inmates of Richard Whittington's almshouse received a similar amount. Bequests were also used for one-off payments to the poor of the fraternity: in 1485 Stephen Trappys left £5 to be distributed among poor householders of the fraternity.[27] Charitable donations were encouraged through the oaths sworn by liverymen, in which they were asked to 'geve and bequethe in your testament to the almesse of Saynt John Baptist more or lesse after your estate and devocion in supportacion and contynuauns of the preestes and poure almesmen of the said crafte'.²⁸

The most impressive charitable achievement of the Company before the Reformation was the construction of its first almshouses, on land near the Hall, and adjacent to the church of St Martin Outwich, which was part of the grant made to the Tailors by John Churchman in 1405 (Col. Pl. XIB). Building work did not begin until after Churchman's death in 1413, and took more than two years. The total cost of more than £120 was partly offset by a levy of members of the livery that raised just over £51. The building itself, in the words of John Stow, took the form of a 'proper quadrant or squared court', and was intended to house seven poor liverymen and their wives. In the extensive surviving building accounts there are references to the construction of a 'cloister', as well as chimneys and a fountain, features that tie in well with the description given by Stow.²⁹ At the time the Tailors' almshouses were unique in London: they predated Richard Whittington's almshouses by almost a decade, and as a purpose-built, quadrangular structure were superior in design to most of the other company almshouses founded in this period. Surviving examples of this sort of design from the fifteenth century include 'God's House', founded at Ewelme in Oxfordshire by William and Alice de la Pole in 1437, and the re-founded St Cross Hospital at Winchester. Indeed, there are notable similarities of design between the Company's almshouses and those at Ewelme, not least the fact that both were located next to parish churches. As we have seen, there were close ties between the Company and St Martin's and there may even have been a door from the almshouses to St Martin's, as there was at Ewelme, through which the almsmen could pass to attend Mass and other divine services. The Company's first almshouses remained in use until the mid-seventeenth century: they were little damaged by the Great Fire in 1666, but thereafter the Company took the decision to lease out the site for development. As each of the seven almsmen died, no further appointments were made. In the meantime (1593) the Company had established a second set of almshouses at Tower Hill on land donated by Richard Hilles (see Fig. 47, below); these were enlarged in 1637 to provide a total of twenty-six houses.³⁰

As mentioned earlier, one of the key functions of all fraternities was the provision of funerals for those members unable to afford one. The Tailors took this obligation seriously, with the result that the accounts of the fraternity record payments for at least two funerals every year during the first three decades of the fifteenth century. In 1414–15, for instance, the burial of John Pampilon cost 6s. 8d. and another 14d. was allocated for a 'wyndyngcloth'.³¹ Funerals were also provided for some of the Company's officials. In 1476–77 the sum of 15s. 10d. was paid for the funeral expenses of Peter Ferrers, who served as Beadle from 1463 until his death. He came to the office fairly late in life after a career in the tailoring industry: he was apprenticed to Richard Nordon (Master 1422–23), and as a young freeman was a member of a contingent of armed men which the Company contributed in 1436 for the defence of Calais against the Duke of Burgundy.³²

By the later fifteenth century the funerals of prominent citizens were increasingly becoming public events, and it was important for the companies to help the relatives and executors to put on a good show. Wills of members of the Company in this period suggest that it was often expected that the Master, Wardens, Clerk and Beadle would attend, and it is likely that on many of these occasions liverymen were also present. In his will of 1485 William Marchall asked for 'men being in the lyvery of the crafte of taylours to bere my body at my decese to the churche and ley my body in my grave'.³³ A slightly different approach was taken in 1503 by Sir John Percyvale, the first member of the Company to be chosen as Mayor of the City, and founder of Macclesfield Grammar School. Like many other testators he asked that the twenty-four large candles that surrounded his coffin during the requiem mass should be held by poor householders of his parish (St Mary Woolnoth), but in his case he asked his executors to make sure that as many as possible were members of the Company. Each man was to have a russet hood and gown, with the name of Jesus embroidered on the right sleeve.³⁴ It is not clear whether all liverymen were required to attend funerals of their fellows in this period: the earliest complete set of ordinances of the Company (1507) states that only those who were specifically summoned were required to attend funerals, so much may have depended on the status of the deceased.³⁵ By the mid-sixteenth century many funerals had become very grand affairs, with the Company taking centre stage, and so there may have been greater pressure on liverymen to attend:

The iiij day of September [1558] was bered in Althermare parryche [St Mary Aldermary] in London master Dalbeney, marchand-tayller . . . and mony morners in blake, and mony clarkes and prestes; and all the compene of the clothyng of the marchand-tayllers, and after home to drynke as the compene, with spycyse bred; and the morow masse, and after to dener.³⁶

The Company possessed all the accoutrements necessary to mount a lavish funeral. The earliest full inventory of the contents of the Hall, dated 27 March 1512, listed not only the many items of plate, tapestry work and statuary given by benefactors over the years, but also wooden boxes containing banners for use on ceremonial occasions. One box held three silk banners each incorporating a different design: images of Our Lady, St John the Baptist, and the Holy Cross. Another contained a 'banner of Saint John' along with two streamers. The third, made of 'estriche borde' (timber from Scandinavia) contained 'the buriyng clothe and half a shete to lay within it', which may be the first documentary reference to the earlier of the two magnificent hearse-cloths which hang in the Hall today.³⁷ This first hearse-cloth, embroidered with scenes of the life of St John the Baptist, is thought to date from the last two decades of the fifteenth century, judging from the costume worn by some of the figures and by similarities with surviving examples from the Ironmongers', Fishmongers' and Vintners' Companies. It also incorporates motifs long associated with the Company: images of scissors denote the working practices of the City's tailors, while the pavilion may refer directly back to John de Yakesley, Edward III's tent-maker, who originally owned the site of the Hall (see Frontispiece and Figs 14 and 15). The representation of the *Agnus Dei* against the sun was incorporated into the Company's first grant of arms in 1481, and by 1512 was being used as a decoration for benches and other items at the Hall. The second hearse-cloth is more elaborate and is

FIGURES 14 and 15. Details from the earlier hearse-cloth (*c.* 1480–1500) of the two belonging to the Merchant Taylors' Company. The first depicts the burial of the headless St John the Baptist, while the second shows an angel carrying the Saint's head on a platter. On either side of these central scenes are motifs associated with the Company, such as a pair of scissors, a pavilion, and the Holy Lamb.
Merchant Taylors' Company

almost certainly of later date, possibly 1520–40. It reveals 'Renaissance' influences in terms of the iconography, costume, and design, but is undeniably pre-Reformation in its highlighting of the life of St John the Baptist. Unlike its predecessor, however, this hearse-cloth incorporates the Company's first set of arms (see Col. Pl. IIB).[38] In both cases the loss of the Company's account books for the period 1484–1545 means that it is not known whether the Company commissioned the hearse-cloths, or whether they were among the many items donated by liverymen.

FEASTING

An annual feast was another important feature of the activities of guilds and fraternities in the Middle Ages, and was maintained with enthusiasm by the London livery companies during the fourteenth and fifteenth centuries. The dinner itself formed just one part of the proceedings which accompanied the elections of the Master and Wardens, an event which, in the case of the Merchant Taylors, took place on the feast day of the Nativity of St John the Baptist (24 June), with the dinner itself often being held the following day.[39] The Company records show the development of this yearly celebration, which became increasingly elaborate (and expensive) as time went on. It became common, for instance, for prominent liverymen to leave substantial items of gold and silver plate to the Company for use or display at the annual feast: the 1512 inventory lists bowls, goblets and other items left by numerous former Masters or other senior members of the Company including John Swan (d. 1492), Richard Adyff (d. 1494–95), John Materdale (d. 1498), Sir John Percyvale (d. 1503), and Owen Boughton (d. 1505).[40]

Amidst this emphasis upon display, there is still evidence of the importance attached to the 'old aunciente ordynaunces and laudable custumes' as a way of drawing people together in a celebration of fraternity and the memory of former members.[41] The religious dimension to the annual feast was one area where continuity was especially important. The patronage of St John the Baptist was central to the celebrations: as early as 1401–02 the accounts record expenses for carving and painting an image of the saint for display in the Hall. Three decades later the Company was able to benefit from the largesse of one its eminent members, Henry Percy, Earl of Northumberland and son of Henry 'Hotspur', who had joined the Fraternity of St John the Baptist in 1419–20. The accounts for 1435–36 include a payment of 10s. to one of the Earl's servants for bringing an image of St John to the Hall. This may even have been the 'gret Image' of the saint which stood in the parlour in 1512, by which time the Company had also commissioned a gilt image which was displayed in a gold-plated tabernacle in the livery hall itself.[42] As well as these 'one-off' expenses, the Company established a regular pattern of expenditure around the time of the feast: large candles, or 'torches', were bought for the chapels in St Paul's and at the Hall, and these were then decorated by painter-stainers with the fraternity's devices of suns and tailors' shears. Meanwhile the linen and table-cloths belonging to the fraternity were washed ready for the celebrations, as were the altar-cloths from the chapels, in preparation for the services held in honour of the patron saint.

The importance of the annual feast was such that in the mid-1420s the Tailors decided to rebuild the kitchen at the Hall. This was an impressive undertaking, similar in scale to the building of the almshouses a decade before: between 1425 and 1433 more than £300 was spent on the new kitchen, although almost half the cost was met by a levy on the membership. The kitchen still survives, to the south-east of the common hall, and is still in use today. The most problematic decision was over the kitchen roof, which was built by a London carpenter named Thomas Winchecombe. Ever ambitious, the Company sent men by barge in 1432 'for to see kennyngton kechyn roof' (Kennington Palace, rebuilt by the Black Prince in the 1350s), to assist with the design of a timber roof, probably steeply pitched to allow smoke to escape.[43] The kitchen was finished the next year, and with it the Company acquired the facilities necessary to entertain in their Hall on a lavish scale. The accounts contain many details of the preparations made for such occasions, particularly for the annual feast of St John the Baptist. As the feast day approached, large quantities of pewter vessels were hired to cater for the guests: in June 1454, for instance, 1200 such vessels were provided by some of the City's pewterers. Other regular purchases included 'sotelteys' (table decorations, usually made of sugar), sixteen of which were bought every year for the feast.[44] Few details are recorded in the Company accounts of the food provided for the annual feast, or the many other dinners and celebrations held in the Hall. An exception is a menu which was written onto a blank page in the Company's earliest account book, and so can be dated to about 1430 (see notes for glossary):[45]

> *Le primer cours*
> *Brawn ove mustard*
> *Blank brewet de Rys*
> *Chynes of pork vel hakel beef*
> *Swan Rosted*
> *Ffesaunt vel capon Rosted*
> *Checons bake*
>
> *Jely vel Penynage*
> *Venison Rosted*
> *Partrich vel Cok rosted*
> *Plover Rosted*
> *Rabettes Soukers*
> *Snytes vel Quayles*
> *Frutur goodwyth*
> *Quynces Bake*

This was the sort of menu that would only have been prepared on very special occasions, and the prominence of small birds such as capon, cock, and partridge was very typical of grand feasts of this period. It can be compared with, for instance, the mutton, cheese, bread, garlic, and onions which were provided for one of the Company's annual 'searches' of tailors' shops in 1406–07, very much a 'working lunch'.[46] Entertainment was provided every year by minstrels, and from time to time money was also spent on trumpeters. The quality of the entertainment may well have varied from year to year, but in 1475–76 the Tailors were able to secure the King's minstrels for the feast. For another occasion, a dinner held at Christmas, the Duke of Gloucester, an important patron of the Company, allowed his 'mummers' to perform at the Hall, while more athletic entertainment was sometime provided by a 'tumbeler'.[47] The focus of the celebrations was the election of a new Master and Wardens for the coming year. We have already glimpsed something of the ritual which took place on election day, as the new Master and Wardens were set in their places by their predecessors after attending Mass in the chapel. The feast itself was a no less solemn occasion: as well as the food and entertainment, it also became an established custom for the new incumbents to be crowned with garlands of roses which they wore during the ensuing festivities.[48] Every effort was made to ensure that the feast was a great success, although it seems that not everyone was as enthusiastic about the celebrations as might have been expected. In May 1493, for instance, the Court of Assistants introduced fines of 20s. for former Wardens of the Company who failed to turn up to sit at the 'wardeyns table' at the annual feast. In condemning this behaviour the Court concluded that:

It is so now a dayes that many and divers persones of this same crafte which have borne thoffice and rome of a wardeyn have not in their myndes the grete othe and promys that they have taken and made unto God and Seint John their patron nether the penaltee that is assessed upon theym that breken thordynaunces nor they fere not as it semeth the grete and orrible peynes that God hath ordeigned for theym that wilfully be purjured, but folow their owne sensualitees and sinistre weyes intendyng by colour and fraudulent excuses to deceyve God and Seint John their foundour and the company.[49]

The need to protect the public image of the Company, when important guests attended the feast, was doubtless what led the Court to use such dramatic language.

The Fraternity of St John the Baptist thus grew from strength to strength in the century and a half before the Reformation. Bequests of property made in exchange for Masses and prayers led to a dramatic increase in the finance available to the Company, and this helped to pay for projects such as the construction of the almshouses, the refurbishment of the kitchen, and other building work at the Hall. An impressive religious framework, centred on the ritual life of the fraternity, underpinned all this. These ceremonials could be conducted in private, at the Hall, or else in the more public spaces of St Paul's and their patronal church of St Martin Outwich. This framework was supplemented by links with religious houses, by the celebration of chantries and anniversaries for the souls of deceased members, and by a remarkably successful policy of admitting members from outside the craft. For the Tailors the benefits were tangible, not just in the creation of an impressive set of buildings for both worship and feasting, but also in the wider recognition of the fraternity as a focus for devotion. As we shall see, the creation of such a prestigious and widely-supported fraternity enabled the Tailors to make their presence felt on the civic stage and beyond.

NOTES

1. GL, Merchant Taylors' Company, Master's accounts, MS 34048/2, fol. 261.
2. GL, MS 34004, fols 17–20.
3. The names on the roll are printed in Clode, *Early History*, I, pp. 293–303.
4. An edition of the Bede Roll of the Fraternity of Parish Clerks is currently being prepared for publication by Dr Norman James for the London Record Society.
5. See *The Register of the Guild of the Holy Trinity, St. Mary, St. John the Baptist and St. Katherine of Coventry*, ed. by M. D. Harris (Dugdale Society, 1935).
6. GL, MS 34048/1, fols 246, 305^v, 313^v, 317^v–19, 325^v–26.
7. These included Hugh Pemberton (Master 1482–83) and Walter Povey (Master 1492–93): *Court Minutes*, ed. by Davies, pp. 297, 300.
8. Translated and printed in Clode, *Early History*, I, pp. 347–50.
9. For the parish fraternities see C. M. Barron, 'The Parish Fraternities of Medieval London', in *The Church in Pre-Reformation Society: Essays in Honour of F. R. H. Du Boulay*, ed. by C. M. Barron and C. Harper-Bill (Woodbridge, 1985), pp. 13–37.
10. GL, Archdeaconry Court wills, MS 9051/1, fol. 179; Commissary Court wills, MS 9171/1, fols 447^v–48; MS 34048/1, fols 9, 38^v.
11. GL, MS 9171/6, fols 53^v–55.
12. *CWCH*, II, p. 272; H. Kleineke, 'Carleton's Book', *Historical Research*, 74 (2001), pp. 117–26.
13. GL, MS 34004, fols 18–19, and see *Calendar of Papal Registers*, V, p. 252. Of the London crafts in this period only the Brewers (in 1466) appear to have obtained a grant of this kind, for a chapel in the hospital of St Thomas of Acon: ibid., XII, pp. 453–54.
14. GL, MS 34048/2, fols 19^v, 247. The fraternity paid for the bread and wine used for the celebration of Mass by the bishop.
15. *CPR*, 1408–13, p. 40; W. Dugdale, *St. Paul's*, pp. 354–57; GL, MS 34048/1, fols 42^v, 49^v, 51, 96^v.
16. Schofield, *Medieval London Houses*, p. 69.
17. GL, MS 34048/1, fols 308^v, 351^v.
18. GL, MS 34004, fols 84^v–86; *Cal. Papal Regs.*, XI, pp. 240–41.
19. *Court Minutes*, ed. by Davies, p. 254.
20. *CPR*, 1405–08, p. 56.
21. *CPR*, 1405–08, p. 56; GL, MS 34048/1–3; *Court Minutes*, ed. by Davies, pp. 297–98.
22. *CPR*, 1401–05, p. 260 (26 April 1403); GL, MS 4158 (cartulary of the Fraternity of St Peter Cornhill); MS 9051/1, fols 274–76; MS 34048/1, fol. 75. The Tailors received 35s. from Bradenham's executors in 1461–62: GL, MS 34048/2, fol. 205^v.
23. PRO, Land Revenue, LR 2/241, fols 12–12^v.
24. *Court Minutes*, ed. by Davies, p. 220.
25. Those outside the livery, known as the yeomen or bachelors of the craft, could expect a limited amount of help from their own organization, also dedicated to St John the Baptist and known as the Bachelors' Company. This had its own 'common box' as early as 1414: see below, Chapter Three.
26. GL, MS 34048/1, fol. 265^v. In 1417–18 'maistir Robert ffitzhugh clerk' had been admitted as a 'confrere'; ibid., fol. 101^v.
27. Davies, 'Charity', pp. 173–74; GL, MS 9171/7, fol. 33^v.
28. GL, MS 34007, fol. 2.
29. GL, MS 34048/1, fols 78^v–79, 86^v.
30. W. H. Godfrey, *The English Almshouse* (1955), pp. 45–75. For Ewelme, see J. A. A. Goodall, *God's House at Ewelme* (Aldershot, 2001).
31. GL, MS 34048/1, fol. 83.
32. GL, MS 34048/1, fol. 276^v; 2, fol. 245; 3, fol. 105.
33. PRO, Probate Records, PROB 11/8, fols 333–35. For a similar will see GL, MS 9171/8, fols 117–17^v.
34. PRO, PROB 11/13, fols 191^v–93^v. Devotion to the Holy Name was popular among some of London's leading citizens and a fraternity was founded in the crypt of St Paul's which was dedicated to this cult: see Elizabeth A. New, 'The Cult of the Holy Name of Jesus in Late Medieval England, with Special Reference to the Fraternity in St. Paul's Cathedral, London *c.* 1450–1558' (unpublished Ph.D., University of London, 1999).
35. See Clode, *Memorials*, pp. 131–32.
36. *The Diary of Henry Machyn, Citizen and Merchant-Taylor of London, from AD 1550–AD 1563*, ed. by J. G. Nichols, Camden Society, 42 (1848), p. 173.
37. Clode, *Memorials*, p. 85. This identification remains uncertain, not least because the inventory does not describe the hearse-cloth in any detail, in contrast to the other items of tapestry work and embroidery that were listed.
38. For discussion, see Clode, *Memorials*, pp. 133–35.
39. See G. Rosser, 'Going to the Fraternity Feast: Commensality and Social Relations in Late Medieval England', *Journal of British Studies*, 33 (1994), pp. 430–46. The yeomen tailors, known from the 1490s as the Bachelors' Company, kept their feast on the Decollation of St John the Baptist (29 August): see below, Chapter Three.
40. Clode, *Memorials*, pp. 89 onwards.
41. *Court Minutes*, ed. by Davies, p. 247.
42. GL, MS 34048/1, fols 113, 271; Clode, *Memorials*, pp. 84–85.
43. GL, MS 34048/1, fols 166^v–69, 179, 221–22, 233, 242.
44. GL, MS 34048/2, fol. 19. £3 6s. 8d. was spent, at 8d. per dozen pieces of pewter.
45. This menu is written on a blank leaf (fol. 212) of the earliest account book of the Company, between the accounts for 1429–30 and 1430–31. Glossary: *Blank brewet* (i.e. *browet*) = a clear soup made of flesh-broth, with a thickening ingredient of rice in this case; *chynes of pork* = the backbone and adjoining flesh of a bacon-pig; *checons* = chickens; *penynage* = not identified; *snyte* = snipe or similar bird; *rabettes soukers* = sucking rabbits; *frutur*

goodwyth = perhaps fritters (*frutours*), using chopped meat from godwits, alternatively fruit of some kind. Source: *OED*.

46. GL, MS 34048/1, fol. 36^v.

47. GL, MS 34048/1, fol. 332^v; 2, fol. 75; 3, fol. 77.

48. Expenses for these garlands are recorded continuously throughout the fifteenth-century accounts: GL, MS 34048/1–3; *Court Minutes*, ed. by Davies, p. 167.

49. *Court Minutes*, ed. by Davies, pp. 245–46.

PLATE I

London, Westminster and part of Southwark in the mid-sixteenth century. First published in G. Braun and F. Hogenberg, *Civitates Orbis Terrarum* (1572), this version was issued in 1574. It still shows the spire of St Paul's Cathedral, although this had been destroyed by lightning in 1561.

Guildhall Library

PLATE II

A. St John the Baptist with the Holy Lamb. This scene is from an illuminated lectionary (Epistles and Gospels) that was owned by Sir Stephen Jenyns and presented to his parish church of St Mary Aldermanbury on the occasion of his election as Lord Mayor in 1508. See also Plate VIII.
British Library, Royal MS 2. B XII, fol. 19

B. The later of the two hearse-cloths belonging to the Merchant Taylors' Company. This one is *c.* 1520–40.
Merchant Taylors' Company

PLATE III

A. The Company's illuminated manuscript, begun *c.* 1510, containing a description of the 'goostly tresoure' of the Fraternity of St John the Baptist. See also Plate VIB.
Guildhall Library, MS 34004, fol. 17

B. The Company's Common Seal, *c.* 1503.
Merchant Taylors' Company

C. A tailor cutting cloth, depicted in a Book of Hours of the Blessed Virgin Mary, *c.* 1320–30.
British Library, Additional MS 6563, fol. 65

PLATE IV

'The Tailor', by Giovanni Battista Moroni (c. 1520/4–1578). White chalk marks or tacking stitches are visible on the cloth he is cutting.

By permission of the National Gallery

PLATE V

A. Transcript, c. 1510, of the first grant of arms to the Company, made by Clarenceux King of Arms on 24 October 1481.
Guildhall Library, MS 34004, fol. 21

B. *Reconciliation of the Skinners' and Merchant Taylors' Companies by Lord Mayor Billesden, 1484*, by Edwin Abbey, RA. This mural was paid for jointly by the Merchant Taylors' and Skinners' Companies and installed in the Royal Exchange in 1904.
By permission of the Mercers' Company

PLATE VI

A. The charter granted by Henry VII on 6 January 1503 which reincorporated the Tailors and Linen-Armourers as the Merchant Taylors' Company.
Merchant Taylors' Company

B. The Company's illuminated manuscript, begun *c.* 1510. These passages were crossed out at the Reformation as they referred to practices and beliefs that were now deemed 'superstitious'. See also Plate III.
Guildhall Library, MS 34004, fol. 11ᵛ

PLATE VII

A. Marian blue dalmatic vestment. This was among the rich collection of vestments and other religious artefacts given to St John's College, Oxford, by its founder, Sir Thomas White.
© *Oxford Picture Library / Chris Andrews*

B. Marian church processional banner, believed to have been given by Sir Thomas White to St John's College, Oxford.
© *Oxford Picture Library / Chris Andrews*

PLATE VIII

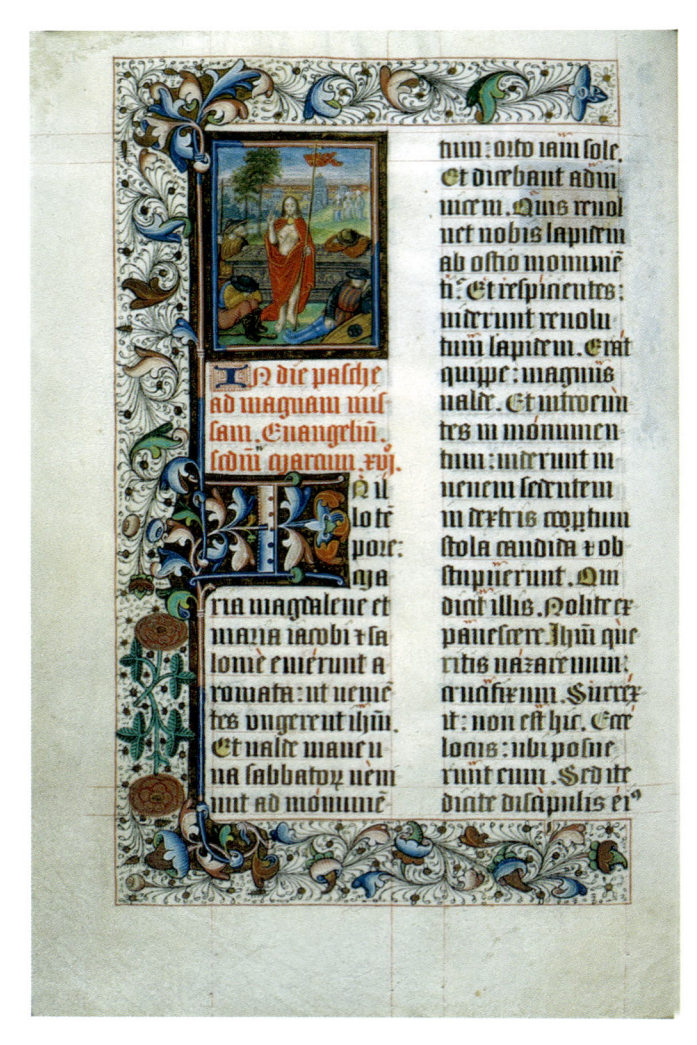

A. A page from the illuminated lectionary (Epistles and Gospels) owned by Sir Stephen Jenyns. It was presented to his parish church, St Mary Aldermanbury, on the occasion of his election as Lord Mayor in 1508. See also Plate II.
British Library, Royal MS 2. B. XII, fol. 14ᵛ

B. The destroyed monument of Sir Stephen Jenyns (d. 1523), formerly in the church of the Grey Friars, London. Drawn by Sir Thomas Wriothesley, Garter King of Arms 1505–34.
British Library, Add. MS 45131, fol. 86

CHAPTER THREE

THE GOVERNMENT OF THE MEDIEVAL COMPANY

THERE ARE many tangible connections between the livery companies of the twenty-first century and their antecedents. Most striking, perhaps, are those organizational features that were originally developed during the later Middle Ages, and which have survived, albeit modified, into the modern era. The division of the 'company' into liverymen and ordinary freemen, for instance, was established in the fourteenth century, and membership of the livery remained both a vital signifier of an individual's status within the craft, and a prerequisite for office-holding both within a company and in the City government. In the case of the Merchant Taylors' Company, the liverymen were members of the Fraternity of St John the Baptist, whose origins, as we have seen, can be traced back to at least 1300. The responsibilities of governing this fraternity, as well as supervising London's largest craft, became increasingly diverse during the course of the fourteenth and fifteenth centuries. The consequences of this diversity can be seen in the proliferation of offices within the Company, of which the most important were those of the Clerk and the Beadle, as well as in the establishment of the Court of Assistants as the governing body of the Company, alongside the existing posts of Master and Wardens. Another notable development was the foundation of a 'fraternity of yeomen tailors', later known as the Bachelors' Company, an association for freemen outside the livery which itself came to play an important part in the government of the Company as a whole.

THE SIZE OF THE COMPANY

Before looking at the way the Company was governed, it is important to have a sense of its size. Accurate figures for the number of members of the Merchant Taylors' Company in the fifteenth and sixteenth centuries are difficult to calculate: there are no complete lists of all the freemen, and so we have to rely upon the yearly admissions of apprentices and freemen to get a sense of the size of the craft and the changes that took place over time. Table 3 shows the average numbers (where known) of apprentices enrolled, and freemen 'presented', that is, admitted, in the 1460s and in each decade from 1560 to 1620. The accounts for the years in between are not sufficiently complete to allow figures to be compiled. Nevertheless, this table shows that between 1560 and 1620 more than 23,000 apprentices and 9,800 freemen were admitted. The expansion of the craft over that period reflected the dramatic growth in the population of London as a whole from the mid-sixteenth century onwards. There were, for instance, an estimated 80,000 inhabitants of the City in 1550, and after rapid growth in the 1580s and 1590s the population total may have reached 200,000 by 1600. Sixty years later, just before the plague of 1665 and the Great Fire of 1666, there were probably around 400,000 people living in London.[1]

To move from these to a figure for overall Company membership at any one point is difficult, as it involves assumptions about life expectancy and migration out of London in a period for which reliable statistics do not survive. Nevertheless, it has been calculated that there were around 8,000 freemen of the Merchant Taylors' Company in the mid- to late seventeenth century, and using the same method one ends up with a Company of about 900 freemen in the 1460s and 3,000 in the 1560s. These figures may well be slight overestimates, but give a sense both of the growth of the Company's membership in the sixteenth and seventeenth centuries, and of its relative size when compared with the other City

TABLE 3
Average numbers of apprentices enrolled and freemen admitted per annum, 1460–1620

Decade	Apprentices enrolled	Freemen admitted
1460s	87	35 (est.)
1470s–1550s	—	—
1560s	130	106
1570s	163	132
1580s	304	138
1590s	487	154
1600s	638	192
1610s	661	261

companies. It is clear that the Company was among the largest in the City: of 1,123 men sworn as citizens in the years 1551–53, no fewer than 148 were sworn as freemen of the Merchant Taylors, more than any other company. The Merchant Taylors and the Clothworkers (108) together admitted a quarter of the new freemen of the City in these two years, a remarkable reflection of the importance of the textile and clothing trades in London.[2]

It should, of course, be remembered that not all new freemen went on to have successful careers, and to speak of the Company 'membership' in these terms can be misleading. In the fifteenth century perhaps a third of those who obtained the freedom by apprenticeship took on apprentices of their own, and a mere twelve per cent entered the livery. These numbers were boosted by those who obtained the freedom by other means, particularly by redemption (through the payment of a fee): these men were generally wealthier, and so more likely to open their own businesses and enter the livery. An average of ten tailors were admitted as liverymen each year, which suggests that membership of the Fraternity of St John the Baptist may have stood at between 80 and 100, perhaps a tenth of the freemen. From the City records we know that the livery of the Company in 1501 was said to number 84, probably an underestimate but a figure which fits well with the pattern of admissions to the livery in the Masters' accounts. A partial check can also be provided by the alms payments of 1s. a year made by liverymen: in 1463, £5 15s. was raised, and if an allowance is made for arrears this would again suggest a livery of about 90. Over the next century or so the livery expanded to perhaps 300. As we shall see in later chapters, the benefits of a large membership were most obvious when it came to participation in civic ceremonial, but it was also useful from the point of view of finance. The Company raised numerous levies in the fifteenth and sixteenth centuries, most notably for projects such as the almshouses in Threadneedle Street and the rebuilding of the kitchen in the late 1420s and early 1430s, and was generally able to count on the support of more than 200 members of the Company.[3]

THE MASTER AND WARDENS

In common with most guilds and fraternities, the Merchant Taylors' Company was governed from day to day by elected representatives, in this case a Master and four Wardens who were drawn from the ranks of its most distinguished members. As the evidence of John Stow, cited in Chapter One, would suggest, the Tailors and Linen-Armourers were supervised by a Master and four Wardens from at least 1300. Their election took place each year on the feast of the Nativity of St John the Baptist (24 June), and this had been confirmed in the charter granted to the Tailors by Richard II in 1390. By the later fifteenth century those who were chosen attended Mass in the chapel at Tailors' Hall in Threadneedle Street and, after swearing their oaths of office, were then 'sette in their romes and places by their said next predecessours . . .', thus completing the ritual transfer of power (Fig. 16). Little else is known of the process of election until 1507, when ordinances record for the first time that the new Master and Wardens were to be elected by members of the Court of Assistants. This had doubtless been the case for some years, but prior to the Court emerging as the governing body of the Company it is likely that the whole livery were involved. The new officers then attended the Company's annual feast at the Hall, wearing their livery robes and garlands of roses which were specially ordered for the occasion.[4]

By the early fifteenth century it was customary for the wife of the new Master to be admitted free of charge as a sister of the fraternity, and this admission ceremony also took place prior to the annual feast. These women were allowed to adopt the title of 'Mistress', corresponding to the prefix of 'Master' which their husbands were permitted to carry for the

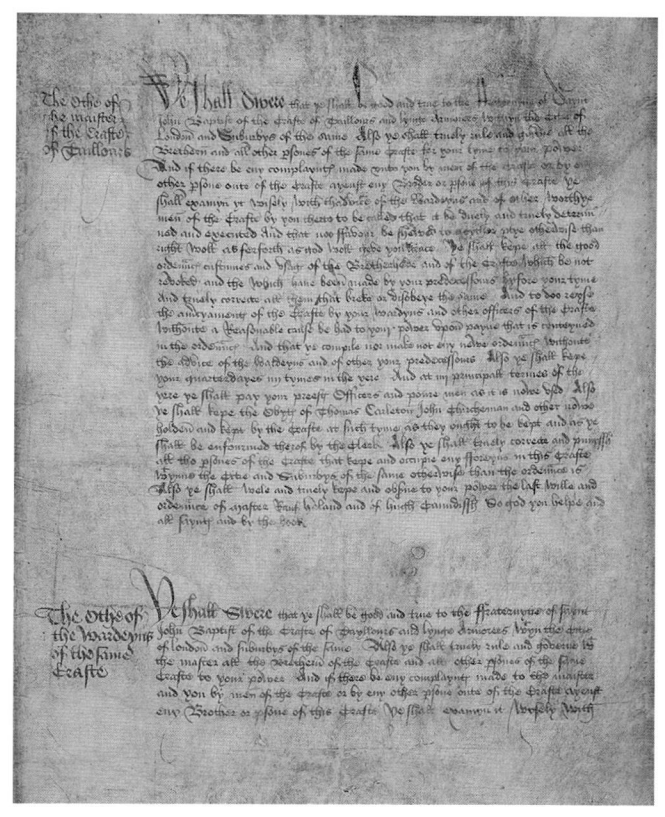

FIGURE 16. The first page from the Book of Oaths, compiled by the Clerk, William Duryvale, in 1491, showing the oaths taken by the Master and by the Wardens of the Company.
Guildhall Library, MS 34007, fol. 1

rest of their days as an indicator of their status within the Company. Widows of former Masters often retained a close connection with the Company. Ellen, widow of John Langwith (Master 1444–45), was just one of a number of wealthy tailor widows who implemented, or even augmented, their husbands' substantial bequests of property to the Company. Shortly after her husband's death in 1467 she drew up a will of her own in which she bequeathed substantial property in the parish of St Mary Abchurch to the Company, in return for an anniversary service for John's soul and, in due course, her own. The Company spent 20s. on the services of a lawyer who negotiated with Ellen on its behalf. Other benefactors included Rose, widow of John Swan (Master 1470–71), who donated the huge sum of 1,075 marks (£716 13s. 4d.) in cash to the Company for a chantry in 1493. Another was Thomasine, widow of Sir John Percyvale (Master 1485–86), who augmented the chantry established by her late husband in the church of St Mary Woolnoth with a bequest of further estates in the City on her death in 1512.[5]

The pattern of office-holding by members of the livery became established during the fifteenth century. Service as Master was normally limited to just one year, although in exceptional circumstances, such as the illness or death of an incumbent, a former Master could be asked to serve again. All Masters were expected to have served previously as one of the Wardens, but until the late fifteenth century it appears that one year as Warden was deemed sufficient. It is only in the early sixteenth century that a pattern emerged whereby a liveryman would serve as a 'lower' and then as an 'upper' Warden before being allowed to proceed to the Mastership. Nevertheless, those who became Master were usually highly experienced individuals, who had had the opportunity to demonstrate their suitability for the Mastership over a period of years. In the same way, the duties of the individual Wardens were being differentiated: by the 1490s, for instance, the youngest Warden was put in charge of supervising the collection of the Company's rents, and repairs to properties. In many ways this gradual consolidation of the procedures and principles of the governance of the Company reflected wider developments in the City, where electoral and governmental structures were in the process of being more clearly defined.[6]

Within the Company, one of the chief duties of the Master was to ensure that the annual accounts of the Fraternity of St John the Baptist were properly drawn up and submitted to the Court of Assistants (see below) for approval. This sometimes proved difficult: in late May 1493 the Court ordered the current Master, two former Masters, and two Wardens to go to the house of William Hert (Master 1491–92) in Fleet Street,

willyng hym in goodly maner bicause he is a sekeman [sick man] to make perfite his accompts which is not yet engroced to thentent that the company may know wether they be advauntaged or no by reason of his office and to thentent also that the M[aister] that now is may suerly and perfectly make and yeld up his accomptes according to the good rules of this place.[7]

Close co-operation between past and present Masters and Wardens was essential to ensure the smooth transfer of power and the effective running of the Company. On one occasion, for instance, the newly elected Master and Wardens, together with their predecessors, as well as the Clerk, Beadle, and rent-collector, were required to meet at the church of St Peter Westcheap at six o'clock in the morning in order to begin 'the viewyng of all the landes perteignyng to this crafte', a task which by then must have been an arduous one. Like the periodic 'searches' for defective workmanship and other offences, however, this would not have been undertaken without recourse to 'mete and drynk' provided at the cost of the Company.[8]

The description given by John Stow of the Master as the 'pilgrim', and the Wardens as the 'purveyors of alms' of the Fraternity of St John the Baptist, has already been noted, but it is worth emphasizing that their responsibilities ranged far wider than the governance of the fraternity. Indeed, with the ceding of important powers of regulation by the City government to the misteries, the Wardens of the crafts inherited the duties of enforcing a host of ordinances concerning working practices, the behaviour of their freemen, and the punishment of offenders. To carry out their duties they relied upon the assistance of officials such as the Clerk and the Beadle, and upon the goodwill and firmness of purpose of the Court of Assistants as the ultimate source of authority and precedent within the craft. From the point of view of the City government, however, the Master and Wardens were the recognized representatives of the mistery, and as such they could expect to be summoned to appear before the Mayor and Aldermen to answer for the behaviour of the freemen of the craft. In October 1441, for instance, the Master and Wardens came before the Mayor in an unsuccessful attempt to secure the release on bail of six unruly tailors who had been involved in disturbances at the mayoral election.[9] More frequent, however, were the occasions on which they presented petitions on behalf of the Company, trying to secure changes in civic regulations which would benefit their freemen. This was the intention in April 1493 when they proposed a bill 'for the reformacion of all foreyns [strangers to the City]', the aim of which was to prevent freemen from employing cheaper, unenfranchised workers, many of whom were migrants from elsewhere in England or from abroad. This bill seems to have come about as a result of pressure from younger freemen who were experiencing problems in finding paid work as journeymen, the usual stepping-stone towards establishing a business and taking on apprentices.[10]

With the day-to-day governance of the craft in the hands of the Master and Wardens, it was inevitable that they occasionally became the focus of resentment on the part of those who had been brought before them for various offences. William Barton, fined for not enrolling his apprentice at the Hall, got himself into deeper trouble by claiming that 'M[aister] Jenyns [i.e. Stephen Jenyns] served hym lyke a falsse Judas when he was M[aister] of the feliship'. The Master who heard Barton's outburst was Walter Povey (1492–93) who, following the end of his term of office, was himself accused of abusing his position: William Gerveys appeared before the Court of Assistants claiming that 'M[aister] Povey dyd unto hym when he was ruler of this worshipfull fraternitee open wrong', and that Povey was 'the [most] covetouse man that ever was in his dayes gouvernour of the said company'. For a final flourish he announced that he would rather quit the country for seven years than have Povey as Master again. Given the frequency of his appearances before the Court, there were doubtless plenty who would have been glad to see him go.[11]

THE COURT OF ASSISTANTS

While the day-to-day administration of the Company was carried out by the Master and Wardens, assisted by their officials, perhaps the most important development in this period was the establishment of the Court of Assistants as the 'governing body' of the Company. Courts were becoming an increasingly important feature of the livery companies by the early fifteenth century, principally because of the additional duties and responsibilities that the companies were taking on. Yet the origins of the company courts may well be found in an earlier period. As we have seen, it was common in the early fourteenth century for the Mayor to draw upon groups of 'better and more discreet' men of the crafts in order to regulate the misteries. This was part and parcel of the City's delegation of regulatory powers to representatives of the crafts, of which the most important was the supervision of admissions to the freedom of the City. The lists of governors of the crafts drawn up in November 1328 are a good example of this: each mistery appears to have had a group of governors in proportion to its size. The Tailors and Linen-Armourers were to have twenty such governors, a number exceeded only by the twenty-one for the Fishmongers and the twenty-four for the Butchers. Likewise, in 1340 the Tailors secured approval for an ordinance which specified that six out of a named group of twenty-four men were to assess the fitness of those who sought the freedom of the City through the craft.[12] These lists suggest that the principle of drawing upon groups of senior craftsmen to help in the regulation of the misteries was becoming well established. By the end of the fourteenth century, a number of London's companies had translated this principle into formally-constituted governing bodies which met together regularly to transact business relating to their crafts. In 1376 the Grocers' Company had a body of six men for 'helping and counselling of the Wardens' for the coming year. In the early fifteenth century this body, known as the 'fellowship associated', met quarterly, its numbers fluctuating between six and ten. The Shearmen of London (who later combined with the Fullers to form the Clothworkers' Company) had a Court by 1452, when they agreed an ordinance for the election by the liverymen 'of twelve persons discrete and well avised . . . for to assist and counsel the said Wardens'.[13]

The earliest reference to the Court of Assistants of the London Tailors and Linen-Armourers comes from a chance survival. Among the manuscript books in the Company's archive are three leaves of a book that was known as the 'Great Register' of the Company. This book was used as an ongoing record of the ordinances and regulations agreed by the Court, and was therefore a vital reference work for the Master and Wardens. The earliest of the surviving ordinances dates from 1429–30, and the first reference to the Court comes from ordinances which were agreed on 1 May 1436 by the Master and Wardens, and 'bi wyse discrecions and good avyse' of a group of senior liverymen, headed by 'my Maister Rauf Holand alderman'. Further on, these men are referred to as the 'seid xvj men', the first indication in the Company's records of the size of the Court at that time. This was to change within six years, however, for by the Mastership of Richard Skernyng (1441–42) ordinances were being agreed by the 'good avyse of xxiiij men', and thereafter membership of the Court was fixed at twenty-four.[14]

Yet, as we have seen, there are indications that records relating to this body may once have stretched back into the fourteenth century. An inventory of the Company's records, taken in 1609, refers to the 'Nyne bookes severally marked with these severall letters viz A, B, C, D, E, F, G, H and I . . . the Booke A begynnyng in the xxviiith yere of King Edward the First, Anno Domini 1299 and the Booke I endyng the xxiiiith day of January 1574'.[15] Of this remarkable series, only Book 'I' survives intact as the first volume (1562–75) of the Company's extensive run of Court minutes, which continues with only a few gaps up to the present day. Whether the very earliest of the nine books were actually dedicated 'minute books' is another matter: the affairs of the Company remained relatively uncomplicated until the later fourteenth century, so it is possible that there was no need until that point for separate books of accounts, minutes and ordinances. Yet by the fifteenth century there is little doubt that proceedings of regular meetings of the Court were being recorded in minute books. Ordinances agreed by the Court were then written up in the Great Register. Much of what we know about the Company's Court before 1562 derives from another chance survival, a run of seven years of Court minutes from 1486 to 1493 which somehow escaped the fate of the rest of the books, lost before the nineteenth century. These minutes, among the earliest records of their kind, contain proceedings of more than 400 meetings of the Court and reveal a great deal about the life of the Company at that time.[16]

THE COMPOSITION OF THE COURT

The surviving fifteenth-century Court minutes reveal important characteristics of the role of the Court. In the first place, much of the routine business was conducted by the Master and Wardens alone, at formal meetings which were normally held on Mondays and Fridays. Full meetings of the Court were much less frequent, perhaps once every three weeks, and it was at these meetings that more important business was transacted relating to Company policy, significant items of expenditure, and serious disputes between members. Second, the surviving attendance lists of these full Courts in the late fifteenth century show that the burdens of Court membership were not shared equally. On average, full Courts were attended by only eleven or twelve of the twenty-four Assistants, and the numbers were not much higher for the four 'quarter-days'. Certain individuals were much more involved than some of their colleagues: two aldermen, Sir John Percyvale and Hugh Pemberton, were among only three men who attended more than 55 per cent of the meetings held between 1486 and 1493. Despite these variations in attendance, membership of the Court of Assistants was an important indicator of a man's status within the Company: nine of the sixteen Assistants of 1436, listed in the surviving fragment of the Great Register, had already served a term as Master of the Company, and two others were shortly to hold that office. This set a pattern for the subsequent history of the Company's Court, and reflected the value placed on the wisdom and experience of past Masters.[17]

THE RESOLUTION OF DISPUTES

The status of the Assistants was particularly important when it came to settling disputes between tailors, as these were frequently put to the arbitration of members of the Court. In most cases this went smoothly: the authority and status of the arbiters ensured that their decisions went unchallenged. However, there were occasions when the authority of the Court was undermined. The most serious dispute recorded in the early minutes involved a former Master, John Heed (Master 1487–88), whose relatively trivial dispute with his apprentice escalated into open rebellion against his fellow Court members in the autumn of 1492. After Heed had refused to co-operate with the first set of arbiters appointed by the Court, it emerged that he bore a personal grudge towards Stephen Jenyns, who was appointed to oversee a second attempt at arbitration, and who, he alleged, 'had caused hym to lose xxxviij li. [£38]'. The only option was for the current Master, Walter Povey, to take over the role himself, and to this end he announced, 'Sir, I most be your juge this yere'. Heed, alluding to his own period in office, responded by making 'grete comparisons with the Maister as in beryng charge in the crafte and other thinges without regardyng or reverencyng his office or the place'. At this point Povey seems to have lost his temper, and declared that it was a pity that Heed had ever been chosen as Master; Heed retorted that Povey himself was far from being a popular choice. The referral of Heed's case to the Mayor was a tacit admission that the limits of the Court's authority to control one of its own members had been reached. It may have been small comfort that, following a spell in prison, Heed returned to the Court to beg its forgiveness.[18]

The fact that the Heed case had to be heard before the Mayor represented a blow to the Company's strict policy of ensuring that 'variaunces and controversies' were dealt with internally: all members of the Court had a duty to preserve the Company's good name in the City. In September 1492 the Master, Walter Povey, came before the Court and claimed that 'the councelles and secretes of the said crafte by som persones beforetyme have ben disclosed and discovered oute of the said crafte wherby grete incovenyences have ensued'. To try and prevent further disclosures, all members of the Court were required to appear at the Hall to swear their oaths of office again.[19] Early the next year a breach of the City's apprenticeship regulations by a member of the Company was deemed so serious by the Master that he feared the

> grete infamy that of lyklyhode myght have growen in tyme to com to the hoole body of the felishyp . . . if the said matier shuld be publisshed and com to lyght affore the Chambreleyn of this citee and ferther . . . affore the mair and aldremen of the same citee.

The culprit himself risked public humiliation by being 'openly shamed with a paper over his hede as untrue citezein', reflecting the common practice of parading wrong-doers through the streets of London with placards around their necks specifying the nature of their offences.[20]

The Court was also keen to regulate the behaviour of members of the Company. This often focused on the enforcement, where possible, of the terms of apprenticeship indentures, which contained strict injunctions against gambling, fornication, and other morally disreputable pursuits. One master appeared before the Court to claim that his apprentice had 'used the company of a woman which was to his grete losse and hynderyng for asmoch as he was so affectionate and resorted dailly unto hyr'. The apprentice, on the other hand, managed to convince the Court that the allegation was false, merely a smoke-screen for the master's own breaches of his duty of care. Indeed, a significant number of the cases brought before the Court dealt with the alleged abuse of apprentices by their masters, a sign perhaps that the elders of the Company were reasonably even-handed.[21] The behaviour of liverymen was also a matter of concern: at one quarter-day it was agreed that members should no longer be allowed to pay their annual alms in the cloistered courtyard of the Hall because 'sum persones goyng there forth have spoken and sayde sum wordes soundyng rather to dishonour than to worship'. Instead they were to pay their dues 'in this place and not in the said cloystre', probably referring to the parlour, a small room next to the common hall where the new Master and Wardens were formally installed.[22] Misbehaviour in public was viewed even more seriously. At a meeting held on 3 February 1490, those present heard that 'a grete cryme and defamacion renneth upon this fraternytie by cause that sum persones of this felaship excede in ther behavour and demeanyng amonges men of worship and other honest persones and namely at Blakwellhall'. As London's principal centre for dealing in woollen cloth, Blackwell Hall was important for those tailors involved in the cloth trade, and so the Court immediately required the two culprits to enter into bonds of £40 and £10 respectively for their future good behaviour.[23]

THE BACHELORS' COMPANY

Another key development within many livery companies in the later Middle Ages was the foundation of associations for freemen outside the livery. The names given to these freemen — 'yeomen' or 'bachelors' — reflected the fact that many of them were at a relatively early stage in their careers, and doubtless hoped one day to be admitted to the livery. What is clear, however, is that for much of their early history these associations were viewed with suspicion. In the late fourteenth century associations of journeymen (wage-labourers) of the Saddlers, Cordwainers, and other crafts were said to have tried to push wages up through collective action. The City government and the Crown were increasingly concerned about their activities at a time of severe labour shortages: a proclamation was made against 'congregations, covins and conspiracies', which was cited in 1387 when the overseers of the Cordwainers complained that several wage-labourers of the craft had organized an illegal fraternity of 'like people' which met on the feast of the Assumption of the Virgin 'to the prejudice of the trade'. These concerns were reflected more widely in a decision taken by the Crown in 1388 to institute a national inquiry into the form and purpose of lay and religious fraternities.[24] Suspicion was still evident in London in 1415, when a complaint was made to the Mayor and Aldermen about the behaviour of a group of 'servants and journeymen of the yeomen tailors' who had 'consorted together in dwelling houses and behaved in an unruly manner'. The charge was investigated and the Master of the Company, Thomas Whityngham, was ordered to come to Guildhall to answer for their behaviour. The ringleaders were ordered to leave a house in Garlickhithe, and to cease wearing liveries at unlawful assemblies.[25] Two years later, in 1417, the City took a similarly firm line when four members of the fraternity of 'yomantaillours' asked permission to meet yearly on the feast of the Decollation of St John the Baptist (29 August) at the priory of St John of Jerusalem in Clerkenwell. Permission was denied by the Mayor and Aldermen, who feared that disturbances would result 'as similar assemblies of the same mistery had done before'.[26]

Yet this negative picture of the yeomen of the Company does not reveal the whole truth. Other evidence shows that their fraternity was already becoming an important part of the Company. In 1414, for instance, John Creek, a wealthy liveryman, drew up his will in which he left 20s. to the alms of the 'fraternitatis valect' cissorum' (valet, or yeomen, tailors).[27] This shows that the yeomen already had their own 'common box' for funds, and that they were well regarded in some sections of the craft. The events of 1415 and 1417 were certainly damaging to the association's prospects, but legal expenses noted in the Master's accounts show that the Company's governors took a keen interest in the success of the petition submitted by the yeomen.[28] By the 1430s the yeomen, although still seen as potentially unruly, had managed to gain permission to hold their annual feast again. The fortunate survival of an ordinance of 1436 reveals that they were allowed to celebrate an annual feast and wear liveries, as long as the festivities were conducted under the watchful eyes of the Master and Wardens of the livery. The yeomen were to attend Mass at the church of St Martin Outwich 'fast bi Taillourshalle' on the feast of the Decollation of St John the Baptist. They were then to proceed to St John's church, Clerkenwell, for their annual assembly 'under the rule and governaunce of the Meister and Wardeins of the Fraternite of Seint John Baptist of Taillours in London', prior to attending an election dinner at Tailors' Hall, at which four Wardens were to be chosen for the coming year.[29] These celebrations were thus officially sanctioned by the livery, and made use of the strong links which the Fraternity of St John the Baptist had with both St Martin's and with the priory of St John of Jerusalem at Clerkenwell. In the meantime, the yeomen had collectively contributed the sum of £6 13s. 4d. towards the roof of the impressive new kitchen at Tailors' Hall (Fig. 17).[30]

By the late fifteenth century, then, the fraternity of yeomen tailors was an integral part of the structure of the Company. It was similar to the Fraternity of the Assumption which was founded by the freemen of the Skinners' Company, and the Fraternity of St Michael established by the yeomen of the Pewterers.[31] The yeomanry adopted the same patron saint, St John the Baptist, as the livery, but in their case chose to celebrate the feast of the saint's Decollation (29 August) rather than his Nativity (24 June). The standing of the yeomen within the craft was shown by the increasing number of bequests made to their fraternity, often by senior members of the livery for whom the yeomanry represented an important stage in their careers. Thomas Parker left 'my best standyng maser [goblet]' to the 'maister taillours', and 'also I biqueth unto the felawship of the yomen my standyng maser next the best', and Robert Colwich in 1480 left 'ii basyns of sylver with myn armes in the bothom' to the Tailors' fraternity, and 66s. 8d. 'to the felaship called the yemanry of the same craft'. Another tailor, Stephen Trappys, bore the less fortunate in mind when he left 20s. 'to the poure almessemen of the yomen Felaship of Taillours', in 1485.[32]

FIGURE 17. A line drawing showing the kitchen of Merchant Taylors' Hall, rebuilt in the late 1420s and early 1430s, bounded on the north by early-fifteenth-century arches.
Guildhall Library

For the governors of the Company, the advantages of having a well-ordered association for freemen outside the livery more than compensated for their occasional insubordination. A reference to the 'five' of the yeomen in 1486 appears in the Court minutes, where these officials received 20d. for assisting the Master and Wardens in their duties. Two years later the Court allowed the yeomen tailors formally to change their association's name to the 'Bachelors' Company', and in August 1489 William Brownyng was sworn as one of the 'sixteen men' appointed to govern it.[33] The Bachelors had the potential to represent and articulate the interests of many ordinary freemen. Several measures passed by the Company's Court in the later fifteenth century could be construed as responses to pressure from below, including the reversal of a three-fold rise in the enrolment fees for apprentices, and restrictions upon the employment of unenfranchized labour. Yet at the same time there is evidence that the Court and the livery were keen to enforce their control over the Bachelors, and thereby reinforce hierarchical values within the craft as a whole. On 25 July 1493, for instance, the Bachelors held their quarter-day 'with licence of the M[aister] and wardeyns'. Their subordinate position within the craft was emphasized when 'divers ordynaunces were redd unto the said company by Henry Mayour, clerk of the M[aisters] clothyng [i.e. the livery]'. Further entries in the minutes show that the Wardens of the Bachelors were often employed to enforce ordinances and collect revenues, tasks which may not have endeared them to their fellow Bachelors.[34]

CLERKS, BEADLES AND OTHER OFFICIALS

On 24 July 1420 John Brynchele, citizen and tailor, drew up his will, asking to be buried in the churchyard of his parish church of St Benet Fink. Among his bequests was the sum of 6s. 8d. to the Fraternity of St John the Baptist of his craft, along with 4d. each to the inmates of the almshouse next to the Hall. This demonstration of regard for his Company was by no means unusual, but what mark Brynchele's will out from those of most of his fellow tailors are his bequests of books. Though evidently not wealthy, Brynchele was clearly learned: he left two copies of Boethius' *Consolations of Philosophy*, one in English, the other in Latin. Not averse to more contemporary reading, Brynchele left to one of his executors, fellow tailor William Holgrave, 'my book called "Tales of Canterbury"' (*librum meum vocatum Talys of Caunterbury*), the earliest known testamentary bequest of Chaucer's great work.[35] These bequests may well have stemmed from Brynchele's position as the first known Clerk of the Merchant Taylors' Company, a post that required literacy in English, French, and Latin, as well as financial acumen and a degree of legal know-how. The important point to note here, of course, is that Brynchele was not a professional clerk: although relatively little is known of his career, he had evidently obtained the freedom of the City as a tailor. The likelihood is that his administrative abilities and education were quickly recognized by the elders of his craft, at a time when many of the City companies were starting to employ paid officials to administer their affairs.

Brynchele's successor, Nicholas Hoper, was also a tailor, but on the latter's death in about 1450 the Company took the decision to recruit from outside the craft, heralding the start of a long tradition of employing Clerks drawn from the ranks of London's lawyers and scriveners. The skills possessed by such men were essential at a time when the London companies were acquiring a large amount of property in the City, were administering an increasing number of chantries and anniversaries, and — largely as a result of these activities — were often embroiled in legal disputes with individuals and institutions. Legal skills were also important in the quasi-judicial context of a company Court, where bonds and other contracts were regularly entered into by freemen. The Clerks also had to be highly numerate, able to assist the Master with the drawing up or 'engrossing' of the annual accounts. From the beginning, the medieval Clerks were relatively well rewarded: Brynchele, for instance, received 53s. 4d. per annum, which was augmented by another 52s. for his 'table' (i.e. board), making a total of £5 5s. 4d. a year. His successor, Hoper, managed to secure a rise in salary to £6 13s. 4d., which put him on a par with the Company's chaplains, but his abilities may have been exceptional: all his known successors before 1500 were paid £5 per annum.[36]

The changing status and role of the Company's Clerks can be seen in the careers of three men, all of whom were responsible for portions of the surviving Court records of the Company from 1486–93. The first of these, Thomas Kirton, spent the first half of his career as a lawyer in the Mayor's Court in London, but had already established links with the Tailors by the late 1450s when he was one of a team of attorneys employed by the Company in a dispute with the church of St Katherine Cree. He evidently impressed the Company's governors, for in the autumn of 1464 he was appointed to succeed Thomas Fillilode as Clerk.[37] Kirton's eventual retirement in the late summer of 1487 may well have been prompted by ill health, for in July that year he drew up his will, describing himself as 'Thomas Kyrton of London, gentleman', and asking to be buried in the church of St Olave Silver Street. Among his bequests was the sum of 13s. 4d. 'to the maister and brethren of the fraternite of Seint John Baptist of Taylors of London to thentent that they shalhave me in ther speciall remembraunce at the quaterdayes among them holden'. Kirton retired from his post the following month, but survived for at least another two and a half years, and his will was finally proved in October 1490.[38] His successor, William Duryvale, also had a legal background of sorts: in January 1488 he took the oath of admission to the fraternity of the London Scriveners, whose members were trained in the skills of drawing up legal documents, although few were active as attorneys. Two years later another entry in the Scriveners' 'Common Paper' lists him with a servant. He left office in October 1492 when his final quarterly wages of 25s. were noted by his successor, Henry Mayour.[39]

Like his predecessor, Mayour was a long-standing member of the Scriveners' Company: he was apprenticed at an unknown date to a Robert Legett and his oath of admission to their fraternity, written in his own hand, is recorded in the Common Paper for 24 November 1481 (see Fig. 18).[40] Five years later, on 26 October 1486, Mayour was appointed to the joint offices of Clerk and Beadle of the Goldsmiths' Company, posts he was to hold for just under six years, and was duly 'sworen and admytted clerk of this felishep'.[41] His departure from the Goldsmiths' in

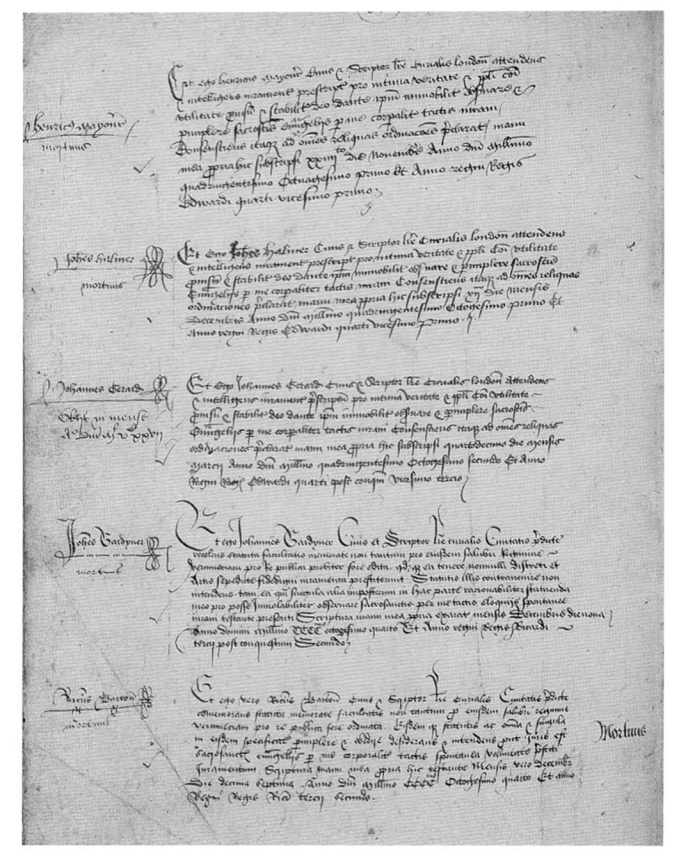

FIGURE 18. Henry Mayour's entry (top) in the Scriveners' Common Paper, 24 November 1481. *Guildhall Library, MS 5370, p. 84*

the summer of 1492 remains something of a mystery. At a well-attended meeting of the Goldsmiths' Court, on 20 July, those present 'were accorded and aggreed and there dismyssed Harry Mayowre of his office that is to saye both of clerkeshipp & also of Bedilshippe'. There is no evidence that he had committed any offence, although it is striking that his removal heralded an immediate reorganization of the Goldsmiths' administration.[42] Less than six months later Mayour succeeded William Duryvale as Clerk of the Tailors and Linen-Armourers, and in March 1493, in a rare reference to his own position, Mayour described himself as 'notary and clerk of this worshipful company'. He held the post of Clerk until at least 1512, when he compiled a detailed inventory of the Hall and its contents (Fig. 19), and was still alive in 1517 when he was left a small bequest by an Essex clergyman. His period in office is

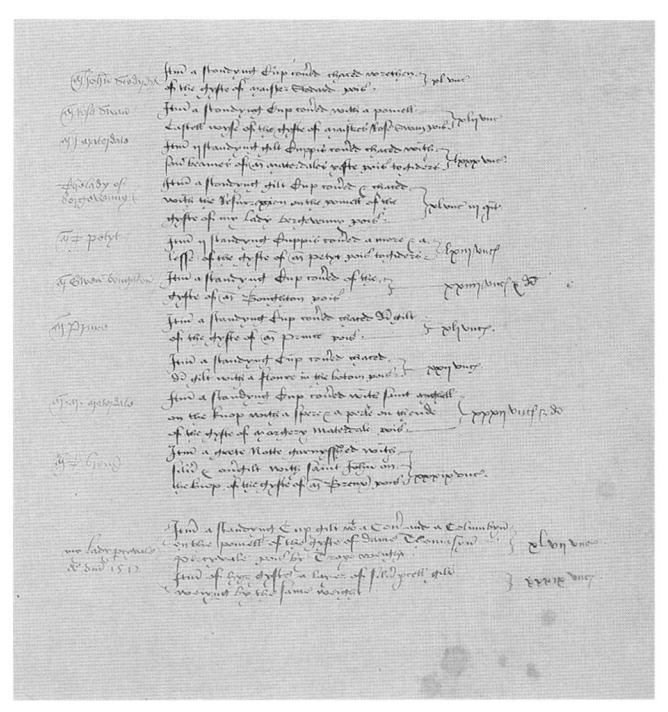

FIGURE 19. A page from the 1512 inventory of the contents of the Hall.
Guildhall Library, MS 34357, fol. 33

especially noteworthy for the remarkable picture of the Company that emerges from his vivid and extremely detailed Court minutes during his first months as Clerk.[43]

The Company's other office-holders also played a vital part in the administration of the Fraternity of St John the Baptist and the regulation of the craft as a whole. The rapid growth of the fraternity's property endowment was noted in Chapter Two, and in 1420 the first entry relating to the 40s. salary of a 'Renter' appears in the accounts. Appropriately enough the entry was accompanied by a marginal 'nota', to emphasize the significance of this addition to the ranks of the Company's officers. The post grew even more in importance during the fifteenth century: from 1459–60 it was held by Thomas Spekyngton, a liveryman, who was paid the sum of £5 13s. 4d. a year until his death in the late 1470s. By the late 1480s, however, this post too had become the preserve of professional administrators, such as Simon Lorymer, a scrivener, who died in 1490.[44]

More established was the post of Beadle which, like that of Clerk, can be traced back to at least 1398,

when the holder was John Wynge. In contrast to the Clerks and rent-collectors, the Beadles recorded in the pre-Reformation records of the Company generally seem to have been tailors, though often men who had reached the latter stages of their careers. Peter Ferrers, for instance, was apprenticed in 1426–27, and had a successful career as a master-tailor in his own right before becoming Beadle in 1463.[45] The duties of the Beadle changed gradually over the centuries, to the extent that by the eighteenth century they centred largely on the administration of the Hall buildings (Figs 20 and 21). In the medieval and early modern periods, however, the Beadles were particularly active in the enforcement of Company rules and regulations in the City. It was as the representative of the Master, Wardens and Court that the Beadle, in his oath of office, promised to seek out miscreants and 'shewe the names of them as sone as ye shall have knoweleche therof to the Maister and Wardeyns', to collect fines, and summon members of the Company to appear before the Court. This put the Beadle in the 'front line', so to speak, of the governance of the craft, and it was common for him to encounter the wrath and resentment of those he had to deal with. In December 1492 the Court ordered the Beadle, Thomas Gresyle, to go to the house of one of their freemen, William Tetford, and seize goods to the value of a fine that had recently been imposed on him. Tetford refused to co-operate, and 'rebuked the said Bedell and called hym carle [churl] and manassed [menaced] hym seiyng that he wold sette his heres [ears] on the poste at his shop dore, with many other unfittyng wordes, if the said Bedell toke any distresse there'. His threats were reported back to the Court who promptly asked the Mayor to intervene, and Tetford was duly imprisoned 'unto such tyme that he knew and sobred hym self better and submytted hymself unto the M[aister] and wardeyns and to the good rules of the crafte'.[46]

The permanent posts of Clerk, Beadle and Renter of the Company were augmented by a host of other individuals who were drawn upon for specific tasks. They included numerous common lawyers who were employed to prosecute the Company's business in the City or the Crown courts, as well as specialist scriveners and illuminators who were paid to draw up documents ranging from petitions to the Court of Aldermen to copies of the numerous royal charters

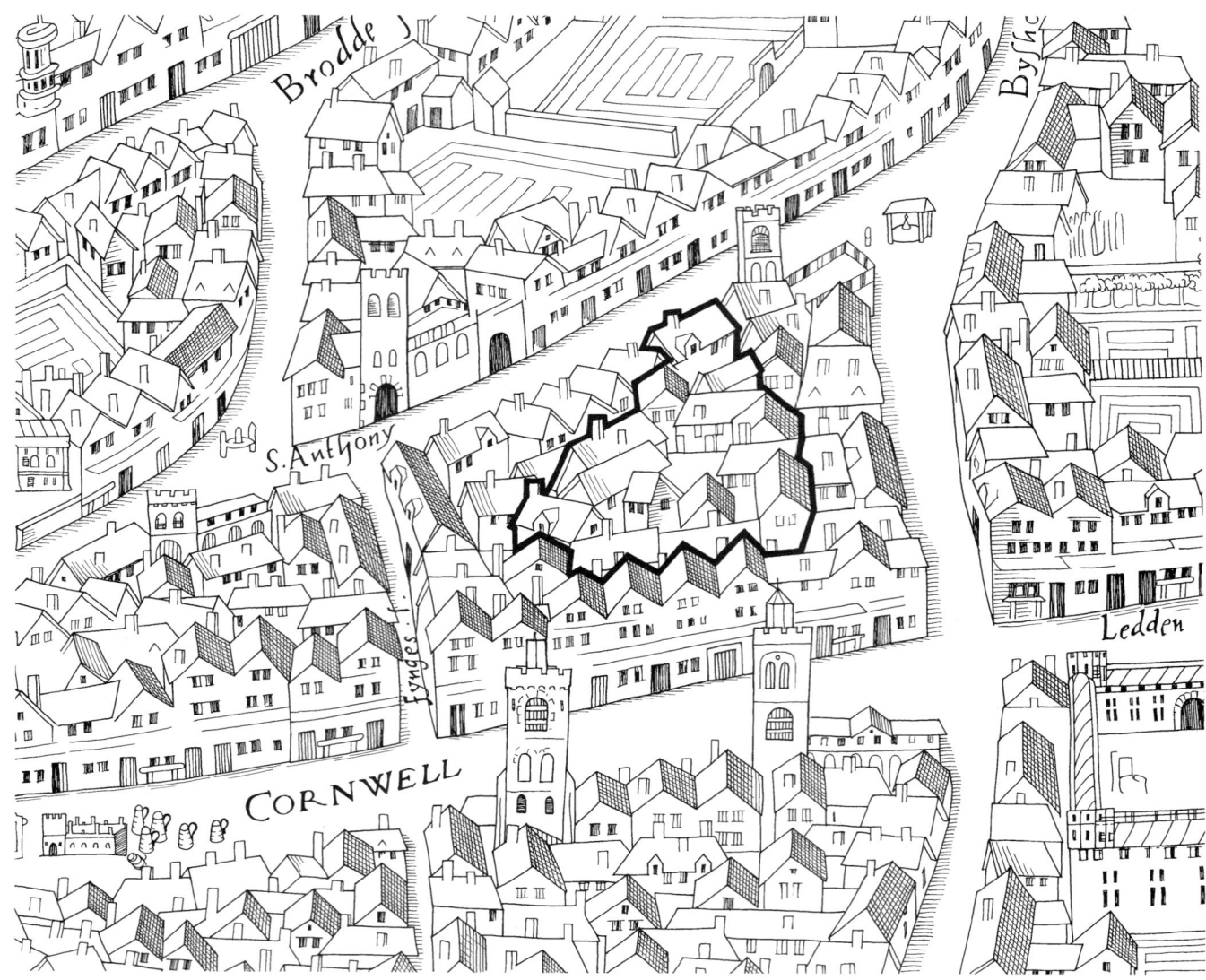

FIGURE 20. A tracing of the Dessau section of the Copperplate Map, showing the approximate area occupied by the Hall buildings in the late 1550s outlined in bold.
Tracy Wellman / Museum of London

acquired by the Company in this period. In 1438–39, for instance, large sums were spent on various 'men of lawe for [t]her labour & counseill dyvers tymes', as the Company lobbied for the grant of a new charter from Henry VI.[47] Many of these lawyers and attorneys were employed on subsequent occasions, for instance during the property disputes that often arose when a bequest of land to the Company was disputed by an heir. In this way the Company built up a network of legal contacts, a network that was paralleled in other areas, notably among the carpenters, builders, and other craftsmen who worked extensively on the Hall and its buildings in this period.

The administrative structures set up by the Company in the later Middle Ages provided the foundations for its activities over the coming centuries. They also provided aspiring members of the Company with career goals, a *cursus honorum* within the Company that for the most successful would

NORTH WEST VIEW OF THE ANTIENT STRUCTURE OF MERCHANT-TAYLORS HALL, AND THE ALMS-HOUSES ADJOINING IN THREADNEEDLE STREET.

FIGURE 21. A somewhat fanciful impression of the frontage of Merchant Taylors' Hall in Threadneedle Street c. 1600, engraved by Robert Wilkinson in 1817.
Guildhall Library

involve admission to the livery, appointment to the Court of Assistants, and election as Warden and then Master. Success within the Company greatly enhanced a man's chance of being chosen for one of the important civic offices, the ultimate position being that of (Lord) Mayor of the City. The next two chapters will look more widely at the activities of the Company, first at its role in regulating the craft, and then at the engagement of the Company and its members with the City and with the Crown.

NOTES

1. These figures are taken from V. Harding, 'The Population of London, 1550–1700: A Review of the Published Evidence', *London Journal*, 15 (1990), pp. 111–28.
2. GL, MS 34048/1–12; MS 34010/1. The admissions of freemen for the 1560s only survive in the Court minutes, which commence in 1562. The overall membership figures were calculated using an average life expectancy of 31.8 years from admission as a freeman: see V. Pearl, 'Change and Stability in Seventeenth-Century London', *London Journal*, 5 (1979), pp. 13–14, 30–31; S. Rappaport, *Worlds within Worlds: Structures of Life in Sixteenth-Century London* (Cambridge, 1989), esp. chapters 7 and 8.

3. M. Davies, 'The Tailors of London: Corporate Charity in the Late Medieval Town', in *Crown, Government and People*, ed. by R. E. Archer, pp. 168–70; CLRO, Journals, 10, fol. 373ᵛ.
4. GL, MS 34004, fols 43ᵛ–70, printed in Clode, *Early History*, I, pp. 357–58; *Court Minutes*, ed. by Davies, p. 254, and see Chapter Two above.
5. C. M. Barron and M. Davies, 'Ellen Langwith, Silkwoman of London', *The Ricardian*, XIII (2003), pp. 39–47; *Court Minutes*, ed. by Davies, pp. 298–99, 302. For Thomasine Percyvale, see Chapter Seven below.
6. Ibid., pp. 15–18; Archer, *Pursuit of Stability*, pp. 18–30. The practice of electing former Masters, i.e. those who had 'passed

the Chair', to subsequent terms as Wardens appears to have been an innovation of the eighteenth century.

7. *Court Minutes*, ed. by Davies, pp. 247–48.
8. *Court Minutes*, ed. by Davies, p. 255.
9. CLRO, Journals, 3, fol. 97^v; C. M. Barron, 'Ralph Holland and the London Radicals, 1438–1444', in *The Medieval Town*, ed. by R. Holt and G. Rosser (1990), p. 170.
10. *Court Minutes*, ed. by Davies, p. 243. Relations with the City government are discussed more fully in Chapter Five.
11. *Court Minutes*, ed. by Davies, pp. 239, 256.
12. *Cal. Letter Bk E*, pp. 231–34; F, pp. 52–53.
13. *Facsimile of First Volume of MS. Archives of the Worshipful Company of Grocers of the City of London, AD 1345–1463*, ed. by J. A. Kingdon, 2 vols (1886), I, p. 21; P. Nightingale, *A Medieval Mercantile Community: The Grocers' Company and the Politics and Trade of London, 1000–1485* (New Haven, 1995), pp. 249, 380; Unwin, *Gilds and Companies of London*, p. 218.
14. GL, MS 34003, fols 8^v, 9^v. Holland was the first tailor to be elected as an alderman. His controversial career is discussed in Chapter Five.
15. GL, MS 34360.
16. The form and composition of these minutes are discussed more fully in *Court Minutes*, ed. by Davies, pp. 6–12.
17. *Court Minutes*, ed. by Davies, pp. 12–15 and Table 1. In the fifteenth century, at any rate, the quarter-days held by the Tailors did not conform exactly to the usual pattern of holding them close to the feasts of the Annunciation (25 March), Nativity of St John the Baptist (24 June), Michaelmas (29 September) and Christmas (25 December). The exact timing and number of quarter-days varied from year to year.
18. Ibid., pp. 207–10, with corrections.
19. Ibid., pp. 203–04.
20. Ibid., p. 237.
21. Ibid., pp. 197–98, 236–37.
22. Ibid., p. 158.
23. Ibid., p. 150. For another incident at Blackwell Hall, see ibid., pp. 227–28.
24. *Memorials*, ed. by Riley, pp. 250–51 (Shearmen, 1350), 495–96 (Cordwainers, 1387), 542–44 (Saddlers, 1396). See also *CPMR*, 1323–64, pp. 225–26, 231, 237; ibid., 1364–81, pp. 54–56, 291–94.
25. *Cal. Letter Bk I*, pp. 136–37.
26. Ibid., pp. 187–88.
27. GL, Archdeaconry Court Wills, MS 9051/1, fols 308^v–09.
28. GL, MS 34048/1, fol. 105.
29. GL, MS 34003, fols 8^v–9.
30. St John's Clerkenwell was one of the religious houses which established 'confraternal' links with the Fraternity of St John the Baptist: see Chapter Two above. GL, MS 34048/1, fol. 227.
31. Veale, *Fur Trade*, pp. 112–15; C. Welch, *History of the Pewterers' Company* (1902), I, pp. 80–81.
32. PRO, PROB 11/5, fols 243–43^v; 11/7, fols 6–7^v; GL, MS 9171/7, fols 33^v–35.
33. *Court Minutes*, ed. by Davies, pp. 76, 115, 137. Unfortunately no records of the Bachelors' Company survive until the very end of the sixteenth century, although there are frequent references to it in the accounts and Court minutes of the Company from 1545 onwards.
34. Ibid., p. 258. Evidence from the records of the Skinners' Company suggests that the subordination of the yeomen skinners to the livery also appears to have been tightened towards the end of the fifteenth century: Veale, *Fur Trade*, p. 114.
35. GL, MS 9171/3, fol. 64^v. See *The Fifty Earliest English Wills in the Court of Probate, London*, ed. by F.J. Furnivall, Early English Text Society, LXXVIII (1882), p. 136.
36. GL, MS 34048/1–3.
37. GL, MS 34048/2, fols 137, 177^v, 259. Kirton was active as an attorney in the City from about 1443 until his appointment as the Tailors' Clerk: see for instance CLRO, Journals, 5, fol. 210; 6, fol. 24. The authors are grateful to Dr Penny Tucker for information about Kirton's career.
38. PRO, PROB 11/9, fol. 63. In the meantime (Lent term 1486/7) Kirton had been specially admitted to Lincoln's Inn where he was permitted to 'have a clerk at the commons as Benchers have'. He was still alive in the autumn of 1489 when he was elected as 'escheator' of the Inn: *The Records of the Honourable Society of Lincoln's Inn, Black Books*, 5 vols (Lincoln's Inn, 1847–1968), vol. 1, pp. 86, 90.
39. *Scriveners' Company Common Paper 1357–1628, with a Continuation to 1678*, ed. by F. W. Steer, London Record Society, 4 (1968), pp. 13, 23.
40. *Scriveners' Common Paper*, ed. by Steer, p. 23. For a general overview of the legal profession, including the many attorneys who were not members of the Inns of Court and had received no formal training, see J. H. Baker, *The Legal Profession and the Common Law* (1986), esp. pp. 87–88.
41. Goldsmiths' Company, London, Minute Book A (vol. 2), p. 268.
42. Goldsmiths' Company, London, Minute Book B, p. 1. The offices of Clerk and Beadle were separated and Mayour's successor as Clerk began to compile a separate 'minute book' of Court proceedings which, though still selective, ran in parallel with the main series of records.
43. I. Darlington (ed.) *London Consistory Court Wills 1492–1547*, London Record Society, 3 (1967), p. 32; *Court Minutes*, ed. by Davies, p. 239. The 1512 inventory (GL, MS 34357, fols 27–35) is printed in Clode, *Memorials*, pp. 84–92.
44. GL, MS 34048/1, fol. 119^v; Spekyngton was evidently a man of some means, for he was himself a tenant of one of the fraternity's most substantial properties, the Saracen's Head in Friday Street, for which he paid a rent of £9 6s. 8d. p.a.: *Court Minutes*, ed. by Davies, pp. 62n., 283.
45. Ferrers's master was Richard Nordon, a wealthy tailor who had been Master of the Company for 1422–23. He enrolled apprentices of his own in 1443–44 and 1455–56: GL, MS 34048/1, fols 172^v, 276^v, 370^v; 2, fol. 62^v.
46. *Court Minutes*, ed. by Davies, pp. 229–30. For the Beadle's oath see the 'Oaths Book', GL, MS 34007.
47. GL, MS 34048/1, fol. 302.

CHAPTER FOUR
THE COMPANY AND THE CRAFT

> Som tyme, afer men myghten lordes know
> By there array, from other folke; but now
> A man schal stody and musen a long throwe
> Whiche is whiche: O lordes, it sit to yowe
> Amende this, for it is for youre prowe.
> If twixt yow and youre men no difference
> Be in array, lesse is youre reverence.[1]

(In days gone by, men could distinguish lords from other folk by their clothing, but now a man must deliberate and ponder for a long while as to which is which. Lords, it is your duty to amend this, for if there is no difference in appearance between you and your men, your reputation will diminish.)

Thomas Hoccleve's warning was delivered in a poem, 'The Regement of Princes', which was written in 1411–12 and addressed to the future King Henry V. Amidst all the advice about the correct exercise of lordly and kingly power, this satirical passage pointed to the importance of clothing as a mark of status. Fashion in clothing was no longer the preserve of the élite, but had become something in which the lower orders in society were interested. In part this was a consequence of the economic changes brought by the Black Death in Europe: the survivors found themselves better off, and able to afford a greater range of consumer goods. It was also a reflection of changes in tailoring techniques and in fashions, which originated with the aristocracy and nobility and, with the aid of the tailor, were adopted by merchants, artisans and the better-off labourers.[2] Criticisms abounded of the 'outrageous and excessive apparel of divers people against their degree and estate', and led to the formulation of sumptuary legislation aimed at regulating what people wore.[3]

The new fashions themselves were sometimes the object of ridicule: long, close-fitting gowns known as 'houpelonds' were becoming common at the close of the fourteenth century, but their long sleeves which trailed along the ground meant that a lord had 'litel need of broomes to swepe away the filthe out of the street'.[4] Yet behind such comments were important developments in tailoring techniques and fashion. Garments were more closely 'fitted', a consequence, so it is believed, of the Hundred Years' War and the demand for clothing that would fit under armour. This placed a greater emphasis on the tailor's ability to 'shape' his cloth according to the fashions, and by the sixteenth century this had led to the production of pattern books to assist in the cutting-out process.[5] Tailoring had become a 'struggle to develop mastery over cloth', which resulted in a great diversity of styles being developed, adapted and then discarded to make way for others.[6] The Merchant Taylors' Company and its members were at the heart of these developments, with London acting as a major source of supply for the households of the great and the good in the City and beyond. This chapter will look at the range of goods made by tailors, the tools that were used, and the involvement of the Company in the regulation of apprenticeship and other working practices.

LINEN-ARMOURERS AND TENT-MAKERS

The manufacture of linen armour was a relatively small part of the tailoring industry, but as we saw earlier, it was of vital importance for the links that were established by the Company with the Crown. By the early fourteenth century the armourers of London were divided into specialisms according to the kinds of armour they made.[7] The main types of armour manufactured in the Middle Ages were plate armour, scale armour, mail armour and finally soft armour. The latter was worn either on its own, or as padding under one of the kinds of metal armour. In 1322 the City government issued ordinances which laid down standards to be applied to all kinds of armour, and these were subscribed to by twenty-eight named 'armourers', some of whose specialisms can be deduced from their surnames and other sources. Hugh le Heaumer, for instance, was almost certainly a 'heaumer', or maker of plate armour.[8] Like other ordinances of this kind, the armourers' regulations have been taken to mean that a guild of some kind, perhaps the forerunner of the Armourers' and Brasiers' Company, exercised authority over the manufacture of all kinds of armour in the City. In fact this was almost certainly not the case. What seems to have happened is that the City government, as it was prone to do, was simply issuing ordinances relating to particular types of goods, in order to address abuses that had been detected. There was no single guild at this time responsible for all kinds of armour, and indeed it is clear that by this time those armourers who made linen armour had already joined with the Tailors, a more natural marriage in many ways. Thus in March 1327 Edward III granted a charter to the 'Tailors and Armourers' of London. At least five of the men who attested the ordinances of 1322 were linen-armourers by trade, and four of those were listed among the governors of the Tailors and Linen-Armourers in 1328.[9] Further evidence of the separation of these specialisms came in 1347, when the Mayor and Aldermen approved ordinances specifically for the heaumers, which were to be enforced by three named Wardens. Recent work has convincingly argued that it was this organization that evolved into the Armourers' and Brasiers' Company.[10]

By the 1330s, therefore, linen-armourers and tailors were united as a single guild, and the rights of search over both were confirmed in the charters granted to them over the next two centuries. The term 'linen armour' covered a number of different kinds of garments, designed to be worn alone or else on top of, or below, metal armour. Garments of this kind typically took the form of quilted coats, known by a variety of names including *gambesons*, *jupons* and *aketons*, depending upon their function. In 1297, for instance, the men summoned from each ward to watch the gates of the City were 'to be properly armed with two pieces; namely with haketon and gambeson, or else with haketon and corset [corslet], or with haketon and plates'.[11] There are few surviving examples of linen armour, but the most famous English example, the jupon of Edward the Black Prince (Edward III's eldest son), now in Canterbury Cathedral, has been subjected to detailed analysis by costume and textile historians. The jupon was constructed in two halves upon a linen foundation, on top of which was a layer of wool padding. Over this was a layer of red and blue silk velvet, used as the background for the embroidered coat of arms. The rows of quilting were put in next, using vertical lines of stitching. Finally, the two halves of the jupon were sewn together (see Figs 4, 22a and b, and Fig. 23).[12]

Of particular importance for the Company's ambitions was the fact that the King's armourer, a key official within the Great Wardrobe, was frequently a linen-armourer with strong links to our emerging London guild. As we have seen, John de Cologne (employed *c.* 1333–55) was probably a member of the Fraternity of St John the Baptist, as indeed was Thomas Carleton (employed 1368–77), who bequeathed property to the Company on his death in 1389. Carleton is also described as an embroiderer, which further confirms the importance of the textile components of armour in this period. Another man with whom the Company was connected was Simon Winchecombe, an armourer and alderman of London. Winchecombe left six suits of armour in his will, as well as the tools of his trade, which indicate that his business focused on the production of metal armour. Nevertheless, he too was connected with the Tailors and Linen-Armourers: he was a trustee of the site of the Hall, and on his death in 1399 left 40s. to the Fraternity of St John the Baptist.[13] Another related craft that had significant royal connections was tent-making, an activity which

FIGURES 22a and b. The Black Prince's jupon, now in Canterbury Cathedral.
By kind permission of the estate of the late Janet Arnold

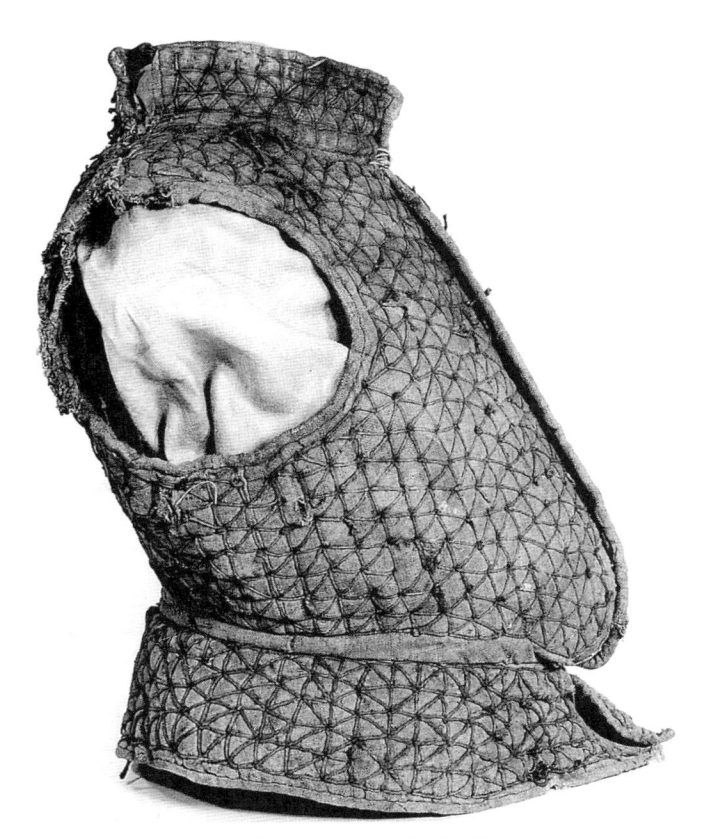

FIGURE 23. A side view of a 'jack of plate', c. 1560.
Royal Armouries Collection, Leeds

was often supervised by the King's armourer. Similar skills and tools were required to make both the elaborate canopies that were used for ceremonial occasions, and the more functional tents that were taken on military campaigns. The incorporation of a pavilion into the Company's first arms, granted in 1481, was a direct reference to the involvement of tailors in tent-making, and to the fact that the site of the Company's Hall had once been owned by Edward III's tent-maker, John de Yakesley (see above, Chapter One). The demand for tents and pavilions was largely confined to royal or noble households, and the need would have necessarily increased during times of war: for instance, tailors and a pavilioner were employed for the Black Prince's expedition of 1355–57 to Guienne (Aquitaine). Under Henry IV John Drayton, the King's tent-maker, employed several London tailors, as well as carpenters and other craftsmen, to manufacture tents for the King's visits to various parts of the kingdom, including the Parliament held at Gloucester in 1407.[14]

Little more is heard of linen-armourers, and even less of pavilioners in London: by the fifteenth century even Henry V's tent-maker, John Cony, described himself as a tailor when he drew up his will in 1417.[15]

However, there is enough evidence to show that these specialist occupations remained alive and well despite the widespread adoption of the designation 'citizen and tailor' as a form of shorthand for the multitude of activities within the garment industry: in 1418, for instance, John Partrich, known to have served as Master of the Fraternity of St John the Baptist in 1393–94, described himself as 'citizen and linen-armourer' in a property conveyance. Six years later, in March 1424, John St John came before the Mayor and Aldermen and stated that he had been admitted to the freedom on 17 July 1402 in the art of 'Lynge Armourers', but had since practised exclusively as a draper and now wished to 'translate' his freedom to the mistery of drapers.[16] Yet although it is difficult to find men described in such terms, there is no doubt that both linen-armourers and pavilioners continued to have a special significance for the Company, largely because of the close connections that they brought with the Crown. Until 1503, for instance, the craft was still officially known as the 'mistery of Tailors and Linen-Armourers', even though 'citizen and tailor' had become a convenient designation for most members.

DOUBLETS, PALTOCKS AND OLD CLOTHES

While linen-armourers and tent-makers had a particular resonance for the Company, it is important to bear in mind that the work of a tailor encompassed a wide range of activities in the garment trade. A number of sources, for instance, suggest that some members of the Company specialized in the manufacture of particular garments such as doublets, 'paltocks' and other items of upper body clothing: in 1378 John Tilneye was described as a 'paltock maker' two years before he was chosen to represent the Tailors and Linen-Armourers on the Common Council.[17] Some tailors diversified into closely related trades: in the mid-fifteenth century Richard Bishop described himself as 'doubletmaker alias hosier alias tailor', suggesting that he recognized the advantages of customers being able to get their 'doublet and hose' from the same shop. John Belham supplied no fewer than 164 pairs of hose to the Great Wardrobe, as well as 32 doublets, between 1442 and 1446.[18] No official distinction seems to have been made in London between those who manufactured different kinds of garments. This was not the case in Bristol, for instance, where the guild of tailors assessed each newly qualified apprentice and determined which kinds of clothes they should be allowed to make: one Bristol tailor was granted permission to make 'a coat, a kyrtyll, a womans gown, hose and doblet and none other but these'.[19]

In London the surviving records of the Company suggest that it was chiefly concerned with two broad areas of the trade: those who made new clothing, and those who refurbished and sold second-hand clothes. Men who made the latter were known as 'botchers', in the days before the term had taken on derogatory overtones, and the Company expended considerable effort in making sure that the two areas of the craft were separate. This was partly in the interests of consumer protection, as the mixing of old and new materials was one way in which customers could be deceived. The Wardens regularly inspected the workshops of the botchers: in 1425 one man was fined 2s. for adding a new lining of buckram to an old gown. Until the early sixteenth century the Company seems to have been happy to leave the second-hand clothing industry in London to unenfranchized tailors, many of them immigrants from elsewhere in England or from the Continent. Only citizens were, officially at least, allowed to make new clothes. A quick check in the Company records would thus make it easy for the Wardens to tell whether or not someone was supposed to be making new clothes, or whether they had found a botcher who was trying his luck. This was to change in the early sixteenth century, when the population of London began to increase for the first time since the Black Death. Although there would have been greater demand for clothing, the number of workshops seems to have increased significantly, to the point where masters feared for their businesses. Freemen could no longer afford to ignore the extensive market in second-hand clothes if they wanted to keep their shops going. In 1518, while reiterating its usual complaint about the numbers of botchers who made 'new apparel', the Company presented a petition to the Mayor and Aldermen in which it pressed the cause of older tailors who, perhaps due to failing eyesight or infirmity, were no longer capable of making new clothes and 'are fain to fall to the said feat of botching' to make a living. Times had changed, and the old boundaries between free and unfree, and between old and new clothing, seem to have been eroded by changing economic conditions.[20]

APPRENTICESHIP

Central to the life of the Company and the craft was apprenticeship. By the fourteenth century this had become the route by which the vast majority of individuals obtained the freedom of the City. Most apprentices came from outside London, placed with craftsmen and merchants by their families, and this helped to perpetuate the City's reputation as both a route to wealth and status and, conversely, as a place where the unwary could be exploited and corrupted.

SIR JOHN HAWKWOOD: A TAILOR'S APPRENTICE?

Alongside the legend of Dick Whittington (who in fact came from a prosperous Gloucestershire family) can be set the story of Sir John Hawkwood, the famous *condottiere* (soldier of fortune), who made both his fortune and his reputation as a captain of the White Company, in the employ successively of the city of Pisa, the Viscontis of Milan, Pope Gregory XI and the city of Florence. He is known to have been born in Essex in about 1330, the son of a minor landowner, and, according to John Stow, writing in the late sixteenth century, was 'bound as an apprentice with a taylor in the City of London'. He then entered the service of Edward III, and subsequently embarked on his adventures on the Continent. He died in 1394: his remains were returned to England and an equestrian portrait of Hawkwood by Paolo Uccello was placed in the Duomo in Florence.[21] His identification as a tailor's apprentice has frequently been doubted, in most instances because it is believed to have been derived from Italian versions of his name, Giovanni d'Acuto or Gianni della Guglia — 'John of the Needle'. However, the fact that Stow made the identification should give us pause for thought: he certainly had access to early records of the Company that no longer survive, and so it is conceivable that among them was a reference to Hawkwood's apprenticeship. Second, there is no doubt that Hawkwood had links with London, and after his death his trustees were in the capital sorting out his interests there, including the reversion of the site of the Leadenhall which they granted to the City in 1411. Finally, we have the evidence of the Westminster Chronicle, compiled in the 1380s and 1390s, which reported the death of 'the famous knight, Sir John Hawkwood, who, from being a poor apprentice of a hosier (*apprenticio caligarii*) in London, went to Lombardy'. Although it does not identify Hawkwood specifically as a tailor (*cissor* in Latin), it is nevertheless important evidence of a connection with the clothing industry in London. As we have seen, tailors frequently specialized in making hose as well as doublets and other garments, and so Stow may well have been right all along in his account of Hawkwood's remarkable career.[22]

REGULATING APPRENTICESHIP

The popularity of apprenticeship as a route to the freedom meant that it was especially important for the London companies to regulate it effectively. By the fifteenth century apprenticeship in London, like most towns and cities, had become subject to a number of rules and regulations introduced by the Crown, the City and by the companies themselves. Apprentices had to be of free condition (i.e. not the children of bondsmen or villeins), of English birth and, by a statute of 1388, at least twelve years old. A property qualification of 20s. per annum for the parents of apprentices was introduced in 1406–07, but London managed to secure an exemption in 1430 after concerted lobbying of the Crown and Parliament.[23] From the early fourteenth century at least, apprentices had to be enrolled at Guildhall within a year of the date of the start of the apprenticeship. The minimum term to be served by a London apprentice was set, from an early date, at seven years, after which the apprentice could be presented at Guildhall by his master in order to become a freeman.[24] The terms and conditions of an apprenticeship were recorded in an indenture, drawn up between the master and the apprentice, or in many cases, the master and the apprentice's father or mother (see Fig. 24). The indenture specified the length of term to be served, and the date when the apprenticeship was to commence, and frequently included clauses against fornication, gambling and the frequenting of taverns.

FIGURE 24. An apprenticeship indenture of 1518. Robert Worston, son of John Worston of Aldenham, Hertfordshire, yeoman, is here apprenticed to John Combe, citizen and merchant taylor of London, for seven years.
PRO, E210/9554

The early records of the Merchant Taylors' Company reveal a great deal about apprenticeship within the craft. From the early Court minutes (1486–93) we learn that the apprentice was formally enrolled at the Hall in the presence of the Master and Wardens of the craft, and a record made of the date of commencement of the apprenticeship, the length of the term, and the fee paid by the master into the common box. The fee charged by the Company for each apprentice was just 3s. 4d., and until the late fifteenth century there was no attempt to raise it in order to control access to the craft. As a result, annual enrolments rose from an average of around 60 in the 1420s to more than 80 in the 1460s, probably helping to expand the size of the craft as a whole. A controversial decision was taken in 1486 to raise the rates for freemen to 20s. and those for liverymen to just 10s., but this was swiftly reversed following protests from the freemen of the Company.[25]

The length of the terms to be served by the apprentices varied from the minimum of seven years — accounting for about half the apprentices — up to ten or even twelve years. One apprentice who was bound in 1486 to serve for twelve years had the unfortunate name of Rowland Lytillskyll, son of John Lytillskyll, and had come all the way to London from Hexham. It should be pointed out, however, that it was common for Londoners when making their wills to release their apprentices from the last years of their terms, so fewer would have actually served these long terms. As the example of Rowland Lytillskyll shows, the origins of the apprentices were often recorded in the Court minutes, along with the occupations or status of their fathers. The pattern that emerges is an interesting one: by the later fifteenth century the Company was recruiting apprentices from as far north as Cumberland and Yorkshire, with a significant number also drawn from the Midlands. Most were the sons of craftsmen, although several were from minor gentry families reflecting a common pattern whereby younger sons came to London to be apprenticed to merchants and craftsmen. It is worth noting that the greater companies, such as the Tailors and Skinners, recruited from further away than most of the other trades, many of whose apprentices were drawn from the Home Counties. This was a reflection of the extent to which the wealthier merchants and craftsmen in London had established trading links with all corners of England, Wales and even Ireland, and also the desire on the part of provincial parents to place their offspring, where possible, with members of the greater companies. Not all arrangements went smoothly: in January 1493 William Cokke was hauled before the Court after it transpired that he had taken on Richard Locan, son of Thomas Locan from Berwick upon Tweed as his apprentice, not being aware that Berwick was 'that tyme beyng Scottysshe and under thobeysaunce of the Kyng of Scottes'. This contravened statutes which laid down that apprentices had to be English subjects, and so the indenture was brought before the Court and cancelled.[26]

How successful was apprenticeship? The answer to this largely depends on the definition of success. On the one hand, no more than around a third of tailor apprentices ever completed their terms and became freemen. Interestingly, the success rate for the apprentices of liverymen was somewhat higher, reflecting the greater assistance which these apprentices probably had in setting up their own businesses. Apart from those apprentices who died during their service — a particular problem when the City was affected by epidemics of plague and 'sweating sickness' — tales of runaway apprentices were legion: the City government was even prevailed upon on occasion to write letters to town governments in the shires to ask for the return of apprentices who had absconded. It is likely that many apprentices left their masters after having acquired sufficient skills to set up some sort of tailoring business, either on the margins of London's economy, or back in their home town or village. It is generally thought that between three to five years was long enough to develop these skills, and thus the last two or three years might have been seen as superfluous for a young tailor who did not want to become a freeman. Many masters were doubtless keen to take advantage of the skilled, but unpaid, labour of their apprentices in the last few years of a term.

The mistreatment of apprentices by their masters is difficult to quantify, but there is plenty of evidence that it was seen as a problem and was taken seriously by company courts in London. On 4 June 1492 a tailor named Robert Archer was charged with a catalogue of breaches of his duties as a master: as well as failing to provide Thomas Godfrey with food and clothing, he had failed to 'find the apprentice to school'. At first, however, the Court accepted Archer's protestations of innocence, and sent Godfrey away. He returned a few days later, but once again the Master and Wardens 'not gevyng credence unto the same apprentice commaunded hym ayen [again] to doo his master service as he was bound to doo'. Some time after this he came before the Court for a third time, 'pyteously compleynyng' of his 'undue chastesyng' at the hands of Archer who had beaten him about the head with a rod described as a 'mete yerd', an iron yardstick used to measure cloth. He also described the verminous state in which he was forced to live. Finally the Court believed him and, 'having respecte to the tendre age of the said apprentice, beyng faderles and moderles, and also of the undue and unreasonable kepyng of the same apprentice', ended the apprenticeship and placed the matter before the Mayor and Chamberlain, who briefly imprisoned Archer.[27] In another case the Court heard that John Bowman

gave unto his said apprentice unlefull and without reason chastisyng as well with wepyns defensyve as with lak of mete, drynke, vitailles and apparaill.

Bowman refused to co-operate with an investigation into his behaviour, asserting that 'he wolde be maister over his own apprentice', and his violent reaction prompted the Master and Wardens to take the unusual decision to send the unnamed apprentice to live with one of the Wardens. The provision of a 'safe house' for the apprentice indicates that the charges against Bowman were taken seriously and that the Company was prepared to intervene.[28] Cases such as these were common to all the crafts in London, and indeed those disputes which came before the Mayor and Aldermen show a similar pattern, in that the master was found to be to blame more often than the apprentice. In many instances it was discovered that the master had abandoned his apprentice, rather than the other way round.[29]

To offset these cases of ill-treatment are the many 'success stories', evidence of good relations between masters and apprentices. As well as releasing their apprentices from the remainder of their terms, masters would also leave them money, goods and occasionally land as a mark of regard. John Snowdon left his apprentice the sum of 20s. 'so that he be trew to

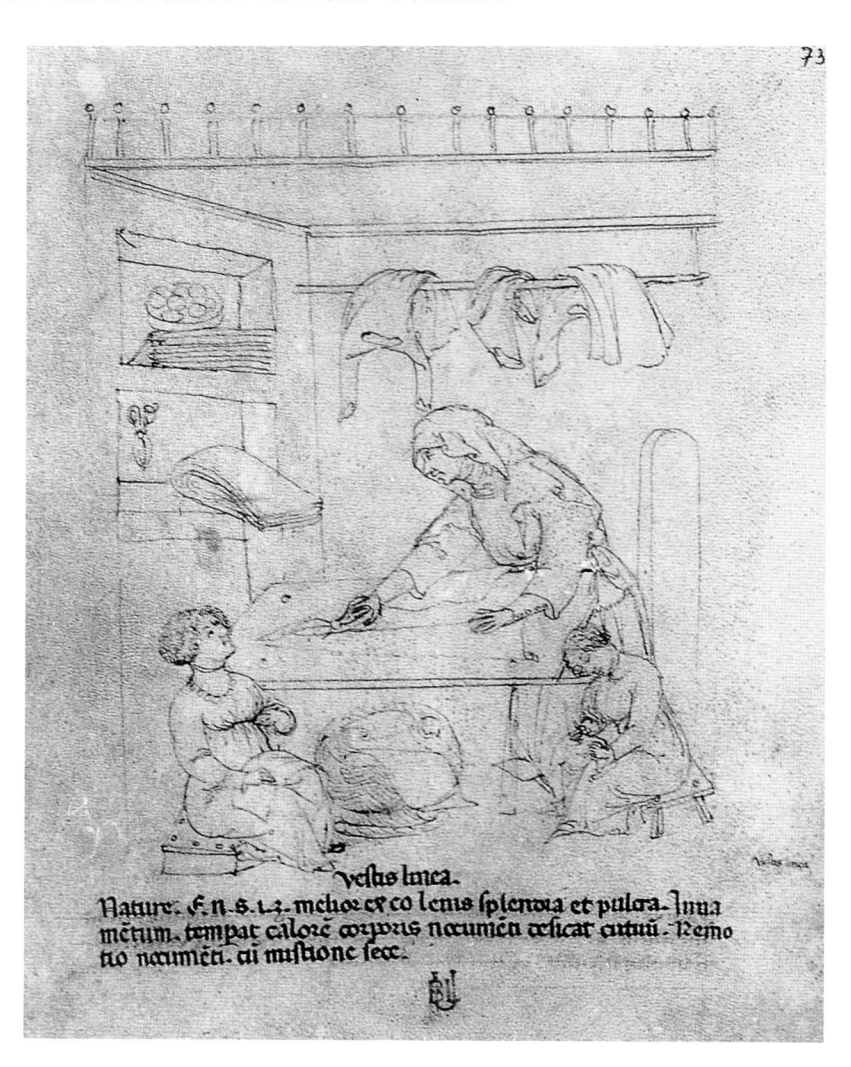

FIGURE 25. A late-fourteenth-century drawing of a tailor's workshop, a rare depiction of a female tailor, from the *Tacuinum Sanitatis* of Liège. The book contains illustrations of many different aspects of medieval life, including cookery, health and medicine, as well as crafts.
Université de Liège, Bibl. MS 1041, fols 73–73ᵛ

my wiffe and myn executors and serve the termes of his apprentesod comyng at my decese'. Hugh Acton (Master 1527), whose own apprentices included (Sir) Thomas White, was among the first members of the Company to establish a 'loan fund' for apprentices wishing to set up their own businesses, and this became a common feature of the charitable provision made by the City companies in the sixteenth century.[30] Naturally, some tailors were in a better position than others to provide for members of their households: in his will proved in 1504, George Lovekyn, Henry VII's tailor and a former Warden of the Company, left his apprentices some fine items of clothing, and his servant Stephen Jasper all the bedding he used to lie on. These bonds could even stretch across three generations: Walter Povey (Master 1492) asked to be buried in the church of St Mary Aldermary 'afore the Roode there in the myddle of the said churche atte the hedde of the buriall of master Raufe Hollande late Alderman deceased'. The controversial Holland (Master 1419) had been master to Povey's own master, Robert Colwich, and was perhaps seen by him as a kind of tailoring 'grandfather figure'.[31]

SETTING UP SHOP

Those who completed their apprenticeships were presented by their masters at Guildhall where, on payment of a fee, they were granted the Freedom of the City. They were also required to come to the Hall and swear an admission oath, promising to be 'good and true to the fraternite of taillours and linen

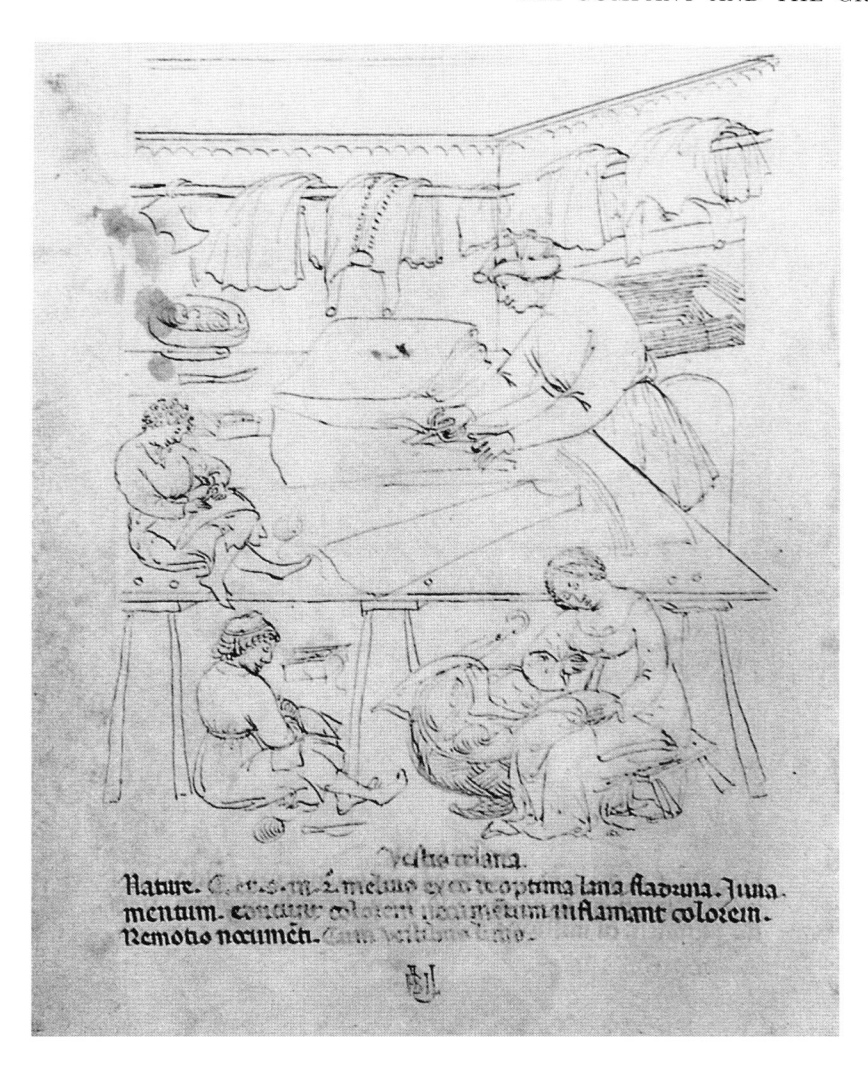

FIGURE 26. A second drawing from the *Tacuinum Sanitatis* of Liège. Details as Figure 25, but this time showing a male tailor, together with his wife and his children or apprentices.

armorers' and at all times to obey the summons of the Master and Wardens. New freemen also had to undertake to obey all the ordinances of the craft and not to disclose the secrets and councils of the craft and the fraternity to anyone. They also promised not to 'forsake this felaship and crafte of taillours for none other in clothyng, goyng and rydyng'.[32] Only around a third of tailor apprentices got this far, compared with about half of all Mercer apprentices — it is likely that the greater wealth possessed by the average mercer enabled them to retain a greater proportion of their would-be members.[33] Having completed their training, new freemen faced the challenge of establishing a viable tailoring business in an already competitive market-place. Some, as we have seen, were aided by their former masters but most were not, and it was for this reason that many of the London companies by the mid-sixteenth century had established schemes of one sort or another to provide capital for apprentices wishing to set up shop.

The kinds of businesses established by tailors varied greatly, largely because some were keen to expand into other related areas, such as the retailing of cloth, while others concentrated on the manufacture of clothes. The prime concern of the Company was to make sure that the Wardens could easily track down and inspect the workshops of its members, and this was one reason why freemen were only supposed to set up shop with the permission of their governors. This was easier said than done: particularly troublesome were those new freemen who decided to set up small workshops in attics or chambers, rather than in the ground-floor shops depicted in most contemporary illustrations (see Figs 25 and 26). These 'chamber-holders' were difficult to locate and their work was often suspected of being sub-standard. One imaginative, but rather ambitious, solution was proposed in 1450: new freemen were ordered to serve as journeymen with established masters until they were in a position to set up a proper business. Those who did not find immediate employment were ordered to live 'in the comons' with other recently qualified tailors so that they could be taken on as servants 'by the day or by the garment'. The ordinance does not, in fact, seem to have been enforced with any vigour by the Company, probably because of the practical difficulties of imposing such a regime upon young men keen to make their own way in the world and who did not necessarily want to do so under the eye of the Wardens. Many new freemen did, nevertheless, serve as journeymen for a period of time in order to raise the capital necessary to set up shop. Such men were known as 'free sowers', and were registered with the Company by their employers, who paid a fee for each one.[34]

Tailoring was not a particularly expensive craft to become involved in: it did not require much in the way of capital investment, unlike the metal-working crafts, nor did it need a reliable water supply or a large labour force. Tailors could justifiably claim that they did not make much noise or generate large quantities of unpleasant waste that could cause problems in built-up urban areas. This made them attractive tenants: the attitudes of many landlords were reflected in a decision taken by the Court of Assistants in October 1486 to grant a lease of one of the Company's many properties as long as it was not sub-let to a pewterer, fuller, shearman, blacksmith or founder, crafts notorious for noise and pollution.[35] Most tailoring businesses were small, comprising the master and perhaps two or three apprentices at various stages and maybe a servant. Although women are generally under-represented in the surviving records, it is clear that they too were very active in the tailoring industry in London. Not being entitled to the freedom, married women could, however, elect to trade as *femmes soles*, with the approval of the City. Others chose to carry on businesses related to the trades of their husbands. Among the latter was Ellen Langwith, married to John Langwith (Master of the Company in 1444), who traded as a silkwoman. The Company's ordinances of 1507 refer at several points to the responsibilities of a 'man or woman of the craft', and among these were the widows of members of the Company who were entitled to take up the freedom on their husbands' deaths. There are numerous examples of widows who continued to run their late husbands' businesses and train their apprentices. Sir John Percyvale's remarkable wife, Thomasine, was already the widow of two tailor liverymen before she married the future Mayor, and in each case she appears to have taken an active part in running their successful businesses.[36]

When it came to equipment, the essential tools were scissors and shears. Surviving examples show that the two were clearly distinct, and it is likely that scissors had become particularly useful for more intricate cutting-out work, while shears remained the best tool for cutting up large pieces of cloth. The form of these tools has not changed in many centuries: shears were made of a single piece of iron bent in the middle to form the two arms and blades, while scissors were made from two pieces of metal joined by a pin to form a central pivot.[37] Both implements are common in medieval iconography: the earlier of the two hearse-cloths belonging to the Company has several fine representations of scissors (see Fig. 15, Col. Pl. IIIc, and Frontispiece), and shears are commonly depicted in portrayals of both medieval shearmen and tailors. Strangely, however, there are very few documentary references to 'scissors'. One of these occurs in the inventory of a tailor, Robert de Kesteven, which was made in 1383–84: he was found to have two pairs of 'sisores' in his shop along with large quantities of cloth, garments, and pewter vessels.[38] On the other hand, examples of 'shears' are plentiful, especially in the wills of members of the Company: in 1470, for example, Benedict Genetas left a pair of 'taylours scheres' to Robert Wadlok, as well as a new doublet of 'musterdevelers' and a 'cote of coton russet'.[39] Another London tailor, James Atkynson, left 'my best pair of shears' to his brother Christopher along with a blue furred gown and a doublet. He left another pair to a second brother, and a third to his apprentice Christopher

Hornby.[40] The solution may lie in the use of 'shears' as an all-embracing term to describe tailoring cutting implements: the Company and its members seem to have regarded scissors as the emblem of the craft (as on the hearse-cloth), yet its chapel was described as being decorated with 'solailes et scheres'. Many individual tailors also seem to have used scissors as visible representations of their craft, some using them on their seals and others painting them on boards outside their shops.[41]

The total cost of a tailor's tools was relatively small in comparison with the cost of the cloth used to make up the garments: the sixteenth-century inventory of John Lumberte, a Southampton tailor, valued his tailoring tools (three pairs of shears and two 'pressing irons') at 2s. 6d. while his stock of cloth was worth £9 5s. 6d. The only furniture in the shop was a set of shelves and a 'shop-board' (worth 3s.) on which a tailor would sit, cross-legged, while stitching together pieces of cloth.[42] As well as pressing irons, tailors' wills and inventories frequently mention 'shaping boards', used to help in cutting out patterns: George Lovekyn, tailor to Henry VII, left several 'shapyng boards' to his servants and apprentices.[43] Other items of equipment mentioned in inventories, accounts and contemporary descriptions include needles, pins, thread, tailor's chalk and strips of parchment, used to measure parts of the body for individual clients in the days before tape measures. Some of these items were imported from the continent: Queen Elizabeth I's tailor took delivery of both 'Spanish needles' and 'Milan needles'. The well-dressed tailor painted by Moroni in the mid-sixteenth century stands with a large pair of scissors, and with the cloth marked out, either with chalk or with tacking (Col. Pl. IV). Yard-sticks made of wood or iron were used to measure lengths of cloth. These had to conform to standard measures, such as the Company's own silver cloth yard, which dates from the reign of Henry VII (see Fig. 27). A 'tailor's yard' was a popularly recognized unit of measure: when an archery competition was held in Calais in 1478, for instance, the distance between the two targets was to be 260 'tayllour yardys met [measured] owt wyth a lyne'.[44]

To open a shop a freeman had first to pay a fee of 10s. to the Company, one means by which it could keep track of its members and ensure that they had the resources to go into business. Shops in London, as in many large towns and cities, were generally small and numerous, particularly in fashionable shopping streets such as Cheapside where many were only four or five feet wide. A single window at the front often contained a counter over which goods were sold.[45] Premises typically comprised buildings of two or three storeys of which the first was given over to the actual workshop, and the rest used as living quarters for the family and any servants or apprentices.[46] Away from London's main shopping streets, houses and shops were larger: a surviving building contract of 1383 provided for the construction of five such buildings in 'Adlane' (Addle Street) in the parish of St Alban Wood Street, which were each to be twelve feet wide and extended fifty feet beyond the street. The ground floor, containing the shop and a parlour, was nine feet in height, the first floor eight feet and the top floor seven feet.[47] In the case of the wealthiest tailors, several premises were needed to fulfil different functions. Thomas Petyt (Master in 1497–98) owned two tenements in London, each with a shop and a warehouse where he stored large quantities of cloth and other merchandise.[48] These 'branches' were often run by members of the family, but also by those apprentices who were sufficiently well qualified and trusted to act on behalf of their masters. In 1444 John Edward obtained a licence from the Master and Wardens of the Company for his apprentice to 'tenir shoppe a son meistres profit within his terme' at a cost of 33s. 4d.[49]

The high cost of renting shops, particularly in the principal shopping streets of London such as Cheapside and the Poultry, encouraged many artisans to set up stalls in off-street bazaars, known as selds. These could be rented far more cheaply than most shops. They were often solid structures, normally single-storeyed, and could contain as many as twenty plots, each with a chest or counter. Selds would frequently become associated with particular occupations: the London tanners, for instance had eighteen stalls for members of the craft in one seld in 1300.[50] Stalls, whether located in selds or not, were generally a popular means of selling goods: in 1375 a jeweller and his wife were granted a ten-year lease on a moveable stall beneath Ludgate at a cost of 40s. per

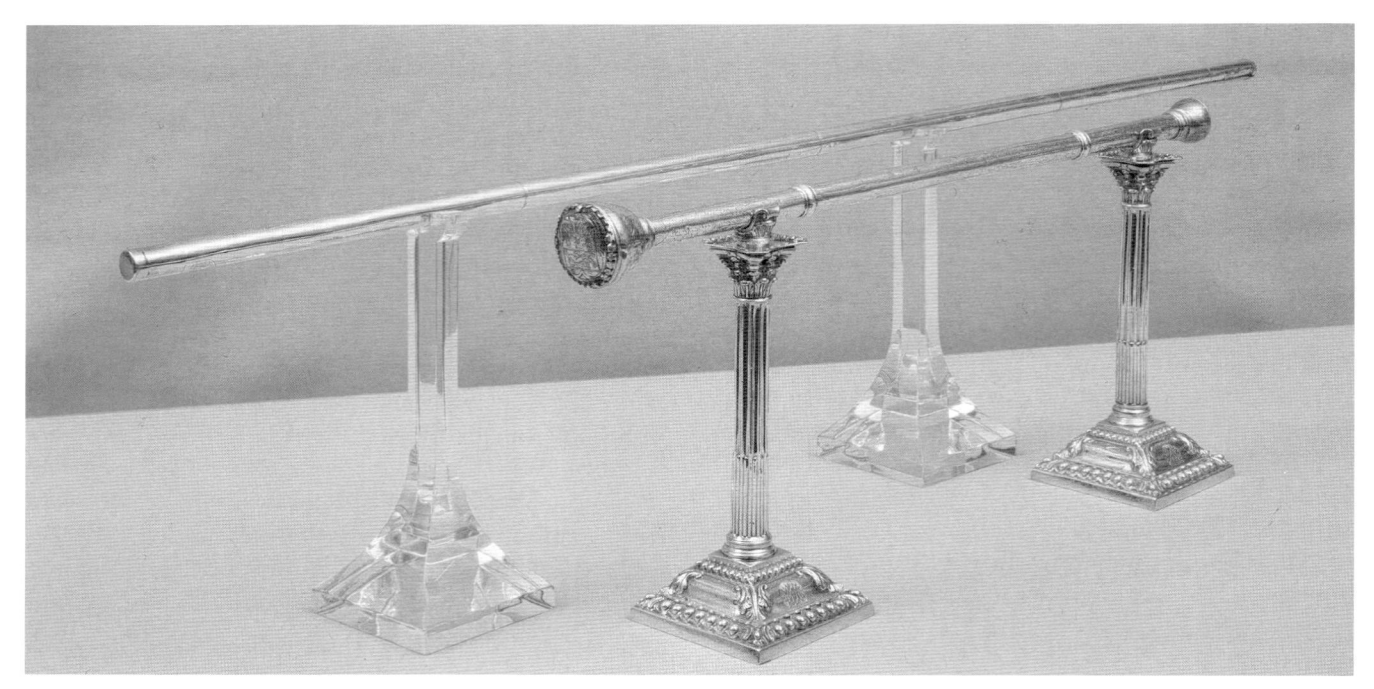

FIGURE 27. The Company's silver Cloth Yard (*c.* 1500), and silver Mace (1512 × 1586). The Company's Arms of 1586, and the Holy Lamb, are engraved on the head and foot respectively of the Mace. The Cloth Yard served as a standard measure for the craft, and was used to check the accuracy of the tailors' own measures in the interests of customer protection.

Merchant Taylors' Company

annum payable to the City Chamberlain.[51] Tailoring examples can also be found. In 1491 the Tailors' Court pronounced judgment in a dispute concerning Rowland Hymeson and his covenanted servant John Langryk. John was to return 'a peyre sheres which the same John toke from the stall of the said Rowland'.[52] The City's desire to regulate stall-holders is again shown in the case of John Clerk, a tailor, who was indicted by the Wardmote of Bread Street in January 1422 for a 'faux' stall, perhaps one which was set up without permission or which took up too much room along the street.[53] In Bristol the operation of illicit stalls seems to have been a matter of concern for the guilds: in 1489 the guild of tailors there ordained that no members of the craft should sell hose 'whatever it be mens or womens in the markett commonly called the Hie strete or market place upon bordes or tressels'.[54]

Finally, it should be remembered that tailors did not operate in isolation. They were part of complex networks of debt and credit, and supply and distribution, not just in London but in the regions as well. Tailoring was particularly closely related to several other crafts: for example, skinners supplied the furs of different kinds and qualities that often adorned clothes at this time. Occasionally there were conflicts between tailors and skinners over the right to work furred garments, as many tailors appear to have preferred to buy the furs from the skinners and attach them to the garments themselves, rather than sub-contract the work to a skinner. Other strong links existed with embroiderers, a number of whom were members of the Company, and with haberdashers, who supplied buttons, buckles and other dress accessories. Finally, of course, there were the suppliers of cloth, together with the dyers, shearmen and fullers who were responsible for the various cloth-finishing processes.[55]

LONDON TAILORS AND THEIR CUSTOMERS

Just as the scale of businesses established by tailors varied a great deal, so too did their customers. At one end of the scale, the 'botchers' were catering for the poorer elements in the capital, people without the purchasing power necessary to afford even the cheapest fabrics for new clothing. At the other end lay the conspicuous consumption of the royal Household and the households of the great and the good. While styles could sometimes cross these boundaries and thus enrage social commentators such as Hoccleve, the materials used meant that clothes made for princes simply could not be afforded by paupers. This next section will look more closely at the extent to which London acted as a centre for the manufacture of high quality clothing, thus attracting the attention of customers from far and wide.

THE GREAT WARDROBE

The highest accolade that could be bestowed on a London tailor was to be a supplier to, or worker in, the 'Great Wardrobe' of the King. The Great Wardrobe emerged in the early thirteenth century, and by the fifteenth had become an independent royal department. By 1366 it was permanently located in a mansion on the site of Baynard's Castle near Blackfriars.[56] The staff of what was increasingly known simply as 'the Wardrobe' included the 'serjeant-tailor', who was paid a wage of 12d. a day and headed a section comprising a small number of 'yeomen' tailors who in the fifteenth century were paid 6d. a day, a good wage by the standards of the time. There were close links with other sections, including that headed by the King's skinner, whose employees worked furs ready to be sewn on to clothing. Tailors also worked in other areas of the Wardrobe: Henry IV's pavilioner, John Drayton, was in charge of ten tailors in 1409–10 when more than £18 was spent on tents for the King's visit to the West Country, including the Parliament which met at Gloucester. The heart of the Wardrobe, though, was the department headed by the serjeant-tailor who, from at least the 1370s, lived in his own house within the rapidly growing complex of buildings at Baynard's Castle. For the Company and its members, the establishment of a permanent Great Wardrobe there was extremely important, for it meant that freemen of the City were increasingly able to monopolize positions within it and to dominate the manufacture of clothing for the royal family. Richard II's tailor, Walter Rauf, was almost certainly a member of the Company, judging by his presence in a list of trustees of the Hall in 1380.[57] So extensive were the links with the London craft that the three serjeant-tailors appointed by Henry V and Henry VI were not only liverymen, but rose to become Masters of the Company. William Tropenell was already a Past Master (1411) when he was appointed in 1413, while his successor John Legge, who had served under Tropenell for several years, was elected Master in 1434, two years after taking up the post in the Great Wardrobe. Legge, in turn, gave way to George Ashton in 1452 and he was elected Master for the year 1455–56.[58]

The victory of the Yorkists over the Lancastrians in 1461, and the succession of Edward IV, was followed by changes to personnel in both the royal Household and the Great Wardrobe. George Ashton was removed from office, although this was less to do with any suspicions about him personally than with more general hostility towards the vestiges of the previous regime. Yet the links with the craft in London continued to be as strong as ever, although a slight change in emphasis is apparent in the choice of two men, William Pault (tailor to Edward IV, 1461–75) and George Lovekyn (tailor to Edward IV, 1475–83, and then to Henry VII), tailors who had come to London from Paris, the capital of European fashion at that time. Both, however, had become freemen of the Company in London: Pault took on a large number of apprentices, including one, Matthew Gregory, who subsequently served under him in the Great Wardrobe, while Lovekyn, born in Paris, rose to become one of the Wardens of the Company in 1486. Lovekyn's long tenure of the office of serjeant-tailor (now increasingly known as 'King's tailor') was interrupted only briefly by the turbulent reign of Richard III when a Londoner, Henry Davy, replaced him. Thus although the Crown seems to have increasingly appreciated the skills that were being developed in northern Europe and brought over to London, the personnel employed in the Wardrobe were still very much drawn from the ranks of the Company. When Lovekyn died in 1504 his own apprentice, Stephen Jasper, succeeded him as King's tailor.[59]

Beyond the permanent staff of the Great Wardrobe, the Crown was also dependent upon the London tailors for the large-scale production of clothing for important state occasions, notably coronations.

The scale of these events made it necessary to recruit large numbers of tailors and other workers for periods ranging from half a day to several weeks in order to produce the many different lavish robes that were needed. Some of the best records survive for the coronations of the ill-fated King Richard III and his consort, Anne, on 6 July 1483. The decision by Richard to seize the throne from his nephew King Edward V in June meant that the Great Wardrobe was a hive of activity. Much had probably already been done in preparation for the aborted coronation of Edward, but the scale of the task meant that no fewer than seventy-three tailors were hired for a total of 412 days' work in order to have everything ready three days before. The following entries from the Wardrobe accounts provide a taste of the finery that was created for the King, and the hundreds of people who took part in the processions and ceremonial:

First a doublett of grene clothe of gold of satyn for the Kyng.
Item a longe gown of purpulle velvett furred with ermyns powdered, opyn at the sides and ermyned abowte the same.
Item for the Kyng ij shertes wherof the oon shalbe launde [lawn: thin linen cloth] and the other of crymsyn tartaryn [= rich silk cloth], the bothe largely opyn byhynde, before and on the shulders and laced with annelettes silver and gilt and with laces agleted [i.e. tipped] silver and gilt.
Item a cote of crymsyn satyn largely opened as the shertes be to the whiche cote his hosen shalbe layced with ryban of sylke.
Item a payre of lynnen gloves to be put on the Kynges handes after he ys anoynted.
Item the Kynges robes of purpulle vellvett.
Item for roobes for lordes, jugez with other officers and lyverey gownes for the Kynges servauntes a gayne [against] the saide coronacion of oure seyde soverayngne Lorde.

The accounts also list a large number of robes of various kinds that were given to archbishops, bishops, dukes, earls and barons and to officers of state such as the Chancellor. The Queen's robes were similarly splendid, and provision was also made for robes for her ladies-in-waiting and members of her household. Again, while many of the key items would have been made by the Queen's own tailor, the scale of the operation meant that a large number of tailors had to be hired by the Great Wardrobe to work day and night in the ten days before the double coronation.[60] A high proportion of these men were London tailors, who appear in the Company's records from the 1460s to the 1490s, enrolling apprentices, paying fines or leaving bequests to the Fraternity of St John the Baptist. The coronations of Richard and Anne, like those of their predecessors and successors, were therefore dependent upon the labour of London craftsmen and the extraordinary results a testimony to their skill.[61]

As well as those members of the Company who provided labour for the Great Wardrobe in 1483, several prominent liverymen were among the chief suppliers of materials to be used for robes and other items of clothing. These included Roger Barlowe (Master 1479), Robert Duplage (Master 1481) and Walter Povey (Master 1492). By this time the fortunes of the wealthier members of the Company were increasingly founded on cloth dealing and other mercantile activity, and their provision of materials for Richard's coronation alongside London drapers and mercers was a recognition of this at the highest level. Two years later the accounts drawn up for Henry VII's coronation, following his victory at Bosworth, listed other prominent Company members as suppliers, such as Hugh Pemberton, who supplied 157½ yards of valuable scarlet cloth at a cost of £75 16s. 8d. This cloth was then used in garments made up under the direction of George Lovekyn, once more drawing on the skills of tailors hired from the City.[62]

This strong link between members of the Company and the monarch continued into the sixteenth century and beyond. London tailors were still seen as being literally at the cutting-edge of contemporary fashions in clothing, and were regularly employed by the Crown and members of the nobility. John Skut, tailor to Queen Anne Boleyn, also supplied clothes to Lady Lisle in the 1530s, and on one occasion was rewarded with a gift of quails. Lord Lisle employed the King's tailor, John Malt, to make him clothes while he was imprisoned in the Tower of London in 1541.[63] As we shall see, one of the most significant royal tailors was Walter Fyshe, Queen Elizabeth's first tailor. He seems to have been employed by her before she acceded to the throne, and continued in her service until 1582, by which time he had been promoted to the post of 'yeoman or keeper of our vesture or apparel'. Fyshe was a liveryman of the Company and member of the Court of Assistants. In 1580 he gave to the Company a tenement in Candlewick Street (Cannon Street), the rent from which was to be used to fund five 'poor studious scholars of St John's Oxford'. He also endowed the almshouses next to the Hall with £7 per annum and an extra 20s. for each of the seven almsmen.[64]

THE NOBILITY AND GENTRY

Away from the wardrobes of the King and Queen, London tailors were frequently employed to make clothes for prominent noblemen and women, and members of their households. Some of them established wardrobes of their own in London: the famous John, Duke of Bedford, brother of Henry V, had a wardrobe in 'Kyron Lane' (now Skinners' Lane) in the parish of St James Garlickhithe. In charge of his wardrobe was David Brecknock, a London tailor.[65] Accounts from the 1390s show several London tailors listed as creditors of the household of Henry, Earl of Derby (son of John of Gaunt, and the future Henry IV), while members of the Company supplied clothing to the household of another prominent fourteenth-century royal earl, Roger Mortimer, Earl of March at about the same time.[66] Less prominent, but equally keen on patronizing the shops of London tailors, were the families of Dinham and Howard, whose family seats lay a long way from the capital in Cornwall and Norfolk respectively. The Dinhams visted London regularly in the 1380s and 1390s to obtain goods from skinners and mercers in the capital, and to be measured for clothes in the house of their tailor, John Bourwell. Fitting sessions were probably convivial occasions: the expenses of John Dinham the younger in 1382 included 'wine at the tailor's house', while ale was provided for Bourwell's servant. The bill came to more than £6, which included quantities of red and green cloth and the costs of making several gowns, probably for the occasion of Richard II's marriage to his first Queen, Anne of Bohemia.[67] The Dinhams were still using London tailors half a century later: Thomas Gay, one of several wealthy Fleet Street tailors, supplied cloth to Sir John Dinham which was used to make banners for the Yorkists at the Battle of Towton (March 1461).[68] Sir John Howard, who was elevated to the dukedom of Norfolk after fighting alongside Henry VII at Bosworth, made good use of London tailors and hatters: Henry Galle (Thomasine Percyvale's first husband) was one of his chief suppliers, but he also bought both cloth and garments from Galle's fellow liverymen Roger Tego and Thomas Parker.[69]

Other gentry families, too, can be found patronizing the shops of London tailors. The remarkable letters of the Paston family of Norfolk, for instance, show that John Paston III established close links with John Lee (Master 1483–84) and even stayed at his house near Ludgate on a visit to London in 1479.[70] In the late 1480s a freeman of the Company named Robert Colson submitted a petition to Chancery in which he complained that he was owed more than £11 by the estate of the late Nicholas Carew esquire, of Beddington in Surrey. In his petition Colson included a full list of the goods which he had supplied to Carew, including short and long gowns and leather jackets for Nicholas as well as for his wife, his children and his servants. The materials included satin, sarcenet (a type of silk), buckram, medley (various colours) and cloth of crimson and green. It represented a substantial investment of time and materials by the tailor and his workshop. It is not known whether Colson was ever repaid; even George Lovekyn, Henry VII's tailor, found himself out of pocket during his time in royal service.[71]

LIVERIES

One of the most colourful developments in fashion in the later Middle Ages was the use of 'liveries', gowns and hoods as indicators of an attachment to a particular craft, to a nobleman, or even to the King. In London the market for liveries was extensive: from at least 1300, representatives of the City would meet the King dressed in red and white parti-coloured gowns, which were also worn at the ceremonies accompanying the election of the Mayor in October each year. By the mid-fifteenth century red and white were no longer being used as a matter of course, but it was still regarded as essential for all citizens who attended occasions such as royal entries to wear liveries of a pre-ordained colour, with badges to identify their crafts. By this time the Mayor and Aldermen commonly wore impressive scarlet liveries for such occasions. Those Londoners elected to Parliament were entitled to an allowance of cloth from the City for their livery: knights, such as Sir William Estfield, a mercer, were granted double the usual allowance.[72] Liveries were also worn by officers of the Mayor's household and the City Chamber, such as the Recorder, Chamberlain, Common Serjeant, Common Clerk and Swordbearer. Normally these men received annual allowances of cloth from the City, which were used to make their gowns. Some of the lesser servants in the Mayor's household were apparently envious of their superiors and were reprimanded in 1486 for wearing livery gowns that were 'so long and so side [low] that they may not do service in this Cittee'. Instead they were ordered to have gowns made that came to at least one foot above the soles of their shoes.[73]

The companies placed liveries at the heart of their ritual and ceremonial lives. The wearing of a common gown and hood was seen as a symbol of brotherhood and as a way of binding members together. Liveries could be changed annually, but as it was an expensive process — liverymen were required to pay for their own gowns and hoods — most companies preferred to change every two or three years. In May 1492, for instance, the Court of Assistants of the Company decided not to order a new livery for the coming year. By the late sixteenth century, although liveries remained of vital importance, there is evidence that there was less variety in the colours that were chosen: John Stow wrote nostalgically of the diversity of colours chosen by the companies in days gone by, noting that 'now of late time they haue vsed their gowns to be al of one colour, and those of the sadest'.[74] Nevertheless, for London's tailoring businesses the popularity of liveries meant a steady stream of work, with members of the Company supplying livery robes to the City government and to the Drapers, Mercers and other livery companies.

TAILORS INTO MERCHANT TAYLORS

The prominent position occupied by the Company in the mid-sixteenth century stemmed in large part from a shift in emphasis away from the traditional artisanal work of making up clothes. At one level this was reflected in diversification into other areas of manufacture. The remarkable 1550 inventory of William Bonyvaunt, citizen and merchant taylor, listed more than two hundred hats of various kinds, as well as gloves, sword girdles and materials 'in the shop on the stretesyde'.[75] Although relatively unusual, Bonyvaunt is a useful reminder that freemen did not necessarily restrict themselves to the craft through which they had obtained the freedom. This was particularly noticeable among those members of the Company who became involved in trade. In the fourteenth and early fifteenth centuries cloth dealing had been the preserve of only the most prominent liverymen of the Company, those who had strong links with wealthy customers. However, a serious dispute with the Drapers' Company in the late 1430s and early 1440s suggests that members of the Company were beginning to pose a severe threat to the Drapers' dominance of the day-to-day retailing of cloth in London. Central to the dispute was the right to 'search' for defective cloth in the City, traditionally the preserve of the Drapers: the Tailors challenged this, most notably by securing a new charter in 1440 that allowed them rights of 'full search' over their members, whatever their line of business. Conflict also arose over St Bartholomew's Fair, again because the Tailors did not want the Drapers to inspect the cloth sold by their members there. By this time several liverymen were being described in non-London sources as 'drapers', referring not to their company affiliation but to the nature of their business dealings. Ralph Holland was one of several London suppliers of cloth in the late 1410s to Thomas, Duke of Clarence. The King's tailor, William Tropenell, was another Master of the Company who was described as a 'pannarius' (draper), along with Robert Fenescales (Master 1420): between 1419 and 1421, for instance, Tropenell supplied cloth worth nearly £90 to the Crown.[76] Over the next century members of the Company became increasingly active as suppliers of fine cloth to the Crown and nobility, to the extent that for the coronations of Richard III and Henry VII they were even as prominent as some of the London mercers. London tailors were supplying cloth to men such as the Earl of Oxford, and to provincial gentry such as Thomas

Carmynowe, a Devonshire esquire, whose executors were sued by Richard Nordon for the non-payment of a bill for £20 worth of cloth.[77]

By the later fifteenth century Blackwell Hall, the centre for cloth-dealing in London, was being used by both tailors and drapers to buy and sell cloth. The Company's Court minutes for 1486 record an agreement between the two companies to regulate trading there: a group of six prominent liverymen was chosen to liaise with the Drapers in case of any disputes or breaches of ordinances.[78] By this time many tailors had built up large stocks of cloth in their warehouses, some of which would doubtless have been made into garments, and some sold on to other craftsmen. A poignant example of this is afforded by the career of Roger Shavelock. He was apprenticed in 1455–56, and after ten years had completed his training and acquired sufficient capital to open a shop and take on his first apprentice. Membership of the livery of the craft duly followed in 1469–70, and the last reference to him in the Company's records shows him enrolling two apprentices in 1476–77.[79] Business was seemingly good, for by the time of his death in 1489 he was said to have cloth worth £1,000 in his shop. However, the manner of his death caused something of a sensation and was reported by the author of the Great Chronicle:

In thys mayers tyme a Taylour namyd Roger Shavelok Dwellyng w'yn ludgate and holdyng there a shopp well storid wyth drapery, kut his awne throte.[80]

The involvement of members of the Company in the domestic cloth trade saw them establish links with suppliers in the provinces and with cloth finishers (fullers, shearmen and dyers). Richard Nayler, for instance, sent his cloth to be fulled in the workshop of a Southwark fuller, while Stephen Trappys pardoned the debts owed to him by two dyers and a shearman on his deathbed in 1485. Another tailor had close links with dyers from Colchester, a noted centre of the cloth dyeing industry in the south-east.[81] The Company kept a beady eye on these activities, for it was damaging to the reputation of the craft if unfinished cloth was sold: fines were often extracted from freemen who sold 'unwet' cloth, in other words cloth that had not been fulled properly. In doing this the Company was heeding Langland's warning that

Cloth that cometh fro the wevyng / is nougt comly to were,
Tyl it is fulled under fote / or in fullyng stokkes,
Wasshen wel with water / and with taseles cracched
Ytouked, and ytented / and under tailloures hande.[82]

Another important development was the growing involvement of members of the Company in overseas trade towards the end of the fifteenth century. A few, notably Stephen Jenyns (founder of Wolverhampton Grammar School) and Thomas Randall, were members of the Company of the Staple, the association of merchants that organized the export of wool through Calais. By this time, however, the trade in wool was in decline and had been superseded by cloth as England's chief export commodity. This appears to have provided greater opportunities for London's tailors, particularly those who were involved in the domestic trade in cloth.[83] Once again there are rare early examples of this: in 1389 John Barton, tailor of London, took twenty-eight dozen woollen cloths from London to Sandwich and thence to Calais.[84] In the early fifteenth century it was the turn of men such as Alexander Farnell (Master 1424) and John Bale (Master 1438). Yet it was not until much later that members of the Company regularly took large quantities of cloth across the Channel, returning with all kinds of consumer goods to sell in London. Walter Povey was typical of the growing band of liverymen of the Company who were engaged in the day-to-day export trade in cloth. Shipments belonging to him, Gilbert Keyes and several others were listed in the customs accounts for the port of London for 1480–81. By the reign of Henry VII members of the Company are found throughout the customs accounts: in the early 1490s for instance, Stephen Jenyns exported large shipments of cloth along with fellow liverymen Hugh Pemberton, James Wilford, Thomas Randall, Thomas Petyt, and Ralph Bukberd.[85] A number of these men were members of the Society of Merchant Adventurers, established to look after the interests of English merchants on the Continent, which held its meetings at Mercers' Hall in London. Using the profits made from the export of cloth, they were able to become involved in trade in a wide range of other commodities, so that by the early sixteenth century some of them could genuinely be described as general merchants. Sir John Percyvale had dealings with a Spanish iron merchant, who owed him for 55 tons of iron, and was also involved in the wine trade with Gascony. His fellow alderman Hugh Pemberton took delivery of a large quantity (635 lb) of raw silk from a Venetian merchant in 1483, and also traded in calf skins with contacts in Genoa.[86] By the reign of Henry VIII the livery of the Merchant Taylors' Company had evolved into a brotherhood of wealthy merchants, more than able to compete with their counterparts among the Mercers and Clothworkers. Indeed the great Sir Thomas White, founder of St John's College, Oxford, and noted philanthropist, was reckoned to be the richest man in London in 1559, having made his fortune during years of prosperity for the Tudor cloth trade.[87] Yet it should be remembered that White owed his start in life to his master, Hugh Acton, one of the new breed of merchant tailors during the reign of Henry VII. Like his contemporaries Pemberton, Percyvale and Jenyns, Acton's wealth was founded upon trade, and his generation of merchants within the Company laid the foundations for the prominence of White and others in the mid- and late sixteenth century.

REGULATING THE CRAFT

Amidst all this activity, the role of the Company and its officials was to ensure that the rules of the craft and the City were obeyed. This was both to protect the consumer from unscrupulous craftsmen, and to ensure that the reputation of the craft did not suffer. Like other craftsmen, tailors were vulnerable to criticism, whether it be about the prices they charged or the misuse of materials supplied by customers. Price was a particularly sensitive issue: tailors in the royal Court were accused by satirists of charging up to twenty times the actual cost of the cloth they were using.[88] In 1493 the Company itself was forced to act when the Court was informed that a preacher had delivered a sermon in which the City's tailors were accused of being 'worsse extorcioners' than men who 'lye in a wayte by a high wey side in robbyng and spoillyng the kynges liege people'. The Court sent the Master, two of the Wardens and two Assistants to speak to the preacher to avoid, in their words, 'a grete infamy and open sclaunder to the hole felliship and body of the crafte of Taillours'.[89]

When it came to regulating the day-to-day activities of the freemen of the craft, the Company's ordinances only tell us the range of legislation that was in place, not whether it was actually enforced. What emerges from the other records of the Company is that there was often a clear sense of priorities, dictated by prevailing economic conditions in London, which determined which ordinances were enforced with vigour. Of central importance was apprenticeship, as this was a means by which the Company could regulate access to the freedom. As we have seen, the Company and its Court of Assistants were active in trying to resolve disputes between masters and their apprentices and punish breaches of the ordinances. Common offences included failing to enrol an apprentice at Guildhall within a year of the date of the indenture, and selling the term of an apprentice to another man without licence.[90] In addition, the right of freemen to work new clothing was seen as paramount, and therefore it was essential to make sure that non-freemen were restricted to the second-hand market as 'botchers'. The results can be seen in the Company's accounts, where there are scores of fines extracted from 'foreyns', both for making new clothes and for mixing old and new materials, offences which could lead to customers being deceived. This reflected a wider concern about the activities of immigrants, whether from abroad or from elsewhere in England, and as we shall see (Chapter Five), this was translated into petitions from several companies asking for restrictions on the employment and retailing activities of such workers.

Other offences punished by the Company's officials included breaches of regulations concerning hours of work. It was widely understood by both the City and the companies that 'no man can work so neatly by night as by day', and this resulted in restrictions on working after sunset and at evening markets, known as 'evechepyngs', where unscrupulous craftsmen might try to pass off faulty goods. The precision needed to shape and stitch garments made this a particular area of concern for the Company, and was one of the reasons why it was so concerned at the activities of young freemen who worked hidden away in attics. For the same reason fines were extracted from those who opened unlicensed shops.[91] Consumer protection was allied to a more general awareness of civic and religious duty in regulations that banned working on Sundays or on feast days. The Company sporadically fined its members for such offences: John Schorter was fined 'pur goodfriday', John Sherpe 'pur Cristes day', and many other tailors 'pur ouverir le sonday'.[92]

It is perhaps surprising that there are few fines recorded specifically for poor workmanship. A rare case was the hefty sum of 6s. 8d. extracted from Robert Simond in 1436 'pur jackes faitz unsuffisauntly'.[93] One probable reason for this was that action was generally taken in response to complaints from customers, rather than as a result of 'searches' of shops. The Court of Assistants, for which we only have a short run of records before the 1560s, generally dealt with such cases, and so the absence of fines in the accounts may be misleading. Second, there is the nature of the market for clothing in the City, which was both extensive and highly diversified. As we saw in a previous chapter, tailors were extremely numerous in London and their shops, as we have seen, served customers from all levels of society. Clothes that a nobleman might not consider, could be sold easily to someone who could not afford to be so choosy. At the same time, reputations mattered: an ordinance promulgated by the Company in 1429 stated that no one was to set up shop unless he was 'of good name fame ... and able to schape and serve the craft truly'. An incompetent craftsman was to be 'put fro[m] the ocupacion of schapyng unto the tyme that he [be] able for to schape and also [be] amytted bi the maister and wardens'. Some years later one of the Company's freemen defended himself against allegations that he had illegally poached another's customers by saying that he 'hadde resonable occupacion as a taillour by meanes of there own free will, by reason of his demeanyng, and his old aquaintance which shall be proved of good disposition'. In other words, he was perfectly able to make a living because of his high reputation amongst his customers, and therefore had no need to steal those of a fellow tailor.[94]

The rarity with which the Company imposed fines for faulty goods may, in other words, indicate that in many cases customers chose tailors who produced goods of a price and quality they could afford. That said, the Court would have been compelled to intervene when customers were dissatisfied, although the actions of the royal government sometimes forced the hands of the companies. A Sumptuary Act of 1463 reflected concern at some of the latest fashions and their adoption by those of inferior rank. Penalties were imposed on the makers and wearers of the popular 'piked' shoes, and on those who made and wore indecently short doublets, unless they were 'of such length that the same may cover his privy members and buttocks'. The Company's accounts for that year show four men fined for making short doublets: this was probably a token effort at enforcing an Act which was detrimental to the interests of many tailors, and the Company thereafter seems to have ignored such 'offences' in order to preserve the opportunities for innovation and marketing for its freemen.[95]

The evidence for the activities of members of the Merchant Taylors' Company shows that their skills were in demand at the highest levels of society. Freemen produced goods for the households of the gentry, nobility and royal family, monopolizing the office of King's tailor from the fourteenth century onwards. The range of goods they produced was vast, ranging from long flowing gowns to short doublets, from linen armour to pavilions and cushions. As time wore on, members of the Company began to extend their interests into trade, starting with cloth but moving on to goods of all kinds which they supplied to the Crown and to the London markets. Amidst all this activity the Company itself maintained a watch over apprenticeship, the means by which the essential skills were acquired, and over the activities of its freemen to ensure that the interests of the consumer and the Company were protected.

NOTES

1. F. J. Furnivall (ed.), *Hoccleve's Works III. The Regement of Princes*, Early English Text Society, extra series 72 (1897), p. 17, lines 442–48.

2. For the economic changes of the period after the Black Death, see esp. C. Dyer, *Standards of Living in the Later Middle Ages* (Cambridge, 1989), pp. 188–210.

3. Stat. 37 Edw. III cc.8–14, *Statutes*, I, pp. 379–82; Stat. 3 Edw. IV c.5, ibid., II, pp. 399–402; Stat. 22 Edw. IV c.1, ibid., II, pp. 468–70.

4. *The Regement of Princes*, ed. by Furnivall, pp. 17 (lines 423–24), 20 (lines 533–34).

5. V. J. Scattergood and J. W. Sherborne (eds), *English Court Culture in the Later Middle Ages* (1983), pp. 15–16; S. M. Newton, *Fashion in the Age of the Black Prince: A Study of the Years 1340–1365* (Woodbridge, 1980), pp. 3–4. The earliest surviving pattern books are from continental Europe: see I. Petraschek-Heim, 'Tailors' Masterpiece Books', *Costume*, 3 (1969), pp. 6–9. Two published examples are: *A Tailor's Book*, ed. by Alessandro Molfino (Venice, 1987); Juan Alcega, *Tailor's Pattern Book*, trans. by J. Pain and C. Bainton (Oregon, 1979).

6. M. Scott, *A Visual History of Costume* (1989), pp. 16–18.

7. See C. Blair, *European Armour, circa 1066 to circa 1700* (1958).

8. Riley, *Memorials*, pp. 145–46.

9. *Cal. Letter Bk E*, pp. 231–34; ibid., *F*, pp. 52–53.

10. Riley, *Memorials*, pp. 227–28. The authors are grateful to Claude Blair for permission to consult material from his forthcoming *A History of the Armourers' and Brasiers' Company*.

11. Riley, *Memorials*, p. 35.

12. J. Arnold, 'The Jupon or Coat-Armour of the Black Prince in Canterbury Cathedral', *Church Monuments*, VIII (1993), pp. 12–24.

13. *CWCH*, II, pp. 272–73, 304; GL, MS 9171/1, fols 431–32, 435a; Davies, 'Tailors of London', p. 57. See also H. Kleineke, 'Carleton's Book: William FitzStephen's "Description of London" in a Late 14th-Century Common-place Book', *Historical Research*, 74 (2001), pp. 117–26; PRO, Chancery, Inquisitions *Ad Quod Damnum*, C143/413/13.

14. H. J. Hewitt, *The Black Prince's Expedition of 1355–7* (Manchester, 1958), pp. 22–23; PRO, Exchequer Accounts Various, E101/404/21; 405/14, fol. 13^v; 405/22.

15. *CPR*, 1408–13, p. 68; GL, MS 9171/3, fols 41–41^v.

16. CLRO, HR 146/45; *Cal. Letter Bk K*, pp. 39–40.

17. *Cal. Letter Bk H*, pp. 67, 42. A 'paltock' was a short coat, sleeved doublet or 'jack' worn by men: *OED*, VII, pt 1, p. 408.

18. *CPR*, 1441–46, p. 484.

19. F. F. Fox, *Some Account of the Ancient Fraternity of Merchant Taylors of Bristol* (Bristol, 1880), pp. 17–18.

20. CLRO, Journals, 11, fols 336–336^v.

21. J. Stow, *Annales, with a Continuation by Edmund Howes* (1632). The classic account of his career is in J. Temple-Leader and G. Marcotti, *Sir John Hawkwood, Story of a Condottiere* (London and Florence, 1890). Earlier, more fanciful, accounts include William Winstanley, *The Honour of Merchan-Taylors [sic], Wherein is Set Forth the Noble Acts [&c.] of Merchant-Taylors in Former Ages* (1668); Anon., *The History of the Taylors; or, The Famous and Renowned History of Sir John Hawkwood, Knight ... To which is Added, A Brief Account of the Original of the Worshipful Company of Merchant-Taylors, their Progress and Success* (1687).

22. *CPMR*, 1381–1412, pp. 257–58, 308–10; A. H. Thomas, 'Notes on the History of Leadenhall, 1195–1488', *London Topographical Record*, XII (1923), pp. 10–15; *The Westminster Chronicle, 1381–1394*, ed. by L. C. Hector and B. F. Harvey (Oxford, 1982), p. 476+n.

23. *CPMR*, 1364–81, pp. xl–xli; *Cal. Letter Bk K*, pp. 87, 105.

24. *Cal. Letter Bk B*, pp. 146, 241; ibid., *D*, p. i; see also Jenny T. Ryan, 'Apprenticeship in Later Medieval London, 1200–1500' (unpublished M.A. thesis, University of London, 1992) pp. 1–3, 14–18.

25. *Court Minutes*, ed. by Davies, pp. 31–32.

26. Ibid., pp. 230–31.

27. Ibid., pp. 197–98.

28. Ibid., pp. 228–29.

29. Ryan, 'Apprenticeship', p. 33.

30. GL, MS 9171/5, fols 367^v–68; R. Tittler, *Townspeople and Nation: English Urban Experiences, 1540–1640* (Stanford, 2001), p. 103.

31. PRO, PROB. 11/14, fol. 48^v; Dean and Chapter of Canterbury, Register F, fol. 200. For Povey's career see *Court Minutes*, ed. by Davies, p. 300.

32. This is among the oaths recorded in the Book of Oaths, c. 1491: GL, MS 34007, fols 2^v–3.

33. For completion rates among the Mercers, see J. Imray, '"Les Bones Gentes de la Mercerye de Londres": A Study of the Membership of the Medieval Mercers' Company', in *Studies in London History*, ed. by Hollaender and Kellaway (1969), pp. 155–80.

34. Davies, 'The Tailors of London', pp. 205–14.

35. *Court Minutes*, ed. by Davies, p. 74.

36. For Thomasine Percyvale's career, and those of her husbands, see M. Davies, 'Dame Thomasine Percyvale', in *Medieval London Widows, 1300–1500*, ed. by C. M. Barron and A. F. Sutton (1994), pp. 185–207. Ellen Langwith at one point in her career supplied silk to make banners for Elizabeth Woodville's coronation in May 1465: Barron and Davies, 'Ellen Langwith', *The Ricardian*, XIII (2003), pp. 39–47.

37. For some iconographical representations see, for example, E. M. Carus-Wilson, 'The Significance of the Secular Sculptures in the Lane Chapel, Cullompton', *Medieval Archaeology*, 1 (1957), pp. 104–17.

38. PRO, C131/31/19. For other inventories see M. Carlin, *London and Southwark Inventories 1316–1650: A Handlist of Extents for Debts* (1997).

39. GL, MS 9171/6, fols 72–72^v (1471).

40. GL, MS 9171/6, fols 272–272^v (1479).

41. GL, MS 34048/1, fol. 127^v (1421–22); a tailor of Westminster used the emblem on his seal, see G. Rosser, *Medieval Westminster 1200–1540* (Oxford, 1989), p. 145.

42. *Southampton Probate Inventories, 1447–1575*, ed. by E. Roberts and K. Parker, Southampton Records Series, 34–35 (1991–92), pp. 270–75, at p. 273.

43. A. F. Sutton, 'George Lovekyn, Tailor to Three Kings of England, 1470–1504', *Costume*, 15 (1981), p. 12, and PRO, PROB. 11/17, fol. 48^v.

44. J. Arnold, *Queen Elizabeth's Wardrobe Unlock'd* (Leeds, 1988), pp. 181–83; *The Cely Letters 1472–1488*, ed. by A. Hanham, Early English Text Society, 273 (1975), p. 267.

45. D. J. Keene, 'Shops and Shopping in Medieval London', in *Medieval Art, Architecture and Archaeology in London*, ed. by L. Grant, British Archaeological Association, Conference Transactions, 10 (1990), p. 34.

46. Schofield, *Building of London*, pp. 88–89.

47. M. Tatchell, 'A Fourteenth Century London Building Contract', *Guildhall Miscellany*, 2 (1962), pp. 129–31.

48. PRO, PROB. 11/11, fols 160–62.

49. GL, MS 34048/1, fol. 369.

50. Keene, 'Shops and Shopping', pp. 38–39; idem, 'A New Study of London before the Great Fire', *Urban History Yearbook* (1984), p. 14.

51. Riley, *Memorials*, p. 382.

52. *Court Minutes*, ed. by Davies, p. 190.

53. *CPMR*, 1413–37, p. 136.
54. Fox, *Merchant Taylors of Bristol*, p. 17.
55. For these networks see Davies, 'The Tailors of London', pp. 239–50. The activities of the London skinners and haberdashers are described in Veale, *Fur Trade*, and Archer, *Haberdashers' Company*. See also G. Egan and F. Pritchard, *Medieval Finds from Excavations in London, 3: Dress Accessories, c. 1150-c. 1450* (1991).
56. See *The Coronation of Richard III: The Extant Documents*, ed. by A. F. Sutton and P. W. Hammond (Gloucester, 1983), pp. 47–73.
57. GL, MS 34130, p. 7.
58. PRO, E101/405/14, 22, 406/9, 30, 407/1, 4, 13, 409/2, 6, 12; E361/6.
59. The career of Lovekyn is particularly fascinating: see Sutton, 'George Lovekyn', pp. 1–12.
60. These entries are extracted from the full list of items commissioned which appears in *Coronation of Richard III*, ed. by Sutton and Hammond, pp. 92–93, 99–101.
61. See also *The Privy Purse Expenses of Elizabeth of York and Wardrobe Accounts of Edward IV*, ed. by N. H. Nicolas (1930); *English Coronation Records*, ed. by L. G. Wickham Legg (1901).
62. *Coronation of Richard III*, ed. by Sutton and Hammond, passim; *English Coronation Records*, ed. by Wickham Legg, pp. 199, 213–14, 217.
63. *The Lisle Letters*, ed. by M. St Clare Byrne, 6 vols (Chicago, 1981), II, p. 229; VI, p. 166n.
64. Arnold, *Queen Elizabeth's Wardrobe*, pp. 178–80. Fyshe's successor as the Queen's tailor, William Jones, was also a liveryman of the Company.
65. J. Stratford, *The Bedford Inventories: The Worldly Goods of John, Duke of Bedford, Regent of France (1389–1435)* (1993), pp. 19–20, 258, 407–08.
66. See W. Paley Baildon (ed.), 'A Wardrobe Account of 16–17 Richard II, 1393–4', *Archaeologia*, 62 (1911), pp. 503–14; PRO, DL28/1/4, 6, DL41/10/43.
67. Cornwall RO, AR 37/41/1, m. 1. The authors are grateful to Dr Hannes Kleineke for this reference.
68. *CPR*, 1461–67, p. 558.
69. *The Household Books of John Howard, Duke of Norfolk, 1462–71, 1481–83*, ed. by A. Crawford (Gloucester, 1992), passim. Galle's widow, Thomasine, later married Thomas Barnaby and, after the latter's death in 1468, Sir John Percyvale.
70. N. Davis (ed.), *The Paston Letters*, 2 vols (Oxford, 1971), I, pp. 617–18.
71. PRO, C1/88/41; Sutton, 'George Lovekyn', pp. 1–12.
72. *Acts of Court of the Mercers' Company*, ed. by L. Lyell and F. D. Watney (Cambridge, 1936), pp. 97–98.

73. A. F. Sutton, 'Order and Fashion in Clothes', *Textile History*, 22 (1991), p. 263.
74. *Court Minutes*, ed. by Davies, p. 196; Stow, *Survey*, ed. by Kingsford, II, p. 195.
75. PRO, C239/15/10.
76. *CPR*, 1413–16, p. 62; PRO, E101/407/1, fols 3–4 (7–8 Hen.V); E101/407/13, fols 5^v–7.
77. PRO, C1/18/61, 19/107.
78. *Court Minutes*, ed. by Davies, p. 50.
79. GL, MS 34048/2, fols 62, 274^v; 3, fols 6, 101.
80. *The Great Chronicle of London, 1189–1512*, ed. by A. H. Thomas and I. D. Thornley (1938), pp. 243–44.
81. PRO, C1/64/561, 886; GL, MS 9171/7, fols 33^v–35; R. H. Britnell, *Growth and Decline in Colchester, 1300–1525* (Cambridge, 1986), pp. 54–57, 74–77.
82. Langland, *Piers the Plowman*, ed. by W. W. Skeat, Early English Text Society, Original Series 38 (1869), Text B: Passus XV, lines 444–47. Glossary: *taseles* = teasels; *cracched* = scratched/scrubbed; *ytouked* and *ytented* = tucked and tented (i.e. spread on a tenter frame for drying).
83. Jenyns and Randall were among a group of Staple merchants who exported wool through Calais in July 1496: PRO, Exchequer Customs Accounts, E122/203/6, fols 21, 23, 25^v, 28, 30, 32, 35–35^v. For the decline of the wool trade and rise of cloth exports, see E. M. Carus-Wilson and O. Coleman, *England's Export Trade, 1275–1547* (Oxford, 1963), and E. Power, 'The Wool Trade in the Fifteenth Century', in *Studies in English Trade in the Fifteenth Century*, ed. by E. Power and M. M. Postan (1933).
84. *Calendar of Close Rolls*, 1385–89, p. 579.
85. *The Overseas Trade of London: Exchequer Customs Accounts 1480–1*, ed. by H. S. Cobb, London Record Society, 27 (1990); PRO, E122/78/9, 80/3.
86. PRO, PROB 11/13, fols 191^v–193^v; W. R. Childs, *Anglo-Castilian Trade in the Later Middle Ages* (Manchester, 1978), pp. 112–19; *CCR*, 1476–85, p. 305.
87. Tittler, *Townspeople and Nation*, p. 103.
88. See, for example, the satirical poem *Mum and the Sothsegger*, ed. by M. Day and R. Steele, Early English Text Society, Orig. Ser. 199 (1936), p. 17, lines 167–69.
89. *Court Minutes*, ed. by Davies, pp. 243–44.
90. The term of an apprentice was regarded as a chattel and could be transferred and even bequeathed to another freeman.
91. Riley, *Memorials*, pp. 246, 532.
92. GL, MS 34048/1, fols 133^v, 192^v.
93. GL, MS 34048/1, fol. 278.
94. GL, MS 34003, fol. 8; PRO, C1/78/5.
95. Stat. 3 Edw. IV c.5, *Statutes*, II, pp. 399–402; a subsequent Act removed the penalties on tailors.

CHAPTER FIVE

COMPANY, CITY AND CROWN 1350–1500

THE FOURTEENTH and fifteenth centuries were times of great change and uncertainty for the City of London and its livery companies, not least for the guild of Tailors and Linen-Armourers, reincorporated in 1503 as the Merchant Taylors' Company. The Black Death of 1348–49, and subsequent outbreaks of pestilence, reduced the City's population from an estimated 80,000 inhabitants to perhaps half that total in 1400, and it was not to begin to grow again until the end of the fifteenth century.[1] London was also affected by political upheaval: Richard II, Henry VI, Edward IV and Richard III were all removed from the throne at a time when the Hundred Years' War was finally and ignominiously lost, and the country plunged into civil war. Each time the City, and its craftsmen, merchants and companies, were forced to come to terms with the new political landscape, and engage with whatever changes were brought by these dramatic events. In the meantime, the companies themselves were growing in size, wealth and importance, and developing their roles as institutions, both in terms of the governance of the crafts and in terms of their relationships with each other, the City government and the Crown. This chapter takes as its theme the political and civic roles of the Company in this period, and its relations with the other companies and with the Crown, concluding with the controversial grant of a new charter by Henry VII in 1503.

The role played by the Company in the politics and government of the City in the Middle Ages is not easily revealed by the sources until the later fourteenth century. Nevertheless, by the reign of Richard II (1377–99) it had already chalked up some significant landmarks, in particular the charter obtained from Edward III in 1327 and the confirmation of this, known as an 'inspeximus' charter, which the Tailors and Linen-Armourers were granted in 1341. Yet despite this the craft remained very much a poor relation, in terms of status at least, of the mercantile companies such as the Mercers, Grocers, and Drapers. Members of those companies were able to make far larger profits from their business dealings than the predominantly artisan Tailors, and to translate this into success on the political stage in London. No Tailor, for instance, became Sheriff of the City until 1429, and only one was elected as an alderman before 1474. Finally, in the autumn of 1498, Sir John Percyvale (Master 1485) was chosen, at the fourth attempt, as the first member of the Company to serve as Mayor of the City.

REFORM AND REACTION: THE REIGN OF RICHARD II

The political outlook of the Company, and the ambitions of its members, can be glimpsed in its involvement in the constitutional debates and conflict that took place in London in the reign of Richard II (1377–99).[2] In 1376 radical reforms were introduced by a 'party' within the City government, headed by a draper named John of Northampton. First, the practice of electing aldermen for life was abolished, and replaced with annual elections. Second, it was decided that the Common Council should henceforth be drawn from the crafts, rather than from the wards. This latter measure was of immediate benefit to those crafts, including the Tailors, whose members were not sufficiently prominent in their wards, compared with members of the mercantile companies, to be chosen as common councilmen. This system was not an innovation, but unlike a number of other European towns and cities, earlier examples of election by craft (such as in 1351–52) had not been translated into long-lasting constitutional practice. Its effect was to give the Tailors greater representation in the Common Council, for they were now able to supply six representatives, the same number as the Grocers, Vintners, Mercers, Drapers, Goldsmiths and Skinners. These measures were incorporated into a new book of customs, known as the 'Jubilee Book'. When John of Northampton himself was elected as Mayor, in 1381 and again in 1382, he continued to pursue his reformist agenda, this time targeting vested interests such as the monopoly enjoyed by the Fishmongers in the retail trade.[3]

The reforms were swiftly reversed in October 1383 with the election as Mayor of Nicholas Brembre, a Grocer, royal favourite, and staunch opponent of Northampton. The Common Council reverted to representation by wards, cutting the Tailors' representation in future Common Councils to a level that was often well below that of the mercantile companies.[4] Yet the reforms seem to have touched a chord among many citizens, particularly, but not exclusively, among members of the artisan crafts. The dramatic events of 1383–84 which saw the election of Brembre and the arrest and trial of John of Northampton provide important evidence of the strength of feeling among certain crafts, and suggest that opposition to Brembre was not simply a consequence of faction-fighting, but reflected a real desire for a say in the City government on the part of some of the emerging artisan companies.

The involvement of the Tailors in these events is striking. The official indictment against John of Northampton alleged that the participants in serious disturbances that followed Brembre's election 'conspired together at the church of St. Thomas of Acon and afterwards at the Hall of the Tailors near the church of St Anthony [i.e. St Anthony's Hospital in Threadneedle Street] in London'. Later that same day they were alleged to have assembled 'in the said Hall of the Tailors and under the choir of St. Paul's and afterwards in the Hall of the Goldsmiths'.[5] One of the inquisitions named eight mercers, five goldsmiths and two tailors, as well as four cordwainers, four saddlers, three drapers and representatives of the leathermongers, bladesmiths and bowyers as having been involved.[6] A few years later a long-running dispute between a mercer, Thomas Austin, and his apprentice, John Banham, referred to these events: Banham accused his former master of complicity with the Goldsmiths, Tailors and Cordwainers on the day of the 1383 election. The involvement of so many goldsmiths may be partly explained by the animosity between Brembre and Nicholas Twyford, a goldsmith, who stood against him in the mayoral election of 1384.[7] The nature of the Tailors' involvement is less clear. The most intriguing possibility is that the guild was linked with Northampton's 'party' through the person of Thomas Carleton, a wealthy embroiderer, who was named in an inquisition as one of the 'principales conspiratores' with Northampton, along with John More, Thomas Usk, William Essex, and Richard Norbury. When Usk produced his famous 'Appeal' he did not accuse Carleton directly, but made it clear that, as Northampton's nominee for Parliament, Carleton was part of Northampton's party.[8] As we saw earlier (Chapter One), Carleton was a member of the Tailors' Fraternity of St John the Baptist: in his will, made in 1382 and proved in 1389, he established a chantry in the Tailors' chapel in St Paul's Cathedral, to be administered by the fraternity out of an annual rent of ten marks from tenements in Wood Street. His surviving collection of statutes and ordinances relating to the City includes documents concerning the chapel in St Paul's.[9]

Subsequent events drew the Tailors further into the conflict, and confirmed their prominence at the head of a reform movement in the City. The arrest and trial of Northampton in 1384 served only to intensify opposition to Brembre. This came to a head at the mayoral election in October of that year in which Brembre triumphed once again, enabling him to begin the reversal of Northampton's reforms. The records of the Mayor's Court list the names of those bound over following disturbances at that election, and once again tailors were prominent among the insurgents. William Rule, Master of the Company, was forced to hand over the names of thirteen freemen of the craft who had taken part in an assembly at St Paul's on election day, before going to Guildhall and creating an uproar. Prominent members of the guild were assigned to be sureties for seven of these men. Similarly, the Wardens of the Goldsmiths, Mercers and Armourers also delivered up members of their respective crafts who were either involved in disturbances, had spoken ill of the Mayor, or were found to have formed congregations. These crafts seem to have formed the bedrock of the opposition to

Brembre. As investigations continued, more craftsmen were arrested and bailed, including more tailors, armourers and goldsmiths, but also several cutlers, cordwainers, saddlers and skinners. In February 1385 William Wodecok, a tailor, was accused of coming to Guildhall on election day and then going back to his shop to fetch a sword, buckler and poleaxe, 'hoping that a riot would arise'.[10]

Brembre's two terms as Mayor were widely resented in London, not merely by those who were supportive of Northampton's reforms, but also by others who had suffered from the iniquities of his rule over the City. Allegations were made in Parliament in 1386 against him, and his successor as Mayor, Nicholas Exton (a fishmonger), by at least fourteen of the crafts. Brembre was accused of manipulating the mayoral elections of 1383 and 1384, and of bringing trumped-up charges against anyone who questioned his government. The Tailors themselves accused him of seizing their charter, the contents of which were rehearsed in detail in their petition.[11] In due course Brembre himself was brought to justice when, in the 'Merciless Parliament' of 1388, he was impeached along with other close allies of Richard II, by the five 'Lords Appellant'. He was found guilty of treason and executed. This contributed to a growing climate of suspicion between the City and the Crown, in which the King's need for finance played a key part over the next four years. Richard took his revenge in June 1392 after his requests for funds were rejected: like previous monarchs before him, he seized the government of the City into his own hands. The citizens' rights were restored three months later, after the Londoners had agreed to supply the King with money, jewels and loans totalling some £30,000.[12]

NEW CHARTERS AND 'INCORPORATION'

Despite these turbulent events, the reign of Richard II nevertheless saw the Tailors and Linen-Armourers consolidate their position in the City, and on 30 July 1390 they acquired their third royal charter. Unlike the second charter, granted by Edward III in 1341, which merely confirmed that King's first grant of 1327, this charter contained new clauses concerning the governing of the craft. First, the charter referred for the first time to a Master and four Wardens, although as we have seen these officials had governed the craft for many years. Similarly, the charter also referred to the celebration of the feast of St John the Baptist for the first time: the grant of 1327 had merely allowed them to 'have and hold their gild' once a year without specifying in whose honour that event was to be held.[13] The Tailors were not the only company to acquire a charter in the early 1390s: grants were made to the Skinners and Goldsmiths in 1393, the Mercers in 1394 and the Saddlers in 1395. One of the reasons for this was the ever-increasing popularity of associations of this kind among groups of artisans and merchants in towns and cities. The Crown, worried about the proliferation of guilds and fraternities, had instituted a full-scale inquiry in 1388, demanding proof of their legitimate aims and functions. More than 500 returns from this inquiry survive from twenty-three counties, including forty-two from London. We do not have returns for most of the greater companies in London, which may mean that they have been lost or else that they were able to provide proof of their legitimacy by presenting their charters or other documents. Nevertheless, it is likely that a number of the companies saw this as a good moment to shore up their positions, and the Tailors may have been among the swiftest to respond. Their rapid reaction may have been a mistake, for the following year (1391) saw the enactment of a statute of 'mortmain' which, as we saw in Chapter One, made it compulsory for fraternities to obtain a licence from the Crown in order to acquire property. In June 1392 the Tailors were forced to purchase such a licence at a cost of £40 in order to gain corporate possession of the Hall and adjoining lands. By the time the Goldsmiths obtained their charter in 1393, it was becoming usual to petition for one which specifically entitled the recipients to hold lands 'in mortmain' to a certain value. These charters are often referred to as charters of 'incorporation' as they granted additional rights, such as the right to hold a common seal and to plead and be impleaded in courts of law.[14]

The Tailors continued to put up with the provisions of the 1391 statute into the reign of Henry IV (1399–1413). In July 1405, for instance, they yet again had to pay the considerable sum of £40 to the Crown so that John Churchman could grant the

Company his property between the Hall and the church of St Martin Outwich, on which the first almshouses were built. This may have proved the final straw for the financially-conscious Master and Wardens, for in the summer of 1408 the Company's efforts were directed at securing a charter which, like the earlier ones granted to the Mercers and Goldsmiths, freed them from the 'mortmain' regulations, as well as bestowing on them other corporate rights. This charter, granted on 2 August 1408, was expensive: £100 was paid into the Exchequer, and a levy of 232 members of the craft raised only £21 13s. Nevertheless, it was clearly felt to be worth it, not only to avoid further expenditure on grants of property, but also to have the Company's status declared publicly. The new and significant clauses permitted the 'Tailors and Linen-Armourers of the Fraternity of St John the Baptist' to be a 'solid, perpetual and incorporate fraternity', to hold property corporately to the value of £100 per annum notwithstanding the statutes of mortmain, to have a common seal, and to act corporately in legal matters (see Fig. 28).[15]

What was the significance of this charter? It is easy to overstate the importance of 'charters of incorporation' for the companies themselves. The Fraternity of St John the Baptist had, after all, been in existence for a century or more, had already successfully established itself within the craft of Tailors and Linen-Armourers in London, and had begun to attract wealthy and important honorary members from all walks of life. It held property, albeit through trustees who acted on behalf of the fraternity, and there is also evidence that a seal of some kind was in use by 1393, well before it gained official sanction.[16] The distinction between 'incorporated' and 'unincorporated' groups was largely a result of the debates of lawyers in the later Middle Ages, rather than the ambitions of such groups for some kind of definable 'legal persona'. Mortmain legislation, and the proliferation of guilds and fraternities, undoubtedly sharpened these debates, as it was vital to be able to fit groups into 'the exactitude demanded of writs and pleadings'. Common lawyers knew that it was essential to be able to identify a defendant, and to be able to say with certainty whether members of groups were responsible as individuals or not. It is true that there was a growing trend in London and elsewhere for charters granted by the Crown to contain the language of 'incorporation', but we should perhaps instead emphasize the practical advantages they brought rather than the creation of a 'legal entity'. It was only in the nineteenth century that legal theories about 'corporations' began to be developed, and these ideas influenced those historians of guilds, such as George Unwin, who gave particular prominence to these charters in the development of the livery companies.[17] The Tailors' charter of 1408 removed the inconvenience and expense of applying for licences every time donors wished to grant property to the fraternity, and made it clear that the Master and Wardens were not acting as individuals, but on behalf of their successors and the craft as a whole.

DRAPERS AND TAILORS: RIVALRY AND RADICALISM

For the City government, the charters acquired by the craft and merchant companies were frequently a cause of concern. This was mainly because negotiations were conducted directly between the companies and the Crown, without reference, in most cases, to the City or to other vested interests which could be adversely affected by any extensions of rights and privileges. A case in point was a charter acquired by the Goldsmiths in 1404, which extended their rights of 'search' and led their rivals the Cutlers to petition Parliament (unsuccessfully) for redress.[18] The Tailors' fifth charter, granted to them in February 1440, caused even more of a storm, and contributed directly to the rise over the next few years of a popular, and sometimes violent, movement in the City in which a number of members of the Company played a leading part.

The Company's political and economic ambitions were intertwined. Perhaps the most significant development of these years was the increasing role which members of the Company were playing in the domestic cloth trade. As suppliers of cloth to the households of the great and the good, and even to the King himself, liverymen of the Company were becoming more and more active as merchants in the first forty years of the fifteenth century.[19] Masters of the Company such as William Tropenell, John Creek and Ralph Holland recognized that much greater profits could be made from dealing in cloth than from the

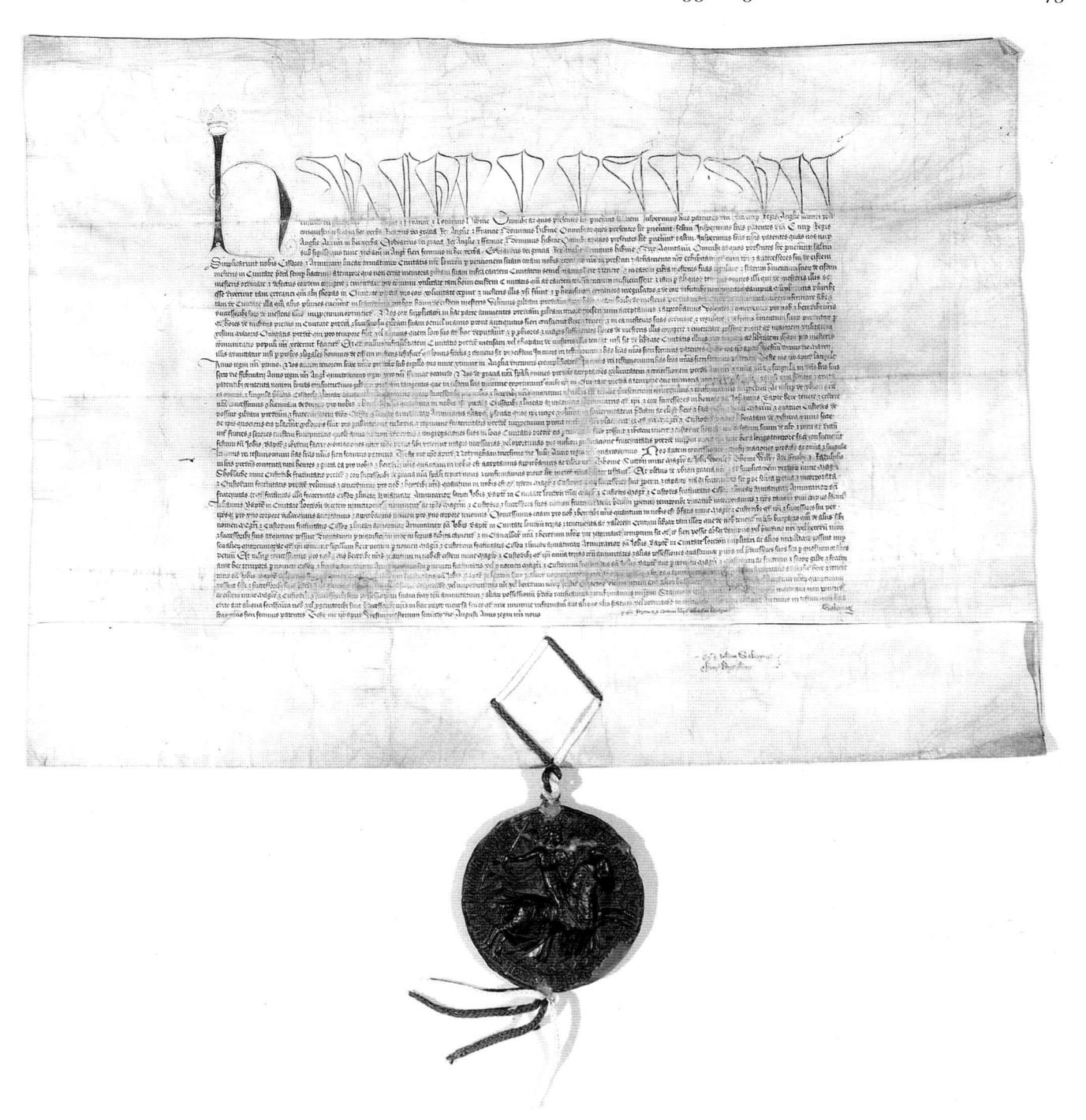

FIGURE 28. The charter of 'incorporation' granted to the Company by Henry IV, 2 August 1408.
Merchant Taylors' Company

manufacture of clothing. It was also true that greater wealth would increase the chances of members being elected to civic offices, and indeed in the first half of the fifteenth century some of the Company's leading men, most of them involved in the cloth trade, were elected to key offices in the City government. Ralph Holland (Master 1419) blazed the trail by becoming the first Tailor to be chosen as Sheriff (1429) and then Alderman (1435). Two other liverymen, William Chapman (Master 1428) and Richard Nordon (Master 1422), served as Sheriff in 1437 and 1442 respectively. Other members of the Company served as City auditors and as wardens of London Bridge. It seemed only a matter of time, therefore, before a Tailor was elected as Mayor of the City.

It was against this background that both the Tailors and the Drapers of London lobbied the Crown for new charters in the late 1430s. Their efforts were prompted by a Statute of 1437, which required the London companies to have their ordinances ratified by the Mayor: several swiftly submitted their existing ordinances for inspection, while some saw this as an opportunity to increase the scope of their privileges. The Drapers acquired their new charter in November 1438, and the Tailors in February 1440.[20] Of the two documents, the charter of the Tailors was the more controversial, largely because of a clause which gave the Master and Wardens increased rights to 'search' the shops and houses of all members of the craft, including those who were involved in the retailing of cloth.[21] The Company spent the large sum of £79 18s. 3d. on the process: the Duke of Gloucester, a member of the Fraternity of St John the Baptist, was a crucial intermediary, and was rewarded with a payment of £30. Adam Moleyns, the Clerk of the King's Council, received £8 6s. 8d.[22] The charter caused consternation among the Drapers: their Wardens had traditionally been appointed by the Mayor to search for defective cloth throughout London. As a result they were able to claim that the Tailors' charter infringed the rights of the Mayor who, in theory, was supposed to appoint searchers himself (although he normally appointed the wardens of the craft concerned).[23] In response to the Drapers' attacks, the Company spent more money to get the charter confirmed. In 1441 the dispute flared up again: the Drapers, worried about the implications of the Tailors' charter for their right of search at St Bartholomew's cloth fair in Smithfield, complained to the Mayor and Aldermen. A compromise was reached whereby the Mayor himself would conduct the search.[24] In the meantime, however, the Tailors had persuaded the King to lend his support to them in the form of a letter to the Mayor asking that they be allowed to remedy defects in their craft, according to their charter. This only served to provoke the Drapers, and as a result of pressure from them and from other elements within the City government the King sent another letter, in which the troublesome clause in the Tailors' charter was declared null and void.[25]

This was more than a petty dispute between two rival crafts. At the same time, Ralph Holland, probably the wealthiest member of the Company and its first alderman, was trying to become the first Tailor Mayor of the City. He was a losing candidate in 1439 and 1440, and made his third bid in October 1441, just when relations between the Company and the City were reaching their nadir. Holland's background made him dangerous to the ruling oligarchy: though himself a member of the 'establishment', he had demonstrated his political credentials as early as 1426, when he was heard to declare that writs which specified who was to be summoned to the mayoral and shrieval elections were fabricated and contrary to the custom of the City. Holland was wrong in his accusation and for his pains was sent to Ludgate prison. His views, however, echoed those of many who were concerned at the tendency of the City government to limit participation in elections to those who were specially summoned, rather than allowing all citizens to take part.[26] The fact that Holland's opponent in 1441 was a draper, Robert Clopton, linked the economic rivalry between the two crafts with these wider political issues. As was customary, the choice between the two candidates was to be made by the Aldermen, meeting in private. Their choice was Clopton, and a contemporary chronicler recorded the events which followed:

And when the mair brought downe the said Robert upon his Right hand, as the custume is, certeyn Taillours and other hand craftymen cried: 'Nay, nay, not this man but Rawlyn Holand', wherfore the mair, John Paddesley, sent those persones that so cried vnto Newgate where as they abide a long while and were punysshed there for their mysse demeanour.[27]

The City Journals record the names of six tailors and five skinners who were declared to have been responsible for breaching the King's peace by shouting 'Holand! Holand! Holand!' in support of their candidate. Some were probably young craftsmen out looking for trouble, but others were liverymen.[28] Even more galling for the Tailors was the fact that during Clopton's mayoralty the offending clause in the Tailors' charter was declared contrary to the liberties of the City.[29]

Over the course of the next two years the City put in place measures to prevent further trouble, including the obtaining of a royal writ which allowed the Mayor and Sheriffs to select those who were to attend the Mayor's election. When John Hatherley, an ironmonger, was elected in 1442, officials stood guard at the doors of Guildhall, ticking off the names of those who had been summoned to attend. Discontent continued, however, particularly with the establishment of a new Commission of the Peace in London in the spring of 1443 that increased the judicial powers of the Mayor and Aldermen. As one chronicler stated, 'a commission was sued for the City of London which was called a charter, and the commons were greatly aggrieved therewith'. Trouble again flared up at the election of the Sheriffs and Chamberlain on 21 September, a few days after Holland himself had attacked the commission in the Court of Aldermen, calling it a 'commission not of peace but of war'. According to contemporary reports a great number of 'inferior' citizens, who had not been summoned, entered the gates of Guildhall. The Sheriffs were elected without incident, but when those present were asked to re-elect John Chichele, who had served as Chamberlain since 1434, 'the greatest number of the commonalty with loud voice and uplifted hands clamoured "Cotisbrok, Cotisbrok"', a reference to their preferred candidate, William Cottesbroke. In response to this challenge the Mayor and Aldermen ordered all those who had not been personally summoned to depart. A new election was held and this time Chichele was elected.[30]

This reversal seems to have spurred the radicals to action during the month which preceded the mayoral election in October 1443. Evidence subsequently presented to the Court of Aldermen confirmed that an armed insurrection had been planned, and it was suggested that Ralph Holland was again involved, along with another prominent Tailor, John Bale. Meetings had been held at houses in several parts of the City with men of various crafts including tailors, saddlers, skinners, goldsmiths and brewers. It was during the mopping up of this attempted revolt that John Bale made a particularly revealing and provocative statement before the Court of Aldermen: the prosperity of the City, he declared, depended upon the artisans and not upon the merchants. Such arguments did not impress the City's governors, and Ralph Holland's leadership of the radicals led to his dismissal from his aldermanry in the summer of 1444.[31]

The disturbances of these years were followed by a return to 'business as usual', although the City government was careful to ensure that civic elections were conducted in an orderly manner. Ordinances were passed which more clearly defined those who were allowed to attend the elections of the mayors and sheriffs: in 1475 it was ordained that elections were to be attended by the Masters and Wardens of the crafts and by the 'good men' of the same, a group which, for the first time, was defined as those who wore the livery. In some senses this represented a compromise, as it allowed members of the 'lesser' crafts to attend. There was also a gradual expansion in the size of the Common Council, from 96 in the later fourteenth century to 187 by 1460. The rivalry between the Tailors and Drapers refused to die down, however. In January 1448, one tailor, John Locok, refused to allow the Wardens of the Drapers into his shop to conduct a search. Another, Luke Sewragh, was even more stubborn, and threatened to break twenty heads if they attempted to enter his premises.[32]

DEFENCE, FINANCE AND PUBLIC WORKS

The involvement of prominent liverymen of the Tailors in the disturbances of the 1440s, and the ongoing rivalry with the Drapers, should not obscure the fact that in most other respects the Company played a full part in the public life of the City. Indeed, as the largest craft in the City, the Tailors were well placed to contribute to many areas of civic life and culture.

The defence of both City and realm was uppermost in the minds of many in the fifteenth century: the Hundred Years' War was in its final phases, culminating in the ejection of English forces from Normandy (1450) and Gascony (1453), leaving Calais as the only English possession on the European mainland. The need for troops and finance placed a twin burden upon the capital city, its merchants, and its increasingly prosperous companies. By the fifteenth century the companies were seen more and more as a convenient means to raise funds and contingents of soldiers to defend the City, or even to go abroad in the King's service. In 1435 the King received an appeal for help from the besieged city of Calais. By July the following year an expeditionary force, led by Humfrey, Duke of Gloucester, was being organized, and writs were sent to the Sheriffs of London requesting them to make proclamations concerning the provision of weapons and food for the army. Meanwhile, 'by the good a-vyse and consent of craftys', the Mayor organized contingents of soldiers who were to join the force at Sandwich at the end of July.[33] The Company's part in the expedition is recorded in its accounts, which noted expenses 'for writyng of indentures and obligacions to Caleys', and then 'les paiementz pur les soudyers a Caleys' which amounted to £28 6s. 7d. These included payments to ten tailors, six of whom were designated as archers, for sixty days' service at a rate of either 16d. or 8d. a day, depending on rank.[34] The surviving Grocers' accounts show that they made a contribution of £14 1s. 8d. 'for the sauf kepyng of Caleys yeinst the seege of the fals pretendyng Duke of Burgoyne'.[35]

In 1459, just after the defeat of the Yorkists at the Battle of Blore Heath, Henry VI ordered the Venetians, the Florentines and the Wardens of the Gunners, Armourers, Bowyers, Fletchers, Mercers, Haberdashers, Joiners, Tailors and Upholders to come to Guildhall to hear his commands. Presumably the choice of these groups was based on the King's need for finance and vital supplies of arms, armour and clothing for the escalating conflict with York.[36] Such supplies as they were able to secure were of no value, however, for the following year the City agreed to allow the Yorkist army to enter London, paving the way for a series of military victories and the eventual coronation of Edward IV in 1461. The City was presented with a similarly awkward situation in 1485, when London awaited the arrival of the victorious army of Henry Tudor following the Battle of Bosworth. Initially the Mayor and Aldermen appear to have contemplated resisting the future King, and asked seventy-three crafts to provide a total of 3,178 men to defend the City. The Tailors, Mercers and Drapers each provided 200, with the Grocers raising a contingent of 220. Conflict was avoided, however, and following negotiations with London's government Henry made an unopposed entry, where he was greeted by thirty horsemen from each of the crafts of Tailors, Mercers, Drapers and Fishmongers.[37]

The companies were also increasingly viewed as a source of finance, especially at those times when the City government chose, or was induced, to lend money to the Crown. In 1487, for instance, the Court of Aldermen drew up a list of crafts that were required to find the sum of £4,000 for a loan to Henry VII. The Mercers, Grocers and Drapers were asked to pay £1,615 between them, while the Goldsmiths, Fishmongers and Tailors had to find a total of £946 13s. 4d. The remaining companies were to provide the residue of £1,438 6s. 8d.[38] Such requests were made in the knowledge that, by this time, the companies were well practised at raising money from their members, albeit normally for their own purposes: the accounts of the Company contain numerous examples of such levies, often to fund building works or the expenses of lobbying for a new charter. In June 1490 the Court of Assistants met to consider another request for money to be lent to Henry VII, this time for £193 6s. 8d. out of a total loan of £2,000. To raise the money the Court selected ten liverymen to act as assessors, with four others as collectors. Like other levies, therefore, this was based upon the wealth of the individual member, not a flat-rate charge.[39] The City itself also asked for money: in July 1493, the Court of Assistants requested that

The M[aister] and wardeyns shuld attempte and take knowlege what every persone of the clothyng of his good will and benyvolence wole gyfe toward the new makyng of thest ende of this hall and the celyng of the Guyhald of London which was moved by my lord the Mayre of this citee.[40]

The works involved were probably connected with the installation of two louvred windows in the roof of Guildhall, the bulk of which had been paid for by a bequest made by a former Mayor, William Heryot (d. 1485). This was the first significant work undertaken at Guildhall since the great rebuilding of the 1420s and 1430s, and was followed by further enlargement in the early sixteenth century. This involved the construction of kitchens there which, for the first time, allowed the Mayor to celebrate his election feast at Guildhall rather than in the halls of the Tailors and Grocers.

Civic ceremonies played an important part in the life of the Company and the City. For the City government, such occasions were welcomed as an opportunity to emphasize civic values and harmony, but were also a cause of anxiety because of their potential for allowing rivalries between the companies to surface. Each year, for instance, the companies escorted the newly-elected Mayor and Sheriffs to Westminster, where they would swear their oaths of office before the Barons of the Exchequer. For many years the procession went on horseback, and the Tailors regularly paid for horses and livery suits for these 'ridings'. Later in the fifteenth century, however, the event transferred to the Thames, and from that point onwards annual payments were made for barges and bargemen: in October 1486 the Company even secured the services of John Savage, the King's bargeman, and his crew, at a cost of 13s. 4d., plus another 12d. for drink for the bargemen.[41] For the Company, a new and welcome addition to its ceremonial came with the elections of its own members to offices in the City. In September 1442 Richard Nordon became only the second member of the Company to serve as a sheriff, and to celebrate this event two tuns of red wine were given him at a cost of more than £10, minstrels were hired for the journey to Westminster, and — less welcome, perhaps — a levy was raised from the livery to pay some of the costs.[42] In October 1498, at the fourth attempt, Sir John Percyvale became the first member of the Company to be chosen as Mayor. This was cause for a double celebration, as Stephen Jenyns had been elected to the shrievalty the previous month. Although little is recorded of the ensuing festivities, entries in the surviving Treasury accounts of the Company show that a gift of £40 was made to Percyvale on his election, with another £26 13s. 4d. given to Jenyns.

Money was also spent on eight 'trumpet banners' for the procession, and these were still in the Company's possession in 1512, along with a richly decorated ceremonial sword, and three scabbards for the same, which was worn by Percyvale in 1498 and by Jenyns on his own election as Mayor in 1508.[43]

The City was frequently the scene of important royal events. The funeral procession of Henry V, for instance, was described in great detail by the Common Clerk of London in the City's Letter Book. The companies provided 300 torches, and these were held by 300 men dressed in white robes who lined the route: the Tailors were asked to provide twelve torches, the same number as the Mercers, Grocers, Drapers, Skinners, Vintners and Fishmongers.[44] A more celebratory atmosphere was planned for the arrival in London in the summer of 1445 of Margaret of Anjou, the intended bride of Henry VI. The Company spent more than £3 on a 'devise for the lyvere ageyns the quene is comyng', made of gold or silver, which may have been a badge of some kind that was worn with their livery suits. Part of this sum was to be spent tracking down those who did not attend. Their concern was justified: fines were subsequently extracted from no fewer than thirty-nine liverymen and ninety-four freemen outside the livery who 'rood not ageyns the quene'. It appears that the process of locating and fining these men took some time, for the accounts record that the Master, Wardens and Clerk were 'sittyng daiely at halle un to the space of a quarter of a yer' in connection with this event.[45]

By the later fifteenth century many of these ceremonial occasions took place on the Thames, and following Henry Tudor's victory at Bosworth in 1485 occasions for the Tailors and the other companies to participate in lavish royal ceremonial were plentiful, as the new king sought to create a favourable image for his dynasty. In the spring of 1486, for instance, the City provided a welcoming party for Henry on his return from a royal tour of towns and cities across England. By 5 June he was back at Sheen and from there journeyed by water to Westminster and was met at Putney by the Mayor and Aldermen of the City and the guilds 'in a great Multitude of Barges, garnyshed with Banners, Penounces, Standers, and Pensells [pennoncel = a short pennon or streamer]'. The Tailors paid 14s. for their barge 'to fette in the kyng Harry the viith', and hired organs and a choir of children under the direction of one 'Crane'. More barges were hired on 23 November 1487 when the livery companies assembled at Greenwich to accompany Henry's bride, Elizabeth of York, to the Tower from where she departed for her coronation two days later.[46] The roles of the companies were normally co-ordinated by the City government. In November 1492, for instance, the Tailors' Court of Assistants received a letter from the Mayor requesting the Master and Wardens to provide 'xxx persones on horssebak in gownes of violet accordyng to thensample herunto annexed to meete with the kyng our soveraigne lord at his next comyng to London from the parties of beyond the see' (see Fig. 29). The occasion was the imminent return of Henry VII from France following the concluding of a peace treaty with Charles VIII of France at Etaples on 3 November. Letters to the companies were sent out on 16 November when, according to an entry in the Goldsmiths' records, the Common Council met and agreed that each craft should provide 'certeyn persones' to ride to meet the King at Blackheath. The precise number was related to the size and prominence of the craft concerned: the Goldsmiths were asked to provide twenty-four riders, compared with the thirty who were to represent the Tailors and the Mercers. The Tailors responded to the Mayor's letter by drawing up a list of riders, and it was agreed that each man would receive expenses of 10s., with former Masters being allocated 13s. 4d. The King eventually landed at Dover on 17 December, from where he proceeded to Greenwich, and on Saturday 22 December, according to the author of the contemporary *Great Chronicle*, he was met at Blackheath by the Mayor and Aldermen, clothed in scarlet, and 'a competent numbyr of the Comoners clothid In vyolet', who together escorted him into the City to St Paul's Cathedral and then on to Westminster.[47]

Not all such occasions went according to plan, and the Tailors seem to have been very adept at tweaking the tails of the other companies. On 27 June 1477 the Court of the Mercers' Company met to discuss the events surrounding the ceremonial entry of the ambassadors of France and Scotland into the capital earlier that month.[48] As was the custom, the City had decided to summon a 'gretter wache [i.e. watch]', or guard of honour, which was to be made up of representatives of the City's crafts. Each man was to wear specially commissioned livery robes of 'oon suet of plunket blew', to emphasize the unity of the citizens. Unfortunately, the Tailors seem to have disregarded this instruction, for according to the enraged Mercers 'the Tayllors had made them Jakettes of cremysyn'. This lapse does not appear to have done them any lasting damage, and indeed it is hard not to admire this *coup de théâtre* as an expression of the Company's self-confidence at that time.[49]

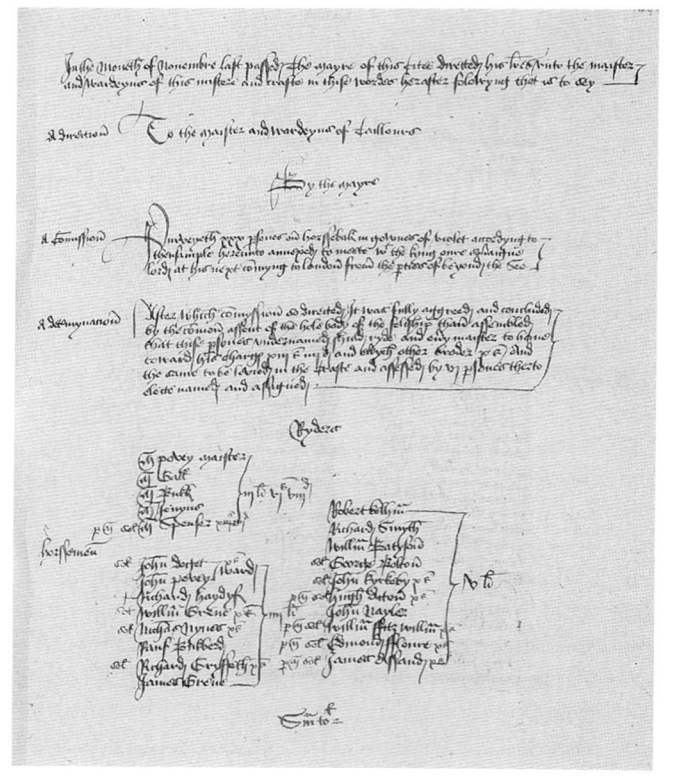

FIGURE 29. Copy of a letter from the Mayor to the Company, asking it to provide 'xxx persones on horssebak' to greet Henry VII, November 1492.
Guildhall Library, Ms 34008/2, fol. 52

LOBBYING THE CITY AND THE CROWN

It would be wrong to see the Tailors and the other companies as perpetually at the mercy of the demands of the City and the Crown. One of the most important aspects of the development of the companies was the way in which they came to represent, and voice, the concerns of their members about a whole range of issues.[50] Lobbying techniques were developed and honed in the pursuit of objectives that reflected particular economic interests. The Tailors were, for instance, one of several guilds that were part of a concerted lobbying campaign in the late 1420s against a statute of 1406 which had restricted the ability of citizens to recruit apprentices from the shires. In the Parliament of 1430 the City secured victory in the shape of an exemption for London that was in sharp contrast to the failure of a similar bid by the city of Oxford.[51]

The single most important issue for the Tailors, as it was for a number of other companies, was regulating access to their trade. As we have seen, the tailoring industry was one of the largest crafts in London, and appears to have been growing steadily during the fifteenth century, to judge from the increased numbers of apprentices being enrolled — from around sixty per annum in the late 1420s to more than eighty-five per annum in the mid- to late 1460s, with several peaks of more than 100. Initially this does not seem to have been a problem: there was no attempt, for instance, to raise enrolment fees to deter masters from taking on more apprentices. This suggests that there was enough work to go round, which may in turn have reflected a buoyancy in the clothing market and in other sectors of London's economy at a time when the population level had not started to recover from the effects of plague. In the mid-1480s the Company made a short-lived attempt to push up enrolment fees to 10*s.* for liverymen and 20*s.* for the rest of the freemen. However the Court of Assistants was forced to abandon this measure after protests from the freemen. In the meantime, the Company had been lobbying for restrictions to be imposed on the employment of non-freemen (known as 'foreigns') in their industry. A petition of 1451, submitted jointly with the Cordwainers, asked that those who employed foreigns should register them and pay 5*s.* for each one.[52] In 1468 several tailors were among a motley group of Londoners who plotted to cut off the thumbs or hands of foreign workers living in Southwark because they 'take away the living of English people'.[53] By the 1490s immigration was perceived to be a serious problem for London's craftsmen. In 1493 the Court of Assistants agreed to submit a petition which called for 'the reformacion of all foreyns that they herafter werke with no freman and citezein of this citee'. This was almost certainly the same petition which was eventually recorded in the City's Letter Book the following year, and which, like one put forward by the Skinners, complained of the lack of opportunities for their freemen and asked for an outright ban on the employment of non-citizens.[54] Concern about the economic activities of non-freemen continued into the sixteenth century, and in many cases drew on xenophobia. The events of 'Evil May Day' in 1517 were a cause of particular concern for the City and company officials: following an inflammatory sermon at the end of April, many 'prentises and other young persons' attacked foreign workers and 'brake the straungers houses'. It was said that as many as 130 'Flemings' and other workers were killed, and at least a dozen of the ringleaders were executed. The remaining participants were led through the streets of London with rope halters round their necks before being pardoned by Henry VIII.[55]

THE BILLESDEN AWARD

The later fifteenth century saw the Tailors continue to cement their position among the leading companies. In terms of their representation in the City government, the going was slow: only Robert Colwich (Master 1460) was elected as an alderman between 1444 (when Ralph Holland was dismissed) and 1481, although other members of the Company served at various times as sheriffs and auditors. A sixth, and less controversial, charter was acquired from Edward IV in 1465. This did not add significantly to the Company's privileges, and was perhaps more important as a sign that the Tailors were keen to engage in dialogue with the newly established Yorkist dynasty. In the years immediately before the granting of the charter two brothers of Edward IV, Richard, Duke of Gloucester (later Richard III) and George, Duke of Clarence, had been admitted as brethren of the Fraternity of St John the Baptist.

By this time it is probable that the rivalry with the Drapers had to some extent subsided, perhaps because members of the Drapers' Company were more intent on expanding their interests overseas, rather than in the domestic cloth market. By the mid-1460s, however, there is evidence of growing tension between the Tailors and the Skinners. In 1464–65, for instance, Henry Clough was sent to Newgate for uttering 'dishonest words about the craft of skinners'.[56] Little else is recorded until 1484 when the Mayor, Robert Billesden, was required to settle a 'variaunce and controversie' between the Tailors and the Skinners, that resulted on 10 April in the famous 'Billesden Award'. Despite the longevity of the settlement, still observed by the two companies today, the precise nature of the rivalry between them is not clear. The immediate cause of the dispute was a disagreement over which craft should have precedence in civic processions: historically the Skinners had been the more successful of the two in terms of having members elected as sheriffs, aldermen and mayors, but by the mid-1480s the Tailors were rapidly gaining ground in terms of the wealth and prominence of their members. Was there an economic dimension to the rivalry? There is no doubt that the work of Tailors and Skinners did often overlap: in the early fourteenth century the City's tailors were specifically banned from working with furred garments. Yet there is little evidence for a rivalry as significant as that between the Tailors and Drapers. It must be assumed, therefore, that the basis of the dispute of 1484 was status, pure and simple. Both crafts had well-established fraternities, to which important people belonged. Both were predominantly artisan in composition, with a growing number of merchants coming to dominate the livery. As such they could not hope to challenge the Mercers, Grocers and Drapers, but were themselves evenly matched. The compromise proposed by Mayor Billesden was ingenious: each company was to take precedence over the other in alternate years. Moreover, the award also required each to invite the other to dinner, once more in alternate years, on the appropriate patronal feast day — Corpus Christi in the case of the Skinners and the Nativity of St John the Baptist in the case of the Tailors (see Fig. 30). By the early sixteenth century the order of precedence of all the 'greater' companies had been fixed, with the Tailors and Skinners occupying sixth and seventh places in alternate years. This gave rise,

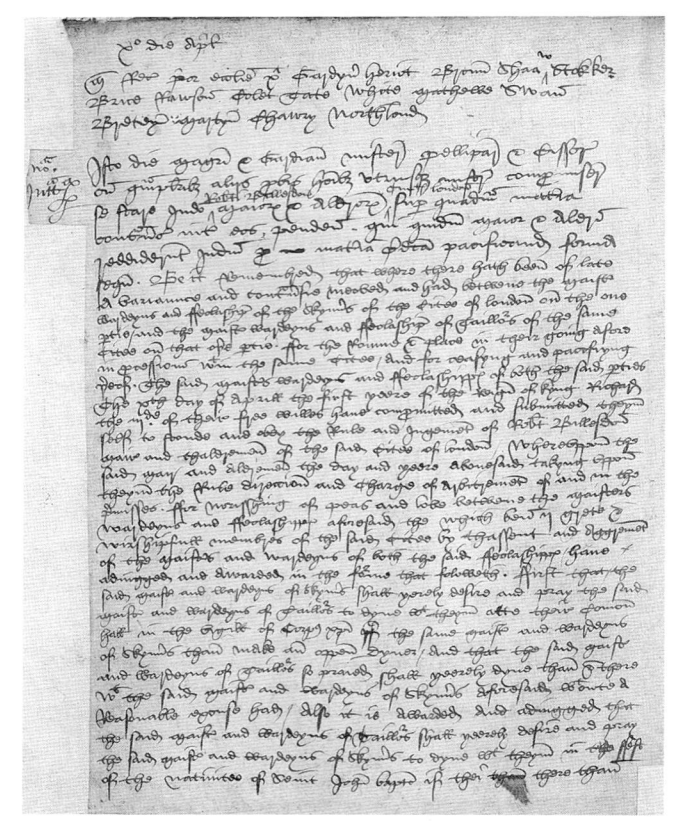

FIGURE 30. The 'Billesden Award' set out in the Journals of the Court of Common Council and Court of Aldermen, 10 April 1484.
Corporation of London Records Office, Journals, 9, fol. 50ᵛ

famously, to the phrase 'at sixes and sevens', implying uncertainty — a meaning which perhaps does a disservice to the flexible approach adopted by Robert Billesden to a tricky dispute (see Col. Pl. VB).[57]

SIR JOHN PERCYVALE: THE FIRST TAILOR MAYOR

The last three decades of the fifteenth century were a period of remarkable success for the Tailors and Linen-Armourers of the City of London, both individually and collectively. In October 1481, for instance, Edward IV granted the guild its first Arms, incorporating symbols associated with the craft and the fraternity, such as the Holy Lamb set within a sun, a pavilion between two mantles, and a portrayal of the Virgin working upon Christ's seamless robe (Col. Pl. VA).[58] No fewer than seven men were chosen as aldermen of the City: Robert Colwich

FIGURE 31. The brass on the tomb of Henry Dacres (d.1530), Master of the Company for 1514–15, in the church of St Dunstan in the West.
National Monuments Record, English Heritage

(1474), Richard Nayler (1481), John Swan (1483), John Percyvale (1485), Hugh Pemberton (1491), Stephen Jenyns (1499), and James Wilford (1500). All those elected from the later fifteenth century onwards were wealthy merchants: both Pemberton and Jenyns, for instance, appear in the customs accounts of the port of London exporting large quantities of cloth. Indeed by the 1480s the Court of Assistants of the Company was entirely made up of men with mercantile interests. Pemberton also had the distinction of becoming the first member of the Company to be chosen as a Member of Parliament for the City of London, in 1487. Their apprentices included men such as Hugh Acton and Henry Dacres who made their fortunes in the cloth trade in the early years of the sixteenth century (Fig. 31).[59]

Despite this, it took some years before a member of the Company was finally elected as Mayor of the City. John Percyvale's rise to prominence as a wealthy merchant was fairly uncontroversial. After ten years as Serjeant-at-Mace in the Mayor's household — an unusual beginning to a mercantile career — he presented his first apprentices as a tailor in 1469–70.[60] His experience as a City official seems to have stood him in good stead, as did his marriage to Thomasine, the widow of two tailor liverymen, and in 1485, the year in which he was elected Master of the Tailors, he became an alderman, first for Vintry and later for Langbourn wards.[61] Two years later he was knighted by Henry VII, one of several London aldermen to be so honoured in that year, but the only member of the Tailors' Company.[62] Like Pemberton, Jenyns and other contemporaries, his wealth was based in large part upon overseas trade, which in his case included dealings in wine from Gascony and links with a Spanish iron merchant.

By the late 1480s Percyvale was well placed to advance to the mayoralty: he was a wealthy alderman who had been singled out as one of London's leading citizens by the reigning monarch. He was a candidate for Mayor for the first time in the autumn of 1489, but a draper, William White, was chosen. This would not have deterred him, for by this time it was becoming customary for first-time candidates to be automatically rejected, on the understanding that they would be elected in a subsequent year. Just like Ralph Holland before him, however, Percyvale was to find success elusive: he was again chosen as a candidate in 1491, and again in 1496 and 1497, but on each occasion his fellow aldermen preferred the other nominee. Finally, in October 1498, Percyvale was elected, at the fifth attempt. For good measure Stephen Jenyns, a future Mayor himself, was chosen one of the sheriffs.[63] The author of the *Great Chronicle of London*, almost certainly the draper Robert Fabyan, provides some helpful, if partisan, evidence as to why Percyvale found it so difficult to become Mayor. Percyvale's rejection, he suggested, was because of the 'hote apetyte which he hadd yerely to that offyce', and because he had been 'verray desyrous to have It, In othir maner than othir of his predecessours mayris beffore hym'. Fabyan's evidence should be treated with caution, for he seems to have been writing at a time when relations between the Tailors and the Drapers were once more at a low ebb. Indeed, Fabyan alleged that after one of Percyvale's defeats the Tailors 'had many Riottous and heynous wordys' to the Drapers, whom they accused of blocking his election.[64] The truth behind these claims is difficult to establish, in part because the earlier Court minutes of the Company end in 1493. Relations between the Tailors and Drapers do seem to have been cordial on the surface: in 1481–82, for instance, the two companies presented a joint petition to the Mayor protesting at the shortcomings of the City's shearmen.[65] Similarly, they acted in concert in 1493–94 when the Wardens of the Tailors met at Drapers' Hall 'for the graining of cloths and to have a potacion'.[66] Nevertheless Fabyan's testimony, and the fact that Percyvale was a losing candidate on four occasions, may well have been a reflection of tensions within elements of London's political élite, and a perception of the ambitions of the Tailors.

FROM TAILORS TO MERCHANT TAYLORS

The nature of the relationship between the Tailors and other elements within the City is revealed most clearly by the reaction to their obtaining their seventh, and most controversial, charter in 1503. By this date the Company had established good relations with Henry VII (Fig. 32), and members of the Company had been prominent among the suppliers of fine cloth for his coronation. Whilst primarily a personal accolade, the knighting of Percyvale would also have been seen in some quarters as a reflection of the standing of his Company.

We know little of the negotiations entered into by the Company with the King, though it is clear from contemporary sources that Percyvale was involved, along with another prominent liveryman, William Fitzwilliam. However, it is likely that the process was similar to that which had produced the 1440 grant, and that it involved the courting of key officials in the royal government, as well as the King himself. The negotiations were complete by December 1502, when the large sum of £87 10s. 6d. (several thousands of pounds in today's terms) was taken out of the well-stocked Treasury at the Hall to pay for the various expenses incurred 'in and about the purchasing of the new grant that the King's grace has given to

FIGURE 32. Monument in bronze of Henry VII by Pietro Torrigiano (1472–1522), in Westminster Abbey. It was probably begun in about 1502, but was not completed until 1517. In January 1503 Henry VII granted the Tailors and Linen-Armourers a new charter which reincorporated them as Merchant Taylors.
National Monuments Record, English Heritage

this company'. The new charter (see Col. Pl. VIA) was granted on 6 January the following year to the Master, Richard Smith, and the four Wardens, Hugh Acton, William Batison, John Skevyngton and James Moncastre. Much of the charter was taken up with setting out and confirming the terms of the charters given by previous monarchs, the earliest being that granted by Edward III in 1327. However this new charter went much further, and contained two important new provisions, both of which were to cause consternation in the City. First, it ordained that the Fraternity of Tailors and Linen-Armourers of St John the Baptist was to be reincorporated 'by name of the Guild of Merchant Taylors of the Fraternity of St John the Baptist in the City of London'.[67] The justification for this title was a bold assertion that members of the guild had 'from time immemorial in many parts and realms of the world frequented, occupied and exercised all and singular kinds of merchandise'. The claim is an indicator of how senior members of the Company saw themselves in the early sixteenth century, and it came hard on the heels of a similar grant to the Haberdashers who, having merged with the Cappers and Hatters, had been reincorporated in 1502 as Merchant Haberdashers.[68] Both the Tailors and Haberdashers wished to emphasize their mercantile credentials, and make a point to their rivals in overseas trade, notably within companies such as the Drapers and Mercers. As well as granting a new title, Henry VII allowed the Merchant Taylors' Company to 'increase and augment' its membership by admitting any person to the guild 'with impunity without impediment or disturbance of any person or persons of any other craft or mistery of the City'. Reference was made in particular to the role that members of the Company played in the cloth trade.[69]

Opposition to the new charters of the Merchant Taylors and Merchant Haberdashers began almost immediately. Status mattered, a fact demonstrated by the earlier rivalry between the Company and the Skinners. In the case of the Haberdashers, the furious reaction from the Aldermen was to lead to the revocation of their new title in a subsequent charter, granted in 1510 by Henry VIII. For the Merchant Taylors such an outcome was certainly on the cards. On 30 January 1503, their new charter was read out to the Court of the Mercers' Company, which was outraged at 'divers thynges theryn that was preiudiciall unto the corporacion of the Citie and also to all felishippes in the said Cite'. The Mercers took the decision to formulate a list of objections to be presented to the Mayor and Aldermen.[70] Opposition within the City's governing élite was again headed by the Drapers' Company which, in early February, put its case before the Mayor and Aldermen. It was then agreed to inform the King 'of the grugges which is tayn by the hole body of thys cite by reason of his letters patent late graunted to the fealeship of taillors'.[71] In a fit of pique the Aldermen decided to boycott the Merchant Taylors' annual feast, a decision which was revoked when it was found that foreign ambassadors were to be present.[72] The City tried on two occasions in 1503 to have the charter annulled. In December, for instance, £5,000 was offered by the City in return for the confirmation of its own charter and the annulling of the Merchant Taylors', an offer which was not taken up by the Crown.[73]

In the meantime the Merchant Taylors were actively seeking to strengthen their links with the King, partly, one presumes, to prevent him from caving in to the City. In December 1503 an important agreement was reached with Henry, under the terms of which the Company, led by the Master, Edmund Flower, agreed to celebrate Mass for his soul in their church of St Martin Outwich. It was further agreed that the Company would celebrate these services in perpetuity, by paying for them to be held on the anniversary of the monarch's death, again in the nearby church of St Martin. The Company fulfilled this obligation until 1548 when the Reformation led to the abandonment of such services. Henry himself was not in a mood to be thwarted by the City, and the opposition to the Merchant Taylors' charter only hardened his resolve to assert himself over the City and its corporations. Of particular importance was an Act passed by Parliament in January 1504. This claimed that the previous legislation (1437) concerning the ratification of guild ordinances had lapsed.[74] This seems to have caused great confusion and annoyance in the City: the new Act flatly denied the Mayor the rights over the companies which had previously been taken for granted. Future ordinances had to be approved by the Chancellor, Treasurer and two Chief Justices.[75] To protect its rights the City asked the King for confirmation of its own royal charter, and for good measure repeated its offer of £5,000 for the repeal of the Merchant Taylors' charter. Although the City secured certain additional privileges, the Company's charter remained intact.[76] Nevertheless, the Company was conscious of the thrust of royal policy and soon after acquiring its charter the Clerk, Henry Mayour, began to compile an illuminated book of privileges, ordinances, and 'ghostly treasure' (see Chapter Two). It was intended to provide royal officials with a lavish and comprehensive statement of the rules and regulations of the craft, together with its ancient privileges, and those that had been recently bestowed, and it contains the earliest full set of Company ordinances written 'within my dwellyng house' by Henry Mayour. These were approved by the Lord Chancellor and his colleagues in December 1507. In some ways the book was an early counterpart to Charles Clode's

Early History (1888), in that it was written at a time when the London companies had to be prepared to explain their aims and purposes to the outside world.[77]

This was not the end of Henry's interventions in the affairs of the City, or his promotion of the Merchant Taylors. In 1506 Henry secured the appointment of William Fitzwilliam, who was held partly responsible for the negotiation of the 1503 charter, to the office of Sheriff. His opponents in the City took their revenge in September 1510 by electing Fitzwilliam as Sheriff again, on the grounds that his earlier election had been invalid. Naturally, Fitzwilliam refused to serve again and sued the Mayor — who happened to be a member of the Drapers' Company, elected against the wishes of the Merchant Taylors. The City in turn took action against Fitzwilliam, fined him more than £600, and deprived him of the Freedom of the City, forcing him to leave London. The case ended up in the Star Chamber where Fitzwilliam managed to get these penalties overturned, but instead of resuming his career in London he spent a period of time in the service of Cardinal Wolsey.[78] In the meantime, in October 1508, another member of the Company, Stephen Jenyns, was elected as the Merchant Taylors' second Mayor, apparently with the support once more of Henry VII.[79]

By the early sixteenth century the newly reincorporated Merchant Taylors were well established among the leading guilds of the City of London. Men such as John Percyvale had blazed a trail which many others were to follow, becoming Master of his company, Alderman and finally Mayor. With the incorporation of the Clothworkers in 1528 the 'Great Twelve' was complete, with the Merchant Taylors and Skinners occupying sixth and seventh places in the order of precedence. The position of the Merchant Taylors in this hierarchy was secured in two main ways. First, the Fraternity of St John the Baptist had given the craft a visible and influential presence in the City, and helped to establish connections with the rich and powerful. Second, just as the wealth of the Company increased, so too did the prominence and standing of many of its members. Involvement in overseas trade was the key to their success, and by the reign of Henry VIII the Company was headed by a formidable array of merchants. The process of advancement was not without its pitfalls, and there is plenty of evidence that the ambitions of the Tailors were not welcomed by their rivals. The charter of 1503 saw relations between the Company and the City at their lowest ebb, but with the support of the King the newly titled Merchant Taylors were able to prevail.

NOTES

1. D. Keene, 'Medieval London and its Region', *London Journal*, 14 (1989), pp. 99–111.
2. The classic study of these events is R. Bird, *The Turbulent London of Richard II* (1949), pp. 73–83. For more recent interpretations, see P. Nightingale, 'Capitalists, Crafts and Constitutional Change in Late Fourteenth-century London', *Past and Present*, 124 (1989), pp. 3–35; C. M. Barron, 'London 1300–1540', in *The Cambridge Urban History of Britain. Volume I*, ed. by Palliser, pp. 405–06.
3. For the Common Council of 9 August 1376, see *Cal. Letter Bk H*, pp. 42–44.
4. See, for example, *CPMR, 1381–1412*, pp. 53–54 (council held 1384: Tailors had 4 members and were in 6th place); *Cal. Letter Bk H*, pp. 237–44 (1384: 12, joint 7th); *CPMR, 1381–1412*, pp. 84–89 (1384: 3, joint 10th); *CPMR, 1381–1412*, pp. 54–55 (1384–85: 5, joint 5th); *CPMR, 1381–1412*, pp. 91–92 (8 Ric. II: 4, 9th).
5. Bird, *Turbulent London*, pp. 134–36.
6. Ibid. Many of these craftsmen were either past or future Wardens of their crafts.
7. See P. Strohm, *Hochon's Arrow: The Social Imagination of Fourteenth Century Texts* (Princeton, 1992), p. 175. For these disturbances see Riley, *Memorials*, pp. 415–16; Bird, *Turbulent London*, pp. 68–69.
8. *The Peasants' Rising and the Lollards*, ed. by E. Powell and G. M. Trevelyan (1899), p. 36; *A Book of London English, 1384–1425*, ed. by R. W. Chambers and M. Daunt (Oxford, 1931), pp. 25–26. For discussion of Usk's 'Appeal' and other texts surrounding these events, see Strohm, *Hochon's Arrow*, esp. pp. 145–60.
9. GL, Commissary Court wills, MS 9171/1, fols 173ᵛ–74ᵛ, calendared in *CWCH*, II, pp. 272–73. Carleton's career is discussed in Kleineke, 'Carleton's Book', pp. 117–26.
10. CLRO, Plea and Memoranda Rolls, A.27, mm.3b-6. Calendared in *CPMR, 1381–1412*, pp. 59–67.
11. Bird, *Turbulent London*, pp. 69, 94–99; *Rotuli Parliamentorum*, 6 vols (1867–77), III, pp. 225–27; *Select Cases before the King's Council, 1243–1482*, ed. by I. S. Leadam and J. F. Baldwin, Selden Soc., 35 (1918), pp. 74–76.
12. C. M. Barron, 'The Quarrel of Richard II with London, 1392-7', in *The Reign of Richard II: Essays in Honour of May McKisack*, ed. by F. R. H. Du Boulay and C. M. Barron (1971), pp. 173–201.
13. Facsimiles and translations of these charters are to be found in Fry and Sayle (ed.), *Charters*, pp. 9–14.

14. For the Skinners' charter, see Veale, *Fur Trade*, p. 70.

15. *Charters*, ed. by Fry and Sayle, pp. 15–18; GL, MS 34048/1, fols 44–45.

16. A deed of 1393, to which the Master and Wardens of the Tailors were party, states that a common seal 'freshly ordained' (*de novo ordinatum*) was attached. This may mean that the Tailors adopted a seal following the granting of their charter of 1390, even though it was not specifically mentioned in the grant: Hopkinson, *Ancient Recs.*, p. 30.

17. These issues are discussed in more detail in S. Reynolds, 'The History of Group Litigation', *UCLA Law Review*, 37 (1989), pp. 421–31.

18. T. F. Reddaway and L. E. M. Walker, *The Early History of the Goldsmiths' Company, 1327–1509* (1975), pp. 93–95.

19. See Chapter Four above.

20. A. H. Johnson, *The History of the Worshipful Company of the Drapers of London*, 5 vols (Oxford, 1914–22), I, pp. 214–15; Fry and Sayle, *Charters*, pp. 19–29 (the charter was misdated here to February 1439).

21. C. M. Barron, 'Ralph Holland and the London Radicals, 1438–1444', in *The Medieval Town*, ed. by R. Holt and G. Rosser (1990), pp. 165–66.

22. Ibid., p.167; GL, MS 34048/1, fols 313ᵛ, 302 (these folios are out of order).

23. *CPMR*, 1437–57, p. 33.

24. Barron, 'Ralph Holland', p. 168.

25. *Cal. Letter Bk K*, p. 260.

26. Barron, 'Ralph Holland', pp. 163–64; *Cal. Letter Bk D*, pp. 24–26.

27. *The Chronicles of London*, ed. by C. L. Kingsford (Oxford, 1905), p. 154.

28. CLRO, Journals, 3, fol. 97ᵛ. Henry Ketelwell was among ninety-four yeomen tailors fined by the Company in 1445 for failing to turn up to greet Margaret of Anjou, while others such as Walter Dolfyn had been liverymen for several years: GL, MS 34048/1, fols 142, 182ᵛ, 246ᵛ, 387ᵛ.

29. *Cal. Letter Bk K*, p. 260. The Drapers spent £10 2s. 11d. in trying to have the charter's controversial clause suspended: Barron, 'Ralph Holland', p. 170.

30. Barron, 'Ralph Holland', pp. 174–75.

31. CLRO, Journals, 4, fol. 10.

32. CLRO, Journals, 4, fol. 205.

33. *Cal. Letter Bk K*, pp. 190, 205–06; *Historical Collections of a Citizen of London in the Fifteenth Century*, ed. by J. Gairdner, Camden Soc., new series, 17 (1876), p. 178. For the impact of this siege, see J. A. Doig, 'Propaganda, Public Opinion and the Siege of Calais in 1436', in *Crown, Government and People in the Fifteenth Century*, ed. by Archer, pp. 79–106.

34. GL, MS 34048/1, fols 271ᵛ, 276ᵛ. Two 'gentlemen' together with the future Beadle, Peter Ferrers, received 16d., while William Lynde, a tailor turned spearman, and the six archers, got 8d. a day. A levy of £28 11s. was raised from 230 tailors who contributed between 4d. and 6s. 8d. each: ibid., fols 268–69ᵛ.

35. *Facsimile of First Volume of MS Archives of the Worshipful Company of Grocers of the City of London, AD 1345–1463*, ed. by J. A. Kingdon, 2 vols (1886), II, pp. 234, 236.

36. CLRO, Journals, 6, fol. 138; C. M. Barron, 'London and the Crown 1451–1461', in *The Crown and Local Communities in England and France in the Fifteenth Century*, ed. by J. R. L. Highfield and R. Jeffs (Gloucester, 1981), p. 95.

37. CLRO, Journals, 9, fols 81ᵛ–82, 85ᵛ. For the City's response to the events of these years, see D. J. Guth, 'Richard III, Henry VII and the City: London Politics and the "Dun Cowe"', in *Kings and Nobles in the Later Middle Ages: A Tribute to Charles Ross*, ed. by R. A. Griffiths and J. Sherborne (Gloucester, 1986), pp. 185–204.

38. *Chronicles of London*, ed. by Kingsford, p. 194.

39. *Court Minutes*, ed. by Davies, pp. 162–63.

40. Ibid., p. 260; C. M. Barron, *The Medieval Guildhall of London* (1974), p. 32.

41. *Court Minutes*, ed. by Davies, p. 73. This custom was said to have been begun by John Norman (Mayor 1453–54) who was made the subject of a popular song which began 'Rowe thy bote Norman ...', although it now seems likely that these waterborne processions had been employed intermittently before his mayoralty: *Chronicles of London*, ed. by Kingsford, p. 164.

42. GL, MS 34048/1, fols 358–59, 365ᵛ.

43. Clode, *Memorials*, pp. 81, 85, 90.

44. *Cal. Letter Bk K*, pp. 2–3.

45. GL, MS 34048/1, fols 387–87ᵛ, 398ᵛ.

46. *Court Minutes*, ed. by Davies, pp. 60, 83; S. Anglo, *Spectacle, Pageantry and Early Tudor Policy* (Oxford, 1969), p. 33; L. Attreed, 'The Politics of Welcome: Ceremonies and Constitutional Development in Later Medieval English Towns', in *City and Spectacle in Medieval Europe*, ed. by B. A. Hanawalt and K. L. Reyerson (Minneapolis, 1994), pp. 220–25; Anglo, *Spectacle*, p. 49. For a description of these events see John Leland, *De Rebus Britannicis Collectanea*, ed. by T. Hearne (1770), IV, pp. 216–33.

47. *Court Minutes*, ed. by Davies, p. 221; *Acts of Court*, ed. by Lyell and Watney, pp. 229–30; Goldsmiths' Company, London, Minute Book B, p. 5; *Great Chronicle*, pp. 247–48. For the treaty, concluded after Henry had besieged the town of Boulogne, see A. F. Pollard, *The Reign of Henry VII from Contemporary Sources*, 3 vols (1914), III, pp. 7–25.

48. The importance of the diplomatic process under way in 1477 made it vital for the City to put on a splendid show for its guests: see C. L. Scofield, *The Life and Reign of Edward IV*, 2 vols (1967), 2, p. 191.

49. *Acts of Court*, p. 97. As on previous occasions it is likely that craft identity was confined to the badges, or 'dyvers dyvysyngs', worn on the robes and which allowed 'every crafte to be knowe from othyr': *Historical Collections of a Citizen of London*, ed. by Gairdner, pp. 185–86.

50. Discussed in more detail in Davies, 'Artisans, Guilds and Government', pp. 125–50.

51. For this, and other examples of parliamentary lobbying by the companies, see M. Davies, 'Lobbying Parliament: The London Companies in the Fifteenth Century', *Parliamentary History*, 23 (2004), pp. 136–48.

52. *Cal. Letter Bk K*, pp. 335–38.

53. CLRO, Journals, 7, fols 178–78ᵛ.

54. *Court Minutes*, ed. by Davies, p. 243; *Cal. Letter Bk L*, pp. 295 (Skinners, 1493), 302 (Tailors, 1494); Stat. 1 Ric.III c.9, *Statutes of the Realm*, II, pp. 489–93.

55. See M. Holmes, 'Evil May-day 1517: The Story of a Riot', *History Today*, 15 (1965), pp. 642–50; *Hall's Chronicle*, ed. by H. Ellis (1809), pp. 587–90.

56. GL, MS 34048/2, fol. 261.

57. CLRO, Journals, 9, fols 50ᵛ–51.

58. For a transcription of the grant, see *Memorials*, ed. by Clode, pp. 96–98.

59. For the careers of these and other prominent members of the Company in the 1480s and 1490s, see *Court Minutes*, ed. by Davies, pp. 285–304.

60. *CPMR*, 1458–82, pp. 22, 47. For this office see B. R. Masters, 'The Mayor's Household before 1600', in *Studies in London History*, ed. by A. E. J. Hollaender and W. Kellaway, pp. 95–114; GL, MS 34048/3, fol. 4ᵛ.

61. For Percyvale's career, see M. Davies, 'Dame Thomasine Percyvale', in *Medieval London Widows*, ed. by Barron and Sutton (1994), pp. 185–207.

62. Stow, *Survey*, II, pp. 187–79.

63. CLRO, Journals, 9, fols 239 (1489), 280ᵛ (1491); 10, fols 79 (1496), 108ᵛ (1497).

64. *Great Chronicle*, pp. 245–46, 288.

65. *Cal. Letter Bk L*, pp. 196–97.

66. Johnson, *Drapers*, I, p. 165.

67. For a survey of these events in the context of the relations between London and the Crown, see H. Miller, 'London and Parliament in the Reign of Henry VIII', *Bulletin of the Institute of Historical Research*, 35 (1962), pp. 128–49; M. Davies, *The Merchant Taylors' Company Charter of King Henry VII, 1503* (Merchant Taylors' Company pamphlet, 2003).

68. I. W. Archer, *The History of the Haberdashers' Company* (Chichester, 1991), pp. 16–17.

69. Fry and Sayle, *Charters*, pp. 34–39.

70. *Acts of Court*, ed. by Lyell and Watney, pp. 259–60.

71. CLRO, Repertories, 1, fols 122, 129.

72. CLRO, Reps, 1, fol. 135 (21 May 1503).

73. See *Select Cases in the Council of Henry VII*, ed. by C. G. Beyne and W. H. Dunham, Selden Soc., 75 (1956), pp. 35–36; Miller, 'London and Parliament', p. 132; CLRO, Reps, 1, fols 148, 149, 150.

74. Stat. 19 Hen. VII, c.7, *Statutes*, II, pp. 652–53; Stat. 15 Hen.VI, c.6, ibid., II, pp. 298–99.

75. The City does not appear to have realized that the 1437 Act had 'expired', a fact suggested by the numerous examples of mayoral confirmation and inspection to be found in the City records from the later fifteenth century, *Cal. Letter Bk L*, passim; Stat. 19 Hen. VII, c.7, *Statutes*, II, pp. 652–53.

76. Archer, *The Pursuit of Stability*, p. 26.

77. GL, MS 34004.

78. *Great Chronicle*, pp. 332–33, 366–67, 375; Miller, 'London and Parliament', pp. 135–36. For Fitzwilliam, see entry in *New Dictionary of National Biography* (forthcoming: Oxford, 2004).

79. CLRO, Repertories, 2, fol. 50; Miller, 'London and Parliament', p. 135. For Jenyns's career, see *Court Minutes*, ed. by Davies, pp. 293–94, and Chapter Seven below.

PART TWO
REFORMATION TO RESTORATION

CHAPTER SIX
THE COMPANY AND THE REFORMATION

MAGNIFICENCE: What, will ye waste wind, and prate thus in vain?
Ye have eaten sauce, I trow, at the Tailors' Hall.[1]

JOHN SKELTON'S moral play, *Magnificence*, was written between 1515 and 1523 when the author was in the service of Henry VIII. Among several London references in the play is this striking allusion to a feast at Merchant Taylors' Hall. As we have seen, the Company's Hall in Broad Street (now Threadneedle Street) was a popular venue for entertainment, not just for other guilds and fraternities in London who hired its facilities, but also for the City government.[2] This reflected the investment made by the Company and its members in the fabric of the Hall, and also the standing of the Company in the City as a whole. There is plentiful evidence that the Company was flourishing in this period, thanks in part to the generous grant of a new charter made by Henry VII in 1503 (confirmed by Henry VIII in January 1512), but also because of the activities and wealth of its members.[3] This chapter will look at the life of the Company in the first half of the sixteenth century, and in particular at the threats posed by the Reformation, not merely to the harmony and brotherhood aspired to within the companies, but indeed to their very existence.

The first half of the sixteenth century was a prosperous time for members of the Company, due in large part to the success of the Tudor cloth industry. A generation of merchants led by Sir John Percyvale and Sir Stephen Jenyns gave way to another in which Sir Thomas White, Sir Thomas Offley, and Sir William Harper took centre stage. In 1522/3 Jenyns's wealth was assessed at £3,500, a figure which was undoubtedly an underestimate given that his testamentary cash bequests alone were to amount to more than £2,600. As well as establishing Wolverhampton Grammar School, Jenyns was responsible for a substantial remodelling of the City church of St Andrew Undershaft. Tax assessments of this period also show men such as Paul Withypool (Master 1523) taking a prominent place among London's leading merchants. In one such tax the 202 Merchant Taylors (more than any other craft) who qualified were assessed as being worth an average of £136 a year each.[4] Thomas White, in his turn, made his fortune in the booming cloth trade in the 1530s and 1540s, and in 1559 was reckoned to be the wealthiest man in London. His remarkable career and charitable activities, discussed in the next chapter, were noted by his near contemporary, John Stow, and were commemorated through the commissioning of at least eighteen portraits, hung in the towns and cities where he established charities (see Col. Pl. IX).

This, however, is one of the few periods for which the Company is not well served by its own records. The financial accounts are missing for the years 1484 to 1545, and the main series of Court minutes does not commence until 1562. Nevertheless, there are some important sources which help to illuminate the life of the Company in this period, particularly inventories of the contents of the Hall, and a run of Treasury Accounts recording monies paid into, and taken out of, the Company's own treasury. Originally, the cash resources of the Company were kept in a wooden chest, to which the Master and two members of the Court had keys, but by the early sixteenth century an entire room had been set aside for housing plate, coin and other valuables. The healthy state of the Company's finances is indicated by the regularity with which the Master paid sums of money into the treasury at the end of his term of office. In 1491 it was reported that coin to the value of more than £140 lay in the treasury, made up of high-value gold coins of the time such as 'Ryals' (worth 10s. each), 'Angels' (6s. 8d.) and 'half-angels' (3s. 4d.), as well as quantities of groats (4d.).[5] The importance of these 'reserves' was that the Company could spend money on one-off events, or invest in its properties. For instance, in the 1490s the Company spent more than £200 on rebuilding its substantial property, the Saracen's Head in Friday Street, as well as further sums on building work on its tenements in the Vintry. Contributions were also forthcoming from members of the Company, such as Sir John Percyvale and Hugh Pemberton who lent £20 between them. Perhaps the best illustration of the use to which these resources could be put came in 1502, when just over £87 out of the previous year's surplus of £114 was devoted to expenses incurred in connection with the Company's new and controversial charter, granted on 6 January 1503.[6]

The Treasury Accounts also show that the success of members of the Company in gaining election to City offices was a cause for much celebration. Sums of money were taken out of the treasury when James Wilford was elected as Sheriff in 1499, whilst Sir John Percyvale's election to the mayoralty in the autumn of 1498 led the Company to purchase banners and hire trumpeters for the mayoral procession. Nor did the Company neglect its civic obligations: as well as contributing to loans made by the City to Henry VII, the Merchant Taylors gave £20 for the building of kitchens and other facilities at Guildhall in 1502. This call for funds was made to ensure that the banquet following the election of the Mayor could, at last, be held properly at Guildhall: it had in previous years been held at Merchant Taylors' Hall or Grocers' Hall as these companies had better facilities. In another year, £50 was given towards a retinue of 'men of armes' which was the City's contribution to an armed force sent to strengthen Calais, England's last remaining French possession.[7]

The inventories of 1491 and 1512 also shed light on the life of the Company in this period.[8] A remarkable collection of plate had been assembled over the years as a result of bequests and donations from members. In 1491 plate worth more than £330 was listed, including gifts from eight former Masters. Many were decorated with devices relating to the Company and were particularly fine: one such item was 'a stondyng gilt cup with 3 Angelles for the Fete, with a lambe and a sonne on the cover, graven with Ecce Agnus Dei on the cover'. Over the next two decades further gifts of plate were acquired, including some from John and Thomasine Percyvale (who died in 1503 and 1512 respectively) and from Hugh Pemberton (d. 1500). These were listed in the inventory of 1512, compiled by the Clerk, Henry Mayour, who undertook a thorough, room-by-room listing of the contents of the Hall. Perhaps the most impressive possession of the Company was a huge tapestry, made up of nine panels of arras, and estimated to be worth no less than £123. This tapestry was paid for through the generosity of several prominent liverymen and, like the earlier of the two hearse-cloths, depicted scenes from the life of St John the Baptist. Too precious to be hung in the Hall on a day-to-day basis, the panels were kept in individual bags in a great chest in the chapel. More mundane, but no less important to the functioning of the Company, were more than thirty tablecloths, some of which were more than twenty yards long, that were listed along with copious quantities of other linen tableware. The list of rooms and contents provides a good indication of the ability of the Company to cater for large gatherings: goods were listed in the kitchen, the larder, the 'pastrye', and the buttery, as well as in a store house.[9]

Sadly, few of the Company's material possessions from the pre-Reformation period survive. Notable exceptions are the common seal and the silver cloth yard, both of which date from Henry VII's reign, and the Company's silver mace, which is probably early sixteenth century in date although it was subsequently adorned with the Company's arms of 1586 (see Fig. 27 above and Col. Pl. IIIB). All these items are kept at the Hall to this day. Of the goods recorded in 1491 and 1512 only two great gilt flagons, weighing some 248 ounces, the gift of Sir John Percyvale, and a standing cup bearing the Company's 'old arms' (i.e. from 1481), were apparently still at the Hall in 1609 when another inventory was taken. The fate of the other items is not known, although by the early seventeenth century the Company had acquired many additional pieces of

FIGURE 33. The Offley Rosewater Dish. This was given to the Merchant Taylors' Company by William Offley (d. 1600) and is one of the few pre-Civil War pieces of plate still owned by the Company. It displays the Company's arms, and those of the Merchants of the Calais Staple.
Merchant Taylors' Company

plate as bequests from some of the great merchants of the later sixteenth century, such as Thomas White, William Harper and William Offley (Fig. 33). It is possible that some of this plate was sold or melted down as a precaution during the Reformation, because of the depictions of saints and other images. However, there is no evidence of this from the surviving records, so the disappearance of the pre-Reformation plate remains something of a mystery.[10]

An important survival from the early sixteenth century is the Company's only illuminated manuscript book, kept today at Guildhall Library (Col. Pls IIIA and VIB). As we have seen, it was compiled in response to an Act of Parliament of 1504 which, controversially, required the companies to have their ordinances inspected by the King and his officers — rather than the Mayor, as was customary. The Merchant Taylors saw this as an incentive to collect together some of their ancient customs and privileges in one volume, and as we have seen the early part of the book contains a remarkable account of the long history of the Fraternity of St John the Baptist and its charitable and religious underpinnings.[11] As we saw in Chapter Two, this religious material was originally put together in 1456–57, when John Prynce was Master of the Company. In addition the book came to include copies of the Billesden Award of 1484, the charter granted by Henry VII in 1503 and the agreement made with the King in December the same year to celebrate an annual 'obit' (anniversary service) for his soul in the church of St Martin Outwich. The Clerk, Henry Mayour, also copied in oaths taken by officers of the Company and, finally, ordinances which were ratified by the Lord Chancellor, on behalf of the Crown, in December 1507. This book, in other words, was a compilation made for the express purpose of explaining the Company's functions to those outside its ranks, particularly in the royal government, thus providing for modern readers some evocative details of the Company before the Reformation.[12]

THE REFORMATION

The illuminated manuscript book created by Henry Mayour in the first decade of the sixteenth century provides a remarkable snapshot of life within a medieval trade guild before the Reformation. The fusion of religious with economic concerns was, as we have seen, a key feature of the development of the livery companies. Yet the book itself is also revealing of the grave threat posed by the Reformation to the very existence of the companies. As Colour Plates IIIA and VIB show, large parts of the text were crossed out, reflecting a religious worldview that no longer tolerated indulgences, papal bulls, or Masses for the souls of the dead. The only section to survive unscathed relates to the almsmen and women aided by the Company. Most of the censored text can still be read, almost certainly because the crossings-out were done by someone within the Company who, whilst conscious of the changing religious climate, wanted to preserve one of the Company's great treasures.

For the City companies the greatest threat was posed by rejection of the Catholic belief in the efficacy of prayers, Masses, and other good works as a way of helping the souls of the dead through Purgatory. Most of the property acquired by the companies had been bequeathed or donated for the express purpose of establishing chantries (priests saying Mass daily) or anniversary services for the souls of the benefactors. The companies could use any money left over from paying for these services for other purposes, and in most cases these 'profits' were considerable. By the mid-1540s the companies were responsible for chantries and anniversary services costing some £960 a year. The Merchant Taylors themselves were paying more than £98 each year for the salaries of nine priests and for twenty anniversaries, including that of Henry VII, more than any other company. The properties used to fund these arrangements generated a gross income for the Company of about £190 a year, a significant proportion of its revenues from real estate, which by this time had risen to £440 per annum. The Merchant Taylors did not rely as heavily as some other companies on the profits from chantry lands, but any attempt to abolish services for the dead, and seize the rents used to pay for them, would still result in a damaging loss of income.[13]

As late as the 1530s, religious opinion in London was still not dangerously hostile to the foundation of chantries and obits. Fraternities of all kinds were still popular targets for benefactions, whilst the Merchant Taylors received bequests for new chantries and anniversaries in 1529, 1530, and in 1538.[14] Yet the climate was beginning to change, first through renewed concern on the part of the Crown at the alienation of land 'in mortmain', that is, into the 'dead hand' of the Church, and then from the 1520s onwards through increased theological doubts about the efficacy of these 'intercessory institutions'.[15] Although total suppression was not yet on the agenda, the 1530s saw a succession of measures which effectively ended the era of the perpetual chantry: in 1532 feoffments to religious use were restricted to periods of twenty years or fewer, and a mere two years later what proved to be the last licence to convey property 'in mortmain' was granted by the Crown.[16]

The Chantries Act of 1545 was, in many respects, a half-hearted attempt at dissolution. Its protagonists stressed the lax administration of many chantries and the poor stewardship of resources meant for alms and charity; as with the monasteries, dissolution was more a solution to fiscal and economic difficulties than a programme for the reformation of doctrinal error, despite an insistence that the revenues be used for 'more godly and virtuous purposes'.[17] Nevertheless the Act, and the subsequent activities of the Chantry commissioners, constituted a warning shot across the bows of the trustees of such intercessory institutions, even those purely lay fraternities and corporations which could not legally be dissolved under the terms of the Act. The Merchant Taylors were visited by the commissioners in early 1546, and payments were made for compiling their return, after which 8*d*. was paid for 'a refeccion made at the marmayde taverne when we put in our boke to the sessers'.[18] The Company was not to emerge entirely unscathed, despite the limited aims of the commissioners and the death of Henry VIII. The Master and Wardens again met the commissioners at the Mermaid 'to take counceill to aunswere Mr. Mildmay and other the Kynges Comyssioners touchyng the last will of Sir Steven Jenyns'.[19] The commissioners' concern was that Jenyns's anniversary, and those of Hugh Acton and Sir John Percyvale, had been celebrated at the now dissolved Grey Friars monastery. This meant that all the rents left to the fraternity for that purpose were now due to the Crown. Hence the same year the Company was obliged to pay 'to the Kynges majestie in arrerage' £52 10*s*.[20] In other words, although the 1545 Act did not pose a significant threat to the companies, the Crown was swift to act on the findings contained in the returns if they proved that monies were owed as a result of earlier legislation.[21]

The death of Henry and the accession of Edward VI brought a new thoroughness to the process of dissolution, led by Protector Somerset. A new Chantries Act, passed by Parliament in December 1547, spoke of 'superstition and errors' and 'vain opinions of Purgatory and Masses', revealing a greater doctrinal rigour and purpose. Although the Act was more lenient than a proposed 'Lords' Bill', which had intended to seize all the assets of guilds and fraternities, it was still a major threat to the London livery companies because of their reliance upon such income.[22] The Crown's commissioners for London and Middlesex visited the livery companies in early 1548, and compiled a new certificate, covering thirty-four London companies, and recording sixty-one chantries and 156 obits administered by them at a total cost of £960 5s. 0½d. a year.[23] The Merchant Taylors took the advice of the Recorder of London 'in makyng our booke of certificate [i.e. the Company's own return] as touchyng what prestes obittes lampes and lyghtes was founde and kepte by the companye and what landes or other thyng was geven for the mayntenance therof . . .'. Realizing the seriousness of the situation, the Company demanded 'a longer daye' to complete their return. The commissioners, who were staying at Haberdashers' Hall, were then presented with the return and entertained to dinner at Merchant Taylors' Hall, in the presence of the Lord Mayor.[24] The Company's return listed twenty obits and nine priests funded in eleven parish churches by the Merchant Taylors at a total cost of £98 7s. 11d. A draft of the return still survives in the Company's archive.[25] These charges were now due to the Crown, and so the Company's accounts record the payment of chantry priests up to the feast of the Annunciation, 1548, after which the rents were paid to the Augmentations office, in half-yearly instalments.[26]

If this had been the extent of the Crown's actions, the Company might have been able to breathe a sigh of relief. However, a far more damaging measure was swiftly introduced. The Crown decided to require the companies to *buy back* their rents, at a rate initially set at twenty years' purchase. Some flexibility may have been used when calculating the precise amounts owed, but despite this the total bill for all the London companies, to buy back their rent charges of £960, amounted to the colossal sum of £18,506 11s. The Merchant Taylors were required to find £2,006 2s. 6d., the third highest sum after those demanded of the Mercers and the Goldsmiths. The Company's success in attracting grants of property, and its reputation as a trustee, had thus become a potential liability.[27] Whatever the doctrinal basis for the Act of 1547, this new measure was a clear attempt by the Crown to swell its coffers, and the companies in 1550 had to react swiftly to raise sums of this magnitude and avoid disaster. The only feasible course of action, other than raising a loan or levy, was to sell property, and in 1549–50 the Master of the Merchant Taylors, Nicholas Cosyn, reported that £2,133 3s. 6d. had been 'by hym received for the sale of the londes late belonging to this misterye'. The purchasers numbered several wealthy and influential members, including Thomas Offley, while Thomas White, Lord Mayor in 1553–54 and founder of St John's College, Oxford, purchased tenements in Watling Street, Friday Street, Tower Street, and elsewhere for £410 6s. 8d. The Company was then able to pay the required amount 'to the Tresorer of the Kynges Courte of Augmentacion'. Canvas was purchased to make bags to put the money in.[28]

It was largely thanks to White and his fellow liverymen that the Company was able to weather this financial storm, and regain its seized rents.[29] The Company tried to avoid significant damage to its corporate finances by ensuring that the loss of rent caused by having to sell property would be mostly offset by the amount that the Company had previously spent on chantries and anniversaries. Nevertheless, the Company experienced a sharp drop in its income from property: it received only £307 13s. 8d. in rent in 1552–53, compared with £440 17s. 10d. previously, having had to sell properties worth some £133 per annum to buy back its rents. Part of this cost was, of course, offset by the ending of the Company's obligation to fund priests and anniversary services, but in some cases it decided to continue to commemorate its benefactors through distributions to the poor.³⁰ One of the few pre-Reformation annual events to survive these upheavals was the annual sermon in memory of James Wilford (d. 1527), which is still preached today. It was fortunate for the companies of London that the 1547 Act was not harsher in its treatment of craft fraternities: parish guilds and fraternities were doomed, but the London livery companies were able to lobby successfully for the protection of the bulk of their assets, doubtless stressing their charitable activities as well as their crucial role as regulators of London's industries.³¹

THE REFORMATION AND MEMBERS OF THE COMPANY

Traditionally, the Reformation has been seen in confrontational terms, with conservatives and evangelicals pitched against one another in a struggle for ascendancy. More recently, greater emphasis has been placed firstly upon the vitality and richness of late medieval religion, and secondly upon the extent to which religious change in London, though undoubtedly traumatic, took place in a way that allowed the City government, the parishes, and the companies to continue to function. As one historian has argued, it was possible for 'a range of religious positions to exist within a common complex of shared civic values and attitudes, preventing serious divisions along religious lines'.³² It is important to bear this change in historical perspective in mind when considering the experience of the Merchant Taylors. Until recently, for instance, it was the norm to suggest that by the 1550s the Company was divided into 'parties', represented on the one hand by the evangelical Richard Hilles, recently returned from exile in Strasbourg, and on the other by the Catholic Sir Thomas White, founder of St John the Baptist's College in Oxford, and Mayor at the time of Wyatt's rebellion against Queen Mary. Whilst not minimizing the differences in religious outlook between such men, it is important to remember that the Company, like the City government, continued to exercise authority and formulate policy. This next section will consider the evidence for the changes brought to the life of the Company, and the religious persuasions of individual Merchant Taylors in this period.

The impact of the Reformation on the corporate life of the Merchant Taylors was significant, although it must not be exaggerated. Depictions of St John the Baptist, such as the statue kept at the Hall, were removed, and it may have been at this time that the nine-piece tapestry portraying the life of the saint was lost and some of the plate disposed of. From the reign of Elizabeth onwards, the quarterly meetings of the full Court of Assistants began with a long prayer that emphasized the attainment of salvation 'through Jesue Christe our Lorde and only Saviour', and counselled members not to 'suffer the enemyes of thy Gospell, the Pope, the Turke or their Adherentes to prevaile'. On 30 October 1578 the Court decreed that 'a bible of the newe forme, lately prynted by Christofer Barker, the Quenes Majesties Prynter, shalbe boughte and sett upp in their Comen Hall'. This was the translation of the Bible undertaken under the guidance of Archbishop Matthew Parker, known as the 'Bishops' Bible'.³³ On the other hand, the Baptist's name continued to be used in official documents, and until new Arms were acquired in 1586 (Fig. 51 and Col. Pl. XIA), the Virgin retained a prominent place as part of the Company's crest. The Company managed to avoid having to sell or destroy its two pre-Reformation hearse-cloths, and the censoring of its books was done very carefully indeed. The main impact on the Company was a change in the way its benefactors were commemorated. The abolition of chantries and anniversaries led to a rise in the popularity of sermons and charitable bequests as means to express piety and corporate identity, as well as to remember donors. Indeed, the period from 1560 to 1640 has been described as the 'golden age' of the London livery companies, not least because they became increasingly involved in welfare provision and acquired large charitable endowments. By the 1590s the Company was spending some £201 per annum on its poor from its corporate and trust sources combined. Even allowing for inflation, this was still an increase on the proportion of income spent on its poor in the latter years of the fifteenth century. By the 1630s almost £1,000 a year was being spent on the Company poor, with a further £400 on charity for non-members, £360 on the schools, and £68 on scholars at St John's Oxford.³⁴ The Company's annual cycle of Masses and prayers was replaced by a modified ritual framework within which commemoration was expressed in other, more 'Godly', ways, with preaching taking centre stage. Charity and education also benefited, with donors remembered through the recitation of lists of names, commemorative sermons, and at dinners for the Company's liverymen.

There is no doubt that for individuals the Reformation was at times a difficult and disorientating process. Belief in Purgatory was the motivation behind not only the foundation of chantries and anniversaries, but also bequests to the poor, relief for prisoners, and the foundation of grammar schools. Indeed, a key part of the duties of the schoolmasters appointed to the grammar schools founded by Edmund Flower and by Sir John and Thomasine Percyvale was to sing Mass for the souls of the founders.[35] The main evidence for religious belief and practice in this period comes from wills. A typical pre-Reformation will is that of James Wilford (d. 1527), who commended his soul 'unto almighty god my creatour and redemer, to his blessid mother our lady seint Mary virgin Immaculate quene of marcy and grace and to all the seints in hevyn'. He recorded in his will an agreement he had made with the Company to fund his anniversary or 'obit' in the church of St Bartholomew by the Exchange 'with placebo and dirige over nyght and Masse of Requiem on the morowe'. Tapers of wax, weighing a total of 12 lb., were to burn about his tomb during the annual services, which were to be attended by the Master, Wardens, Clerk and Beadle. Among the other arrangements for the health of his soul was a Good Friday sermon in the same church, which was the only part of the agreement to survive the Reformation: sermons to commemorate benefactors and spread moral and religious values were popular amongst evangelicals, and so Wilford's sermon could easily be accommodated in the changed devotional framework.[36]

The Reformation involved the denial of the existence of Purgatory and the effectiveness of prayers, Masses, and good works. Salvation could only be obtained through divine forgiveness, not through the sacraments and other rites of the traditional Church, and the preambles to Protestant wills often made a point of expressing this belief. Chantries and anniversaries were abolished. Churches were stripped of images and relics. The culmination of these changes was the establishment of the Church of England by statute in 1559. Yet it took some time for the religious changes of the Reformation to percolate down to the daily lives of the laity. A study of the wills of aldermen and common councilmen who held office in the period 1520–47 has revealed that none of the Merchant Taylor aldermen, and only three of the common councilmen, Ralph Davenant, Stephen Kirton, and Emmanuel Lucar, displayed evangelical tendencies. Henry VIII's reign was one in which the Reformation only gained so much ground. Yet even in the reign of Edward VI, when the Reformation acquired momentum, Kirton and Thomas Rowe are the only obvious evangelicals out of the seven Merchant Taylor aldermen. There was a similar proportion among the Company's twenty-eight common councilmen.[37]

On the other hand, there is evidence that some members of the Company at least were involved in heretical movements, or sympathetic to some of the evangelicals' ideas. The influx of religious texts in English into London from the Continent was starting to gather pace in the early sixteenth century, going far beyond the conservative reformism of Henry VIII's government. This intermingled with an attachment to older forms of heresy, such as the teachings of John Wycliffe. At various points members of the Company appear in the records, associated with heretical groups and practices. Among them was William Russell, whose house in the parish of St Stephen Coleman Street was used in the 1520s as a meeting-place for followers of Wycliffe's teachings. Later in the same decade two other members of the Company in Abchurch Lane and Budge Row were identified as members of a group that met together to read the Bible in English as well as 'Lollard' texts.[38] Little else is known of these 'proto-Protestants', but there were other members of the Company whose activities were to ensure them a prominent place in histories of the Reformation.

RICHARD HUNNE: A MERCHANT TAYLOR 'MARTYR'

Richard Hunne's fame, and his place in John Foxe's *Acts and Monuments*, stem from his clash with the

Church authorities and his violent death on 3 December 1514 in Lollards' Tower in the south-west corner of St Paul's Cathedral, where he had been imprisoned on charges of heresy.[39] Hunne ended up in prison as a result of a dispute with the Church authorities that began in 1511 with the burial of Hunne's infant son, Stephen. Hunne refused to hand over a christening gown to the priest as the customary fee for performing the service. The Church authorities backed the priest, but the dispute escalated into a *cause célèbre* when Hunne, having been refused communion at church, brought a suit under the provisions of the statute of *praemunire*. This little-used but potentially explosive statute made it treason for an Englishman to appeal in law to any power higher than the King. In theory, all those who had opposed Hunne's rights in common law — including Richard Fitzjames, Bishop of London, and Cuthbert Tunstall, then Chancellor to the Archbishop of Canterbury — were vulnerable. The case was thus much more significant than a simple dispute over a christening gown: whose law took precedence, that of the Pope or that of the King?[40]

The Church's response was to accuse Hunne of heresy, and in October 1514 he was arrested. He was interviewed by the Bishop of London about the withholding of tithes due to the Church, but was also accused, according to Foxe, of having 'in his keeping divers English books prohibited and damned by the law; as the Apocalypse in English', as well as 'epistles and gospels in English' and others of John Wycliffe's 'damnable works'.[41] He was also accused of defending Joan Baker (wife of a fellow Merchant Taylor) who had admitted that she believed images were a device to extort money from the deluded. The following morning, however, Hunne was found hanged in his cell. Immediately the story was put about by the bishop and his Chancellor, William Horsey, that Hunne had committed suicide. The Church authorities saw it as essential to have Hunne's guilt confirmed, and so the bishop decided to go ahead with a post-mortem trial for heresy.

The pre-trial depositions included testimony from a servant, who claimed that his late master had asked him to fetch an English Bible and other religious texts 'which the said Richard Hunne was wont to keep under lock and key in his own keeping'. A second witness confirmed that Hunne possessed an English Bible, formerly owned by one Thomas Downe, and had kept it in the church of St Margaret Bridge Street when he was parish clerk there. The trial itself then took place before a court presided over by Bishop Fitzjames, along with two other bishops, and with Archbishop Wolsey and Sir Thomas More in attendance — an imposing line-up indeed. More later boasted that he knew the case 'from top to toe'.[42] Thirteen charges were laid against Hunne, mostly relating to the possession of a Wycliffite 'Great Bible' that contained a prologue that challenged the sale of indulgences, pilgrimages, the use of images and the doctrine of transubstantiation. Witnesses also confirmed that he kept a heretical Bible about his person. The trial concluded at St Paul's on 16 December 1514, less than a fortnight after Hunne's alleged suicide. The inevitable guilty verdict was read, and Hunne's corpse was carried to Smithfield four days later and burned at the stake. More was involved throughout: 'I was also myselfe present at the judgement given in Poules wheruppon his bokes and his body were burned.'[43]

In the meantime it had become clear that Hunne had in fact been murdered (see Fig. 34). In January 1515 a coroner's jury in London was presented with the confession of one Charles Joseph, who had taken sanctuary in Exeter after Hunne's death. Joseph had been a lowly-paid church court official in the employ of William Horsey. Although Joseph had refused to torture Hunne, and was dismissed for his pains, Horsey subsequently persuaded him to take part in an even more grisly deed. According to the confession, Horsey led Joseph and another man into Lollards' Tower,

And when all we came up, we found Hunne lying on his bed. And then Master Chancellor said 'Lay hands on the thief!' And so all we murdered Hunne. And then I, Charles, put the girdle about Hunne's neck. And then John Bellringer and I, Charles, did heave up Hunne, and Master Chancellor pulled the girdle over the staple. And so Hunne was hanged.[44]

Other evidence was presented to show that Hunne could not possibly have hanged himself, including the fact that both his stool and his table were too far away to allow him to attach the girdle to the staple in the wall. The jury ruled that Hunne had

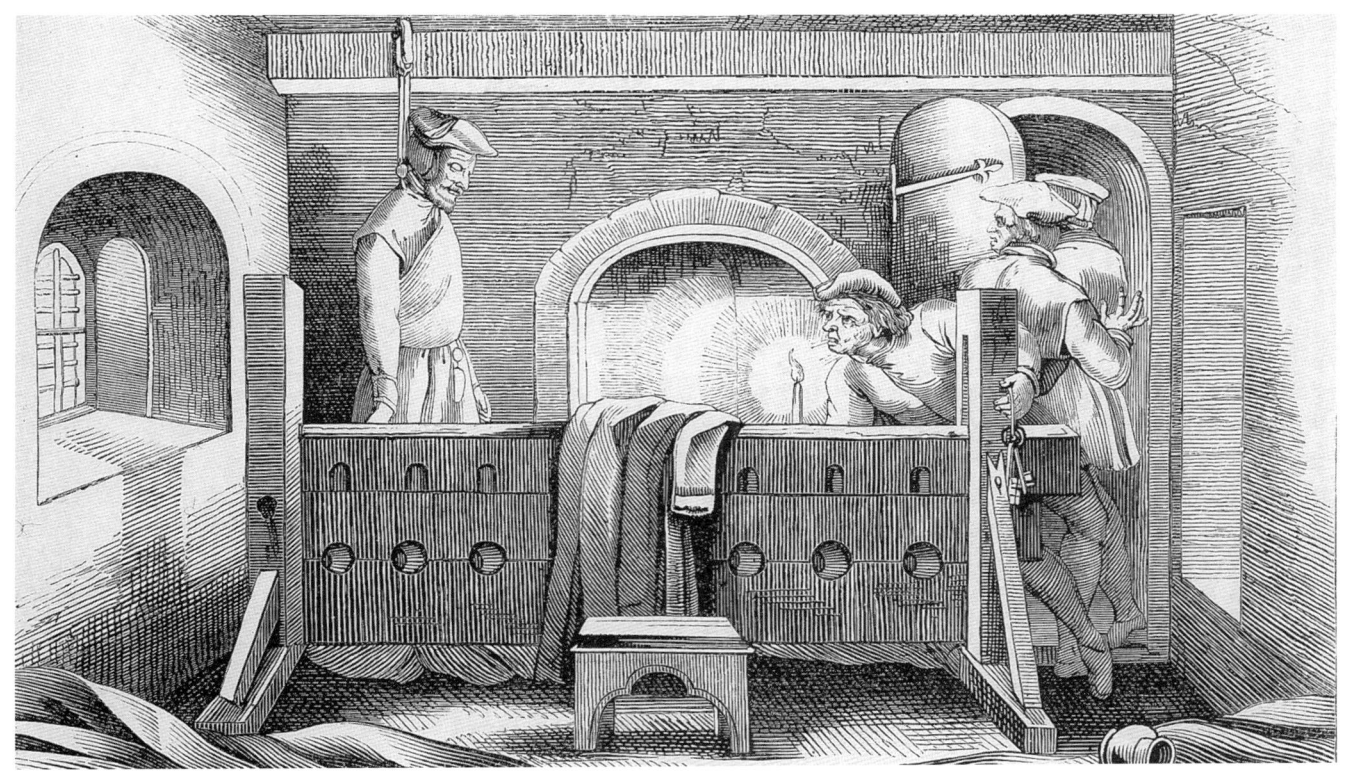

FIGURE 34. An engraving depicting the murder of Richard Hunne, Merchant Taylor, in Lollards' Tower.
The Acts and Monuments of John Foxe, ed. by S. R. Cattley, 8 vols (1837–41), IV, facing p. 184.
Guildhall Library

been murdered, and issued indictments against the three alleged perpetrators. This caused an outcry in London, where there was already deep unease about the persecution of Hunne. Although the three men were never put on trial, popular disquiet about the case eventually led Parliament in 1523 to pass a bill in which Hunne's property was restored to his remaining children. At least one of the alleged murderers was asked to make financial restitution.

A postscript to this tale was added very recently, when a small Wycliffite Bible appeared for public sale in 1999. Keen-eyed researchers noticed that it was inscribed on one page (in Latin) with: 'This is the book of Thomas Downe of Haloghton.' Soon afterwards the connection was made between this Bible and the allegation made in 1514 that 'the Englishe Bible which Richard Hunne had was one Thomas Downys.' Presumed burned along with his other books, this Bible provides a tangible link to the early days of the Reformation in London, and the activities of men such as Richard Hunne, Merchant Taylor. It is now in a private collection in California.[45]

THE COMPANY DIVIDED?

The assertion that the Company was divided into 'Romanist' and 'Reformist' parties during the reigns of Edward VI and Mary stems from the traditional bi-polar view of the Reformation, and the prominence of Richard Hilles, Thomas White and Thomas Offley in the events of those years. This is not surprising, as all held office within the Company and in the City government, with White and Offley being elected Lord Mayor in 1553 and 1556 respectively.

The career of Richard Hilles is worth summarizing briefly. In 1533, then the apprentice of Nicholas Cosyn 'at the sygne of the anker' on London Bridge, he wrote from Roone in Flanders to Thomas

Cromwell asking for help after his master had cut off his funds. Hilles had offended the Bishop of London by writing a tract 'on that part of St James's Epistle how Abraham was justified by works'. Cosyn had offered Hilles the choice of returning to the faith or having his financial support withdrawn: 'he would not for 100*l*. help me with 1*d*. for fear of the Bishop'. The outcome of Hilles's appeal is not clear, but on his return in 1535 he obtained the freedom of the City and set up in business as a cloth worker. However, he soon fell out with his fellow parishioners in St Margaret Bridge Street, having refused to contribute towards a light before the rood in the church. As we have seen, London was still overwhelmingly conservative in religious persuasion, and he was seen as undermining the parish community by his actions. The churchwardens threatened to report him to the Bishop of London. Soon afterwards Hilles and his family were investigated by Bishop Stephen Gardiner of Winchester, who questioned local inhabitants about his behaviour. In 1539 Hilles left London again, this time going to Strasbourg, where his ideas on religion and education were influenced by fellow exiles who included Miles Coverdale, translator of the Bible (see Fig. 35), who later rented a tenement belonging to the Company in the parish of St Benet Fink, close to the Hall. English Protestants often fled not to Lutheran Germany but to Strasbourg, Frankfurt, and Switzerland, where they came under the humanist influences of Calvin and Zwingli. Like other English Protestants there, Hilles was eager to discuss his faith with like-minded people, and he soon struck up a correspondence with the Zurich reformer Heinrich Bullinger. Hilles's twenty-two letters to Bullinger survive, revealing much about his religious views and about his career both in London and on the Continent. He passed on news from his contacts in England, including some of the remarkable events of the latter years of Henry VIII's reign, such as the Northern Rebellion, the King's repudiation of Anne of Cleves, his marriages to Katherine Howard and then to Katherine Parr, and finally the death of the King and the accession of the young Prince Edward. His letters also reveal a sharp sense of humour: a fortnight after Henry VIII's marriage to Katherine Parr, in July 1543, three Protestants were burned at the stake in one day.

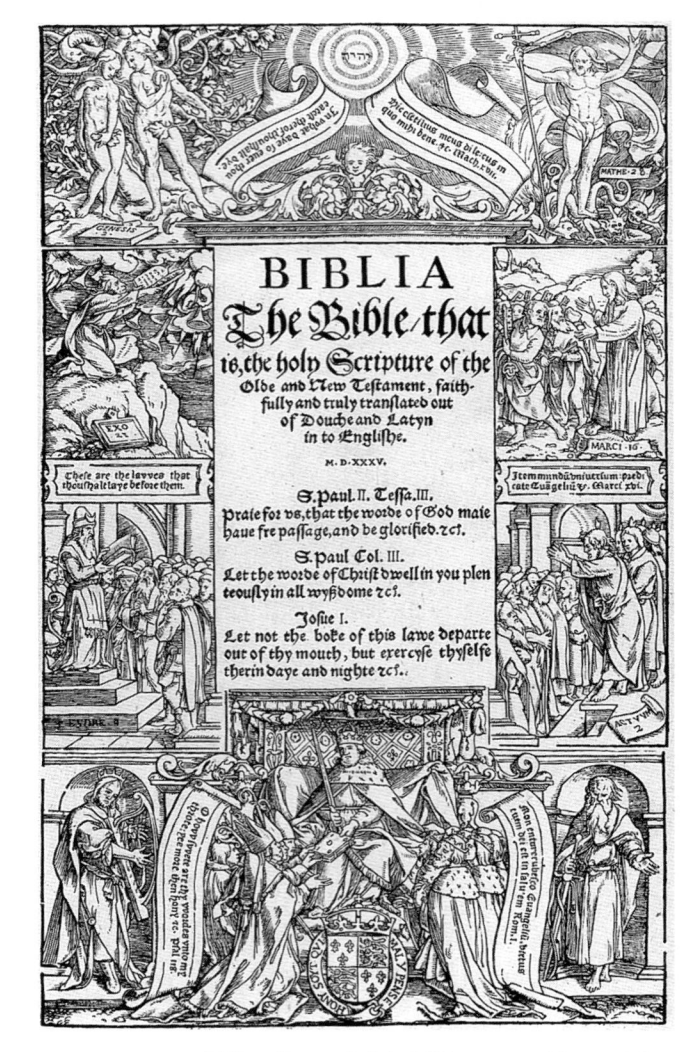

FIGURE 35. Miles Coverdale's Bible, 1535. Coverdale was an associate of Richard Hilles and later a tenant of the Merchant Taylors' Company.
Cambridge University Library, pressmark BSS. 201. B35. By permission of the British and Foreign Bible Society and the Syndics of Cambridge University Library

Hilles commented to Bullinger that Henry 'is always wont to celebrate his nuptials by some wickedness of this kind'.[46]

THE DEATH OF EDWARD VI AND THE ACCESSION OF MARY

When Hilles eventually returned to England in 1549, with Edward VI now on the throne, the climate of opinion was much more sympathetic to his views. That year saw the passing of the first Act of

Uniformity, and the issuing of Thomas Cranmer's Book of Common Prayer. Yet it is important to remember that the progress of reformist ideas was often 'hesitant and faltering', and most Londoners were content, as we have seen, to fall in with the prevailing orthodoxy — at least as far as their testamentary provisions were concerned. Hilles no doubt arrived back to find a range of opinions accommodated within the Company, from his own strong evangelical leanings to those of Thomas White, who remained firmly attached to the Catholic faith. Hilles himself was admitted to the livery in 1550 and in March 1553 obtained an Act of Parliament ensuring that his children, although born on the Continent, could inherit his estate.[47] There is no evidence to show that the life of the Company was seriously disrupted through religious disagreements in these years, notwithstanding the changes that, as we have seen, were forced upon it. However, the death of Edward VI in the summer of 1553 precipitated a political and religious crisis. The problem was that Henry VIII's Act of Succession (1544) was still in force, allowing Mary to succeed, and so at the instigation of Guildford Dudley, son of the Duke of Northumberland, 'Letters Patent for the Limitation of the Crown' were signed before Edward's death, which excluded his half-sisters, Mary and Elizabeth, and installed Dudley's wife, Lady Jane Grey, as Edward's heir. The signatories included the Lord Mayor of London and prominent supporters of a Protestant succession, including Hilles, Emmanuel Lucar, and Thomas Offley. In a letter to Bullinger, Hilles described Jane as 'a truly learned and pious lady', whilst accusing Mary of being 'ill-disposed to the pure doctrine of the gospel'.[48]

The proclamation of Lady Jane Grey was by no means popular in London: when she made her entry to the City on 10 July many of the citizens stood silent, with 'sorrowful and averted countenances'.[49] It was only a matter of days before another noble conspiracy had secured the agreement of the royal council to the accession of Mary, which was proclaimed on 19 July (Col. Pl. XII). The City soon fell into line, despite the fact that thirty-two of its governors had signed the letters patent, and this was probably because of the residual strength of Catholicism in the capital, and apprehension at the prospect of further reform.[50] The apparent joy and excitement in London was recorded by Henry Machyn, Merchant Taylor and funeral furnisher, who wrote of the 'belles ryngyng thrugh London, and bonefyres and tabuls in evere strett and wyne and bere and alle'. His description of the celebrations was matched by other witnesses, including one who wrote that 'others, being men of authority and in years, could not refrain from casting away their garments, leaping and dancing as though beside themselves'.[51] Thomas White, perhaps the wealthiest Londoner of the time, was one of five leading citizens who rode out on 29 July to greet Mary on the outskirts of London.[52]

At the end of September the City and its inhabitants began to prepare both for Mary's coronation and for the election of a new Lord Mayor. The coronation took place on 1 October in Westminster Abbey, with full Catholic rites and ceremonial. The previous day a magnificent pageant had been held in the City, during which the Genoese, Florentine and Hanse merchants erected a triumphal arch in Cheapside. On 13 October the Aldermen of the City chose Thomas White as the Lord Mayor, and this honour was augmented by a knighthood bestowed on him by the new Queen. His mayoral procession to Westminster was enthusiastically described by Machyn:

Hevere (every) craft wer set in [array]: furst wer ij tallmen bayreng ij gret stremars [of] the Marchand-tayllers armes, then cam one [with a] drume and a flutte playng, and a-nodur with a gret f[ife?] all they in blue sylke . . . and then cam in [blue] gownes and capes and hosse and blue sylke slevys and evere man having a target and gayffelyn (javelin) to the nombur of lxx . . . and then cam the bachelars all in a leveray . . . and then cam the pagant of Sant John Baptyst gorgyusly with goodly speches.[53]

THOMAS WHITE AND WYATT'S REBELLION

There is no doubt that Mary relied heavily on White to maintain the City's support for her rule during the first year of her reign. As if a restored Catholic Church was not enough, the Queen then announced her intention to marry Philip of Spain, a move that was bound to inflame tensions in London and elsewhere. White was not only required to implement controversial policies in the City, such as the expulsion of Protestant intellectuals, but was also charged with making London ready for the arrival of the Spanish prince. Orders were given in early January 1554 that London Bridge was to be painted 'against the coming of the King of Spayne' and, in anticipation of rioting, a twenty-four hour watch was ordered and all weapons and gunpowder seized.[54] Interestingly, it was Richard Hilles who was put in charge of the adornment of London Bridge, an example of the way in which civic loyalties could come to the fore at times of crisis. In the meantime, however, opposition outside the City to Mary and her policies had erupted into rebellion, led by Sir Thomas Wyatt, who raised a large force in Kent. Later that same month, with 3,000 rebels closing on London, the City companies were ordered to provide 600 men for the defence of the City. Unfortunately these troops, arrayed in white coats with St George's crosses on their backs, defected to Wyatt at Rochester Bridge, with shouts of 'A Wyatt! A Wyatt!'. It is possible that they included the thirty men 'sent into Kent' whose equipment was provided by the Company at a cost of £14 17s. 1d. on 27 January.[55]

The road to London lay open. At this crucial moment Mary herself came to the City, on 1 February. She entered Guildhall and addressed the assembled companies in a speech which was in many ways a foretaste of the speech that her sister Elizabeth was to deliver at Tilbury more than thirty years later:

> I am your Queen, to whom at my coronation ... you promised your allegiance and obedience ... My father, as ye all know, possessed the same regal state, which now rightly is descended unto me, and to him always ye showed yourselves most faithful and loving subjects: and therefore I doubt not but ye will show yourselves likewise to me ... I cannot tell how naturally the mother loveth the child, for I was never the mother of any, but certainly if a prince and governor may as naturally and earnestly love her subjects, as the mother doth love the child, then assure yourselves that I, being your lady and mistress, do as earnestly and tenderly love and favour you. And I, thus loving you, cannot but think that ye as heartily and faithfully love me; and then I doubt not but we shall give these rebels a short and speedy overthrow.[56]

After making this rousing, and evidently successful, appeal, Mary joined White for a cup of wine, and then departed by barge from Three Cranes Wharf, a property owned by the Merchant Taylors. Under White's leadership the City had already begun making further preparations for the imminent arrival of Wyatt's rebels, including the raising of another levy from the livery companies, this time of 1,200 men. Householders in London were ordered to wear armour, and White himself went armed about Guildhall. The rebels arrived at Southwark in early February, but were unable to cross London Bridge, which was guarded night and day by 300 men. The Company was closely involved in the defence of the bridge: the accounts record expenses of £59 9s. 7d. for equipment for sixty men 'which kept London bridge contynually duryng the tyme that the Rebelles of Kente laye in Southwerk'.[57] After looting the Bishop of Winchester's mansion, Wyatt turned west and was forced to journey upriver before crossing at Kingston. His forces then turned back towards London and, by-passing Westminster, advanced down Fleet Street to Ludgate. There they met the force assembled by Lord Mayor White and the Aldermen: a warning shouted by John Harris, 'a merchant taylor of Watling Street', ensured that that gate was barred against Wyatt. The rebels, realizing that they would not be able to enter the City, turned away and, after a pitched battle at Charing Cross, were surrounded and captured.[58]

The aftermath of the rebellion saw members of the Company once again involved. Particularly striking was the role played by Thomas Offley (Col. Pl. XIIIA). As one of the Sheriffs for 1553–54, his duties included organizing the trials and executions of some of those involved in the rebellion. According to Machyn, forty-six were hanged, with gallows erected 'at evere gate in Lundun', as well as at Cheapside and eleven other locations, including 'Hyd parke corner'. The reprisals continued until 22 February, but Wyatt himself was not executed until 11 April (Fig. 36). Offley's most notable role was in the trial of Sir Nicholas Throckmorton, who was charged with plotting the capture of the Tower and the deposition of the Queen. During the trial, many of the original jurors were replaced when the defendant successfully challenged their appointment. The new jurors included Simon Lowe, Emmanuel Lucar, and Walter Young — all well-known evangelicals and members, like Offley, of the Merchant Taylors' Company.

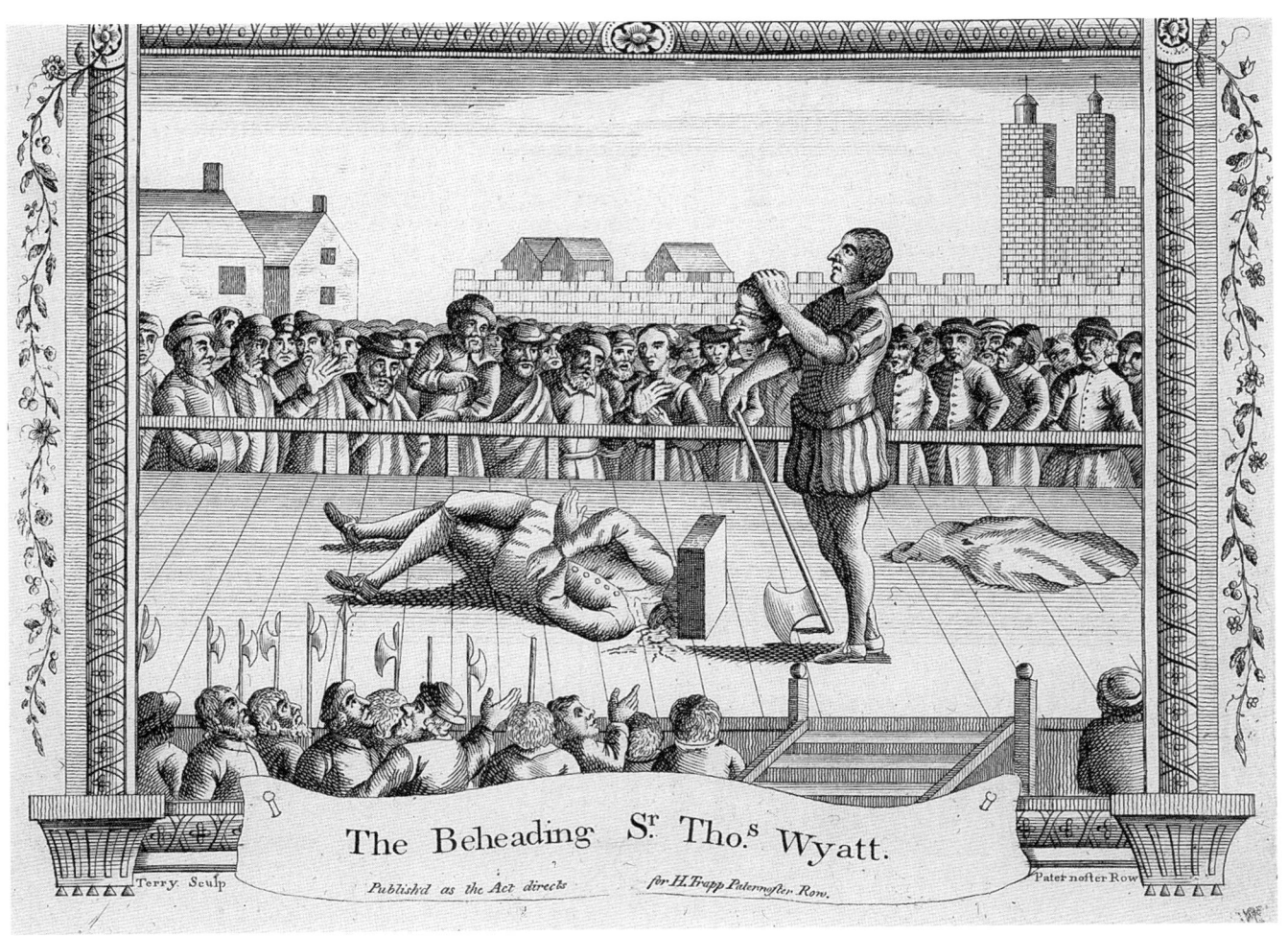

FIGURE 36. The Beheading of Sir Thomas Wyatt, depicted in an engraving in Foxe's *Acts and Monuments*, 1776 edition, facing p. 5.
Gresham College collection, on deposit at Guildhall Library

Throckmorton's acquittal caused a sensation in London, and contemporary writers hailed the jurors (who were imprisoned for their pains) and the character of the defendant. It is quite likely that Offley played a key part in the acquittal, given that his office allowed him considerable influence over the choice of jurors. He was connected with some of the reformist jurors, not only through his Company and trading activities, but also in his capacity as a governor of Christ's Hospital. Offley indeed was rumoured later to have 'saved many who should have died', among them his brother Hugh whom he sent into exile.[59] The aftermath of the rebellion was a tense time in London, and the Lord Chancellor, Stephen Gardiner, Bishop of Winchester, warned White that 'the City of London is a whirlepoole and a sinke of all evil rumours'. There was a general inquiry into those who had not helped in the defence of the City, and it was found that the Clothworkers' armed contingent 'went not whither they were sent'.[60]

Wyatt's rebellion brought some of the simmering tensions in London to the surface. There is no doubt that the Reformation created divisions amongst London's inhabitants: between fellow parishioners, between family members, and between those who belonged to particular livery companies. Yet remarkably, despite the turbulence, the City and the

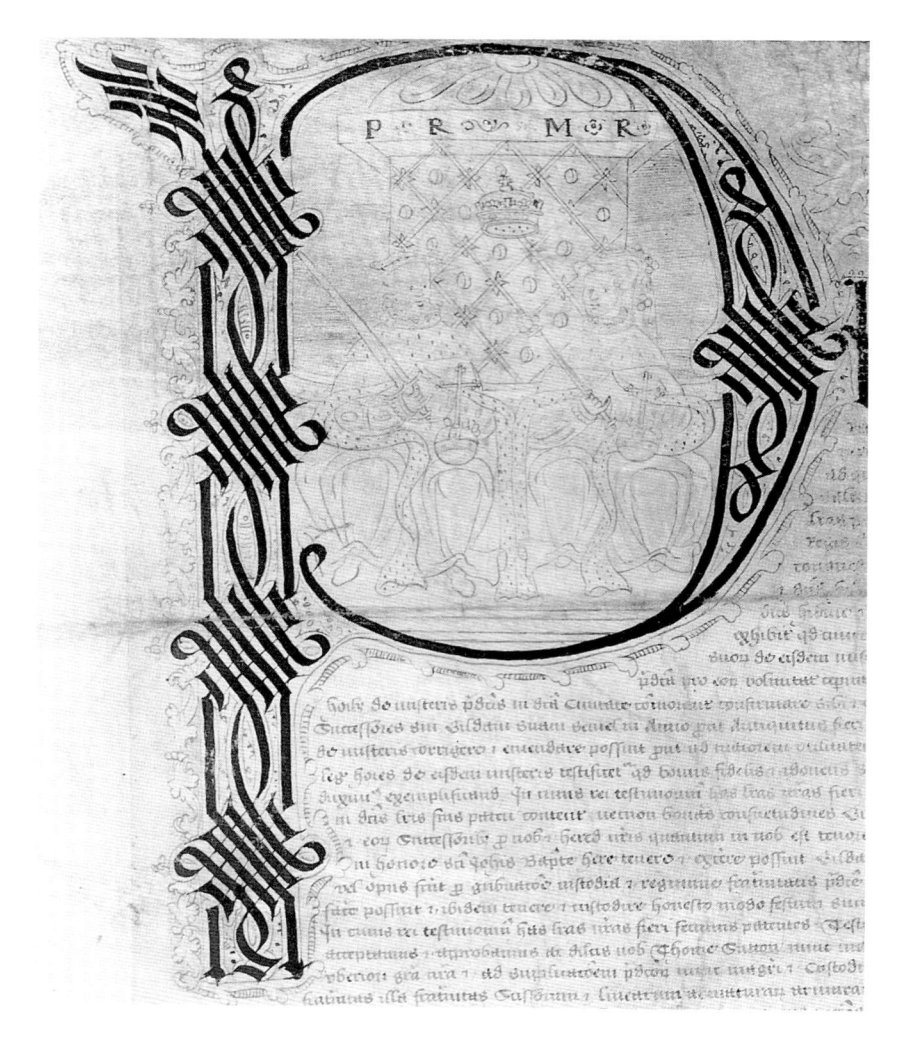

FIGURE 37. A detail from the charter granted to the Company by Philip and Mary, 10 June 1558, showing the Queen and her consort enthroned.
Merchant Taylors' Company

companies survived intact. Whatever their sympathies for Wyatt and his rebels, White and his fellow aldermen were able to secure the support of the majority of citizens to defend the City against attack. This testifies both to the spread of reformist values, and also to the extent to which the restoration of the old religion was welcomed by many citizens. Many simply conformed for appearance's sake, among them Hilles who, to the consternation of his servant, attended Mass again in 1554.[61] It was during the Marian years that White established his College of St John the Baptist in Oxford, creating a link with the Merchant Taylors' Company that is maintained to this day (see Col. Pls VIIA and B). The Company also displayed its willingness to engage with the Crown by obtaining yet another royal charter, issued by Philip and Mary on 10 June 1558. This was little more than an endorsement of previous letters patent, but is notable for its fine line drawing of Mary and her consort (see Fig. 37).

There is little evidence that the contrasting religious views of Hilles and White, and other members, created problems for the Merchant Taylors' Company. Indeed, in several respects the foundations of St John's in 1555 (White) and of Merchant Taylors' School in 1561 (led by Hilles) drew their strength from the common values and impulses that drove many merchants to make charitable and educational benefactions. White's remarkable charitable schemes in Coventry and in other clothing towns in the Midlands and West Country show that not just Protestants could exhibit a social conscience. His loans to apprentices and journeymen were 'not only interest free, but prayer free as well'. Likewise,

White did not let his adherence to the Catholic faith prevent him from serving as a governor of Christ's Hospital from 1556 until his death eleven years later.[62] To see the Company as split into 'parties' by the Reformation is a poor reflection of the diversity of the beliefs held by freemen, and of the ways in which the Company, through its insistence on the old principles of reconciliation and brotherhood, was able successfully to adapt. That is not, of course, to minimize the extent of the changes, described above, to the religious and social life of the Company. These changes were finally 'embedded' during the reign of Elizabeth (1558–1603), a period when Protestantism finally became the prevailing orthodoxy among the City's ruling élite and among members of the Company.

NOTES

1. John Skelton, *Magnificence*, ed. by P. Neuss (Manchester, 1980), pp. 151–52.
2. Stow, *Survey*, ed. by Kingsford, I, p. 273.
3. The 1512 charter no longer survives in the Company's archive, but like other letters patent its text is preserved among the records of the royal Chancery: see *Charters*, ed. by Fry and Sayle, p. 46.
4. PRO, Exchequer Lay Subsidy Returns, E179/251/15b. The authors are grateful to John Oldland for his analysis of this tax return, made — it is believed — for the two forced loans of 1522–23.
5. Seven 'Angels' from the reign of Edward IV (1461–83) were found in the major Spitalfields excavation in London in the spring of 2002. The values of Angels and Ryals increased during the reign of Henry VIII with the rise in the price of gold.
6. The Treasury Accounts are in GL, MS 34357. They are printed in Clode, *Memorials*, pp. 69–81.
7. Clode, *Memorials*, pp. 69–81.
8. The inventories are in GL, MS 34357, fols 65–68, 71 (1491) and fols 27–35 (1512). They are printed in Clode, *Memorials*, pp. 82–92.
9. Ibid., pp. 82–92.
10. Ibid., pp. 92–96.
11. See above, Chapter Two.
12. The manuscript is GL, MS 34004.
13. GL, MS 34048/4, fols 53, 66; PRO, E301/34, mm. 38, 38d. The chantry certificate of 1548, showing the revenues and expenditure of the London companies on chantries and anniversaries, is calendared in C. J. Kitching, *London and Middlesex Chantry Certificate 1548*, London Record Society, 16 (1980). The assets used to fund the expenditure of £960 on chantries and obits yielded a gross income of just over £1,050 a year.
14. Brigden, *London and the Reformation*, p. 389; Davies, 'Tailors of London', pp. 51–53. These were the chantry of Henry Hill, a haberdasher, and the anniversaries of Hugh Acton and Sir Stephen Jenyns.
15. A. Kreider, *English Chantries: The Road to Dissolution* (Cambridge, MA, 1979), pp. 79–89, 93–104.
16. Ibid., p. 85.
17. Stat. 37 Hen.VIII c.4; Kreider, *English Chantries*, pp. 165–85.
18. GL, MS 34048/4, fols 5^v, 18^v.
19. Ibid.
20. Ibid., fol. 6. The other arrangements made by Percyvale (1503), Jenyns (1523) and Acton (1530) were as yet unaffected by the Crown's actions.

21. Kreider, *English Chantries*, p. 179. The chantry certificate of 1546 is PRO, LR2/241 fols 7^v–19.
22. Stat. 1 Edw.VI c.14; Kreider, *English Chantries*, pp. 190–91, 197.
23. PRO, E301/34, mm. 36–40, and see Kitching, *London and Middlesex Chantry Certificate 1548*.
24. GL, MS 34048/4, fols 84, 84^v (1547–48).
25. GL, MS 34168A. The fair copy of the return is untraced, but its contents are reproduced in the commissioners' certificate, PRO, E301/34, mm. 38, 38d. The rents of all the companies put together came to £1,050 4s. 8d. (m. 40d).
26. GL, MS 34048/4, fol. 104, 'Salarye[s] of preestes' (1547–48): compare this with the £110 18s. 6d. from the same properties paid in 1548–49 to one of the King's collectors, ibid., fols 137, 137^v.
27. Brigden, *London and the Reformation*, p. 390. £2,000 in the mid-16th century had a purchasing power approximately equal to that of £500,000 in 2002 (Economic History Society data).
28. GL, MS 34048/4, fols 164^v, 167^v, 168. For a list of the properties sold and their purchasers see Clode, *Early History*, I, p. 151.
29. *CPR*, 1549–51, pp. 386–401 (4 July 1550). A smaller grant, made in December 1549, included some of the Merchant Taylors' rent charges: ibid., 1549–51, pp. 86–87.
30. Clode, *Early History*, I, p. 371; GL, MS 34048/4, fols 176–77, 264–65^v, 269–70.
31. Kreider, *English Chantries*, pp. 199–205.
32. D. Hickman, 'The Religious Allegiance of London's Ruling Elite, 1520–1603' (unpublished PhD thesis, University of London, 1996), pp. 17–19.
33. GL, MS 34010/1, pp. 152, 307; 2, fol. 2^v; 3, fol. 36^v. The prayer is printed (with modernized spelling) in Clode, *Memorials*, pp. 128–29; Clode, *Early History*, I, p. 237.
34. I. W. Archer, 'The Livery Companies and Charity in the Sixteenth and Seventeenth Centuries', in *Guilds, Society & Economy in London 1450–1800*, ed. by I. A. Gadd and P. Wallis (2002), pp. 15–28. By comparison, the Grocers were spending £80 on their poor in the 1590s, and £242 in the 1630s, and the Clothworkers £86 and £289. If company size is taken into consideration, these figures represent a per capita expenditure on company poor in the 1630s of 6s. 4d. for the Merchant Taylors, compared with 9s. 6d. for the Grocers and 3s. 4d. for the Clothworkers.
35. See Chapter Seven below.
36. Wilford's will is abstracted in *Archaeologia Cantiana*, 48 (1936), pp. 32–36. The original is PRO, PROB 11/22, fols 102^v–05^v. It is also fortunate, perhaps, that the sermon is no

longer delivered at the time specified by the founder, between 6 and 9 a.m.

37. See Hickman, 'Religious Allegiance', Appendix I.

38. Brigden, *London and the Reformation*, pp. 103–05.

39. The full account by Foxe, including the charges against Hunne and the subsequent investigation into his death, can be found in *The Acts and Monuments of John Foxe*, ed. by S. R. Cattley (8 vols, London, 1837–41), 4, pp. 183–98.

40. What follows is derived from the accounts in R. Wunderli, 'Pre-Reformation London Summoners and the Murder of Richard Hunne', *Journal of Ecclesiastical History*, 33 (1982), pp. 209–24; J. Fines, 'The Post-mortem Condemnation for Heresy of Richard Hunne', *English Historical Review*, 78 (1963), pp. 528–31. See also W. R. Cooper, 'Richard Hunne', *Reformation*, 1 (1996), pp. 221–51.

41. For John Wycliffe and the 'Lollard' heresy see, amongst others, A. Hudson, *The Premature Reformation* (Oxford, 1988); J. A. F. Thomson, *The Later Lollards, 1414–1520* (1965).

42. T. M. C. Lawler, G. Marc'hadour and R. C. Marius (eds), *Complete Works of St. Thomas More, vol. 6: A Dialogue Concerning Heresies. 2 parts* (New Haven, CT, and London, 1981), pp. 318–19.

43. Ibid.

44. *Acts and Monuments*, 4, p. 192.

45. The identification was made by Dr William R. Cooper and Valerie Offord. The text of the Bible is the so-called 'Later' or 'Purvey Version' of Wycliffe's translation of the New Testament. This information is taken from an unpublished paper, 'The Discovery of Richard Hunne's Wycliffite Bible', delivered by Dr Steven Sohmer of UCLA to the Tyndale Conference in Geneva in 2001. The authors are grateful to Dr Sohmer for allowing them to read the paper. See also C. de Hamel, *The Book. A History of the Bible* (2001), pl. 132 and p. 336.

46. See H. Robinson (ed.), *Original Letters Relative to the English Reformation* (Cambridge, 1846–47), I, esp. pp. 241–42; Clode, *Early History*, II, pp. 58–97.

47. *Lords Journal*, II, p. 438.

48. *Original Letters*, ed. by Robinson, I, p. 273.

49. Brigden, *London and the Reformation*, p. 520.

50. Ibid., p. 523.

51. A. De Guaras, *The Accession of Queen Mary* (1892), p. 96; *The Diary of Henry Machyn, Citizen and Merchant-Taylor of London, from AD 1550-AD 1563*, ed. by J. G. Nichols, Camden Soc., 42 (1848), p. 37.

52. R. Tittler, *Townspeople and Nation: English Urban Experiences, 1540–1640*, p. 104.

53. *Diary of Henry Machyn*, pp. 47–48.

54. CLRO, Rep. 13, fols 116–23.

55. GL, MS 34048/4, fol. 290. Near-contemporary accounts can be found in J. Stow, *Annales* (1631), pp. 618–22; *The Chronicle of Queen Jane and of Two Years of Queen Mary*, ed. by J. G. Nichols, Camden Soc., 48 (1850), pp. 39–52.

56. *Acts and Monuments of John Foxe*, 6, pp. 414–15.

57. GL, MS 34048/4, fol. 290ᵛ.

58. This is an abbreviated version of the account of the rebellion in Brigden, *London and the Reformation*, pp. 534–45.

59. Brigden, *London and the Reformation*, pp. 551–53; Thomas Fuller, *The Worthies of England* (1662), Cheshire, p. 291.

60. Clode, *Early History*, II, p. 128; T. Girtin, *The Golden Ram* (1958), p. 34.

61. *Original Letters*, ed. by Robinson, I, pp. 345–46.

62. Tittler, *Townspeople and Nation*, pp. 116–17.

CHAPTER SEVEN

THE COMPANY AND EDUCATION IN THE SIXTEENTH CENTURY

Both before and after the Reformation, education was of great interest to the citizens of London. The renewed interest in founding grammar schools in the late sixteenth century continued in part at least along the path blazed by pre-Reformation founders, who provided educational opportunities at the same time as providing for their own souls through the establishment of chantries. The Merchant Taylors' Company and its members occupy a unique place in the history of education, mainly because of the sheer number of foundations established in London and elsewhere from the early fifteenth century by prominent Merchant Taylors such as Sir John Percyvale, Sir Thomas White and Sir William Harper, as well as by the Company itself. Some came to be administered in one form or another by the Company, whilst others were less closely connected. All however are in some sense part of the Company's educational 'family', reflecting a connection that has remained durable for more than five hundred years.

EDUCATION IN THE LATER MIDDLE AGES

The period after the Black Death saw an unprecedented rise in the demand for education of all kinds amongst the laity of England. Standards of living were rising, and it became increasingly important for young craftsmen and merchants in towns and cities to obtain at least an elementary education.[1] English was being used more and more as a language of written communication, and institutions such as guilds and urban governments were gradually adopting the vernacular in their own records. The Goldsmiths of London in 1469 bemoaned the fact that they had been taking on apprentices who could not read or write, 'which is a practice damaging not only to the fellowship, but also to the master taking such apprentices and to the apprentice himself . . . also, for want of such literacy, members of this fellowship are not held in esteem by merchants of the City of London or favoured by lords and gentlefolk as are literate men of other fellowships of the City'.[2] Apprenticeships themselves were gradually becoming associated with the acquisition of reading and writing skills, in addition to expertise in the chosen craft. In 1492 the Merchant Taylors' Company's Court heard Thomas Godfrey complain that his master, Robert Archer, had failed to send him 'to scole contrary to thendentures and covenauntes bytwene the said Archer and his apprentice'. On another occasion a boy was apprenticed to a tailor in the hope that he would also be taught to 'rede, write and lay Accomptes suffisauntly'.[3]

Education in late medieval London took place at different levels, in informal and formal environments, and under the jurisdiction of both lay and ecclesiastical authorities.[4] Many informal opportunities for education in London sprang up in response to a rising demand for learning. Chantry priests, for instance, frequently seem to have acted as teachers, providing a service to parishioners and their children. Scriveners and parish clerks too possessed the education and training to pass on skills to the sons and daughters of craftsmen and merchants. Formal opportunities in London, however, remained limited. 'Song schools', providing elementary education in Latin and English, equipped younger boys to sing services at parish churches or religious houses. There were at least eight song schools in the City, including one at St Paul's and three attached to parish churches. Grammar schools, for older boys, were fewer in number: until the mid-fifteenth century there were just four approved schools, at St Paul's Cathedral, and the churches of St Mary le Bow, St Dunstan in the East, and St Martin le Grand. In 1441 these were joined by a fifth, when John Carpenter, then Master of St Anthony's Hospital, founded a grammar school, as well as another song school, at the hospital in Threadneedle Street, opposite Merchant Taylors' Hall, where Sir Thomas More was to be a pupil.[5] This provision was clearly inadequate, and a parliamentary petition of 1447 submitted by four distinguished rectors of City churches argued for the foundation of more grammar schools in the capital because of the numbers of people who flocked to London 'for the lake of scolemaistres in their own country'. The petition was a failure, partly, it seems, because of the reluctance of the Church authorities to extend provision beyond the five existing licensed grammar schools.[6]

THE COMPANY AND THE CORNHILL SCHOOL

The control exercised by the Church in London over the foundation of approved grammar schools could not prevent the growth of unlicensed schools of various kinds in the capital. This trend was noted in 1391 when concern was expressed at the activities of 'strange and unqualified masters of grammar', who were holding 'general schools of grammar' in London. By the early fifteenth century the Cornhill area of London was an important centre for the teaching of grammar. John Seward, a noted scholar and layman, ran a grammar school in Cornhill from about 1404 until his death in 1435. He was associated with another schoolmaster, William Relyk, who established a school nearby at the Cardinal's Hat in Lombard Street.[7] References to these and other schoolmasters who lived and taught in this part of London indicate that Cornhill had become an important centre for education in the City, regardless of the fact that the City and Church authorities did not recognize these 'schools'.

It is notable, then, that as early as 1417 the Company was renting out one of its properties close to the Hall, in the parish of St Peter Cornhill, to a schoolmaster. The property concerned seems to have been the *viell' hostiell'*: as we have seen, this may have served as the first meeting place of the Company before the building of the livery Hall in the later fourteenth century.[8] This reference is the earliest known connection between the Merchant Taylors and education, and hitherto unknown to historians of the Company's schools. It was far from being a casual or temporary arrangement, for the Company's records show that schoolmasters occupied the property for at least the next sixty years. Moreover the Company regularly spent money on repairs to 'le scolemaysters', and the detailed accounts suggest that the property had been sub-divided into a tenement for the schoolmaster himself and another known as the 'scolehouse'. By the 1450s the schoolmaster was one Robert Killingholme, who paid rent of 13*s*. 4*d*. for his tenement and the larger sum of 16*s*. 8*d*. for the schoolhouse. He remained there until 1472, when he may have died, whereupon the Company let the property to 'Master Stephen, schoolmaster', showing its continued commitment to this use of the buildings.[9] Like the other informal 'schools' in Cornhill and elsewhere in London, this enterprise was small-scale and was presumably funded by fees paid by parents. Yet the Company's involvement in a school on its own doorstep is striking, and it was in precisely this period that liverymen such as John Percyvale, Edmund Flower, and Stephen Jenyns were formulating their own plans.

THE FOUNDATION OF GRAMMAR SCHOOLS BY LONDONERS

In 1432 William Sevenoak, grocer of London, founded a school and almshouses at the town of his birth, Sevenoaks in Kent. Sevenoaks school appears to have been the earliest of the foundations established by London merchants outside the City. As time went on, more Londoners came to express their educational ideals and aspirations — as well as their piety — by founding grammar schools in the counties of their birth. As we have seen, this may have owed something to the reluctance of London's authorities to allow new schools to be established in the City. A remarkable attempt to break the mould was made by the wealthy draper, Simon Eyre, who made complex and expensive arrangements for a 'chapel and scoles' to be established at the Leadenhall, whose building he had overseen. Sadly the scheme was never implemented, for, had it been, 'London would have had an educational establishment as fine as any of the colleges then being built at Oxford or Cambridge'.¹⁰ Yet it was an important moment nonetheless, both because of its scale and because — unlike previous foundations — it would have been administered after his death by his company, the Drapers. For London's merchants, the City companies had become an important means by which they could ensure the success of their testamentary provisions, and over the next two centuries education became an important aim for many of them. Further foundations in the fifteenth century that marked the way ahead included John Abbot's school at Farthinghoe in Northamptonshire (1443), administered by the Mercers' Company, and, perhaps most significantly, the foundation of Stockport Grammar School in Cheshire (1487) by Sir John Shaa, a Goldsmith and Mayor of London, who also entrusted the administration of the endowment to his company. At that time another Cheshire man, John Percyvale, was rapidly making his mark among the Tailors and Linen-Armourers, soon to be Merchant Taylors, and would have taken a particular interest in Shaa's foundation.

SIR JOHN AND LADY PERCYVALE: THE SCHOOLS AT MACCLESFIELD AND WEEK ST MARY

Sir John Percyvale's career has been alluded to in previous chapters, not least because in 1498, after serving as alderman for Vintry and Langbourn Wards, he was the first member of the Company to be chosen as Mayor of London. Unusually, he had begun his career as an official in the household of the Mayor, but was admitted to the livery of what was still known as the Tailors' Company in the 1460s, rising to become a prosperous merchant. He acquired a substantial amount of property in the City, including a mansion in Lombard Street which he left to the Company. In the mid-sixteenth century this house was suggested as the location for the new Exchange, but the City and the Company failed to reach an agreement.¹¹ After his mayoralty it is likely that Percyvale turned his attention to the foundation of a grammar school at Macclesfield in Cheshire, 'fast by which Town I was borne'. The foundation deed, dated 25 January 1502 (1503 in modern reckoning), spells out in detail not only how the school was to be run, but also the discussions that Percyvale had had with some important men with Cheshire connections. In particular, he claimed to have benefited from the 'good and holsome counsell' of Sir Richard Sutton, a member of a prominent Cheshire family. Sutton was a co-founder of Brasenose College, Oxford, in 1512, and made sure that its statutes included a provision which enabled the college to draw some of its scholars from the Macclesfield area. He also remembered the school at Macclesfield in his will. Percyvale also claimed to have been 'moche stered' by conversations with another Cheshire man, Thomas Savage, then Archbishop of York, whom he appointed as one of his executors. Savage was not a noted benefactor of education, although he had been educated in Oxford, Bologna and Padua, but he no doubt provided Percyvale with further encouragement to found a school.

Percyvale's motivation for the foundation is also apparent from the foundation deed:

... God of his haboundant grace hath sent and daily sendeth to the inhabitaunts there Copyous plentie of Children To whose lernyng and bryngyng forth in Conyng [learning] and vertue right fewe Techers and scolemaisters been in that Contre whereby many Children for lak of such techyng & draught in conyng fall to Idlenes And so consequently live disolately all their daies.¹²

Percyvale was not alone in pointing out the moral purpose of educating the young, and he was also reflecting a wider concern about the lack of educational opportunities in the shires. To address these problems, and help his own soul into the bargain, he set out a scheme for a 'fre gramer scole' in Macclesfield, to be run by a priest who was also to 'syng and pray for me and my freends'. Like other foundations before the Reformation, therefore, the school had a dual purpose, both educational and spiritual. Although characterized as a 'free' grammar school, Percyvale made it clear elsewhere in the document that his attentions were focused primarily on 'Gentilmens sonnes and other good mennes Children of the Towne & Contre thereabouts'. This was not a school for the poor as such, therefore, although his words do seem to suggest that he had a wider constituency in mind than just the sons of gentlemen.

The practical arrangements for the foundation were straightforward. An endowment of lands in

Macclesfield and in nearby parishes worth 10 marks (£6 13s. 4d.) a year was purchased by Percyvale from Thomas Savage at a cost of £90 7s. 2d., and was augmented by further property that increased the annual income of the school to £10 a year. The endowment was to be conveyed to a group of eighteen trustees who were to employ the schoolmaster-priest and a rent collector. The trustees, an impressive group, included not only the Archbishop, but also Sir Richard Sutton and the latter's nephew John Sutton. All were men with strong Cheshire connections, and it is interesting that Percyvale chose this path rather than settle the endowment on an institution, such as the Company. On the one hand this might make the trustees more responsive to the needs of the school, and avoid some of the disputes that occurred in relation to Wolverhampton Grammar School in the sixteenth and seventeenth centuries. On the other, there was pressure on the trustees to ensure that their numbers were not allowed to fall to the point where the future of the school could be in doubt. Although Percyvale did not involve the Company directly in his foundation, he stated that one copy of the deed (now lost) 'remayneth In the taylours hall In the Cite of London'.[13]

The school itself, according to a document of 1544, comprised a tenement and a garden located in the heart of the town of Macclesfield in a place known subsequently as 'School Bank', adjacent to the parochial chapel of All Hallows (now St Michael's church). This was the location for the daily services for the souls of John and Thomasine Percyvale, almost certainly in a side chapel built by Archbishop Savage between 1505 and 1507. Percyvale's deed also provides the only early evidence of how the school was to be run. Masses and prayers, attended by the pupils, were to be celebrated every day by the schoolmaster for the souls of Percyvale, his wife Thomasine, and Richard Sutton. A suitably solemn atmosphere was to prevail: the boys were to attend services 'without Janglyng or talkyng or other Idell occupacion'. The first schoolmaster, William Bridges, was a kinsman of the founder. Sadly, little is known about him. However Percyvale clearly had high standards, and demanded that the schoolmaster be a 'vertues preest conyng in gramer and graduate', and so we can assume that Bridges was suitably qualified.

Bridges was Master of the school until his death in 1538. Thereafter little is recorded of it until the late 1540s when, like the Company, it was visited by the chantry commissioners. As a chantry school, whose endowment was dedicated in part to the celebration of services for the dead, its future was in the balance. Fortunately, the fact that the original deed of foundation was for a school, with chantry attached, was in its favour. Nevertheless it seems likely that the school was forced to close for a few years after 1547 while arrangements were made to secure its future. Pressure from local residents, no doubt including the trustees, helped to move events forward, and on 25 April 1552 a charter of refoundation was granted by Edward VI, 'upon the humble petition as well of the Inhabitants of Macclesfield . . . as of many other of our subjects of the whole neighbouring country to us presented for a Grammar school to be erected and established in Macclesfield within the parish of Prestbury'. The endowment of the school, now known as 'the free grammar school of King Edward VI in Macclesfield', included not only the original lands purchased by Percyvale, but also further property from a dissolved college of priests in Chester. It now had an endowment worth some £20 a year, a substantial sum, that enabled it to go from strength to strength. Moreover, the charter of 1552 conferred corporate status on the school for the first time, enabling it to hold property as an institution rather than being dependent on trustees.[14]

The emphasis on the teaching of grammar continued. The first Master of King's School, John Bolde, was described as 'a discreet man, skilled in grammar', and as the 'gymnasiarchum sive pedagogum' (gymnasiarch or pedagogue) of the 'liberi gimnasii sive scole gramaticalis' (free 'gymnasium' or grammar school). His stipend was £13 6s. 8d., although in return he was reminded that he would be liable for dismissal for immoral behaviour or drunkenness. Bolde's successor in 1561 was a noted classical scholar, John Brownswerd, who was previously Master of Wilmslow School. He held the post at Macclesfield until shortly before his death in 1589, and during his period of office several pupils went on to continue their education at Oxford or Cambridge. A brass in the church celebrated his achievements: 'the first of poets, the chief among grammarians, the flower of pedagogues is here buried in the ground.' The final Master appointed in the sixteenth century was similarly well qualified. William Legh's brass states that he not only taught Latin, Greek and Hebrew — a mark of a successful school in that period — but was also skilled in Spanish, French and Italian. The school remained on its site next to the church until December 1748, when it moved to Back Street, now King Edward Street. An Act of Parliament of 1774 allowed it and its governors greater freedom to buy and sell property in order to expand the range of activities of the school. Just over a century later, in 1856, King's School became established on its present site in Cumberland Street.[15]

John Percyvale died on 10 April 1503, and was survived by his remarkable widow, Thomasine. She was to found a school herself, at Week St Mary in Cornwall, and is notable as the earliest female commoner known to have founded a school. Legend later made much of her apparently humble origins, describing her as a poor shepherdess who, whilst tending her flock on a moor in her native Cornwall, captured the heart of a travelling London merchant who took her to London as his wife. She married three times, each time more advantageously, finally ending up as Dame Thomasine Percyvale, Lady Mayoress.[16] Despite the flowery language often used to describe her Whittington-like story, elements of the legend are true. She was born Thomasine Bonaventure in the village of Week St Mary, a few miles north of Launceston in Cornwall. However, her family was not poor: she was related to a gentry family, the Dinhams of Lifton, and thus to Thomasine Dinham, prioress of Cornworthy. Her brother was an Oxford graduate who became rector of a church in Kent. That she was in London by the early 1460s is clear, and it is possible that this was as a servant. This was a path often trodden by young men and women, for whom a period in service was a prelude to marriage or setting up a business. What is not in doubt is that her first husband was Henry Galle, a liveryman of the Company, who was tailor to Sir John Howard, later Duke of Norfolk. Galle died in 1466, whereupon she married another member of the Company, Thomas Barnaby, who did not survive their first year of marriage. Both men lived in Fleet Street, at that time home to a number of prominent members of the Company. It was probably in the late 1460s, therefore, that she married Percyvale, who had recently become a liveryman after serving in the Mayor's household.[17]

Like her husband, Thomasine was an important benefactor of the Merchant Taylors' Company. In her will, proved in 1512, she left substantial property in the parish of St Martin in the Vintry to augment an estate in Lombard Street already given to the Company by John to fund their chantry in the church of St Mary Woolnoth. She remained childless, but during her final widowhood took an active role in bringing up poor children in her own household: her will refers to three boys 'which I have brought up of almes', and two girls 'maide children which I have also brought up'. All were to have 'mete, drynk and lernyng' until the age of twenty-one, or until they married or became apprentices. This interest in education was undoubtedly one of the inspirations for her own school foundation, although her husband's school at Macclesfield provided the model. The deed of foundation was drawn up on 10 July 1506. Like John, she cited a lack of teachers in Cornwall that was responsible for many children falling 'to idleness & diuerse other vices', many of the phrases exactly matching those in her late husband's deed. Once again, the endowment was to be placed in the hands of trustees, nineteen in all, of whom four were to act as governors of the school. She was even more insistent on the quality of the man appointed to run the school, specifying that he was to be 'sufficiently lerned in Gramer, Graduated in one of the universities of Oxford or Cambriege So that he be a maister of Arte or a maister of Grammer atte least'. Like his counterpart in Macclesfield, the Master was to say Mass every day for the souls of herself and her three husbands, whilst undertaking to teach the pupils 'without asking or demaundyng of the said children or of the freends eny money or other reward for such techyng'. He was also required to celebrate other services in the church 'for the lake of pristes'.[18]

The first Master was to be John Andrew, educated at Winchester College and at New College, Oxford.

FIGURE 38 a & b. Thomasine Percyvale's school at Week St Mary, Cornwall.
Woolf/Greenham collection

He had returned to Winchester as the Usher there before being recruited by Thomasine. When the chantry commissioners visited in 1546 they were seemingly enthusiastic, claiming that 'they that list [likest] may sett their children to borde there & have them taught freely'.[19] The school building still survives, close to the parish church in Week St Mary (see Fig. 38). A substantial early Tudor domestic building, it was able to provide accommodation for the scholars as well as the Master. An illuminated copy of the foundation deed still hangs on the wall in the kitchen. The school probably opened in late 1508, the year in which Thomasine made her will. She had already in May 1506 purchased the manor of Simpson in Devon, as well as 270 acres of land at Holsworthy, from Sir John Lisle for £220, and these were conveyed in December 1508 to John Andrew, pending the transfer of the estate to the trustees on her death. On 6 November 1508 she also obtained a royal licence approving the new chantry at Week St Mary. In the event, Thomasine lived on for almost four years, and so, unlike her husband, would have been involved in running the school in its early years. In her will she entrusted the supervision of the school and chantry arrangements to her cousin, John Dinham, 'requiringe hym to see every thinge concernynge the same to be parfite and sure as nigh as he can accordyng as he knoweth my mynde'.[20]

Little is recorded of the school until 1536 when it was part of an attempt to exclude chantry schools from taxation under the First Fruits and Tenths. Its annual income at that time was said to be £11 11s. 3d.[21] The final fate of the school was determined after the visits of the chantry commissioners to that remote part of Cornwall in 1546 and 1548. There they found a school that was 'a grete comfort to all the countre'. William Cholwell, aged forty-five, was the schoolmaster, 'a man well learned and a greate setter forthe of Gods worde'. In the meantime they also visited Launceston, a few miles away, where two schoolmasters, attached to a chantry in the parish church, were supported out of an endowment originally conveyed to the Mayor and Corporation in 1409. During these visits a scheme was proposed

Sir Thomas White (1492–1567), artist unknown. The portrait hangs in Merchant Taylors' Hall. It is thought to be one of perhaps two originals that were the progenitors of the eighteen or more portraits that exist in the towns and cities that benefited from his remarkable charities.

Merchant Taylors' Company

PLATE X

A. The monument to Robert Graye (1574–1638) in St Mary Magdalen church, Taunton, where he had founded almshouses.
Photograph by John Bentley, reproduced by permission of Mrs Anne Bentley

B. John Vernon (d. 1616), artist unknown. Presented to the Company by Vernon in 1616. An anniversary service is still held each December in his memory.
Merchant Taylors' Company

C. Robert Dowe (1523–1612), artist unknown. The portrait was in the Company's possession by 1609. Dowe was an exceptionally generous benefactor; he particularly encouraged John Stow.
Merchant Taylors' Company

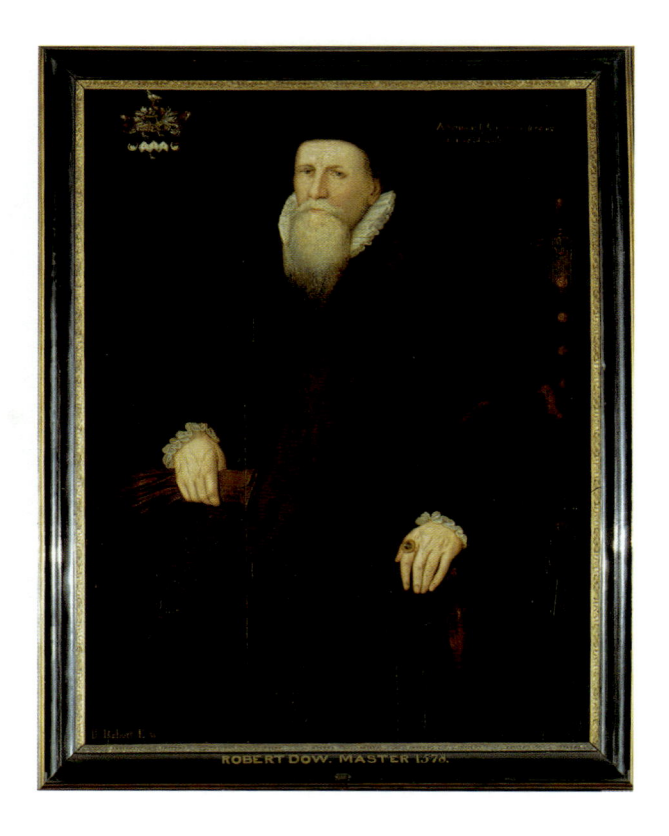

PLATE XI

A. Grant of arms to the Company, 1586 (detail of Fig. 51).
Merchant Taylors' Company

B. View of the parish of St Martin Outwich, attributed to William Goodman, showing Merchant Taylors' Hall and the almshouses in 1599. From an eighteenth-century printed copy of the lost original.
Merchant Taylors' Company

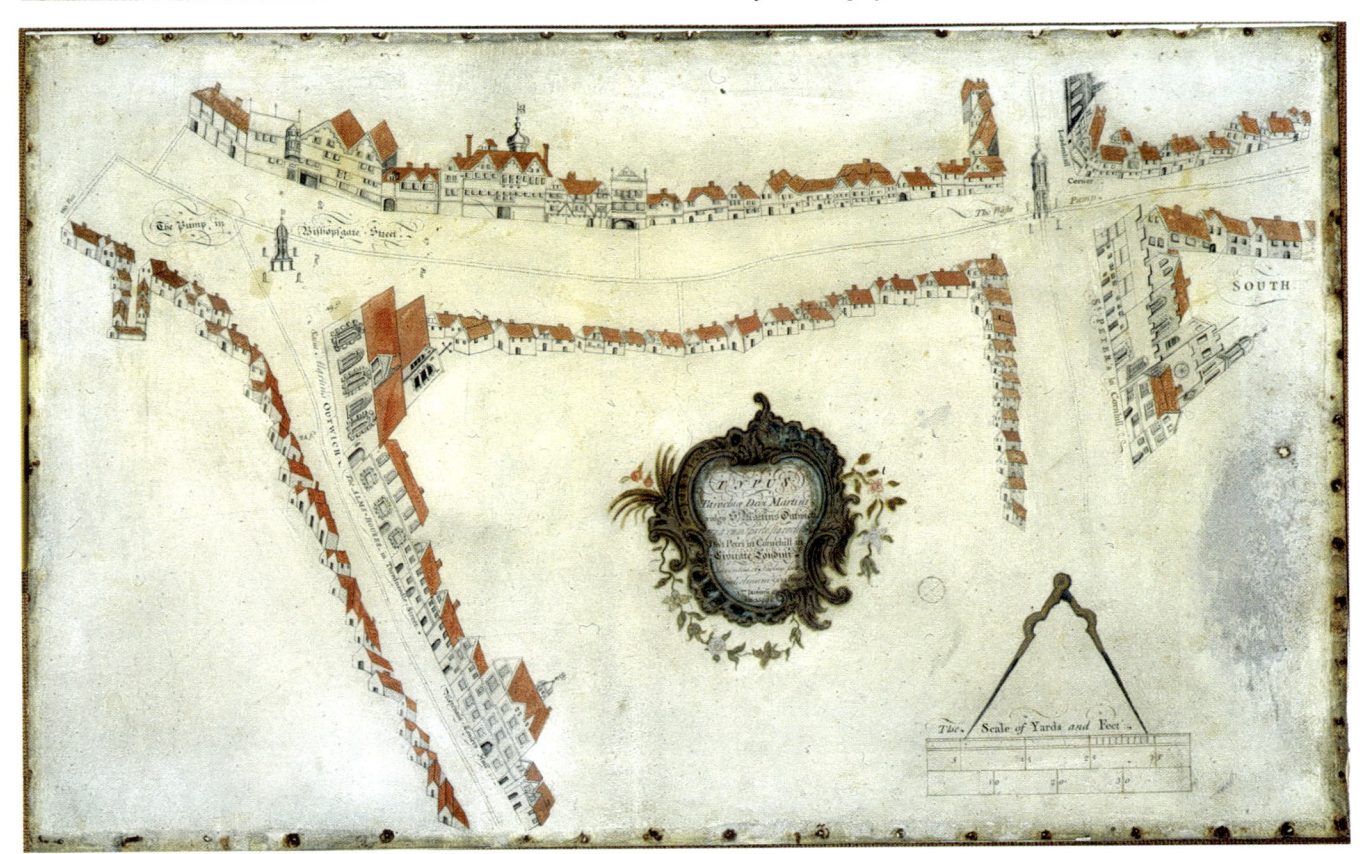

PLATE XII

Queen Mary I, by Hans Eworth, 1554, painted before her marriage on 25 July — she is not wearing a wedding ring.
By permission of the Society of Antiquaries

PLATE XIII

A. The funeral monument of Sir Thomas Offley, Lord Mayor in 1556, died 1582, in St Andrew Undershaft. Drawn by Thomas Fisher, *c.* 1810.
Guildhall Library

B. Robert Dowe's funeral monument in St Botolph Aldgate, sculpted for the Company by Christopher Kingsfeild in 1622.
National Monuments Record, English Heritage

PLATE XIV

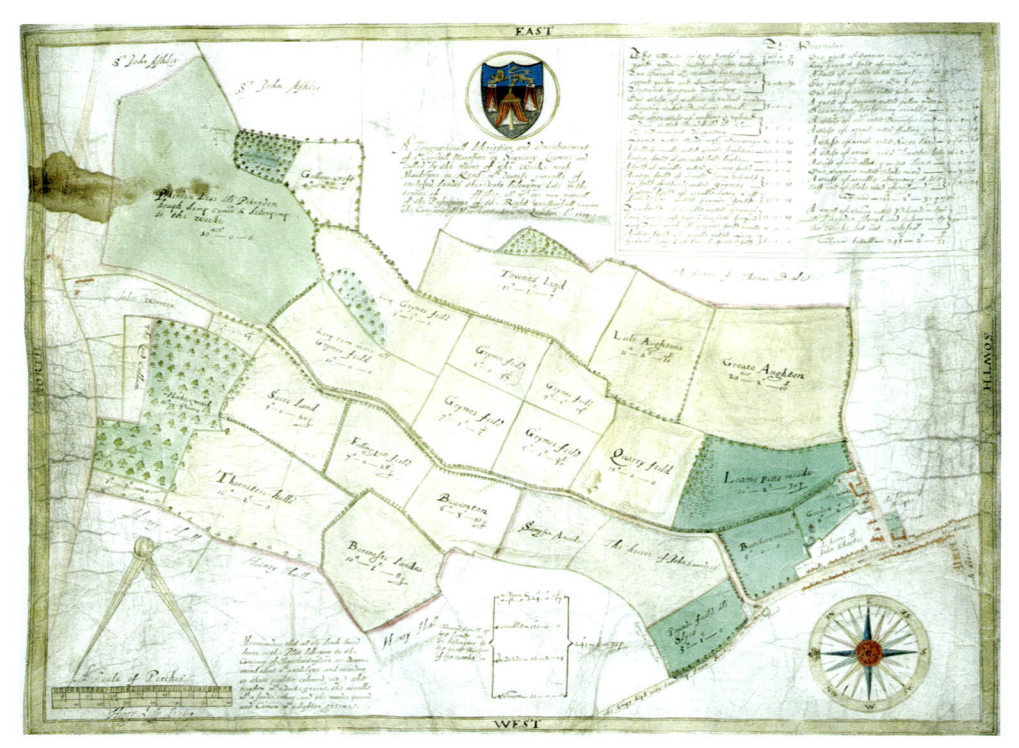

A. The Company's Maidstone estate, 1619, drawn by Henry Lilly.
Guildhall Library, MS 34215

B. The Company's Irish estate, 1622 (Carew MS 634, fols 52ᵛ–53ʳ).
By permission of Lambeth Palace Library

PLATE XV

The Company's Irish estate, 1622 (Carew MS 634, fols 55ᵛ–56ʳ).
By permission of Lambeth Palace Library

PLATE XVI

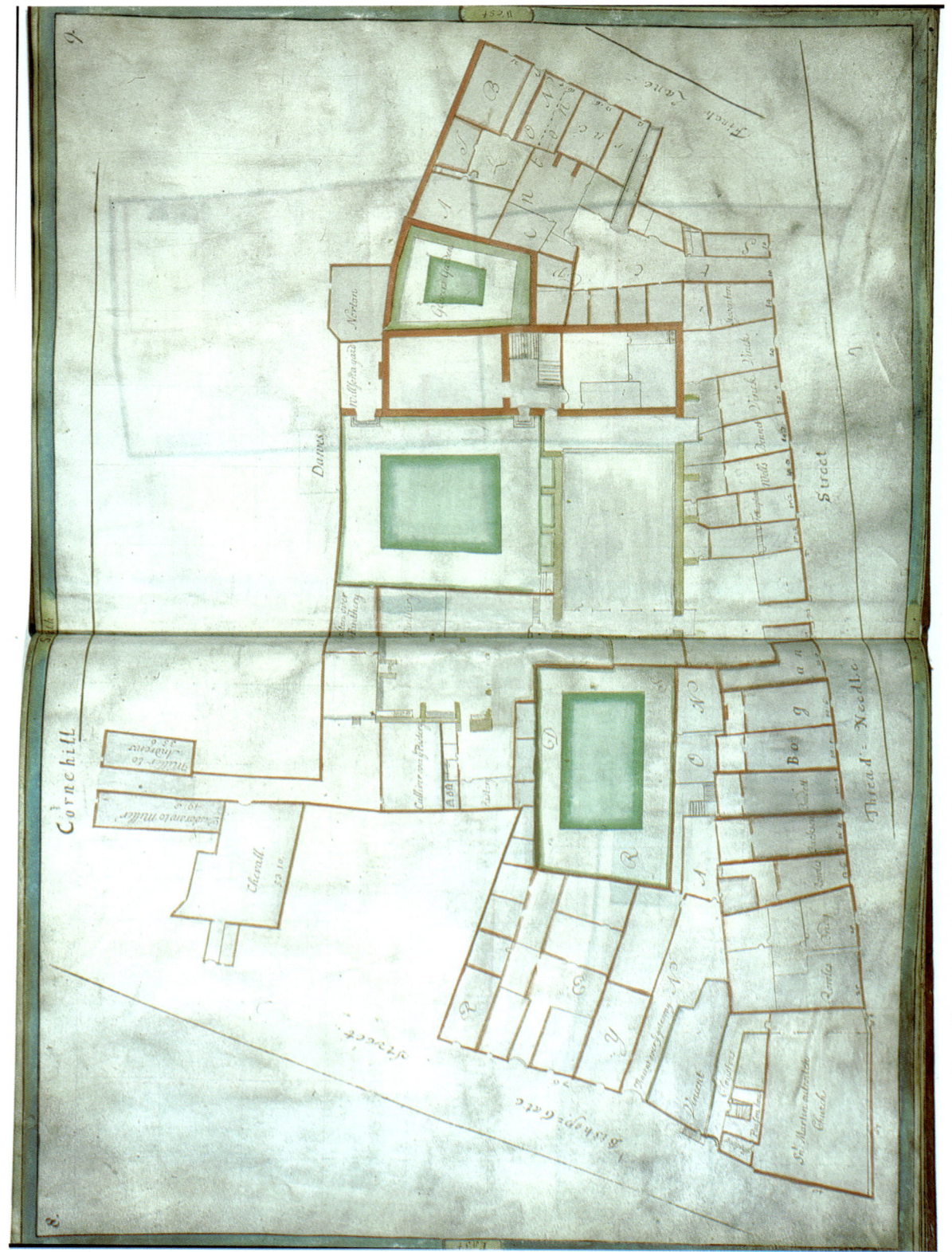

Post-Fire plan of the Hall and surrounding buildings as far as St Martin Outwich. Probably by John Oliver and William Leybourne, c. 1680. The Hall itself can be seen clearly; the expanse of lawn to the south is now the Courtyard. The frontage along Threadneedle Street is already built up with smaller properties.
Guildhall Library, MS 34216

whereby the school at Week St Mary would be transferred to Launceston. This seems to have had the support of the citizens of Launceston: they stressed the need for a school in the town, and argued that the school at Week was in decline and so should be moved. The commissioners' account of the Week school in 1548 endorsed this opinion by remarking that 'the said scole is in decay by reason yt standith in a desolate place and far from the markett for provision of the said scolers'. The Government was consulted, and Protector Somerset agreed that the Week school be moved to Launceston, almost certainly intending that it should replace the existing school there. This scheme was implemented between 1549 and 1552, with the Crown paying the salaries of the staff out of the revenues of the Week St Mary endowments seized at the Reformation: Cholwell continued as Master, although for a while a half-salary was paid to one of the Launceston grammar teachers, Stephen Gourge.[22] The new Free School at Launceston then had a continuous existence until 1824, after which it suffered a series of closures, amalgamations, and refoundations. It emerged in January 1965 as Launceston College, a mixed comprehensive school.

The removal of the school to Launceston was both the end of Thomasine's school as she originally envisaged it, and also a new beginning. Like other founders, she wanted to establish a school in the parish of her birth, but it seems clear that this was not sustainable given its small size and remote location. On the other hand, like her late husband, she made sure that it was properly endowed, and run by highly qualified and effective staff, so that by the time of the Reformation there was no doubting its quality. Both Macclesfield and Week St Mary schools were able to survive, albeit under different names, and are testimony to a remarkable couple whose two foundations are a unique reflection of early Tudor interest in education.

WOLVERHAMPTON GRAMMAR SCHOOL

The foundation of Wolverhampton Grammar School marked the Company's first foray into direct management of an endowed school. Whilst the schools of John and Thomasine Percyvale were administered by groups of trustees with little or no connection to the Company, Sir Stephen Jenyns made the Company itself responsible for the endowment and for appointing the staff. Jenyns's career has been well documented, but is worth recalling here in its essentials. He was probably slightly younger than Percyvale, having come to London in 1462 from his native Wolverhampton to be apprenticed to Thomas Pye. He entered the livery and became a Warden of the Company at an unknown date (probably in the early 1480s), and Master in 1489–90. A wealthy cloth merchant, he enjoyed a similar level of success on the civic stage, serving successively as Alderman for the wards of Castle Baynard, Dowgate and Lime Street from 1499 until his death in 1523. He was Sheriff in 1498–99, and was the first Lord Mayor of Henry VIII's reign, having been chosen for that office in the autumn of 1508. He was married to Margaret, the widow of a fellow Merchant Taylor, William Buck, demonstrating — as with Thomasine Percyvale — the connections between Company members. The occasion of Jenyns's election as Lord Mayor was a joyous one for both husband and wife, and the couple used the occasion to donate a lavishly illuminated two-volume lectionary (Epistles and Gospels) to their church of St Mary Aldermanbury (see Col. Pls IIA and VIIIA). It still survives in the British Library, and includes a Latin inscription at the front of each volume that reads:

Pray for the good estate of Stephen Jenyns, knight and Alderman of London, and Lady Margaret his wife, for as long as they live, and for their souls when they shall have migrated from this light ... For the said Stephen and Margaret gave this book to the church of the Blessed Virgin of Aldermanbury, to remain there for ever, in the year of Our Lord 1508 and in the 24th year of the reign of Henry VII, during the time when the said Stephen was Mayor of London aforesaid.[23]

Margaret predeceased her husband on 15 March 1520, and there exists an unusual description of her last hours and funeral, contained in an early-sixteenth-century compilation of funerary and heraldic practices. It was said that she 'went to bed in good helthe and aftir her first slepe such humours arysse on her that ... it stopped her brethe'. Her body was laid out at their home in Aldermanbury in a chamber hung with black, four tapers burning around the coffin. On the Sunday following, the funeral procession went to St Mary's church, where her arms and those of her two husbands were displayed amidst more black hangings. The funeral, which was said to cost more than 300 marks, was described as being 'as honourable and sumptieux as well in lyveres, wax, almes and vitailles as of any bacheler knights wiff had been sien [since] a good wille before'.[24] It was probably shortly after his wife's death that Jenyns paid for substantial building works in another City church, St Andrew Undershaft, including the roofing of the north aisle, glazing in the windows of the south side, and new pews in the south chapel.[25] Jenyns himself was buried in the monastic church of Grey Friars, and a representation of his monument — lost at the Reformation — survives in the same manuscript as the description of his wife's funeral (see Col. Pl. VIIIB).

Perhaps encouraged by the success of the schools established by the Percyvales, Jenyns took the first steps towards the establishment of his own foundation at Wolverhampton on 22 September 1512, some years before his death. At his instigation the Company obtained the necessary licence from the Crown enabling it to acquire property to the value of £20 a year to maintain a school. In April the following year he himself received a licence to grant the manor of Rushock in Worcestershire, worth some £15 a year, to the Company, which would enable it to pay the stipends of a Master and an Usher.[26] The manor was eventually conveyed to the Company in 1515. The rest of the endowment comprised the school-house, with accommodation for the Master and Usher, in John's Lane (later St John's Street), apparently built on the site of Jenyns's own family home. These transactions having been completed, the Company returned Rushock to Jenyns rent-free for life, and the governance of the school rested with him until his death in 1523, whereupon his son-in-law John Nicholls, Merchant Taylor, took it over. Other property was conveyed to the Company in 1528 to fund Jenyns's chantry and anniversary.[27] It was only in 1531, on Nicholls's death, that the Company gained control of the school, and from that date until 1784 the Company administered the Rushock estate and appointed the Masters and Ushers. As we shall see in subsequent chapters, relations between the Company and the local community were not always harmonious, and at various points the Company had to dismiss staff or take other steps to ensure the school's survival. Nevertheless, the school soon came to occupy an important place in the life of the Company (see Fig. 39), particularly when set alongside the other schools founded by members in the first half of the sixteenth century, and the Company's emerging plans for a grammar school of its own in London.

CUCKFIELD GRAMMAR SCHOOL

Perhaps the least known of the pre-Reformation Merchant Taylor foundations is the school established by Edmund Flower in the parish of his birth, Cuckfield in Sussex. Although not as celebrated as some of his contemporaries, Flower was a prominent member of the Company, and the first Master to be elected under the terms of the charter granted by Henry VII in January 1503. Like other Masters, he made gifts of plate to the Company, which in his case included a 'gilt cup, with one cover with a columbyne, weiyng 28 oz'.[28] In his will, dated 11 July 1521, occurs the first reference to his school:

> I certaine yeres past at my costes and charges have caused a Free gramer Scole tobe mayntened and kepte at Cukfeld aforesaid for the erudicion and lernyng of poore scolers thedur resortyng to the honor of God in that behalf.

The composition of the school was similar in many ways to those founded by the Percyvales, in that Flower specified that 'a secular prest and a sufficient man to teche gramer maye be alway resident there to teche gramer'. He made it clear that he was to be known as the 'first founder' of the school, and desired that the priest/schoolmaster should pray for his soul for ever. He placed the endowment of the school in the hands of the Master and Wardens of the Fraternity of Our Lady in Cuckfield church: this endowment comprised property in Kent, together with other property worth at least £5 a year that the trustees were to buy with £100 from his estate. To make sure that the school did not fail, Flower made the Merchant Taylors' Company responsible for issuing a 'monycion or warnyng' to the fraternity if it failed to appoint a new schoolmaster, or otherwise allowed the school to be 'unkept' for a year. If the fraternity

FIGURE 39. The gallery in St Peter's church in Wolverhampton. This was erected in 1611 by the Merchant Taylors' Company to accommodate the boys from Wolverhampton Grammar School. It bears the arms of the Company and of the founder, Sir Stephen Jenyns.
From the collections of Wolverhampton Archives and Local Studies

then failed to act, the endowment was to be sold and the proceeds applied by the Merchant Taylors to the provision of 'ffarthyng brede' for the inmates of City prisons. Two members of the Company, Richard Cornhill and Robert Shether, were chosen by Flower as the executors of his will.[29]

The will was proved in August 1521, and three months later property in three Sussex parishes was purchased and conveyed to the school trustees. However, it soon became apparent that this endowment, worth just £6 10s. a year, was not sufficient. In October 1528 a three-way agreement was drawn up between the Vicar and Churchwardens of Cuckfield, the Master and Fellows of St Catharine's College, Cambridge, and William Spicer, parson of Balcombe in Sussex. Spicer, a member of St Catharine's College, was the prime mover behind the agreement, promising to increase the value of the endowment by another £5 a year. He asked, in turn, to be recorded as the school's second founder, after Flower. The documents provide the earliest information about how the school was to be run, and of particular interest is Spicer's insistence that the scholars be taught 'after the form order and usage used and taught in the grammar School at Eton next Windsor'. First, the scholars were to be taught from Lady Day (25 March) to Michaelmas from 6 a.m. to 6 p.m., and from Michaelmas to Lady Day from 7 a.m. to 5 p.m. These hours were those that were kept by Eton College. A detailed description of the curriculum also survives, setting out the requirements for each form, and emphasizing the need to learn, construe and recite Latin. Saturday was the day when the scholars were to 'rehearse and render by heart all the lessons they have learnt all the week'. This is thus an important indication of the extent to which Eton College's curriculum served as a model for some of the early Tudor grammar schools, another example being Saffron Walden School which adopted its curriculum two years later.³⁰ The first schoolmaster, probably Edmund Molyneux, was to say Mass at least three times a week for the souls of the founders, and in the evening before departing the scholars too were to say 'De Profundis' for their souls.³¹ One change to Flower's foundation is immediately noticeable: there is no longer any mention of the Merchant Taylors' Company as the body responsible for making sure that the parishioners did not neglect their duty. Instead, Spicer was able to insist that this power be given to St Catharine's College, which in extreme circumstances could seize the rents and profits from the endowment and use them to fund a Fellow at the college.

The subsequent history of the school saw it escape the attentions of the chantry commissioners of 1548, when the endowment was said to be worth £11 8s. a year, with a salary of £10 paid to the current schoolmaster, Robert Hedon. However the school's long-term viability was placed in doubt following the sale of a large part of the endowment, most of it to a Thomas Pelham, in exchange for fixed rent-charges. These amounted to some £28 8s. a year in 1588, but their value in real terms was to decline dramatically over the ensuing centuries. Nevertheless schoolmasters continued to be appointed until the early nineteenth century, although by that time the demand for instruction in classics had declined. The costs of running the school now far exceeded the income from the endowment, and so in 1846 the endowment was applied to the 'National' School in Cuckfield.³²

SIR WILLIAM HARPER AND THE FOUNDATION OF BEDFORD GRAMMAR SCHOOL

A school may have existed at Bedford as early as the twelfth century, probably supervised by Newnham Priory, although nothing is known of its form or subsequent history. It is likely, however, that educational provision continued in the town into the sixteenth century, when there is reference to a 'scole lane'. The opportunity for more substantial arrangements came with the dissolution of the chantries under Edward VI, perhaps ironically given the dangers that the same phase of the Reformation had posed to the Company and the other schools discussed so far. The involvement of William Harper, Merchant Taylor, was crucial to the various stages of foundation.³³ Originally from Bedford, by the late 1540s he was making his mark in London as a wealthy merchant: he and his wife Alice rented from the Company the mansion in Lombard Street — 'the largest and stateliest house of this citie' — that Sir John Percyvale had bequeathed to the Merchant Taylors in 1503. Harper was nominated to the shrievalty in 1552, but asked to be allowed to refuse on the grounds that his 'substance and goods were out of his hands'. It is possible that he was contemplating becoming Master of the Company, to which he was chosen in the summer of 1553, an office which came with its own financial burdens. He promised to accept a subsequent nomination, however, and duly became Sheriff in 1556–57. Early accounts of Harper's career characterized him as a staunch Catholic, who was said by Foxe to have abused his position as Sheriff in the examination and burning of thirteen Protestant martyrs at Stratford-le-Bow in June 1556. In fact Harper was not chosen as Sheriff until the autumn of that year, and in general terms seems to have been pragmatic in his religious life, conforming to the Catholic faith under Mary but accepting the Elizabethan settlement.³⁴ The lavish pageant that accompanied his election as Lord Mayor in 1561 included orations from legendary harpists ('harpers'), with King David giving the following speech:

> For why your gentle Harper may
> With myldenes bringe aboute
> As moche touchinge good governement
> As they that be right stoute.
> Wherefore rejoice, ye Londoners,
> And hope well of your mayre,
> For never did a mylder man
> Sitt in your chiefest chaire.³⁵

It is not known precisely when he first became interested in establishing a school at Bedford, but evidence of his intentions may perhaps be glimpsed in 1548, when he made an attempt to purchase the property of the dissolved Fraternity of the Holy Trinity, perhaps hoping that it could be used as an endowment. Although this purchase did not go ahead, it may be no coincidence that in the same year a fellow of New College, Oxford, Edmund

Grene, is noted as having gone to 'teach boys in the county of Bedford'. Grene was subsequently described by Harper as the first headmaster of Bedford School, and it is possible that William paid his salary out of his own pocket, pending the acquisition of a suitable endowment.[36]

This came a step closer on 15 August 1552, when royal letters patent were issued by Edward VI in response to the humble petition of the Mayor and Citizens of Bedford for the establishment of 'a free and perpetual grammar school . . . for the institution and instruction of boys and youths in grammar, literature and good manners'.[37] The Corporation was permitted to hold lands worth up to £40 a year as an endowment, but the choice of the Master and Usher of the school was reserved to the Warden of New College. The involvement of New College again is striking, and suggests a connection either with Harper himself, or with the earlier school at Bedford. Harper's own role is not alluded to, but later documents make it clear that the school was located in a house that Harper himself had built, already known as the 'scoole house', which he still owned. In the meantime Harper was busy with his civic career, and so it was not until the early 1560s that he made perhaps his most significant contribution to the refounded Bedford School. In the autumn of 1564, two years after his term as Lord Mayor (during which he was knighted), Harper and his wife Alice bought for £180 an estate of some 13½ acres in the Holborn area of London from Dr Caesar Adelmare, Queen Mary's physician. Two years later they conveyed the estate to the Mayor and Corporation of Bedford for the 'sustentacion of the master and ussher' of the school. He also conveyed to the Corporation the school-house itself, 'now in the tenure or occupacion of the said Edmond Grene'. In contrast to the letters patent of 1552, Harper's deed gave the power to appoint the Master and Usher to the Corporation of Bedford.[38]

The foundation of Bedford Grammar School was now complete. Alice Harper died in October 1569, and William married his second wife Margaret less than a year later. He died in February 1574 and was buried in St Peter's church, Bedford. His widow caused the Merchant Taylors some trouble, for she refused to vacate the house in Lombard Street that William and Alice had rented from the Company. Proceedings were initiated by the Clerk, Nicholas Fuljambe, and after prolonged negotiations (during which Fuljambe died of plague) Margaret was persuaded to vacate the mansion. Of the school's subsequent history, little is known until the early seventeenth century beyond the names of some of the Masters. Many of them were Fellows of New College, reflecting a continuing connection between school and college. The Corporation remained closely concerned in the running of the school, ensuring that it retained its links with the locality: boarders were not admitted until 1656. The school eventually became a leading public school: under the headmastership of J. S. Phillpotts (1874–1903) it grew from 250 to 800 boys and moved to its present site in 1891. By that time the endowment of the school had grown significantly in value, and the Harpur Trust now administers four schools as follows: Bedford School (the former Grammar School); Bedford Modern School; and two girls' schools, Bedford High School and Dame Alice Harpur School, both opened in 1882. The magnificent façade of 1838 by Edward Blore of the Trust's former complex of buildings can still be seen in Bedford town centre.[39]

SIR THOMAS WHITE AND ST JOHN THE BAPTIST'S COLLEGE, OXFORD

Sir Thomas White was one of the most significant figures in sixteenth-century London. Born in Reading, he had made his fortune in the cloth trade by the 1530s and was chosen as Master of the Merchant Taylors in 1535. He was an alderman from 1544, Sheriff in 1547–48 and, as we have seen, was chosen as Lord Mayor during the first, and eventful, year of Mary's reign in 1553–54. His civic achievements were impressive, but it is White's philanthropy that sets him apart from most of his contemporaries, and it was for this reason, above all, that his career was celebrated by his fellow Merchant Taylor John Stow, and by Richard Johnson in his *Nine Worthies of London* (1592), in which the figure of White recounts in verse his own achievements:

> The English Cities and incorporate townes
> Doe beare me witnesse of my Countrys care
> Where yearely I doe feede the poore with crownes

> For I was neuer niggard yet to spare,
> And all chiefe Burrowes of this blessed land,
> Have somewhat tasted of my liberal hand.[40]

White began his charitable work as early as 1542, with the city of Coventry, when he gave the Mayor and Burgesses the huge sum of £1,400, to be used to buy property that would generate income 'to relieve and prefer the Comon Wealth of the said City of Coventry being now in Greate Ruine and decay'. The city's declining fortunes were well attested at the time, and were caused in part by severe problems with its broadcloth industry. The Corporation agreed that after White's death the income from the endowment would be used to give £2 a year to twelve poor men, and also to establish a loan fund whereby four young freemen of Coventry would receive £10 a year (interest-free) for nine years. As capital came to accrue from the estates, the scheme would be extended one at a time to four other cloth towns, Northampton, Leicester, Nottingham, and Warwick. White then entrusted the supervision of these arrangements to the Merchant Taylors' Company, and used the scheme as a model for two additional loan funds, with the Company once again overseeing them. One of these focussed on Coventry, Worcester, York, and Lincoln, and this time loans of £25 were made to young men who 'woll promys to make clothe'. Most impressive, however, was White's scheme, administered by the City of Bristol, for charitable provision to clothiers from twenty-three different towns. It was a complex scheme, both practically and financially, and involved gifts from White to the City of Bristol that amounted to some £2,000. The agreement was confirmed by a deed of July 1566 to which White, the Mayor, Commonalty and Burgesses of Bristol, and the Merchant Taylors' Company were parties. The initial phase of the scheme was concerned with providing loans of £50 to merchant tailors in Bristol, and the purchase and resale of corn to Bristol's poor, but from 1576 onwards the fund was sufficient for the larger plan to take effect. This involved a rotating and perpetual charity, administered by Bristol, that would provide interest-free loans to young clothiers in twenty-three towns, and among the Merchant Taylors. Each of the towns and the Company would benefit at intervals of twenty-four years in rotation, and on St Bartholomew's Day every year at Merchant Taylors' Hall representatives of the Corporation of Bristol would hand over £104 to representatives of the recipient town: £4 was for administrative costs, with the rest intended for four loans of £25. Loans were to be repaid at the end of ten years, and lent out again immediately. Those who received the loans were to be 'of honest name and fame, occupyers and inhabitants within the sayed Citie and ffreemen of the same . . . And Clothyers to be preferred aboue all others to be named'. The first city to start its twenty-four year rotation was York in 1577, with Canterbury and Reading following in 1578 and 1579. In 1580 it was the turn of the Merchant Taylors' Company, followed successively by Gloucester, Worcester, Exeter, and Salisbury.[41] In view of this remarkable charitable venture, much of which still operates to this day, it is little wonder that at least eighteen portraits of White were commissioned to hang in the places of his benefactions, with the portrait at Merchant Taylors' Hall being one of the first, and a likely model for the others (see Col. Pl. IX).

Despite being engaged in such complex plans, White also found time to indulge his interest in education through the foundation of an Oxford college.[42] He took the first step towards this in July 1554, during his mayoralty, when for £1,908 16s. he purchased extensive estates in Oxfordshire, including the manors of Fyfield and Long Wittenham. In December that year an 'article of agreement' was drawn up in which the Dean and Chapter of Christ Church undertook to grant White the premises of the dissolved 'St Bernard's' or 'Bernard' College in Oxford for the purposes of founding and endowing a college of students of divinity and art. The story goes that White saw the site of his future college in a dream, when, passing St Bernard's College, he saw two elm trees springing from the same root. There is, it seems, some truth in this for Edmund Campion stated in his funeral oration for White that the founder had spoken to him of his dream. Campion revealed that White had been considering St Bernard's for his college, and when he visited the site had recognized from his dream an ancient building, two decayed walls and a row of trees, which had convinced him that his choice of St Bernard's College was divinely ordained. Letters patent were granted by Philip and Mary on 1 May 1555, enabling White to establish a college in a house called 'Barnard Colledge', for the study of arts, philosophy and theology, consisting of a President and thirty members, or more or less, according to the statutes that White himself was to draw up. It was to be known as St John the Baptist's College, echoing the dedication of the Company, and could hold lands to the value of £600 a year.[43] Later that month the Dean and Chapter fulfilled their part of the agreement, granting to White, at a rent of 20s. a year, the 'house commonly called Bernerd Colledge'. On 29 May, therefore, White was able to draw up his first foundation deed, settling his Oxfordshire estates on the college and appointing Alexander Belsyre as the first President.

Much remained to be done, however, before scholars could be admitted and in 1556 White had a considerable amount of work carried out on the buildings, including the completion of the eastern side of the quadrangle, and the construction of a new kitchen. He was in Oxford on 10 October that year, when the University presented him with a pair of gloves, and the next month he had some 'little organs' installed in the college chapel. The college came into existence on St John the Baptist's day (24 June) 1557, and the chapel was probably dedicated on 3 October: it is likely that both occasions made use of the handsome banners and vestments still owned by the college, whose iconography suggests that they were made during Mary's reign, rather than under the Protestant Elizabeth (see Col. Pls VIIA and B). A second foundation deed was drawn up in March 1558, which enlarged the curriculum to include canon and civil law. Among the new members of the college were Campion, and Francis Willis, who was to be the sixth President. Further estates were also added to the endowment. The first statutes of the college no longer survive, but those of May 1562 suggest that White borrowed heavily from those of Corpus Christi College, founded by Richard Foxe in 1517. A striking feature of the 1562 statutes was the retention of provisions in Foxe's statutes for religious services and compulsory confession, a reflection of White's Catholic faith and perhaps his hope that the old religion would be restored. On the other hand, White pressed ahead with his college during Elizabeth's reign and was able to accommodate himself to the new order, whatever his private thoughts may have been.

The formal link between the Company and the college developed gradually over the next ten years. In White's first will, drawn up in December 1558, he ordained that four places at the college were to be reserved for poor scholars from London, elected by the Mayor and Aldermen. The implication was that these were to be chosen from the pupils at Christ's Hospital. Every fifteen years, however, the college was to find money for two further scholars, to be chosen by the Merchant Taylors from all the schools in London. The next development took place in May 1562 when the earliest surviving statutes were drawn up: this time White reserved twelve places in the college to 'London school', although it is unlikely that this referred to Merchant Taylors' School as this had only recently been founded. By the autumn of 1564, however, the school had been in existence for three years and the relevant statute was rewritten: the twelve places were now to be filled by the Merchant Taylors' Company, and if possible the scholars were to be taken from Merchant Taylors' School itself. White's third will, of April 1565, increased the number of Company nominations to twenty, and in 1566 the fifty places at the college were allocated as follows: one to Tonbridge School (founded by his friend Andrew Judde), two each to schools in Coventry, Reading and Bristol (sites of his other benefactions), six to White's kin, and thirty-seven to Merchant Taylors' School. The Company's quota could rise to forty-three if there were no more descendants to take up places.

White was closely involved in the running of the college until his death in 1567. He himself chose the scholars who were admitted between 1557 and 1567, and he even removed the first President, and some of the Fellows, being convinced of their dishonesty. He had trouble too with some of the commoners, because 'they would not abide chastisement': flogging was allowed at the college, although limited to those under the age of nineteen. In the meantime, he enlarged the college site through the acquisition of several plots of land adjacent to the existing site, including the site of the former Gloucester College, and managed to obtain several important gifts of books for the library and various legacies. An agreement was made with Trinity College to erect a wall between the two colleges, with a door through which 'it should be lawfull for the presidents of eather . . . at all tymes to have free passadge'. However the early years of the college were difficult, largely because the endowment, worth around £230 a year, was not sufficient. In September 1564 White gave £144 from his own pocket to enable the college to meet its deficits for the next six years. White died on 12 February 1567, having spent nearly £4,000 on endowments for the college and probably another £1,000 on repairs to the buildings, but in the 1560s he was able to do little beyond shore up its finances. After his death a series of disputes arose over his estate, the most serious of which involved his widow Joan's jointure, and her right under the custom of London to half of White's goods and chattels: if she were to claim all she was entitled to, there would not be enough money left to augment the endowment of the college, as White had optimistically intended. In June 1570 the matter was settled, when Joan — very generously in the circumstances — agreed to pay £3,000 to the college in instalments, and over the next two years further manors were purchased that helped to place the college's finances on a firmer footing. It also allowed the Company and the school to begin in earnest their close and enduring relationship with the college.

MERCHANT TAYLORS' SCHOOL, SUFFOLK LANE

By the 1560s the Company and its members had displayed an unrivalled interest in education that can be traced back to the early fifteenth century. The foundation of Merchant Taylors' School was a natural next step, all the more so because the Company had recently acquired the right to choose boys from London to attend St John's College — a school would instantly give the Company a pool of talent from which to choose, and a role in devising an appropriate curriculum. The foundations established by members of the Company elsewhere in the country provided exemplars of varying kinds, whilst in London the school at nearby St Anthony's, and the re-founded St Paul's School (1509), provided models closer to home.[44]

The Master of the Company in 1561 was no less than Richard Hilles, reformer and erstwhile exile, who had returned to England during Edward VI's

FIGURE 40. A plaque marking the original site of Merchant Taylors' School in Suffolk Lane.
Merchant Taylors' Company

reign. Although he should not be counted as the 'founder' of Merchant Taylors' School, there is little doubt that the project was actively promoted by him within the Company. The first step was to secure suitable premises, and these were found in April 1561 when the Company purchased part of the site of the 'Manor of the Rose' in Suffolk Lane in the parish of St Lawrence Pountney (Fig. 40). The site and its buildings had once belonged to Sir John Pulteney (or Pountney), five times Mayor of the City in Edward III's reign, and had subsequently belonged to a number of prominent courtiers. In 1561 it was held by William Hettie, who agreed to sell for £566 13s. 4d. the west gate house, together with all the adjacent rooms and premises, including two galleries on the south side, with part of the chapel, and a large courtyard leading down to the Thames. Hilles contributed £500 to the purchase price, and the remainder was supplied by Sir Thomas Offley,

Emmanuel Lucar and Stephen Hayles. A quarter-day meeting of the Court was held on 24 September that year, with Hilles presiding along with the Wardens, Sir Thomas White, Lucar and William Harper and ten other prominent liverymen. The main purpose of the meeting seems to have been to agree to the setting up of the school 'for the better education and bringing up of children in good manners and literature': forty-five statutes were drawn up setting out the aims and nature of the school. It was to be a school of 250 boys, with 100 of the places offered free of charge. The curriculum was to concentrate on the usual Latin and Greek, although Hebrew was also to be taught, as at Macclesfield. As we have seen, Thomas White then began to make arrangements for the election of a number of scholars, eventually fixed at forty-three, from the school to St John's College.

The Company made an impressive choice for its first headmaster. Richard Mulcaster had been educated at Eton and King's College, Cambridge, and at university had been taught by the Provost, John Cheke, who presented his scholar with works by Euclid and Xenophon. He was teaching in London by 1558, and when Elizabeth made her formal entry into the City on 14 January 1559 he prepared a book, on the City's behalf, 'conteynynge and declarying the historyes set furth in and by the Cyties pageauntes at the tyme of the Quenes highnes commyng thurrough the Cytye to her coronacion'.[45] He was persuaded to be the first headmaster of the school after the stipend of £10 a year offered by the Company was augmented by another £10 from Hilles's own pocket. He had three under-masters or ushers to assist him, each of whom was paid £10 a year.

Mulcaster was more than simply an imparter of classical knowledge. He had an active interest in the processes and purposes of education. During his years as headmaster he wrote a book on the subject, *Positions wherin those primitive circumstances be examined, which are necessarie for the training up of children, either for skill in their booke, or health in their bodie* (1581) (Fig. 41). His writing, although prolix, reveals an awareness of the dangers of spoiling children by 'to[o] fond cokkeryng', but also the damage caused by vain parents in pushing their children too far. Individual attention was essential in order to bring out the best

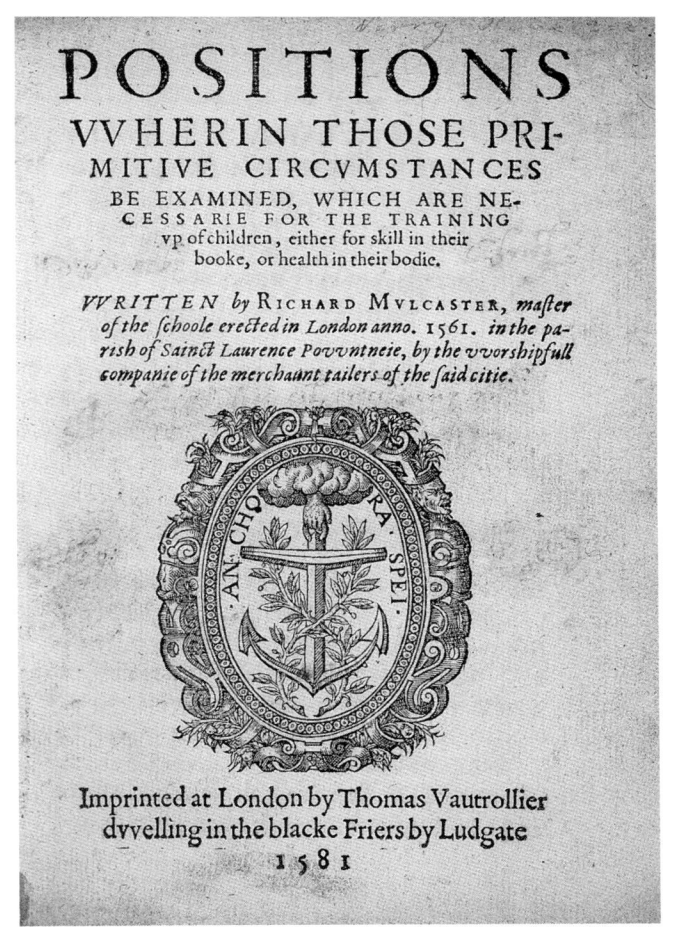

FIGURE 41. The title page from Richard Mulcaster's *Positions . . . for the training up of children* (1581).
Merchant Taylors' Company

in each child. His book, which was dedicated to Queen Elizabeth, whose learning he praised, also shows an interest in the education of girls, stating at one point '[I] am for them with toothe and naile'. However, no girls were among the pupils of Merchant Taylors' School in his day. Mulcaster wrote a second volume soon afterwards, on the teaching of English, which he felt to be of prime importance: 'I love Latin but worship English.' He also wrote plays for the boys of the school, to teach them 'good behaviour and audacitie'. Performances were given in the Company's Hall and at Court, although they were suddenly abandoned in 1574 because of the 'tumultious disordered persones repayringe hither [i.e. to the Hall] to see suche playes as by our scholers weare here lately plaide'.[46]

The Company naturally took a close and active interest in the progress of the school. Regular inspections were held, the first taking place on 21 August 1562 when the Bishop of London, Edmund Grindal, accompanied by other clergy and the Lord Mayor, William Harper (the founder of Bedford Grammar School), examined the boys and the masters. They reported that the 'schole master of the said schole . . . had moche profyted the schollers there & [was] therefore worthy of greate commendacon'.[47] The only criticism was that the boys spoke indistinctly, but they put this down to the fact that Mulcaster was from Cumberland, and that most of the ushers were from the north of England, and 'therefore did not pronounce so well as those that be brought up in the schole of the south partes of the Realme'. Inspections such as these lasted from nine in the morning until five in the evening, and usually concluded with satisfactory reports of the school's progress. Among the boys who were attending the school in these early years were three future translators of the Authorized Version of the Bible, Lancelot Andrewes, Giles Thompson and Ralph Huchenson. Another who was to make his mark was the future poet, Edmund Spenser.

The pupils were drawn from a variety of backgrounds. In February 1569, for instance, four boys were admitted, one a son of a bowyer, another the son of a gentleman, whilst the other two were the sons of an innholder and stirrup-maker respectively. All were admitted at a fee of 5s. a quarter. In October 1572 seven boys were awarded free places: the fathers of two were clothworkers, while the fathers of the remainder comprised a minister, saddler, labourer, fletcher and yeoman.[48] The school was thus, by and large, fulfilling the Company's intention of providing a sound grammar school education that was accessible to the sons of tradespeople and craftsmen, as well as to the offspring of the mercantile and gentry élites.

Relations between Mulcaster and the Company were not always smooth. In January 1569, when the school had filled its 250 places, he was rebuked for trying to admit still more pupils. He was ordered to send away those boys not admitted by the Master and Wardens on penalty of 'dismyssing and avoydynge of hym oute and frome the roome and place of scholemaistershippe of the saide schole'. Mulcaster complied, and for a while matters went calmly, but in 1574 when visitors were in the school Mulcaster lost his temper and was later admonished by the Court for his 'Injurious and quarelinge speache as he used to the visitors'. He later apologized, admitting that he had spoken 'meerly of collor [choler]'. Worse was to come, however, when Hilles decided, by 1580, to withdraw the £10 a year he had contributed to Mulcaster's salary. The Company was able to lend him £50, which was later converted into a gift, but this may have been the final straw, for Mulcaster resigned in 1586. Nevertheless he remained on friendly terms with the Company, and was present on several occasions when examining boards were held to choose boys to go up to St John's. As we have seen, under the terms of White's final will of 1567 the school was entitled to send up to forty-three scholars to the college. None were elected until 1572, which may have been because of the college's financial circumstances at that time. In that year Mulcaster wrote to the college, and a selection board was held in June 1572 at which a distinguished panel heard Latin orations from the head boy and other pupils before making their decision.[49]

Relations between the Company and St John's were strained when Mulcaster resigned. There were six candidates for the vacant headmastership, two of whom were former members of the college. President Willis wanted the college to have a much greater say in the choice of headmaster, and in elections to exhibitions to the school. However the Company, after deliberating for some time, chose as the next headmaster Henry Wilkinson, a man who had himself been chief usher of the school in the early 1570s. He served for six years, and on his retirement Edmund Smith, a former pupil, was chosen to succeed him. During the latter's six years as headmaster, once again punctuated by occasional disputes with St John's over elections, the pupils included the future Bishop of London, William Juxon, and Matthew Wren, uncle of the architect. Gradually, however, the relationships between the Company, the school and the college settled down, so that by the early seventeenth century they had come to embody the remarkable, and enduring, commitment of the Merchant Taylors of London to education.

NOTES

1. For studies of education in the pre-Reformation period see, amongst others, A. F. Leach, *The Schools of Medieval England* (1915); N. Orme, *Education and Society in Medieval and Renaissance England* (1989); N. Orme, *English Schools in the Middle Ages* (1973).
2. Reddaway and Walker, *Goldsmiths' Company*, pp. 261–62.
3. *Court Minutes*, ed. by Davies, p. 198; PRO, Early Chancery Proceedings, C1/66/66.
4. For a recent discussion of educational provision in London see C. M. Barron, 'The Expansion of Education in Fifteenth-Century London', in *The Cloister and the World: Essays in Medieval History in Honour of Barbara Harvey*, ed. by J. Blair and B. Golding (Oxford, 1996), pp. 219–46.
5. A school-book containing Latin and English vocabularies and hymns, possibly belonging to a pupil from St Anthony's school, survives as British Library, Add. MS 37075.
6. *Rotuli Parliamentorum*, V, p. 137.
7. Barron, 'Expansion of Education', pp. 227–31.
8. See Chapter One.
9. GL, MS 34048/1, fols 104^v, 177, 209, 231, 274^v, 299, 311, 311^v; 2, fol. 27^v; 3, fol. 42^v.
10. Barron, 'Expansion of Education', p. 236; M. Samuel, 'The Fifteenth Century Garner at Leadenhall', *Antiquaries Journal*, LXIX (1989), pt 1, pp. 119–53.
11. See Chapters Two, Three, Five and Nine. For the careers of John and Thomasine Percyvale see M. Davies, 'Dame Thomasine Percyvale, "the Maid of Week" (d. 1512)', in *Medieval London Widows, 1300–1500*, ed. by C. M. Barron and A. F. Sutton (1994), pp. 185–207.
12. The deed is transcribed in its entirety in G. E. Wilson, 'A History of the Macclesfield Grammar School in the County of Cheshire from 1503–*c*. 1890' (unpublished MEd thesis, University of Leeds, 1952), pp. 264–71. See also J. P. Earwaker, *East Cheshire, Past and Present*, 2 vols (1877–80), II, pp. 511–18.
13. Wilson, 'Macclesfield Grammar School', p. 271.
14. *CPR*, 1550–53, p. 361.
15. Earwaker, *East Cheshire*, II, pp. 515–18.
16. The earliest account of the legend can be found in Richard Carew's *The Survey of Cornwall* (1602), fols 119–19^v. It was embellished by subsequent writers, including R. S. Hawker in his *Footprints of Former Men in Far Cornwall*, ed. by C. E. Byles (1908), pp. 139–57.
17. A full account of Thomasine's life can be found in Davies, 'Thomasine Percyvale', pp. 185–207.
18. The foundation deed is printed in full in P. L. Hull, 'The Endowment and Foundation of a Grammar School at Week St Mary by Dame Thomasine Percyvale', *Journal of the Royal Institution of Cornwall*, New Series, VII (1973), pp. 43–48.
19. PRO, E301/15, fol. 47.
20. *CPR*, 1494–1509, p. 604; PRO, PROB 11/17, fol. 221.
21. *Letters and Papers Foreign and Domestic of the Reign of Henry VIII*, 1536, nos 679, 810, 954.
22. N. Orme, *Education in the West of England 1066–1548* (Exeter, 1976), pp. 148–50, 180–81; A. F. Robbins, 'John Aylworth and the Launceston Free School', *Notes and Gleanings for Devon and Cornwall*, III (Exeter, 1890), pp. 161–67.

23. BL, Royal MS 2. B. XII, XIII.
24. BL, Add. MS 45131, fol. 87^v.
25. Stow, *Survey*, ed. by Kingsford, I, p. 145.
26. *Letters and Papers Foreign and Domestic of the Reign of Henry VIII*, 1509–14, nos 1415 (19), 1804 (25).
27. *Court Minutes*, ed. by Davies, pp. 293–94.
28. GL, MS 34357, fol. 34^v.
29. PRO, PROB 11/20, fols 56^v–58.
30. The authors are grateful to Mr Brian Cutler for transcripts of the Bede Roll and Ordinances of the school (late-eighteenth- or early-nineteenth-century copies of the originals) and of the Spicer indenture: West Sussex RO, PAR 301/25/67; East Sussex RO, SAS A/9.
31. *VCH Sussex*, II, p. 417.
32. Ibid., pp. 420–21.
33. Words ending in '-er', including surnames, were often spelled '-ur' in this period. Harper's surname thus appears as 'Harpur' in some sources, and it was probably for this reason that this spelling was adopted by the Harpur Trust. However, for consistency 'Harper' is preferred by most writers.
34. For Harper's career see Clode, *Early History*, II, pp. 240–70; J. G. Nichols, 'The Biography of Sir William Harper, Alderman of London, Founder of the Bedford School Charities', *Transactions of the London and Middlesex Archaeological Society*, IV (1875), pp. 70–93.
35. Clode, *Early History*, II, p. 269.
36. For a detailed account of the early history of the school see *VCH Bedfordshire*, II, pp. 152–65; J. Wyatt, *The Bedford Schools and Charities of Sir William Harper* (Bedford, 1856).
37. *CPR*, 1550–53, p. 405.
38. *VCH Bedfordshire*, II, p. 160.
39. See J. Godber, *The Harpur Trust, 1552–1973* (Bedford, 1973); *VCH Bedfordshire*, II.
40. Quoted in R. Tittler, *Townspeople and Nation*, pp. 118–19.
41. For full details of White's various schemes see Tittler, *Townspeople and Nation*, pp. 104–09.
42. Unless otherwise stated, this account is derived from W. H. Stevenson and H. E. Salter, *The Early History of St. John's College, Oxford*, Oxford Hist. Society, new series, I (1939).
43. *CPR*, 1554–55, pp. 322–23.
44. The earliest history of the school is H. B. Wilson, *The History of Merchant-Taylors' School, from its Foundation to the Present Time*, 2 vols (1812–14), which runs to some 1,254 pages. More accessible is F. W. M. Draper, *Four Centuries of Merchant Taylors' School, 1561–1961* (1962).
45. CLRO, Rep. 14, fol. 143; Draper, *Merchant Taylors' School*, p. 11.
46. GL, MS 34010/1, p. 699; R. Mulcaster, *The First Part of the Elementarie Which Entreateth Chefelie of the Right Writing of Our English Tung* (1582).
47. GL, MS 34010/1, p. 12; Draper, *Merchant Taylors' School*, p. 12.
48. GL, MS 34010/1, pp. 376, 613.
49. Draper, *Merchant Taylors' School*, pp. 14–19.

CHAPTER EIGHT
DAILY LIFE IN ELIZABETHAN LONDON

THE COMPANY'S AFFAIRS

THE MAIN RUN of Court minutes begins on 1 July 1562 and continues, with occasional breaks, to the present day. A short run exists for 1486–93,[1] but time, damp, mischance, fire and mice have done their damage; previous volumes, which once existed, have vanished; and it is not until the early years of Queen Elizabeth's reign that we can begin to form a clear picture of the day-to-day activities of the Company. These early minutes are exceptionally full and detailed — a whole section of sixteenth-century London seems to be scurrying across the pages, though the information is often elusive and the accounts of undertakings, charitable actions, quarrels, law suits, musters and celebrations often tail off, unfinished to our eyes, whatever happened in reality, since the participants found it unnecessary to set down the various outcomes.

Appropriately enough, the first entry is for the election of a new Master, Richard Whethill, and his Wardens, Ralph White, Thomas Browne, Thomas Haile and Christopher Marlour. The keys to the Hall and treasury were duly handed over, the valuables — an 'ale pott of sylver with a cover of sylver all gilte together with an old masour bound aboute with sylver gilte' — were inspected, obligations to the Company carefully noted. A month later, the Bachelors' Company, the association of ordinary freemen, respectfully asked for permission to hold their feast as usual; the bill of fare survives:

> Rabbittes stewed
> Gese roste
> Venyson bake
> ffresshe sturgeon
> Custarde.

The minutes deal with the regular daily concerns of the Merchant Taylors. These include admission to the freedom of the Company, the overseeing of apprentices, discipline in matters of misbehaviour, employment of foreign workers or quarrelling between members, the inspection of work considered to be below standard, the care of the Hall itself and the administration of a considerable amount of property in London and elsewhere, the dispensing of charity, inspection of the Company's school nearby in Suffolk Lane and of other schools, and negotiations with St John's College in Oxford. The minutes also cover relationships with other companies, with the City itself, with the Crown, and with the wider world beyond; these will be discussed in the next chapter.

Although the rewards — good fellowship and civic advancement — could be great, the burden of involvement was heavy in terms of both time and money. Once the Master and Wardens had donned their garlands at the annual Election Dinner, they would have to devote a considerable proportion of their energies to Company affairs. In addition to the four quarterly meetings and the regular Court meetings (usually once a month), there were 'Ordinary' meetings attended by the Master and such Wardens as were available; these were normally held on a Monday or a Friday — sometimes both — but could be on any day of the week as required. It was a good thing that the City, even though it had spread outside its walls, was still small; for a middle-aged Master, hurrying between the Hall in Threadneedle Street, the Guildhall itself, and his own place of business, it must often have seemed too large.

A young man's entry into the Merchant Taylors was a prime concern both for the applicant and for the Company. When matters were done in their proper order, an employer was meant to present a new apprentice, by this date aged not less than sixteen,[2] to the Master and Wardens and to pay 2s. 6d. into the common funds; when a seven-year apprenticeship was completed satisfactorily, the young man was made free before the Court and 3s. 4d. was

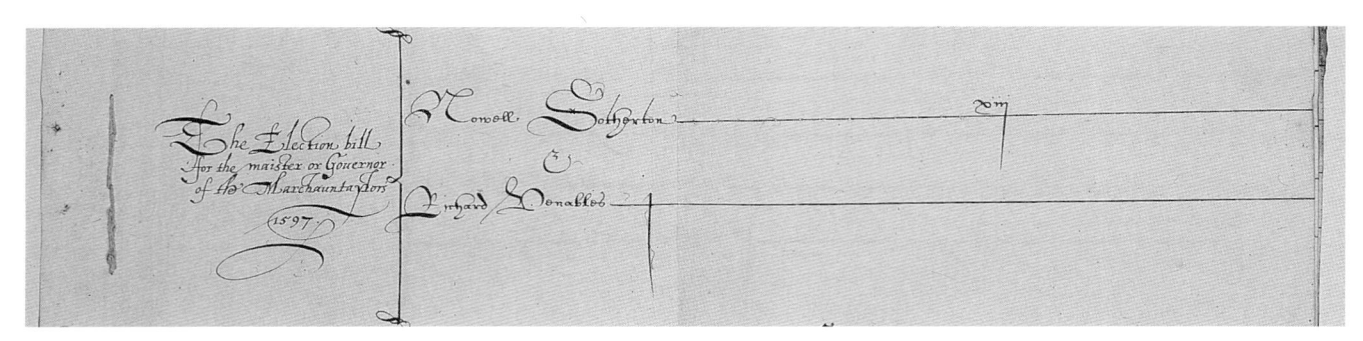

FIGURE 42. Rare survivals – voting slips from the late sixteenth and early seventeenth centuries. In this first example, Nowell Sotherton is elected Master in 1597 over Richard Venables.
Guildhall Library, MS 34100/118, Misc. Docs A8

added to the Company's resources. Soon after, the new freeman would have gone with his master and possibly his father, or a close relative or friend, to Guildhall to be admitted to the freedom of the City itself. Thereafter, he could seek employment as a journeyman and, perhaps, one day, set up on his own.

The Company was zealous and attentive in its care of apprentices. An employer could be fined for non-presentment,[3] and each setting-on or transfer of an apprentice to a new master was carefully noted. This could happen for all sorts of reasons, the death of an employer being the most common. In such cases, it was the widow's responsibility to see that the boy's training was completed or to find him a new master and to report the arrangement. The Company paid proper attention to its young intake; when Richard Haryson abandoned his apprentice, George Swoytell, the Master arranged for George to be set on to Robert Whithande.[4] When an unprincipled employer, Richard Crofte, wanted Francis Gibsone to 'purloyne other mens goodes which is unlawfull', the lad was transferred to Stephen Tenante.[5] Discipline could be harsh; on 9 February 1573, John Davy was publicly commanded to serve William Phellipps faithfully and, if his master had cause to complain again, 'correction of this howse' would be meted out 'in oppen Hall to the example and Terrore of other lewed and frowarde servantes'.[6] When Tristram Basford walked out of William Dodworth's shop, leaving it unattended, and went off to Flushing, a careful note was made of his misdemeanour,[7] and on 4 February 1566 Thomas Thomas was fined by the City for marrying while still an apprentice.[8]

But the Court were not always on the side of the employers. On 2 April 1563, they committed Thomas Palmer to prison 'for that he hath broken Henry Bowcefelde his apprentice hede without eny juste cause', and, though he was released, he was fined a heavy £3 6s. 8d. and ordered to bear the medical expenses, while the boy was told to appeal to the Court if there were 'further argument'.[9] When Henry Cooper refused to free George Cragge, who had served him honestly for seven years, the Master sent Cooper to prison and freed Cragge by his own authority. Though in June 1577 Henry Buckett was ordered to serve his employer Walter Slyfelde till Christmas and then for a further year if he 'lyke' it, Slyfelde was told firmly to 'use him as a m[aste]r oughte to use his Apprentize servante',[10] while two years earlier, when Cliff — no Christian name is given — was changing employment for some unspecified reason, the Master, Arthur Dawbney, 'delivering to him his Apparrell and gevinge his good worde for his furtherance', took charge of all important documentation, the boy's indenture and his father's bond.[11] The reference to apparel is significant; to maintain a clean, neat appearance was part of the apprentice's training, while his master was responsible for seeing that his lads were properly and warmly clad. Humfrey Humfrey was discharged from his apprenticeship to Thomas Vernam because he 'did lacke bothe learning & Apperrell', the Company retaining his indenture 'untill his frendes can provide him a m[aste]r'.[12] On 3 September 1574, Thomas Figge and Robert Huberstey were presented by their respective employers, but Thomas was 'putt of[f] for his apparell and not sworne',

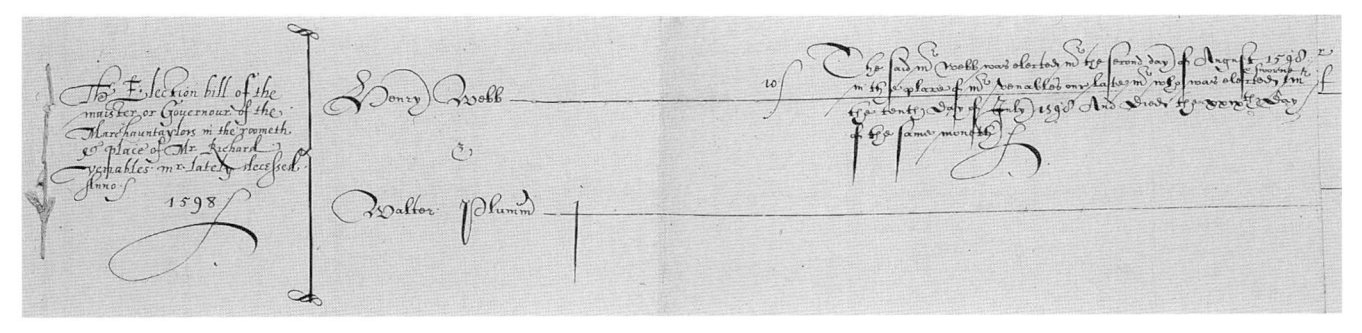

FIGURE 43. Henry Webb is elected Master in August 1598 over Walter Plummer in the place of Richard Venables deceased.
Guildhall Library, MS 34100/118, Misc. Docs A8

while Robert was 'put of[f] to reforme his Apparreill and after admytted'.[13]

There were other ways of joining the Company than serving a long apprenticeship. If a boy's father had been a Merchant Taylor at the time of the child's birth, then the son could be admitted by patrimony for a payment of 3s. 4d., though when Simon Meeke, son of John Meeke, was so admitted in February 1569, he paid only 2s. 4d., and was forgiven the last shilling 'in respecte of his povertie'.[14]

There was also admission by redemption. This was expensive — a down-payment of 20s. and usually the promise of a 'fat buck' against the Master's feast on St John's Day — but, if a man was accepted, it was a worthwhile investment for the future, since freedom of a company meant freedom of the City and the right to trade in any commodity or to follow any craft for which one had the skill. A candidate needed a recommendation, generally from a senior member of the Company, the Court of Aldermen or the Lord Mayor, but sometimes from an individual of much greater importance, in which case the fee was often waived. Between 1562 and 1577, the Company accepted, among others, John Carys, servant to Mr Gerard, the Queen's Attorney-General;[15] William Coverdale, at the request of 'Mr Coverdale, late bysshop of Exceter', who was none other than Miles Coverdale, translator of the Bible and, presumably, William's relation;[16] John Hides, at the Queen's own request;[17] Pierce Evans, at the Chamberlain of London's request — he promised a firkin of sturgeon as well as a buck;[18] James Wolton, recommended by the Dean of St Paul's, Alexander Nowell, who was punctilious in paying 3s. 4d. to the Company Clerk and 2s. to the Beadle;[19] John Smythe, at the suggestion of the Archbishop of Canterbury's steward, Mr Wendesley;[20] John Owthwayte, another recommendation from the Queen;[21] John Stacye, put forward by Mr Secretary Walsingham;[22] Philip Twiste, nominated by 'Mr Christofer Hattone, Captayne of the Quenes Majesties Garde';[23] Laurence Drewe, at the request of Sir Thomas Gresham;[24] while Henry Bayne, dwelling in Southwark, and recommended by the Court of Aldermen, at the request of the Earl of Warwick, pledged a 'sugar loffe of x^{li}'.[25] Back in August 1568, there had been a little confusion when the Earl of Sussex, himself a freeman, proposed Thomas Fletcher and was told, rather smugly, that admission was only by servitude or patrimony; the Court soon realized the unwisdom of this reply and Fletcher was duly admitted. There was no problem when, on 24 January 1578, the Earl presented the composer and organist John Bull as his apprentice; just over two decades later, Bull would become the first Professor of Music at Gresham College.[26]

Occasionally, other delicacies in lieu of or in addition to the customary buck were offered by newly-redeemed freemen. John Philipps provided a 'hoggeshed of good gascon wyne',[27] Thomas Woodwarde added a 'Rondlett of sack conteynynge x gallondes' to the venison,[28] and John Anderson proposed a cygnet,[29] while Nicholas Bodlowe offered a 'suger loffe of fyne suger'[30] and John Brettar (alias Cooke) promised another 'suger lofe'.[31] One redemption was an act of charity: Sir James Hawes proposed Morrys Pleyman in respect of 'his disabilitie'; he was accepted.[32]

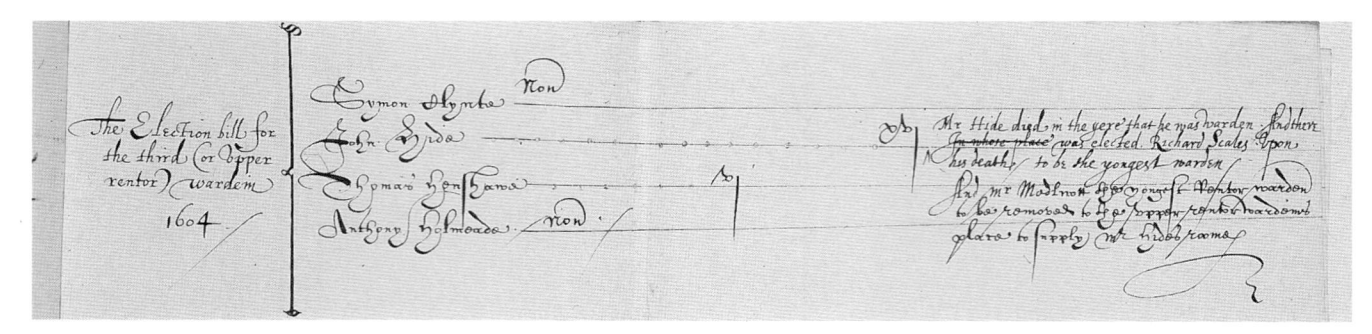

FIGURE 44. 1604. John Hide is elected Upper Renter Warden, but dies 'in the yere that he was warden'. Mr Medlicott takes his place and Richard Scales is elected as the youngest Warden.
Guildhall Library, MS 34100/118, Misc. Docs A8

It is hard to determine the full size of the Company during Elizabeth's reign; it certainly was exceptionally large. Between 1545–72, judging from the accounts, 1,718 lads were apprenticed and 1,332 went on to be admitted to the freedom. Over the same period, sixty-two joined by redemption, and the same number were elevated to the livery. At its largest, in the late sixteenth and early seventeenth centuries, the Company might have numbered 8,000;[33] of these, between 200 and 300 were liverymen, while the Court of Assistants had twenty-four members from whom the Master and Wardens were chosen each year. It was a long climb from apprentice boy to freeman to liveryman to Assistant and — perhaps, eventually — to becoming a Warden and, at last, Master of the Company.

The size of the Company was conditioned by the essential human need for clothing, especially in a cold climate. A lot of cutting and stitching was required to provide apparel for the population of London, both resident and in transit. A solicitous parent would have known that, even in hard times, the need for clothes is constant. That parent would also have been aware that the work was clean, varied and dependable.

The apprentice had to be healthy and to have good eyesight, but the craft did not require exceptional strength. Nimble fingers were more important. Fine sewing requires skill and patience, but is not extraordinarily difficult to learn. As we have seen (p. 59), the capital costs were low: scissors, a cutting board, needles, thread, and a pressing iron[34] were — and are — the necessities; unlike, for example, brewing, no costly equipment was needed. An enterprising young journeyman might venture to set up on his own, especially if he were fortunate enough to be granted a modest loan by the Company.

In the Royal Exchange, opened by the Queen herself in 1571, there were seventeen shops run by Merchant Taylors, along with fifty-five Haberdashers, twenty-five Mercers and twenty-one Painter-Stainers.[35] If a man worked hard and was favoured by fortune, there were good prospects ahead.

The size of the Company made for financial strength and encouraged a willingness to admit many who were not practising tailors. There was indeed considerable variety of occupation among those admitted as freemen; some, like John Fisher, Gentleman of the Chapel Royal to both Henry VII and Henry VIII, may have provided useful social and political contacts.[36]

Admission to the livery was another matter. It was a great honour, though normally an expensive one. The initial outlay was 20*s*., to be paid into the common fund, but it did not stop there if a man went on to become a Warden or the Master. Meetings were frequent, duties onerous, and not everyone was willing to serve. In August 1568, Emmanuel Lucar begged that he might be allowed to give up the keeping of the Treasure House key

for that he findethe hym self not so well able to travell hither as heretofore he hathe done by reason of his greate age and debilytie.

The key was passed on to Robert Rose.[37] On 30 June 1572, Thomas Shottesham was elected Master in his absence. Over the previous few months, he had

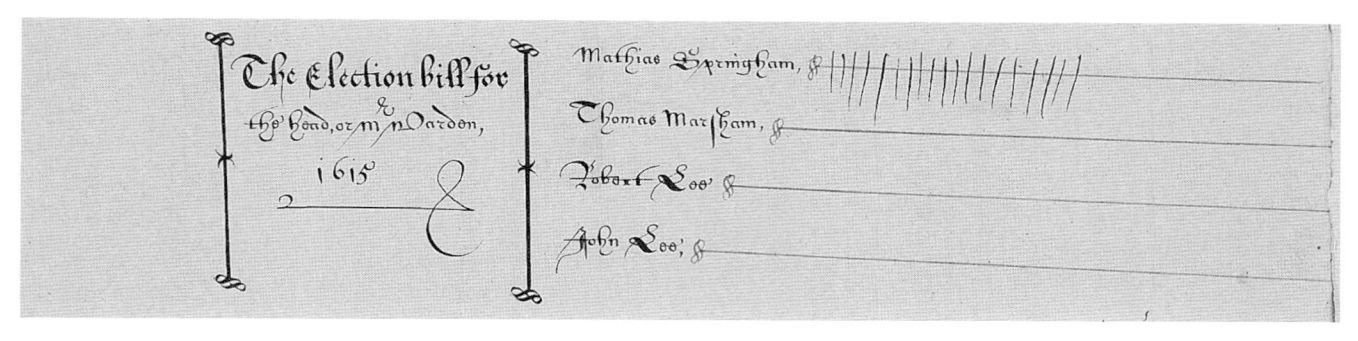

FIGURE 45. 1615. Mathias Springham is elected Senior Warden.
Guildhall Library, MS 34100/118, Misc. Docs A8

secured the lease of a desirable property in Thames Street, but now he was unwilling to serve. At the next meeting, on 7 July, Mistress Shottesham presented herself to the Court to explain her husband's inability to attend. The Court wrote to him a long letter, urging him to do his duty; his reply was read out to the Court of Assistants on 12 July. He thanked them for their 'lovinge gentilnes' but pleaded that 'habilitie in substance lacketh'. 'I am aged', he lamented, 'remembrance faileth me, utterance in speech I lack.' Recalling his eagerness to obtain the Thames Street lease, the minutes noted tartly:

(notwithstandinge that he is well able to kepe the rowme and office) [he] hathe wilfully reffused [showing] greate contempt of his dutie

and they fined him £40. For the next year, he whined, wriggled and begged for a reduction, but in the end he was forced to pay up.[38] He was not the only one to find the cost of office a problem; in July 1574, Thomas Offley, the Senior Warden, announced that he would accept the Mastership only if he could fulfil it 'with worship'.[39] The same obligations were felt at all levels in the Company. In January 1577, the Wardens Substitute and the Sixteen Men, those who spoke for the Bachelors' Company, petitioned for help. The position carried an allowance of £3 6s. 8d. or five marks, a mark being 13s. 4d., but the sum was

nothinge in comparrisone of the charges which a warden substitute bearethe besides his greite and paynefull Trayvell and losse of Tyme.[40]

Nothing very much seems to have been done to ease the burden although, if a man achieved high office such as Mayor, Sheriff or Alderman, he might expect a certain amount of subsidy.

In all these labours, the Master and Wardens were supported by the full-time employed staff. In 1562, when the minutes open, the Clerk was John Huchenson, with Francis Yomans as the Beadle. Huchenson died in 1571 and was succeeded by Nicholas Fuljambe. After Fuljambe's appointment, the Earl of Sussex protested that he had wanted the place for Henry Evans, and a tactful deputation, consisting of Richard Offley and Robert Dowe, was instructed to call on the Earl to explain that the election had taken place before his letter arrived.[41]

For the four years that he held the Clerkship, before he died of plague in the late summer of 1575, Fuljambe served the Company well and truly. Having established that his wages were to be £20 a year — a very fair sum — he applied himself to his duties. He was a precise and careful man, delighting in the detail of his office. From his minutes, we learn something of how the meetings were organized; the entry for 18 October 1572[42] begins:

Fyrste at this daye the comen clarke according to the lawdable order of this howse redd the Actes paste at the laste Courte of Assistantes ... The comen clarke exhibited to the saide Master a Breviat of sundry matters Chiefly to be determyned at this presente Courte of Assistantes in hec verba ...

and on 9 March 1573 he tells us that the minutes of the last meeting were read out 'accordinge to the good custome of this howse'.[43] Clearly the Court of Assistants was regularly provided with minutes and an agenda as it would be today, although the minutes were not supplied as individual copies but were read out loud, and the Breviat or agenda would have been

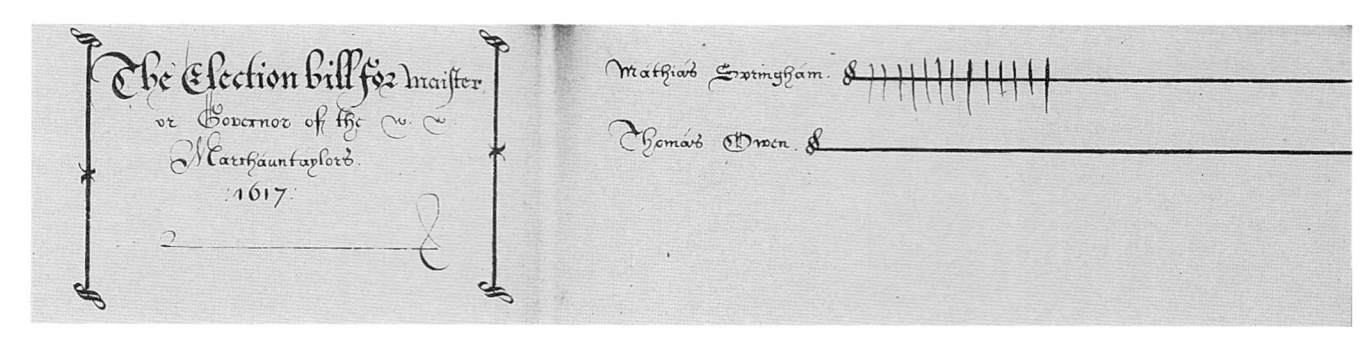

FIGURE 46. 1617. Mathias Springham is elected Master.
Guildhall Library, MS 34100/118, Misc. Docs A8

a single sheet placed on the table or held in the Master's hand. On the one occasion that he made an error in recording the rental of a property, Fuljambe did not seek to hide his mistake, but noted contritely that it had been mis-written 'by the necligence of the Clarke'.[44]

Fuljambe's watchfulness served the Company well. In July 1572[45] the Grocers' Company laid claim to the 'ypocrise house',[46] lying in the south part of the garden adjacent to the Hall. The Master demanded their evidence. Fuljambe searched through the back registers (demonstrating thereby that the minutes missing today were in existence then) and found that in 1514 John Sandforth of Thorpe Salvin in Yorkshire had sold lands to the value of £226 3s. 4d. to Mr Dacres the Master, and that even earlier, in 1491 and 1497, money had been laid out for a new lock on the door and for three days' work by a carpenter. Fuljambe's memorandum continues:

Also in the tyme of Mr Jamys Wilford Master [1494–95] it apereth in an olde register writton with thand of Henry Maiour notary then Comen Clark . . . how many messes of meit [meat] were placed in the Hall and the other howses & romes therabowt to the nombre of iij^c vi [306] whear amonges other he noteth vj metz of loving frendes to be placed in the garden chamber wherby it may apere that the Company have longe enjoyed the said howse before the grocers' interest so that the said company of grocers can have no just title to the said howse which I have thought good here to note for better manifestacion therof.

Fuljambe's attentiveness paid off; no more was heard from the Grocers.

He did well financially out of his post. In December 1572[47] it was agreed that he should be paid for each apprentice's indenture that he drew up, and in May 1574[48] his salary was increased by £10. His son John, a 'poor scholar' at Merchant Taylors' School, was granted an exhibition, and his second boy, William, also enjoyed a free place. After Fuljambe's death in 1575,[49] his widow Agnes, pleading 'greite povertie', was granted a pension of £4 a year, a sad diminution from her husband's substantial income, though probably adequate for modest needs.

In his duties Fuljambe was assisted by the Beadle, Francis Yomans, whose duty it was to go round all the Assistants to remind them of any imminent meeting. Yomans was clearly getting old; in September 1572, being of 'great age (which beinge a contynewall sicknes of it self cuttith hym of from all other gaynes and encreasith charges)', he was granted £4 a year for life, but seems to have continued in his post, for in March 1575[50] he petitioned the Quarter Day Court that the 'presente derthe of victualles . . . dothe pynche the purses of us poore men'. He received a lengthy lecture on his duties to the Company, at the end of which the Court, 'wayinge and tenderly consideringe that oure saide officer is an olde man', decided to grant Yomans an additional £6 out of which he could pay a younger deputy if he needed help.

The Court were staunchly supportive of their employees. When in March 1575 Nicholas Harrisone complained that Fuljambe had attempted to arrest him for some unspecified misdemeanour, the Master roundly told him to go away 'untill he hadd more cause to complayne'.[51] When Fuljambe died later that summer, Thomas Haselfoote was elected in his place.

FIGURE 47. The almshouses on Tower Hill. Detail from a copy of Haiward and Gascoyne's survey of the Tower and surrounding area, made by Robert Whitehand in January 1713.
Public Record Office, Work 31/836

'THE ONE SHALL FORGIVE THE OTHER'

A heavy responsibility on the Master, Wardens and Court was the settling of 'variances' between the membership; there were few meetings in which there was no 'controversie' to be pacified. No man could seek a remedy at law till he had brought his complaint before the Court; to do so was a serious offence. In an argument over a house in Southwark,[52] the complainants were told firmly that litigation would be too costly and protracted, and that they had better accept the judgement of the Court. There was a real determination to keep the peace within the Company; its members were to be 'loving brothers', all arguments 'from the beginning of the worlde to this presente day' were to be healed — 'the one shall forgive the other' — and it was the responsibility of the Court to maintain control and, if need be, to impose good behaviour. Stability was all-important.

Most disagreements were over money. The usual remedy was to lay down that the debt was to be paid in instalments, their size and frequency being specified by the Court; it was the Clerk's responsibility to see that the payments were kept up. The size of the sums involved varied; in March 1572 Thomas Sutton owed Nicholas Peale £9,[53] which was to be paid off at the rate of 5s. the quarter,[54] while widow Elizabeth Younge was told in December 1575 to clear her 10s. debt to William Bonde before Easter, paying up in 2s. instalments.[55]

Apart from money, the most frequent cause of controversy was the exchange of 'ill words'. William Heton called Thomas Wylford a 'pratynge boye'; he was ordered to deposit a gold ring worth 40s. against future good behaviour.[56] In March 1565 one of the Wardens, Thomas Browne, was insulted by Edward a Ley, who had said that Browne was 'but a shyfter . . . and in thende it shulde appere that he is worthe a grote [4d.], with other lyke wordes of infamy'. Ley denied it utterly, but Mrs Anne Smythe was called as a witness; she took oath that Ley had called Browne a shifter, and had added that he 'lived only by the making of shifts'. Ley was put in gaol till he made submission and apologized.[57] John Stempford was in trouble for calling Gilbert Lylly a slave and a knave,[58] and there were regular complaints of 'indecent and unsemely words' and 'unfyttinge woordes and unorderly dealinge'.[59] Fighting between servants was another problem, though even Merchant Taylors might come to blows. In January 1569, Miles Exilbe was sent

. . . to warde [i.e. prison] for that he in the presense of the Master and Wardens openlie in the Streete did streke [strike] and drawe blud upon Luys Lloyde, a brother of this Mistery, contrary to the Ordenaunce of this house and also to the infringinge of the Quenes peace . . .[60]

Matters far more domestic came before the Court as well, for its jurisdiction extended to the wives of freemen. When Plomer's wife 'receyved' from the 'wyf' of Anthony Humfrey certain pewter vessels and did not return them, Plomer was ordered on 28 July 1564 to produce in the Hall

before Sonday next . . . ij pewter dysshes, iiij porrengers, a quarte wyne pott and a bason of pewter and that in consideracion thereof the said Umfrey shall pay to the said Plomer before Sonday next xx^d in full payment of suche money as the wyf of the said Umffrey did bowow [borrow] of the wyf of the said Plomer upon the said pewter. And further it is agreaed that the said Umfrey shall at his costes and charges withdrawe all suche accon [action] and sutes as he hathe commensed agaynst the said Plomer before Sonday next.[61]

We may deduce that Plomer's wife had lent 20 pence, and had taken the vessels as security; when the money was not returned, she hung onto the dishes, and the Court was needed to sort matters out. There were many other wranglings. Harry Reignoldes

. . . ys committed to warde, for that he will not paye suche money as by him is owinge unto a poore woman who kepte hym in the tyme of the Plage he lienge sicke thereof for the space of a quarter of a yeare or there aboutes.[62]

Presumably Reignoldes paid up, as did Thomas Pratt who had run up an exorbitant ale score and other debts to the sum of £4 with Thomas Berry; he was ordered to pay it off, the ale score before Easter and the rest at 20s. at a time, at quarterly intervals.[63] David Powell was ordered to pay Alice Wrighte 'xx^s for the carrying of a childe gotten [in Wales]' back into Wales to be nursed.[64] Powell was released from any further claims; one wonders what became of the child. Two disagreements related to travel charges. John Carringtone had hired a horse from Robert Wolle but, the journey safely completed, refused to pay up; the Court assessed the charge at 4s. and commanded that 'the sayde controversie be clerely ended'.[65] In September 1576, William Singleton complained that John Park owed him 14s. 7d. but, when the Court heard that Park 'had brought him [Singleton] up frome Whitboke [Whitbeck] in Cumberlande . . . and [did] defraye his charges uppon the waye', they decided the debt was fully paid.[66] When widowed Mrs Thomas complained on 9 February 1573 that Peter Legate was trying to turn her out of her 'now dwelling house' (no address is given), on which he had been granted a lease, the Court ruled that she might occupy the lower rooms, and Legate offered to provide her with food for the rest of her life.[67]

The great controversy which rumbled on for years was between John Toppe and John Eden: there had been a partnership between the two men, but in the first half of 1570 they seem to have fallen out. Early entries give no details, but the Court minutes for 5 July 1570 include a letter from someone of no less importance than Sir Nicholas Bacon, strongly advising all those concerned to refrain from going to law. His wise words were ignored. On 14 and 18 July 1572, the parties presented their suits separately to the Master and Wardens, Toppe alleging that John Eden '. . . did of late practize with dyverse his confederates to have entered [Toppe's] shoppe', and that he had been obliged to board up the premises. Eden counterclaimed that Toppe had 'conveyed his clothes owt of his shoppe' to the value of £1,000. The Master, William Hodgson, asked whether the complainants would accept his award. Eden refused, there being no 'lerned counsell for better advise in the makynge' of the decree, and went to complain to the Lord Mayor, who told him to go back to his Company. This he did, but was told the matter had been settled, so he appealed to the Court of Common Pleas. This took time, but in January 1577 a letter arrived from the Privy Council,[68] signed, among others, by Sir Francis Walsingham, expressing surprise at having been bothered by so trifling a matter — surely the Master and Wardens could deal with their own liverymen? It was decided that the case should be re-heard before the Master, the Wardens and nine senior liverymen; on 3 May a report went back.[69] The investigating panel had held fourteen separate meetings with Eden and Toppe. Eden's own stock in the shop — unfortunately, no detailed inventory appears to survive — amounted to £1,164 6s. 11½d. He had been paid in full for this – indeed, overpaid by £23 0s. 5d. which he still owed to Toppe. He had also received £650 as his share of Henry Suckley's former property, with an additional £100 a year later, but nothing would content him.

He had been to the High Court of Chancery. The Master said that Eden had repeatedly returned to the Company

> requyringe and desyringe us to make an ende betwene them, and what order, Judgemente, Determinacyon or ende whatsoever wee made, whether wee gave him anythinge or nothinge, muche or lytle, he wolde be contente to stonde to obey and performe the same, yet now [is] denyinge that ever he hadd so submytted himself to our order . . . Oure ende is no ende unto him which we cannot fynde nor thynck to be as he allegeth.

Failing to get the satisfaction for which he yearned, Eden appealed again in October 1577 to the Privy Council and then, in 1581, to the Star Chamber, and was told soundly by Sir Thomas Bromley, the Lord Chancellor, to return to his Company and 'acknowledge and confess that he hath rashly, unadvisedly and untruly charged the . . . defendants', and that he should beg for forgiveness. This Eden did, on 11 November 1581; his substance being expended in a useless law suit, the Company generously granted him a pension of £5 a year and conferred on him a place in the almshouse, though when he died they refused to continue the same protection to his unfortunate widow. John Toppe prospered and became Master of the Company in 1587, having previously served as Warden in 1580 and 1584.[70]

THE MAKING OF CLOTHES[71]

Another area of Company jurisdiction reveals what the craft members were actually doing to earn their livings. By this time the senior members, those who had reached the livery, were merchants trading in goods generally, but particularly in cloth; of the craftsmen, some were in fact clothworkers (see pp. 141–42) but most others were truly tailors, making and mending garments. Sometimes, there were complaints over bad workmanship, the ill-making of garments ordered by individual clients. In March 1565,[72] Mistress Agnes Onesley complained that Laurence Tompson had lost

> . . . a frock of fyne clothe containing ij yardes di [2½ yards] garded with velvett which she did delyver to hym to new garde with velvett and for that the same Laurence cannot delyver the same frocke to the said Agnes for that he alledges that the same frocke is stollen frome hym.

The Court ruled that Tompson must pay 33s. in compensation and must return such scraps of velvet as remained; the guarding for which the rich fabric had been intended was the broad band of trimming down the open front and round the hem of the skirt. Thomas Warden complained that Richard Selby had marred his wife's cassock but was still trying to charge him 7s. 11d.: the price was reduced and Warden told to accept the garment as it was, though when Margery Stacy complained that Thomas Taylor had made her cassock too small, she got 40s. compensation for the cloth and Taylor was told to get what profit he could from the sale of the garment.[73] A cassock was a loose full-length overgarment usually worn by women; when Richard Bell was £3 in debt to William Petingale in April 1575, he was told that before midsummer he must make Mistress Petingale a cassock worth 33s. 4d., or settle the debt in full.[74] The minutes carry laments about a 'cloke not made so orderly', or about garments such as a 'paire of gascoynes of cloth' (loose baggy breeches) for which David Fludd was to pay 10s. to Lewis ap Williams at the rate of 4d. every Saturday,[75] or a canvas (probably linen) doublet which William Tobbyn, an apprentice, had 'loste by his necligence and other his Defaltes', and for which he was to pay 20s. to Evan Joans, his master.[76] In passing, we may note how many apprentices seem to have made the long journey from Wales to get their training in London; the well-travelled wool-routes from the West Country must have been a factor here. Richard Brynningham brought an anguished appeal from Sir John Desmond and Denis Case in far-away Limerick; they had left velvet with Richard Tysdall to make a 'short gowne', but it had not been sent; Tysdall was ordered to complete the work and hand it over.[77] Some of the work undertaken was costly; Richard a Vane, a gentleman in Kent, ordered from Daniel Symsone

> . . . one woman's gowne of blacke taffytta gardid with two gardes of black velvett and one foreparte of a kertill of chaungeable taffitta cut and lyned with ashe cullour sarssnett and laide over with a lace of silke blacke and asshe cullour withoute anie alteracion of the saide gowne and kertill even as the same was shewn before the saide Master and Wardens. Uppon the delyvery thereof the saide Master and Wardens doe . . . determyne that . . .

Richarde a Vane . . . shall paye . . . Daniell . . . vj^{li} xiij^s iiij^d [£6 13s. 4d.].[78]

We do not know who was going to wear this finery.

There are frequent references to textiles and furnishings, sometimes lodged as security for loans; we get references to 'a bedestede a fetherbedde a coveringe of rede Rugge and a cheste',[79] and to

. . . a cassock of sheepes colour welted and lyned with cotton, a kyrtle of mory [deep purple or red] clothe, with a welte of vellett. A vallaunce for a bed, and cortayns of white lynnen clothe to the same, a course Table clothe and a course Towell to the same.[80]

In two instances, tailoring equipment is mentioned. In September 1573, Nicholas Dicke was ordered to return a shopboard, a stall and a pressing iron to Henry Bollen and was found guilty of slandering Bollen, saying that he had stolen a cloak, and of suborning a maid servant to bear false witness.[81] In another case John Noxe was told to return to Henry Northall his 'presse and suche other thinges as he hathe of his and so all things to be clere betwene them'.[82] One wonders whether these small-time craftsmen had any knowledge of the sophisticated continental tailoring manuals such as Juan de Alcegar's *Libro de Geometria, Pratica, y Traca*, published first in 1580 and then again, in an enlarged edition, in 1589. It seems unlikely, though those at the top of the Company's hierarchy, with Court connections, may well have done. Walter Fyshe, Master in 1576, and Tailor to Queen Elizabeth from 1558 until near his death in 1586, would have been fully aware of the increasing sophistication of Spanish and French attire, and would have cut his cloth to produce similar results.

Occasionally, we get a reference to industrial processes. In April 1565 Thomas Ryckemour, skilled in 'calendryng of fustyans', agreed to employ only his own apprentices in his techniques.[83] In May of the following year, the Governors of Bridewell, 'for the better settinge of worke of such persons as heretofore have bene vacabondes', offered to supply woollen cards at 12d. the dozen; the Company took fifty dozen in all, of which ten dozen went to Sir Thomas White and four dozen to Richard Hilles.[84] In the spring of 1575 a dyer called Bayly begged for access to the newly-built stairs on Three Cranes Wharf in order to 'wasshe his clothes'; the Court prudently agreed to a temporary arrangement, and were soon receiving objections from Company members who said the stairs had been constructed for their use but

. . . the sayde complaynantes were willed to be quiett untill they hadd more cause to complayne and in the meane seasone to suffer the sayde Bayly to enjoye his saide Lycens.[85]

THE COMPANY'S PROPERTY

The management of their property continued to be one of the serious and regular concerns of the Court. Their first care was for the Hall itself. On 15 March 1572, an agreement was made with Richard Ridge, joiner, to

. . . make and set up A Sealinge of good and well seasoned and sorted wenskott in the newe parlour before the first daye of June next ensuynge after the patrone [pattern] of one large panell in the parlour beneth, set at the toppe of the stonework of the chymney theire on the side towardes the dore of the sayd parlour with crestes etc accordingly for every yard wherof he is to be paid fyve shillinges at the fynishing of the same and moreover [is] discharged of the yron work goinge to the setting up and sure makinge of the same.[86]

Ridge was, we may assume, a son or grandson of the Richard Ridge who had carved the pendants of Henry VIII's hammerbeam roof at Hampton Court, and had sculpted some of the heraldic beasts set along the bridge over the moat. Next, it was the exterior of the Hall that needed attention. Thomas Lymly, the Lord Mayor's 'paynter', was told he would receive £10 when he

. . . fynishe his worke to be done upon the Tarras in the comen garden in suche maner and forme as was and shalbe appoynted to him.[87]

In August of the next year he was needed

. . . to stoppe the Ryffes [cracks] of the raylinge and oyle all the leade colour of the same so as yt maye be fresshe.

Any defects found over the ensuing two years were to be remedied at Lymly's own expense.[88]

Then the garden needed attention; an item in Nicholas Fuljambe's Breviat on 18 October 1572 runs, 'To remember the decaye of your Garden necessaryly requieringe to be amended'. In December the Master agreed to take action, but it is not until September 1574 that we find the entry:

William Yonge Gardyner ... admytted to kepe the comen garden [of] this Companye ... For his paynes to be taken in dressinge, plantinge and weedinge of the saide garden and kepeinge of the Bowlinge Alley in reparacions and fyndinge from tyme to tyme all thinges neadfull ... xl^s [40s.] quarterly.[89]

Then there was trouble with the well in the kitchen, it was '... newe in ruyne ... lyenge open, diverse noysome things have fallen into the same'.[90] It had to be covered in and converted into a pump at the Company's expense. The entry runs on:

Also ... the Southe Alley in the garden, beinge nowe unpavid and after anye rayne noysome to goe throughe shalbe pavid with Purbeck stone at the costes and Charges of this house and ... the lytell plott under the Tarras shalbe pavid.[91]

Altogether, these were expensive years for the Merchant Taylors. But there was help to hand in rents from numerous smaller and several substantial properties, and from the fines when a lease was renewed. Although the Company had been forced to sell some fifty-four properties in 1549–50 to meet Edward VI's extortionate demands,[92] much remained and more was going to be given. There was property in Trinity Lane, Shoe Lane, Rood Lane, Lombard Street, Broad Street and Fenchurch Street; there were tentergrounds on Moorfields and at least one house on London Bridge wherein one Swallowe, a 'forren' [ie foreign], dwelt and for which he at last succeeded in securing a proper lease; there were wharfs at Stonehouse, in Ratcliffe, and on Three Cranes. Although brethren of the Company were to be preferred as tenants,[93] anyone might apply for a vacant house and would-be tenants were only too willing to offer venison, French wine and rondletts of sack in addition to the required rents or fines. All in all, the Company owned at least 67 properties within the City, as well as lands beyond, often acquired or held in connection with the various school foundations. Usually the houses were let on full repairing leases, though in May 1572 James Butson was given £4 towards the repair of his dwelling 'so as it be well and effectually imployed upon the same'.[94] Again, in June 1575,

Richarde Offley and Roberte Hawes are appoynted to viewe William Body's howse and to have with them a Bryckleyour and a Carpenter to see what remedy maye be founde for water which falleth into A Cellour their to the greite Annoyanc of the saide Body.[95]

Sometimes tenants were truly distinguished people; not long before his death, Miles Coverdale, 'professor of holly divinitie', transferred the lease of a house in the parish of St Benet Fink to Edward Babington, gentleman; four years earlier, as we have noted, he had obtained the freedom of the Company for a relation, William. Sometimes, a lease includes much detail about the property. When, in August 1568, Arthur Gardner subdivided his premises with Edward Cutler, haberdasher, the parts of the property assigned to Cutler comprised:

A shoppe with an entry leading into the Yarde of the Backsyde. A parlour lyenge nexte the saide Yarde, the sayde Yarde, A kytchen, a colehouse & well therein, with a shedde Roome by the same kytchen, A chamber over the same kytchen, with a chymney therein, Two chambers directly over the saide parlour, and Two garrettes directly over the sayde parlour and chambers and over other back Roomes of the saide Artour lyenge under the sayde Garrettes, An other shedde or roome in the weste ende of the foresaide yarde, A payre of stayers leading uppe to the same Shedde Roome and two Jake stooles for the Tunnell of the prevye in the same, and a lytle cellour betwene the same Shoppe and parlour.[96]

The property was in Ludgate, rented out at £7 a year; the detailed description needed to make clear the subdivision suggests that the premises were used as commercial or industrial premises, workrooms and sheds squeezed into a yard, perhaps like those at 77 Wood Street, surveyed by Ralph Treswell for the Clothworkers' Company, where one large out-building is labelled 'The Callender House'.[97]

Sometimes there were multiple applications for a particular property, as in May 1573 when four liverymen — Thomas Wilforde, Richard White, William Kympton and Warden Jacob — competed for the lease of a house in Thames Street on behalf of various relatives or former servants.[98]

Sometimes a substantial bequest seemed to be more trouble than it was worth. Sir William Harper, founder of the still thriving school in Bedford, had rented the mansion in Lombard Street bequeathed to the Company by Sir John Percyvale (see p. 111); Alderman Kympton begged the use of it during his shrieval year; Alderman Olyff withdrew his claim; but Richard Hilles, Gerard Gore and Sir

Thomas Offley all tried to outbid each other for the lease. Lady Harper, however, upset everybody's plans by stubbornly refusing to move out; she was Sir William's youthful second wife, a vigorous and emphatic lady, and she had friends in high places. Summoned before the Mayoral Court, she produced letters from Lord Burghley. The Merchant Taylors stood firm and she was finally ejected, but the effort required had been great.[99]

CHARITABLE WORKS

The dispensing of charity was a more agreeable duty. The well-built and well-endowed almshouses have already been described, but the selection of the inhabitants needed constant responsible attention. Richard Holte, a Merchant Taylor and a liveryman, 'fallen into decaye and grete povertie' in the autumn of 1574,[100] was given a place, and three years later, room was found for Thomas Sutton although he was a carpenter.[101] A merry inmate, William Jenkyns, was allowed to marry in January 1567 'for his further comforte',[102] though Almsman Wilson was turned out for begging in the street which was something no respectable resident needed to do; Edward Burbeck, an aged plaisterer, had the vacant place, 'his sight and lyons [lines] being faltie'.

Appeals for help were seldom made in vain. William Firman, blind and dwelling on London Bridge with his wife and a maidservant, all of them suddenly struck sightless, was instantly relieved with 20s. from the common box, and was promised the fines for non-attendance at meetings and further help if needed.[103] In September 1564, the Company was unexpectedly bequeathed the remainder of the lease of tenements and tenter-grounds in Moorfields. Four poor souls benefited thereby — Widow Cockerham and Widow Standysh, and

a poore man named John Cooke and his wyf ... who hathe as yet nothing and yet is an overseer to the groundes there ... The said two wydowes are very holde and have ... viij^d [a week], and the poore man and his wif ... have nothing as yet but as they can get by theire daies labour, he by portage of burdens and she by wasshing of the clothes in honest mens howsyng.[104]

The widows' incomes were increased by 4d. a week and John Cooke and his wife were given 4d. Some of them at least stayed on in the humble property, for in March 1569, John Lynne, citizen and Merchant Taylor, and Elizabeth his wife, 'who are of late fallen and come into greate povertie, necessitie and mysery as is well known', were allotted 12d. a week and 'the little tenement and garden in Moorefields where the late widow Cockerham late dwelt'.[105]

The Company was responsible for a number of charitable bequests, in particular under the wills of Mrs Agnes Suckley (or Suckliffe — the spelling varies), Sir Thomas Rowe and Robert Donkyn. Agnes, presumably the widow of Henry who left four properties at Pie Corner, Smithfield, to Christ's Hospital,[106] was a practical and resourceful lady. When she died in 1569, she left £400 to be held by the Company to dole out in loans of £25 0s. 0d. to young men setting up on their own and needing capital to lay out in stock; the money was to be repaid within two years. Sir Thomas Rowe, dying in 1570, left substantial funds and specified that £4 each was to be given every year to ten poor men, being drawn from the companies of Clothworkers, Carpenters, Armourers, Plaisterers and Tylers.[107] A few months later, Robert Donkyn died as well, leaving the Company a considerable amount of property in Bell Alley off Bishopsgate; his benefaction was practical too.[108] Every year, twelve poor men and twelve poor women were to be provided with clothing, the men receiving a 'gowne of welshe freze', a 'sherte' and a 'paire of showes', and the women a cassock, a smock and shoes. The garments were to be distributed from the Hall each Christmas and the recipients were to carry them out openly in their hands, thereby demonstrating their gratitude and the beneficence of the donor and the Company. They were surely glad to do so; warm clothing was worth having.

NOTES

1. See *Court Minutes*, ed. by Davies.
2. GL, MS 34010/1, p. 653.
3. GL, MS 34010/1, p. 612.
4. GL, MS 34010/1, p. 640.
5. GL, MS 34010/1, p. 724.
6. GL, MS 34010/1, p. 634.
7. GL, MS 34010/1, p. 592.
8. GL, MS 34010/1, p. 213.

9. GL, MS 34010/1, pp. 57, 63–64.
10. GL, MS 34010/2, fols. 41ʳ, 65ᵛ.
11. GL, MS 34010/2, fol. 15ʳ.
12. GL, MS 34010/1, p. 171.
13. GL, MS 34010/1, p. 744.
14. GL, MS 34010/1, p. 376.
15. GL, MS 34010/1, p. 22, 16 October 1562.
16. GL, MS 34010/1, p. 144, 1 December 1564.
17. GL, MS 34010/1, p. 565, 15 March 1572.
18. GL, MS 34010/1, p. 578, 10 May 1572.
19. GL, MS 34010/1, p. 611, 13 October 1572.
20. GL, MS 34010/1, p. 679, 6 November 1573.
21. GL, MS 34010/1, p. 686, 4 December 1573.
22. GL, MS 34010/2, fol. 32ᵛ, 13 January 1576.
23. GL, MS 34010/2, fol. 45ᵛ, 12 October 1576.
24. GL, MS 34010/2, fol. 47ᵛ, 19 December 1576.
25. GL, MS 34010/2, fol. 67ᵛ, 15 July 1577.
26. GL, MS 34010/1, pp. 351, 357; 34010/2, fol. 73ʳ.
27. GL, MS 34010/1, p. 191, 20 July 1565.
28. GL, MS 34010/1, p. 330, 3 April 1568.
29. GL, MS 34010/1, p. 648, 22 May 1573.
30. GL, MS 34010/2, fol. 40ʳ, 14 May 1576.
31. GL, MS 34010/2, fol. 50ʳ, 18 March 1577.
32. GL, MS 34010/2, fol. 36ʳ, 9 March 1576.
33. See S. Rappaport, *Worlds within Worlds* (1989). Also I. Archer, *The Pursuit of Stability* (Cambridge, 1991).
34. But remember the pressing iron, 14 lb in weight, used to batter out the brains of Thomas Arden on St Valentine's Day, 1551. This celebrated murder provided the material for *Arden of Faversham* which some, probably erroneously, attribute to Shakespeare.
35. See Ann Saunders (ed.), *The Royal Exchange* (1997), p. 89.
36. *A Biographical Dictionary of English Court Musicians, 1485–1714*, ed. by Andrew Ashbee and D. Lasocki (Aldershot, 1998), II, pp. 423–24. See also Fiona Kisby, 'The Royal Household Chapel in Early Tudor London, 1485–1547' (unpublished Ph.D., London, 1996). I am most grateful for Dr Kisby's generous help. Fisher lived in the extra-mural parish of St Dunstan in the West, where there were several working Merchant Taylors; may we guess at a connection between the Royal Wardrobe and the Chapel Royal?
37. GL, MS 34010/1, p. 350.
38. GL, MS 34010/1, pp. 586–89, 631, 637, 645, 662; MS 34048/5, pp. 199, 261, 325.
39. GL, MS 34010/1, p. 733.
40. GL, MS 34010/2, fol. 52ʳ.
41. GL, MS 34010/1, pp. 555–57.
42. GL, MS 34010/1, p. 613.
43. GL, MS 34010/1, p. 641.
44. GL, MS 34010/2, fol. 11ʳ. A lease in reversion granted to Alderman Kympton of two tenements called Copthall, now occupied by assigns of Sir Thomas White 'of worthy memory'. The yearly rent should have been 40s., not 33s. 4d.
45. GL, MS 34010/1, p. 593.
46. Hippocras was a sweet wine; the name suggests that the garden or summer house was somewhere to go to take a glass with a friend, and that it could be used as an overflow area when the Hall was crowded.
47. GL, MS 34010/1, p. 628.
48. GL, MS 34010/1, pp. 712–13.
49. GL, MS 34010/2, fol. 64ʳ.
50. GL, MS 34010/2, fol. 8ʳ.
51. GL, MS 34010/2, fol. 6ᵛ.
52. GL, MS 34010/1, pp. 559, 561.
53. The debt was £9, but Sutton had to give a bond for £10 that he would keep up instalments.
54. GL, MS 34010/1, p. 564.
55. GL, MS 34010/2, fol. 32ʳ.
56. GL, MS 34010/1, p. 96, March 1564.
57. GL, MS 34010/1, p. 170.
58. GL, MS 34010/1, p. 395.
59. GL, MS 34010/2, fol. 68ʳ, 26 July 1577.
60. GL, MS 34010/1, p. 371.
61. GL, MS 34010/1, p. 128.
62. GL, MS 34010/1, p. 523, 18 May 1571.
63. GL, MS 34010/1, p. 563, 4 Feb. 1572.
64. GL, MS 34010/2, fol. 50ʳ, 16 March 1577.
65. GL, MS 34010/2, fol. 49ᵛ, 1 March 1577.
66. GL, MS 34010/2, fol. 44ʳ.
67. GL, MS 34010/1, p. 634.
68. GL, MS 34010/2, fol. 52ʳ.
69. GL, MS 34010/2, fols 54ᵛ–55.
70. GL, MS 34010/1, pp. 456, 458, 589, 591–94, 641, 666; MS 34010/2, fols 48–49, 52, 53ʳ–55ᵛ, 63–64, 157; MS 34010/3, fols 14ᵛ, 15–18, 25ᵛ–27, 35ᵛ–36ᵛ, 62ᵛ, 68–69, 74, 77, 92ᵛ, 159ᵛ.
71. An expanded study of this subject can be found in Ann Saunders, 'A Cloke not Made so Orderly', in *The Ricardian*, XIII (2003), pp. 415–19.
72. GL, MS 34010/1, p. 170.
73. GL, MS 34010/1, p. 178, 13 April 1565; p. 560, 14 January 1572.
74. GL, MS 34010/2, fol. 9ᵛ.
75. GL, MS 34010/2, fols 49ʳ, 70ʳ.
76. GL, MS 34010/2, fol. 4ʳ.
77. GL, MS 34010/1, p. 638.
78. GL, MS 34010/2, fol. 85ᵛ, 4 November 1578.
79. GL, MS 34010/1, p. 97.
80. GL, MS 34010/1, p. 318.
81. GL, MS 34010/1, p. 670.
82. GL, MS 34010/2, fol. 43ʳ.
83. GL, MS 34010/1, p. 178.
84. GL, MS 34010/1, p. 227.
85. GL, MS 34010/2, fols 11ʳ, 12ᵛ.
86. GL, MS 34010/1, p. 565.
87. GL, MS 34010/1, p. 685, 25 November 1573.
88. GL, MS 34010/1, p. 741.
89. GL, MS 34010/1, pp. 613, 628, 747. This neglect was only recent, for in the accounts for 1569 we find an entry for Francis Yomans, two men and two women, brushes and brooms, plants and seeds, and 'wyre to bind up the Rosemary', amounting to 2s. 2d.
90. GL, MS 34010/2, fol. 62ʳ.
91. GL, MS 34010/2, fol. 62ᵛ. An interesting paper, by John Schofield, on City gardens, appeared in *Garden History*, 27 (1999), pp. 73–88.
92. Clode, *Early History*, I, p. 151.
93. GL, MS 34010/1, p. 99.
94. GL, MS 34010/1, p. 578.
95. GL, MS 34010/2, fol. 14ʳ.
96. GL, MS 34010/1, p. 347.
97. *The London Surveys of Ralph Treswell*, ed. by John Schofield, London Topographical Society, Publication No. 135 (1987), p. 135.

98. GL, MS 34010/1, p. 650.
99. GL, MS 34010/1, pp. 703, 704, 712, 751, 762; MS 34010/2, fols 5^v, 8^v, 15^v, 19^r, 19^v, 25^v, 27^r, 30^r, 30^v.
100. GL, MS 34010/1, p. 751.
101. GL, MS 34010/2, fol. 59^r.
102. GL, MS 34010/1, p. 285.
103. GL, MS 34010/1, p. 673.
104. GL, MS 34010/1, pp. 133–34.
105. GL, MS 34010/1, pp. 382–83.
106. Treswell, *Surveys*, ed. by Schofield, p. 85.
107. GL, MS 34010/1, pp. 478–79.
108. GL, MS 34010/1, pp. 500–02.

CHAPTER NINE

THE CLOTHWORKERS, THE CITY AND THE CROWN

THE COMPANY AND THE CLOTHWORKERS

THE MERCHANT TAYLORS' relationships with other livery companies and with the City Corporation are worth examining. Inevitably, the information to be found in the Court minutes is one-sided, and must be supplemented from the archives of other companies, from the Corporation records, and from government muniments. Apart from one complaint in April 1566,[1] that the Merchant Taylors were 'furring of garmentes', there were no squabbles with their earlier rivals, the Skinners and the Drapers; in the early years of Elizabeth's reign, most of the disagreements were with the Clothworkers.

To understand the situation, we must realize that though in earlier centuries England's chief export had been raw wool (which is why, even today, the Chancellor still sits on the Woolsack), by the late fifteenth and throughout the sixteenth centuries this had been largely replaced by woven cloth. In the very early 1500s, perhaps 30,000 lengths of cloth were shipped abroad yearly; by the 1530s, average annual exports had risen to 80,700 lengths; by the 1540s, to 108,000 lengths, a peak being reached about 1554 with 136,000 lengths exported.[2] Thereafter the demand fell sharply, largely due to Spanish invasion of the Netherlands, and many skilled men found difficulty in finding work. 'Foreigns' — that is, any craftsman from outside London or from abroad — were more unpopular than ever; it was a finable offence to employ one of them, though highly skilled craftsmen were flooding in from overseas, driven from their homes by the horrors of war, and desperately eager to find work.

Now, many of the Merchant Taylors were clothworkers by profession rather than tailors, and thus presented a threat to the more recently formed Clothworkers' Company. In March 1545, the Clothworkers had initiated six years of frustrating legislation with a Bill of Petition to the Lord Mayor, that all apprentices engaged in making fabrics should belong to their company and none other. Understandably the Merchant Taylors protested, hired counsel, and fought the Bill all the way till it was finally rejected by a Committee of Arbitration on 21 April 1551. The legal costs amounted to £26 4s. 9d. in 1550–51, with additions of £1 10s. 0d. for bailing out freemen and apprentices committed to prison on accusations from the Clothworkers of employing foreign craftsmen, and of £4 13s. 0d. for bringing shear-grinders from Suffolk and Reading when the Clothworkers refused to grind the shears of any save of their own company, with a final legal bill of £21 2s. 6d. for professional support in 1551–52.[3]

The importance of this becomes clear when in 1566 the Clothworkers approached Parliament with another Bill over the dressing and finishing of cloth, and for the sole right to search premises within the City and three miles around.[4] The Merchant Taylors drew up a list of their craft members most likely to be affected, arranging them by address and with a note in the margin to show each man's particular skills.[5] They divided into rowers and shearers, though a man might possess both skills. The nap of the fabric was raised by the rower,[6] passing teasel heads set in a frame across the surface of the cloth. The shearer, equipped with a pair of broad shears, made the surface smooth again — a highly skilled operation where one careless snip could ruin hours of labour.

The annotations on the list make it clear who had both skills, and who specialized in the shearing of kerseys or lighter cloths. One hundred and sixteen names are given, thirty-eight of them master craftsmen, sixty-six apprentices and twelve journeymen. All the masters were householders, most of them spread out in a line in parishes parallel with the river. They were clearly among the less well-off members of the Company. Only one name, that of Nicholas Spencer, appears among the seventy-six members of the livery who subscribed to the building of the Royal Exchange,[7] or the sixty-eight who contributed to the grain levy.[8] There was a firm, though not impenetrable, line drawn between the merchants who made up the livery, and the working craftsmen who belonged to the Bachelors' Company.

The Company again hired legal advice, and a committee met at the house of Sir Ambrose Cave, Chancellor of the Duchy of Lancaster, who held that both companies should have the right of searching premises, checking in particular the quality of work and that no 'forren' workman be employed. The Clothworkers offered to turn over all their handicraftmen to the Merchant Taylors, who were willing to accept such an increase provided they were granted land to help them shoulder such a responsibility. The Mayor set up another committee, but on 4 December the Clothworkers withdrew their offer. Both companies retained right of search, and comparative tranquillity prevailed.

THE COMPANY AND THE CITY

To have a Merchant Taylor as Lord Mayor was naturally a matter for jubilation. As we have seen, the first of the Company to be so honoured was Sir John Percyvale in 1498. He had been escorted with rejoicing to his oath-taking at Westminster and to Guildhall; the Company had eased his expenses with £40 0s. 0d., and spent £6 4s. 0d. on 'trumpet banars and waytes and wages'.[9] He was followed in 1508 by Sir Stephen Jenyns, founder of Wolverhampton School and a benefactor of St Andrew Undershaft, then by Sir Henry Hubbathorne in 1546 and by Sir Thomas White in 1553. Henry Machyn, himself a Merchant Taylor, observed and noted 'ij tallmen bayreng ij gret stremars [of] the Marchand-tayllers armes', and that there were 'goodly speeches'. It was Sir Thomas Offley's turn in 1556, and Sir William Harper's in 1561. His pageant was very grand indeed, 'trymed and fornysshed as well or better in all thynges as hath bene done at any tyme heretofore'. The verses written for the pageant made great play with the Mayor's name, the speakers being King David, Orpheus, Omphion, Arion and the Trojan Topas, all celebrated for their skill on the harp. John Stow walked in this procession, his duty being

... to attend upon the pageant to see that it be not borne against penthouses & to attend upon the children and theire apparell and to see it be safely sett up within the hall accordingly ...

The children were from 'the late monastere of Westmynster' and had their choirmaster, John Tayllour, with them; it was they presumably who represented Orpheus and the other characters.

Then, in 1568, it was Sir Thomas Rowe's turn, and for him the pageant was devised by Richard Mulcaster, headmaster of the Merchant Taylors' own school, and spoken by the boys, which must have been gratifying to the whole Company. Once again, punning was the order of the day and Sir Thomas became the 'Roe, the swyft in chase'. He was married to Mary, cousin to Sir Thomas Gresham, and the mother of eleven children. Understandably, the Rowes needed a large house; they did rather well out of Sir Thomas's mayoralty, for he was given a benevolence of £66 13s. 4d.

towarde the trymmynge and beawtyfyenge the roof of his parlour with frettes, and of newe makynge of the apparell for the chymney in the sayde parlour, to be sett oute with the Quenes Majestie her Armes, and the Armes of the sayde Mr Alderman Rowes, in free stone, with collers correspondent to the sayde Armes. As also for the makinge oute of a Baye Wyndowe oute of his Chamber, to have prospecte into his Garden, and for the raylinge in of his Garden, and roughe castynge with morter the wall aboute the same garden, and also for and towardes the payntinge and trymmynge of his house, and suche other housinge which he hathe by lease of this House, As maye make the same house and houses in and by all thinges apte, decente and mete to serve his purpose, for the kepynge of the Roome of Mayrealtie, when it shall please almightye god to call hym to the saide Roome and place of Lorde Mayour of this Honorable Citye.[10]

There was then a long gap before the Company could boast of another Lord Mayor. Sir Robert Lee was chosen in 1602 with John Swinnerton, also a Merchant Taylor, as one of his sheriffs. The verses for this pageant are not recorded, but the Accounts show that they were written by Anthony Munday, poet and playwright, and that he was paid 30s. for 'prynting the bookes of speeches', and £30 for 'provyding apparell for all the Children in the pageant, shipp, Lyon, and Camell', the animals, of course, being those on the Company's coat of arms. Besides his own literary works, now mostly lost, Munday was going to be John Stow's executor and was responsible for the 1618 edition of the *Survey*. Stow himself, by now a very old man, joined in this pageant, being paid 10s.

... for great paynes by him taken in serching for such as have byn Maiors, Shereffs and Aldermen of this Companie.

Such shows were expensive — Rowe's had cost £317 7s. 7d., Lee's £747 2s. 10d. — but the demand was irregular and the honour great. The ship and the camels proved to be a good long-term investment.

Less agreeable calls on the Company's funds were made by the City authorities for provision of corn in time of dearth. The Merchant Taylors were assessed at £350 in January 1563, when there had been 'abundance of rayne',[11] and in February 1565 £575 was demanded,[12] with another call for money a year later. The next seven years must have been blessed with good harvests, but in the early autumn of 1573 the Lord Mayor wrote to say that the Company was assessed at £300, though £175 would suffice.[13] However, in November the demand had increased to £437, of which £137 was to be raised from the Bachelors' Company, and in March of the following year the Lord Mayor was asking for an Easter benevolence for the 'poore, needie and impotent'. The money had been collected by the summer of 1574, but in November 1575 the Mayor had to make an urgent call for charity. The harvest had been unseasonable, and because of 'contrary wyndes, foule wether and longe lyenge on the waye', the grain supplied was 'mustye and not holsome', 'mete for no use'. Representatives were to come to Guildhall to discuss what should be done. The Court decided that the loss must be borne somehow, that they would accept a share of 2,000 quarters of 'swete grayne in Sussex' against the City's debt to the Company, and that it could be sold on to the bakers.[14]

Then there were individual, extraordinary demands to be met, the most significant being the building of an Exchange or Bourse by Sir Thomas Gresham.[15] The lack of such a facility had been recognized as early as 1538, when Sir Richard Gresham, father of Thomas, had been Lord Mayor, but nothing had happened. Now, on 4 January 1565, Sir Thomas sent his servant, Anthony Stringer, to the Court of Aldermen with an offer

for the erecting and building at his only costs and charges of a comely burse for merchants to assemble upon, so that the City at their charges will provide and appoint a meet and apt place for the same.

The Aldermen were swift to accept the offer and a committee was appointed to select a site. Their choice fell upon Lombard Street, which had for generations been the chosen meeting place of merchants. A deputation, headed by the draper Sir William Chester, who had himself been Lord Mayor only three years before, arrived at the Hall. The Merchant Taylors knew the reason for the visit; Alderman Thomas Rowe, himself married to Gresham's cousin Mary, had already told them, and they had made up their minds to refuse the request. The choice of the site would have meant the demolition of the house of Sir John Percyvale, the Company's first Lord Mayor, a bequest too precious to sacrifice to any City project, however important. Nevertheless, on 12 January they received the embassy courteously, listened to the plans 'to build a burse more fair and costly builded in all points than is the burse of Antwerp', asked the delegation to withdraw, kept them waiting an hour, and then said that they needed more time for deliberation. That evening they sent round a tactfully phrased refusal to sell the land, though they assured the Court of Aldermen they would support the venture on another site.

The next day, Saturday 13 January, the Master and Wardens were summoned to the Inner Chamber of Guildhall, and there were urged by the Lord Mayor and Aldermen to part with the land. They refused. Sir John Percyvale had left the houses for charitable purposes; to sell them would be to break his will, which would discourage other benefactors. The Recorder told them they should have other lands to supply the same good purposes; they still refused. The Recorder suggested calling in the Bishop of London or the Dean of St Paul's to quiet their consciences; the Company stood firm and on 18 January delivered a final refusal. The City was forced

FIGURE 48. Queen Elizabeth. An engraving from John Thane's *British Autography* (1819).
Private collection

to acquire land between Cornhill and Threadneedle Street, being the greater part of the site on which the Royal Exchange stands today. The Merchant Taylors contributed £183 3s. 4d. towards its building, Rowe giving £10, more than anyone else except Past Master Sir Thomas Offley; perhaps he thought it wise to support his cousin by marriage. Indeed, the Company as a whole advanced more than any other, except the Grocers who contributed £281 13s. 4d.; the Mercers' share was only £144.

Two other demands for money, one local, the other more unusual, may be noted in these early years of the minutes. On 1 August 1569, the summer heat being at its height, the Lord Mayor sent a demand for £30 towards the cleansing of the 'towne dyche'; the Company played for time — had the work been properly authorized by the Court of Common Council? Another, more peremptory, letter came on 19 August, and the Company paid up, anxious not to offend Sir Thomas Rowe, the Mayor, who had helpfully given £100 to provide interest-free loans to eight poor Merchant Taylor householders.[16]

The exceptional appeal for money came on behalf of the town and harbour of Yarmouth. On 11 June 1577, the Mayor wrote to say that Yarmouth had invested £10,000 in repairing and developing its harbour, that he had promised £1,000 towards the costs, and perhaps the Merchant Taylors would advance £100? The expenditure was immediately queried. What was the Mayor's authority? Had Common Council been consulted? Were other companies going to contribute? In July, the Merchant Taylors paid up, noting in the minutes that

> they doe not yealde to this presidente that suche paymente be made upon a precepte or Comaundment of the Lorde Maior where no assente of the boddy of the Cittie [has been given],

but, because the Queen's Majesty was anxious that support should be given, and because it was to the advantage of the 'Common Welthe', they would advance the money.[17]

On the whole, relationships were cordial with the City authorities, typified perhaps by the annual gift of £13 6s. 8d. to George Heton, the City Chamberlain. This he discreetly declined in March 1573, 'God havinge otherwise well provided for him'; however, the Company gave him £3 6s. 8d., all the same.[18]

One civic expense in particular was cheerfully borne — the cost of the Watch held at midsummer, on St John's Day. The most elaborate was the Marching Watch when, according to Stow, bonfires were made in the streets, doors were garlanded 'with greene Birch, long Fennel, Saint John's wort, Orpin, white lilies and such like', and lit with oil lamps, while

FIGURE 49. Robert Coulthirst's monumental brass of 1631 in Kirkleatham parish church, Yorkshire. The Company's arms are proudly displayed in each of the four corners. He was the grandfather of Sir William Turner, a distinguished post-Restoration Lord Mayor. Robert himself reached the age of ninety, having lived during six reigns.
Monumental Brass Society, from a rubbing by Patrick Farman

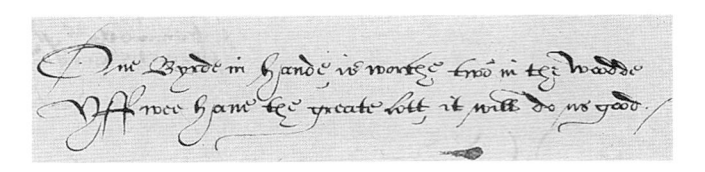

FIGURE 50. The verse chosen by the Court for their lottery application in 1567.
Guildhall Library, MS 34010/1, p. 353

tables with food and drink were set out by such as could afford to do so, and to which all were welcome. Every able-bodied man joined the parade, 'all in bright harness', and the Watch

> in every ward and streete of this Citie and Suburbs passed through the principal streets thereof, to wit, from the litle Conduit by Paules gate, through west Cheape, by the Stocks, through Cornhill, by Leaden hall to Aldgate, then backe downe Fenchurch streete, by Grasse church, aboute Grasse church Conduite, and vp Grasse church streete into Cornhill, and through it into west Cheape againe, and so broke vp.

Each livery company provided blazing iron cressets, strong men to bear them, and bag bearers to hold the spare coal for the cressets. Sometimes, the Company's arms were borne aloft — the minutes for 15 June 1571 lay down that this should be done. The Standing Watch, when the streets were simply lined with men supporting cressets, and there was no parading about, was a quieter affair but still impressive. Those who formed the Watch on these occasions were the fathers or grandfathers of the generation which would make up the City's Trained Bands in the next century.

THE COMPANY AND THE CROWN

The Company's personal relationship with the Queen was most amiable. At each Court meeting, those assembled prayed for her health. In November 1600, the Court called for thirty Merchant Taylors 'whose bodyes are hable to endure the extremitie of the wether', to escort Elizabeth from Chelsea to Whitehall; we need not doubt that there were plenty of volunteers.[19]

In a way, the relationship was almost intimate. Throughout her reign, the Queen's personal tailor was a member of the Company. First it was Walter Fyshe, Master in 1576, benefactor of St John's College,[20] who may already have been making clothes for her whilst she was Princess.[21] He certainly made the Coronation robes, and continued to be 'Our Tailor' until April 1582, when his name is joined with that of William Jones, another Merchant Taylor. Fyshe's name disappears from the Wardrobe Warrants, but he continued to attend the Company's Court almost until his death early in 1586; a quarter of a century's service at the royal Court, to a Queen who could turn political indecisiveness into an art form, must have been enough. The responsibility for the rich fabrics measured out from the Great Wardrobe in the house that had belonged to Sir John Beauchamp,[22] and for the jewels that bedizened the garments made from them, was a heavy one.[23] Jones took over the office from Fyshe, and continued to serve until Elizabeth's death on 24 March 1603.

The day-to-day responsibility for the royal fabrics rested with another member of the Company, Ralph Hope. A single quotation from one warrant gives some idea of what was laid on these faithful servants:

> First to Walter Fyshe our Taylour . . . Item for making of a frenche gowne with a shorte Traine of carnacion cloth of silver the gowne lyned with white sarceonett the bodies & slevis lyned with taphata and cloth of silver cutt chevernewise and bounde with lase of venice silver the cuttes drawen oute with lase lawne the ruffes lyned with buckeram and Rolles of bent coverid with fustian the skyrtes being a rounde kyrtle of our store of the chardge of Rauf Hope yeoman of our warderobe of Robes with eighte yerdes of like cloth of silver of our store.

To be the Queen's tailor was not a light charge, but it could be a profitable one, though payment was not always prompt.

Inevitably, some royal requests were uncomfortable. In December 1562, the Queen needed to 'borrow' £100 from the Company.[24] It was given readily, but does not seem to have been repaid. There was a little more hesitation five years later, when a licence to hold a lottery was granted to two entrepreneurs, and the Company was instructed to invest in it.[25] Rather unwillingly, fifty-three members were persuaded to subscribe collectively, and a motto was chosen (Fig. 50):

> One Byrde in hande is worthe two in the woodde
> Yff wee have the greate Lott it will do us good.

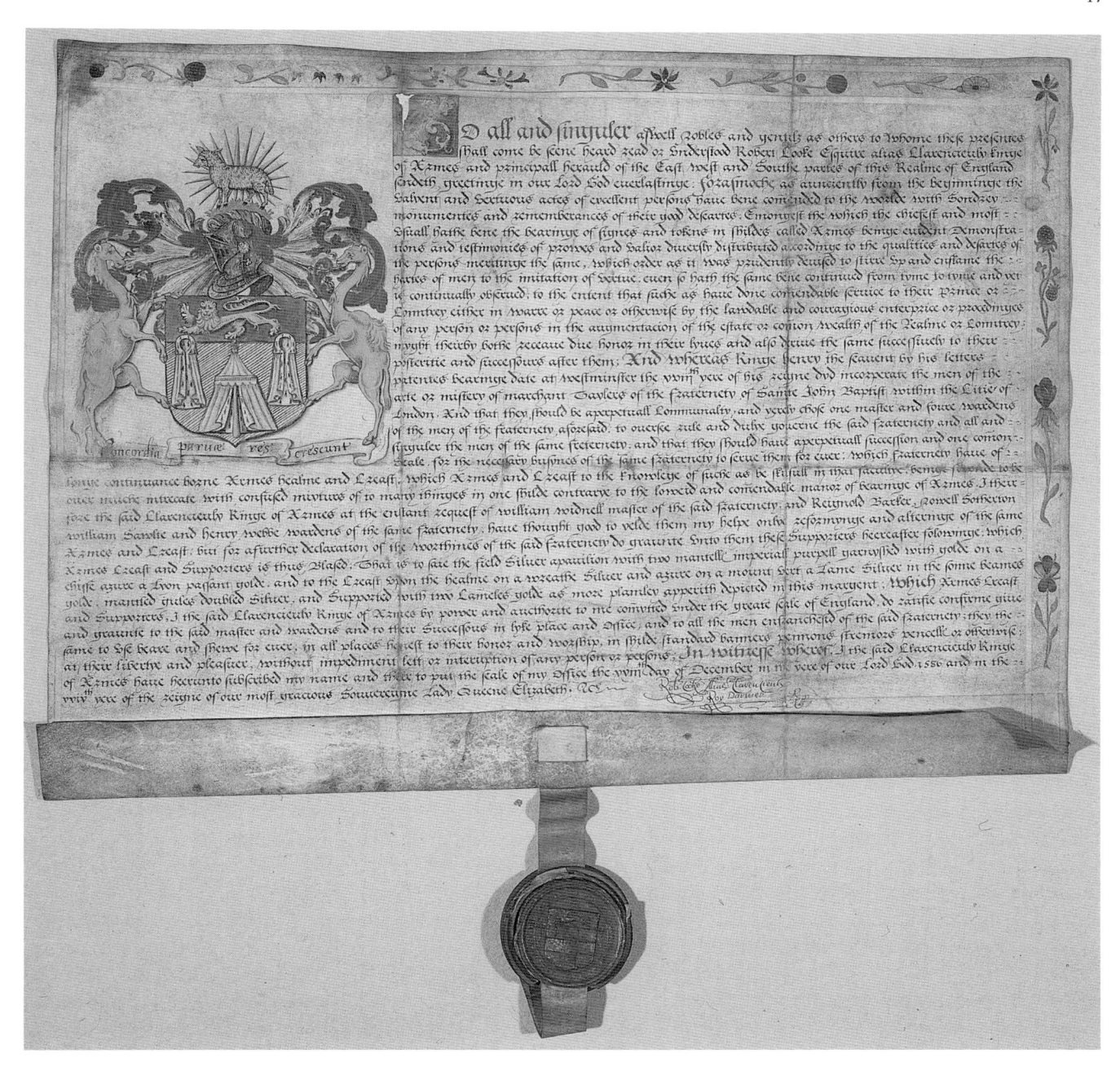

FIGURE 51. Grant of arms to the Company, 1586. The authority of the grant resides in the text; the illustration is for pure delight and can be varied as fashions change (see p. 149, and Col. Pl. XIA).

Merchant Taylors' Company

The Company does not appear to have profited.[26]

Some calls on the Company seem to smack of backstairs diplomacy. A request in February 1573 from the Bishop of London and from the Lord Mayor, Sir Lionel Duckett, must have been prompted by a higher authority. They asked that supplies of 'wyne and salte' should be sent to the embattled French Protestants, the Huguenots, in La Rochelle; it was suggested that the Merchant Taylors should advance £300, and William Kympton and Walter Fyshe were asked to enquire into the matter.[27] Some money was lent, but had eventually to be written off as a bad debt.

Harder than requests for money were demands for men. In the early years of Elizabeth's reign, France was torn by wars of religion. Loath though the Queen was to shed blood — or to spend money — it seemed an opportunity to regain Calais, lost a few years before in Mary's reign. That port was now strongly garrisoned by the French, but an expeditionary force of some 3,000 men, led by Sir Adrian Poynings and the Earl of Warwick, was despatched to hold Le Havre. Among them were thirty-five men, some of them Merchant Taylors, others — possibly — recruited in the Company's name.[28] Eleven of them were 'gonners' (gunners), armed with an arquebus, a morion, a sword and a dagger, and equipped with a white leather jerkin and a cloak. There were seventeen pikemen, who were each provided with a corslet (a light half-armour), pike, sword, dagger and cloak, and seven billmen, similarly equipped but with bills rather than pikes. The cloaks were hastily shaped and cut out in the Hall, and the men were assembled at 9 a.m. on 17 August 1562 outside Guildhall. Thirty-three men had already been conscripted from the Clothworkers' Company; they crossed from Newhaven on 19 September.[29]

The money to equip them was raised from seventy individual members, the Company's three knights, Thomas White, Thomas Offley and William Harper heading the list, with £3 13s. 4d. apiece, and Thomas Rowe and Harry Suckley close behind with £3 6s. 8d. each. Most of the rest gave 20s; the Bachelors' Company contributed £33 6s. 8d.

Through the winter and spring of 1562–63, the troops at Le Havre worked on the fortifications. Warwick was proud of his men, reporting that:

... this is as noble a garrison as ever served a prince. They fight like Hectors, labour like slaves, are worse fed than peasants, and are poorer than common beggars.[30]

But with spring, plague struck the force, and soon the men were dying at the rate of 200 a week. Reinforcements were despatched, but on 24 July 1563 control of the harbour was lost, and Warwick decided to parley. Honourable terms were granted, the remnants of the force hauled down the flag, and with it and their arms embarked for England. Once again, France controlled her own territory.

In July 1566 an ominous order arrived from the Mayor that six soldiers should be provided to serve in Ireland,[31] where there was rebellion under Shane O'Neill, and then in the late autumn of 1569 came the unexpected Rising in the North, prompted by religion and a desire to see the succession to the throne settled on the imprisoned Mary Queen of Scots. London groaned, but raised money, men and equipment; this time the Merchant Taylors had to send no fewer than sixty men with 'Calyvers'. They took £100 from the Company chest, and levied nearly another £100 on the livery.[32]

That emergency safely past, the City decided in March 1572 to demonstrate its loyalty by a great May Day Muster of 3,000 men at Greenwich.[33] The Company was to provide 188 men variously equipped with corslets, calivers, pikes, halberds and morions; there would be a rehearsal — one of many — for the muster on 25 April at seven o'clock in the morning at St George's Fields. At once everything was activity. John du Boys was to organize the collection of weapons; Robert Hulson, William Kympton and Nicholas Spencer were to assist the Master; William Merick and Thomas Wilford were to obtain gunpowder. Another letter from the Mayor assured the participants that there would be victuallers on hand at Greenwich on May Day, so that there would be no need to carry food supplies, only military equipment; flasks of gunpowder were to be filled and ready.

The Muster met with mixed success. Some companies, the Goldsmiths among them, were rehearsing frequently:

To these were appointed diverse valiant Captains, who, to traine them up in warlike feats, mustered them thrise everie weeke, sometimes in the Artillerie Yard, teaching the gunmen to handle their peaces, sometimes at the

Mile's-end, and in Saint George's Field, teaching them to skirmish, In which the skirmish on the Mile's-end the tenth of April, one of the gunners of the Goldsmith's Companie was shot in the side with a peece of a scouring sticke left in one of the calivers, whereof he died, and was buried the twelfe of Aprill in Paul's Church-yard; all the gunners marching from the Mile's-end in battell raie, shot off their calivers at his grave.

On Maie daie they mustered at Greenwich before the Queen's Majestie, where they shewed manie warlike feats; but were much hindered by the weather, which was all daie showring; they returned that present night to London, and were discharged the next morrow . . .[34]

It sounds like a typically unhelpful wet London day.

One royal relationship, however, gave the Company great satisfaction. In 1586, the College of Heralds made a visitation and inspection throughout the land of pedigrees and armorial bearings. The Merchant Taylors took advantage of this to secularize their coat of arms (Fig. 51). The religious emblems, Our Lady and Child with St John, vanished, robust camels became the supporters, and a motto, taken from Sallust, was added:

CONCORDIA PARVAE RES CRESCUNT.

The Company has followed that advice ever since.

NOTES

1. GL, MS 34010/1, p. 224.
2. These figures are taken from S. Rappaport's study of late sixteenth-century London, *Worlds within Worlds* (1989), pp. 88–90. See also G. D. Ramsay, *The English Woollen Industry, 1500–1750* (1982), and B. Dietz, *The Port and Trade of Early Elizabethan London: Documents* (London Record Society, vol. 8, 1972).
3. There are no Court minutes from this period; the lack has been supplied from the Clothworkers' archives. See Thomas Girtin, *The Golden Ram* (1958), pp. 29–31, 42–45.
4. GL, MS 34010/1, pp. 245–47, 252–54, 256–74, 276–80.
5. GL, MS 34010/1, pp. 248–52.
6. Today the term usually appears as *roving*.
7. GL, MS 34010/1, pp. 210–11.
8. GL, MS 34010/1, pp. 216–17.
9. The superb series of accounts running, with remarkably few breaks, from 1398 to the present day, yields much information about early Lord Mayors' pageants. Relevant entries were abstracted and published by Past Master R. T. D. Sayle in 1931 as *Lord Mayors' Pageants of the Company*.
10. GL, MS 34010/1, p. 316.
11. GL, MS 34010/1, pp. 41–42.
12. GL, MS 34010/1, pp. 166–67.
13. GL, MS 34010/1, pp. 671–72.
14. GL, MS 34010/2, fols 28^r–28^v. Some of the mouldy grain had been purchased from Denmark.
15. A detailed account of these negotiations has been published by Jean Imray. It is to be found in *The Royal Exchange*, ed. by Ann Saunders (1997), pp. 20–35.
16. GL, MS 34010/1, pp. 407, 410, 417–21.
17. GL, MS 34010/2, fols 56^v, 57^r, 59^r–59^v.
18. GL, MS 34010/1, p. 641.
19. GL, MS 34010/3, fol. 425^r.
20. See Clode, *Memorials* (1875), pp. 290–91.
21. See Janet Arnold, *Queen Elizabeth's Wardrobe Unlock'd* (Leeds, 1988), p. 177.
22. The church, St Andrew by the Wardrobe, takes its name from this department of state.
23. See Janet Arnold, *Lost from Her Majesties Back* (Costume Society, 1980).
24. GL, MS 34010/1, p. 34.
25. GL, MS 34010/1, pp. 314, 348, 353.
26. C. L'Estrange Ewen, *Lotteries and Sweepstakes* (1932); R. R. Sharpe, *London and the Kingdom*, 1 (1894), pp. 506–08.
27. GL, MS 34010/1, pp. 633–4, 637, 670; 34010/3, fols 411^r, 429^r, 429^v.
28. GL, MS 34010/1, pp. 9–11, 28–29.
29. T. Girtin, *The Golden Ram* (1958), p. 47.
30. Quoted in J. B. Black, *The Reign of Elizabeth*, 2nd edn (1959), pp. 56–62.
31. GL, MS 34010/1, p. 235.
32. GL, MS 34010/1, pp. 426–9, 432–5.
33. GL, MS 34010/1, pp. 568–75.
34. John Nichols, *The Progresses and Public Processions of Queen Elizabeth*, 3 vols (1823), 1, p. 296.

CHAPTER TEN

THE TURN OF THE CENTURY

> . . . now I remember,
> We met at Merchant-Taylors-hall, at dinner,
> In Thread-Needle Street.
>
> Ben Jonson, *The Magnetick Lady*
> Act V, Scene vii

It was hard to be a Londoner in the 1590s. Though the Spanish Armada had been repulsed, there was always the fear of another attempt at invasion from the Continent. The events of 1588 had cost enough in terms of men's lives, shipping and hard cash — the Queen had called on the City for a loan of £50,000, and the companies had been charged with the provision of sufficient gunpowder for the fleet — but the next decade would exact a still heavier toll.[1] There were three main problems — famine across Europe, plague, and an increasingly fragile political situation. London was by far the largest city in the kingdom, with a population of perhaps 200,000 compared with 15,000 in Bristol and Norwich and perhaps 20,000 in York. A city cannot feed itself; it must rely on its hinterland for supplies. For seven years, the harvests failed throughout Europe. The City Corporation did its best. It called on the Aldermen to fast twice a week and on the companies to set aside their feasts and dinners. It laid special taxes on all the larger public buildings. It set up granaries and levied contributions to fill them with grain for distribution to the poor. The Company's figures for Corn Money, abstracted from the volumes of accounts, tell the tale of a terrible decade more clearly than any words.

In 1586–87, the Company had contributed £450 7s. 3d.; the next year the figure had risen to £737 11s. 1d. Then it fell back for three years, but in 1591–92 it was above £500, with low receipts in the treasury, while in 1596–97 and 1597–98 the call was for £1,066 7s. 5d. and £938 14s. 11d., and in each of the next three years above £500 was required. It is not clear how the Company contrived to meet such demands, but somehow the money was raised and some comfort was given to the poorest. Harvests improved in the new century, but the 1590s remained a grim memory.[2]

One set of documents which tells the tale of those hard years is the inventories of the possessions of defaulting mercantile debtors, now held in the Public Record Office. Small businesses were particularly hard hit. A recent analysis of these records shows that more clothworkers, drapers, haberdashers and tailors were affected than any other of the craft-related companies.[3]

When the crops failed, sections of the rural population trailed into the capital, hoping to find some support, charity, human kindness there. Plague and disease, ever present, throve on the overcrowding. Even as early as September 1563, the Clerk was writing in the minutes that the calling over of the livery was omitted for danger of plague, 'that so sore here contynuethe amongeste us whiche God for his Chryste sake ceasse yt and withdrawe his heavye wrathe frome us. Amen.' A generation later, the city was larger and the mortality higher.

To dearth, sickness and overcrowding we must add the political uncertainty of the times. The Queen was old — there was no denying it — and the succession was uncertain. Elizabeth might paint her face, pad out her sagging cheeks — she had lost her teeth long ago — wear wigs and jewels and magnificent gowns made by Walter Fyshe and William Jones, while the whole livery was ready to provide the Queen with an escort within London. The Court might celebrate her birthday each November with fantastical joustings which were almost masquerades, and the citizens might throng the tilt-yard of Whitehall Palace to marvel and cheer, but everyone knew, though they

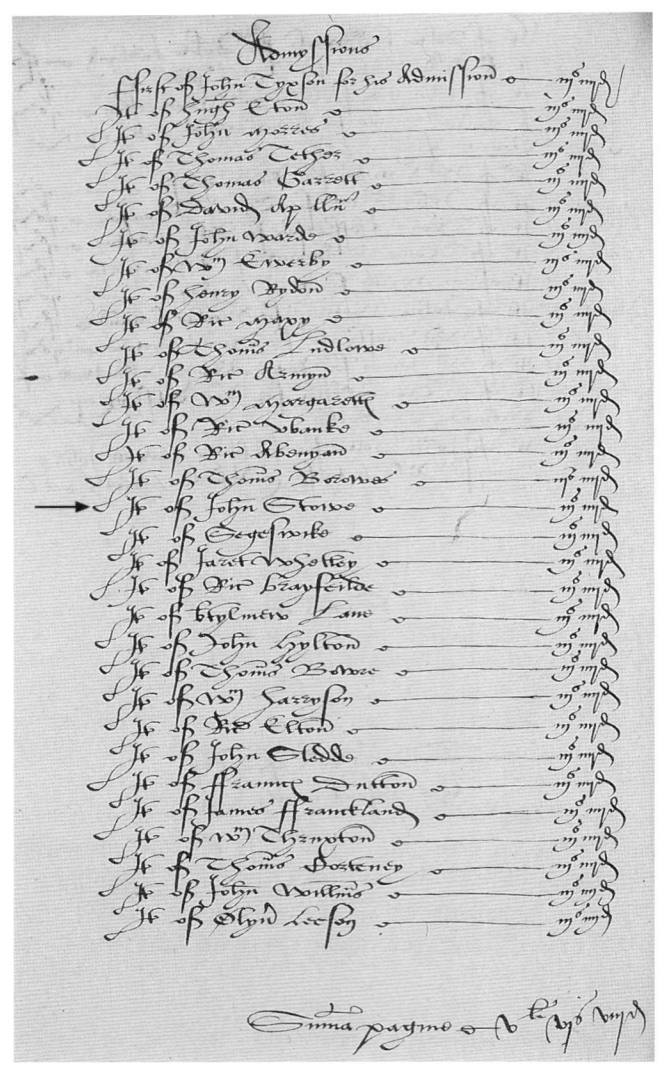

FIGURE 52. The freedom entry for John Stow.
Guildhall Library, MS 34048/4, fol. 79

— John Stow the chronicler,[4] John Speed the cartographer, and William Fleetwood, Recorder of the City.

Stow was probably born in 1525, the eldest son of Thomas Stow, tallow chandler and supplier of candles to St Michael Cornhill. Thomas lived in that parish and he and his wife were buried in its 'little green churchyard' alongside earlier generations of the family. John did not follow his father's craft, but was apprenticed to John Bulley and admitted to the freedom of the Merchant Taylors' Company on 25 November 1547 (Fig. 52). Not long after, he set up shop in Aldgate, by the well lying between Leadenhall and Fenchurch Streets, and it was on the pavement before his house that he witnessed and recorded the summary execution of the Bailiff of Romford, who was said to have spoken treasonous might not say it, that Death was edging ever nearer towards Gloriana. The war in Ireland, the back door into England from the Continent, and the rebellion of the Earl of Essex in 1601, when he felt that his efforts in the sister-island were under-valued, all added to the uneasiness of the capital, and maimed soldiers from the Irish and European wars increased the city's overcrowding.

THREE EMINENT BRETHREN

Amidst all this unrest, the Company could boast of three exceptional men among its membership

FIGURE 53. John Stow.
Guildhall Library

words in those uncertain times, but who died asserting his innocence.

Stow's wife's name was Elizabeth — we do not know her maiden name — and by her he had three daughters; he earned their living with his needle. Throughout his life, he remained a member of the Bachelors' guild; he was never admitted to the livery and so never held office in the Company, though as we have seen, he participated enthusiastically in the Lord Mayors' pageants for Harper and Lee. He took his younger brother, another Thomas like their father, as apprentice.

Stow seems to have led a troubled life, both professionally and domestically. He fell out with his brother over their mother's will. She, poor soul, went in her widowhood to live with Thomas and his wife. One day in the summer of 1568, she visited John and, over the 'best ale and bread and a cold leg of mutton', they gossiped unwisely about Thomas's wife, John lamenting that his brother was 'matched with a harlot'. When old Mrs Stow returned home, Thomas and his wife interrogated her to know all that had passed and when they heard John's unwise remarks, they forced the old woman to change her will, leaving a mere £5 to John, but £10 to each of her other children and making Thomas beneficiary of the remainder of her goods. Family bitterness ensued but the fragmentary surviving documents deny us the end of the story.

Soon afterwards, possibly egged on by a neighbour, William Ditcher alias Tetforde became convinced that Stow had complained to the wardmote that Ditcher was setting up his featherbed-frames in the open street. Though assured that Stow had done no such thing, Ditcher and his wife took to shouting abuse 'too shameful and slanderous to be spoken', to throwing tiles and stones at Stow's apprentice, to accusing Stow's wife of having had two children out of wedlock, and to calling Stow 'prick louse knave, beggarly knave, rascal knave, villain and lying knave, adding more over that the said John hath made a chronicle of lies'. This last insult must have been especially painful; 'prick-louse' was a common coarse epithet for a tailor, but there is nothing more hurtful to a writer than to have his books abused. At least this document tells us that Stow was still busy at his craft after he had begun to write and publish. Once again, the surviving evidence is fragmentary, but a third controversy concerning the Stow family, recorded in the Court minutes for 20 October 1570, has a more satisfactory ending. Thomas Holmes's wife had slandered Mrs Thomas Stow, the unkind daughter-in-law, with 'undesent and unseemly words'; she was made to apologize publicly before the Court assembled in the Hall, where Mrs Stow forgave her and Holmes was required to pay Thomas Stow 20s. as compensation for the wrong done. We have here another example of the Court's authority extending to quarrelling wives.

With such professional and domestic problems, it is not surprising that John Stow turned to books and the past for solace and stimulation. Matthew Parker, Archbishop of Canterbury, encouraged him in his studies and in 1561 he prepared a new edition of Chaucer's *Works*. Four years later he published *A Summarie of Englyshe Chronicles*, which embroiled him in argument with the antiquary Richard Grafton. The *Summarie* ran through several editions and abridgements, and was followed by *The Annales of England* in 1592. The author presented a copy to the Company 'as a small monument . . . in token of his thankfulness'.

But even these literary pursuits brought him trouble. Naturally enough, Stow accumulated books, and the range of his library was broad. In an age when the unlucky Bailiff of Romford was not the only man to be hanged for a chance remark, Stow's enquiring mind was enough for him to be regarded with suspicion. In January 1569, the Spanish Ambassador circulated a manifesto defending the conduct of the Duke of Alva in the Netherlands; Stow possessed two copies, and was required to explain himself to the Lord Mayor. A month later, the Bishop of London ordered that his house should be searched, where his library was found to hold 'a greate sorte of old written English Chronicles both in parchement and in paper, som long, som shorte'. The inspectors — theological thought-police — also found 'old phantasticall popishe bokes' and — more dangerously — recent recusant printing brought in from the Continent. However, the authorities do not seem to have pursued the matter, though a year later, in 1570, Stow was hauled before the Ecclesiastical Commissioners on seventeen trumped-up charges which a servant, dismissed for dishonesty, had brought against him. Stow refuted the accusations and went free.

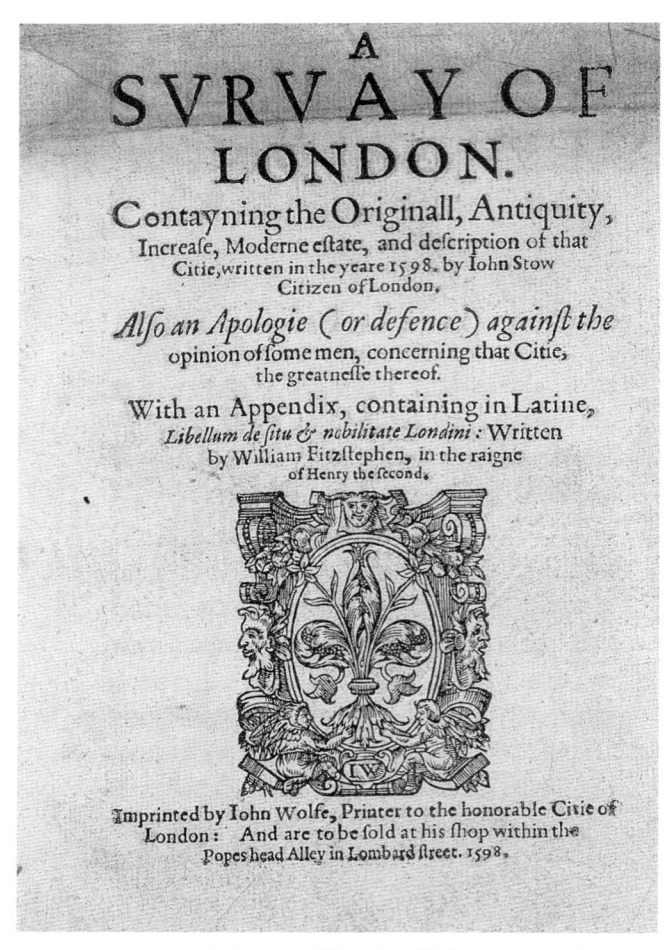

FIGURE 54. *A Survay of London*. Title-page of John Stow's masterpiece. First published in 1598, a second, definitive edition appeared in 1603.
Merchant Taylors' Company

For most writers, to live by the pen alone is to live leanly. The Company recognized this, and in 1578–79 we find a first reference in the Company accounts to a grant of £4 a year to Stow. In 1593, this sum was doubled through the generosity of Robert Dowe, Master in 1578, and this continued till 1600 when the Company raised the overall figure to £10 a year. Stow had good reason to give a copy of his *Annales* to the Merchant Taylors.

Thus supported, as old age advanced on him, Stow began his masterpiece, *A Survey of London* (Fig. 54). It was published in 1598 — the year before the Globe Theatre opened in Southwark — with a second edition following in 1603. It is an extraordinary work. Starting with some general chapters on the antiquity of London, on its water supply and geographical position, and on the 'Honour of Citizens and worthines of men in the same', he goes on to describe it in detail, ward by ward and street by street, so that as we read it we are transported back to the sixteenth-century City. No other European capital has received such loving examination. And Stow not only tells us about what he could see as he walked the streets in the 1590s; at the end of a long life, he packs in the contents of an unusually retentive memory, and adds tales and details that he was told by his grandparents' generation. As we read him, we can see London changing; let one example suffice — he is describing the Minories near the Tower where, before the Reformation, there had been a Convent of the Sorores Minores or Poor Clares:

By this time he had given up tailoring and was living by his pen; before long, he and his wife moved to a house in Lime Street ward, near to the Leadenhall and St Andrew Undershaft church. He had an established reputation among his fellow-citizens and in particular, as we shall see, within his own Company. He was invited to join the original Society of Antiquaries, founded by Archbishop Parker in 1571, and there he found the companionship of like-minded men such as William Camden, Sir Robert Cotton and William Lambarde, the historian of Kent; men who had been to university, who had travelled abroad, who were recognized as scholars, and who treated him, a London craftsman, as their peer and equal.

A farme by the Minories wherein hath beene sold 3. pints of milke for one halfe pennie in memorie of men liuing.

Neare adioyning to this Abbey on the South side thereof, was sometime a Farme belonging to the said Nunrie, at the which Farme I my selfe in my youth haue fetched many a halfe pennie worth of Milke, and neuer had lesse than three Ale pints for a half-pennie in the Sommer, nor lesse than one Ale quart for a halfe-pennie in the Winter, always hote from the Kine, as the same was milked and strained. One *Trolop*, and afterwardes *Goodman*, were the Farmers there, and had thirtie or fortie Kine to the paile. *Goodmans* sonne being heyre to his fathers purchase, let out the ground first for grazing of horse, and then for garden plots, and liued like a Gentleman thereby.

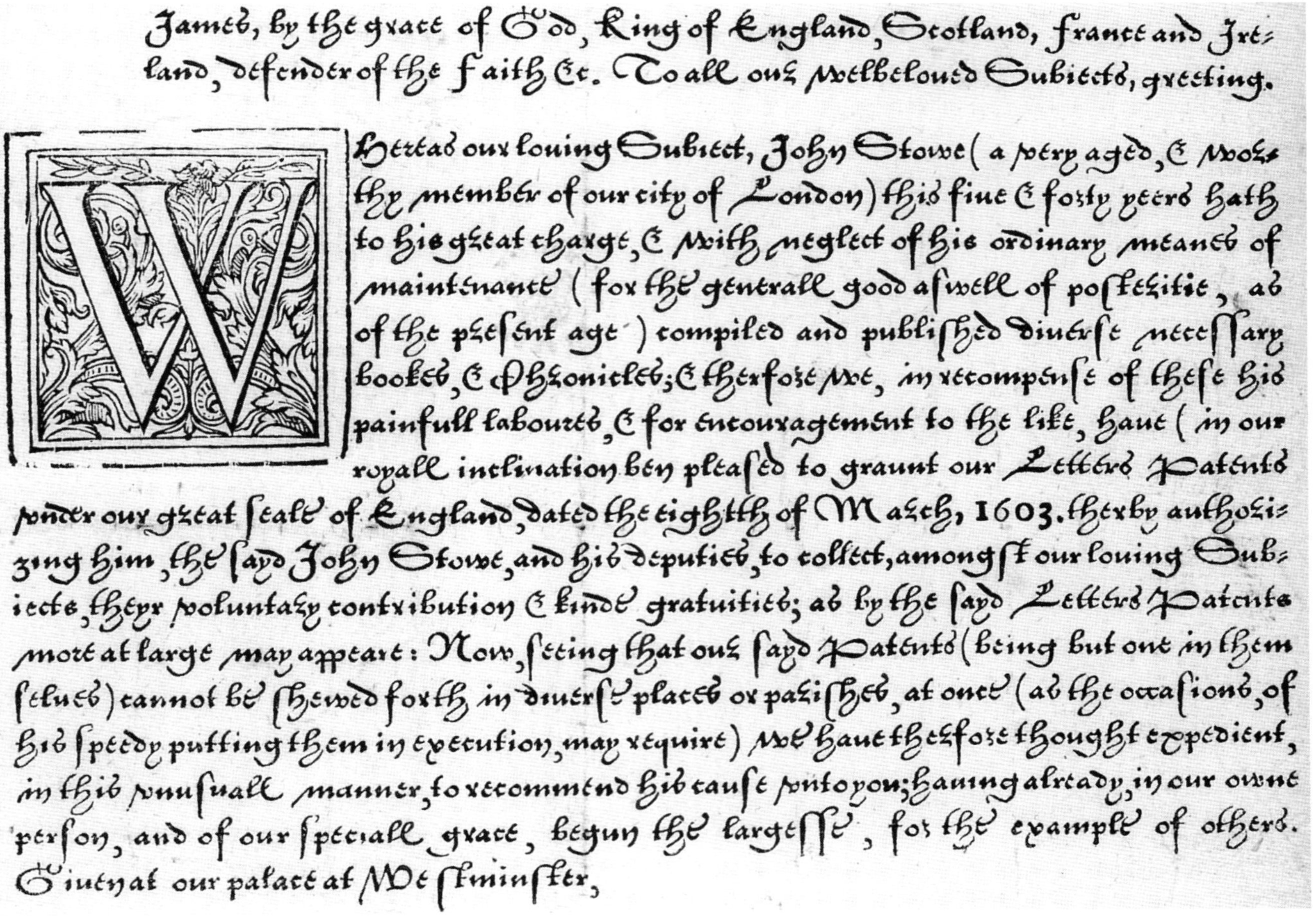

THE TURN OF THE CENTURY

> James, by the grace of God, King of England, Scotland, France and Ireland, defender of the faith &c. To all our welbeloued Subiects, greeting.
>
> Wheras our louing Subiect, John Stowe (a very aged, & worthy member of our city of London) this fiue & forty yeeres hath to his great charge, & with neglect of his ordinary meanes of maintenance (for the generall good aswell of posteritie, as of the present age) compiled and publiſhed diuerſe necessary bookes, & Chronicles; & therfore we, in recompenſe of theſe his painfull labours, & for encouragement to the like, haue (in our royall inclination) ben pleaſed to graunt our Letters Patents vnder our great ſeale of England, dated the eighth of March, 1603, therby authoriſing him, the ſayd John Stowe, and his deputies, to collect, amongſt our louing Subiectes, theyr voluntary contribution & kinde gratuities; as by the ſayd Letters Patents more at large may appeare: Now, ſeeing that our ſayd Patents (being but one in them ſelues) cannot be ſhewed forth in diuerſ places or pariſhes, at once (as the occaſions of his ſpeedy putting them in execution, may require) we haue therefore thought expedient, in this vnusuall manner, to recommend his cauſe vnto you; hauing already, in our owne perſon, and of our ſpeciall grace, begun the largeſſe, for the example of others. Giuen at our palace at Westminſter,

FIGURE 55. John Stow's begging licence.
British Library, Harleian MS 367, fol. 10

Stow writes with tenderness of a world that was changing as he wrote; we may guess that his sympathies lay with the old religion. He was not the only Merchant Taylor to regard the new century with wariness; on page 159 of the fourth volume of Court minutes, at the entry for 21 March 1603, the Clerk Richard Langley[5] wrote

Here endeth all the Courtes that were kept in the lief tyme of our late noble Queene (of famous memory) Queene Elizabeth

and everyone waited to see what would come next.

For Stow, it was going to be disappointment. He petitioned the new King for support and was rewarded, not with an additional pension, however small, but with a licence to beg (Fig. 55); the parishioners of St Mary Woolnoth collected 7s. 10d. for the old man. The Company continued its financial support until his death on 5 April 1605,[6] when Thomas Berry began to receive alms in Stow's place. His position as London's chronicler was taken up by Edmund Howes, whom the Company encouraged with a grant of £10 in February 1608.

Then a surprising thing happened. Stow's widow Elizabeth erected a handsome monument to her husband in St Andrew Undershaft, their parish church (Fig. 56). Search the records as we may, there is no mention of it among the Company's archives. We do not know whether the Stows had taken up residence in the almshouse (wives might accompany their husbands), or whether they still lived on in their own dwelling near the Leadenhall, in which case she might have been able to raise the capital to

FIGURE 56. John Stow's monument, St Andrew Undershaft.
National Monuments Record, English Heritage

commission such a work. It is a wonderful monument. A full-length marble figure of the antiquary sits at his desk in a stone niche, writing away, busy perhaps with his survey of the city he loved so well. He wears a gown and a ruff, and is intent on what he is doing.

The identity of the sculptor responsible for this handsome work is a mystery. One yearns to attribute it to Nicholas Stone, who carved John Donne's monument in St Paul's Cathedral, but Stone was abroad in Flanders, perfecting his skills as a master craftsman, at the time when Stow's memorial was probably set up, and there is no reference to it either in his Journal or in his Account Book.[7] Had it been he, the charge would have been something over £50. We will say more of the monument's place in the Company's later history in a future chapter.

One of Stow's younger contemporaries was John Speed, antiquary and cartographer, probably born in 1552 (Fig. 57).[8] His father was a tailor, being admitted to the Company on 5 April 1556; he kept a shop in St Paul's Churchyard and his son was apprenticed to him, being made free and admitted to the Company on 10 September 1580. He leased property from the Company, built on it, speculated with it and prospered. In his new-found leisure, he set to drawing maps, presenting some to the Queen in 1598 and three others to the Company in 1600. One of these was probably *The Invasions of England and Ireland with all their Civil Wars since the Conquest*, and another may well have been the outsize version of a similar map which gives the whole of southern Scotland as well. The Court immediately instructed that curtains should be made to hang before the maps, 'of such stuffe as they shall thinke fitt and convenient'. This precaution, coupled with the reference in the 1609 Inventory, to '3 Great Mapps in 3 great Frames, with three large Silk Curtains to them', suggest that the maps were manuscript water-colour drawings, Speed's cherished originals. Not long after, Speed begged the Company for a lease of a house in Fenchurch Street but, though the Court set down that he was a man whom they

doe much respect . . . because he is a man of very rare and ingenious capacitie in drawing and setting fourth of mappes and genealogies and other very excellent invencions,

they were unable to gratify him since the house had been bespoken by the Queen herself for Thomas Lovell. However, through the good offices, it was said, of Sir Fulk Greville, Speed was granted a lease of part of the prebendal estate of Mora, which the Company held from St Paul's Cathedral; he had already enjoyed, since 1598, a post in the Customs House. Speed recognized his obligations; in the Introduction to his *Theatre of Great Britain* (1611), he writes that Greville's patronage had set 'this hand free from the daily imployments of a manuall trade, giving it full liberty thus to express the inclination of my mind'.

By his wife Susanna he had eighteen children, twelve sons and six daughters. The eldest boy, William, had a free place at the Company's school,[9] as did another son, John, who went on to St John's College, was admitted to Gray's Inn and, when he died, was buried in St John's College chapel.

The third of our trio is William Fleetwood (1535?–94), Recorder of London.[10] The son of Robert Fleetwood, he studied at Brasenose College but left Oxford without a degree, transferring his studies to the Middle Temple. On 21 June 1557, he was admitted to the Company by patrimony. This admission is significant, indicating that the Merchant Taylors were no longer solely a craft guild, but that a man might follow what profession he might choose, once he was a freeman of the City. Fleetwood sat as MP for Marlborough in the last Parliament of Mary's reign, and for Lancaster in the first two of Elizabeth's. In 1571 he became Recorder of London, a high and honourable post which continues to this day; it was said that he achieved it through the influence of the Earl of Leicester, but it is certain that for twenty years he fulfilled his office with integrity, with great learning, and with exceptional zeal for law and order.

His relationship with the Company was most friendly. In the summer of 1563, he was chosen as Reader of the Middle Temple. This would entail much entertaining, so the Company helpfully voted him a hogshead of wine. When the Clothworkers' Company sought, in 1566, to bring a Bill to Parliament whereby all those concerned with clothmaking must belong to their company, Fleetwood prepared the Merchant Taylors' answer to the suit. He read it out to the Master, Wardens and Assistants on 23 November 1566, and it

> was of all the foresaide assystantes well lyked and thereupon agreed that [it be presented] as there full and absolute answer.[11]

It was successful, and the Company continued to number clothworkers as well as tailors and general merchants among its membership.

The Company turned again to Fleetwood for advice when St John's College, pleading poverty and under-endowment, was unwilling to give the full number of free places to pupils at Merchant Taylors' School. Twice, in March 1572 and April 1573, Fleetwood was one of a deputation to the Master of the Rolls, and in the end all matters were settled cheerfully between the school and the college.

In all his undertakings, Fleetwood would have had a staunch ally in a fellow Merchant Taylor, Robert Smith, who had come to London from Market Harborough soon after the middle of the century and who, by the 1570s, was serving Robert Hodgeson, an attorney of the Mayor's Court and a member of the Company.[12] Smith married Mary Robins, heiress to Hodgeson's estate, was made free of the Merchant Taylors despite having married before his apprenticeship was completed, and went on to become City Solicitor and, at last, Comptroller of the Chamber. In July 1580, he proposed and undertook a reorganization of the City's records, labouring away for thirty years at calendars and indexes which would have been of great usefulness to Fleetwood. It is good to know that Smith, who seems to have come from a poverty-stricken background, became a rich man, a director of the Virginia Company, and, in the best Merchant Taylor tradition, founded a school in his home town which still survives.

During his Recordership, Fleetwood certainly pursued his duties vigorously. A series of letters and reports to Lord Burghley, preserved at Hatfield, shows how severely — one might say harshly — he pursued the 'roogs' and 'strumpets' who crowded the streets of London. He ordered floggings, and any beggar or vagrant was sent back to his home parish, if it could be proved that the poor wretch came from outside the City. On one occasion, in his zeal, he over-reached himself. The Charterhouse was then the property of Philip, Earl of Arundel, who had inherited it on the execution of his father, the Catholic Duke of Norfolk. Arundel had leased the buildings to the Portuguese Ambassador, who was within his rights to have Mass celebrated in his own chapel for himself and for members of his staff. Word went round that London citizens went secretly there to hear the old service which they loved. Fleetwood determined to make an example. The Senior Sheriff was William Kympton, another Merchant Taylor, and the two went to the Charterhouse with a strong guard one night in November 1576. The Portuguese door-keeper refused them entrance and when Fleetwood tried to insist on his authority, slammed the metal gate shut on the Recorder's leg, bruising him sorely thereby. The rest of the party forced their way in, and a number of the congregation were conveyed to the Fleet prison for hearing Mass. What Fleetwood had forgotten — or perhaps did not know — was that such behaviour constituted a trespass on diplomatic property, and the Queen was very angry indeed.

Perhaps because of this incident, the highest legal offices eluded Fleetwood, and he retired in 1591 with a pension of £100 per year granted by the City Corporation. He settled in Great Missenden in Buckinghamshire, and passed his old age agreeably enough. Back in 1583, he had presented the Lords of the Council with a treatise on how all London's ills could be remedied: no new houses were to be built, so that the City might grow no larger. There should be fewer ale-houses, and strict regulation of temporary market buildings and stalls. The apprenticeship system needed reformation, with more difficult terms of entry, and admittance to the freedom by redemption was to be restricted severely — for too long it had been a perquisite which a great lord could demand as a reward for a servant at no cost to himself. Those sick of the plague should be placed in infirmaries, and all open spaces about the City should be preserved as open ground for fresh air and recreation for the citizens. There have always been plans for an ideal London.

The honour of Queen's Serjeant was conferred on him in 1592, and he presented to the City a book of legal judgments, preserved to this day in the Corporation of London Records Office where it is known as Liber Fleetwood. He died at his home in Noble Street on 28 February 1594, but was buried in Great Missenden.

FEASTING THE KING

The last decades of the sixteenth century had not been an easy time for the Company, but with the turn of 1600 men hoped things would improve. There had not been a Merchant Taylor as Lord Mayor for thirty-four years, but in 1602 Sir Robert Lee was called to the highest office. His was a magnificent and costly pageant (see p. 142–43), and the ship made by 'Mr Hearne the paynter' to be carried through the streets had, at the end of the day, been strung up to the roof in the Company's Hall, at a cost of 30s., the work being carried out by Mr Thornton and his men (Col. Pl. XVIIB). That ship was soon going to be useful.

The next Merchant Taylor to be Lord Mayor was Sir Leonard Halliday — his name gave opportunity for punning on holy-day and holiday. His was an especially significant mayoralty, for by 1605, not only did England have a new King but the country was now to be ruled by a new dynasty and — though no one could see into the future on that rain-beaten November day in 1605 — the relationship between that dynasty and the City of London was going to be of paramount importance.

All possible pains were taken with the planning of Halliday's pageant. Anthony Munday wrote *The Triumphs of Re-united Britania*, which told how the Trojan Brutus came to Albion, renamed the island Britain, and divided it between his three sons, Locrine, Camber and Albanact, thus creating the kingdoms of England, Wales and Scotland. Now these kingdoms were reunited in the person of the new monarch, James. The pageant concluded with a recital of all the previous kings who had honoured the Merchant Taylors by joining the brethren, and a hope that James might do likewise:

> PHEME
> But sacred Lady, deigne me so much grace,
> As tell me, why that seat is vnsupplied,
> Being the most eminent and chiefest place,
> With State, with Crowne and Scepter dignified?
>
> EPIMELEIA
> Haue our discourses *(Pheme)* let thee know,
> That seauen Kings haue borne free brethrens name,
> Of this Societie, and may not time bestow
> an eight, when Heauen shall so appoint the same?
>
> PHEME
> I finde recorded in my Register,
> Seauen Kings haue honord this Society:
> Fourteene great Dukes did willingly prefer,
> Their loue and kindnesse to this Company,
> Threescore eight Lords declarde like amitie,
> tearming themselues all brethren of this band,
> The verie worthiest Lordes in all the Land.
>
> Three Dukes, three Earles, foure Lords of Noble name
> all in one years did ioyne in Brother-hood:
>
> I finde beside great Lords from France there came
> To hold like league, and do them any good:
>
> Yet no imbasing to their heigth in bloud:
> For they accounted honor then most hie,
> When it was held vp by communitie.

The procession had to be repeated a second time since the rain was torrential — the only time that a Lord Mayor's Show has been given a second performance.

The delicate invitation of the crowned but empty chair was soon to be accepted. On 12 June 1607, James I dined with the Lord Mayor, Sir James Watt, a Clothworker, and accepted membership of that company. A fortnight later, on 27 June, the King announced his intention of dining with the Merchant Taylors, when they kept their Election Feast on 16 July. The notice was short; from thereafter, it was all frantic preparation and it was fortunate that the Company was well provided with table linen since, in the previous year, a 'Drawer' had been paid 11s. to design a 'Holy Lambe' to be embroidered, and Mrs Hurdis, the Beadle's wife, had been paid £3 4s. 4d. for hemming and for working the lamb on each of twenty-five and a half dozen 'Damask and Diaper napkins', with a further 10s. for hemming and marking 'three long clothes for the hall, three towells and three cowchers, and six breaking board clothes'.

Otherwise it was all scurry and bustle. Anything up to three hundred guests might be expected — this was corporate entertainment on the grandest scale. Sir John Swinnerton was Master, with Richard Wright, Andrew Osborne, Edward Atkinson and William Albany as his Wardens — all men of experience; those who would be their successors were John Johnson as Master with Thomas Owen, Richard Scales, John Wooller and Randulph Woolley. A special committee was appointed consisting of the current officers, the four Merchant Taylor aldermen, Baron Sotherton, John Vernon and 'all the old Masters', 'to determyne, direct and appoynte all matters concerninge the said greate and noble entertaynement'. Entertainment on such a scale and of such dignity required professional guidance, so 'Lansdale the Lord Maior's Cater, and Sotherne, one of the Sheriffs' Caters' were called in to provide it.

The first concern was to prepare the Hall. The body of it was handsome enough, but the little separate chamber at the west end which had been used by earlier monarchs when they visited the Company, it being the custom for kings to dine in private, needed modernizing and the insertion of a new large window. It was worth spending money on the garden for such an occasion, and it was thought advisable to raise the brick wall on the side adjoining 'the Taverne', presumably one of those in Finch Lane, 'to take away the prospect of such as use to walke upon the leades of the Taverne and thereby woulde overlooke the Garden'. With such a gathering, there would be shortage of equipment, and various of the livery were charged with the hire of plate, glasses, ewers, chairs, cushions and kitchen equipment. They were exhorted to be as economical as possible; 'it is not doubted but they will deale carefully and frugally', runs the minute. In the end, the plate cost £25 14s. 9d. and the pewter £9 15s. 6d.; the Lord Chamberlain was prevailed upon to lend the royal silver vessel for His Majesty's own use.

Entertainment must be provided for the guests. Sir John Swinnerton was

> entreated to conferr with Mr. Benjamin Johnson the Poet aboute a speeche to be made to welcome His Majestie, and for musique and other inventions which maye give likeing and delight to His Majestie

since they doubted whether 'their Schoolmaster and Schollers be not acquainted with such kinde of Entertainements'. Jonson did well out of it, being paid £20 for his verses; Dr John Bull, Gresham Professor of Music, and Nathaniel Giles, Master of the Chapel Royal, gave their services free of charge.

Then there was the crucial, the all-important matter of the food. The Company's chef, Henry Beamond or Beamont, was assisted by thirty-two cooks and forty-six labourers; the Great Kitchen is large, but it must have seemed over-crowded. There was £40 14s. worth of beef to be roasted, along with fourteen bucks, presented by the Wardens and by the Prince of Wales, who was also invited. The fish cost £22 19s. 4d., the poultry, including ten owls for a pie, was £104 9s. 3d., the groceries came to £32 9s. 10d. and the greengroceries to £30 2s. 8d., including 15s. 1d. for 'herbs and nosegaies', and £2 10s. 0d. for 60 lb of potatoes at 10d. a pound; these had only been introduced into this country a few years before from South America, and so were a rare and costly delicacy. One thousand three hundred eggs were used, costing £2 3s. 4d. at 3s. 4d. per hundred. The bill for fuel amounted to £7 7s. 8d. The wine, costing £61 12s. 7d., was the responsibility of Mathias

FIGURE 57. John Speed, cartographer and Merchant Taylor.
Guildhall Library

Springham, one of the livery, who also laid out £12 9s. on beer and £16 7s. 6d. on hire of butlers. Waiting at table was to be the duty of the younger and more 'personable' members of the Company, but thirty-six professional waiters had to be engaged at 4s. each, so the total for that came to £7 4s. 0d.[13]

An awkward question of protocol then arose. Should the Lord Mayor and all the Aldermen with their ladies be invited as well? The Court of Assistants met specially on 9 July to deliberate the matter:

severall delyvered their conceite and opynions, some holdinge opinion that it would be an honour and grace to the Company to see soe many sitt togeather in their Scarlet Robes: other being of opynion that it would much derogate from the private Companie who should be at the whole charge, and soe make it seeme as an entertainment done at the charge of the whole Cytty.

Some feared that it would offend the noble guests if the Lord Mayor were entertained in a proper manner, while there were others

houlding it the duty of us citizens to have a very special care to give satisfaccon and preferr the Governours of the Cytty.

However, some of the Merchant Taylors had suspicious minds. The Lord Mayor was a Clothworker; that company had already fêted His Majesty in the last month, when James had been graciously pleased to become a Brother of the company. A Clothworker Lord Mayor would

doe his endeavour to crosse our Companie of that honour which wee understand the Prince's Highness meaneth to conferr upon our Company.

In the end, a vote was taken and it was decided not to invite the Corporation.

This was an insult that could not be passed over, and on 15 July the Recorder arrived with 'many perswasive speeches' to urge the Company to change its mind, but in vain. Another vote was taken, 'and soe by scruteny yt was agreed that they should not be invyted at this tyme'.

The great day, 16 July, arrived. 'The Companie made great haste to Church to the Sermon', which, since there was plague near to St Michael Cornhill, was given in St Helen Bishopsgate. The preacher was Dr Buckeridge, the President of St John's College and a relative of Sir Thomas White; he finished 'in convenient time' and the Company hurried to the Hall to make sure that all was ready. To their surprise, the Lord Mayor and all the Aldermen were there before them, and insisted on staying till the King and Prince arrived — the Queen did not come. They joined in the welcome at the gate, where the Lord Mayor ceremoniously delivered up his sword to the King, and then withdrew, having made their discontent obvious. Then Swinnerton reasserted himself as host and led the King through the garden into the Hall where

at the upper end of the Hall there was sett a Chayre of State where his Majestie satt and viewed the Hall, and

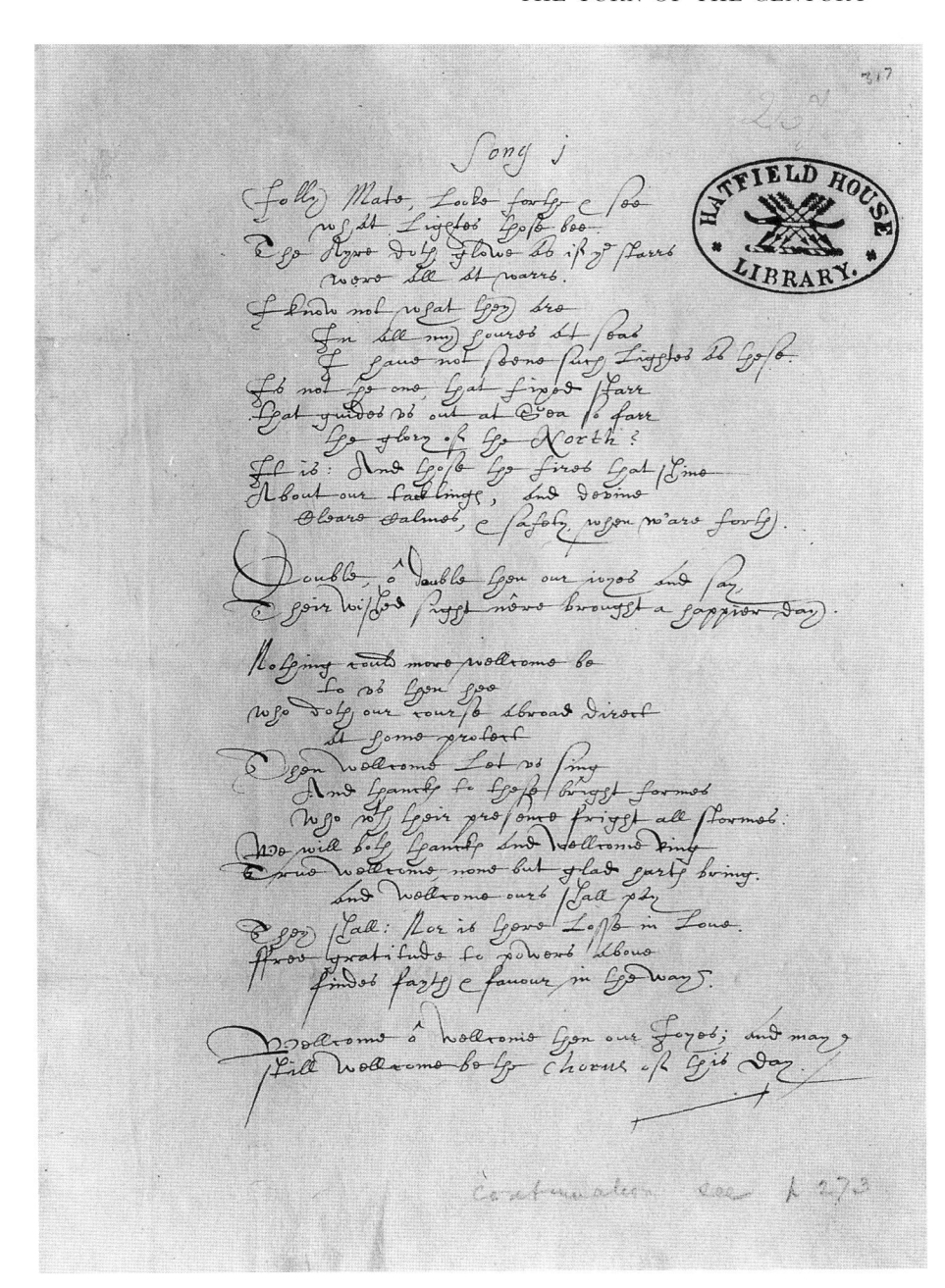

FIGURE 58. Song of salutation to James I, when the Company entertained the monarch in their own Hall. Written for the occasion by Ben Jonson, the King was so delighted by it that it had to be repeated again and again.

Hatfield House, by kind permission of the present Marquess of Salisbury

a very proper Child, well spoken, being clothed like an angell of gladness with a Taper of Ffrankincense burning in his hand, delivered a short speech contayning xviii verses, devised by Mr. Ben. Johnson the Poet, which pleased his Majestie marvelously well.

The child, John Rise, was rewarded with 5s., while Mr Hemmyngs for his direction of the boy received £2. We may assume that this was the John Hemming of Burbage's Company at the Globe who, with Henry Condell, gathered together and published Shakespeare's plays in the first folio edition. The entertainment continued with music:

Upon either side of the Hall in the Windowe neere the upper end were Gallories or Seates made for Musique, in either of which were seaven singular choice musicions playing on their Lutes.

Previously, the pageant ship had been hung from the rafters of the Hall, and from it 'three rare men and very skilful sung to his Majestie'. They were John Allen, who received £4, Thomas Lupo, His Majesty's Musician, and John Richards; the two latter had £3 each and the trio were considered to have 'exacted unreasonable somes [sums]' of the Company.

Meanwhile, in the minstrels' gallery at the far end of the Hall, the wind instruments were doing their best:

over the skreene, cornets and loud musique wherein it is to be remembered that the multitude and noyse was so greate that the lutes nor songs coulde hardly be heard or understoode.

The clamour must have been deafening, and it did not cease even when James went up into the King's Chamber, probably hoping to dine in peace, for Dr John Bull serenaded him throughout on 'a very rich paier of Organs' hired from the Rucker family, celebrated makers of musical instruments, while in the Hall Nathaniel Giles, Master of the Chapel Royal, had brought the Children of the Chapel Royal with him to the Hall, and their young, sweet voices delighted the Company.

When James had dined, Swinnerton and his Wardens came to the little upper room and presented the King with a 'faier purse wherein was one hundreth pounds in gould', and a roll listing all those who had been chosen honorary members of the Company. Since these included seven kings, one queen, and an impressive list of prelates, nobles and other dignitaries, Richard Langley, the Company's Clerk, must have spent a satisfactorily busy time searching for names. Perhaps the work that John Stow put into the preparations for Lee's pageant back in 1602 provided him with a basis.

James could not be invited to join the Company since he was already a Clothworker, but the young Prince was a very suitable candidate. While his father sat in the King's Chamber, Henry had dined at a separate table in the Hall with the main assembly. He was only thirteen, and this may have been the first big public occasion which allowed him a solo part. Like his father, he received a purse, this one containing £50 in gold. When it came time for last year's Master and Wardens to yield their garlands to the next year's officers, Henry put the Master's garland on his own head, at which the King, watching from the window above, 'did very harteley laugh'.

The Prince insisted that all those nobles who had accompanied the royal guests, and all his personal attendants, should become Merchant Taylors too. Three ambassadors from the Netherlands begged to be admitted as well, which they were with great good will.

James came down into the Hall and prepared to depart. The singers in the ship, 'apparelled in watchett [pale blue] silke like seamen',[14] sang him a

melodious song of farewell . . . which song so pleased his Majestie that he caused the same to be sung three times over. And his Majestie and the noble Prince, and Honourable Lords gave the Company hearty thanks and so departed.

The text of that song has recently been recognized among the archives of the present Marquess of Salisbury, at Hatfield House (Fig. 58).[15] These are Ben Jonson's words that so delighted the monarch:

> Jolly Mate, Looke forthe & see
> what Lightes those bee.
> The Ayre doth glowe as if the starrs
> were all at warrs.
> I know not what they are
> In all my houres at seas
> I have not seene such Lightes as these.
> Is not the one, that fixed starr
> that guides us out at Sea so farr
> the glory of the North?
> It is: And those the fires that shine
> About our tacklinges, and devine
> Cleare Calmes, & safety, when w'are forth.
>
> Double, O double then our joyes and say,
> Their wished sight ne're brought a happier day.
>
> Nothing could more wellcome be
> to us then hee
> who doth our course abroad direct,
> at home protect.
> Then wellcome Let us sing
> And thanckes to these bright formes
> who with their presence fright all stormes:
> We will both thanckes and wellcome Ring
> True wellcome, none but glad hartes bring
> And wellcome ours shall pay.

They shall: Nor is there Losse in Love.
Free gratitude to powers above
findes fayth & favour in the way.

Wellcome O wellcome then our Joyes; and maye
still wellcome be the Chorus of this day.[16]

Now it only remained to reward those who had laboured, and to pay the bills. Henry Beamont the chef received £5, and he and his thirty-two cooks were given dinner, 'there being noe cold meate left for them'. John Bull and Nathaniel Giles, who had given their services freely, were admitted to the livery without paying redemption. The total cost came to an amazing £1,061 5s. 1d. — the equivalent of at least £1,000,000 in today's money. Money was taken from the common box and Sir John Swinnerton contributed £140, so that the Company should not be in debt, though the Court noted sourly that they thought he should have given still more.

The glory day passed, as such days do, and became the stuff of legend. The Company settled down to the harder realities of the new century and the new dynasty.

NOTES

1. R. R. Sharpe, *London and the Kingdom*, I (1894), pp. 534–46.
2. See also Ian Archer, 'The Livery Companies and Charity', in *Guilds, Society & Economy in London 1450–1800*, ed. by Ian Gadd and Patrick Wallis (2002). I am most grateful to Stephen Freeth for his help with the figures.
3. Martha Carlin, *London and Southwark Inventories, 1316–1650: A Handlist of Extents for Debts* (1997).
4. Stow's *Survey of London* has remained in print, in one form or another, since it was written. The best edition is that of Charles Lethbridge Kingsford, published by OUP in 1908 in two volumes; all references are to that text. The account of Stow's life given here is drawn from Kingsford's Introduction, supplemented with information from the Company's minutes (GL, MS 34010/1 and 2). See also Clode, *Memorials*, and *Early History*, chapter XX, and Julia Merritt (ed.), *Imagining Early Modern London* (Cambridge, 2001); the first three essays, by Patrick Collinson, Julia Merritt and Ian Archer, are particularly devoted to Stow's *Survey*. Among the Merchant Taylors' archives, GL, MS 34125 is in Stow's own hand. It is a copy of Robert of Gloucester's *Chronicle*. The contemporary binding has 'IS' stamped in gold. See *Notes and Queries*, 248 (2003), pp. 384–85.
5. Langley was a great one for re-organizing the Company's records; later generations owe much to his exemplary care and skill in re-ordering documents and volumes.
6. He was buried on 8 April 1605. An example of his begging licence has just been recognized in the British Library, Harleian MS 367, fol. 10 (see above, Fig. 55).
7. *Walpole Society*, VII (1919).
8. For John Speed, see Clode, *Early History*, chapter XXII, and R. A. Skelton, *County Atlases of the British Isles, 1579–1850* (1970), p. 30 onwards.
9. GL, MS 34010/2, fol. 298, 10 February 1595.
10. For William Fleetwood, see Clode, *Early History*, chapter XIX, and P. W. Hasler, *The House of Commons, 1558–1603* (1981), II, pp. 133–38.
11. GL, MS 34010/1, pp. 267–71.
12. For a fuller account of Smith's career, see P. Cain, 'Robert Smith and the Reform of the Archives of the City of London, 1580–1623', in *London Journal*, 13, no. 1 (1987–88), pp. 3–16.
13. The entire cost of the banquet is given in detail in Clode, *Memorials* (1875), pp. 147–82. Also in Clode, *Early History*, I, pp. 275–318.
14. The taffeta for their costumes had cost £13.
15. We are most grateful for permission to quote the song here. Copies were distributed to the honoured guests, so possibly this is Lord Salisbury's own copy; Clode, *Memorials*, p. 177.
16. There is nothing to give the setting of the words, but there has long been a legend that among the music with which John Bull entertained the King was an early version of what is now the national anthem, *God Save the King*. There is no hard evidence for this; the first recorded performance of that paean was at Drury Lane Theatre on 28 September 1745, when the words were sung to Thomas Arne's arrangement. Bull did, however, leave a manuscript, keyboard composition remarkably similar to the anthem, so there is always hope but no certainty. A most interesting paper by Prof. Ross W. Duffin of Case Western Reserve University, Cleveland, USA, has recently been published in *Music & Letters*, 83, no. 4 (2002); it suggests other songs that may have been sung at the feast.

CHAPTER ELEVEN
PRELUDE TO THE CIVIL WAR

The monarch's attitude to the Company — and indeed towards the whole City — was not always going to be so friendly. James may have 'laughed heartily' at the feast, but his banqueting humour was the exception, not the rule. The relationship with the new dynasty was going to be such that people would look back on Elizabeth's reign and remember it — with whatever false nostalgia — as a golden age.

Most of the problems facing the new King had already been there in Elizabeth's day. They came under two main headings — money and religion. Inflation throughout Europe was steady and seemingly endless; the complaint of Beadle Yomans, that the times did 'pynche the purses of us poore men', might have been echoed by many other London citizens. The Spanish invasion of the Netherlands had effectively ruined the centuries-old wool trade with north-western Europe; the outbreak of the Thirty Years War in 1618 was going to make matters worse. The search was on for new markets. The East India Company had been established in 1600; a first, unsuccessful attempt had been made to colonize Virginia in North America in 1606. The will, the navigational skills, the indispensable capital were all there, but new markets are not opened up overnight.

Then there was religion. The Church of England, as established at the outset of Elizabeth's reign, held a middle course between the old Catholic faith and the zeal of new-found Protestantism, and at first men and women, remembering the fires of Mary's years, were glad to accept this seemly and moderate faith. But before Elizabeth's death, more extreme forms of Protestantism were becoming widespread, especially in the cities and townships; by 1600 there was a sizeable and vocal minority, anxious for the abolition of the Prayer Book and of all bishops. James, having been brought up in the rigours of Calvinism, was content to accept the Church of England; not all his subjects agreed with him.

In this age of change, the machinery of government was inadequate to bear the demands and burdens placed upon it. The Bank of England only came into being in 1694; it was going to be another century beyond that before Income Tax was proposed. Parliament might vote money, willingly or unwillingly, against the threat of the Spanish Armada, or when faced with the drain of the wars in Ireland, but it was still assumed silently that the Queen would manage her Court and the government of the kingdom on the income from the royal estates, with a little help sometimes, perhaps, from her loyal subjects. By the end of her reign, it was only the strength and magnetism of Elizabeth's personality that held in check the increasing demand for change. Faced with a Parliamentary storm over monopolies, Elizabeth remedied the worst problems by proclamation and then summoned the Commons to Whitehall, received them in state, and told her listeners:

This I account the glory of my crown, that I have reigned with your loves.

James had no such command of language, nor of men's hearts.

To be fair to him, he was in a different position from his predecessor. Elizabeth's whole policy had been based on her single state; it was natural for her courtiers to bring her gifts, lengths of fine cloth, fabrics which could be made into resplendent garments by skilful tailors such as Walter Fyshe and his team of craftsmen.

James's household was of a different kind; he had a wife and three surviving children. The Court increased, quite literally, overnight. A new Banqueting House was built for Whitehall Palace;

the King did not like it, finding it dark and with too many obstructive pillars. When it burnt down accidentally in 1619, Inigo Jones designed the magnificent structure which still stands today, open, light, almost buoyant in its airiness. Until the very end of Elizabeth's reign, maintenance of royal buildings — she initiated no new ones — amounted to little more than £4,000 a year; in eighteen months, between 1607–09, James needed £23,000, which mounted in the next year and a half to £51,800.[1] Strict accounting was imposed, but clearly, Court finances had moved onto a different scale. Similar escalation applied to most departments.

In such circumstances, the Crown did the best it could by whatever means were to hand. Monopolies came back whereby a man, for a substantial downpayment or as an especial royal favour, had the sole right to trade in particular goods, and might set what price he pleased on them which the public either had to pay or do without. Salt, and starch for ruffs and lace, had been great irritants in Elizabeth's day. James granted Robert Cecil a monopoly on the import of fine fabrics, and the Earl of Essex the right to export undressed cloths, thereby cutting straight across the interests of such City companies as were concerned with textiles. Then such taxes as there were could be farmed out. The Customs farm was notorious. But in the absence of an effective civil service, what was a monarch to do? It was not unreasonable to make use of the organizational skills of the business community. Parliament might growl and flex its muscles and complain of corruption, but things went on as they had always done. The pieces needed to be rearranged in a different pattern; the question was whether this could be achieved peacefully, or whether there would be bloodshed.

All this needs to be in our minds as we study the Company's records. The nature of the Court minutes is beginning to change; they have become more formal, there are tidy headings in the margin to indicate the matters under discussion, there are separate volumes now — one for the meetings of the Master and Court of Assistants, and another chiefly as a register for the binding and freeing of apprentices, though urgent matters, such as school places, or settlement of disputes, are often included. The main matters under discussion are the renewal of leases, the payment of corn money, the election of Masters and Wardens and, at the other end of the scale, of alms men and women. Human stories still appear, however. Mrs Bellew, the widow of the Company's butler, may live rent-free in a house near Three Cranes Wharf with her 'poore impotent daughter'; we do not know whether the child was crippled in body or in mind.[2] John Horsley, a lately-freed apprentice, gives on 3 January 1612 a gilt spoon weighing 1½ oz, 'out of his poore ability . . . as a token of his love, and thanckfulnes, for his said freedome'.[3] Gerson Hilles is dead;[4] the poor soul was 'decayed in his sences', and has been looked after by Joan Gibbs; he was the son of Richard Hilles, instigator of the School; great care was taken of him over many years. There are violent quarrels. Richard Johnson uses 'uncivill wordes . . . unfitt to be recorded in any book', while Richard Veale calls Humfrey Markham a 'varlett and a loggerhead with other such disdainfull words'. For that, the Court fines him 40s., whereupon he repeats himself publicly before everyone in the Hall, but then apologizes and is let off with a 5s. fine. Robert Cooper, sent from the school to St John's, is observed to be lame. The college, ever short of money and so ready to turn away a scholarship boy, insists that all students must be perfectly whole, physically as well as mentally. The Company protests and finally the matter is referred to the Bishop of Winchester as Visitor who, mildly but firmly, lays down that, while it might be better not to have a lame student, this should have been noticed before Cooper was accepted and that he should stay.[5] Later, the boy was awarded a scholarship. But the Court of Assistants concerns itself for the most part with everyday matters such as the lending out of modest sums of capital — £12 10s., £25, £50, occasionally £100 — to serious young tradesmen, each of whom has to produce three guarantors. The details of these guarantors provide fascinating material for analysis, for they emphasize that by now a man was not necessarily following the trade of the company to which he belonged. Arthur Juxon, a Salter living by Walbrook, earned his living as a sugar baker; Daniel Tannar, Girdler, was practising as a haberdasher in Friday Street. The nearer a man could be to St Paul's, the better he knew his pitch to be; Roger

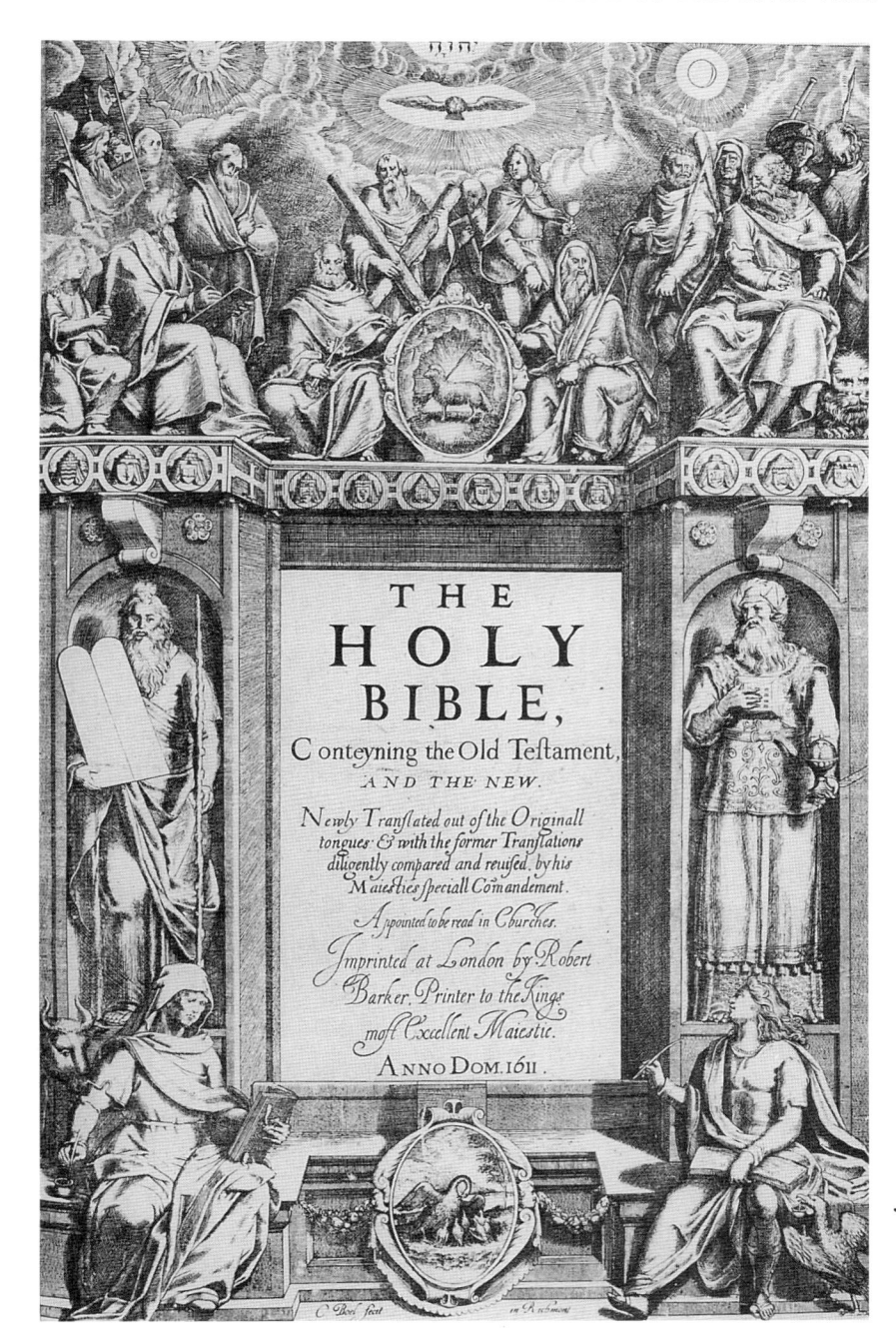

FIGURE 59. Title-page to the Authorized Version of the Bible. Six former pupils of Merchant Taylors' School contributed to the work of translation. They were Lancelot Andrewes, Ralph Ravens, John Spenser, John Peryn, Giles Thompson and Ralph Huchenson.
Cambridge University Library, pressmark BSS. 201. C11. By permission of the British and Foreign Bible Society and the Syndics of Cambridge University Library

Price, a Tallow-Chandler, had set up as a woollen draper at the sign of the Golden Key in the Churchyard there. Of thirty guarantors whose names are given in two and a half pages in May 1647, ten are in or around St Paul's, another ten on or immediately off Cheapside, and the remaining third spread out in the eastern half of the City.[6]

Three matters beside day-to-day finance which did concern the Merchant Taylors were the well-being of the schools under their care, the establishment of a colony in Ireland, and the regulation of the Bachelors' Company.

Their own school was running satisfactorily enough under a sequence of headmasters, several of them

— Edmund Smith, William Hayne, John Edwardes and William Staple — having been pupils at the school. In 1606, Robert Dowe advised that there be a 'probation' or examination of the whole school three times a year, and this was instituted, undoubtedly with good results if the comments in Beaumont and Fletcher's play, *The Knight of the Burning Pestle*, are evidence. A lively citizen's wife describes a youthful character, Humphrey:

Did you ever see a prettier child? how it behaves itself, I warrant ye, and speaks and looks, and perts up the head! — I pray you, brother, with your favour, were you never none of Master Moncaster's scholars?

Mulcaster had retired in 1586 and the play was not produced till about 1610, but the first headmaster's fame and good repute lived on.

The Company was rather hard on him when, now an old man, he petitioned for 'some remembraunce of their good willes' and was refused, being warned 'not to presse' them. Mulcaster was presumably waiting outside the door. He had gone from the Company's school to St Paul's, and the feeling was that the Mercers should support their former headmaster, since they were rich under Dean Colet's will, while the Merchant Taylors were less well endowed.[7]

There was the occasional problem, as when in 1624 John Foy, a liveryman of the Company who had not paid his son's fees, made complaints against William Hayne which resulted in the headmaster's dismissal, but since he had run the school successfully for a quarter of a century, and since the Company paid him £130 compensation, we may better judge his headmastership by the quality of his pupils. Those pupils included the dramatist James Shirley, the theologian and geographer Peter Heylyn, the brilliant Parliamentarian lawyer Sir Bulstrode Whitelocke (or Whitlocke) (Fig. 60), William Juxon who, as Bishop of London, would stand beside Charles I on the scaffold, and two brothers, Matthew and Christopher Wren, who would both enter the Church. Matthew became Bishop of Ely and spent eighteen years in the Tower for his Royalist principles; Christopher suffered too, though less severely, and would become the father of another Christopher, the architect of St Paul's Cathedral. The brothers owed their advance in life to Lancelot Andrewes who, when about to

FIGURE 60. Bulstrode Whitelocke. Once a pupil at Merchant Taylors' School, he became the leading lawyer of the day and served as Cromwell's ambassador to Sweden.
John Thane's British Autography *(1819). Private collection*

become Dean of Westminster, had made the annual inspection of the school on St Barnabas' Day, 11 June 1601.[8] Matthew Wren had then delivered a 'Greeke' oration which had caught Andrewes' attention; though it did not earn him a coveted place at St John's, the boy was given one at Pembroke College, Cambridge, whither his younger brother followed him. In the following year, Dean Andrewes was joined as examiner by the school's first headmaster, Richard Mulcaster, and by Ralph Huchenson, son of a former Clerk to the Company, and now President of St John's, and by Matthew Gwynn, a former pupil and now the first Gresham Professor of Physick. This was a special occasion. 'Very bountifull provision of fishe' was laid on; everyone made speeches; and the Company departed 'in farr more quyett sort then in former eleccions they were accustomed'.[9]

By this time, the school's relationship with St John's was getting better.[10] The college's financial affairs were becoming more settled and it was easier to admit scholarship boys. Sir Thomas White's good works of half a century earlier now bore fruit. William Laud, the future Archbishop of Canterbury, was a further source of good will. He was the son of a Reading cloth merchant and had gone to St John's on one of White's scholarships. He may have felt an instinctive friendliness towards Sir Thomas's company — had his father been a Londoner, he might well have belonged to the Merchant Taylors — and towards the Company's school. In 1611 he became President of St John's College, and when possible attended the school on St Barnabas' Day. The Company's accounts for 1615–16 show the Master, two Wardens and two Past Masters taking him out for a meal at the Ship tavern at the cost of 23s. 4d.

Matters, however, were less equitable with Sir Stephen Jenyns' grammar school at Wolverhampton. The rent from its endowment of the manor of Rushock was meant to keep the school building in good repair, and to provide a Master with a stipend of £10 a year and an Usher who only got £2, though this was later increased to £5. The townsmen of Wolverhampton seem to have been a fastidious and critical group. In 1573, there had been unspecified objections to Mr Raby, appointed about 1569, and he had been replaced by Thomas Madox, whom the Company spared, unwillingly, from their own school in the City. He remained in charge until his death thirty-three years later and seems to have been the perfect headmaster, for the local inhabitants, writing to the 'wurshipfull' company to solicit an increased salary for Madox, described him as

A man not only of good and honest life but also Learned, and not only of good life and Learninge but also A man bothe willinge Diligente and as paynefull in his good trade of teaching as ever any hathe ben in the roome and Office.[11]

The Merchant Taylors, rather grudgingly, gave him an additional five marks (£3 6s. 8d.) and suggested that the townsmen should do the like, which they, ever parsimonious, refused to do. However, Mr Madox stayed on and gave the school a set of statutes, no doubt modelled on those in use in St Lawrence Pountney.[12] A boy — all the pupils were boys — needed to be able to read and write before being admitted, and would be sent away if he proved 'unapte' for grammar school training. For those children continuing in the school, their parents were to be 'contente that your childerne shall have due and reasonable correction either for mysusinge them selfes in mannours or negligence in lerninge'. School started at seven in the morning and continued till five, with a two-hour break between eleven and one so they could run home for a meal. Children had also to be provided with books, and with 'candils' in winter, and to say their prayers 'distynctly' before and after lessons. Their parents were also to allow them to attend church services 'uppon the Sabbothe and holly dayes'. Therein lay future trouble, for there were still many in the area who loved the old religion.

Thomas Madox died in July 1605 and was succeeded by Richard Barnes of Oxford, second usher at Merchant Taylors' School. At first, all seemed to go well, though there was some wrangling with the former headmaster's son over 'reparacions' and removal of what should have been fixtures, including some wainscot and some painted cloths, the poor man's equivalent of warm tapestry wall-hangings. Then in a letter of February 1606 Mr Barnes asks for guidance:

There is a further matter wherein I desire to knowe your worships pleasure, and that is concerning Recusants Children with whose parentes I have often delt, to let them com to the Church but they say flatly that they shall not, obiecting (as I am perswaded moast untruly) that Mr Madox my predecessor had aucthority from some of the Company to suffer them and others, which cannot be, for that it is contrary to the Articles and Statutes of the Schoole.

The Master and Wardens wrote, most emphatically, to tell Mr Barnes that he must stand firm over recusants' children; if parents wanted the benefits of free grammar school education for their children, those children would have to attend the parish church regularly. All went quiet for the next three years; necessary repairs were done to the schoolhouse, and Mr Barnes' salary was raised to £20 and the usher's to £10. The earliest list of pupils survives from Barnes' headmastership — sixty-nine boys in all. John Normansell was recommended for, and received, a scholarship of £4 a year to study at university,[13] and Mr Barnes wrote to assure the Company that the children were studying Horace, Virgil, Terence, Cato and Cicero.[14] Then on 9 October 1609 the Court received a letter filled with troubles; 'the usher is not yet determyned to followe such a course of teaching as I shall prescribe', lamented Mr Barnes. His letter goes on to list the boys who had done well under his tuition, though he had found some of them 'very rude, and coulde doe almost nothing before I tooke them'. Then the writer bursts out with the real trouble:

I knowe not through whose default it is come to passe, nor howe, but wee have had an hurly burly with the Townsmen in Woolverhampton: I meant peace, and sought peace, God is my witnes. They are nowe bending them selves against your worships and against me, and out they will haue me, for soe goeth the Common cry of all inhabitantes in Woolverhampton and neere thereaboutes; theire malice and envy is greate and only for Papists sakes ... [I] have behaved my self kyndly towardes my schollers, towardes all men putting upp many insolent abuses and wronges from tyme to tyme, which I have not deserved. I have likewise ordered my self soberly and discreetely which is much envied at. I have bene loyall and conformable to my most Soveraigne King, his lawes ecclesiasticall and temporall, cheerefully and willingly, and will soe still contynue, God willing, to th'end of my lief.

Before the Company could reply, the townspeople made their feelings known in a letter to Randulph (or Randle) Woolley, one of the Assistants. The complaints were vague and unspecific, save that they believed Mr Barnes to be deaf; otherwise 'better were it for us, there were noe free schoole att all, then such a one as nowe it is'. A hundred and two townspeople signed the letter.

The Company sent a copy of the letter to Mr Barnes, who replied with an impressive testimonial with 120 signatures of the more substantial inhabitants; the encomium described him as 'a godly learned discreete peaceable and modest man sufficiently furnished with knowledge in the Tongues'. It was decided to seek the advice of the Archbishop of Canterbury, but before the prelate could reply there was another pathetic appeal from the beleaguered headmaster:[15]

I was never in all my lief convicted of any cryme or scandall to the world, I doe intreate yow to deale with me in these my trobles, as with a Christian man, by admonycion first and not by extremyty; protesting to your worships, that I have not done any of them such wronge that they should soe maliciously oppose themselves against me, or goe about uniustly to traduce me in these theire courses and proceedinges as a man soe untractable, as that I would not have lent a patient eare to any reasonable man, especiallie to any that is grave and religiouslie wise, or indifferent and conscionable. And seing that my adversaries doe not alleadge against me any enormyties, nor are not able to convince me of insufficiency or crymes in lief and conversacion I cannot perceave any reason why you should proceede to any extreame course, or eiection, the which is used by noe lawe but in case of extremytie, when as a man hath highly and extraordynarily offended.

The Court decided they had better see for themselves. Accordingly, Randulph Woolley and Thomas Johnson, Wardens, Richard Wright, Assistant, and Richard Langley, the Company Clerk, set out for the distressed school and town early in August 1610. With them went a learned minister, Dr Foster, to give an academic opinion. The party's expenses came to £50 9s. 6d. for the round trip. They found the school itself in a state of disrepair and the town still in a 'Hurly-Burly'. Clearly, Mr Barnes would have to go elsewhere — there would be no peace while he stayed in office, whether or not he was at fault. Assured of this, and promised that a 'gallory' should be erected in the church for the sole use of the school, parents of all religious persuasions were happy to allow their children to attend services. The visit ended with everyone happy and content, except poor Mr Barnes.

The school was repaired, the gallery built at the cost of £40 (see Fig. 39, p. 117), Mr Barnes was dismissed, and William Wilson of Queen's College, Oxford, appointed in his place at a salary increased to £30 a year. Wilson was a kindly soul. He allowed Barnes to shelter through the winter while the poor creature wrote desperate letters to the Company begging them to find him a teaching post or a living somewhere, for he had committed no real fault. In the end Randulph Woolley, who as one of the deputation had presumably seen the true state of things, spent £36 of the Company's money in buying him the living of Sellindge, south-east of Ashford in

Kent.[16] There he remained till his death nearly a quarter of a century later; his parishioners seem to have been perfectly satisfied with him.

* * *

Far larger sums of money than those required for Wolverhampton's repairs had to be found from time to time. At the outset of his reign, James I had demanded money from the City: in August 1604 there had been a peremptory request for £15,000, of which the Merchant Taylors' proportion was £1,350. It was hard to raise the sum. On 5 October, the Lord Mayor wrote again; the money was to be brought to Guildhall before the next night:

Yf you shall faile hereof, I shall doe to you that which will greatlie discontent you,

threatened the chief citizen. A hundred pounds was taken out of the Bachelors' Company's funds, to be replaced when the King paid back. Needless to say, there was no repayment.

That year also saw considerable costs in connection with the King's triumphal procession through the City (Fig 61); hundreds of yards of azure blue cloth were required for gowns and to decorate and cover the raked temporary 'standinges' (seating) for the livery to occupy along the route. That pageant should have taken place a year earlier but plague in the City had postponed it. In addition, the Speaker and a hundred Members of Parliament were entertained at a 'friendly and loving meeting' in the Company's Hall to which feast the King contributed a buck and a hogshead of wine, and thirty uninvited guests managed to crowd onto the tables where everyone marvelled at the *pièce de resistance* of the evening — a marchpane (marzipan) model of the House of Commons assembled and seated.[17] Three years later, the Company entertained the King himself at an amazing cost, and the demands continued, the monarch writing in July 1614 that he had need of

great somes of money whereof our Coffers at this tyme are unfurnished ... not knoweinge where to fynd a more speedie supply then in our Chamber of London.

The merchants groaned but they paid up.

The most bottomless outlay of all was in Ireland. The wars which had darkened the later years of Elizabeth's reign had been brought to a bitter end by Lord Mountjoy. An uneasy peace reigned, the Earls of Tyrone and Tyrconnell, who had been prime movers in the years of rebellion, having been pardoned and restored to the greater portion of their estates. And then, early in September 1607, the two earls, with their wives, families and retainers to the number of nearly a hundred, took ship from Rathmullan and made for Europe, settling eventually in Rome where many of them died of the local fever. They were immediately declared to be guilty of High Treason and their estates, which amounted to the whole of Ulster, were forfeited to the Crown. It was decided that the land should be colonized by English and Scots farmers, artisans and craftsmen, thereby simultaneously guarding against another invasion by a Spanish army, advancing the cause of Protestantism, and promoting the modernization of agriculture.

Such colonization had been attempted before in Elizabeth's reign, most notably in Munster, but such efforts had failed to establish themselves. Edmund Spenser, once a pupil at Merchant Taylors' School, had gone there as Lord Grey's secretary and had acquired Kilcolman Castle, where he wrote much of *The Faerie Queene*, but the castle had been burnt in an insurrection in October 1598 and he had been forced to flee with his wife and children. This new venture was going to be different. James I would allow the City of London the opportunity of settling the area. The province would be divided between the twelve great companies, each of which might associate itself with several lesser companies. It would be the responsibility of the companies to recruit suitable settlers, and to see to it that they laid out streets with strong, snug houses, built a church and, where necessary, fortifications, and employed modern methods of husbandry. The indigenous Irish were to be persuaded, by one means or another, to resettle themselves elsewhere. The capital sum to be invested by the City was £60,000, payable in three instalments of £20,000, each company paying its own share and accepting a proportion of land, to be distributed by lot.[18]

This is not the place to attempt a detailed history of the Ulster Plantation; we are concerned only with that proportion of it which fell to the Merchant Taylors. At the beginning, the Company was enthusiastic about the venture; the first two instalments were paid with very little hesitation, and a poor man,

FIGURE 61. An Arch of Triumph erected to welcome James I on his entry into the City of London. Designed by Stephen Harrison, it was originally intended for 11 May 1603, but the ceremony had to be postponed until 15 March 1604 for fear of plague. Above the double archway are models of the buildings on the riverfront from St Bride's church to Fishmongers' Hall. The tower of pre-Fire St Paul's Cathedral crowns the City, while the arched steeple of St Mary le Bow and the tower of Gresham's Royal Exchange with its grasshopper can be identified.
By kind permission of the Society of Antiquaries of London

Edmund Wolverstone, who had a wife and five children, was given £4 on 10 March 1610 to help with his moving expenses.[19] The Company was allotted 18,700 acres for an investment of £6,186; within the next sixteen years £1,836 18s. 6d. would be spent on buildings, on vital equipment — agricultural implements, carpenters' tools, domestic utensils — and on arms and munitions. The first two tenants, Valentine Hartopp and his son-in-law, Ralph Wall, were profoundly unsatisfactory, simply not paying their rents, being put in prison, promising to reform, coming out — and continuing with their non-payments. George Costerdyne, in charge of building works at Macosquin, the main settlement, was a steady and reliable man and Mathias Springham, Master of the Merchant Taylors' Company in 1617, who was one of the City's Commissioners for Ireland, decided in the year of his Mastership to build a school in Londonderry at his own expense.[20] Though the name and the site have both changed, the school still flourishes today as Foyle & Londonderry College.

The Company's estate (Col. Pls XIVB and XV) adjoined that of the Clothworkers' Company, and the two worked together, employing the same surveyor, Simon Kingsland, to draw a map of the two portions in 1613. So close together were the lands that a 1616 survey by Thomas Raven of the Clothworkers' lands gives a detailed layout of Macosquin, the Merchant Taylors' chief little township.

Further contributions were required towards a second attempt at a settlement across the Atlantic in Virginia. On 28 March 1609 the Court studied a letter from the Lord Mayor.[21] It was blunt, saying that such a plantation would

> ... ease the Citty and Suburbs of a swarme of unnecessary inmates, as a contynuall cause of dearth and famyne, and the very originall cause of all the plagues, almost that happen in this kingdome ...

The Court conferred with the Bachelors' Company and agreed to send £100 out of the common stock, with an additional £54 3s. 4d. out of the Bachelors' funds. Individuals contributed a further £39 12s. 6d., and the Bachelors rounded it up with £6 4s. 2d. to give a total of £200. In addition, some twenty-two members, hoping for an eventual profit, advanced £586 13s. 4d., the Company in all making a substantial showing.

* * *

There was restlessness to contend with nearer to home, in the ranks of the Bachelors' Company. This was, as it were, a company within the main Company, made up of the ordinary freemen outside the livery (see above, Chapter Three). The livery was for a couple of hundred of the senior membership; the others belonged to the junior Bachelors' body. It was governed by its own four Wardens Substitute, and its seniors were the Sixteen Men. Their duties were to collect quarterage, to keep an eye on apprentices and, when such regulations were in force, to make sure that no one had more apprentices than his entitlement, to search out the employment of foreign — that is, non-London — labour, and to adjudicate in quarrels over the ill-making of clothes.

A post as Warden of the Bachelors was laborious, time-consuming and no doubt often expensive and frustrating, but it did confer considerable status on the holder among the Company at large, and make it more likely that a man would be invited to join the livery. Not every one wanted to do that — invitations to serve were sometimes turned down — but a Warden certainly carried as much responsibility as most men were prepared to bear. The lesser Company needed its own salaried Clerk and Beadle, which is some indication of how much work there was to be done. They also had an informer, whose duty it was to search out alien tailors and to warn the Company of such misdemeanours, and a full-time cook.[22]

In the autumn of 1608 relationships between the Bachelors' Wardens and the Sixteen Men became very uncomfortable indeed. The Wardens complained to the livery that the Sixteen would not obey them, and the Sixteen growled that they 'must governe their Wardens or els there wilbe noe quiett with them', and announced that 'they have much busines which must be concealed from their Wardens'. The wrangling and arguing went on till the following year. The Wardens retorted tartly that there had been 'too [two] severall idle meetinges in one moneth and lesse in tavernes', which had cost the Company £3 12s. 0d. and £2 4s. 0d. In the end, duties were set down in the Court minutes[23] and a loving dinner was held. One wonders, apart from the tactlessness of individuals, whether some of the friction may not have come from those in the lower ranks who had felt that the livery had taken too much of the limelight at the feast for James I in the summer of 1607, but this is only conjecture.[24]

Before turning to the violent history of the century's middle decades, in which the Company played its part, we may consider two outstanding mayoral pageants, and the lives of some exemplary Merchant Taylors.

The pageants were those for Sir John Swinnerton in 1612, and for Sir John Gore in 1624.[25] What distinguished them so particularly was that the verses for each of them were written by a poet who was connected with the Company — Swinnerton's by Thomas Dekker, author of *The Shoemaker's Holiday* and once an apprentice tailor, and Gore's by John Webster, who wrote *The White Devil* and *The Duchess of Malfi*, and was free of the Company. Dekker's four tableaux for Swinnerton showed Neptune in a watery chariot; Arete or Vertue enthroned and surrounded by the Liberal Sciences and by actors representing the Twelve Great Companies; a 'Forlorne Castle, built close to the little Conduit in Cheapside', assailed by Envy and her attendants, all put to flight as Vertue passes by; and finally Fame, who greets the Mayor beside Cheapside Cross and shows him all the monarchs, nobles and prelates who have been free of the Merchant Taylors. There were several displays of fireworks, and a last, long poem to be spoken by Justice as the new Mayor returned home after his banquet in Guildhall.

Webster's pageant, entitled *Monuments of Honor*, was opened by speeches from Oceanus and Thetis, and included a Temple of Honour set up in St Paul's Churchyard. As might be expected from a poet, the Temple was peopled by Chaucer, Gower, Lydgate, Sir Thomas More and Sir Philip Sidney, with Henry de Ryall, the Company's first known Pilgrim — or Master — and John de Yakesley, who purchased the Hall and was Edward III's pavilion maker. Speeches were delivered by that monarch, each verse ending with the Company's motto: *By unity the smallest things grow great*. Anne of Bohemia, Richard II's wife, the first Queen of England to be a member of the fraternity, was represented in this gathering of the great and the good.

Other displays included the Knights of St John of Jerusalem (who protected pilgrims in the desert), the *condottiere* Sir John Hawkwood, and Sir Thomas White sitting in a garden beside an elm tree with twin trunks springing from one root, with a model of St John's College and twelve representatives — 'for more would have over-burthened it' — of the twenty-four cities and towns to which the good knight left money to help young tradesmen set up in business. It must have been an especially popular pageant.

The Company was rich in benefactors in these years. One of the most distinguished was William Craven (Col. Pl. XVIIIA), born about 1548 in Appletreewick in the parish of Burnsall, near Skipton in the West Riding of Yorkshire, the son of William Craven and his wife, Beatrix Hunter. The story goes that at the age of about thirteen or fourteen, he was put on the carrier's cart and sent up to London to accept the offer of an apprenticeship with Robert Hulson, Merchant Taylor of Watling Street. He served his time, was admitted to the freedom of the Company on 4 November 1569, and entered into partnership with his master, but after a while they disagreed and submitted their differences — 'from the beginning of the world to this day' — to the Court of Assistants on 9 November 1583. The problem seems to have been over a shop 'late in the occupation of William Craven'. The Master gave judgment that Hulson should pay the young man £10, and then 'have unto himself the said shoppe to use at his pleasure'. The disagreement cannot have been too serious, for Hulson bequeathed three years' occupancy of a shop at the intersection of Bread Street and Watling Street to Craven after his own death. In 1588, now in partnership with Robert and John Parker, Craven took from the Mercers' Company the lease of 'a great mansion house' in the parish of St Antholin, where he remained in business till the end of his life, bequeathing the tenancy of it to the Parker brothers.[26]

On 4 July 1593 he was elected one of the Wardens of his Company, being then about forty-five years of age. That was a bad year for London — the plague 'hot in the city', Stow tells us — but Craven was judged to have 'borne and behaved himself commendably' and was invited to join the Court of Assistants, on which he served with the utmost diligence, though he was excused service as Master. He gave generously to the almshouses, on one occasion,

15 May 1593, laying down £20, and on another undertaking the maintenance of an almswoman at 16d. a week. He gave £50 towards the provision of a library for St John's College. On 2 April 1600 he became alderman for Bishopsgate Ward, and a year later was chosen Sheriff. The Company presented him with £30 'out of the common box' to help with the expenses of office, and was willing to loan him plate — faithfully returned later — so that he might make a good showing on his buffet when entertaining formally. One of the knighthoods, bestowed by James I at his accession, fell to Craven in July 1603; when the King dined with the Company in 1607, Craven was among those active in the organization.

In 1610 he was elected Lord Mayor, the Company bestowing one hundred marks on him for the 'trymmyng' of his house. It so happened that Christian, the Prince of Anhalt, was visiting London that autumn — he arrived at Dover on 29 October — so he was invited to the banquet in Guildhall where he declared

There was no state nor cittie in the world that did elect their magistrates with such magnificence, except the cittie of Venice, unto which the cittie of London commeth very neere.[27]

The accounts for Craven's pageant are less full than others, but we know that Anthony Munday again provided a text, for which he was paid £126, though some of that fee went to 'Mr Grinking the Painter', who adorned a chariot with the Company's arms and newly painted 'the Shipp', and another portion of the money went to the printing of the text, though apparently no copy survives. From the accounts, we know that the pageant, presumably mounted on a wagon, was 'kinges that sate in the Rock on the Thames', that there were gilded statues, and guns saluting, and thirty-two trumpeters, and drums and fifes, and six Green Men with fireworks, while sixteen armed professional fencers were needed to control the crowds. A hundred and sixteen poor men had blue gowns with crimson mockadoe sleeves;[28] their breakfast cost 58s. It took a hundred porters to carry the pageant, the chariot and the ship through the streets on 'the Triumph Day'. The ship was, presumably, the one from which the azure-clad seamen had sung to the King three years before at the great banquet. With all that and a full-scale mayoral feast, it is no wonder that the Prince of Anhalt was impressed.

Securely established in the City hierarchy, Craven acquired a fine new house for his own use in Leadenhall Street. The property had recently been redeveloped by another Merchant Taylor, Sir Robert Lee. It had sixty-two rooms, external courtyards, blue and white marble paving, carved chimneypieces and a fine hall screen, a flower garden and a summer pleasure house. Later, in 1648, the house became the London headquarters of the East India Company.[29]

In 1611, Craven became President of Christ's Hospital, a position which he held till his death; in July 1613 he bestowed on St John's College the advowson of Crick in Northamptonshire, and he contributed to the subscription of £1,000 for the repair of St Antholin's church. He did not forget his birthplace, for he founded a grammar school at Burnsall in Yorkshire which still exists (Fig. 62).[30] His last public act was on 26 May 1618, when he laid the foundation stone for the new Aldgate, and he attended his last Court in Threadneedle Street on 1 July. On the twenty-ninth of that month, his will was read out to the Court, and over 500 mourners attended his funeral in St Andrew Undershaft, where he rests modestly without a memorial. On the Company, he had bestowed the Pope's Head tavern in Lombard Street, with adjacent buildings.

He married, possibly in 1605, an alderman's daughter, Elizabeth Whitmore. In 1616, this sensible City couple were called upon, by James I, for a full year to entertain Lady Elizabeth Coke, the termagant — if sorely provoked — wife of Sir Edward Coke; later, James wrote them a letter of thanks. The Cravens had five children, three sons and two daughters. The second son, John, attended Trinity College, Oxford, founded the Craven Scholarships in the two universities, and was created Baron Craven of Ryton in Shropshire by Charles I. The elder brother, William, gave shelter to the widowed Elizabeth of Bohemia, James I's daughter, when she returned to England.[31]

Our second example, Robert Dowe (Col. Pls XC and XIIIB), led a less public but equally honourable life.[32] He was born in 1523, the second son of Henry Dowe of Stradbroke in Suffolk and his wife, Alice

FIGURE 62. Burnsall School, near Skipton in Yorkshire, celebrated its fourth centenary in 2002.
Burnsall School

Nowell. Coming to London, he was apprenticed to Nicholas Wilford and became free of the Company on 9 August 1550. Working as a tailor, he settled in Houndsditch near Aldgate, and married Laetitia Bull. By her he had five sons who all predeceased their parents, so Dowe turned his wealth and charity towards the Company, bestowing upon it in his later years an amazing total of £2,958 10s. 8d. We have already noticed the support he gave to John Stow but, besides that, he gave money for the almshouses and their inmates, and, to out-pensioners, £6 3s. 4d. for each of thirteen men over sixty years of age, with a warm gown every third year. This garment was to have a dove embroidered upon it — a play upon the benefactor's name. He sponsored individual almswomen and organized a regular 'proving' or examination of the school, with refreshments laid on for the examiners. He left money to Christ's Hospital and to the City's prisons. His most memorable bequest was for the ringing of a hand-bell outside the condemned cell at Newgate on the night before a public execution (Fig. 63). The ringer was then to recite a verse in a loud voice:

> All you that in the condemned hold do lie,
> Prepare you, for to-morrow you shall die;
> Watch all, and pray, the hour is drawing near
> That you before the Almighty must appear;
> Examine well yourselves, in time repent,
> That you may not to eternal flames be sent,
> And when St Sepulchre's bell to-morrow tolls,
> The Lord above have mercy on your souls.
> Past twelve o'clock.

Such disturbing of a condemned man's last hours may seem barbaric cruelty to twenty-first century sensibility, but Dowe's intention was not to torment, but to save a soul that might otherwise be lost. The bell survives and is still displayed in St Sepulchre's church.

Dowe was indefatigable in his Court attendance. He presented the Company with gilt spoons, each with a dove on its handle; he established a convivium dinner, and in September 1611, at the age of eighty-eight, attended its celebration at the Angel. He died peacefully on 2 May in the following year and was buried in St Botolph Aldgate, where his monument can still be seen. Anthony Nixon preached an eloquent and lengthy funeral sermon which was published under the title of *London's Dove*, with an engraving of a coffin covered with a pall on which is seated a dove holding a little banner inscribed *Alta Peto*, meaning 'I seek higher things'.

Not everyone appreciated him, however. The Record Book of St Botolph's for 1598 records that Mrs Linkes and Widow Tomkins were committed

FIGURE 63. The Newgate Bell, instigated by Robert Dowe. It was rung during the night before an execution. It is now kept in the church of St Sepulchre, Newgate.
National Monuments Record, English Heritage

to Bridewell for casting 'certen fowle bowles of beastlynes' against Dowe's back door.[33]

Another substantial Merchant Taylor was Robert Graye (Col. Pl. XA). Baptized in Taunton in October 1574, he came to London, served his time as apprentice to Ralph Hamer, set up in business with an interest-free loan of £100 from the Company in December 1601, and subsequently did well as a silkman dealing in fine cloths, employing numerous 'workfolkes', some of them 'callenders and cottoners', which implies that he was involved in at least some cloth-finishing. He was admitted to the livery in 1610, served as Warden in 1628 and 1631, and as Master Elect in 1633, but he was excused office, promising a substantial bequest in his will. He was elected a Common Councilman in 1626, but paid a fine rather than serve as Sheriff. He married Anne Preistley in November 1606 at All Hallows, Bread Street; she died in May 1614 and Graye then lived on alone till his own death in October 1638, when he was buried in the chancel of the same church. He left £500 to the Company, to be used for loans to young freemen, but his heart was in his native town, to which he left £2,000 to found almshouses which still flourish today, fulfilling their original purpose. The Company was asked to act as trustee but felt that Taunton was too far away, so a local committee was set up. A handsome memorial was erected in St Mary Magdalen church, Taunton, with a standing figure of Graye in a long gown with hanging sleeves, and verses beneath:

> Consecrated to the blessed memory
> of Robert Graye Esq and Founder.
> Taunton bore him. London bred him.
> Piety trained him. Virtue led him.
> Earth enriched him. Heaven carest him.
> Taunton blest him, London blest him.
> This thankful town, that mindful city
> share his piety and his pity.
> What he gave and how he gave it
> ask the poor and you shall have it.
> Gentle reader, Heaven may strike
> thy tender heart to do the like.
> Now thine eyes have read the story.
> Give him the praise and Heaven the glory.

It would be gratifying to claim another West Country man, Robert Baker, as a member of the Company.[34] Such he may have been, but the hard evidence is lacking. He came to London from Staplegrove near Taunton, having served his apprenticeship there; the year must have been near 1588, for later witnesses in a law suit recalled that he had been 'a souldier at Tilburie Camp'. He married a flax-woman, Elizabeth Nightingale, at St Martin-in-the-Fields in November 1600; she was a 'verie careful good woman and wiffe' to him. Together they set up a business near Lord Salisbury's New Exchange in the Strand — Charing Cross Station occupies the site today — which, being close to the Court in Whitehall, prospered, Baker and his wife employing some twenty men in making piccadills or overmantle collars, a dozen and a half of which were supplied, for £21 12s. 0d., for the wedding of James I's daughter, the Princess Elizabeth, to Frederick, Count Palatine of the Rhine, in December 1612. Later, Baker launched into land speculation and property development; the name of his original speciality attached itself to a country lane across the fields, giving London its Piccadilly.

And then there was John Vernon (Col. Pl. XB), who had come to London from Chester and who served his apprenticeship with Richard Offley, a distinguished Merchant Taylor. Vernon was made free of the Company in 1572 and became Master in 1609. Growing old and his sight failing, he wisely decided to give outright those things which he most valued, rather than trust to the reliability of executors, so two days before the annual election, as was reported on 26 July 1616, he presented to the Company his own portrait and seven small pictures, since he could no longer see them. Later, he gave his 'best tapestry carpet and a faire salt', instructing the Court that the carpet should be kept carefully and never lent out of the Hall. The portrait still hangs in the Court Room, but the carpet has vanished. He devised to the Company property in Lombard Street, and each year, close to Christmas, a service is held in his name at St Michael Cornhill, where he was buried on 23 December 1616 in the same vault as his friend, Alderman John Houghton. He had prepared a joint memorial which was destroyed in the Fire of 1666; the Company set up a bust to Vernon some thirty years later.[35]

These were the men of London with whom James I had had to deal. They were substantial men, not proud, not top-lofty, but aware of their own dignity and their rightful place in society. They were men who would be respectful to proper authority courteously exercised, but they were also men whom it would be hard to cow.

NOTES

1. Howard Colvin (ed.), *History of the King's Works*, III (1975), pp. 107–09.
2. GL, MS 34010/5, p. 165, 21 June 1615.
3. GL, MS 34010/5, p. 29.
4. GL, MS 34010/4, p. 452.
5. GL, MS 34010/4, p. 234, 2 August 1606.
6. GL, MS 34010/7, fols 255ᵛ–256ᵛ.
7. GL, MS 34010/4, p. 368, 29 April 1609.
8. GL, MS 34010/3, fol. 433ᵛ.
9. GL, MS 34010/4, pp. 30–31.
10. W. C. Costin, *The History of St John's College, 1598–1860* (Oxford, 1958).
11. GL, MS 34010/1, p. 684, 25 November 1573.
12. GL, MS 34010/1, p. 636; Mander, *The History of the Wolverhampton Grammar School* (Wolverhampton, 1913), Appendix 6.

13. GL, MS 34010/4, p. 308, 30 May 1608.
14. GL, MS 34010/4, pp. 408–09, 9 October 1609.
15. GL, MS 34010/4, p. 441, 24 March 1610.
16. GL, MS 34010/5, p. 62, 12 November 1612.
17. Clode, *Memorials*, p. 147; Sharpe, *London and the Kingdom*, II (1894), p. 12.
18. For fuller information, see James Stevens Curl, *The Londonderry Plantation, 1609–1914* (Chichester, 1986), and Nicholas Canny, *Making Ireland British, 1580–1650* (Oxford, 2001).
19. GL, MS 34010/4, p. 438.
20. For more information on Springham, see W. S. Ferguson, 'Mathias Springham, 1561–1620', in *Transactions of the London and Middlesex Archaeological Society*, 23, part 2 (1972), pp. 194–203. I am most grateful to Mr Magill, the present headmaster, for much help and information.
21. GL, MS 34010/4, pp. 363–64.
22. GL, MS 34010/4, p. 449, 7 May 1610.
23. GL, MS 34010/4, pp. 333–59.
24. N. Sleigh-Johnson, 'Aspects of the Tailoring Trade in the City of London', *Costume*, 37 (2003), pp. 24–32.
25. The full texts and descriptions of these pageants, with the accounts for them, are to be found in R. T. D. Sayle, *Lord Mayors' Pageants of the Merchant Taylors' Company* (1931). For the association of John Webster and his father, also John, with the Company, see Charles R. Forker, *Skull Beneath the Skin: The Achievement of John Webster* (Carbondale, Il., 1986). I am grateful to Jean Tsushima for this reference.
26. For Craven's career, see *Dictionary of National Biography*; Sayle, *Lord Mayors' Pageants* (1931); and Clode, *Early History*, chapter XXI.
27. Sayle, *Pageants*, p. 86.
28. Mockadoe = a stout woollen cloth with a pile, manufactured in Norwich; M. C. Linthicum, *Costume in the Drama of Shakespeare and his Contemporaries* (Oxford, 1936).
29. See John Schofield, *Medieval London Houses* (1994), pp. 194–95.
30. It is now a junior school, still flourishing in the original handsome stone building.
31. P. Croot, 'Before and After Drury House', *London Topographical Record*, XXVIII (2001), pp. 43–44.
32. For Dowe's life, see Anthony Nixon, *London's Dove, or a Memoriall of the Life and Death of Maister Robert Dove, Citizen and Marchant-Taylor* (1612). Also many references in Clode, *Memorials*.
33. William Kent, *London Worthies* (1949), p. 135.
34. See Francis Sheppard, *Robert Baker of Piccadilly Hall and his Heirs* (1982), London Topographical Society, publication no. 127.
35. See Hopkinson's pamphlet on Vernon (1922), and F. M. Fry, *A Historical Catalogue of the Pictures . . . at Merchant Taylors' Hall* (1907), pp. 67–71. The carpet had vanished by Fry's day.

CHAPTER TWELVE
THE COMPANY IN THE CIVIL WAR

James I's reign ended uneasily; Charles I's closed in tragedy, the country torn with civil war and bloodshed, the King himself lying prone on the scaffold to meet his end. Charles became King on 27 March 1625. He was as old as the century, having been born on 19 November 1600, three years before his father became King of England. He was a delicate child from birth, suffering from rickets, unable to walk unaided till he had turned four years of age, and always undersized. He had a slight speech impediment, a hesitation which became worse in moments of stress. He was very unlike his elder brother Henry, who had joyfully, so boisterously, attended the Merchant Taylors' great banquet in 1607 and who had so willingly joined the Company, insisting on his entire entourage doing the same. England had looked upon Henry as the hopeful future, a true Protestant leader, unlike his drunken, unmannerly father. And then, suddenly, Henry was dead, a month before his sister's wedding to Frederick of the Palatinate. Rumours of all sorts were rife, but the cause was typhus, a common enough killer in the seventeenth century. In spite of it, the wedding went ahead with Robert Baker's dozen and a half of piccadills in the bride's trousseau; James was too heavily in debt to consider postponing the marriage till after a lengthy royal mourning, for that would have meant entertaining the bridegroom and his train for several more months. Charles became the heir apparent; perhaps there were those who never forgave him for not being his elder brother.

The new King was a slight figure, very formal in his manner and address. He had considerable style and was interested in his clothes. Van Dyck's splendid portraits have made his appearance familiar to us; the garments depicted were mostly made in the Royal Wardrobe,[1] in Sir John Beauchamp's old house near St Andrew's above the river Thames, by Patrick Black, who had come south and had been admitted to the Company by redemption on 27 October 1606 as Prince Henry's tailor. Queen Anne's man, James Ducane (or Duncane), had been similarly admitted on 18 November in the previous year. The King's embroiderer was a Londoner, Edmund Harrison, whose contemporaries described him as 'the ablest worker living'.

Good clothes do not come cheap; the accounts for 1633–35 show expenditure of £4,058 1s. 8½d. in the first year and £5,195 7s. 9d. in the second.[2] For this, the King got fifty-three suits of clothes, ten of them black, seven cinnamon, six faun, and four bright green, with single outfits of willow, lemon, carnation, peach and honey. The material used was almost always satin; it is not impossible that the three suits, in black, carnation and a purplish-brown, which the King wears in Van Dyck's triple portrait (Fig. 64), were all wrought by Black's team of craftsmen. Beside the suits, these accounts include substantial supplies of boots and shoes, hats, gloves and underwear, and all the packing and transport of the royal garments when travelling. The bills were met out of the Customs farm on imports of 'currants and all sorts of wine'. The years 1633–35 come right in the middle of Charles' eleven years of personal rule; farming out the Customs was one of the ways by which the King could meet his debts.

Charles was a connoisseur to his elegant fingertips. He delighted in court masques, in handsome architecture — it was at his insistence that the Earl of Bedford employed Inigo Jones to lay out Covent Garden in the Renaissance manner, thereby giving London its first example of town planning — and above all in painting. His collection was incomparable. But he was not interested in money, excepting to spend it. The steadfast, thrifty accumulation of

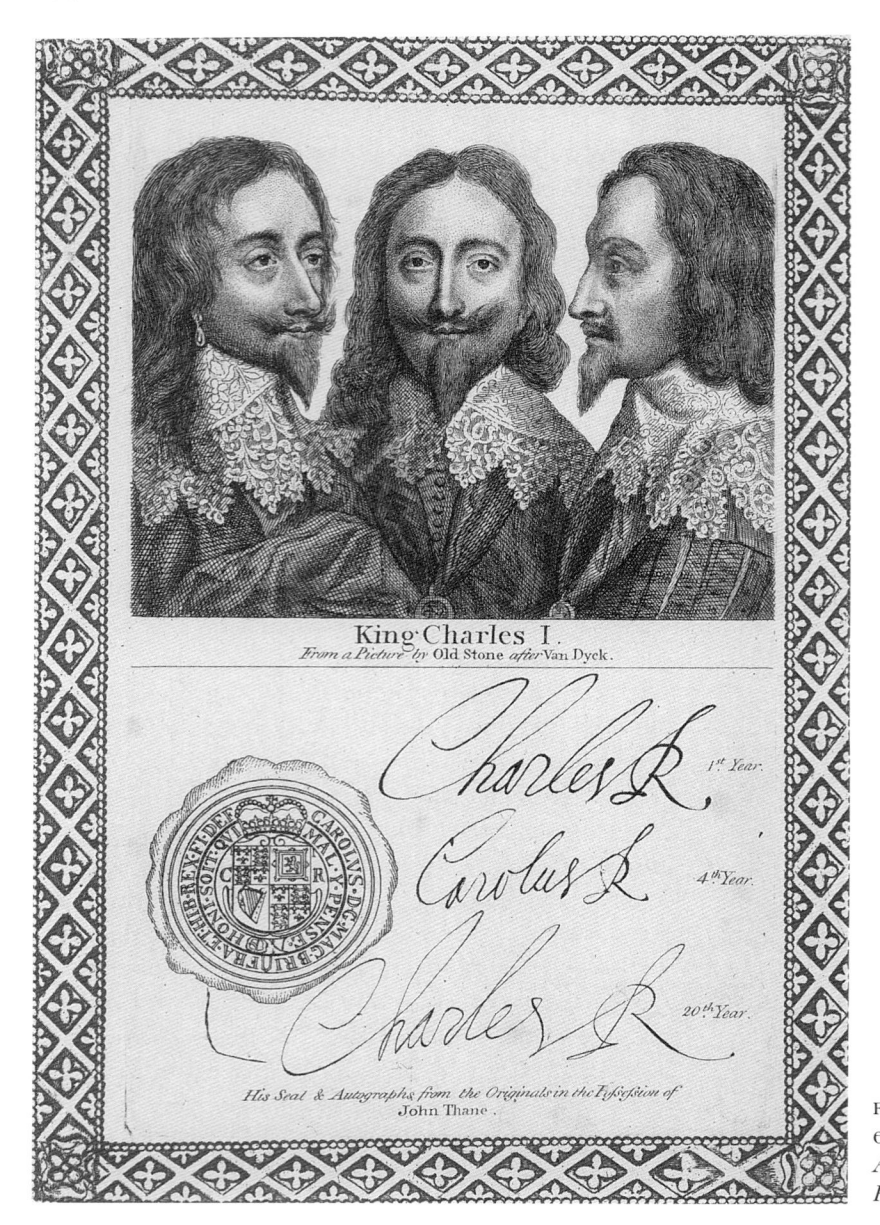

FIGURE 64. Triple portrait of Charles I, engraved by John Thane for *British Autography* (1819).
Private collection

wealth in the City of London, the measured laying-out of it, were alien to him. He had little sympathy with the City merchants, excepting for the few on the edges of the Court circle like Sir Nicholas Crispe, who lent him money without clamouring for its return. As far as the City was concerned, Charles' Court was a withdrawn Court — there was no spontaneous *bonhomie*, no friendly relationship between it and the City. The young monarch had even avoided making the traditional coronation procession along Cheapside, though that was perhaps a sensible precaution since, once again, the plague was rampant. At least the citizens gave Henrietta Maria a hearty welcome when she and Charles sailed up the Thames a few days after their marriage in Canterbury.

There was just one, unexpected occasion in 1634 when the four Inns of Court put on a masque to entertain the King and Queen. The masque, by James Shirley, a former pupil at the Company's school, was *The Triumph of Peace*, but all the organization was left to the young lawyers, two for each Inn being chosen to form a committee. The pair for the

Middle Temple were Edward Hyde, later Lord Clarendon, and Bulstrode Whitelocke, another Merchant Taylors' pupil (see Fig. 60); two decades later, he was to be Cromwell's ambassador at the court of Queen Christina of Sweden.[3] He was particularly responsible for the music, insisted on proper rehearsals, and sometimes had forty lutes, all playing together, at his house in Salisbury Court, off Fleet Street. The masque was performed at the Banqueting House in Whitehall and was such a success that Henrietta Maria begged to see it again, so a second performance was organized at Merchant Taylors' Hall, which Whitelocke would have known well, and was equally applauded, with the Lord Mayor and, presumably, the Master and Wardens in the audience, though there is no mention of the occasion in the Court minutes. The whole entertainment cost £20,000, but everyone present judged it to be well worth the money, though there must have been others who were aghast at the expense.

In the first months of the reign, the City lent £60,000 to the King, of which a large proportion fell to the Merchant Taylors. The money must have been especially welcome since, from the very first, Parliament showed itself suspicious toward Charles and restrictive in the supplies it granted. By the beginning of 1628, Charles's need for money was such that he agreed to convey to the City a proportion of royal lands for £120,000, to be paid in two instalments of £60,000. Of all the companies, the Merchant Taylors' contribution was the highest — £6,300.

Matters did not stop there; in particular, there was trouble over the Irish estates. In trying to colonize them, the City companies were attempting the impossible. Early in 1635, the Court of Star Chamber brought charges that insufficient houses and fortifications had been built, too few able-bodied settlers had gone out, and that the native woodlands had been cut down wantonly and sold off for personal profit. The City attempted to make a financial settlement, but in 1639 all the Irish estates were declared forfeit to the Crown. The management of the property had been a burden and certainly required a huge financial outlay, but the City felt, justifiably, that it was being forcibly deprived of a long-term investment. In spite of all this, the more substantial merchants at least remained loyal to the Crown, though not uncritical.

There was, so far, no thought of the disasters that came upon England during the Civil Wars, yet military matters were very much in men's minds. The struggle against Spain continued in the Netherlands, with English volunteers in the Dutch forces, while the Thirty Years War (1618–48) went on, with increasing violence, in the Holy Roman Empire. That conflict had begun when James's daughter, Elizabeth, and her husband, both firmly Protestant, had accepted the throne of Bohemia, had insulted the Emperor's ambassadors, and had been thrown out of their domain. There was strong feeling that an English army should be sent to support the Princess, but James had refused to send troops and Charles had continued his father's policy, in this instance a wise one. So much experience of conflict brought in new military techniques, and the Guild of St George, otherwise the Artillery Company, which in 1537 had received a charter of incorporation from Henry VIII, was the body through which such information filtered into the minds of Londoners. There was no thought of applying such skills, but men were interested in military matters; in the years to come, the training provided by the Artillery Company would be of real significance.

On 28 August 1638, the Court of Assistants received a request from the Artillery Company for 'leave to exercise their Armes in the Common Hall and Garden'.[4] The request was 'lovingly graunted', and accordingly on 18 October the exercise took place; a description of it was published later as *Mars, his Triumph* by William Barriffe, who had devised the whole display. The account is dedicated to Alderman Thomas Soame, Colonel and President of the Artillery Garden, to John Venn, the Vice-President, and to William Manby, the Treasurer. Now John Venn was an active member of the Merchant Taylors' Company, and was to serve as Warden in 1641–42; it was presumably he who negotiated the use of the Hall, and certainly he who played a role in the tournament as leader of the Christian Captains.

The display was impressive. Eighty men took part, demonstrating the precision of their drill and their skill with musket, pike and sword, the manoeuvres accompanied by fife and drum.⁵ As a final enlivenment, 'a Sentinel gives fire without in the Yard', and 'one comes crying into the Hall Arme, Arme, the Saracens are landed'. Some thirty-eight of the Artillerymen, now disguised as Saracens with turbans on their heads and scimitars in their hands, engaged the Christian Captains in a complicated mock battle till at last — as might have been expected — they submitted, worsted, but were treated with such kindness that they converted to Christianity and 'are now either Merchants or Shopkeepers'.

The display had been watched by the Mayor, many of the aldermen and other important persons. The Artillery Company had its reward, for three years later they were granted the field which they still hold today, the Artillery Ground. By that time, many of these civilian soldiers were about to see action in earnest. William Barriffe, who had devised the spectacle, went on to write *Militarie Discipline*, which ran through six editions and served as a manual for both sides in the Civil War.

We might dismiss, or at least gloss over, the Civil Wars with a few carefully chosen sentences as if they were no direct concern of the Merchant Taylors, as if they were something of such huge importance that they should only be considered on a national scale, outside the scope of the history of a single City company. But however far away from London the main military actions might be fought, the initial explosion occurred in London, and John Venn and other Merchant Taylors played significant roles in the early stages. London was the key to the whole development of the conflict.⁶

In 1636 Charles I made one of his disastrous mistakes. Urged on by Archbishop Laud, he decided to impose the Church of England Prayer Book on his father's ancestral kingdom of Scotland, a place which he had left at the age of three and had visited only once since, for his second coronation there in 1633. However, the Reformation had come about very differently in the two countries. In England it had, initially, been imposed from above, to lend respectability to Henry VIII's marriage plans. It was only gradually that this essentially Lutheran brand of Protestantism took root in men's hearts and flourished there. In Scotland, a sterner, Calvinist faith was accepted first at a humble level in society and then spread rapidly. Charles can have had no realistic idea of how he was challenging his northern kingdom.

In spite of warning, the order was given that the Prayer Book should be read in St Giles Cathedral in Edinburgh on 23 July 1637. Scarcely had the service begun than a woman called Jennie Geddes stood up shrieking and hurled her little seating stool at the clergyman's head. A howling, screaming riot broke out, and the service was only completed with soldiers guarding the doors. Charles decided to march north to subdue his recalcitrant subjects, but to raise and equip an army required money. Rather than summon what he knew would be a highly critical Parliament — he had ruled without one for eleven years — he turned in January 1639 to the City yet again, but met with a cold response. The Aldermen were ordered to collect money, each from his own ward; less than £5,000 was scraped together, and that unwillingly. After an abortive attempt by the King to march on Scotland, which failed for lack of funds, Parliament was summoned, but sat for less than three weeks (13 April–5 May 1640) without agreeing to anything. Once again the King turned to the City, requiring £100,000 and the names of the wealthiest men in each ward. The information was refused, and a week later the King increased his demands to £200,000. Whilst matters were still debated, the King set out for the north, leaving London on 20 August 1640, the very day that the Scottish forces crossed the Tweed and marched south, taking Newcastle without a shot being fired on 30 August, occupying Durham and Northumberland, and halting at last at the river Tees. Charles was forced to sign the Treaty of Ripon by which, until a permanent religious and civil settlement could be negotiated, the Scots might continue to occupy the northern counties, being paid £850 a day maintenance to guarantee peaceful behaviour. There was nothing to do but to call Parliament, and accordingly the Long Parliament, which was to sit until 1660, assembled on 3 November 1640.

The King was in London, but travelled north again in the late summer of the following year to engage in further futile dealings with the Scots. On his return to London, on 25 November 1641, he was entertained with a magnificent banquet, the new Lord Mayor, Richard Gurney, a Clothworker, being a staunch royalist. Charles showed himself gracious as he had never done before. He knighted the Lord Mayor, the Recorder, the Sheriffs and five aldermen and promised the restoration of the Irish estates. This was something of an empty gesture, for savage rebellion had broken out in Ireland a month before, while Parliament had already declared the Ulster sequestration illegal, and had reversed the Star Chamber's sentence by abolishing that much-hated court.

While the King was being feasted in the City, a mob assembled at Whitehall shouting for the abolition of the episcopate and a 'root and branch' reform of the Church of England. Many, including the Venetian ambassador, thought that the demonstration was far from spontaneous:

There was a kind of discipline in disorder, tumults being ready on command, upon a watchword given.

Venn, who had recently been elected one of the City's four Members of Parliament, was recognized as a ringleader. By this time in his mid-fifties (he had been born in 1586), of substantial Somerset yeoman stock, he had come to London in 1602, had served his apprenticeship, and had been made free of the Company in 1610. He was a founder member of the Massachusetts Bay Company — an institution with strongly Puritanical leanings — and traded in wool and silk from a shop in Bread Street. He had served on Common Council from at least 1638 and, as we have seen, was Vice-President of the Artillery Company and an active participant in its exercises. He was not especially wealthy, but was certainly a man of authority who took life and politics seriously.[7]

Now his wife sat in their shop, sobbing and wringing her hands, crying out that he had sent her a message from Westminster that he was likely to be killed. Her neighbour, a grocer, tapping his sword-hilt and brandishing a pistol, assured her that, should such a thing happen, he and others would take revenge. Venn, however, came home safely, and published a calming address which he said he had delivered to the rioters. He may have made such a speech, but there were those who felt he had made others of a different tenor, and in a pamphlet published two years later by the King at Oxford, Venn, along with Alderman Isaac Pennington, Alderman John Fowke and Thomas Manby, was named as one of the chief instigators of the troubles.

On 21 December 1641, the elections were held for Common Council, and it was at once clear that that body had been largely taken over by the radical element, while the Court of Aldermen remained substantially royalist. Parliament, which had been in recess over Christmas, reassembled on 3 January 1642. Charles refused its request for a guard, but the Commons sent a message to the Lord Mayor to have the Trained Bands in readiness 'for the safety of the King's person, the City and the Commonwealth'; the reference to the King's safety was probably politic rather than heartfelt. On that day, Charles attempted the impeachment of the five Members most critical of his policies, Pym, Hampden, Holles, Hazelrigg, and Strode. That failing, ignoring the centuries-old rule that the monarch does not enter the House of Commons, he came to demand them in person. By then the five were safe in the City, probably in property in Coleman Street belonging to Alderman Pennington, and Speaker Lenthall, on his knees, declared that he

had neither eyes to see nor tongue to speak in this place but as this house is pleased to direct me, whose servant I am here.

The King, looking round, realized that 'the birds had flown', and sought them the next day in Guildhall, where Common Council was sitting, but without success. He invited himself to dinner with Alderman Garrett, a Draper and a supporter of the Parliamentary Opposition, made his way through an over-excited mob, and later returned to Whitehall with people screaming 'No bishops! No bishops!' around his coach. The next day, Common Council petitioned the King not to proceed against the Five Members other than in accordance with the privileges of Parliament. Parliament itself was invited to meet in Guildhall, since men feared that Westminster was too conveniently close for a royal attack; Committees of the House met in Merchant Taylors' Hall, though there is no mention of this in the Court minutes.

The City put itself in readiness lest the King's supporters should make a night assault. In the words of Nehemiah Wallington, a turner in Eastcheap, 'there was great bouncing at every man's door'. The Trained Bands were armed, a double watch equipped with muskets and halberds, and chains strung across the streets to impede charging horsemen.

Older citizens, well acquainted with Antwerp, recalled the sack of that city by the Spaniards in 1576 — the 'Spanish Fury' it was called — when 7,000 citizens were butchered in a single night; in 1631 Magdeburg had been left a smoking ruin by Imperial troops, particular violence having been shown to the women, and the number of dead being given at 20,000 at the lowest estimate; more recent stories, of horrors committed within the last few weeks, of massacres of babies and young children, were coming from Ireland. If an attack on the City were planned, the citizens were going to put up a hard fight.

No attack came. The long January nights passed without alarm. On 10 January 1642, Charles made his worst mistake. Despite, men said, the heartfelt entreaties of the Royalist Lord Mayor, the King and Queen left the capital for Hampton Court with their three eldest children. On the following day, the Five Members stepped into a barge at Three Cranes Wharf — a Company property — and were rowed up to Westminster accompanied by a veritable Lord Mayor's Day water procession, while crowds cheered all the way from the banks. Popular support had now swung behind the more radical elements in Parliament. A generation later, Edward Hyde, by that time Lord Clarendon, described London as 'the sink of the ill-humours of this kingdom', and an anonymous pamphlet, published in the summer of 1643, laid responsibility for the conflict firmly on the City:

Could Saye or Pym and their beggarly confederates have found money to levy an army against their liege Lord, that had not money to pay their own debts, had not [London] furnished them? ... If ... posterity shall ask ... who would have pulled the crown from the King's head, taken the government off the hinges, dissolved Monarchy, enslaved the laws, and ruined their country; Say, 'twas the proud, unthankful, schismatical, rebellious, bloody City of London.[8]

London knew its own importance, and others recognized it too.

Through all this, Company matters had gone on as usual at the Hall. On 7 December 1641 prayers had been read in 'reverent manner', and the Court had heard that John Escott, a woollen-draper at Launceston in Cornwall, was too far away to serve as a Warden Substitute. They contemplated a new lease of the Company's farm near Maidstone, and then went to dinner. On 8 January 1642, £200 was voted for the relief of sufferers in Ireland; the Court, noting that the Master, Clement Mosse, was out of pocket because the Company had lent so much money to the King, decided to borrow £1,000 at the lowest possible interest rate. They also ruled that the Quarter Day Dinner should be cancelled because of 'the sadnes of the tymes'. At the next meeting, on 9 March, they agreed that the King's Day Dinner should be treated similarly, because it fell on a Sunday — a diplomatic excuse. On John Sictor, a 'poore Bohemian' refugee in this country for religion's sake, they bestowed 40s.; they gave him more money five years later. George Langham and Warden John Venn, now both Captains, were instructed to check the arms and armour stored in the Hall, to make the suits of equipment up to 200, and to prepare a list of the weaponry.[9] At the next meeting, on 1 April, the Wardens were instructed to meet with other Wardens in Guildhall to confer over the £5,000 already lent to the King. The Court agreed to provide two 'peeces of Artillery' for Londonderry in the form of two demi-culverins. School business took up most of the May meeting; wider issues were to be discussed on 10 June. A year later Langham, on campaign with the Parliamentary army and sick of a fever, wrote to say that he could not accept the honour of being Master; a week later, the fever had killed him.

Throughout the earlier months of 1642, matters had been growing steadily worse in Ireland. The King was in no position to send help; Parliament ordered Venn and Pennington to see how money might best be raised from the livery companies. Venn commanded the Lord Mayor — still the Royalist, Sir Richard Gurney — to summon Common Hall; Parliament was asking for £100,000 for Ireland, to be raised from the companies and repaid with 8 per cent interest 'out of the first and next moneys to be graunted by Acte of Parliament'.

The Court of Assistants and some of the Bachelors assembled at the Hall on 10 June 1642.[10] The Master, Clement Mosse, recited the circumstances in which previous royal loans had been raised. But this was different — Mosse was one of the foremost lawyers of his day and perceived the danger. The money — £10,000 as the Merchant Taylors' share — was being sought by Common Hall, the general assembly of the liverymen of the City. To accede would put the Company's resources into the hands of a popular assembly. The Company had already met one demand after another for cash. Could not Captain Venn — for such he now was — win back the £5,000 already lent to the King? He promised his 'best endeavor therein'. Mosse then pointed out that the larger sum would either have to be lent by such individuals as trusted the word of Parliament, or raised as a loan on the Company's seal. He would himself prefer the former course, 'alleadging that hee had rather loose such parte of his owne then the Companies moneys, yett it was agreed that it should bee put to the question'. The meeting was becoming more than Mosse could control. A vote was taken, and it was agreed that the money should be raised on the common seal of the Company, that the lenders should be restricted to members of the Company, and that they should receive interest from the Company at eight per cent. For their security, if needs be, the Company's lands, plate and goods should be sold. The money was paid over in two instalments, on 20 June and 22 August. The latter was the day — a miserable, wet, rainy one — on which the King raised his standard at Nottingham. Full-scale warfare was now unavoidable. By this time, Sir Richard Gurney had been deposed as Lord Mayor and his place taken by the radical Fishmonger, Alderman Isaac Pennington.

The first major action of the war was fought at Edgehill in Warwickshire on Sunday, 23 October 1642. Both sides claimed victory. The Parliamentary army drew off northwards, leaving the road to London open. Though urged by his nephew, Prince Rupert, to make a quick dash for the capital, the King proceeded in a leisurely manner, marching first to Oxford and then turning eastwards towards London.

Fearing the threat from the King's forces, the City decided to throw up eleven miles of defences around the capital. This met with an immediate popular response and the livery companies turned out in full force. William Lithgow, a Scottish traveller visiting London, observed how the Londoners were

wondrous commendable, in marching to the fields and outworks (as merchants, silk-men, mercers, shopkeepers, &c) with greate alacritie, carrying on their shoulders yron mattocks and wooden shovels; with roaring drummes, flying colours, and girded swords; most companies being also interlarded with ladies, women and girles . . . carrying baskets, for to advance the labour . . . The greatest company which I observed to march out . . . were the [guild of] taylours, carrying fourtie-six collours, and seconded with eight thousand lusty men.[11]

Feminine participation made a particular impression on the beholders. The Lord Mayor's wife, Abigail Pennington, was there with the foremost, wielding an entrenching tool, while behind her the women of London

> March'd rank and file with drum and ensign
> T'entrench the City for defence in;
> Rais'd rampires with their own soft hands,
> To put the enemy to stands;
> From ladies down to oyster-wenches
> Labour'd like pioneers in trenches,
> Fell to their pick-axes and tools,
> And help'd the men to dig like moles.[12]

On 28 October, Venn was ordered to seize the royal castle at Windsor, which he did; a few days after, he fought off a sharp attack by Rupert's advance guard, and the castle withstood a seven-hour bombardment. On Friday, 11 November, the London Trained Bands under Philip Skippon marched along the Thames Valley to meet the royal forces. Early in the morning of 12 November, Rupert and his cavalry attacked Brentford, surprised the defenders and did a good deal of damage. Parliamentary pamphlets described it as worse than the sack of Magdeburg, but no civilian life seems to have been lost, just a great deal of property smashed. The two armies faced each other, but the Londoners twice out-numbered the Royalist forces, and moreover were kept well supplied by their womenfolk from the capital. The King's hungry supporters drew off, Charles making his headquarters first at Reading and then at Oxford.

Venn remained as Governor of Windsor Castle. He was a disciplinarian, who kept his men under tight control. For a few weeks, horses were stabled in St George's Chapel but, compared with the desecration done at St Paul's Cathedral, there was comparatively little damage — the heads remain on the 203 stone angels, and the glass survived unbroken. However, Venn was ordered to take into his custody the insignia and records of the Order of the Garter, which were in the keeping of Dr Christopher Wren, Dean of the Chapel and father of a ten-year-old boy, the future architect of the post-Fire St Paul's. Understandably, the Dean refused to give up his charge, his study was broken into, and the treasures removed, though some of the records were later returned to his keeping. Venn moved into the Deanery, making it his headquarters and office, and the Wren family moved out, settling at last at Bletchingdon in Oxfordshire where the Dean's eldest daughter, sixteen-year-old Susan, was married to the rector, William Holder, who began to teach mathematics to his small brother-in-law.

There were Royalist prisoners within the castle; towards them Venn behaved firmly but fairly, though his conscience forbade him to permit prayers to be read at the funerals of any who died, since such a practice was considered Popish. He had more trouble with the Fifth Monarchy men, an extreme group who believed that the end of the world was nigh. One of them, Christopher Feake, refused to stop preaching from his prison window; Venn organized a drummer to drown the sound at intervals. The Royalist journal, *Mercurius Aulicus*, commented on his governorship from time to time, alleging that Mrs Venn had abandoned the shop in Bread Street and would only sleep in the Queen's apartments. This sounds like propaganda, for Venn himself was certainly in the Deanery.

* * *

Before long the City began to realize that, if royal demands for money had been heavy, those of Parliament were no better. The Court of Assistants was careful to set down the demands made upon the Company — £5,000 to the King, £10,000 for the relief of Ireland, and £4,050 for the defence of the City. Interest at 8 per cent was due on all these sums, but little of it was paid, and by 1647 £24,731 8s. 2d. was due to the Company.[13] Nevertheless, having made its choice, the City stood by Parliament, and Common Council entertained both Houses of Parliament to a public dinner at Merchant Taylors' Hall.

Inevitably there were some among the Company who profited from the troubles of the times. Both armies needed equipment — guns and swords, boots and uniforms — and uniforms are made by tailors. Records are scanty, but a few survive in the Public Record Office; none of the names can be tied securely to a member of the Company, but connections there must have been.[14]

Things were difficult out of London, too. The manor of Rushock, intended to provide an income to maintain the school at Wolverhampton, was assailed at intervals by Parliamentarians, Royalists and the Scots, and it was not only money that was demanded. Provisions had to be sent to Hartlebury Castle on two occasions,[15] as well as to 'the Scotts army lying at Wyche [Wick, near Pershore]', 'to them at Bewdley', and to Worcester; the cost was assessed at £20 3s. 2d. Then free quarter was demanded on thirteen occasions, the sums involved ranging from 15s. for putting up two officers, five men and ten horses for one night, to £12 10s. 0d. for '1000 of Sir William Wallers men in his martch from Stowrbridge to Huesham [Evesham] after the King', and £21 0s. 0d. for quartering '70 Horse of the Lord Mollineux his reformadoes 4 daies and nights, his Lordshipp and his brother being then there'. Money spent by the Company's tenant, Francis Finch, totalled £406 13s. 11d., but that takes no account of the trouble involved in finding sheets, bedding, food, straw and hay; the housewives must have felt particularly harassed.[16]

The Court minutes thereafter become more and more bland, increasingly non-committal. Those of the Mercers' Company do the same, and so do those of the Joint Grand Gresham Committee for the Royal Exchange. These were dangerous times and were recognized as such; it was safer not to say too much publicly. However, a significant number of individuals, realizing the importance of what was happening around them, kept diaries. One of them was Thomas Juxon, a member of a leading Merchant Taylor family. Born in London on 24 June 1614, he was baptized in his parents' parish of St Stephen Walbrook. His father was a Merchant Taylor but earned a prosperous living as a sugar baker and refiner. Thomas attended the Company's school as a boy, and was bound apprentice to William Allott, a liveryman of the Company, on 29 November 1630, though in the end he obtained his freedom by patrimony on 25 October 1637. He was admitted to the livery on 8 July 1646. He then went into partnership with his maternal uncle, Matthew Sheppard, another

FIGURE 65. St John's College, Oxford, founded in 1555 by Sir Thomas White, Merchant Taylor. Canterbury Quad, shown here, was added in 1631–36 by Archbishop Laud who had been President of the College from 1611 to 1622; it is the finest building of its date in Oxford.
National Monuments Record, English Heritage

sugar baker, and later made a successful marriage to Elizabeth Carent, a well-connected young lady from a Somerset family. As a convinced Parliamentarian, though in no way fanatical, Juxon was active in the Green Regiment of the City Trained Bands, and saw action at the first Battle of Newbury in October 1643, when his elder brother John was mortally wounded and he himself injured. His diary, or rather journal, which he wrote up at intervals, opens on 1 January 1644, contains little that is personal, and makes no mention of the Company. It is, however, of great interest for public events. Juxon clearly recognized the importance of the times in which he lived, and through his family and business connections was possessed of much inside information about the religious and political manoeuvrings of the day. Unfortunately, the journal ends abruptly on 6 August 1647,[17] though Juxon lived on to serve as MP for Helston in Cornwall in Richard Cromwell's only Parliament, to see the Restoration, to be elected a junior Warden of the Company in 1669–70, and at the same time to be appointed to the Court of Assistants on which he served until his death on 2 October 1672.

Thomas Juxon, like many others, had relations on the King's side, among them William Juxon, a future

Archbishop of Canterbury. Though he himself strongly disapproved of the episcopate, Thomas was fair-minded enough to record another Archbishop, William Laud, 'dying in a most calm and composed manner' when he was executed on Tower Hill on 10 January 1645 by the orders of Parliament. As President of St John's College (Fig. 65), Laud had been closely associated with the Company, and had given time generously to school inspections; we have already noted that, after one such occasion, he dined with the Master and Wardens at the Ship tavern. His body was carried into All Hallows church by the Tower where a courageous clergyman, Thomas Fletcher, dared to read the forbidden funeral service over the coffin. His body remained there till after the Restoration, when St John's welcomed it and buried him before the high altar, where he remains. His tortoise lived on for another 108 years, and was only killed through a gardener's carelessness.

By early 1647, the defeated King had been sold to Parliament by his hereditary subjects the Scots. It became obvious that Charles would never consent to any settlement that would satisfy Parliament, and that he would stand by the Church of England and his royal prerogative, come what might. Cromwell and his supporters in the army began to think the unthinkable: that the only solution was to charge the King with all the deaths and miseries of the Civil War, to bring him to public trial, and to condemn and execute him.

Accordingly, negotiations with the King were broken off. On 6 December 1648, Colonel Pride stood at the door of the House of Commons and turned away or arrested all those Members who might have expressed support for the royal cause, while on 23 December the Commons appointed a committee 'to consider how to proceed by way of justice against the King and other capital offenders'. When those few Lords who were still sitting demurred, the Commons declared that they 'were the supreme power in the nation'. By this time Fairfax, with substantial portions of the army, had entered the City, had seized all he could find in the treasuries of the Goldsmiths', Haberdashers' and Weavers' Companies, and was quartering his soldiers in St Paul's, in Ludgate, in Blackfriars or in private houses. By express order, Merchant Taylors' Hall was spared from billeting either horse or foot, since Quartermaster-General Gravenor was free of the Company; on 2 January 1649 the Court gratefully voted him £20 and rewarded his man, who brought Fairfax's letter, with 10s.

In the previous autumn, as was customary, a new Lord Mayor had been elected. The choice had fallen on a Merchant Taylor, Abraham Reynardson (Col. Pl. XVIIIB). Born in 1590 at Plymouth, he had come to London, been apprenticed to Edmund James, had served his time, and had become a freeman of the Company and of London on 5 October 1618. He had married twice, first with Abigail, daughter of the profoundly royalist Sir Nicholas Crispe, and then, on her death in 1632, to Eleanor Wynne; the surviving sons from both marriages attended the Company's school. In December 1625, Reynardson was elected a Warden Substitute of the Bachelors' Company, and was taken onto the livery in the following year. He prospered, was active in the East India and Levant Companies, bought a substantial house on Tottenham Green, and in 1640 leased from the Company a mansion in Bishopsgate which had once belonged to Henry VIII's chancellor, Lord Wriothesley.

In 1639, his name was put forward as Sheriff, but he fined rather than serve at that time. However, he was elected Master of the Company in the following year, and at the same time was required to serve his turn as Sheriff. Clearly well-organized, he contrived to fulfil both offices. In the autumn of 1648, he was elected Lord Mayor, his Company loyally voting him on 18 October one hundred marks to 'trim up his Lordship's house', and offering him the loan of any plate that he might care to borrow. He was going to need all the support he could get.

Common Council was to be elected, as usual, on St Thomas's day, 21 December. On the 18th and 20th of that month, Parliament passed an ordinance disenfranchizing anyone who had recommended negotiations with the King. The City pleaded in vain that this would disqualify so many that it would be impossible to carry on the administration, but the House of Commons was adamant.

With the army now in general control, and any formal protest apparently effectively stifled, the new Common Council were due to assemble on 13 January. Reynardson had already forbidden any to take his seat unless he would take the oath of allegiance;

the House of Commons had promptly suspended all such oath-taking. With the preparations for the King's trial already going forward, it was vital for Cromwell and his supporters to appear to act with the approval of the people; the City's consent to the King's trial and execution was essential. Reynardson denied it to them.

On 13 January 1649, Common Council assembled at eight o'clock in the morning, a usual enough hour in those days. Normally the Lord Mayor, accompanied by as many aldermen as happened to be available, and preceded by the civic Mace and Sword, would join them immediately. But on that particular day, Reynardson kept the Council waiting till eleven o'clock and, when he arrived, had only two aldermen with him. He refused to acknowledge the authority of a Council so composed, or to allow the minutes of the last meeting to be read. The Council passed over this and asked leave to read a petition to the House of Commons which they had been considering in committee. Reynardson knew perfectly well what that petition contained, and refused to let it be read. A debate, or rather an argument, followed, but the Lord Mayor stood firm. The altercation continued for several hours — in Reynardson's funeral sermon, the preacher claimed eight[18] — till finally he rose, followed by his mace-bearer, and led the two aldermen from the chamber. The gathering was no longer an official body.

Those present demanded that the Town Clerk or Common Serjeant should take over the meeting, but they refused and left as well. Colonel Owen Rowe then took the chair and the petition was read and passed. It called upon the House of Commons

to advance the interest of impartial justice, so you would vigorously proceed in the execution thereof upon all the grand and capital authors, contrivers of, and actors in, the late wars against the Parliament and Kingdom, from the highest to the lowest. That the wrath of God may be appeased, good men satisfied, and evil men deterred from adventuring upon the like practices for the future

and declared that

the Commons of England, in Parliament assembled, have the supreme power of this nation.

On 15 January, it was presented to the Commons and received with much satisfaction.

However, Reynardson's withdrawal meant that, whatever might be claimed, the petition did not have the authority of the City behind it. By his stand, he kept his own conscience clear, and saved the City from formal assent to the King's execution. According to his funeral sermon, he went still further, tearing and burning any documentary evidence of those who had striven to make some sort of treaty with the King — it was said that he destroyed full two reams of paper.

The King was brought from Windsor to London on 19 January, and his trial commenced the next day. It lasted a week, Charles steadfastly refusing to acknowledge the legality of the court. The verdict was a foregone conclusion; John Venn was one of the fifty-nine who signed the death warrant (Fig. 66). Three days later, on 30 January, the King was executed before his own Banqueting House in Whitehall. Beside him on the scaffold, sustaining the monarch to the last, stood William Juxon, Bishop of London, once a pupil at Merchant Taylors' School and a student at St John's College. He was among those who accompanied the coffin to Windsor and saw it lowered, still covered in its velvet pall, into the royal vault, to lie close to that of Henry VIII. In Juxon's hand was a closed copy of the Book of Common Prayer, for he was forbidden to read the funeral service and refused to extemporize in a Puritanical manner. By this time, the Governor of Windsor Castle was Bulstrode Whitelocke; two former pupils of the Company's school were obliged to confront each other.

* * *

Until 2 January 1649, the Court minutes invariably begin with the relevant date coupled with the King's regnal year. After the execution, there was no meeting till 7 March, when the date alone is given. The Company was ordered to destroy the royal arms and to take down any painting of the late monarch; wisely, it obeyed. The kingly office was abolished by Act of what remained of Parliament on 17 March. Alderman Pennington had a copy delivered to Reynardson's house in Bishopsgate Street. His wife refused to give the bearer a drink, as was the custom, 'bidding him to return to his masters for his wages'.

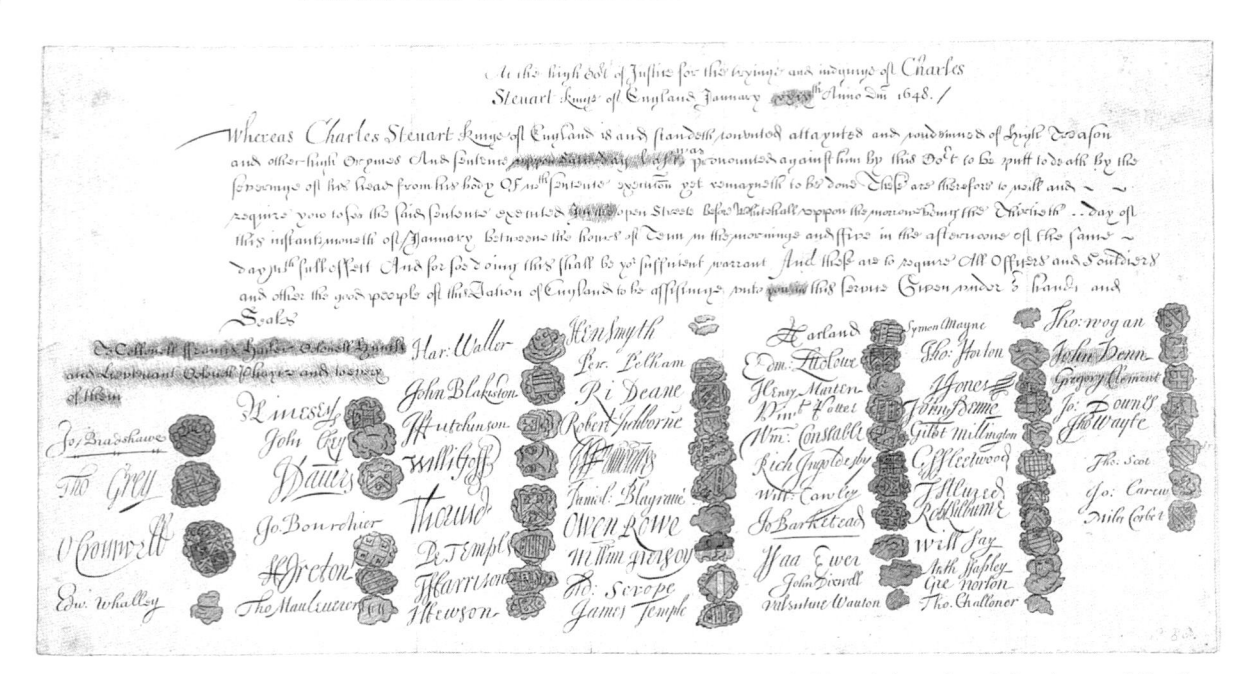

FIGURE 66. Charles I's death warrant, 1649, signed by Cromwell and fifty-eight other Members of Parliament, including John Venn, Merchant Taylor. His signature is in the right-hand column, near the top.
Guildhall Library

Reynardson, fully aware of what the consequences would be, determined not to proclaim the Act. On 29 March he presided over his last civic Court, and on 2 April was summoned to the House of Commons to answer for his obduracy. He declared he was acting according to his conscience, and the House deprived him of his mayoralty and his aldermanry, shut him in the Tower and fined him £2,000. This he refused to pay, so his goods were distrained and sold by auction in 1651. On his release from prison, he resumed his place on the Merchant Taylors' Court of Assistants, being present on 19 January, 9 February and 16 November 1653, and on 1 March and 20 July 1654, besides acting as auditor in 1655–56. The Court minutes cease in July 1654 and do not resume till 1663; we must turn to other evidence for the history of those years. But before 1654, one name has vanished from those on the Court of Assistants — John Venn's. In 1648, he had been elected Master, but had refused — his Parliamentary duties were too demanding. The man who had been brave enough to sign the King's death warrant — and to do so must have required much thought and much courage — was now dead himself. On 28 June 1650, his friends noted, he had been cheerful enough. He had gone to bed with his wife at their usual time, but when she awoke in the morning he was dead beside her, though she had neither heard nor sensed anything untoward. The Royalists put it about that there was something sinister in the death, or that it was suicide, but the most likely explanation is heart failure or a stroke. Venn was sixty-six, and in later life had exerted himself beyond all reason for a man of his years. It was fortunate for him that he did not live to see the Restoration.

THE COMPANY'S SCHOOLS

During the Interregnum, the Company's chief concern was with the schools under its care. From the very beginning of the Civil War, once the King had made Oxford his headquarters, it became almost impossible for St John's College to send assessors to the school in London to select future students. Nevertheless, students continued to go to Oxford on the Company's recommendation, and the links with the College remained strong.[19]

Wolverhampton and Great Crosby had long provided the Company with much unrest and anxiety. We have already recounted the story of Mr Barnes and his 'hurly-burly' with the townsfolk of Wolverhampton in 1609–10. His successor, William Wilson, held the headmastership for eighteen years and then accepted a good living in the vicinity, possibly accounting the care of souls less exhausting than the care of young boys. During his term of office, William Burton, the Usher or second master, had to be dismissed in the summer of 1619 for unspecified reasons, but was given a pension on which he lived in humble comfort for another seventeen years. His place was taken by William Smith, for whom a separate house was built with additional rooms in it so that boys who lived too far away could board.

In 1626, the townspeople became convinced that the Company was failing to spend the full income from the manor of Rushock on the school, but was instead diverting the money into its own coffers. This was completely untrue; hearings in Court demonstrated that the Company was heavily out of pocket in its administration of the school and care for the buildings, but the wrangling dragged on and on.[20]

The next headmaster, Gervaise Needham, only lasted two years before he too moved to a good living. His tenure must have been satisfactory, for the Merchant Taylors voted him a gratuity of £13 6s. 8d. He was succeeded by Daniel Rawlett, who ran the school to everyone's satisfaction for nearly thirty years from 1629 to 1658, being buried at last in the churchyard of the parish which he had served.

During his headmastership, the school was visited in 1629, 1640 and 1648 by deputations of Merchant Taylors. It was no light undertaking, even in the best of times, to travel more than a hundred miles from London. It meant four or five days' steady riding each way with attendant dangers, especially during the Civil War, and is some measure of the seriousness with which the Company undertook its responsibilities towards its schools.

It was a good thing that Daniel Rawlett was a calm, strong headmaster. As usher, he had Francis Storr, appointed at almost the same time as himself. The younger man's Puritanical sermons pleased his congregations and his teaching was satisfactory, but when a Royalist force occupied the town in the summer of 1642, Storr was turned out of school and pulpit, and replaced by the local curate. At such a time the Company could only send £5 to Storr, and a severe letter to the authorities in Wolverhampton. When Parliamentarian troops occupied the town in March 1643, Mr Storr resumed his duties, only to be ejected again when the fortunes of war changed and the King visited Wolverhampton. A few months later, in January 1647, on the advice of William Dugard, headmaster of the London school, Samuel Crosse was chosen as usher, and travelled north, but within eighteen months the local inhabitants were complaining about him too, accusing him of unspecified 'scandalous crimes', and Francis Storr was reinstated yet again. He occupied the usher's house, newly completed at a cost of £282 13s. 4d., and wrote humbly to the Company, begging that his floor might be paved, and that he might have a little piece of the school ground set aside as a garden for his house. Both were granted to him, and he remained in post, contentedly, till his death in 1661.

The country being quieter by the spring of 1648, a deputation set out from the Hall. It consisted of the Master, George Nash, the Wardens Nicholas Jerrard and Ozias Churchman, an Assistant, John Stone, and Mr Dugard, headmaster of the London school, together with the Clerk. They went first to Coventry, since that city was in receipt of Sir Thomas White's perambulating bounty for young freemen, which the Company administered. There they found the accounts in good order, and were made very welcome at the Guildhall. They then travelled on to Great Crosby School, and finally, on their return journey, to Wolverhampton. There they recognized, perhaps rather grudgingly, that Mr Rawlett was doing his best in 'these distracted times', though there were a mere forty pupils in the school; they agreed that the salaries were far too low, that the schoolhouse was in much need of repair, that a new house was needed for the usher and for boarding students, and that books must be provided for the pupils. Then they had a very unpleasant experience:

While we were att Woolverhampton, many of the Townesmen came to us demaunding an Accompt of much money (as they pretended) to bee in the Companies hands which should be imployed there according to the Decree of the Court of Chancery.

The deputation produced an account which showed that the Company was out of pocket over the school but, realizing the strength of feeling in the town, thought it wise to recommend higher salaries and to put the building work in hand straight away. The Company thanked its deputation for the labours undertaken, and approved of all that had been done, raising Mr Rawlett's salary to £40 and the usher's to £26 13s. 4d., with an additional £3 6s. 8d. for teaching the younger children to write, thereby making it £30 in all.

The deputation had already met with problems at Great Crosby. The origins of these went back almost thirty years, to the very foundation of the school and, like the Company's deputation, we need to be aware of the details. The school at Great Crosby had been founded in 1620 under the will of John Harrison, cloth merchant, who had been admitted to the Company by patrimony on 9 August 1591, and had been advanced to the livery on 10 July 1602. He had bequeathed the Company £500 with which to build a free grammar school there, together with property in Crane Court, in Old Change and in St Swithin's Lane, to provide an endowment.[21] The work was put in hand, a schoolhouse and dwelling for a master half-built, and a headteacher appointed. He was John Kidde, a former student of Emmanuel College, Cambridge, which indicated that his religious views were likely to be fairly strongly Puritan. Unfortunately for him, many of the families in the area still clung to the old religion, and there was at once friction between them and the newly appointed headmaster, especially over the teaching of the catechism. Kidde wrote the Company asking for advice. He was instructed to stand firm, but with discretion, so that the boys might be 'drawn to be conformable to good orders'. Before long, Kidde had thirty boys in the school, and in December 1622 the Company appointed an usher, Thomas Carter, who had been servant to Richard Baldock, the Clerk. Though not a graduate, Carter had been examined by William Hayne, the headmaster of the London school, and was considered well able to teach the younger children. He travelled north and soon after married; the Carters moved into the more-or-less completed house with Kidde and his wife, and before long the two couples were bickering with each other. By the summer of 1627 the Company, with firm if lengthy letters, was having to step in to keep the peace and to admonish 'Mr Carter to carry a better respect to Mr Kidd, the Cheife Master'. Carter was instructed to find lodgings in the town, for which the Company would pay the rent. Friction continued and the Company wrote again to Carter:

It is a generall observacion and custome in all free schooles whatsoever, that the Ushers are subordinate and directed in the teaching of the scholers by the cheife Master of the said schoole . . . Carry your selfe towards him in a more respectfull manner then formerly you have done, and . . . take and observe such direccions and orders from him for the governing of the schoole as shalbe expedient and as may redound to the honor thereof . . . Your manner of living with Mr Kid wilbe more loving and correspondent then in tymes past it hath.

Carter sent his wife and small son, John, to argue his case with the Court, but by March 1628 it was clear the situation was beyond remedy. The Court dismissed him, and appointed in his place John Fell, of Pembroke College, Cambridge, on the advice of their London headmaster, Dr Nicholas Gray.

In the July of the following year the Company decided to make an inspection of the school, and in September the immediate Past Master, Robert Draper, set out, accompanied by another former Master, Ralph Gore, and three Court members, Bartholomew Elnor, George Benson and Simon Beardall, together with the future Master, Clement Mosse, who was then serving as Clerk. They found the school to be 'very fair and substantially builded in freestone', but that it was

verry slenderlie furnished with schollers, and many of those schollers the children of poore people, and some of them papistes.

Messrs Kidde and Fell were struggling to teach the children simply to read and write; there was very little studying of Latin and Greek. The Company nevertheless provided the school with an impressive library of Latin dictionaries, a Graeco-Latin lexicon, and a good collection of classical authors and anthologies.

All went smoothly for a few years, but by January 1635 steady inflation was making life difficult for the Kidde family, which now had stretched to six children. The Company,

In respect of the hardnes of the times [and] the dearth of corne and other necessaries for household provision in those partes allowed Kidde 15s. a year to rent three acres of land on which to grow wheat, barley and fodder for his cattle — he presumably hired someone to till and sow the ground, but it must have diverted his attention from the school, and his usher, John Fell, became lax in his teaching. By the outbreak of the Civil War, the school was in poor shape.

The situation now became more difficult for Kidde; he was a Puritan in an area which was strongly Royalist. Between the two forces, the whole countryside was ravaged, and at intervals Kidde was forced to abandon the school and take refuge in the Parliamentary stronghold of Bank Hall, the home of Colonel John Moore who was to be another who signed the King's death warrant. Once the Royalist forces were expelled from the area Kidde, instead of returning to his charge with renewed zeal, decided to take upon himself the ministry of the chapel at Crosby, and the school continued to suffer.

In 1648 the Company's inspection team arrived. Mr Dugard examined the thirty children and found the results most unsatisfactory — 'not above two scholars in the schoole which could perfectly read a chapter in the Bible'. Mr Fell, 'a very deboshed man and very scandalous in his life', was dismissed; he had held the post for twenty dangerous and difficult years, and we may feel that the quarter's salary allowed to him, with an additional £5, was not particularly generous. A local Committee of Visitors was organized, who reported adversely on Mr Kidde; his religious views had never accorded with those of the neighbourhood. He defended himself with a powerful letter to the Company, for he and his wife now had eight children, 'one whereof is a creeple', but in vain. In September 1651 he moved out of the school house into rented lodgings, but continued as minister to the chapel. He died in 1654 and was buried there. His place at the school was filled by Dr John Stevens, once headmaster of the Company's school in Suffolk Lane, and with his name, we must return to London, for the Merchant Taylors' worst educational problems were on their own doorstep.

In October 1634, the Company had appointed a new headmaster, William Staple, who had attended the school as a boy and was now a Fellow of St John's. Archbishop Laud had assured the Company that he was a 'fitt and hable schoolemaster'. There was plague raging in London in 1636–37, the junior forms were closed, and the younger boys had been sent home, but Staple kept the senior form together and managed to send a scholar to St John's in spite of the college's refusal to visit London. All seemed to be going well, but on 18 October 1643, Parliament, determined to extend its control of education, set up a Committee with 'power to enquire after malignant Schoolmasters'. Staple, known to be staunchly Royalist, was summoned to give an account of himself, failed to appear, and was dismissed. The Committee appointed Nicholas Augar, 'Schoolmaster at Mercers Chappell', in his place, but the Company, feeling their authority to be abused, temporized, and finally on 10 May 1644 appointed their own man, William Dugard, on condition he should not 'attend or follow anie other calling during his continuance of cheife schoolemaster'.[22] Little did they know.

For the first few years, all went well. The headmaster's learning was beyond question, and the discipline good — so good, in fact, that the pupils begged for a little respite. *The Scholars Petition for Play-Dayes* was published on 21 March 1645, 'being the day of their publick Examination'. The anonymous poet assured the Company that

> A Bow, a while unbent, will after cast
> His shafts still farther, and them fix more fast.

He continued

> Thus your poor Orators devoutly pray
> That you sequester would some time for Play.
> O let not then our Masters be our Jailors!
> So shall we ever pray for MERCHANT-TAILORS.

It seems doubtful whether Dugard took any notice.

His relationship with the Company remained good. As we have seen, he accompanied the deputation to Great Crosby in 1648, and he was afterwards voted £20 as a reward. On his advice, books were added to the school library, and the headmaster began to write textbooks specifically for use in the school, though employed by other establishments as well. He also set up a register of boys admitted to the school, with details of their parentage, age and achievements. But then the situation began to change. At the end of 1647, or early in 1648, Dugard acquired a printing press from Robert Young, and on 10 February 1648 he was, without charge, made free of the Stationers' Company, 'hee being a gentleman well deserving and may bee helpfull in the correction of the Companies School Bookes'. On the premises of the school, he began both to print and to publish; between 1648 and 1661 he was responsible, in whole or in part, for 171 volumes, thirty-three of them relevant to his own calling, and seventy-seven concerned with theology, science, medicine and economics. However, the remaining sixty-one were political, and there the trouble began.

The King was executed on 30 January 1649, and the next day a small volume appeared, *Eikon Basilike*, purporting to have been written by Charles himself. It was more likely, at least in an editorial sense, to have been the work of John Gauden, whom Charles II later made Bishop of Worcester, and only parts of it by the dead monarch, but whatever the authorship, it was political dynamite, and Dugard was probably the printer. Later in the year, Claude de Saumaise wrote *Defensio Regia*, condemning the King's execution, which appeared in two Latin editions both printed in Leiden, and a third, printed and published in English by Dugard from the school premises. John Bradshaw, President of the Parliamentary Commission which had condemned the King, had Dugard arrested and thrown into Newgate; he also wrote to the Company, demanding the headmaster's instant dismissal. The Court of Assistants complied — they must have known about the printing press, and probably disapproved. In Dugard's place, on 20 February 1650, they appointed John Stevens, of Trinity College, Oxford, who held the position only till 25 September of the same year, for Dugard spent no more than a month in prison; he had a friend in a high place, Sir James Harrington, who presumably represented to the authorities that the new régime needed a competent printer. Dugard was willing to change his loyalty. He was released from Newgate and set up his own school in St Peter's Hill, Doctors Commons, whither a good number of Merchant Taylors boys followed him. Bradshaw wrote to the Company again, demanding the headmaster's reinstatement. At the third letter, the Company gave in, dismissing Stevens, who wrote bitter Latin verses in the School Probation Book; Dugard was once again in charge of both boys and printing press. A little over a year later, the luckless Stevens was appointed headmaster to Great Crosby School.

Dugard busied himself with Commonwealth propaganda, most notably John Milton's *Pro Populo Anglicano Defensio*, a reply to Saumaise's treatise, for the printing of which Dugard had been imprisoned in the first place. For a decade after 1650, he began to issue a politically acceptable news-sheet in French, *Nouvelles Ordinaires de Londres*. He was recognized as 'Printer to the State' and 'to His Highness the Lord Protector'. In 1651 he was in trouble again, when his press issued an anti-trinitarian tract, the *Racovian Catechism*, all copies of which were burnt at the Exchange and in New Palace Yard. This must have outraged the Merchant Taylors, but the political climate of the times prevented them from doing more than imploring Dugard that

It wilbe very acceptable unto the Company if he shall leave his printing and apply himselfe wholy and solely to the duty of the Schoole.[23]

The headmaster took no notice. For the Council of State, he published Milton's Latin text of the *Declaration of War against the States of Holland*, and — of exceptional importance — John Selden's *Mare Clausum, or Of the Dominion, or Ownership of the Sea*. By the end of 1654, he ceased to print for the Government, but continued to work his printing press, issuing three of his own textbooks, besides the *Pharmacopia Londiniensis* and such important works as William Harvey's *Exercitationes de Generatione Animalium* and the mathematician William Oughtred's *Dialling Performed Instrumentally*. His last effort was *The Schools Probation; or Rules and Orders for Certain Set Exercises to be Performed by the Scholars on Probation-Daies*; it was published by 'William Dugard, late of Merchant Taylors, now Master of a Private School in Coleman Street'. The Company had acted at last, dismissing him from his post after seventeen years. Once again, a number of his former pupils joined him.

Dugard had one last flamboyant fling. Careless to the last of authority, though loyal to his friends, in December 1660 he sheltered Sir James Harrington, to whom he owed his release from Newgate, from Charles II's officers. Dugard's home at Newington Butts was searched, and Harrington arrested, but Dugard stood bail for him to the tune of £5,000. The credulous officers left Harrington in Dugard's care; he promptly fled in disguise, but was apprehended and committed to the Tower. No one seems to have demanded the £5,000 from Dugard; they must have realized that he had not got it. He died a year later, on 3 December 1662, undoubtedly one of the more original headmasters.

It has been worth recounting the Company's involvement with its schools at such length in order to demonstrate with what seriousness such responsibilities were taken. It cannot have been easy to make the school inspections of 1610, 1629 and 1640, but to have made one in 1648 smacks of an almost reckless devotion to duty. Through the years of Cromwell's supremacy, the Company kept its head low; perhaps it is no accident that the Court minutes break off after a meeting on 25 July 1654, and do not resume till 20 May 1663. Their lack may be due to chance, the Great Fire, or the ravages of mice, but there may have been deliberate censorship. Even the City Corporation records from 1641 to 1659 have been crossed out, page after page, though mercifully the leaves have not been torn out and are still there as a record.

The Merchant Taylors may well have decided that discretion was the wiser part.

NOTES

1. The site is now marked by Wardrobe Court.
2. PRO, AO3/910. For an analysis, see Roy Strong's 'Charles I's Clothes for the Years 1633 to 1635', in *Costume*, 14 (1980), pp. 73–89.
3. For Bulstrode Whitelocke's extraordinary career, see *The Improbable Puritan: A Life of Bulstrode Whitelocke, 1605–1675* (1975) by Ruth Spalding, who has also edited Whitelocke's *Diary* (1990), British Academy, Records of Social and Economic History, New Series, vol. XIII. The account of the masque is given in Spalding, pp. 47–50.
4. It was not the Honourable Artillery Company until 1700. For the performance, see G. Goold Walker, *The Honourable Artillery Company, 1537–1987* (1986), pp. 48–51. There is a copy of William Barriffe's *Mars, his Triumph* (1639) in the Company's library at the Hall.
5. One of the historical re-enactment groups has revived the drill and still performs it.
6. There are many books on the English Civil Wars, beginning with Lord Clarendon's *History of the Great Rebellion*. For the years immediately before, and the complexities and intricacies of City politics, I have relied on Valerie Pearl's *London and the Outbreak of the Puritan Revolution, 1625–1643* (Oxford, 1961). For the course of the strife, John Kenyon's *The Civil Wars of England* (1988) seems to me to be the clearest account; it should be read in company with *The Civil Wars* (Oxford, 1998), edited by Kenyon and Jane Ohlmeyer. Veronica Wedgwood's three volumes — *The King's Peace, 1637–1641* (1955), *The King's War, 1641–1647* (1958), and *The Execution of Charles I* (1964) — are invaluable. From the Parliamentarian side, anything by Christopher Hill or Conrad Russell is of interest and value, and there are two older books still worth reading — Reginald Sharpe's *London and the Kingdom*, II (1894), and C. M. Clode's *London during the Great Rebellion* (1892).
7. Details of Venn's career are to be found in the forthcoming volume of *The History of Parliament, 1640–60*; I am most grateful to the History of Parliament Trust for having been given access to the material.
8. *A Letter from Mercurius Civicus to Mercurius Rusticus* (Oxford, 1643), reprinted in *Somers' Tracts*, IV (1810), pp. 580–98, esp. pp. 582 and 598.
9. There were 153 swords, 60 head-pieces for muskets, 52 muskets, 70 pikes, 50 corslets, 40 musket rests, 32 halberds, 3 hundred-weight of musket balls, 3 hundred-weight of match, and 40 barrels of gunpowder; R. T. D. Sayle, *A Brief History* (1945), p. 23, and GL, MS 34010/7, fol. 144^r.
10. The proceedings are given in full transcript in C. M. Clode's *London during the Great Rebellion* (1892).
11. William Lithgow, *The present Surveigh of London and Englands State* (1643), reprinted in *Somers' Tracts*, IV (1810), pp. 534–45.
12. Samuel Butler, *Hudibras*, part ii, canto ii, ll. 801 seq.
13. Court minutes, GL, MS 34010/7, fols 252^v–53^r.
14. See Peter Edwards, *Dealing in Death: The Arms Trade and the British Civil Wars, 1638–52* (Stroud, 2000), chapter 6. Gerald I. Mungeam has transcribed several contracts in 'Contracts for the Supply of Equipment to the "New Model" Army in 1645', in *Journal of the Arms and Armour Society*, VI (1968–70), pp. 53–115.
15. £2 4s. 0d. to provision the castle, and then £5 12s. 0d. to supply those besieging it.
16. GL, MS 34010/7, fols 250^v, 251.
17. The manuscript diary is now in Dr Williams' Library in Gordon Square, and was published in a careful transcript in 1999 by Keith Lindley and David Scott as *The Journal of Thomas Juxon, 1644–1647*, Camden Society, Fifth Series, vol. 13. It ends so abruptly that the student cannot help wondering whether, somewhere, other volumes may still survive.
18. Given as Appendix III in C. M. Clode, *London during the Great Rebellion* (1892).
19. W. C. Costin, *The History of St John's College, 1598–1860*, Oxford Historical Society, New Series, XII (1958).
20. G. P. Mander, *The History of the Wolverhampton Grammar School* (Wolverhampton, 1913), chapter 5.
21. H. M. Luft, *A History of Merchant Taylors' School, Crosby, 1620–1970* (Liverpool, 1970).
22. The fullest account of Dugard is by Leona Rostenberg, 'William Dugard, Pedagogue and Printer to the Commonwealth', in *Proceedings of the Bibliographical Society of America*, vol. 53 (1958), pt 3.
23. Court minutes, GL, MS 34010/7, fol. 419^v, 14 July 1653.

CHAPTER THIRTEEN
RESTORATION, FIRE AND REBUILDING

ON 5 MAY 1660, the unthinkable happened. Charles II was restored to his father's throne amid general rejoicings. On 29 May, his thirtieth birthday, London greeted its monarch with the wildest enthusiasm (Fig. 67), and the past conduct of Abraham Reynardson meant that the Merchant Taylors were in high favour.

Both Court minutes and accounts are missing for the period, but from the Corporation records we know that Reynardson was restored to his aldermanry[1] and that in October 1660 he was re-elected Lord Mayor. He declined the office on grounds of ill health, and Sir Richard Browne was chosen in his place. Reynardson died just a year later, on 4 October 1661, at his house at Tottenham. His body lay in state for a fortnight at Merchant Taylors' Hall and he was then buried in St Martin Outwich, his funeral sermon being preached eloquently by the Reverend George Smallwood.[2]

Sir Richard Browne, who had begun his career as a wood merchant, had been a staunch Parliamentary soldier, in command of two regiments and instrumental in the Parliamentary victory at Alresford (29 March 1644). On becoming a major-general, he made his headquarters at Abingdon and joined grimly in besieging Charles I's headquarters in Oxford. When the King was betrayed by his Scottish subjects into Parliamentary hands in January 1647, it was Browne who had charge of his person at Holmby House in Northamptonshire, whence the King was snatched and brought south by those with more extreme political views. Browne's religious opinions proving insufficiently radical, he was imprisoned in various places for five years and was harshly treated. Released at last, he was excluded from Parliament and lived quietly till the Restoration, when he was knighted along with others who greeted Charles II at Blackheath. He became a Merchant Taylor in December 1656, by patrimony since his father had belonged to the Company.[3]

The selection of Browne as Lord Mayor is characteristic of the general determination that peace must be restored at all costs, whatever contradictions or injustices it might entail. Blood had been shed between members of the same family; it was as if England had lost her innocence. The years of civil war had been so frightful, so barbaric, had so engulfed and battered all four parts of the kingdom — England, Scotland, Wales, and Ireland — that men were determined that the past must be shut away. It was not so much a denial of past horrors as a clear resolution that a fresh start had to be made. Even before Charles reached England, a Bill of Indemnity and Oblivion was being debated, and was speedily passed. There were fewer than a hundred exemptions, and only nine regicides were executed, with four others too deeply implicated to be forgiven. Cromwell's body and those of thirteen of his deceased supporters were dug up, exhibited at Tyburn, and thrown on dung heaps. Otherwise, the stability of society was what counted. The Chancellor, Lord Clarendon, summed up matters with his hope that the country would return to 'its old good manners, its old good humour, and its old good nature'.

On 29 October 1660, Browne's mayoral procession set off from Merchant Taylors' Hall. An entertainment was devised by John Tatham, the dramatist and writer of City pageants. The procession, announced by kettle-drums and trumpets, marched through the streets to Three Cranes Wharf where barges were waiting to waft the company to Westminster, with guns saluting and bells ringing. At Whitehall — the water-stairs are still visible behind the Ministry of Defence building — was moored a floating stage, with a ship, fully rigged and manned, at one end of it and a rock at the other. From this, an actor attired as Oceanus made a speech of welcome,

FIGURE 67. Charles II's entry into the City of London.
Guildhall Library

and the new Lord Mayor disembarked to take his oath. On his return, he was met in St Paul's Churchyard by another pageant, which could boast two camels, the supporters of the Company's arms, and eight actors dressed as those kings who had been free of the Merchant Taylors' fraternity, with Henry VII, holding the first charter to the Company as *Merchant Taylors*, sitting before all the rest. In deference to the new Lord Mayor, an actor, attired as a Senator and Soldier, holding a gauntlet in one hand and a book of laws in the other, made a long speech, and the procession then moved on to Cheapside, where a Royal Oak had been contrived — a delicate compliment to the new King, who had hidden in the leafy branches of such a tree when pursued by Cromwell's soldiers after his defeat at Worcester in 1651. Around the tree Woodmen and Wood-Nymphs disported themselves, and addressed speeches to the Lord Mayor in a 'Rustick Dyalect'. Then at the east end of Cheapside there were more speeches, by Sylvanus, by Time, and by Peace, until at last 'the Companies hasten to their Hall, the Gentlemen of the Artillery tak[ing] leave by several Vollies'. Everyone concerned must have been very tired and ready for a meal.[4]

Samuel Pepys watched from the window of

Mr Isaacson's, a linen draper at the Key in Cheapside, where there was a company of fine ladies, and we were very civilly treated, and had a very good place to see the pageants, which were many, and I believe good for such kind of things, but in themselves but poor and absurd.

The diarist was contemptuous, but most people enjoyed it.[5]

Browne was going to have a trying year of office, for in January 1661 a religious zealot, Thomas Venner, a Fifth Monarchy man intent on setting up the reign of King Jesus, tried with about fifty followers to seize London. He shot and killed a passer-by who declared his loyalty was to King Charles. With a Lord Mayor like Browne, Venner was soon arrested and was subsequently hanged. His was the last head to be stuck on a pike over London Bridge.

The camels that had been objects of wonder in the mayoral pageant were useful again on 23 August 1662 when Charles and his bride, Catherine of Braganza, came down the Thames from Hampton Court to Whitehall. Fantastically arrayed, the barges of the Great Twelve City companies floated out to greet the new Queen (Fig. 68). John Tatham was again in charge of the spectacle. In the centre of the Merchant Taylors' barge was a wilderness where John the Baptist sat attended by Faith, Hope and Charity, while the camels stood in the prow and stern, mounted by grooms attired as Indians and bearing shields with the arms of England and Portugal. John Evelyn was deeply impressed:

I this day was spectator of the most magnificent Triumph that certainly ever floted on the *Thames* ... far exceeding in my opinion all the Venetian Bucentoros &c. on the *Ascention*, when they go to Espouse the *Adriatic*.[6]

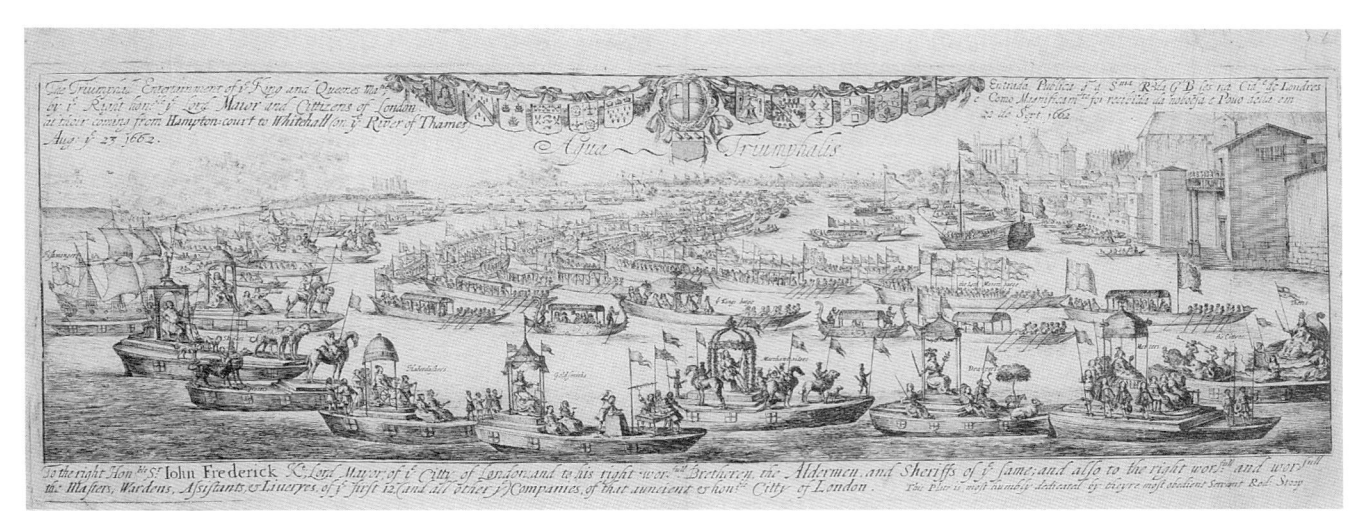

FIGURE 68. London welcomes Catherine of Braganza, Charles II's bride. Drawn and engraved by Dirck Stoop, 1662. The royal barge is about to land at Whitehall Stairs. The barges of the Great Twelve accompany it, the Merchant Taylors in the centre.
Guildhall Library

It was not the first time the magnificence of London had been compared favourably with that of Venice — the Prince of Anhalt had said the same in 1610. A seven-plate panorama of the procession was engraved by Dirck Stoop; there are animals on the Merchant Taylors' barge, though it takes the eye of faith to see them as camels.

The Court minutes resume on 20 May 1663 in the Mastership of Nicholas Delves. Business was much as usual — renewal of leases, election of almsmen and women, consulting Dr Smallwood, who had preached Sir Abraham Reynardson's funeral sermon, about the usher's place at Great Crosby, the repair of highways in Surrey under the will of James Wilford. One week later, a stubborn Yorkshireman, Patience Ward, who had served his apprenticeship from 1646–53 and was now trading on his own in Lawrence Pountney Lane, refused to take the livery, though he changed his mind a few weeks later. Almswoman Dorothy Triminges was reported as bearing herself with an 'unquiet and unhansome carriadg', but had promised reformation and was on probation. In May 1664, Mr Coles, the headmaster at Wolverhampton, complained that his and the usher's salaries had not been paid for several months; the Court agreed that matters should be put right and in October of that year increased his wages by £5 a year, with an additional £1 3s. 4d. for the usher. In August and September, there were difficulties with the Clothworkers, who had searched Mr Everard's shop without any right to do so, and with Ralph Heygate, who was not paying proper fees for his apprentices. Loans were doled out to worthy young men setting up in business. The school was examined satisfactorily on 5 October 1664, and in March 1665 put on Beaumont and Fletcher's play, *Love's Pilgrimage*, in the Company's Hall, to general applause and at a cost of £17 10s. 9d. for the staging and seating. Two years later it was agreed that each newly-elected Assistant should subscribe 40s. to the school library fund. In November 1664, £2,000 had been raised for the King, and in the following spring the Lord Mayor wrote soliciting contributions to provide His Majesty with a ship; a committee considered it but nothing happened for the time being.

Plague, ever present in London, increased disastrously in the hot summer of 1665. Intervals between Court meetings became longer, and none were held between 20 July and 16 December. Five men refused the Mastership, preferring to pay fines; Nathaniel Lavendor wrote from Cheshunt that he was passing 'black blooddie water and voyding many cloddes of blood', and that in any case he could not afford to be Master because his tenants were all dead. The death rate rose alarmingly in the almshouses, with fifteen vacancies in a matter of months; the Company's porter and cook also died, as did thirty out-pensioners. A place was given to Mr Alport who had formerly been an Assistant; he promptly petitioned, without success, to be allowed to fashion the material for his almsman's cloak into a suit for himself. Later, he was found to have a son, daughter-in-law and grandchildren living with him and the whole family were ejected, though rented accommodation was eventually provided for him.

Meetings became more regular in 1666. On 20 June, the Lord Mayor demanded £1,000 as a contribution towards the King's ship, now referred to by name as the *Loyal London*, and it was decided to borrow the money. She had already been launched on 10 June though in an unfinished state; she saw scarcely a year's service, being burnt out by the Dutch in their attack up the Medway in 1667. The Company's contribution rested at £700.

At the July elections, Nathaniel Withers became Master; John Coles, headmaster at Wolverhampton, presented a book, dedicated to the Company, which he had written, and was rewarded with £5; Jane Tarbock, now aged but once laundress to the Merchant Taylors, was granted a pension of £4 a year and promised the next out-pension; it was no more than her due, for she had been most careful to lay lavender and sweet herbs among the linen. It was decided to re-slate the roof of the Hall, and Mr Elwood the bricklayer was consulted.

And then, in the small hours of the morning of Sunday, 2 September, the Great Fire broke out in a baker's shop near the north end of London Bridge.

The flames reached Threadneedle Street on Tuesday, and crept eastwards along it. That day saw the worst destruction of all. Prompt action on the part of John Milner the Clerk, Simon Baylie the Beadle and Thomas Mordeyne the Porter, saved most of the Company's charters, minutes and account books.[7] It cost £23 5s. 8d. in cart hire and labour which, remembering Pepys's comments on how the hire of a cart rose by the hour as the danger increased, seems more than reasonable. Much of the plate in the treasury had to be abandoned, for fused silver to the value of £286 1s. 9d. was recovered afterwards from the debris, and a further £4 19s. 6d. worth was swept up later from the dust. A fortunate change of wind spared the main walls of the Hall, even though the interior was gutted. The almshouses beyond were scarcely damaged, and St Martin Outwich escaped altogether. The school, however, in Suffolk Lane was in the direct path of the fire; the headmaster, John Goad, managed to rescue most of the books in the library, but the building was beyond repair.

The Master, Nathaniel Withers, the Upper Warden, Robert Hall, and twelve others of the Company including Thomas Nevill, Past Master, and Sir William Bolton, Alderman, assembled, presumably in some less damaged part of the building, on 21 September. They gave orders that Mr Elwood the bricklayer should be paid for his labours which had most likely been destroyed, that the melted plate should be assessed by 'Mr Taylor att the Tower' or one of his subordinates, that only such pensions as were guaranteed by bequests should be paid unless there were serious poverty, that everything possible should be done to encourage rebuilding both of the Hall and of such other properties as paid rent to the Company, and that a committee with power to act should meet weekly each Friday morning at nine o'clock. Finally, the Master and Wardens were required to inspect the garden behind the Hall, since several holes had been broken though the walls.

The next Court meeting was not until 12 October. Sir William Bolton, who was not present, had been elected Lord Mayor. It was usual to present any Merchant Taylor so honoured with a hundred marks (£66 13s. 4d.), but it was hoped that he would excuse the gift in view of the emergency. It was decided that the almshouses near the Hall should be made 'wind tide and water tide', that the melted lead from the school roof should be kept safe, and that the parlour at the Hall and the garret above it should be made fit for Court meetings.

The future Lord Mayor was not pleased with the economy. He was offered £46 13s. 4d. but insisted on the full hundred marks; they were given to him. He seems to have been a most unworthy member of the Company, for he was later accused of embezzling £1,800 collected for poverty-stricken victims of the Fire and was forced to resign his aldermanry.[8] He continued, however, to sit on the Company's Court and to join in the general life of the Company.

The rebuilding of the Hall was a protracted business, probably undertaken in two campaigns and not complete till 1675/6. It was not that the Master and Wardens were dilatory, but timber and other materials were in short supply, and skilled craftsmen were hard to be had. At the Court meeting of 8 February 1667, it was ordered that the parlour be finished 'with all convenient speed', and that an estimate be prepared for rebuilding the school; if such an estimate was made, it has now vanished.

Over the next few years, we can trace the restoration of the premises from the accounts. A Mr Lock was paid £9 1s. 8d. for 'draughtes and viewes'. This must have been Thomas Lock, a member of the Fishmongers' Company but a Master Carpenter by trade, who was employed by Sir Christopher Wren on St Magnus the Martyr, St Mary at Hill and St Mildred Poultry; when Edward Jarman, City Carpenter and one of the City Surveyors appointed after the Fire, died in November 1668 from overwork, Lock took over the rebuilding of the halls of the Fishmongers and the Apothecaries. The Company was employing a first-class craftsman.

A careful analysis of the accounts indicates that the damage to the Hall, though serious, was comparatively superficial. The initial outlay amounted to £3,186 18s. 1d., though more would be spent in the following decade. Materials — bricks, timber, lime, tiles, stone and metalwork — came to £594. Another £886 13s. was for bricklaying, with £187 9s. 0d. for plastering, £63 11s. 9d. for glazing, £99 5s. 0d. for plumbing and £27 4s. 0d. for painting. The chief expenditure was for carpentry and joinery — £1,328 15s. 4d., which suggests that the main damage had been to floors and panelling; judging by the outlay on deals (load-bearing timbers) and 'youfers' (long, substantial sections of wood), the opportunity may have been taken to give the Hall, Parlour and upper rooms a better quality of flooring. Much of the carpentry work was done by Thomas Dorebarr, while Mr Whiting, a joiner, fixed presses, presumably for storage, to the walls of the Hall. Thomas Elwood the bricklayer died before the task was complete; he was replaced by Joseph Lem, who also worked on Mercers' Hall. John Oliver, whose firm did most of the glazing, was one of the City Surveyors; he became Wren's right-hand man on St Paul's. The greater part of the masonry work fell to James Florey, so he may have been responsible for the imposing stone entrance with the Company's arms above which proclaimed the Hall's existence to the street and the world outside;[9] might the ladder, purchased from him in 1672/3 for the Company's use, have been to keep the coat of arms clean? Other masonry work went to Thomas Cartwright (d. 1702), twice Master of the Masons' Company, who worked for Wren on three City churches, rebuilt four other Halls, and completed the Royal Exchange. Little is known of the three other stonemasons employed; only their names are recorded — Mr Shorthose, Daniel Norris, and Robert Waters.

But, even if the repair of the Hall was a manageable proposition, the Company's losses were almost stupefyingly large. On 22 November 1667, the new Master, Edmund Lewin, reported to the assembled Company that the Fire had deprived them of about £1,400 in annual rental income. The total loss was even worse, since many of the leases were due to be renewed which, in many cases, would have meant a substantial fine in addition to the rent. Between them, the Wardens had responsibility for collecting rents from 199 properties, large and small, spread across the parishes and streets of the City; of these, forty-seven paid their rent — the rest had gone in the flames. The Company was in no position to borrow from anyone, and the assembly prudently decided to spend nothing on the Hall till all of the debts, which had built up in earlier decades, were repaid, and to start repaying capital to its creditors immediately, in stages.

This restrained behaviour was insufficient to meet the regular demands on the Company's resources. The almsmen and women still needed pensions on which to live, and proper burial when they died. The schoolmasters at Wolverhampton and Great Crosby needed their salaries, and there were always repairs to those buildings. Mr Ashworth at Great Crosby heard in April 1667 that the houses in John Harrison's bequest which should have paid his wages were destroyed; when he petitioned again in July, he was told grimly that he would have to exist on half of what was due to him, and that he must dismiss Mr Barker the usher and manage the school singlehanded. He finally got his arrears a year later, in July 1668, after the expense of a journey to London to beg

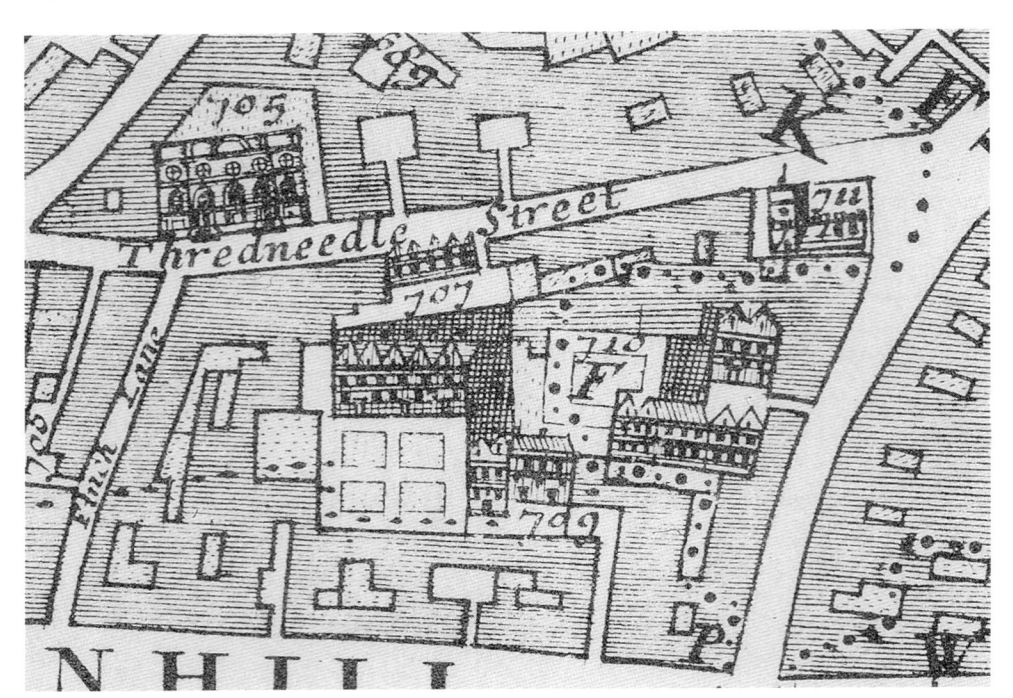

FIGURE 69. William Morgan's map of London, 1682. An enlarged detail of the buildings making up Merchant Taylors' Hall. The garden is clearly visible. Notice how the frontage on Threadneedle Street is being filled up with post-Fire buildings.
Guildhall Library

FIGURE 70a and b. Morgan's London again. These details show the heart of the City from St Paul's to Threadneedle Street. Wren was only beginning on the rebuilding of the Cathedral, so Morgan had to guess what it might look like when finished.
Guildhall Library

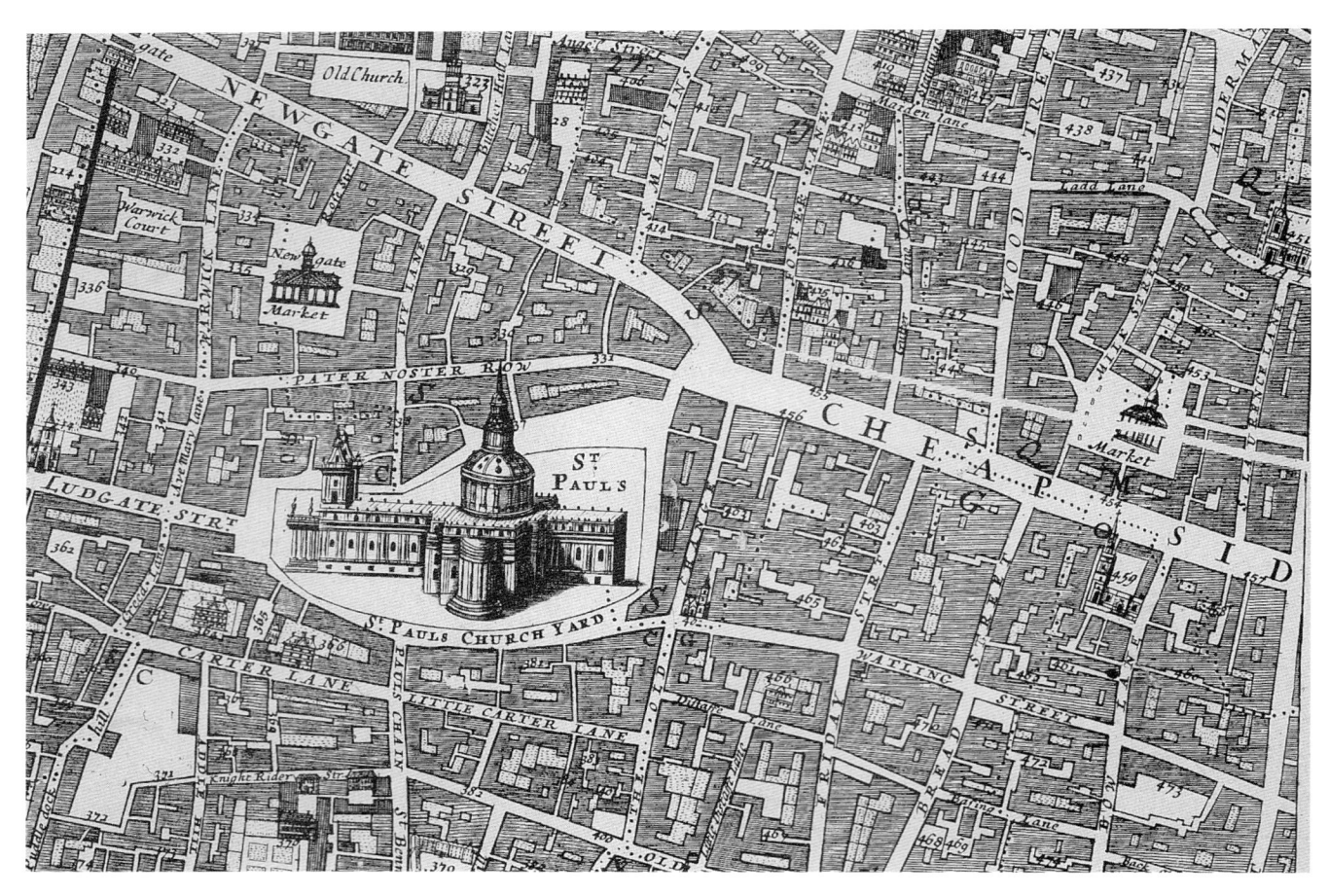

for them; the Company did not pay his costs. Mr Barker eventually got his arrears, too.

Anyone who had money and energy for rebuilding was able to make an excellent bargain for themselves with the Company. In 1667, Colonel Mew was told that he could have the remains of the Kitchen for five years at a peppercorn rent, provided he put a roof over the ruins and paid a fine of £20. In desperation, long leases were granted, without any fine, at ridiculously low rents for long periods. Richard Griffith, citizen and gunmaker, undertook to build 'one good and substantiall house' on a site in Elbow Lane which was his for 51 years at £3 per annum; Thomas Onley, merchant taylor, had a 99-year lease in Thames Street for £6 a year, and John Steventon, grocer, had three sites in Threadneedle Street and Finch Lane at £11 a year for 90 years; Dame Honora Watkins had land in Candlewick Street and Sherborne Lane on which to build four or five houses at £10 for 92 years. Michael Rolls, merchant taylor, and John Bridge, painter-stainer, had a 71-year lease of the temporarily repaired almshouses beside the Hall for £5, a good fat buck for the Master's Feast, and a fine of £300; by November 1668 the almsmen were petitioning that, since their former home was 'to be rebuilt into substantiall dwelling houses fitting for persons of quality', they needed some additional support; they were each awarded an extra £5 a year 'dureing the Companies pleasure and noe longer'. John Oliver the surveyor picked up a bargain, with an 81-year lease of two sites in Trinity Lane for a total of £9 a year. Scores of such agreements were made; the Company was laying up trouble for the future, but there was nothing else to be done at the time. It made the Irish estate look like a good investment, even though it was the cause of much wrangling.

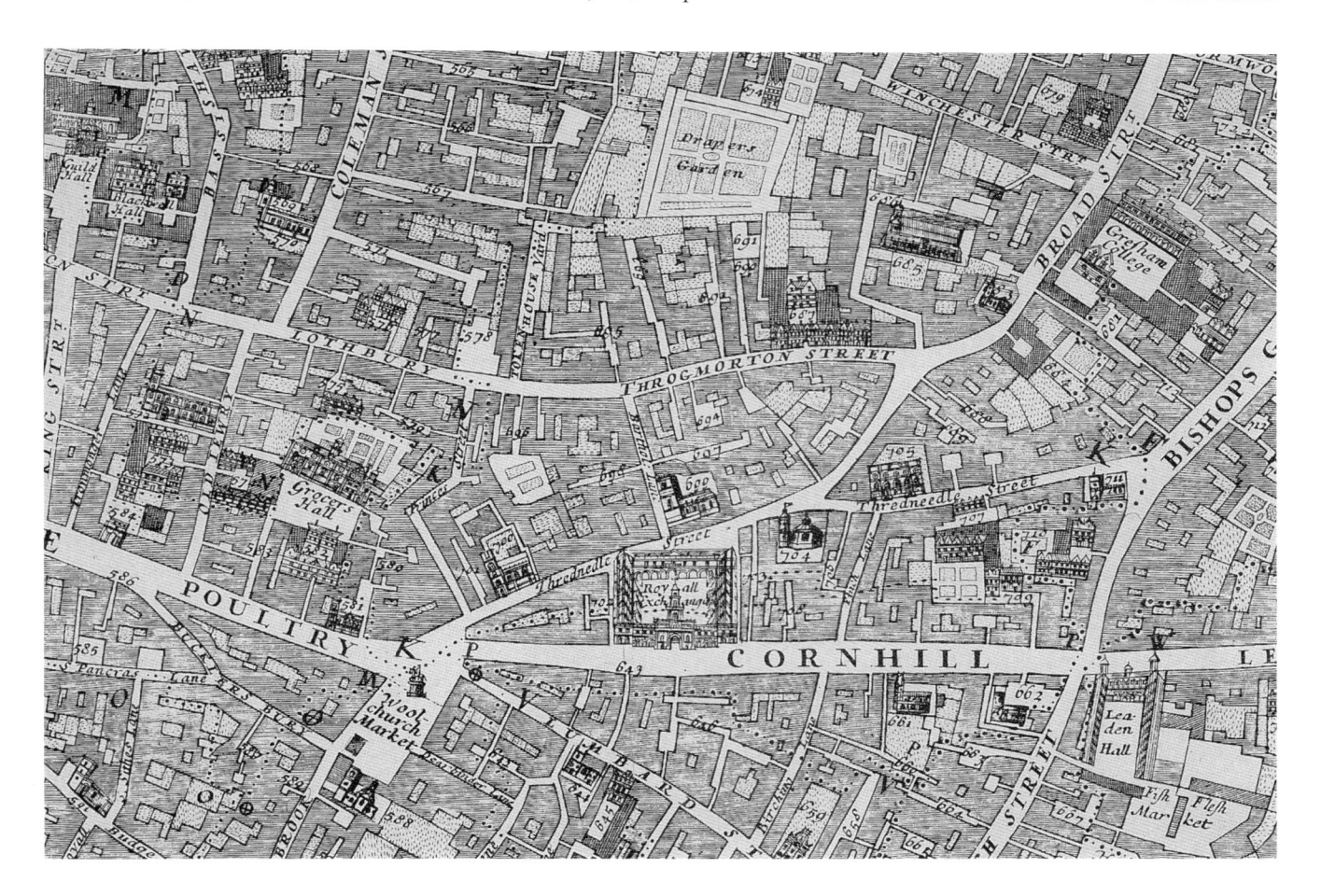

In addition to all this, there were constant frictions, some minor, some acrimonious, over the post-Fire settlement of boundaries. Land was taken for the widening of streets, and compensation had to be agreed; there were regular squabbles about the small shops and tenements in Pope's Head Alley and Shepherd's Alley, and over the buildings along Three Cranes Wharf; there was a dispute over two feet of land in Bread Street between Sir Walter Plumer and Mr Strange. Mr Allestry wanted six inches of Mr Harris's ground on Fleet Street, and would pay £20 for it, of which the Company demanded £10. And there was a long-running battle between the Company itself and Mr Thoroughgood, who was rebuilding his tavern against the wall of the Hall's garden and was determined to make windows through it to lighten his own rooms. Committee after committee of senior members went out to view site after site, and John Milner the Clerk trudged backwards and forwards between the Hall, still undergoing repairs, and the Fire Court, set up to adjudicate in all disagreements. It was an exhausting time for everyone. Nevertheless, the Company struggled to keep up appearances and put on a good show when there was occasion for rejoicing. Somehow, probably under an improvised roof, a dinner was held for Lord Mayor's Day in 1667. Somehow, the almsfolk received their pensions and allowances of coal in winter weather. Somehow, money was found for the poor of St Mildred in the Poultry. The Court made time on 25 November 1668 to hear a recommendation from Mr Bedford of Ashwell that Robert Bland, graduate of Magdalene, Cambridge, was a fit and proper person to be appointed schoolmaster in Hertfordshire (see pp. 216–17). He was interviewed and awarded the post on 12 March in the following year.

The election as Lord Mayor of a popular merchant taylor, Sir William Turner, was a reason for celebration in 1668. Eighty-five brethren were raised to the livery, eighty-eight were made Rich or Budge Bachelors, and another thirty-five became Gentlemen Ushers. They paid for the privilege, and those who refused to join in were fined. It was one way of raising money.[10] Even so, there were none of the usual shows and pageants. The old barge was repainted, and with so many new liverymen, it was necessary to hire a tilt-boat, a large boat with an awning, in order to accommodate everyone; neither children nor servants were to be allowed to join the voyagers, though the seventeen watermen were to have new sky-blue plush caps, costing £5 10s. 0d., and the Company's arms on their sleeves. Economically, only half the usual number of banners were painted up by 'Mr Nowers the Herald Paynter', but Thomas Edwards of Shads Key was paid £30 for providing and twice discharging thirty pieces of ordnance, as the new Lord Mayor arrived at and returned from Westminster, Mr Shadbolt the mason erected the Company's arms, and the order was given that 'tables be set up and sheds [sheds] made over whereby the Companie may entertaine the whole Livery on the Lord Maiors Day'. No matter how much improvisation might be needed, the Company was determined to cut a good figure when one of their own was called to the highest office.

The Court wasted no time in taking advantage of this fortunate circumstance. On 18 December 1668, it was decided to consult Sir William about the 'great debt'. The accounts are provokingly uninformative, but in the following January the Clerk, John Milner, was instructed to draw up particulars of all the Company's lands and an account, which has unfortunately disappeared, of all monies owing by and to the Merchant Taylors.

A few years later, John Oliver, assisted probably by William Leybourne, set about drawing up plans. The results can be seen in MS 34216, commissioned in May 1680, which outlines property held by the Company on around fifty City streets, occupied by over 100 different tenants. These plans give us the first clear view of the Hall and its surroundings; if we could go back in time, some spaces would seem familiar (Col. Pl. XVI). The size of the Hall has scarcely changed, though to the south on the garden side there was an open cloister. To the south-west was the Great Parlour with a staircase leading up from it, and another large room or entrance hall to the north between it and Threadneedle Street. On the colder east side lay the Kitchen with other domestic offices. The frontage onto the street was already let out in narrow tenements.

As soon as his mayoral year had ended,[11] Sir William Turner gave his attention to his Company and began to organize the completion of the Hall. Members were invited to contribute and subscriptions were taken up. The sums were not large in themselves, 10s. to £20, depending on a man's circumstances, but they totalled up, year by year.[12] Small refinements began to be added; Major

FIGURE 71. Hall screen designed by Robert Hooke in 1673 at Sir William Turner's request. Drawn in 1904 by L.G. Detmar.
Guildhall Library, MS 34214/5, no. 13

Mallory was commissioned to paint a portrait of Walter Pell, Master in 1649, at a cost of £11 3s. 0d., and in December 1674 an iron chest was purchased to lock up the Company's plate. Assistant John Short presented a portrait of Charles I on 28 June 1672.

Money was laid out generously on upholstery; Warden Spence provided chairs and hangings for £74 0s. 0d. The almshouses at Tower Hill were given a new watercourse at a cost of £72 5s. 0d., 'pales, broomes, Mopps for the Comp[ies] use' were provided for £3 15s. 3d., and £24 0s. 0d. were laid out on books, though these were almost certainly for the school. When we consider that the complete rebuilding of their Hall had cost the Mercers some £13,716 12s. 4d.,[13] and that the Fishmongers spent nearly as much, then the Merchant Taylors had escaped lightly.

The final touches for the time being were put to the Hall when an oak screen was inserted at the east end (Fig. 71). Its design was by Robert Hooke, City Surveyor, Gresham Professor and friend to Sir Christopher Wren; after a visit to the Hall on 1 August 1673, Hooke drew the screen roughly and presented the sketch to Sir William Turner.[14] A careful, measured drawing was made by George Pawley, joiner, who was paid £3 for it, and the construction was undertaken by Mr Whiting for £200. He accepted the commission in August 1673 and had it finished by Lord Mayor's Day that autumn. £100 towards the cost had already been subscribed by the previous Master in lieu of holding a public dinner. The final bill, for £111, was settled in the accounts for 1674. That screen adorned the Hall until the bombing of 1940. The total cost of the post-Fire restoration cannot have exceeded £4,500.

The screen was not the only matter in which Hooke guided the Company.[15] He advised about paving, and on 1 October 1673 'gave Milner the Draught of Merchant Taylors Garden'. Early in the New Year, on 28 January, he was at the school in Suffolk Lane, advising on the rebuilding, and met Joseph Lem the bricklayer there the following day. Always a prompt and efficient worker, Hooke delivered a plan to Sir William Turner five days later, and his diary records three subsequent visits to the Hall and school.

In the immediate post-Fire years, the school had survived as best as it could. Whilst the building was in ruins, teaching had gone on as and where the staff could find a place in which to assemble a class. Hector Forde, the Undermaster, taught some boys in the Vestry of St Katherine Cree, a partition being erected to prevent the children running about the church.[16] In the spring of 1668, the devoted headmaster John Goad obtained permission to use the schoolhouse in St Mary Axe, and the accounts for

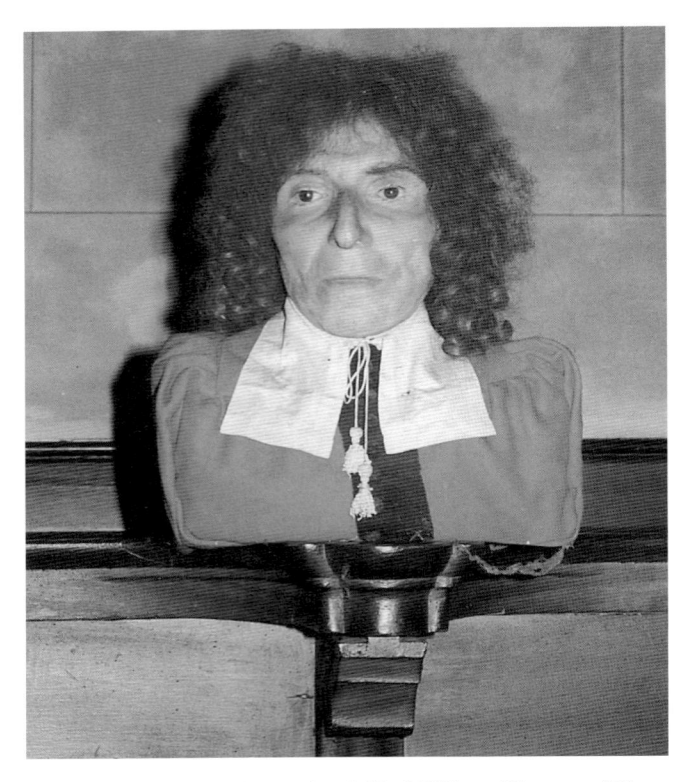

FIGURE 72. Death mask of Sir William Turner. (The wig is thought to have been his own property.) It rests in the chapel of his Hospital at Kirkleatham, North Yorkshire.

By kind permission of Sir William Turner's Hospital, Kirkleatham

1669–70 indicate that accommodation was found as far away as Kentish Town. Teaching went on, somehow, somewhere, and William Gibbons was accepted as a scholar at St John's in 1668, with four more boys in 1669 and another two in 1670.[17]

In that year Patience Ward, who had so unwillingly joined the livery in 1663, was elected Sheriff. His premises adjoined the site of the school, and he set to work to have built a handsome room wherein he might undertake the inevitable official entertaining. His plans encroached on the school's territory; as soon as the Company realized, they ordered that the rebuilding of the school should be put in hand and appointed a committee to deal with the matter.[18] Once again Sir William Bolton was on the committee; this time Sir William Turner was treasurer. Money was borrowed, and individual merchant taylors were invited to subscribe; members of St John's College gave generously. Joseph Avis was given the commission for the carpentry work, Joseph Lem for the bricklaying, and William Barton for the smith's work; Avis and Barton both belonged to the Company. The work went forward so diligently that the boys were able to assemble in the new building by the summer of 1672, and the St John's Day Election was held in the chapel in 1674.[19]

The much-needed new school building, which should be ascribed to Hooke rather than to Wren, had its main frontage on Suffolk Lane. It was of brick, eight windows wide, with a round-headed doorway to the north and brick pilasters between the windows to the upper storey. It was plain — severe, even — but had its own dignity (Col. Pl. XIXB) The premises contained a chapel, a library, separate rooms for the headmaster and each of the three ushers, and classrooms; heating in winter was by open fires. The schoolyard was distinguished by a cloister with pairs of pillars, one round but its companion square; generations of boys played games about them (Fig. 73). An excavation of the site, carried out in 1969, retrieved from the drainage system fragments of broken toys and marbles, reminders of the children who once played there.[20]

The school had had a struggle to hold on to its own library. Nathaniel Withers, who had been Master of the Company in the year of the Fire, had taken the volumes for safe-keeping into his house, which stood unscathed in Seething Lane, where Samuel Pepys, whose father had been a merchant taylor, was his neighbour. Withers seemed profoundly unwilling to part with them, and on 14 June 1668 it needed an order of the Court of the Company, instructing Colonel Thomas Nevill and the Wardens to procure if necessary a warrant from the Lord Mayor or the Lord Chief Justice, before the books were returned, presumably to the Hall since the school was still in ruins.

At last, a decade after the disasters of plague and fire, the Company was able to draw breath, to look proudly at its refurbished Hall and rebuilt school, to regard its almshouses on Tower Hill, which had remained safe, with satisfaction, to contemplate the streets all around being reconstructed and filled with life once more. The Company had even been able to afford a modest new barge, costing £197 1s. 0d., from Henry Forte of Lambeth, in place of the old, decayed

FIGURE 73. The Suffolk Lane playground with cloister, 1827.
Guildhall Library

vessel.[21] Precious land on Lombard Street and other thoroughfares had had to be sold, building sites had had to be let out on disadvantageous terms, but the Company itself was still here, intact. It had survived.

NOTES

1. CLRO, Journal 41, fol. 240b.
2. Text of Smallwood's sermon given in C. M. Clode, *London during the Great Rebellion* (1892). Dr Smallwood would one day become Dean of Lichfield.
3. GL, MS 34018/4, Presentment Book.
4. John Tatham, *The Royal Oake* (1660), reproduced complete in R. T. D. Sayle, *Lord Mayors' Pageants* (1931), p. 129 onwards. I am inclined to think that the camels were carved from wood, not living creatures.
5. Samuel Pepys, by this time a rising man at the Navy Office, was the son of John Pepys, a not very successful tailor and a humble freeman of the Company. Affectionate and solicitous letters from the father to the son can be found in Helen Heath's *The Letters of Samuel Pepys and his Family Circle* (Oxford, 1955). This fascinating book also gives the inventory of John Pepys' shop, goods which he had lent to his elder, unsuccessful son, Thomas. It is headed 'An Inve[n]tarye of all the goods that is Left'. The only professional item is the cutting board, mentioned twice. Thomas died in debt to the tune of £300. Regrettably, Samuel chose to join the Clothworkers' Company; he served as Master in 1677 and presented that Company with three magnificent gifts — a silver-gilt cup and cover, and a silver-gilt ewer and salver.
6. E. S. de Beer (ed.), *The Diary of John Evelyn* (1955), III, p. 333.
7. This, presumably, is when the eight volumes of Court minutes, 1299–1562, were lost, along with the accounts for 1445–53 and 1484–1545.
8. J. R. Woodhead, *The Rulers of London, 1660–1689: A Biographical Record of the Aldermen and Common Councilmen of the City of London* (1965). See also Pepys' *Diary* for 3 December 1667.
9. Florey or Flory, active 1663–76. He estimated for repairs to St Christopher le Stocks in 1666–67, and paved the chapel of Emmanuel College, Cambridge, with marble in 1676. D. Knoop and G. P. Jones, *The London Mason in the Seventeenth Century* (Manchester, 1935), p. 42.
10. These honorific titles seem to have been attractive. 'Budge' is lambswool, used to trim a gown, and so distinguish its wearer. The figures are as follows, taken from GL, MS 34048/23, 24:

1666–67	15 admitted to livery, all at £25, except for two who offered part-payment only, at £10 and £15. There were no fines for refusals. The total came to £350.
1667–68	6 admitted plus the balance of one of the part-payments; no fines for refusals. Total: £160.
1668–69	85 admitted, 62 at £25, 22 at nil, plus one more part-payment of £15, and the balance of the second part-payment of 1667, at £15. Fines for refusals amounted to £460. Total: £2,040.
1669–70	26 admitted, 24 at £25, one at £10, and one part-payment at £20. Fines for refusals: £295. Total: £925.
1670–71	7 were admitted, two with part-payments, and some were fined. Total: £200.

11. Turner, who kept his mayoral year at 73 Cheapside, a mansion said to have been designed by Wren, had a tough term of office. Invited to dine at the Inner Temple, he had gone in full regalia with his mayoral sword borne aloft. The law students objected, saying the City had no control over the Temple, and there had been a riot. Turner was related by marriage to Samuel Pepys, see note 5. An account by the present author of an imaginary day in Turner's life is due to be published in Mireille Galinou's *City Merchants and the Arts* (forthcoming 2004).

12. The subscription lists are as follows:

1671/2	92 people offering £10 down to 10s., a total of £250 3s. 4d.	
1672/3	68 people offering £20 down to 10s., a total of £188 13s. 4d.	
1673/4	67 people offering £20 down to 10s., a total of £185 3s. 4d.	
1674/5	61 people offering £10 down to 10s., a total of £156 13s. 4d.	

13. Jean Imray, *The Mercers' Hall* (1991), p. 43.

14. H. W. Robinson and W. Adams (eds), *The Diary of Robert Hooke MA, MD, FRS* (1935), pp. 53, 55; GL., MS 34010/9, 15 August 1673.

15. Robinson and Adams, op. cit.; Hooke's laconic entries indicate that he and Sir William Turner were on friendly terms and that he worked for Turner on his Hospital at Kirkleatham, Yorkshire.

16. GL, MS 1196/1, St Katherine Cree, Vestry minutes, 7 October 1666.

17. H. B. Wilson, *History of Merchant-Taylors' School*, 1 (1812), pp. 350–53.

18. GL, MS 34010/8, 23 September 1670; 11 January 1671.

19. H. B. Wilson, *History of Merchant-Taylors' School*, 1 (1812), pp. 354–64; F. W. M. Draper, *Four Centuries of Merchant Taylors' School, 1561–1961* (1962); GL, MS 34010/8–9, 20 January, 24 February, 7 April 1671; 5 November 1673, St Barnabas Day [11 June] 1674.

20. J. Schofield and C. Maloney, *Archaeology in the City of London, 1907–91* (1998), p. 96.

21. R. T. D. Sayle, *The Barges of the Merchant Taylors' Company* (1933), p. 13.

PLATE XVII

A. Interior of a tailor's workshop. English school, *c.* 1750.
Museum of London

B. Pageant decoration for the Fishmongers' Company, 1616. The Merchant Taylors' ship, hanging from the roof of the Hall, may have looked like this. A Victorian re-drawing of the original design.
Fishmongers' Company/Guildhall Library

PLATE XVIII

A. Sir William Craven (1548–1618), Lord Mayor in 1610, attributed to Marcus Gheeraerts the Younger.
Guildhall Art Gallery

B. Sir Abraham Reynardson (1590–1661), possibly by Cornelius Janssens. Purchased by the Company in 1876 for 100 guineas.
Merchant Taylors' Company

PLATE XIX

A. The Merchant Taylors' school room, drawn by Augustus Pugin, engraved by J. Stadler, for Ackermann's *History of the Colleges*, 1816.
Merchant Taylors' School Archive

B. The entrance to Merchant Taylors' School from Suffolk Lane. From a lithograph by J. Fahey, 1864.
Guildhall Library

PLATE XX

A. Suit worn by the Duke of York, later James II, to greet his bride, Mary of Modena, in November 1673.
By permission of the Victoria and Albert Museum

B. Dress suit of very fine brown wool, English workmanship, *c.* 1700–20, said to have been worn by Thomas Severne, Gentleman of the Bedchamber to William III.
By permission of the Victoria and Albert Museum

PLATE XXI

A. Interior of Merchant Taylors' Hall, *c.* 1860, artist unknown.
Merchant Taylors' Company

B. Entrance to the Hall from Threadneedle Street. Watercolour by George Shepherd, *c.* 1810.
Guildhall Library

C. Charles Mathew Clode (1818–93), Master 1873–74, first and most detailed historian of the Company. A posthumous painting by Alexander Macdonald, *c.* 1894.
Merchant Taylors' Company

PLATE XXII

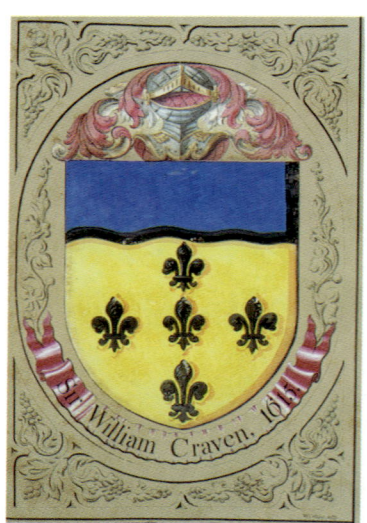

Heraldic glass, designed for the Hall in 1836.
Merchant Taylors' Company

PLATE XXIII

A. Staircase mural by Janet Shearer, painted 2001.
Merchant Taylors' Company

B. The Great Hall, 2003.
Merchant Taylors' Company

PLATE XXIV

A. The Parlour, 2003. Note the portrait of Queen Elizabeth, the Queen Mother, Honorary Freeman, painted by Sir Gerald Kelly, KCVO, PRA.
Merchant Taylors' Company

B. The Courtyard, 2003. This has replaced the garden of earlier times, but is still a delight to all who visit it.
Merchant Taylors' Company

CHAPTER FOURTEEN
TROUBLED TIMES

AFTER THE TUMULT of the Civil Wars, the long drawn-out strain of Cromwell's Protectorate, and the traumas of plague and fire, the Merchant Taylors, along with London's other livery companies, might fairly have hoped for a time of respite, a spell of tranquillity in which to recuperate, to enjoy the restored Hall with its new screen, to build up the academic prowess of the handsomely rebuilt school, and to watch, with relief rather than complacency, as overstretched finances gradually rebalanced themselves.

The past quarter-century had left men nervous, determined to preserve the peace, and yet anxiously suspicious, ready to see a threat almost anywhere. The extraordinary expansion of manufacture at home, and trade overseas, which had begun by the end of Elizabeth's reign, was starting to accelerate. The 1670s and 1680s, for those not a part of the silken whirl of Court life, were years in which to be cautious and hard-headed, for a man might need to look warily at his neighbour. Life was precarious. Political and religious differences were still there, only just out of hearing. The King might have sired a whole brood of children by various mistresses, but had failed to beget any with his sweet-tempered Portuguese wife. His brother James, Duke of York, had openly chosen the Catholic faith, and it was rumoured that Charles's own inclinations lay that way too. Beneath the surface, as London rebuilt itself indomitably, the times were uneasy. It so happened that the actions of a one-time pupil of Merchant Taylors' School were going to turn that uneasiness into tragedy.

At some time during 1649, the year that saw the execution of Charles I, a son was born to Samuel and Lucy Oates. He was named Titus. His family came from Norfolk; his grandfather occupied himself as a weaver and brewer in Norwich. Samuel attached himself to the Parliamentary army as a preacher, became chaplain to Colonel Pride's regiment, contrived to be ordained into the Church of England, and settled down for some years as vicar of All Saints, Hastings. Here Titus grew up.

He was an unprepossessing infant, subject to epileptic fits in his early years, and with a perpetually running nose.[1] His father 'could not endure him . . . and would jumble him about' to his mother's great distress, for she treasured her frail offspring. However, he grew up, and early in 1665, at the fairly advanced age of sixteen, was admitted to Merchant Taylors' School on the recommendation of Nicholas Delves, Master of the Company in 1662–63, and MP for Hastings in the Parliaments of 1659 and 1660. Delves, who traded from Friday Street in the City, came from the Hastings area, where his father farmed, and in 1659 had bought the manor of Hoseland, three miles inland to the north, which is presumably how the connection came about.

At that time, the headmaster was John Goad. Oates was received by one of the ushers, William Smith, whom he contrived to cheat of the entrance money which he should have handed over. His time at the school was short for, within a year, he was expelled for some unknown reason, and returned home to attend a local school at Sedlescombe, six miles from Hastings. From there he went first to Caius College, Cambridge, and then to St John's College; there is no record of his having obtained a degree, but somehow he managed 'to slip into holy orders', obtaining first the living of Bobbing in Kent, in March 1673, and then becoming his father's curate at Hastings. Here he chose to bring false accusations of sodomy against William Parker, a local schoolmaster whose post he coveted. These were discredited and Oates went on the run, serving as a naval chaplain and then turning up in London,

FIGURE 74. Charles II, engraved by John Thane for *British Autography* (1819).
Private collection

penniless, but somehow obtaining a post in the household of the Catholic Duke of Norfolk. Converting to Catholicism, Oates went abroad to train as a Jesuit, returning to England in the summer of 1678 having caused general distress wherever he went.

In London again, he became acquainted with a fanatical preacher, Dr Israel Tonge. Between them, they hatched what came to be known as the Popish Plot. On 14 August 1678, they alleged to the Lord Treasurer, the Earl of Danby, that there was a conspiracy to murder Charles II, and that the Jesuits would take over the country. An English St Bartholomew's Day Massacre was being planned. On 6 September, Oates made a deposition about the plot to Sir Edmund Berry Godfrey, a Justice of the Peace. Godfrey was last seen alive on Saturday, 12 October; his body was recovered the following Thursday from a ditch beside Old St Pancras church near Primrose Hill. He had been run through the heart with his own sword; now everyone believed in a plot to murder the King and overthrow the nation.

This is not the place to relate in detail the insanity of the next nine months, during which at least thirty-five innocent men were executed, the evidence against them depending on Oates's accusations and ramblings. The only person who disbelieved him from the first was the King, who seemed powerless to hold back the wave of public hysteria and prevent the judicial murders. Oates also had a score to settle with Merchant Taylors' School, and in March 1681 charges of Catholic sympathies were brought against John Goad (Fig. 75), the headmaster who had held the pupils together after the Fire and who must have been partly responsible for the successful rebuilding of the school. In spite of the twenty years' service he had given them, the Company reluctantly dismissed him, voting him £70 as a parting gratuity.[2] Dr Goad, who later did join the Roman Catholic Church, set up a school in Piccadilly whither a number of his pupils followed him. Among those whom he had taught at the school in Suffolk Lane was Peter Le Neve, the future Norroy King of Arms and first President of the Society of Antiquaries.

Dr Goad was not the only schoolmaster to be attacked. The Court minutes for 20 July 1681 set out letters from Oates, from a certain Elias Best, and from William Smith, the usher who had admitted Oates to the school fifteen years earlier and who was now allied with him, against Isaac Backhouse. Formerly Goad's pupil, Backhouse had gone on to St John's, had then returned to teach at the school, and was now headmaster at Wolverhampton. The Court were prepared to dismiss him, but Backhouse fought back stoutly, supported by testimony from the minister, the churchwardens, the constables and twenty-nine residents of Wolverhampton, which declared him to be 'a very fitt and able Schoolmaster, a very honest good man, and a true son of the Church of England'. The Court rescinded its decision, and Dr Backhouse continued to teach at Wolverhampton till the autumn of 1685, when he became rector of Northop in Flintshire.

FIGURE 75. Dr John Goad, headmaster of Merchant Taylors' School, 1661–81. He managed to save the library from the Great Fire, held his pupils together in the months and years that followed, and was much involved in the rebuilding of the school.
Merchant Taylors' Company

Later hands have made entries against Oates's name in the School Probation Book.[3] The first, presumably written about 1678, describes him as 'the Saviour of the Nation; first discoverer of that Damnable, Hellish Popish plot', but a second entry declares him to be 'Perjur'd upon Record, and a Scoundrel Fellow' (Fig. 77). Oates was indeed, on 9 May 1685, found guilty of perjury and for it was twice flogged through the streets, from Aldgate to Newgate and then, two days later, from Newgate to Tyburn; he was stood in the pillory five times a year and remained in prison for the next four years. He died at last in July 1705. He was that rare thing — a discreditable pupil of Merchant Taylors' School. Perhaps, if he had not been expelled but had stayed for his full term of education, he might have become a better and more stable man.

* * *

During these years of public turmoil and tragedy, the Company's affairs went on as steadily as possible at the Hall. A Court meeting was held on 15 December 1671, when it was reaffirmed that no apprentice should be bound till he had first been formally presented to the Master and Wardens on an appointed day. Thereafter, apart from a brief Assembly on 6 September 1672, only Court meetings are recorded, and such members as were regular in their attendance found themselves grouped and regrouped into one committee or another. The minute for 3 November 1671 reads, 'So greate a worke of restoring this desolate state is very heavy upon a small number', and it was decided to try to find another twenty liverymen willing to serve on the Court. Seven years later, the entry for 13 September 1678 makes clear that a general feeling of harassment and confusion still prevailed. Committees were set up to determine what land and property the Company owned and where it was. Moreover, they needed to know what leases, made before or after the Fire, were still operative, and with whom these leases were made, for how long and for how much rental. Once the properties were identified, the Company's arms, cast in lead, were to be set on each house, asserting ownership.

To this end, two books of plans were drawn up,[4] the first, undertaken in 1680, by John Oliver and William Leybourne, and the second in 1694–95. Oliver was one of the three surveyors appointed by the Corporation to supervise the rebuilding of the City, and from 1676, for twenty-five years, he was Wren's assistant surveyor for St Paul's Cathedral, while Leybourne[5] was regularly employed by the City authorities. The Merchant Taylors were employing the most experienced men available.

This earlier volume is very large — 1 foot 10 inches by 1 foot 5 inches — and consists of sixteen sides of vellum with maps of varying completeness giving the Company's property within, or just outside, the confines of the City. Some of the plans are full of detail; that showing Threadneedle Street with the Hall itself repays long study (see Col. Pl. XVI).

FIGURE 76. Titus Oates, engraved by John Thane for *British Autography* (1819).
Private collection

FIGURE 77. Page from the Probation Book of Merchant Taylors' School, with Titus Oates' name and comments about him.
GL, MS 34282/2, p. 633.

Other plans give little more than a bare outline. All are executed in pen and watercolour; the pressure of work, to which both men would still have been subjected, presumably accounts for the incompleteness. There was time, however, to paint a magnificent Company coat of arms, in full colour, as a frontispiece. The surveys indicate the positions of the George Inn in Aldersgate and the Saracen's Head in Friday Street, both of which the Company owned, as well as Mr Phillips's Coffee House down by the Tower in Little Minories — an early date for such business, for coffee had only recently been introduced into England.

The second volume is easier to handle and much more detailed. Undertaken in 1694–95 by a Captain John Stad, of whom nothing else is known, it measures 1 foot 3 inches by 10 inches. The maps are drawn with pen and watercolour, on sheets of substantial paper, now mounted on linen. There are fifteen surveys, identifying property in some fifty streets. Around 125 names of leaseholders are given, of whom twenty-three held two properties, with three — Milner, Oliver and Steventon — holding three each. We may guess that the Company's former Clerk, John Milner, and its Surveyor, John Oliver, had been taking a legitimate interest in the properties. Plan 6 makes clear the layout of the school in Suffolk Lane, with a chapel, a library, four separate rooms for the headmaster and the three ushers, classrooms, the school yard for playtime, and a cloister for wet weather. The courtyard of the former almshouses in Threadneedle Street can be made out, but the Coffee House seems to have gone. Plan 10 shows Pope's Head Alley, overcrowded with tiny shops and tenements; it is no wonder that there was constant squabbling over premises.

In the immediate aftermath of the Fire, the Hall had been restored as best as possible and had at least been adorned with Hooke's screen (Fig. 71); now it was time to improve the rest of the premises. In the spring of 1681, it was decided to deal with the western side of the property, rebuilding the Parlour, staircase, King's Chamber and rooms above, Avis and Lem once again undertaking the work.[6] An underground storage vault was dug, the northern section of which was let out at £3 10s. od. a year to a Mr Wilson, who already had the bulk of the space for £22 a year, but who was soon complaining that the wines he stored there were much 'dampnified by reason of the water falling into the same'.[7]

Lem's estimate for the digging of the vault had been £160, and £670 for the rebuilding work, but the final bill came out at £1,631.[8] The Company settled with him for £1,550 and went on doggedly, deciding on a costly lead roof, fitting out the Parlour with wainscoting, installing a marble fireplace, paid for by four generous liverymen,[9] in the King's Chamber, and providing seats in the garden, now tended on a regular basis by John Darling, who was to have £4 a year for 'finding all things necessary'.[10]

On 13 July 1687 it was ordered that the ship hanging from the rafters was to 'bee taken downe . . . [since] it obstructs the Beauty of the Hall'.[11] Was this the vessel from which the three sailors clad in light blue silk so successfully serenaded James I in 1607? Was it somehow miraculously spared by the Fire? What became of it? We shall never know. In its place came portraits of worthy members of the Company, Sir William Turner, Sir William Pritchard, Sir Patience Ward and — most proudly — one of His Majesty Charles II.[12] All were the work of 'Mr. Kneller', later to be Sir Godfrey; they cost the Company £180, though the price included the frames.[13] An inscribed stone was set up in the Kitchen to mark the date of its rebuilding. The Hall remained the focus of the Company's efforts.

Various other properties, acquired chiefly by bequest, needed attention too. In the rebuilding of the City, streets had been widened and necessarily Company property had been sacrificed to the public good. Compensation came at 5s. for each lost foot of ground. Mr Lewin, who had substantial premises in Poultry, was particularly vociferous and won the lion's share of the money doled out. There were constant squabbles over shops and leases and party-walls in Pope's Head Alley, and a temporary panic in March 1682 that the City meant to take over all the tenter grounds in Moorfields for use as a market, though this came to nothing.[14] Ground levels had altered with the post-Fire rebuilding. Some tenants tried, mistakenly, to take advantage of the Company. Alderman Sir George Waterman surreptitiously tapped two pipes into the Company's water supply and drew off the precious liquid for his own use; the Clerk, John Milner, was instructed to call and threaten to report it to the New River Company.[15]

The various charities for which the Company was responsible must have consumed a great deal of the Court's time and energy. The most demanding were the almshouses on Tower Hill, and the pensions distributed from various bequests and known by the benefactors' names — Reynardson, Dowe, Craven, Chadwick, Woolley, Dandy, Vernon, Rowe — a whole litany of those who had been Merchant Taylors and who had wished the Company well. Every time an almswoman, or a pensioner still living in his or her own home, died, another had to be chosen from the eager applicants; those disappointed were usually comforted with a dole of £2 10s. od. apiece. The fortunate inmates, however, even when provided with extra supplies of fuel in winter, simply would not behave themselves as the high-minded Company expected them to do. Sometimes, contrary to all regulations, they went begging round the streets, or fought amongst themselves; on 9 June 1680 Margaret Lucas and Mary Lawrence were dismissed for brawling, thereby forfeiting their pensions. In early August, a properly penitent Margaret was re-admitted, and Mary was allowed to creep back into shelter a month later, both vowing henceforth to keep the peace.

An additional responsibility for succouring the elderly was accepted in June 1683, when Christopher Boone, friend to John Evelyn the diarist, asked the Company to become trustees of his almshouses and a small school at Lee in Kent, and the offer was accepted. We shall consider Boone's Charity again in a later chapter.

The Court had also, under James Wilford's will, to provide money for the upkeep of roads in Streatham in Surrey, and at Northiam in Sussex. The parishes of St Giles Cripplegate, St Antholin, and St Andrew Undershaft could ask for help, which was never refused, for the binding of orphans or particularly poor children as apprentices, and there was money to be doled out to free fellow Merchant Taylors imprisoned for small debts, usually about £3 0s. 0d. a time. Modest handouts were made to industrious scholars at Oxford and Cambridge so that they might buy more books.

Altogether, the Company upheld valiantly the English tradition of social support by voluntary effort.

But the main concern, as always, was for the schools under the Company's care. With Dr John Goad in Suffolk Lane, the boys were well looked after, besides being well educated. When there was a heatwave in June 1680, awnings were spread over the narrow courtyard that served as a playground.[16] A new house of easement was made sweet for them; and when autumn storms brought the rain through the roof, he was swift to appeal to the Court:

The defect of our Tyling is so greate that we have been washed 4 or 5 times in our bed chambers, the rain finding it [sic] way through 2 or 3 flowers [floors] under it.[17]

The inspection hatch in the door had given way and robbers could burst in, warned Dr Goad, 'but I am silent least I should incurre the Charecter of a bold beggar'. The Court told Mr Lem to hasten to the aid of the school.[18]

Usually, the boys behaved well, occupying places at St John's with credit, but on one occasion just around the time of Dr Goad's unfair dismissal in the spring of 1681, some lads were heard uttering 'prophane words and sweareinge'. The Court was grieved and threatened expulsion, but perhaps there were those who felt that, if Dr Goad had still been in charge, such behaviour would not have happened.[19]

Attention was also paid to the schools at Wolverhampton and Great Crosby. Repairs were done, salaries paid more or less punctually. In August 1672 John Coles, headmaster at Wolverhampton, was awarded an extra £50.[20] He wrote a pathetic letter of thanks, begging to receive the money regularly — he had served faithfully for twenty years. He pleaded:

You have heard no complaints of me .. I am likely to receive but small encouragement from any here ... make my life a litle comfortable ...

Five years later he was dead. His successor, Samuel King, volunteered to give the widowed Joyce Coles £10 a year for five years out of his own salary — the Coleses had a sizeable family. Grudgingly, the Company added £5 a year for the same period. In the following year, 1679, Mrs Coles petitioned for additional help, was given £20 and told not to trouble the Company again. Samuel King died in the following March but his successor, Isaac Backhouse, continued his generosity. In January 1684, Wolverhampton took up cudgels on Mrs Coles's behalf; the lady was in 'meane and forlorne condicion', she should have been given an annuity for life. And then the town council showed its real anxiety:

... you assume to yourselves the power and authority of sending downe and placing School Masters amoungst us without our approbacions and without any Security given to indempnify oure said Towne ...

In short, the town was as unwilling as the Company to provide Mrs Coles with a proper pension, even though her late husband had been 'such a worthy person'. The Company reconsidered the matter and granted Mrs Coles £10 a year for the next three years, after which she vanishes from the records. Perhaps she moved away to live with relatives, or perhaps she died; we do not know.[21]

The Company's new educational venture in the seventeenth century was the founding of a charity school at Ashwell in Hertfordshire.[22] During the Commonwealth period, Henry Colborn (or Colbron) had made a will. He left his goods to his son, provided the young man did not marry before the age of twenty-one. Should he do that, or should he die, then £1,000 was to go to the Merchant Taylors with the specific obligation that they were to establish and maintain a school in Ashwell. Young Colborn did die; it took a protracted suit in Chancery before the Company obtained the legacy, though by now it only amounted to £701. A schoolmaster, Robert Bland,

FIGURE 78. Ashwell School, built 1681–83.
Photograph by kind permission of David Short

was appointed and began to teach in the church in 1669 on a salary of £20.²³ The parishioners urged that a proper school should be built, and at last the Company bought a site for £90. A local bricklayer, Walter Love, built a school with accommodation for the schoolmaster, for £170 (Fig. 78).²⁴ Robert Bland had been replaced at Michaelmas 1677 by Thomas Edwards; he sealed his bond at the Hall on 4 January 1682. The parishioners continued grumbling that the Company had been unreasonably slow in providing the building and, led by Walter Love — who had been paid for his work — brought a suit in Chancery against the Company, alleging that the school was too small and should be better endowed. The Company defended itself, maintaining with reason that the troubles stemming from the Fire obstructed it from doing more sooner, but it was called upon to pay all legal costs. Provision of education was not always rewarded with gratitude.²⁵

A second mid-seventeenth-century gift established yet another school, this one at Wallingford in Oxfordshire.²⁶ Walter Bigg, born in that pleasant town about 1605, had been apprenticed to a relative in London and had become a Merchant Taylor. He prospered and acquired land around St Giles in the Fields. During the Civil War, he fought with Parliament and took part in the siege of Basing House. By 1646, he had become a liveryman of the Company; by 1653, he was on the Court, had become an alderman and was serving as Sheriff; the following summer, he was elected Master of the Company. In 1658, he moved back to Wallingford, leaving his property in St Giles to finance a school in his home town; six poor boys were to be educated free of charge. The early years of the school are obscure, but the Merchant Taylors were involved and regularly doled out £10 a year towards the schoolmaster's salary.

* * *

With so many duties to perform and obligations to fulfil, it is surprising that brethren could be found, willing to spare the time, voluntarily, away from their own concerns. During the latter years of the seventeenth century, though Londoners were still anxious to become free of the Company, it became harder to recruit any willing to take the step of joining the livery, and often more difficult still to persuade individuals to serve as Master or as Wardens. Nevertheless, the Company continued to exist, though cutlers, distillers, bodice-makers, perfumers and harness-makers were now joining its ranks. There was a steady intake of copperplate engravers and of map printers; perhaps they were following John Speed's example. They included the silver engraver, Ellis Gamble, to whom William Hogarth was apprenticed on 2 February 1715.[27] London was changing, the whole pattern of trade was changing and, inevitably, the Company was changing too.

There was restlessness within the Company itself, an uneasiness that centred around the Clerk, John Milner, who had been so resolute in saving the records from the advancing Fire. The first recorded sign of trouble is in the Court minutes for 6 December 1671; Milner had gone absent without leave and had sent a 'letter to the Master importuning a pretence of a right to his place for life'. There was an enquiry in the following April, throughout which Milner continued 'a contemptuous demeanour'.[28] The Court dismissed him, confining him and his family to his room and forbidding them entrance to the Hall, where watchmen were posted till a substitute could be found. No such person was forthcoming, so Milner, abating his *hauteur* a little, was re-appointed, but the tension remained and the charade was repeated at intervals till Milner finally retired in December 1685, and Thomas Ange was appointed in his place. Perhaps — and with some justification — Milner felt himself to be the sole true professional, and resented taking orders from the ever-changing Master and Wardens and all the members of the Court.[29]

Other employees gave trouble, too. Richard Farewell, appointed in December 1680 to collect quarterages at a salary of £8 a year and certain perquisites, failed to deliver the money and had to be discharged two years later; the Company was not out of pocket, for Farewell's brother paid his debts.[30] Thomas Wharton, the Under Beadle, sent out in 1680 to summon the livery to dine with the Lord Mayor and the Sheriffs, used 'unhansom and sawcy expressions' about Sheriff Slingsby Bethel, and was made to apologize.[31]

The background to all this was anxiety over money. In the aftermath of the Fire, in sheer desperation, sites for rebuilding were let on long leases for extremely low rents. This had a double effect on the Company's income. Not only were annual rents low, but the long leases meant that there were far fewer fines to come in on renewal. The Company took up one short-term loan after another; in November 1682 the Master lamented that he had to raise £1,500 at once, but from where might he get it?[32] In February 1684, the Company had to borrow £350 from their own builders, Joseph Avis and Joseph Lem, and eighteen months later they were considering leasing out almost the entire rent roll of the Irish estate at £150 p.a. for twenty-one years in return for a lump sum.[33] At least the Merchant Taylors did not get involved in any harebrained financial venture. The Mercers, similarly embarrassed, as were all the City companies, took up Dr William Assheton's Annuity Scheme,[34] and found themselves in serious trouble. The Merchant Taylors struggled on, existing from hand to mouth.

* * *

The suspicious atmosphere within the Company was echoed in the wider political world outside. Discontent with the prospect of the Catholic Duke of York becoming King was growing. On 21 October 1679 the Artillery Company dined at the Hall, with the Duke as their guest of honour. An unseen hand fixed a notice on the gate declaring that all the guests were 'Papists in Masquerade'. There was, however, more conviviality in the Hall on 9 August 1682, when a feast was provided for apprentices known to be of a Tory persuasion. The King provided three brace of bucks for the celebration, the Dukes of Ormonde and Albemarle were present with the Earls of Sunderland and Halifax, and music was laid on:

The Kings Kettle drums and Trumpets and most of the Kings and dukes Musick attending them all the while they were at dinner.[35]

The Hall must have echoed with the noise of it, and several long doggerel accounts of the occasion appeared.[36] In these difficult years, the Lord Mayors for 1680–81, 1682–83, and 1693–94 were Merchant Taylors. Sir Patience Ward was installed on 29 October 1680 with protracted and elaborate pageantry devised by Thomas Jordan. Sir William Pritchard's inauguration on 30 October 1682 was a quieter affair, coming, as we shall see, at a time of political crisis in the City, though a small collection of 'new Loyal Songs and Catches' was published for it.

In May 1679 and again in October 1680, Parliament had brought in Bills to exclude the Duke of York from the succession to the throne. Charles, determined that the rightful line should be maintained, dissolved Parliament before the first Bill could be passed, and the House of Lords rejected the second attempt. However, Charles realized that he needed greater control over those elected to public office, and decided on what amounted to a general confiscation of municipal charters.[37] The idea was not a new one — it had happened occasionally during the Middle Ages,[38] and Charles I and Cromwell had used it too — but this was on an unprecedented scale. In all, the charters of 240 boroughs and companies were confiscated, and those bodies were told that they might sue for new ones which would give the King greater control over the officers elected. Only the Corporation of London dared to contest the case, which was heard between February and June 1683; inevitably, the City lost. 'The King of England is likewise King of London', said Judge Jeffreys.

Wisely enough, after consultation with the Attorney-General, the Merchant Taylors handed in their precious charters with the seals attached and thirty-two assistants resigned their places.[39] A petition to the King was prepared:

... your Peticioners haveing been lately served with a writt, upon a Quo Warranto, gives us great Cause to feare that wee are under your Majestie's displeasure by our Misgovernment, than which nothing in this world can be more grevious and troublesome to your Petitioners; in the sence whereof, wee humbly presume to prostrate ourselves at your Majesty's Royal Feet, beging your Majestie's gratious pardon, and in all humility beseech your Majesty to accept of the Surrender of our Charter, Most Humbly imploreing your Sacred Majesty ... to regrant to your peticioners a Charter, with such reservacions and restrictions, as your Majestie, in your great wisdome, shalbe pleased to thinke fitt.

On 14 April 1684, a committee of eight was nominated to deliver the deed of surrender and the petition to the King; among them were Sir William Turner, Sir William Pritchard, and Alderman Peter Paravicini. Thereafter no meetings could be held, and the Court minutes cease till 17 January 1685 when, a new charter with restricted powers having been received, the Court at last reassembled, ready to thank the King, to spend £3 on a case for the charter, and to consider 'how to put a stop to the growing debts'. The Master, Thomas Wardall, being seriously ill, begged to stand down from office, and Sir William Turner agreed to stand in for the remainder of the official year. Notwithstanding the debts, the Court voted to present a piece of silver to a value of £100 to Chief Justice Jeffreys's lady, since the brutal judge had praised their submissiveness. John Milner delivered a set of silver fire-irons, perhaps like those which still adorn the fireplace at Ham House and which once belonged to the Duke and Duchess of Lauderdale.[40]

Charles II died, suddenly and unexpectedly, from a stroke on 6 February 1685, and James succeeded peacefully enough. The Merchant Taylors voted to be responsible for his statue in the Line of Kings around the courtyard of the Royal Exchange, and Alderman Paravicini, who was to be the next Master, was instructed to 'discourse some artists'. The choice fell on Grinling Gibbons;[41] urged on by visits from the Wardens, the statue was completed, gilded and put in place by the spring of 1686. The sculptor had already had £20 and now was paid another £40 to settle the account. Eighteen months later the King promised his portrait to hang beside that of his late brother. This was delivered to the Hall in October 1688, and 'Mr Kneller's man' was rewarded with 20s., so presumably James, too, honoured the Company with his image executed by the Court painter, who would become Sir Godfrey Kneller under the next monarch.[42]

James's reign was already drawing to a muddled and undignified close. The King was well aware that feeling was running against him. In February 1688 some twenty liverymen had been ordered to stand down; in October, they were all restored. But it was too late; everyone realized that something extreme was going to happen, and on 2 November the Court decided that the Company plate had better be put into safe keeping by Mr Michael Rolls, the Senior Warden.[43] The royal religious policies, though probably misunderstood and possibly misrepresented, were unwise. On 10 June 1688 a son, James Edward (the 'Old Pretender'), was born to Mary of Modena, James's second wife, and baptized into the Roman Catholic Church. On 5 November 1688, by invitation, his son-in-law, William of Orange, landed an armed force on the Devon coast and began to march, in a most orderly fashion, towards London,

FIGURE 79. James II, engraved by John Thane for *British Autography* (1819).
Private collection

which he reached on 18 December. James fled to France and was assumed to have abdicated; Parliament offered the throne jointly to William and to Mary, James's elder daughter, who accepted it.

The fragility of the situation is demonstrated in the written record. Until 18 January 1689, the Court minutes are still dated in James's regnal year, but in the brittle months following, a gap is left where a king's name should appear, and William and Mary are not acknowledged till 10 May 1689.[44]

While all this was going on in the public arena, there was unrest within the Company itself. The gap between those on the Court and those who earned their living with their scissors and needles was widening. The story can be pieced together from the Court minutes, the Repertories (the records of the Court of Aldermen, stored in the Corporation of London Records Office), and other miscellaneous documents.

In January 1678, a group of 'Master Working Taylors' petitioned the Court of Aldermen to help them obtain an Act of Parliament 'against aliens exercising the said trade';[45] support was graciously promised. A further petition was presented in June 1680; the tailors were told to report any strangers, and complaints were lodged against someone called Dormibee who was not free of the Company. The Court minutes record that on 31 August 1683 Edward Haines complained that some Clothworkers had entered his shop, searched the premises, taken away two of his cloths, and fined him 13s. 4d. The Court promised to settle the fracas and no more is heard of it.[46]

Then matters took an unexpected turn. Another petition was presented to the Aldermen by 'divers Inhabitantes, Handicraft Taylors of the Same Citty', begging that a master might employ whom he wished, whether or not a man were a native Londoner,[47] despite an Act of Common Council passed long ago under Philip and Mary. Six reasons were given for this proposed reversal of policy. First, the suburbs around the City had spread out so far, and so many foreign masters had set up beyond the walls, that it was now difficult to find a young man willing to serve an orthodox apprenticeship or to take up the freedom, since he could prosper equally well without either. Secondly, tailoring was a seasonal trade, the main demand being in the spring. Otherwise, it was for an emergency — a funeral, or a wedding — which meant that many hands might be needed suddenly and must be sought wherever available. Thirdly, the severity of the ancient Act had persuaded many skilled workers to put themselves beyond the boundaries of the City authorities, especially since the 'late lamentable fire'. Fourthly, any English tailor travelling in other kingdoms could work there freely; if the same liberty were offered in London, a master might more easily find skilled journeymen when he needed them. Fifthly, many retailers of ready-made garments for men, women and children had set up shop, and there was increasing specialization so that it was becoming hard to find a man with all-round skills, but the only alternative was for senior tailors to be 'perpetually tormented with Informers, arrests and vexatious suites' because of the said Act. Finally, those who had set up businesses in the outer suburbs paid none of the main taxes, neither did they undertake civic duties which, with the dwindling size of the inner city's population, fell more and more heavily on those willing to serve. Such incomers

have swallowed upp all the trade & devoure the bread of us, our wives and Children and make a scorne & contempt of us.

This unorthodox petition is neither signed nor dated, but the Aldermen agreed to set up a committee of seven, with James Fletcher in attendance as Clerk, to consider the proposition.[48]

Before long, complaints began to come in about such a liberal attitude, and in September 1687 the Company asked for a copy of the petition.[49]

In the following February, the working tailors tried another approach. They asked the Court if the Bachelors' Company or Yeomanry might be revived — it had been in virtual abeyance since the emergency of the Fire. They wanted the right to search premises for unfree workmen, and to have once more a meeting place in the Hall, for their gatherings had lapsed. The Court assured them they were welcome to meet in the Little Parlour but regretted they felt they had no legal right to authorize searches.[50] Nevertheless, in March 1688, the Bachelors reported triumphantly that Alexander Holmes was working as a tailor, though not free of the Company. Holmes was quite ready to join, and the cases of some more humble craftsmen and women, Bardwell and [illegible] and their wives, were set aside for consideration later.[51]

Encouraged by this, the Yeomanry asked for full re-establishment and the right to elect once again their Wardens Substitute. This was accepted on 20 June 1688, but in August the Bachelors were told that they could have no access to Court minutes nor any other papers save the Books of Ordinances,[52] and that they must ask permission before holding a meeting. Next March, the Court relented and conceded that the Bachelors could also have the Silver Yard at their meetings as a symbol of authority, and look at whatever books they needed in the presence of the Clerk.[53]

They were to regret it, for by August 1689 the Bachelors were protesting that the Court were failing to fulfil all the duties laid down in benefactors' wills. There could have been some truth in this, but circumstances had changed since those wills were made, some of them more than a century earlier, and the schools, almshouses, road repairs, and most other responsibilities were well maintained. A committee was set up to consider the charges, but its assembly was regularly postponed. At last, on 29 October 1690, it did meet, and announced abruptly that the Yeomanry was 'burthensome and prejudiciall to this Company', and that the Wardens Substitute should not be sworn in. A month later, the Court declared that the Yeomanry had no right to inspect any Company records whatsoever, though they added, graciously and probably most irritatingly, they would of course always defend any working tailors.[54]

The Yeomanry appealed against the decision to the Court of Aldermen, who agreed to hear the case, postponed it twice, and then at last, 'after a long heareing', declared that

... the said Wardens and sixteen men have bin of late Altogeather Useless and only a charge to the said Company. [The Aldermen] were of Opinion that the Master, Wardens and Assistants ... ought not to be Obleiged [*sic*] by this Court to sweare the said four Wardens of the Yeomandry.[55]

The seam between the Company and its craft had been unravelled. Whether or not anyone realized it at the time, the Merchant Taylors were becoming primarily a charitable fraternity.

NOTES

1. The fullest account of Oates is by Jane Lane, *Titus Oates* (1949). Other information has been gathered from C. M. Clode's report on Oates and the Merchant Taylors' Company, presented to the Master of the Company in 1890, and from the *History of Parliament* (volume in preparation).

2. GL, MS 34010/10, pp. 111, 114, i.e. 13 and 27 April 1681.

3. GL, MS 34282/2, p. 633.

4. GL, MSS 34216 and 34217.

5. See Betty R. Masters, *The Public Markets of the City of London Surveyed by William Leybourn in 1677*, London Topographical Society, no. 117 (1974).

6. The rebuilding entries read:
GL, MS 34010/10, p. 102, Court meeting, 4 March 1681. Avis and Lem to rebuild 'a Councel Chamber [or Parlour], a King's Chamber, a large Staire Case and roomes over the said King's Chamber with Seiling Mouldings and pannells floated' by the end of July for £670. This did not include mason's work or wainscoting. Subscriptions to be raised.
GL, MS 34010/10, p. 119, 14 May 1681. Various changes to the agreed design at an extra cost of £420.
GL, MS 34010/10, p. 143, 3 August 1681. A new lead roof.
GL, MS 34010/10, p. 245, 20 April 1683. Wainscoting agreed. Sir William Turner to be treasurer of the same.
GL, MS 34010/10, p. 246, 27 April 1683. Assistants Rolls and Clarke offer to pay for this. Offer accepted.
All this work may well have involved the demolition or reconstruction of the parlour rebuilt in the late 1660s and early 1670s. It seems likely that it was at least altered and improved. (*Note supplied by Stephen Freeth.*)

7. GL, MS 34010/10, pp. 121, 123, 185, 186, 254.

8. GL, MS 34010/10, p. 232.

9. Daniel Baker, George Torriano, Peter Proby, and John Brett, GL, MS 34010/10, p. 265, 31 August 1683. The Company installed another fireplace in the 'Court roome or Parlor' by 'Mr Cartwright', GL, MS 34010/10, p. 248, 11 May 1683.

10. GL, MS 34010/10, p. 247.

11. GL, MS 34010/10, p. 394.

12. GL, MS 34010/10, pp. 393, 395; 34010/11, fol. 7ᵛ. Also Master's accounts, 1686–87, and 1690–91, in GL, MS 34048/29 and 30.

13. F. M. Fry, *A Historical Catalogue of the Pictures . . . at Merchant Taylors' Hall* (1907), pp. 29, 61–62, 72, 80–82.

14. GL, MS 34010/10, p. 189.

15. GL, MS 34010/10, pp. 198, 202.

16. GL, MS 34010/10, p. 61.

17. GL, MS 34010/10, p. 20, 7 November 1679.

18. GL, MS 34010/10, p. 20.

19. GL, MS 34010/10, p. 110, 8 April 1681.

20. GL, MS 34010/8, pp. 479ff.

21. GL, MS 34010/9, pp. 402–03 and /10, pp. 11, 48, 281–82. Gerald Mander, *History of the Wolverhampton Grammar School* (1913), pp. 156–58, 168–70.

22. I am most grateful to Mr David Short of Ashwell for generously providing information.

23. GL, MS 34010/8, p. 214.

24. GL, MS 34010/10, pp. 50, 116.

25. GL, MS 34010/10, pp. 275, 284–89.

26. A history of Walter Bigg and his school is being prepared by Mrs Judy Dewey of Wallingford. I am most grateful for her generous assistance.

27. Laurence Worms, 'Maps, Prints, Presses and the Merchant Taylors in the Seventeenth Century', in *London Topographical Record*, XXVIII (2001), pp. 153–66. William Hogarth's apprenticeship is in the Apprentice Binding Register for 1696–1718, now GL, MS 34038/18, p. 330.

28. GL, MS 34010/8, pp. 413, 443.

29. GL, MS 34010/10, p. 336.

30. GL, MS 34010/10, pp. 94, 210–28, 256.

31. GL, MS 34010/10, p. 91.

32. GL, MS 34010/10, p. 223.

33. GL, MS 34010/10, pp. 223, 291, 331.

34. See Ian Doolittle, *The Mercers' Company, 1579–1959* (1994), chapter VII.

35. Bodleian Library, MS Don b.8, p. 597, quoted in T. Harris, *London Crowds in the Reign of Charles II* (Cambridge, 1987), pp. 107, 177.

36. For example, *Horns, Make Room for the Bucks with Green Bowes* (1682). The political innuendoes are now so obscure that I think it better not to quote the text. It is clear that those invited ate well and that many got drunk.

37. For a full discussion, see Jennifer Levin, *The Charter Controversy in the City of London 1660–1688, and its Consequences* (1969).

38. See R. R. Sharpe, *London and the Kingdom* (1894–95).

39. See William Herbert, *The History of the Twelve Great Livery Companies* (1834–37, reprinted 1968), vol. I, pp. 212–20, vol. II, pp. 407–09. Also GL, MS 34010/10, pp. 297–98, 300.

40. GL, MS 34010/10, pp. 303, 305, 314, 316. Also see *Mundus Muliebris*, a poem written by John Evelyn and his witty daughter Mary, who died when she was only eighteen; Costume Society, Extra Series No. 5 (1977). It contains a reference to silver fire irons.

41. GL, MS 34010/10, pp. 308, 324, 337, 345, 346.

42. GL, MS 34010/11, fol. 11ᵛ.

43. GL, MS 34010/10, pp. 423–24, and MS 34010/11, fols 11ᵛ–12, 14ᵛ.

44. GL, MS 34010/10, fol. 20.

45. CLRO, Repertories 83, fols 56ᵛ, 62ᵛ; 85, 171ᵛ; 86, fol. 3ᵛ; Clode, *Memorials* (1875), pp. 22–29.

46. GL, MS 34010/10, p. 266.

47. CLRO, Alchin Papers, Box C12, no. 70. I am most grateful to Dr Nigel Sleigh-Johnson for telling me of this petition.

48. CLRO, Repertory 91, fols 110, 141ᵛ.

49. GL, MS 34010/10, p. 398.

50. GL, MS 34010/10, p. 421.

51. GL, MS 34010/10, p. 425.

52. i.e. GL, MSS 34006 and 34020.

53. GL, MS 34010/11, fols 5ᵛ, 9, 19.

54. GL, MS 34010/11, fols 30ᵛ, 45, 46.

55. CLRO, Repertory 96, pp. 17, 45, 100–01, 10 November, 1 December 1691, 14 January 1692. Thirty years later, there was similar restlessness in the Clothworkers' Company; see T. Girtin, *The Golden Ram* (1958), chapter 10.

PART THREE

THE COMPANY IN THE MODERN WORLD

CHAPTER FIFTEEN
THE LONG EIGHTEENTH CENTURY

Though the link with the craft had become tenuous, the Company was still a powerful force within the City. It was during Sir William Ashurst's mayoral year, 1693–94, that the Bank of England was instituted, and he went on to serve as Director several times in the new century. In the first half of that century, no fewer than four Lord Mayors were Merchant Taylors. They were Sir Robert Bedingfield (1706–07), Sir John Ward (1718–19), Sir John Salter (1739–40), and Sir Robert Westley (1743–44). Each of them had already served as Master. Sir Robert Bedingfield, a woollen draper, had married as his second wife Anne, the widowed daughter-in-law of the Company's Royalist hero, Sir Abraham Reynardson.[1] Sir John Ward sat twice as MP for the City in 1708–10 and 1715–22, and once again for Dunwich in Suffolk from 1722 until his death in 1726. He was a well-known man — first Director and then Governor both of the Bank of England and of the East India Company.

One fellow Merchant Taylor, whom Ward must have known only too well, was John Blunt, whose cunning provided the mainspring of the South Sea Bubble, the financial scandal of the century.[2] In the early days of the South Sea Company, its meetings were held in the Hall,[3] and when, at the height of his success in June 1720, Blunt was created a baronet, the Company invited him to be Master.[4] Fortunately, he refused; the Bubble collapsed in 1721 and Sir John was arrested for fraud. His estate, valued at £183,349 10s. 8¼d., was confiscated save for £1,000.[5] He retired to Bath, where he lived out his remaining fourteen years; we may guess that he had managed to salt away sufficient to make those years comfortable enough.

After Westley's mayoralty, no other Merchant Taylor filled the highest civic office till 1807, but that did not mean that the Company withdrew into obscurity; the brethren knew their own worth, and were ready to sing it aloud:

> To sing the Renown of the brave *Merchant-Taylors*
> Come blow a fresh Gale, Boys, and Hey jolly Saylors.
> For weell merrily troll
> All around round the Pole;
> Weell cut the Sea through;
> And bring home the Wealth of the Indian *Peru*.
> For the World has no Lord but the Merchant alone,
> And the whole *Phenix* Nest, Boys, is all but Your own.
> Then ith' Triumphs of the Day,
> To the Merchants weell pay
> Our heartiest Zeal and Devotion:
> Weell sing, and weell laugh,
> And the Bowls that we quaff
> Shall hold a whole Little little Ocean.
>
> Weell cut through the Line, Boys; then hey merry Saylors,
> From *Cancer* to *Capricorn* bold *Merchant-Taylors*:
> 'Tis for You the North Swain
> Drives the Great *Charles* his Wain:
> The Star at the Pole
> For You lends the Needle her whole Life and Soul;
> Whilst the Sun in the Skyes, and the Stars in their Glory
> Are all but Your Linkboys to travel before You.[6]

The Company also revelled in the glory of its barges.[7] There had already been three of these, built in 1640, 1669 and 1687; the first had survived long enough to join in the water pageant welcoming Catherine of Braganza, Charles II's bride, in August 1662 (see Fig. 68). All three had been comparatively small vessels, though the barge house had been enlarged in 1687 and the entrance to it made easier in 1718. The fourth barge gave good service for forty-four years, but then sprang a leak so that 'it was with difficulty the Company was landed in safety'.

Its replacement was built in 1764 by Thomas Searle of Lambeth, shipwright, to an estimate of £660 (Fig. 81). Rowed by eighteen oars, she was to be built from white English oak, with a House amidships to shelter the passengers in foul weather. A carving of the royal arms was to be set above the Master's seat, with 'Sea Lyons' on either side as armrests, and a handsome shield at the stern with the

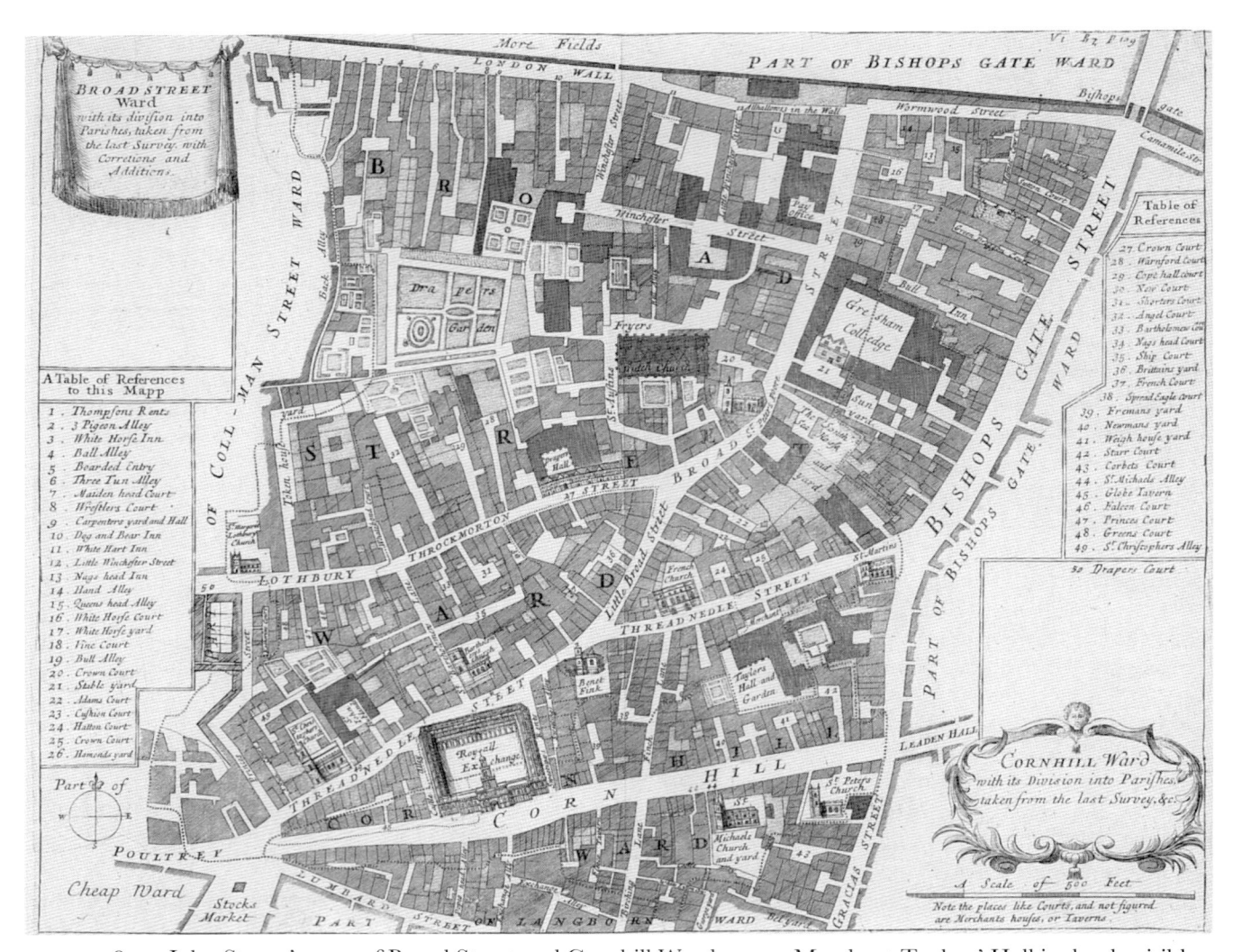

FIGURE 80. John Strype's map of Broad Street and Cornhill Wards, 1720. Merchant Taylors' Hall is clearly visible, set between the Royal Exchange and Gresham College.
Guildhall Library

Company's arms and supporters. Nathaniel Clarkson, a liveryman, decorated the barge with 'Emblematical representation[s] of the Four Quarters of the World' and with scenes from the history of the Company, Henry VII presenting the Charter which renamed it, and Prince Henry inspecting the membership roll at the Feast given to James I.

Another and still longer vessel, 'Seventy Nine feet in length and fourteen feet in Width', was ordered in 1799, at a cost of £1,300, from Richard Roberts of Lambeth. Clarkson's decorations were probably reused to adorn her, and she had the honour of joining in Nelson's funeral procession down the Thames from Greenwich to Whitehall on 8 January 1806. On this occasion, the weather was so rough that the Company's Colours were damaged beyond repair and had to be replaced. The victory of Trafalgar had been celebrated in the November of the previous year with a banquet in the Hall. The barge continued to serve the Merchant Taylors till 1846, when it was decided to discontinue so expensive an instrument of pageantry. The carved Company arms from that last vessel can still be seen on the Hall staircase. The barge was purchased

FIGURE 81. The Merchant Taylors' Company barge of 1764, built by Thomas Searle of Lambeth.
GL, MS 34340

by Oxford University Boat Club for £180, and eventually became the property of University College.

The Company's greatest pride was the Hall itself, with the handsome new screen, grand main staircase wainscoted a yard high, and elegant marble fireplaces in the Parlour and King's Chamber. Comparatively little maintenance was needed through the first half of the eighteenth century. An accidental fire on 7 November 1765 (Fig. 82)[8] meant that repairs and redecoration had to be undertaken, but little was done to change the character of the Hall or the adjacent rooms.[9] There were others, too, who appreciated the Hall's stylishness and the facilities it offered. From 1723–26 and then again in 1729 and 1730, the Freemasons held their annual Grand Assembly and Feast there. When the Duke of Norfolk was installed as Grand Master in 1730, he was met with a

Band of Musick viz. Trumpets, Hautboys, Kettledrums and French Horns to lead the Van and play at the Gate till all arrive.[10]

By this time, the Court minutes have become almost entirely concerned with the management of the Company's property and with the welfare of the schools and almshouses. The school in Suffolk Lane continued its steady existence throughout the century with John Criche as headmaster from 1730 to 1760; he had been a boy at the school and had served as usher for nineteen years before taking control. During Criche's long tenure, a boy was admitted briefly to the school; he was Robert Clive (1738–39), an obstreperous lad who would join the East India Company as a writer and go on to conquer India. Criche's successor, the Revd James Townley (1760–78), was a more innovative man.[11] Having attended the school himself, he came back to it from teaching at Christ's Hospital where mathematics had been on the curriculum since 1673, the subject having been introduced at the instigation of Charles II to train boys for the Navy. Very soon after his appointment, the new headmaster wrote to the Court suggesting mathematics should be part of the boys' studies at Merchant Taylors' School too, but the Court 'deferred the consideration of the same for the present', and it was not mentioned again. Townley, however, was a man of many parts; he had written a play, *High Life below Stairs*, which had been produced at Drury Lane in 1759 with great success, the theatre then being under David Garrick's management. In 1762, Townley asked permission for the boys to put on a Latin play; the piece chosen was the *Eunuchus* of Terence, and 2,000 tickets were sold for the three performances. Garrick was in the audience; he had provided the scenery for the play,

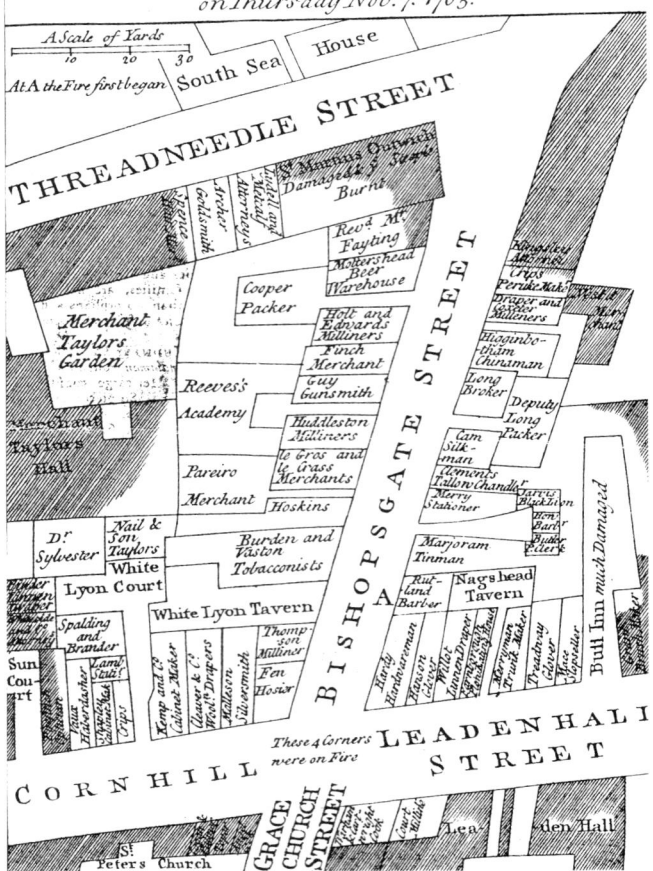

FIGURE 82. Plan showing damage done by a fire on 7 November 1765. From *The Gentleman's Magazine*.
Private collection

and he offered one of the young actors, Nathaniel Moore, an engagement at Drury Lane. Two other productions were put on in the following year, but thereafter the Court became anxious about the amount of school time spent on drama, and there were no more performances. Richard Mulcaster, that first unparalleled, remarkable headmaster, would have supported Townley; he believed that through acting, a boy would learn 'good behaviour and audacity'.[12]

Townley died in 1778 and was succeeded, after the brief headmastership of the Revd Thomas Green, by Samuel Bishop, who held the post for the next twelve years. He was considered to be a poet, though perhaps versifier would be more accurate. The Revd H. B. Wilson, the first historian of the school, speaks of Bishop's

> simplicity of manners, strength of penetration, integrity of conduct, depth of learning, and brilliancy of imagination[13]

but this eulogy should perhaps be tempered by the reminiscences of Charles Mathews, the actor, one of the most celebrated of Bishop's pupils. In his *Memoirs*, he recalls how the headmaster wore an enormous bushy wig, which the boys would shoot full of paper darts, the wearer remaining oblivious.[14] Mathews complains of the cruelty with which the boys were flogged, in particular by two masters called Rose and Lord. He tells that an Old Boy — he does not name him — returned to the school to horsewhip Rose in retribution and how, with this example before them, the next time that Lord attempted chastisement, the whole school rose, fell on the master and ripped the birch in pieces. Nothing of this appears in the Court minutes, nor in early official histories of the school.

At Wolverhampton matters were in their usual state of friction between Company, town and headmaster. The town, in spite of the Company's protests, was convinced that the income from the manor of Rushock should be sufficient to provide them with better school buildings and more able teachers; in 1685 the townsfolk brought a suit in Chancery against the Company, and an answer was prepared. No judgment seems to have been reached and the matter appears to have been dropped.[15]

Isaac Backhouse retired in 1685 and was succeeded as headmaster at Wolverhampton by John Plymley, a graduate of St John's, who had taught for six years in Suffolk Lane. He was inspected by a deputation from the Company in 1692, when he persuaded them to have additional classrooms built on at a cost of £30,[16] but his salary remained pitifully low. His enthusiasm for his duties began to fail and by 1710 the townsfolk were protesting again.

> Mr. Plymley is very Antient and for some yeares last past has to a very great degree Neglected the Said Schoole . . . Many of the Scholars have themselves complained that they had more hours of play than of Learning.[17]

Mr Plymley, who had served the school for a quarter of a century, retired with a pension from the Company to the rectory of Ham near Sandwich,

FIGURE 83. A merchant tailor's shop in 1777; detail from a writing sheet prepared to give practice in writing to the young. The border of vignettes, showing the Twelve Great Companies, is intended to demonstrate to what an apprentice might aspire, through industry and application.
Guildhall Library

where he died in 1734. His son John, educated at Wolverhampton, and a student at Brasenose College, had in 1708 been favoured with 'fifty shillings out of Mr. Juxons gift to poor scholars'.[18]

Plymley's place was taken by Robert Daubrie, of Pembroke College, Oxford. He was an energetic and forceful man; shocked at the state of the school buildings, he agitated for a visit from the Company. An expedition up the long, dusty roads was made in May 1712, and its members reported in February 1713[19] that a new schoolhouse was indeed essential. Fortunately, the lease of Rushock had just been renewed with a fine of £860. The work was put in hand by 'Mr Wm Smith the builder', and a handsome new school, with accommodation for master and usher, was built fronting St John's (or John) Street. The Company's arms were set up above the door, with a Latin inscription beneath.

Mr Daubrie resigned in 1729, to become rector of Aldridge near Walsall, and was succeeded by the Revd Robert Cartwright, whose usher, the Revd John Downes, forbade the headmaster to flog the boys under his care, since that was his prerogative. The Company upheld the headmaster and the affronted usher resigned.[20] Later headmasters included Dr William Robertson, who was appointed in 1768 and who oversaw £241 18s. 8½d. worth of repairs to the buildings in the next year. He lived frugally on his small stipend, relieved only by a welcome anonymous benefaction of £500 in 1773, and had the misfortune to outlive all his twenty-one children. Among his pupils, from 1773 to 1778, was John Abernethy, who became a distinguished surgeon.

During his headmastership the townspeople again commenced a suit against the Merchant Taylors, and this time the Company thankfully surrendered responsibility for the school. It had done its best for 250 years to maintain the foundation over which, by sheer force of distance, it had little hope of keeping proper control. The severance was made final in the summer of 1783. The responsibilities now lay with the Trustees, chosen chiefly from the townsfolk of Wolverhampton.

Matters proceeded with somewhat more tranquillity at Great Crosby. From 1677 to 1711 the Revd John Waring held the headmastership, and was succeeded by his son, Gerard. Both men had good relationships with their neighbours, who were charged with the inspection of the school, and they cheerfully taught reading, writing and arithmetic to their charges; there were not many who desired a classical education though a few went on to university. The salaries remained unaltered from those laid down in 1619.[21] John Waring managed all the teaching himself, taking boarders to eke out his finances and also serving as curate for the chapel at Great Crosby. When he died in October 1711, his son took over the duties till his own death in 1730. He maintained the same good local relationship and a wealthy widow,

Anne Molyneux, left money to the school which still funds a Divinity prize named after her.

Their successor was the Revd Anthony Halsall, who came with his sister, Catharine, from the Isle of Man. They settled happily into local society and seem to have had sufficient private means to employ an usher. The school prospered and the number of boarders increased. When Miss Halsall died in 1758, three years after her brother, she left a small estate to found a free school for girls where they might be taught reading as well as knitting and sewing; that school, now attached to St Luke's parish, still receives grants from the Halsall estate. A plain, dignified wall tablet in Sefton church commemorates the brother and sister.

For the three years after Dr Halsall's death, the school was sustained by acting headmasters, until in 1758 the Revd Wilfred Troutbeck was appointed, to begin a reign of nearly thirty years. He was well liked and conscientious, and shrewd in business dealings, raising the money to rebuild the fifteenth-century local chapel — 'ruinous and decayed in every part thereof' — though there is no indication that the Company contributed to the restoration fund. He also acquired land in and around the parish, including in 1770 the strip behind the school which previous headmasters had rented, and he managed to persuade the Company to pay out the £20 stipend for an usher.

It was one of these ushers, a young clergyman called Matthew Chester, who took over the school when, suddenly and unexpectedly, Dr Troutbeck died on 22 October 1787. Chester ran it until his own death in 1829, by which time there were some forty boys in the school. The age range was wide, too much for one master to manage, but the Company would allow no more than the meagre £20 for an usher, adequate perhaps in 1620 but far too little a century and a half later. By this time, one of the Company's Court of Assistants, John Beatson, who served as Warden in 1788, was frequently visiting the Liverpool area, and on the Company's behalf regularly called at the school. He saw no reason to employ an usher — clearly he had never been a teacher himself — but he did recognize a need to repair the building, and the Company was persuaded to spend £92 7s. 10½d.

The school maintained its level of pupils and Dr Chester, desperate for assistance, decided that, since John Harrison had intended that his school should be a grammar school for the teaching of Latin and — just possibly — Greek, he could fairly charge for instruction in writing and arithmetic. Accordingly, in 1804, he instituted charges of 5s. a quarter for writing alone, and 7s. 6d. if arithmetic was studied as well. The parents were outraged; for sixteen years Dr Chester had provided free education and few of them were willing to pay up now. When a local farmer, John Lurtin, absolutely refused to contribute, Chester brought an action at law against him and the Company supported the headmaster. Lurtin lost the case, but Dr Chester had lost something more valuable — the goodwill of parents and parish. The number of pupils began to decline.

In May 1822, the Master, Edward Complin, with John Buswell, a Warden, and William Bovill, the Clerk, came to inspect the school. Afterwards, they wrote a long and most sensible report,[22] declaring that the salaries were 'a very inadequate compensation for the duties to be performed', and indicating that some increases were needed; a young usher, Lancelot Sanderson, who had endured the £20 stipend, had just moved to the Royal Grammar School in Lancaster as writing and mathematical master on a salary £100 higher. His place was taken by George Chester, the headmaster's seventeen-year-old son, who was presumably living at home.

If the Company had seen fit to act upon Edward Complin's Report, the school might well have been saved from the slow decline into which it fell on Matthew Chester's death in 1829. His successor, Joseph Clark, was also a clergyman, but his story must wait for another chapter. What Great Crosby really required was not the grammar school, dispensing dead languages, of which John Harrison had dreamed, but a practical school teaching the Three Rs, with drawing, surveying and other useful studies available. What it needed most of all was a properly remunerated and enthusiastic master, with an adequately paid usher, but it was going to have to wait for that.

Matters went on peaceably enough with St John's College. Between 1667 and 1871 eight of the eleven Presidents had been pupils at Merchant Taylors'

FIGURE 84. Jane Skrimshaw, who lived to the age of 126 in the Company's almshouses.
Guildhall Library

School; of the fourteen headmasters, ten had been educated at the school and had gone on to St John's. It was a closed, orderly world, in contrast with the first half of the seventeenth century. After the traumas of the Civil War, all that most people wanted was peace, and Oxford was peaceful. We may note that Dr William Stuart, Chancellor of the diocese of Exeter, left money so that a suitable boy, who was excluded from a foundation scholarship by being just too old when a vacancy came up, might nevertheless have an assisted place at St John's. William Holmes when President invited 'one Handel a foreigner' to play at Oxford, and the great musician performed in the Music Room at Holywell. Jane Austen's father, George Austen, was admitted to a fellowship as Founder's kin through his mother, Cassandra Leigh; the link with the Company is tenuous, but the slightest association with the author of *Pride and Prejudice*, *Emma* and *Sense and Sensibility* is something to treasure.[23]

Care of the almshouses took up much of the Court's time and attention. Those adjacent to the Hall in Threadneedle Street had received some damage from the Great Fire; an attempt was made to patch them up, but soon the valuable site was reused, and thereafter the Company's only resident pensioners were the poor women in the Rosemary Lane buildings on Tower Hill. As the years went by, an increasing amount of money was spent on maintaining the buildings. The most celebrated of the residents was Jane Skrimshaw, the daughter of a woolstapler. Born in the parish of St Mary le Bow on 3 April 1584, she was still hale in 1710 when her portrait was engraved (Fig. 84).

In 1825 it was decided to transfer the almshouses to Lee in Kent, and the Tower Hill site was sold to the Blackwall Railway Company for a goods station. The Company already had almshouses at Lee, put under their guardianship by Christopher Boone who had established them in 1683. Boone and his wife lived in Lee Place; John Evelyn, who held Boone among his closest friends, described their stylish way of life. The house, he declared, was 'a most prety place, which he [Boone] has adorn'd with all maner of curiosities, especially Carvings of Mr [Grinling] Gibbons', and some pictures by Streeter.[24]

Boone's almshouses faced on to Lee High Road, and consisted of a chapel and accommodation for six 'ancient almspeople' and a schoolmistress 'to teach poor children to read and work'. The design of the chapel is traditionally attributed to Sir Christopher Wren, who was indeed an honorary freeman, but there is no hard evidence to confirm that he ever lent a hand in so practical a manner; Robert Hooke, Wren's friend, who designed the screen in the post-Fire Hall and advised over the school buildings in Suffolk Lane, is at least as likely a candidate.

In Ireland, after the Company's hopeful and energetic co-operation with James I's scheme for settling Ulster, matters had lapsed into sullen stalemate.[25] The Merchant Taylors had paid up promptly,

£6,186 in all, subscribing so magnificently that they were granted an interest in the Clothworkers' land adjacent to their own. As required, they built a bawn or fortified stone mansion, a church and smaller houses, while a school was erected at the expense of Mathias Springham, Master in 1617. George Costerdyne, related by marriage to Springham, went out to supervise the building programme and proved an honest and energetic Agent.[26] He strove to encourage craftspeople and able-bodied farmers to come from England to settle in the new lands; we know the names of some of them — Edmund Hayward, John Roe, John Mathews, Anthony Lipsett, and William Parratt, who later prospered, building St Columb's Cathedral in Londonderry and becoming Mayor of Coleraine in 1642 — but it was hard to find such pioneers. Of the succession of tenants who leased the estate from the Company, each seemed more unreliable and feckless than the last. What with the Rebellion of 1641, the Civil War, invasion, the Restoration and the final struggle between William III and James II, when the apprentice boys of Londonderry slammed the city gates against their former monarch, an estate in Ireland was not an easy or even desirable responsibility. Rents remained unpaid, but when, in 1720, the Clothworkers offered to buy out their proportion, the Merchant Taylors declined to sell. Nine years later, they leased the land to William Richardson for £20,640 and an annual rent charge of £150 a year, and ceased to have much to do with the luckless estate, though they retained their financial interest in the Clothworkers' property.[27]

For sixty-four years, from 1743 till 1807, no Merchant Taylor was chosen Lord Mayor. Throughout the second half of the eighteenth century, they dissociated themselves from City politics. Other companies might applaud William Beckford for having — most tactfully and gently — reproved George III; they might cheer for John Wilkes and Liberty, or be aghast at the Gordon Riots of 1780; they might remonstrate on behalf of the American colonists, since war with America affected London's trade; they might shudder at the brutalities of the French Revolution, and support the Younger Pitt throughout the wars against Napoleon despite the Prime Minister's introduction of Income Tax; they might rejoice in George III's restoration to health in 1789, lament his later illnesses or, in the next century, take the part of George IV's unfortunate Queen, Caroline; the Merchant Taylors remained apart. Safe within the sheltering walls of their medieval Hall, they rode out the storm of City and national politics. In the previous century, they had counted among their brethren both Abraham Reynardson, who, as Lord Mayor, had defied Common Council in defence of his King and had suffered imprisonment for his loyalty, and John Venn, who had taken up arms in Parliament's cause, had occupied and held Windsor Castle, and had readily signed his monarch's death warrant. In the next century, the Company would again move to the forefront of civic activity, but for sixty-four years its members lay low. They had had enough excitement.

The only indication in the Court minutes of the Company's involvement in national affairs is a donation of £200 on 20 December 1745 for 'the relief of His Majesty's forces'. Those forces, trying to suppress Bonnie Prince Charlie's rebellion, must have needed some comfort; by 6 December — 'Black Friday' — the Highland army had reached Manchester and looked set to march on London, but the Prince's command wavered and the enterprise ended in the bloodiness of Culloden, and Charles Edward Stuart's flight to the Isles and back to exile in France. The Clothworkers gave a banquet in rejoicing, but there is no indication that the Merchant Taylors did anything of the sort. Nearly half a century later, in 1789, the Company lent the Hall without charge to 'Eminent Merchants of the City of London' to celebrate George III's recovery from his first attack of porphyria, which was then interpreted as madness — 'so joyful an event' — but held no banquet of their own, even though they had just purchased a quantity of Queen's Ware white china plates, manufactured by Mr Wedgwood, on which to regale the livery.[28] Four years later, the country now at war with revolutionary France, the Company deferred a petition for help from the 'suffering clergy of France' who had found refuge in England, but gave half a guinea to each almswoman and pensioner in view of 'the dearness of provisions'.[29] Mr Jupp, the Company's Surveyor, was insisting on a

FIGURE 85. A tailor's shop, by Louis Philippe Boitard (*c.* 1733–*c.* 1767). Notice the pattern hanging behind the door, from which a coat may be cut.
The Royal Collection. © *HM Queen Elizabeth II*

new roof to the Hall, so perhaps they were right to be careful.

Though the links with the craft had been severed, tailoring skills moved on, reaching ever loftier heights of elegance (Col. Pl. XXA and B). Robert Campbell, in his invaluable 1747 volume, *The London Tradesman*, devotes nearly thirty pages to the making of clothing; he knew that a good tailor needed intelligence, flair and skill:[30]

... According to the vulgar saying, it takes nine Taylors to make one Man, yet you may pick up nine Men out of ten who cannot make a compleat Taylor.

His Fancy must always be upon the Wing, and his Wit not a Wool-gathering, but a Fashion-hunting; he must be a perfect *Proteus*, change Shapes as often as the Moon, and still find something new: He ought to have a quick Eye to steal the Cut of a Sleeve, the Pattern of a Flap, or the Shape of a good Trimming at a Glance; any Bungler may cut out a Shape, when he has a Pattern before him; but a good Workman takes it by his Eye in the passing of a Chariot, or in the Space between the Door and a Coach.

He must be able, not only to cut for the Handsome and Well-shaped, but to bestow a good Shape where Nature has not designed it; the Hump-back, the Wry-shoulder, must be buried in Flannel and Wadding, and the Coat must hang *de gage*, though put over a Post: He must study not only the Shape, but the common Gait of the Subject he is working upon, and make the Cloaths sit easy in spite of a stiff Gait, or awk[w]ard Air. His Hand and his Head must go together; he must be a nice Cutter, and finish his Work with Elegancy.

Since Campbell's book was intended for parents deliberating which trade might be most appropriate to a child's innate abilities, he goes on to discuss workshop conditions and future prospects:

In a Taylor's Shop, there are always two Sorts of Workmen; first the Foreman, who takes Measure when the Master is out of the Way, cuts and finishes all the Work, and carries it Home to the Customer: This is the best Workman in the Shop, and his Place the most profitable; for besides his Cabbage,[31] he has generally a Guinea a Week, and the Drink-Money given by the Gentlemen on whom he waits to fit on their Cloaths. The next Class, is the mere working Taylor; not one in ten of them know how to cut out a Pair of Breeches: They are employed only to sew the Seam, to cast the Button Holes, and prepare the work for the Finisher. Their Wages, by Act of Parliament, is twenty Pence in one Season of the Year, and Half a Crown the other; however, a good Hand has Half a Crown and three Shillings: They are as numerous as Locusts, are out of Business about three or four Months in the Year, and generally as poor as Rats.

A memory of the Company lingers when Campbell describes the successful tailor:

The Master's Profit is very considerable, arising not so much from the Price he gets for the Labour of his Journeymen, but from the high Prices he charges for the Furniture and other Goods he buys for the Use of his Customers: The Article of Buckram, Stay-tape, and Binding, with the many *Etceteras* in a Taylor's Bill, is much heavier than the Article of making. They are in this Shape Merchants, and many of them affect to be called Merchant Taylors. As such, they furnish Gentlemen, not only with Trimmings, but with whole Suits, and of this they make a handsome Penny, and would raise Estates soon, were it not for the Delays in Payment among the Quality.

Young William Farington, about to attend a reception in the recently built Norfolk House in the south-west corner of St James's Square in February 1756, wrote home to his sisters:

I heard one Single Shop sold above a Hundred Suits, so you judge what Numbers were bought; mine was a Figur'd Velvet of a Pompodore Colour which is the Taste, an entire Silver Wastecoate with a lose Net trimming waved over the Skirts & my Hair dressed French — don't you think your Brother is growing very youthfull?[32]

In the opening painting of Hogarth's sequence, *The Rake's Progress*, the young squire's first step on his downward path shows him being measured for a suit of clothes, and in the second, while instructors and hangers-on fawn around him, he wears a tangerine or 'Pompodore colour' full-skirted coat. By the next century, Ingres was recording exquisite young gentlemen who had been to London for their suits and 'redingotes' (overcoats); 'le style anglais' swept Europe.

Shops were changing, too (see Fig. 85 and Col. Pl. XVIIA). The cramped premises along Cheapside or round the Royal Exchange, where the standard booth was a mere 5 feet wide and only 7½ feet deep,[33] survived, but fashionable trade was moving away. With the Restoration, the Court was centred on St James's Palace, and the Fire accelerated the move westwards. New streets marched northwards from Piccadilly, which took its name from the trimmings sold by the tailor Robert Baker;[34] Bond Street became the most fashionable of shopping enclaves. Jane Austen was there in April 1811,[35] buying dress materials at the premises of Wilding and Kent in Grafton House, 164 New Bond Street. She wrote to her sister Cassandra that 'the whole counter was thronged and we waited *full* half an Hour before we could be attended to', but — happily — 'I am getting very extravagant and spending all my Money'. She was in London for the publication of *Sense and Sensibility*, so she may well have felt able to spend a little.

The long wars with France appeared to have ended with the forced abdication of Napoleon in April 1814. The leaders of the Allies came to London to celebrate. Tsar Alexander, the King of Prussia, Field-Marshal Blücher, Prince Metternich, Chancellor of Austria, and Count Platoff, the Cossack commander, were fêted across the metropolis with the Prince Regent as their host. This time, the Merchant Taylors joined in. The Hall had been borrowed on 10 June by the Merchants and Bankers of London to feast the Emperor of Russia, the walls had been adorned with sumptuous hangings, and the Company had invited the Tsar and the King of Prussia to become freemen, though they did not accept the compliment.

Within three days, the royal visitors had returned to Europe, and the Company decided it was time to honour the British commander of the allied forces, the Duke of Wellington. He accepted an invitation for 13 July, and the freedom of the Company as well, and the Court determined that the festivities should

FIGURE 86. The Duke of Wellington; marble bust by Edward Physick.
Merchant Taylors' Company

approach as nearly as circumstances and a due regard for practical economy will admit to the nature of a Royal Banquet.[36]

The hangings for the Tsar's entertainment were retained, but yards and yards of costly scarlet cloth were used to carpet the whole floor area of the Hall and staircase and to provide an awning under which the 'First Hero of the World' might enter. Thirteen additional chandeliers were borrowed and installed; the long tables were adorned with

> rich and costly Silver Gilt Candelabras and Candlesticks — Vases — Tureens — Cups — and every other Article in Plate that could add Splendour and Richness.

The recess at the western end of the Hall was lined with a display of plate, and a 'very handsome Venison Dinner . . . with Port, Madeira, Hock and Claret' was prepared.

It was decided to invite the Princes of the Blood Royal — the Dukes of York, Kent and Sussex — the Duke of Norfolk, the Government ministers, the Speaker of the House of Commons, the Lord Mayor and Sheriffs, numerous foreign ambassadors, the Governor of the Bank of England, the Chairman of the East India Company, and Wellington's comrades in arms, Field-Marshal Blücher and Count Platoff, who were still in the country.

On the great day, the Court assembled early, and the livery prepared to line the entrance and stairs. Some 150 'Beautiful and Elegant Females', wives and daughters of liverymen, filled the balcony. The Clerk, Richard Teasdale, delivered an address, assuring Wellington that the Merchant Taylors would

> consider this, my Lord Duke, one of the proudest Days in the History of the Company, and so it will be considered by their Children's Children . . . [*They could say much more, but*] feelings of delicacy are inseparable from the Breast of a Hero; they are unwilling to oppress your Mind by an Address which can add nothing to your Grace's fame.

The Duke, to a 'profound and respectful silence', assured the Company that the victory was due to the 'Gallantry' of his soldiers. The band of the Foot Guards, 'accoutered in their full dress uniform', struck up *Hail the Conquering Hero*, and the ladies on the balcony waved their handkerchiefs. The Revd Cherry said Grace, and trumpeters of the Life Guards, positioned at either end of the Hall, proclaimed the arrival of the meal. The heat in the Hall must have been intense. At the end of the meal, a group of singers, led by Mr Sale, sang *Non Nobis Domine*, and toasts were drunk to Church and King, the Prince Regent, the Queen and the Royal Family. The Duke was at last able to slip away. It had been an evening to rival the Feast given two centuries earlier, to James I.

The Court reassembled on the following day and resolved to offer the freedom to the Duke of Norfolk. The Master and Wardens were applauded for their 'indefatigable Labour, Diligence and Skill'. Andrew and George Nash, two of the Wardens, were thanked for lending so many of the chandeliers. *The Times* devoted nearly a column to the occasion.

The Merchant Taylors were once more in the forefront of London's activities.

NOTES

1. J. R. Woodhead, *The Rulers of London, 1660–1689* (1965), has supplied many of the details given here.
2. J. Carswell, *The South Sea Bubble*, 2nd revised edition (2001).
3. GL, MS 34010/11, fol. 296ᵛ, 4 October 1711.
4. GL, MS 34010/12, pp. 117–19, 12 July 1720.
5. *The Particular and Inventory of Sir John Blunt* (1721). Copy available in Guildhall Library.
6. E. Settle, 'The Triumphs of London, Performed on Monday, Octob. 30th 1693 . . . for Sir William Ashurst, Knight, Lord Mayor', in R. T. D. Sayle, *Lord Mayors' Pageants* (1931).
7. A full account of these vessels is given in R. T. D. Sayle, *The Barges of the Merchant Taylors' Company* (1933). Embarkation was from stairs at a Company riverbank property in the Vintry; leases of the site in question are GL, MS 34100/87 and 147 (no. 15).
8. GL, MS 34010/13, pp. 206–07.
9. H. L. Hopkinson, *The History of Merchant Taylors' Hall* (Cambridge, 1931) gives much detail on the development of the building.
10. Archival material at Freemasons' Hall. I am most grateful for permission to consult the documents.
11. F. W. M. Draper, *Four Centuries of Merchant Taylors' School* (1962), pp. 99–110.
12. Sir James Whitlocke, *Liber Famelicus*, Camden Society Publications, no. LXX (1858).
13. H. B. Wilson, *History of Merchant-Taylors' School*, I (1812), p. 520.
14. Anne Mathews, *Memoirs of Charles Mathews, Comedian* (1838–39), I, pp. 32–34.
15. G. P. Mander, *History of the Wolverhampton Grammar School* (Wolverhampton, 1913); GL, MS 34010/10, p. 339.
16. GL, MS 34010/11, fols 70ᵛ, 103ᵛ. The visit was in 1692; it was three years before the new building was added.
17. Mander, op. cit., pp. 175–76.
18. GL, MS 34010/11, fol. 254ᵛ.
19. GL, MS 34010/11, fols 301ᵛ, 307ᵛ.
20. Court minutes; also GL, MS 34100/119, no. A 13.
21. The original salaries were £30 for the master and £20 for the usher. In the aftermath of the Fire, these were reduced to £30 6s. 8d. for both posts in 1672; the full salaries were reinstated in 1741.
22. Printed in full in H. M. Luft, *A History of Merchant Taylors' School, Crosby, 1620–1970* (Liverpool, 1970), pp. 130–35.
23. For further information on the college and the Company in this period, the reader should seek out W. C. Costin, *The History of St John's College, 1598–1860* (1958); Mark J. Simmonds, *Merchant Taylors' Fellows of St John's* (1930); R. H. Adams, *Memorial Inscriptions in St John's College* (1996), the author of which attended both the school and the college; Mr Adams, when a schoolboy, also contributed to *Merchant Taylors' School* (1929). For the Austen connection, see C. Tomalin, *Jane Austen* (1997), and D. Gilson, 'The Austens and Oxford: Founder's Kin', *Jane Austen Society Report* (1977), pp. 43–45.
24. E. S. de Beer (ed.), *The Diary of John Evelyn* (1955), IV, pp. 180, 288.
25. See above, pp. 171–73.
26. *London and Middlesex Archaeological Transactions*, vol. 23, pt 2 (1972). I am grateful to Mr W. J. Magill, headmaster of Foyle & Londonderry College, for the help he has given me.
27. The story of the livery companies' involvement with Ulster is, quite simply, tragic. For further reading, I would recommend two books by James Stevens Curl: *The Londonderry Plantation, 1609–1914* (Chichester, 1986) and *The Honourable The Irish Society and the Plantation of Ulster, 1608–2000* (Chichester, 2000). There is also T. W. Moody, *The Londonderry Plantation, 1609–41: The City of London and the Plantation in Ulster* (Belfast, 1939) and Nicholas Canny, *Making Ireland British* (2001). The rent charge was seldom paid and was extinguished altogether in 1901 (GL, MS 34101/12, bundle 131).
28. GL, MS 34010/14, pp. 285, 351. The same Court, in an unusually extravagant mood, authorised the purchase of a 'New Hat laced with Gold for the Bargemaster'.
29. GL, MS 34010/14, pp. 445, 447.
30. R. Campbell, *The London Tradesman* (1747), pp. 191–94; '. . . the Coat must hang *de gage* [*dégagé*]' (the coat must hang easily, without constraint).
31. Cabbage is a left-over length of cloth, the foreman's perquisite — the word is still in use.
32. Desmond Fitz-Gerald, *The Norfolk House Music Room* (1973), pp. 48–49.
33. Ann Saunders (ed.), *The Royal Exchange* (1997), p. 89.
34. See above, p. 178.
35. A. Adburgham, *Shops and Shopping, 1800–1914* (1964), and *Shopping in Style: London from the Restoration to Regency Elegance* (1979); F. Chenoune, *A History of Men's Fashion* (1993), provides fascinating reading.
36. All the details given in the following pages will be found in the Court minutes, GL, MS 34010/16, pp. 319–39.

CHAPTER SIXTEEN

THE NINETEENTH CENTURY

ONCE THE LONG WARS with France were over, England turned to expansion of trade overseas and to reform at home. By the end of the fourth decade of the century, the Reform Act had been passed for the re-organization of Parliament, and there was a new, young Queen on the throne.

Throughout the previous century, the population of the country had increased steadily, but the administration of the swelling cities and towns was still largely that laid down in the Poor Law Act of 1601, dependent on voluntary parochial administration. In February 1833, the reformed Parliament set up a select committee on municipal corporations; by July, this had become a Royal Commission, and the Report, calling for a 'thorough reform', was complete by March 1835.[1] A Bill was before the House by June, proposing uniform town government based on a ratepayer franchise and regular local elections; its terms applied to 183 corporations but London was not among them. The able Chairman, John Blackburne, MP, and the Secretary to the Commission, Joseph Parkes, were shrewd enough to realize how strongly the City would resist any change: they decided

The importance of that city is so great and its institutions are so peculiar, that it will be necessary to make them the subject of a special Supplementary Report.

The Report on London was published in 1837 in five volumes. No government action was taken with regard to the City, but it was made clear that the Corporation would be wise to set about reforming itself, a suggestion that did not meet with the approval of the livery companies; the Merchant Taylors promptly declared their 'unqualified resistance'. Over the next fifteen years, those within the Corporation whose instincts were more liberal and more forward-looking succeeded merely in reducing the freedom fine, while in 1835 Common Council decided a man could be free of the City without belonging to a company. In 1849, after much effort, the franchise for ward elections was redefined to include all those occupying property rated at £10 per annum or more. Attacks on the City continued, some of the most vociferous coming from Francis Place, a tailor and breeches-maker, who had no connection with the Company, from William Carpenter, with a volume entitled *The Corporation of London, as It Is, and as It Should Be* (1847), and, a generation later, from J. F. B. Firth with *Municipal London* (1876).

While all this was going on in the political world, the Company was concerned with its own affairs. Masters and Wardens came and went annually, charity was distributed, properties were leased and repaired, and parts of the Hall were redecorated on the advice of George Dance, the City Surveyor.[2] Stoves were installed for winter warmth, plate glass doors, costing £300, were fitted to alleviate the draughts,[3] a new entrance was suggested from Threadneedle Street,[4] two new marble fireplaces, costing up to £100, were ordered for the Drawing Room,[5] paintings of George III and Queen Charlotte by Allan Ramsay were purchased,[6] and portraits commissioned of the Duke of Wellington and Lord Eldon, who had both accepted the freedom of the Company.[7] John Thane, the celebrated engraver, was paid ten guineas to clean and restore Sir Thomas White's portrait, and particular attention was given to the well-being of the records and muniments, extra staff being employed for the task, while a china closet was adapted as a strong room for their storage.[8] Special care was taken of the hearse-cloths and tapestries. Additional expenses included four new ottomans with cushions and new chandeliers for the Hall, though the gilding on them turned black and they had to be repolished. A new carpet was laid in the Dining Room, and curtains, dyed with 'real cochineal scarlet', were made for the windows.[9] As might have been expected, the refurbishment cost a great deal of money, but the Court felt it was well spent (Col. Pls XXIA and B, XXII).

The membership remained large, and the professions of the livery within it varied as much as ever, with practising tailors few and far between. By the 1870s, out of 273 apprentices bound, only three had any connection with tailoring.[10] Indeed, Company and craft by now had no relationship, though there were significant developments in the manufacture of clothing, with ready-made apparel increasingly available from the late seventeenth century onwards. By the beginning of the nineteenth, sizing and cutting systems began to be developed, and methods of pattern construction were explored in print, thereby becoming more easily available.[11] By the 1860s, the sewing machine had been introduced; by the end of the century, it had become a significant factor in the production of clothing. There was a wide rift between the dignity of the Hall in Threadneedle Street, and the discomfort of an overcrowded sweatshop in the East End of London.

In the early decades of the century, those admitted to the Company included a corn merchant, an insurance broker, a hop merchant, a silk merchant, a pawnbroker, a coal merchant, a hatter, a vintner, a miller, a dyer, an engraver and several gentlemen. A more unusual liveryman was the sculptor, Henry Rossi, one of the sixteen children of John Charles Felix Rossi, an artist who had designed some of the imposing monuments erected in St Paul's to the heroes of the Napoleonic Wars. Henry was admitted to the livery on 20 December 1814 on payment of £52 10s. 0d. In October 1827, he was obliged to apply to the Company for a loan of £80 or £100; as surety he offered his sculptures of the Cricketer and the Wrestler, but was sternly turned away. However, ten years later, after a second appeal, the Company bought plaster casts of the Bowler and Batsman, and of Mary Magdalene Washing the Feet of Jesus, for £42.[12] They have all vanished, presumably in the bombing of 1940; a marble Bowler can be seen at Woburn and is a handsome piece of work.

So diverse was the livery that it was proposed to strike a silver medal for 'identification at Dinners'. This might have been useful when, in November 1829, George Hope got so drunk that he broke a chandelier; he apologized humbly once he was sober.[13] We may note that, in the accounts rendered by each Master at the end of his year of office, the payments to Mr Birch the caterer, and to various wine merchants, were always the most substantial items. In June 1832, Mr Birch was summoned before the Court to be told that his charges were inordinate — the bills were usually over £800 — but he replied calmly that if the Company wished to give such sumptuous dinners, they could not be done more cheaply; however, if they cared to settle on a fixed price meal, he would do his economical best to comply. The Court instructed him to omit the sweetmeats for the next Billesden Award Dinner, and matters went on much as usual.

Considering the generosity of the entertainment, it must have been a shock to the Court when four rebellious brethren — Robert Hugh Franks, George Machin, Charles Fox Smith, and John Atkinson — created a disturbance at a dinner on 4 August 1830. They queried the propriety of the election of the Master and Wardens, asked to see the early charters, and demanded an opportunity to inspect the accounts. The request was refused and battle was joined. On 11 August a meeting of the livery was called at the London Tavern. Franks and Smith complained that the Company's revenues were misemployed in 'frequent and extravagant feasting'. They spoke of 'lavish and expensive entertainments', and reminded their audience that the previous Clerk, Richard Teasdale, had had to resign in January 1822 because of a deficit in the accounts of 'several thousand pounds'. A letter of complaint, requesting access to the muniments, was signed by fourteen members; among them was George Clode, father of Charles Mathew Clode, who was to become the Company's first and most devoted historian. The argument continued; the Company remained obdurate. Then on 17 April 1833 a Special Court was called; the Master broke the news that Franks had published a pamphlet entitled *Corporation Abuses*. It accused the Merchant Taylors and other companies of misuse of funds and of wild culinary extravagance, speaking — for once, not of turtle soup but — of 'green peas at Christmas at two guineas per quart'. The Court felt betrayed by its own brotherhood. The insurgents had gone still further; before the end of

FIGURE 87. The Company's almshouses at Lee; the foundation stone was laid in 1825.
GL, MS 34214/19

1830 they had challenged the Court in the King's Bench, seeking a *mandamus* to compel inspection of the records. It was refused, so they then demanded that the Master and Wardens should be elected by the whole Company and not simply by the Court of Assistants, but once again the judges ruled against them.[14] They then tried to petition the House of Commons, but general support was lacking[15] and the protest died away. It was however a warning to the senior members and, although no immediate action was taken, it was not ignored.

* * *

In truth, the Merchant Taylors were concerning themselves with many other matters besides epicurean dinners. In the winter of 1816, land on Three Cranes Wharf, Thames Street and Queen Street was compulsorily purchased from the Company to provide the foundations for Southwark Bridge. There was wrangling over compensation but eventually £19,617 10s. 0d. was accepted.[16] The valuable site of the old almshouses on Tower Hill was sold off, and in 1825 land was purchased immediately to the north of Christopher Boone's almshouses in Lee (see p. 231). Neither Mr Cubitt nor Mr Peto, two distinguished builders of the period, wished to estimate for the work, but eight others were eager. The choice — almost inevitably — fell on the lowest estimate offered, that of Mr Samuel Cooper. The foundation stone was laid on 7 July 1825, the Master,

Richard Jennings, being present, while the Revd John Joseph Ellis offered up 'a most impressive and appropriate Benediction' which was recorded in its entirety, filling a page and a half of the minutes.[17] The number of inmates was increased to thirty. Half a century later, in 1874, Boone's almshouses moved to new buildings on a new site; the Company purchased the seventeenth-century houses, demolished them, and added the land to the delightful gardens in front of their own almshouses. Boone's chapel was retained in the south-east corner of the grounds. The Company has always been distinguished for its humane and supportive conduct towards the elderly; the original almshouses, built in 1413 beside the Hall in Threadneedle Street, are believed to have been the earliest such provision in London.[18]

As always, the Company's chief care was for its educational work. Merchant Taylors' School continued to occupy its original site, with the schoolhouse rebuilt after the Fire (Col. Pls XIXA and B). In 1819 Thomas Cherry resigned the headmastership on grounds of ill health. There were four candidates for the post — J. J. Ellis, Lancelot Sharpe, H. B. Wilson, and J. W. Bellamy; all were in holy orders, the first three already teaching in the school, but Dr Bellamy was the previous headmaster's son-in-law and he was appointed, to the intense chagrin and disgust of the others. By way of compensation, Ellis was made chaplain to the Company, and Sharpe resigned with a gratuity of 250 guineas, while the school educated his nine sons.[19] Wilson, author of the school's first — and most massive — history, remained for a while on the staff, and then continued as rector of St Mary Aldermary until his death in 1854.

Dr Bellamy was a modernizing man, capable of handling the Court in a gentle but persuasive manner. Each term, he submitted a report, hinting at improvements, indicating in the most delicate manner the direction in which the school should be moving. A major one was presented in April 1821 and, on 27 June 1828, he told the Court that there was an 'increasing demand for a more general education', persuading them to contribute £200 to the 'proposed University, to be called King's College London'. University College, already established in Gower Street, received no such largesse, but then its antecedents were radical and, unlike King's, it had no intention of establishing a theology school. A year later, he was urging the 'enlargement of the present system ... Mathematics are now properly considered necessary', and he referred to King's and to UCL as 'two great modern establishments'. The Court agreed to the teaching of mathematics, fees were raised to two guineas a quarter, and two maths masters were appointed. A year later, Bellamy lamented 'we suffer much from want of room', which was no exaggeration. All the boys, over two hundred of them, were taught in the one hall, with its eight tall windows on either side grimy with London's dirt (Fig. 88).[20] They sat on forms, not at desks, so that for written work it was necessary to kneel on the floor and rest the exercise book on the form. Illumination was provided by candles, so the boys worked in pairs, taking turns to hold the flickering light. The only area for play at break-time was the narrow, cramped schoolyard; lunch was not provided, so those whose homes were far from Suffolk Lane — and that was an increasing number — frequented a pie shop and then wandered about the City streets, thereby acquiring an intimate knowledge of that quarter of London. Till the introduction of mathematics, instruction was confined to Latin and Greek with some Hebrew in the upper forms. Bellamy succeeded in adding a Writing Master to the staff, but the introduction of French was too much for the Court. English literature was simply ignored, and one wonders what Mulcaster would have thought; 'I honour the Latin, but I worship the English' was his tenet. Bellamy managed to persuade the Company to convert into classrooms space that had once been living accommodation for masters, and to box in the cloister along one side of the play yard to gain a little more teaching area, but conditions were cramped and dirty with, by now, warehouses around and a brewery nearby; there was nowhere for sport — not that that was on the curriculum — and the school cannot have been a healthy place for children. There seemed, however, no real solution at that time.

Discipline was severe, though no more so than in any other school of the period. One parent, a Mr Barber of the Remembrancer's Office, Guildhall, complained vigorously in October 1823 that his child

FIGURE 88. Speech Day, St Barnabas' Day, 1864, in Merchant Taylors' School, Suffolk Lane, painted by James Fahey.
Merchant Taylors' Company

had been hit so violently on the head with a cane by Mr Roberson, the third master, that the boy was deprived of speech for two months.[21] The Court set up an inquiry which

> received such ample testimony to the mild and aimiable disposition of the Rev. J. Roberson as to convince them he is incapable of harshness or severity.

Nevertheless, £100 was paid to Mr Barber and the Court ruled that in future only the headmaster might inflict corporal punishment. This was probably ignored, for six years later Capt. John Fisher of the Harbour Master's Office was protesting that his son had been beaten so cruelly that his testicles had been damaged,[22] and an Old Boy, the novelist Albert Smith, described the inexorable caning in *The Fortunes of the Scattergood Family* (1845), while W. C. Hazlitt, grandson of the essayist, could remember frequent chastisement. Such conduct would not be condoned today, but, in spite of everything, the school was always full of pupils and Dr Bellamy's own son went on to become President of St John's.

Wolverhampton Grammar School had broken away from the Company in the previous century, but close relationships were maintained with Ashwell and with Great Crosby, which may have been happier places of instruction, perhaps because there was more space and air than in the confines of Suffolk Lane, and because neither school followed a classical curriculum. The rustic pupils, sons of farmers and labourers, were taught to read and write English, and to keep accounts, as the Master, Upper Warden, and Clerk reported when they visited Great Crosby in May 1822, the journey having taken five days.²³ They made many recommendations which unfortunately were disregarded, but matters were more satisfactory at Ashwell. When Mr Peacock retired from the headmastership there, he was granted a pension of £31 10s. 0d., and in his place came a young man, John Thomas, who received a month's training and a certificate from the National School Board, and settled in happily. His salary was, at intervals, increased by £5, and he was allowed a similar sum to buy books for the pupils. The local vicar reported regularly on the young man's conscientiousness. The schoolroom was substantially enlarged in 1848 so that seventy-five pupils could be accommodated, and Mr Thomas remained in charge till his retirement in 1862, though twice in the previous decade he had had to answer to the Master and Wardens when parents complained of his beating their sons.²⁴

Thomas was succeeded by John Goffage, a young schoolmaster from nearby Guilden Morden. He, unfortunately, was elected Assistant Overseer of the Poor with responsibility for collecting the Poor Rate. Money went missing over the next ten years; he was forced to resign in 1874, and decided to emigrate to Australia. The Company sent him £150 just before he left, to pay off his debts.

When the Education Act of 1870 was passed, the Company had to decide whether to bear the expense of upgrading the school to take 150 pupils, or to hand it over to the local board. They inclined to the latter course but were dissuaded by the villagers. The classroom space was increased again and a bell-tower built at the Company's expense, though no bell was ever hung in it. When the Master and Wardens visited Ashwell on 26 May 1876, they were given an enthusiastic welcome, and the school continued satisfactorily with Albert Chote, a local man from Hitchin, as teacher. When the 1902 Education Act was passed, the management of the school was taken over gradually by the County Council.

In addition to educational and charitable concerns, the Company was still involved, at one remove, with Ireland. The Merchant Taylors' own 'proportion' of land had been rented in the previous century (see p. 232) but, since they had subscribed so whole-heartedly to the original scheme, they also held a share in the Clothworkers' land. That Company decided to take the administration of its property back into its own hands in 1840 and set about a vigorous course of improvements — land drainage, shoreland and riverside embankments, church and school building, road building, tree planting, and before long the laying out of railways — so much so that the Merchant Taylors became worried about the cost and considered selling out their share; but nothing came of it for the time being, and they remained as sleeping partners.²⁵ Eventually, in 1871, the Clothworkers sold their proportion and the Merchant Taylors received £31,142 2s. 8d. as their share. The money would be put to good use.

* * *

By 1848, the antiquary and printer John Gough Nichols had transcribed the manuscript of the diary of Henry Machyn, Merchant Taylor, covering the years 1550–63; it was published by the Camden Society. This diary, from which we have quoted in earlier chapters, was — and is — a most extraordinary survival. It was part of the library of Sir Robert Cotton, which became one of the core collections of the British Library; it escaped severe damage in a fire in 1731, and tells us an amazing amount about the London of the mid-sixteenth century. The Company, as far as we know, had no hand in the publication of the manuscript, though the transcriber had attended the school, but once the diary was in print and easily accessible, it must have fascinated the more historically-minded members.

That some members were so inclined was demonstrated most handsomely when a Past Master, Charles Mathew Clode, published his *Memorials of the Guild of Merchant Taylors* in 1875. Clode, a member of a family for long — and still — associated with the Company, was a distinguished lawyer living in Phillimore Gardens on Campden Hill; he was Solicitor to the War Office and author of several official publications (Col. Pl. XXIc).²⁶ Years, if not decades, of study must have gone into the compilation of the Merchant Taylors' volume, which sets out the texts of the Company's charters, ordinances, and oaths with copious extracts from the Court minutes and the accounts. Thirteen years later, Clode followed up the *Memorials* with two volumes on the early history and personalities of the Company, and when he died in 1893 the Court set up a handsome brass to his memory in St Helen Bishopsgate.[27]

The Company admired Clode, but not everyone was quite so appreciative. Benjamin Disraeli, honorary freeman, after dining at the Hall, wrote to the Earl of Zetland:

> I did not escape from the Hall of the Taylors till midnight, and exhausted, not by the words I uttered, but by sitting for hours at a banquet of which I couldn't partake, in a Hall of gas like the Hall of Eblis in Valhalla, listening to the inane observations of the Master Taylor, who felt it his duty as a host to inundate me with his platitudes.[28]

Clode's researches were a direct reaction to the series of bills begun in 1856 by the Home Secretary, Sir George Grey; these bills were intended to reform the City Corporation. Feeling against them ran high in the City; Alderman J. C. Lawrence described the first attempt as an 'April Fool's bill' — it had come in on 1 April — and declared that it showed

> the moderation of the border plunderer, who took away as much as he could in one foray, leaving the remainder for a future incursion.[29]

In the end, nothing direct came of the Government's efforts to reorganize the City and to integrate it with the rest of the vast area covered by the Metropolitan Board of Works, but the Corporation realized that something would have to be done by way of modernization. The qualification to vote in ward elections was made dependent on property rather than on freedom of the City; Smithfield meat market was rebuilt hygienically; Holborn Viaduct was constructed, and so was Blackfriars Bridge, while, at the victorious close of an eleven-year battle, Epping Forest was reclaimed as the City's own land, to be preserved as open countryside. The Corporation and sixteen livery companies combined to establish the City and Guilds of London Institute in 1877–78; the Company was not among the original supporters — the Clothworkers, Drapers and Mercers were particularly active — but later it helped financially. The Merchant Taylors, however, were busy with their own special attempt at educational improvement. In 1861, the Clarendon Commission had been set up to examine the nine chief public schools of England, and Merchant Taylors' had been considered alongside Eton, Winchester, Westminster, Charterhouse, St Paul's, Harrow, Rugby and Shrewsbury.[30] The Commissioners' findings had been favourable, though inevitably they had commented on the cramped conditions in the old school, and considered that it was understaffed for the number of pupils.

On 4 April 1866 a special General Court was summoned, and the Master, William Foster White, informed the members that he had called it

> in consequence of an intimation having been privately made to him that the Governors of the Charterhouse were willing to sell a portion of their Estate in Goswell Street to the extent of about 5½ acres under the impression that this Company would like to remove their School to that site.

The conditions in Suffolk Lane had finally become intolerable; Charterhouse School had resolved on a removal to Godalming, leaving their much larger, if somewhat medieval, premises vacant, and the Merchant Taylors acted briskly, if not without heart-searching. The asking price was £120,000; in the end, the site was purchased for £90,000, the money from the sale of the Irish lands going a good way towards the cost. The Revd James Hessey, who had taken on the headmastership aged thirty-one, at the retirement of Dr Bellamy in 1845, realized that, at fifty-six, he was too old to oversee such a fundamental reorganization; he wisely retired, and was succeeded in 1870 by the Revd William Baker, OMT and tutor at St John's, who was four days short of his twenty-ninth birthday and who was to guide the reborn school for the next thirty years.

The old Charterhouse buildings on the west side of the Great Cloister were pulled down, not without the destruction of much medieval fabric, and a new, more spacious school erected to the designs of the Company's architect, Edward I'Anson. The foundation stone was laid on 16 June 1873 by the Duke of Edinburgh, accompanied by the Archbishop of York, and the work was complete in less than two years. It was opened on 6 April 1875 by the Prince of

FIGURE 89. Merchant Taylors' School in the Charterhouse, designed by Edward I'Anson, and opened in 1875.
Merchant Taylors' School

Wales, the future Edward VII, himself a Merchant Taylor, accompanied by Princess Alexandra; the day was gloriously fine and the head monitor, Montague Shearman, recited a Latin poem, composed by the headmaster, declaring that, though the school was changing its abode, it was not changing its character. Staff and pupils looked back on Suffolk Lane with affection, but the improvements in space, light and air were too great to allow much room for regret.[31] John Gibson, a former day boy, remembers that the journey to school involved a tram ride to Farringdon and then a walk past Smithfield meat market 'along pavements wet with blood and the odd calves' heads', before the safety of Charterhouse Square could be reached.[32]

The new school buildings had cost a great deal of money, but there was now space for 350 boys, with the intention of increasing the intake slowly to 500 — double the number that could have been squeezed into the old premises — and provision was made to teach Modern Languages, science and drawing. Among the boys admitted in the early years of the re-established school were Gilbert Murray, the classical scholar,[33] Sir James Jeans the physicist and astronomer, and Lord Hailey the colonial administrator; all three received the Order of Merit.

* * *

The changes that came about at Great Crosby were as significant as those wrought by the move of the London school.

Although matters had been satisfactory when an inspection was made in 1822, Matthew Chester's successors were unfortunate appointments. The Revd Joseph Clark (1829–49) pocketed both his own and the usher's salaries, but admitted fewer and fewer pupils until at last there were none. A fresh start was made under the Revd John Burnard (1850–61), but his headmastership was still more unsatisfactory. He 'frequently adjourned the school in the afternoon to go rat-hunting', and used the cane excessively; his morals were dubious and his honesty was suspect.[34] He was dismissed, and a new director, the Revd Robert Carter, was appointed in 1861. Though he only stayed for two years, he succeeded in turning the school around, and was followed by another

FIGURE 90. Boys working in the laboratory, an early-twentieth-century photograph.
Merchant Taylors' School

clergyman, the Revd Samuel Crawford Armour, who stayed for forty years. An inspiring teacher and a first-class administrator, he transformed the school.

Under his aegis, the school began to grow. There were forty pupils when he took over, but seven years later there were at least seventy-five, all still crammed into the little seventeenth-century building. It was obvious that more space was needed. Land was found along the Liverpool Road and a ten-acre site acquired in 1874 for £3,500. Messrs Lockwood and Mawson of Bradford and London were the architects, Samuel Webster of Bootle the builder. It took another £20,574 18s. 5d. to build and equip the school and lay out the grounds, but it was money well spent. Masters and boys marched in procession from the old to the new school on 27 June 1878, and it was opened by the Countess of Derby; there were now ninety-six boys, and nine members of staff besides the headmaster. After an initial hesitation, the numbers continued to increase so that by 1893 they exceeded 200, new classrooms had to be added, and a steady stream of boys began to go up to Oxford and Cambridge.

In the meantime, the old dilapidated building had been refurbished for £1,425 and reopened as a school for girls on 30 June 1888 with forty-five girls — a most respectable size, with another twenty-five joining in the following January. The first headmistress was Isabel Bolton, second mistress at Liverpool Ladies' College, who had taken the Cambridge Local Examinations and had spent four months at Merton Hall, which would eventually become Newnham College. To open a school for girls was a far more radical move than rehousing the boys' school, and it might well not have happened at all had it not been for James Fenning, Master of the Company in 1882–83, who supported the idea strongly and urged it on to realization. The girls were taught English, history, geography, French, German, mathematics and Scripture, with Latin added later, and botany. Drawing, singing and music were part of the curriculum, as well as cookery and needlework. At first, the pupils felt the old building was a place to be endured, 'like a prison', the boys' 'cast-off', the building that 'men had condescended to leave to us', but as time went by, they came to love it and to treasure its venerable stones. The headmistresses who succeeded Miss Bolton — Miss M. H. Shackleton (1911–21), a relative of the explorer, and Miss Emily Fordham (1922–40) — were also pioneers in the education of women.[35]

* * *

Since the early years of the century, at first a select committee and then full-scale commissions, periodically revived, had been enquiring throughout the country into the state of education and of charities, many of them established during the Middle Ages and which were intended to provide instruction as well as to ameliorate the condition of the poor. Such an inquiry was undoubtedly needed; by 1834 the team of twenty commissioners had examined 26,751 charities and by 1840, when the final report was published in six volumes, they had looked into very nearly 30,000 endowments.[36] Trollope immortalized the condition and dilemmas of one such institution in *The Warden*, where the almshouse of St Cross in Winchester appears as Hiram's Hospital.

Among the eighty-five charities which the Merchant Taylors were administering, one received particular attention. In 1570, Robert Donkyn[37] had left property in Bell Alley, in the parish of St Botolph without Bishopsgate, to provide clothing each Christmas for twelve poor men, 'of honest fame and most in need', and twelve poor women, 'of honest conversation'. In the nineteenth century, the Company was still doggedly dispensing clothing and giving an extra 5s. to each individual in order to provide better shoes. But railway development first nibbled and then swallowed Bell Alley, although the money from the sale of the land was carefully invested. The Charity Commissioners recommended that property should be purchased in Bognor, since the air there was considered especially restorative, and that a convalescent home be opened for sick men and women where they might go to recuperate on being discharged from a London public hospital. Fitzleet House near Waterloo Square in Bognor opened on 5 July 1870, and ten years later a similar refuge for ladies in Hothamton Place.

All of this expenditure on education and good works was going to be of maximum support to the Company when, in 1880, a Royal Commission into the Livery Companies was set up. It began to hear evidence in 1882. This Commission was an outright attack on the companies, and the munitions for it were provided by the Reports of the Charity Commissioners. The assault was led by J. F. B. Firth, author of *Municipal London* (1876). The accusations were that charitable funds were no longer spent on their proper purposes, but on outrageously luxurious dinners at the various halls, that liverymen were paid generously for services which should have been given freely, and that company properties were let to members on advantageous terms. Firth's lieutenant, James Beal, contributed letters to the *Weekly Dispatch* and to the *Echo* under the pseudonyms of 'Nemesis' and 'Father Jean', calling the City Corporation a 'fathomless court of corruption', and castigating the companies as dens of 'gluttony and fraud'. The hearings promised to be lively.

Their findings were published in five substantial volumes in 1884. The livery companies were found to possess more wealth than the universities of Oxford and Cambridge put together. However, Lord Selborne, Lord Chancellor and a leading Mercer, declared that the companies owned their property in a manner as absolute and unqualified as a private individual, though they might spend it with greater discretion on charitable objectives. The reformers urged that all company property should be confiscated and thrown into a 'hotch-potch or into one mass': Parliament should use the money chiefly for educational purposes, with particular care for technical and elementary schools, while as for the company halls, exclaimed J. R. Phillips, one of the most vehement critics, 'I would sell the Halls, every one of them! I do not think they are wanted at all!'. The Merchant Taylors, with their particular interest in and care for schools, and their beloved and remarkable Hall, felt especially threatened.

They were defended stoutly by James Fenning, Master in 1882–83, who drew frequently on Clode's *Memorials* for evidence of the true nature of early bequests, and the way in which they had been interpreted to fulfil the trust as the centuries passed. The Company ended its evidence with a dignified statement:[38]

We should rather be disposed, from a lengthened experience of things as they are, to congratulate the State and the public upon the existence of an administration which, while eminently venerable, paternal, and practical, conducts its operations with more than ordinary regard to efficiency, utility and economy.

The Commission's inquiry closed without direct action being taken, but its effects were generally beneficial. Its pressure enabled — indeed, spurred on — the Company to redefine itself, thereby becoming, once more, an active force for good in the twentieth century.

NOTES

1. PP Cmd 239 (1837), XXV. The best and clearest accounts of the reform movement are I. G. Doolittle, *The City of London and its Livery Companies* (Dorchester, 1982), and John Davis, *Reforming London: The London Government Problem, 1855–1900* (Oxford, 1988).
2. GL, MS 34010/16, p. 390, 13 August 1816.
3. GL, MS 34010/18, p. 241, 19 December 1828.
4. GL, MS 34010/18, p. 196, 27 February 1828. The idea was soon dropped as too expensive. The new (western) entrance was not to be built until 1843.
5. GL, MS 34010/18, p. 227, 17 October 1828.
6. GL, MS 34010/18, p. 203, 22 April 1828.
7. GL, MS 34010/19, pp. 207–08, 20 December 1831.
8. GL, MS 34010/18, pp. 312, 314.
9. GL, MS 34010/18, p. 239, 19 December 1828.
10. Report of the Livery Companies Commission, 1884, vol. 2, p. 431. The Report states that the number of freemen was uncountable, but that there were 195 liverymen, of whom thirty-one served on the Court.
11. Much research is currently being done in these fields. For further reading, see Margaret Spufford, *The Great Reclothing of Rural England: Petty Chapmen and their Wares in the Seventeenth Century* (1984); Beverly Lemire, *Dress, Culture and Commerce: The English Clothing Trade before the Factory, 1660–1800* (Basingstoke, 1997); James Schmiechen, *Sweated Industries and Sweated Labor: The London Clothing Trades, 1860–1914* (1984); Richard Walker, *The Savile Row Story: An Illustrated History* (1988); and Katrina Honeyman, *Well Suited: A History of the Leeds Clothing Industry, 1850–1990* (Oxford, 2000); the journals *Textile History* and *Costume* will also be found informative. *The Tailor's Guide* appeared in 1810, G. Walker published *The Tailor's Masterpiece* in 1838, and J. Couts issued his splendidly illustrated *Practical Guide for the Tailor's Cutting Room* in 1843. There is a substantial archive on the subject in the library of the London College of Fashion: see Janine Odlevak's article in *Costume*, 34 (2000).
12. GL, MS 34010/18, pp. 179, 195; MS 34010/20, pp. 298–99, 302, 318.
13. GL, MS 34010/18, pp. 330–31, 349, 360.
14. Clode, *Memorials*, pp. 656–57; GL, MS 34109/1–7. There are seven boxes of material relevant to the case.
15. Hansard, vol. XV, 3rd Series, pp. 1030 and 1114.
16. The financial details were very complex: see GL, MS 34138, p. 75.
17. GL, MS 34010/18, pp. 37–39. It was later published.
18. See above, p. 29.
19. One of them, R. R. Sharpe, became the City Corporation's first archivist.

20. The first history of the school was by the Revd H. B. Wilson, published in 1812–14 in two volumes and running to 1,254 pages. By 1936, Mrs E. P. Hart had compiled *Merchant Taylors' School Register* in two volumes, and in 1962 F. W. M. Draper published *Four Centuries of Merchant Taylors' School, 1561–1961*. The most imaginative approach to the school's history is a collection of essays, *Merchant Taylors' School*, undertaken by the sixth-form members of the Archaeological Society and published in 1929; the opening chapter was written by Reginald Adams, who later became head monitor.
21. GL, MS 34010/17, pp. 319, 325, 338.
22. GL, MS 34010/18, p. 304.
23. GL, MS 34010/17, p. 264.
24. I am most grateful to Mr David Short of Ashwell for his generosity in giving me access to his researches into the history of the school, and to Mrs Eileen ten Hove for showing me round the buildings.
25. James Stevens Curl, *The Londonderry Plantation, 1609–1914* (Chichester, 1986), pp. 384–88.
26. For example, *The Administration of Justice under Military and Martial Law* (1872); *The Military Forces of the Crown: Their Administration and Government* (1869), 2 vols; *The Statutes relating to the War Office and to the Army* (1880).
27. GL, MS 34010/37, 15 December 1893; Clerk's general out-letter books, GL, MS 34087/12, pp. 272–73, 297–98, 372.
28. Quoted in 'A Family Mosaic', by Col. W. N. Nicholson, unpublished manuscript in the possession of Mr Walter Clode, giving a history of the related Clode and Nicholson families.
29. For further reference, see note 1 above.
30. The Commission took its name from its chairman, Lord Clarendon; the findings were published in two volumes in 1864. Its work, and the report on the Company's school, are considered more fully in F. W. M. Draper's *Four Centuries*, chapter XIV.
31. For a pupil's account of the move, see the anonymous contributor to *Merchant Taylors' School* (1929).
32. Personal communication.
33. In *An Unfinished Autobiography*, Murray gives a brief account of the school. He found the students far less courteous than those he had known in Australia where he was born. *Blood for the Ghosts: Classical Influences in the Nineteenth and Twentieth Centuries* (1982), by H. Lloyd-Jones, describes and evaluates Murray's scholarship.
34. H. M. Luft's excellent *History of Merchant Taylors' School, Crosby, 1620–1970* (1970), tells the whole unsavoury story.

35. The history of the school is well told in Sylvia Harrop's *The Merchant Taylors' School for Girls, Crosby: One Hundred Years of Achievement, 1888–1988* (Liverpool, 1988).

36. The best and clearest book on this tangled subject is D. E. Owen, *English Philanthropy, 1660–1960* (Cambridge, USA, and London, 1964). Victor Belcher's *The City Parochial Foundation, 1891–1991* (Aldershot, 1991) is also valuable.

37. See p. 138. There are twenty minute books (MSS 34243–44) besides much other archive material (MSS 34245–60) concerned with Donkyn's charity and the Homes in Bognor. See also Clode, *Memorials*, pp. 53, 289, 389–401. In 1864, the Company published a list of all those charities under its care.

38. Report of the Livery Companies Commission, vol. II, p. 457.

CHAPTER SEVENTEEN
THE TWENTIETH CENTURY

THE MERCHANT TAYLORS entered the twentieth century with a flourish by participating in three major artistic undertakings in the City of London: at the Royal Exchange, in St Paul's Cathedral and in a pre-Fire City church.

The second Exchange had vanished in a conflagration on the night of 10 February 1838; a third, larger building was designed by Sir William Tite. As soon as it was completed, he recommended its decoration with sculpture and with wall and ceiling painting.[1] First attempts proved unsatisfactory, but the desire for some sort of adornment remained. The antagonism of the newly formed London County Council during the 1890s towards the City, and its livery companies, revived the idea, and with first Lord Leighton and then Sir Lawrence Alma-Tadema — both of them successively Presidents of the Royal Academy — the Joint Grand Gresham Committee set about the scheme enthusiastically.[2] The intention was to emphasize all the good qualities and strengths of the City, and the brotherly harmony and mutual supportiveness of the livery companies. In 1895, the ageing Lord Leighton painted and donated the first panel, *Phoenicians Trading with the Early Britons on the Coast of Cornwall*. Nine years later, *The Reconciliation of the Skinners' and Merchant Taylors' Companies by Lord Mayor Billesden in 1484* was painted by Edwin A. Abbey RA and presented jointly by the two companies. This representation of the historic award was welcomed by *The City Press*, which declared the judgement was

... perhaps the most remarkable piece of arbitration the City of London has ever experienced, inasmuch as the award has been faithfully fulfilled for a period of over four centuries.[3]

The artist was also a stage designer for Sir Henry Irving, and the painting provides a dramatic scene, with Mayor Billesden seated high in judgement, the City arms and insignia displayed around him, and the Masters of the two companies about to share a loving cup. It is a glorious reconstruction of a true event in a golden, somewhat idealized, past (Col. Pl. VB).

Throughout the nineteenth century the clergy and staff of St Paul's had struggled to keep the vast, cavernous building warm and clean. The windows and fabric once repaired, under the zealous wardenship of Canon Hale, discussion began again about the adornment of the interior, and a scheme of mosaic decoration for the choir, the apse and the spandrels of the dome was conceived, chiefly by Sir William Blake Richmond.[4] The considerable cost of the work was largely borne by the City companies, notably the Merchant Taylors, the Mercers, the Goldsmiths and the Fishmongers. Their reward was the insertion of their coats of arms into the design of the westernmost saucer-dome above the choir, the Merchant Taylors being on the north. Each company also took a particular responsibility for one of the quarter-domes; the powerful Crucifixion fell to the Merchant Taylors.

The third undertaking was of a more domestic nature — the restoration of Stow's monument in St Andrew Undershaft. The Court minutes for 17 December 1903 record a request for assistance from the Vestry Clerk, and the matter was delegated to the good judgement of the Master, the Wardens and F. M. Fry, a Past Master, who was cataloguing the Company's paintings. Help was promptly given and the monument refurbished. The custom of renewing the quill in the effigy's hand at a special church service was already well established; Thomas Allen, in his *History and Antiquities of London*, published in 1828, mentions it in his text, and it still, in the twenty-first century, continues to delight London enthusiasts.[5]

The voluminous minutes record the steady but undramatic existence of the Company during the

Edwardian era. As always, the Merchant Taylors' dearest care was for the schools, and their own, now in the old buildings on the Charterhouse site, was going through a difficult stretch. The headmaster was John Arbuthnot Nairn; in 1901 he had succeeded William Baker, who had held the post for thirty years. Nairn had excelled in Classics at Cambridge, winning the Chancellor's Gold Medal;[6] he was twenty-six years old — young to be appointed to such a post — and he soon became anxious about the state of the school. The curriculum had been broadened under Baker, partly in response to the criticisms of the 1864 Royal Commission on Public Schools, but there was still a heavy emphasis on the teaching of Latin, Greek and Hebrew. Much of the school building was old and cramped, and far from bright and encouraging. The families of the boys likely to become pupils no longer lived in the City but in the suburbs, with a preference for north and north-west London, which meant a long journey to and from school, on top of a liberal amount of homework. Playing fields were rented at Willesden and then acquired at Bellingham in south London, but these necessitated even more travelling. The best scholars were still as good as ever, but standards had fallen among the mass of the pupils. Around Easter 1902, newspapers began to snipe critically at the school; Nairn reported on this and on the shrinkage in numbers to the Committee in November 1903. He urged the introduction of a preparatory department, but no action was taken.

Matters were going better in the more distant schools. Wolverhampton had dissociated itself from the Company in 1783, but it still remained in the old premises in John Street. Under the Revd Thomas Campbell (headmaster 1855–63), the curriculum was broadened, mathematics, Modern Languages, and drawing being added and better provision made for gymnastics and cricket, but when he suggested moving the school to a larger, healthier site, the governors refused and Dr Campbell resigned and set out, with his whole family and the usher, for New Zealand, to become headmaster of Dunedin School. They never reached their destination; there was an accident on landing, the Campbells drowned, and the usher became headmaster at Dunedin.

The new headmaster at Wolverhampton was Thomas Beach, who engaged the Revd Henry Williams as usher. Both men were inspiring teachers, and Beach was possessed of such drive and enthusiasm that he soon persuaded the governors to purchase six and a half acres of farm land off what is now Compton Road, where a new school was built; a shopping centre now covers the original site of Sir Stephen Jenyns' school. Beach resigned when the introduction of science teaching was promoted, but he was succeeded by Dr Williams who was more open to new ideas. Links with the Company were renewed on an informal basis, the school went on to become one of the best grammar schools in the country, and Sir Stephen would be satisfied and delighted with the atmosphere and achievements of his foundation today.[7]

The Company continued to dispense charity in its usual attentive, but still generous, manner. It gave to individual hard-luck cases — a widow with children to educate would probably receive help. It looked after the almshouses, doling out small pensions secured on the generosity of past great members of the Company. It maintained the convalescent homes at Bognor, gave open-handedly to St Bartholomew's Hospital, and £2,000 a year to the City and Guilds Institute. There was an annual scholarship to a choirboy at St Paul's Cathedral and — almost shyly — small links to the original craft began to be picked up again. Premiums were paid for girls taking up apprenticeships in dressmaking. On 15 July 1907, £5 5s. was set aside for tailoring prizes to be awarded by the Sir John Cass Foundation.[8] Mr Jennings Temple wrote in October 1909 to propose a scheme for the registration of tailors' cutters; he felt there should be an 'Incorporated Institute for British Tailors and Cutters', and that they should be considered to be professional men. Two and a half years later, in April 1912, Mr F. A. Stacey wrote with a 'draft Scheme for a National Guild of Merchant Tailors and Foremen Cutters'; the Court decided to do nothing till the plan was made more definite.[9]

In January 1911, under the Mastership of Henry Lennox Hopkinson, it was decided that sundry ancient deeds and documents should be photographed, transcribed and arranged in a convenient form for reference.[10]

FIGURE 91. The new Wolverhampton School, c. 1885.
Wolverhampton School Archives

The work was set in hand at once, with the two Misses Martin being entrusted with the labour of transcription; it proceeded to the highest standards, for they were the daughters of Charles Trice Martin of the Public Record Office and author of *The Record Interpreter*, a handbook still in use today. With their help, by 1915 Hopkinson had completed his *Report on the Ancient Records of the Guild of Merchant Taylors*, an indispensable volume and the first really scholarly attempt to set in order the wealth of documents cherished so lovingly by former guardians and students, from the Clerks, Nicholas Fuljambe, Richard Langley and John Milner, to Charles Mathew Clode, the Past Master and first historian of the Company.[11]

The school in Charterhouse now seemed to be more settled. Those boys on the science side were treated to visits to Price's candle factory, to Beckton gas works, the soap factory at Silvertown, the White Lead Company at Brimsdown and the British Oxygen Company — experiences that would have demonstrated the practical applications of what they were studying in the classrooms and laboratories of the school. On the modern language side, in October 1913, a group of German schoolboys came to London. They spent time at Merchant Taylors' School and, along with English schoolfellows, were entertained on 2 November to a banquet at Guildhall. Each boy was presented with a handsome pocket-knife, and toasts were drunk to the present and future friendship between the two countries.

On 28 June 1914, Archduke Franz Ferdinand, heir-apparent to the thrones of Austria and Hungary, was murdered in Sarajevo. On 2 August, Germany declared war on Russia, and by the next day on France. On 4 August, England entered the war, to protect Belgian neutrality. A meeting was held at the Hall and 200 former pupils enlisted. By the time of the Armistice in November 1918, 1,836 OMTs had served in the forces; 299 had been killed, 350 wounded. Three VCs had been won, with thirty-eight DSOs and 116 MCs; 198 individuals had been mentioned in dispatches.[12] The VCs were awarded to Midshipman George Leslie Drewry RN, to Lieutenant John Cridlan Barrett, Leicestershire Regiment, and to 2nd Lieutenant A. O. Pollard, Honourable Artillery Company.[13] On 25 April 1915, at the Dardanelles landing, Drewry, though already wounded, had swum between vessels and shore with mooring ropes; three years later, through the cruelty of chance, a block swinging from a derrick struck him on the head, fatally shattering his skull. Barrett, on 24 September 1918, had successfully attacked a machine-gun post almost single-handedly, while Pollard, 'with an utter contempt of danger', had led a counter-attack at Gavrelle near Arras in April 1917; both men survived, and Barrett was presented with a gold watch by the residents of Leamington, his home town. Deaths were reported in the school magazine, *The Taylorian*, with photographs, when available, of heart-breakingly young faces. Five masters were killed, and on 11 June 1917, Edward Raphael, pupil at the school from 1896 to 1901, probably the greatest all-round sportsman of his generation, excellent at both cricket and rugby, died of wounds received some days earlier at Messines Ridge. He was buried at Poperinghe in Belgium; his headmaster, Dr Nairn, unveiled a memorial to Raphael at St Jude-on-the-Hill, Hampstead Garden Suburb,[14] while a memorial window in All Saints church, Forest Gate, was dedicated to Drewry's memory by his brother officers.

Throughout the War, the Company gave to a variety of relief funds, while the school organized gifts of tobacco and chocolate for all serving OMTs; letters expressing delight and thanks appeared in *The Taylorian*. The London school was not the only one to suffer; 105 former pupils at Wolverhampton were killed, and 155 of those who had attended Great Crosby. Funds were set up for the education of those who had lost their fathers, and war memorials were erected, some in the schools, and one, the names of the fallen carved by relatives, in the pavilion at Teddington where a sports ground was purchased for OMTs.

After 1918, everyone tried to get back to the way of life which had once been normal, in a world that had changed for ever. The Company continued to dispense its usual charity: 500 guineas went to the School War Memorial Fund,[15] needy individuals were supported, and in any year, between 200 to 300 institutions received encouragement. But a new watchfulness was beginning to appear. A Report[16] of 6 March 1918 emphasized the need to keep the Corporate and Trust Funds clearly separate, and spoke of the threat of 'disestablishment'. The Ladies' Convalescent Home at Bognor was felt to be much under-used and was closed down; economies were made in the diet provided in the Men's Home. Nevertheless, money was found to renew the armorial stained glass in the Hall windows.[17]

Probably unconsciously, the unease that was felt in these difficult years led to a revived interest in the Company's own history. R. T. D. Sayle (Master 1938–39), who had taught history at the school, produced *A Brief History* of the Company, an account of the Company barges (1933), and a superb volume on *The Lord Mayors' Pageants* (1931) of such Lord Mayors as had also been Merchant Taylors. Only a very short run was printed, with limited distribution, but that book, consisting largely of high quality archival material, is a tribute to London's ceremonial prowess over the centuries. H. L. Hopkinson added to his account of the Company's records with a history of the Hall (1931). The Merchant Taylors were beginning to re-examine and redefine their role in a changing world.

The school continued in its congested quarters at Charterhouse Square. Morale was still high, the sporting record was good, with particular success in fencing, and Ronald Cove-Smith proved to be an exceptional athlete, going on to be capped for

CHANGING LONDON.

Merchant Taylors' School with the Charterhouse and Elizabethan cloister. The Great Hall on the right was built in 1873 on the removal of the School from Suffolk Lane to its present site. The School will remove to Moor Park, Rickmansworth, in about three years' time.

[*Specially drawn for the* SUNDAY TIMES *by Hanslip Fletcher.*]

FIGURE 92. Merchant Taylors' School in the Charterhouse. All that survives is the headmaster's house, just in sight on the extreme left of this drawing by Hanslip Fletcher, 1930.
Guildhall Library

England twenty-nine times for rugby. A collection of essays about the Company, the school and its surroundings was written by the senior boys[18] and judged to be of such excellence that it was published in 1929. Exchanges of boys were arranged with Lycée Condorcet in Paris. But the overcrowding remained, the buildings were old, dingy, inconvenient and poorly lit, the playing fields at Bellingham a full hour's journey away, and the number of pupils began gradually to fall away.[19]

In 1914, the Oxford and Cambridge Schools Examination Board had made a first inspection of the school and had found a good deal to criticize. There was no proper library, no music, and little attention to English literature; the boys were urged into specialization far too young; in the reading of the Classics, the emphasis was on grammar and composition rather than on literature, and it seemed strange that no use was made of Gilbert Murray's translations of Euripides, since Murray himself was an OMT. There was an exceptional emphasis on the teaching of Hebrew, but far too little time given to science. Mulcaster, that great and liberal teacher, would have been disappointed in the school he had helped to form.

The masters were unhappy too and, with justification, complained of low pay. Some attempt was made to meet their request, but matters were not improved when the headmaster wrote, first asking for more money to cover his two daughters' fees at Roedean, and then offering to vacate his official residence, since it was costing £520 a year in domestic staff, but desiring the right to leave his furniture *in situ* rather than pay the cost of storing it. Understandably, the Company was irritated.

It was obvious that something needed to be done about accommodation for the school, but everyone hesitated. The association with London and, above all, with the City was so very strong. Then in 1923 Charles Roche Finnis became Master. He was a man with exceptional clarity of vision, and soon produced a Report[20] setting out the alternatives — to stay at Charterhouse, to find another site in London, to move into the country, thereby becoming a boarding school, or to find a convenient site and to continue as a day school. Though fairly balanced, the Report made it clear that a move was the only proper choice. Another report from the Oxford and Cambridge Schools Examination Board reinforced the Master's opinion:

Very little attention appears to be paid to the aesthetic side of education . . . It [the school] has not yet adapted itself completely to the scope and purpose of modern education . . .[21]

The headmaster replied somewhat defensively, and for the moment nothing obvious happened, excepting that Mr Finnis, his year of office as Master completed, became Clerk to the Company.

In 1926, Dr Nairn resigned the headmastership. He had held the post for twenty-five years and had prepared some brilliant pupils, two future archbishops, Donald Coggan and Joost de Blank, among them; he — and the school — had weathered the wartime years, but he and the Company had never really been comfortable with each other.

The post was advertised in the usual manner, but it seems probable that a decision had already been made privately. In a Report on 18 October 1926, details were given of the three most promising applicants. Humfrey Grose-Hodge of Charterhouse, and Charles Russell, headmaster of Edward VI School at Southampton, provided several impressive testimonies apiece; the third, Spencer Leeson, sixth-form master at Winchester, provided only one from his headmaster, which said, rather coldly, that since Leeson had 'after all, decided to stand for the headmastership', he was sure 'he [Leeson] will do admirable work in the future'. Leeson was appointed to the post.

Born on 9 October 1892, the son of a distinguished doctor, he won a scholarship to Winchester and in 1911 went from there with another scholarship to New College, Oxford. He joined up in the first days of the War, saw service at Ypres, was invalided out, and was eventually appointed to the Naval Intelligence Division of the Admiralty. After the War, he joined the Board of Education and then, in 1924, was asked to return to his old school to teach. This he did for a bare two years. It is not surprising that his headmaster's letter of reference was terse.[22]

Leeson took up his duties on 23 January 1927. In spite of the fact that a new science block was opened on the Charterhouse site in that year, the new headmaster, undoubtedly supported by Mr Finnis, soon realized that the need for removal was imperative. Nevertheless, his first Report to the Court (30 September 1927) was directed to immediate improvements; they included a proper careers advice scheme, the introduction of a scout troop in addition to the OTC, increased emphasis on music and art, and better salaries for the staff, with a less breathlessly overcrowded teaching timetable for them — Jeffries, the history master, was in the classroom for twenty-six periods out of twenty-nine. Music and art were, he felt, of particular importance:

Our boys, living as they mostly do in uncultured homes, spending two or more hours a day in trams and tubes, and coming to a school situated in rather ugly surroundings . . . must suffer a degrading and coarsening effect on their minds.[23]

On 10 October 1928, Leeson — tireless man that he was — produced another Report, which effectively recommended the acquisition of a new site and the removal of the school.[24] In March 1929 the Master, Ernest Prescott, himself an OMT, recommended 'that the School be moved from its present position if a suitable site can be obtained'.

Such a site was found, at Sandy Lodge near Rickmansworth in Hertfordshire. Purchase of 250 acres was completed in November 1929, and a month later W. G. Newton, Professor of Architecture at the Royal College of Art, was appointed as architect, with Sir Giles Gilbert Scott as consultant.[25] Plans were drawn up, and the foundation stone was laid on St Barnabas' Day, 11 June 1931, by the Duke of York, who would become George VI, accompanied by his Duchess, the future Queen Mother.

All this did not happen without strong opposition, particularly from the OMT Football Club. Leeson called a meeting at the school in the lecture room of the science block; it was packed with critics, most of them positively hostile. Supported only by a large-scale map of London pinned to the blackboard, the headmaster explained the necessity of a move if the school were to survive; by the end of the evening, even the most antagonistic, even those most determined that the school should remain within the City of London, were persuaded and convinced, and supported the headmaster.

The choice of Newton as architect was both bold and inspired.[26] He had become profoundly affected by the dramatic developments in architecture taking place at the time in Scandinavia and Holland. The impact of the work of Gunnar Apslund and Sven Markelius had begun to extend across northern Europe, and the Stockholm exhibition of 1930 proved to be hugely influential. Ragnar Östberg's magnificent Stockholm Town Hall had been completed only in 1923, and proved to be particularly popular with romantically-minded architects in England. A preference for natural materials, and the modest domestic scale on which even many larger buildings were conceived, gave the Swedish brand of modern architecture a more human

FIGURE 93. The school on the new site at Sandy Lodge, Northwood, Middlesex.
Merchant Taylors' School

character, which appealed strongly to those who preferred the break with the past to be softened by reference to valued tradition. The dramatic expression of function, however, was regarded as absolutely appropriate, as was evidenced by Newton's friends and contemporaries, such as Charles Holden, who produced the universally praised station designs for London Transport, and Elizabeth Scott, Gilbert Scott's cousin, who designed the Royal Shakespeare Theatre at Stratford. Following his achievement at Sandy Lodge, Newton, in particular, gained significant influence as a designer of education buildings. More of his fine work can be seen at Marlborough and elsewhere.

The new Merchant Taylors' School generated exceptional interest. The buildings were arranged around two quadrangles, the smaller containing the 'academic' facilities and being formal in its layout, the larger being more informal and containing such facilities as the gymnasium, squash and fives courts, the workshop block, changing rooms and accommodation for the Scouts and the OTC. The smaller, main quadrangle is enclosed on the north and south sides by two-storey classroom blocks served by wide internal corridors. Newton's innovation was to group nearly all these teaching spaces to face south with huge windows, often the whole width of the classroom, whilst most of the science laboratories had a cooler northerly aspect. His concern was to ensure that the overall planning should be clear and coherent, that there should be an abundance of natural light, and wherever possible, cross-ventilation. He succeeded brilliantly, and those aspects of his design have always made an immediate and enduring impact on the building's users. John Gibson can still remember the scent of wallflowers drifting in from the flower bed outside as he sat in class, and what a contrast it was with the buildings in Charterhouse.

Newton invested the new school buildings with much subtlety of both form and detail. The 'academic' main quadrangle appears at first sight to be a simple rectangle. Closer inspection, however, shows that the slightly splayed classroom blocks exaggerate the perspective of this space along its north–south axis, a device used by architects for hundreds of years. In the splayed wings, it is not too fanciful to see the plan of the school as a keyhole, opening the door of learning. The symmetry thus created is reinforced by the central positioning of the arcaded clocktower at the west end, and the grand massing of the Great Hall at the east. At that end the Great Hall rises dominantly above a fully arcaded brick cloister linking the teaching blocks and supporting an exterior roof terrace, from which the space of the quadrangle can be fully appreciated. Behind the cloister and under the Hall is a large undercroft, designed originally to contain lavatories and cloakrooms. At either end of the undercroft and of the two teaching wings are entrance halls, accessed from the external paved quadrant with its central porch which was intended to form the main entrance to the school. It was opposite this porch that it was proposed that the school's chapel should be constructed; it remains unbuilt. In the north-east corner of this group of buildings stands the dining hall, linked to the main body of the school. It, too, is an impressive space, in which the entire school community can sit down to eat together.

In the 'academic' quadrangle, the symmetry of the design is completed on the cross axis by the formation of central blocks to both the teaching wings, that to the south containing an examination hall, the library and reading rooms, whilst that to the north contains the common rooms, museum and music rooms. For many boys the examination hall, inevitably a place of some apprehension, soon took on a more benign character in summer with its delightful south-facing terrace as the setting for the annual sixth-form ball.

The headmaster's house is also linked to the school in the south-east corner of the main group of buildings, but the boarding house for fifty boys whose parents were abroad, or whose homes were too inconveniently placed for them to be able to reach the school on a daily basis, was located in a separate block to the south-east. It was called the Manor of the Rose, after the property which had first housed the school at its foundation. The grounds provided great tracts of space for playing fields and pitches, as well as water meadows running down to the nearby lake and river. There was also plenty of space for field days; John Gibson can

FIGURE 94. The original building of John Harrison's school, still in good use as the library of Merchant Taylors' School for Girls, Crosby.
Merchant Taylors' School for Girls, Crosby, Archives

remember his delight when he came upon a lark's nest, well concealed.

The buildings were constructed to very high standards, using only the best quality materials, including brick, stone, and metalwork, all assembled by skilled craftsmen. Whilst, at first, the buildings appear quite austere, Newton incorporated subtle detailing and many witty, sometimes allegorical, features in the fabric. On the outer wall of the library block he introduced stone reliefs of seven seminal figures: Newton, St Paul, Goethe, Shakespeare, Dante, Socrates, and David, all the work of Alan Durst. There are other carvings, and also delightful wrought-iron grilles, often incorporating musical and sporting motifs. In the small court between the headmaster's house and the south end of the Great Hall, for instance, is a grille based upon the outline of the opposing forces of a rugby scrum!

The Great Removal was planned for April 1933. Well before that date, happily, the Company had been approached by St Bartholomew's Hospital, who wanted to redevelop the Charterhouse site as a medical college; it was probably no accident that the Dean of the Medical School was the surgeon Girling Ball, himself an OMT.

The logistics of the move were planned by the school secretary, E. P. Hart, whose wife was the author of the school *Register*.[27] It went smoothly. An Old Boys' committee had listed those treasures that might not be abandoned — the monitors' table and prompters' benches with their carved names, the old school bell, the statue of Sir Thomas White, the war memorials of the South African and First World War. A service of farewell to the City was held in St Paul's on 20 March 1933; 3,000 attended. Dr Guy Warman, OMT and Bishop of Manchester, preached the sermon, with texts from both the Old and the New Testaments: 'The place is too strait for us' (II Kings, vi. 1), and 'God giveth the increase' (I Corinthians, iii. 7). He emphasized that the school itself was something far more than any of its buildings, that what mattered was what the boys learned and took out into the world with them — character, willingness to serve, and comradeship.

The last day at Charterhouse was 25 March 1933; Sandy Lodge opened on 4 May, with a short service and addresses in the Great Hall by the

FIGURE 95.
Merchant Taylors'
Hall, bomb damage,
September 1940.
Merchant Taylors' Company

Master of the Company, the Hon. W. D. Gibbs, and the headmaster, after which the Bishop of St Albans, within whose diocese the new school lay, led a smaller group for the dedication of the temporary chapel, while everyone else explored the new buildings with excitement and then took tea in the dining hall. After that, the school settled down to adjust itself to its new surroundings, which it did with admirable speed.

Leeson gave further service by instigating a revision of the Company's scholarships tenable at St John's. They were now opened up to a broader range of subjects — mathematics, history, and Modern Languages, as well as Latin, Greek and science; Hebrew slipped out of the curriculum in 1937, Merchant Taylors being the last secular school in England to teach it as a regular subject. Late in 1934, however, Leeson was offered the headmastership of Winchester College, his own old school, and felt unable to refuse; after eleven years there, six of them in wartime, he was ordained and eventually became Bishop of Peterborough, dying on 27 January 1956. He had quietly achieved extraordinary changes at Merchant Taylors' School.

He was succeeded by Norman Birley from King's School, Canterbury. He had seen hard work and distinguished service in the First World War, winning both the MC and the DSO. He was a first-class administrator with a great understanding of and sympathy for his pupils. He consolidated the benefits of the move to Sandy Lodge, and brought the school successfully through the 1939–45 war, making arrangements for it to function effectively as a boarding school for those boys who needed accommodation. Teaching went on much as usual and university places continued to be won.

The Company's other schools also struggled to maintain normal teaching conditions, though the girls' school at Crosby suffered grievously when, in an early air raid on 29 August 1940, a bomb killed the former head girl, Cynthia Smith, just as she was about to take up a scholarship to Somerville College, Oxford. Her mother and brother died with her; her father gave a prize to the school in his daughter's memory.

FIGURE 96.
Merchant Taylors' Hall, bomb damage, September 1940. The King's Chamber (now the Drawing Room), looking north. Its floor, of steel and concrete, was not destroyed.
Merchant Taylors' Company

Otherwise, the schools survived the war in better trim than the Company's Hall. Hostilities started on 3 September 1939; it was obvious from the beginning that air attack on major cities was probable. The Blitz started on the night of 24–25 August 1940 and, in earnest, on 7 September; the Hall was an early casualty.[28] About 1 a.m. on the night of 17 September, at least eight incendiary bombs struck the building. The Beadle and his wife had left for Windsor a few days before; the early days of the bombing were particularly frightening, though later Londoners became hardened to it. The only people on duty were two young porters, aged seventeen and eighteen; following instructions, they had taken shelter in the nearby Bank of New South Wales, so there was nobody to stifle the bombs as they fell. The panelling and timbers of the Great Hall and Hooke's screen were ideal fuel for the flames. By the time the porters had been alerted — they came, fearlessly, at once — and the fire services arrived, there was nothing anyone could do. The Hall, Grand Staircase, King's Chamber, Parlour, the West and East Entrances, and the Beadle's and Assistant Beadle's offices were destroyed, though the Court Room, Library, offices, the Beadle's flat, and the bedrooms above were saved. Hoses were trained on the rest of the building, as best as low water pressure permitted, but this had its dangers, too, for the water ran down to the cellars and threatened the precious Muniment Room. The vestibule carpet was rolled up and deployed, with sandbags, to form a dam; the water came within an inch of the Muniment Room door but mercifully did not penetrate it — and the records remained unharmed. Duncan Liddle, the Office Clerk, who was serving as an ARP Warden at Beckenham, was alerted by his wife by telephone, but travelling conditions were such that it took him until 7 a.m. to reach the Hall. He was joined there by the Master, Robert Turner, and together they did what they could to get the Company's treasures to safety. Seven portraits had been utterly destroyed, three of them by Kneller;[29] the Poor Box, which had served the Company since its installation was ordered on 18 August 1647, was

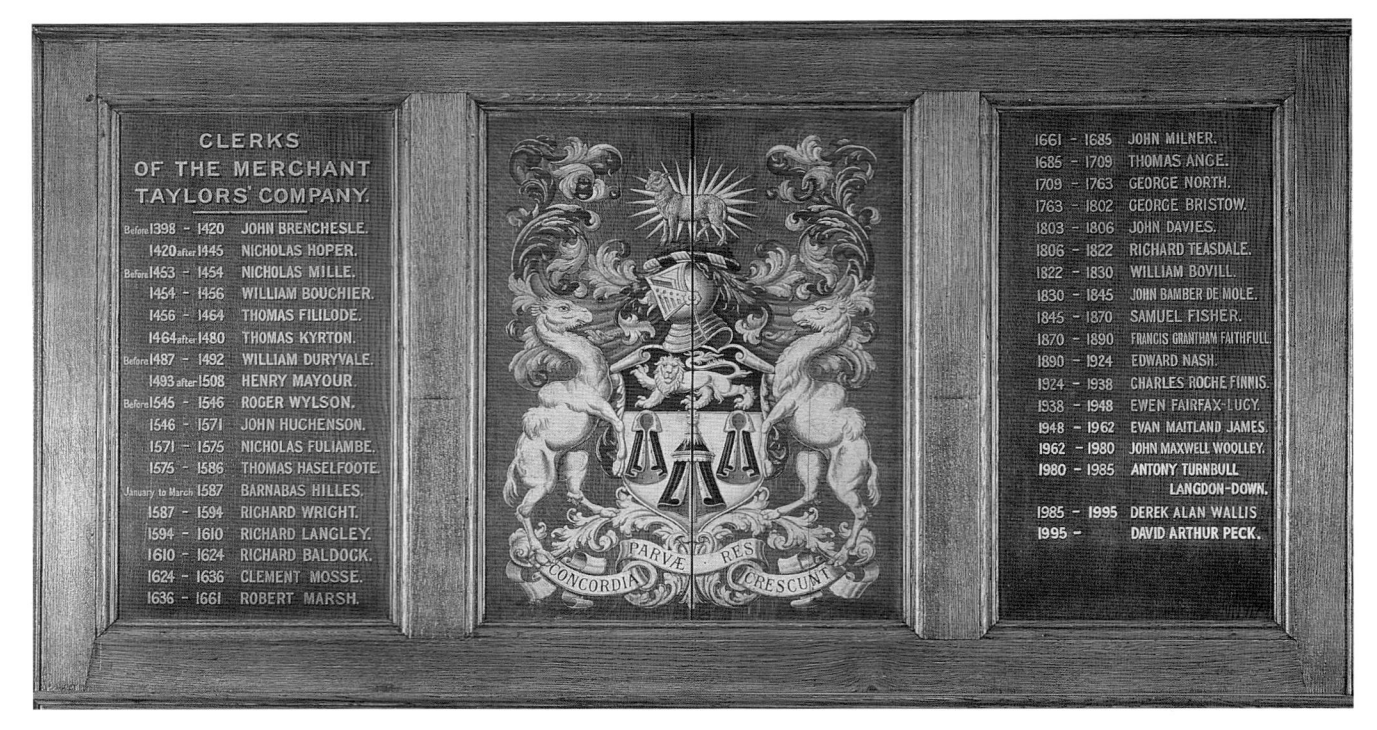

FIGURE 97. The Clerks of the Merchant Taylors' Company. The overmantel of the Clerk's room lists the names of those who have held office before him. New research since has improved the list.
Merchant Taylors' Company

burnt, nine marble busts had gone, and ten inches above the hem of one of the hearse-cloths were soaked, but most of the portraits were in safety in the Muniment Room or, if elsewhere, were capable of restoration.

Successful efforts were made to find temporary accommodation in the Banca Commerciale Italiana, at 32 Threadneedle Street, and to make the less damaged portions of the building usable. In June 1941, some muniments were transferred to the Public Record Office in Chancery Lane, where they remained till January 1946; another section went to the strongroom in Brighton of the solicitors, T. M. Eggar. Two nightwatchmen were appointed, as their forerunners had been after the Great Fire of 1666; one of them had had a leg amputated but in spite of that, when four more incendiaries struck on the night of 10/11 May 1941, the pair succeeded in extinguishing them.

Whilst the war continued, and before the destructiveness of the V1 and V2 weapons had made itself known, representatives of the City's livery companies had set up a Joint Committee for War Damage. They felt that the company halls were all special cases, and guessed — perhaps fairly — that the War Damage Commission might not view matters in quite the same way as they did. Dr Watney of the Mercers' Company took the chair, E. A. R. R. Fairfax-Lucy, Clerk to the Merchant Taylors, acted as Secretary, and W. A. D. Englefield of the Painter-Stainers was particularly helpful. As matters worked out eventually, the War Damage Commission acted most responsibly towards the halls, but it was just as well to have such a committee.

The war in Europe ended on 7 May 1945, and with Japan on 14 August. Now it was time to begin the rebuilding of London and the restoration of the Hall.

A special Reconstruction Committee was set up, and in November 1948 it was decided that the Great Parlour should be restored first, with Sir Hubert Worthington FRIBA as architect. His offices were in Manchester, but it was generally felt that

FIGURE 98. St John the Baptist. A bronze statue by Barbédienne after Benedetto da Majano, presented by C. M. Clode, Master 1873–74, the first historian of the Company.
Merchant Taylors' Company

he was the proper person for the responsibility. It must be remembered that, for more than a decade after the war, shortages of materials and of skilled labour were such that the actual rebuilding often seemed the simplest part of the undertaking. Any change of plan required a fresh set of permissions. However, any architect in charge needed to be close at hand and constantly watchful, or at least he needed a clerk of works to exercise constant supervision. Manchester is a long way from London.

The Great Parlour was restored, handsomely, and began to be used for entertainment of limited numbers. The Governing Bodies of Public Schools gave a dinner there in 1954, and in 1957 the Eton Old Collegers gave another, with the Prime Minister, Harold Macmillan, as guest of honour. But work on the rest of the property was making no perceptible progress, and H. D. C. Whinney, architect to three of the Hall's neighbours, was finding it increasingly difficult to work with Worthington or with his deputy, T. W. Sutcliffe. In January 1954, the Master wrote to Sir Hubert enquiring whether he really had enough time to supervise such an undertaking; the Court found it hard to believe his assurance:

It was generally argued that in the light of past experience this statement was not reassuring, and that no useful purpose would be served by calling for a written assurance as to the amount of time which Sir Hubert Worthington would himself be able to devote to the work ... It was doubted whether he had an adequate knowledge of the special problems affecting building in the City.

A year later, no perceptible advance had been made. On 20 January 1955, one Court member (not named) suggested abandoning any proper restoration, but patching up the Hall to re-open as a luncheon club. The rest of the Court, however, declared this to be

too pusillanimous and unfair to posterity ... As the centre and a symbol of their corporate life, the Hall was essential to the nature of the Company. A City Company without a Hall is like a snail without a shell.

A vote was taken, that the Hall must somehow be rebuilt, and that a replacement would have to be found for Worthington.

The Reconstruction Committee, at a meeting on 16 December 1954, had already authorized one of its members, Austin Blomfield, to make an informal approach to Professor Sir Albert Richardson, President of the Royal Academy. The Professor was already seventy-four years of age and very busy, but he responded at once, with his usual charismatic enthusiasm; matters were arranged equably if a little regretfully with Sir Hubert, and the Court voted for Richardson as their architect.

They had the right man. This was a task to Richardson's heart, and the work began to move forward at once, with the reconstruction of the Hall and the East and West Galleries, of the Grand Staircase and of the Drawing Room all entrusted to the Professor, to his partner and son-in-law E. A. S. Houfe, and their assistant, S. Holland. It was agreed to dispense with any formal contract, but that Richardson should be paid 12 per cent of the total cost, to be advanced by quarterly payments of £1,250. Preliminary sketches were ready by April 1955. It was decided that the formal entrance to the Hall should be from the western doorway, that the Grand Staircase should be turned to make more graceful use of the space, and that a ladies' cloakroom should be constructed at basement level. The Hall was to be in the proportions of a double cube, with square-headed windows three feet higher than before. Preliminary drawings were shown in the Royal Academy Summer Exhibition. Messrs Dove Bros were selected for the construction work, with an estimate of £197,111, against which the War Damage Commission allowed £147,500; the task began in earnest at last.

In May 1957, the Reconstruction Committee were informed that Sotheby's were offering forty-six rolls of hand-painted, Chinese wallpaper for sale; the estimated price was £5,250. The discovery had been made by W. M. L. ('Mac') Escombe, the Master-elect and one of the members; the Committee agreed to bid to the limit, and so were pleased to secure the prize for £2,500. The precious rolls make the Drawing Room a place of delight. Other adornments have continued to be purchased, such as marble busts of the Younger Pitt by Nollekens and the Duke of Wellington by Physick.

Francis Spear provided stained glass for the Hall, with the armorial bearings of past benefactors and patrons. Bronze chandeliers were designed by Sir Albert; the detailed drawings for them were the work of Mr Holland. Sound equipment, heating and ventilation were installed. The Hall, in its glory, was declared open once more with a Livery Dinner on 19 March 1959. Though the equipment on which the food was cooked was modern, the banquet was prepared in kitchen premises which had been installed five centuries before and in constant use ever since.

In January 1960 the Court offered membership of the Company to Queen Elizabeth, the Queen Mother, and she graciously accepted, the first Queen of England to be a Merchant Taylor since Anne of Bohemia, Richard II's Queen. A luncheon was held to welcome her, and Her Majesty was presented with four shell-shaped silver salt cellars designed by Leslie Durbin. She seemed delighted.

In less than three hundred years, Merchant Taylors' Hall had twice been burnt and destroyed. Although it had taken eighteen years to restore the Hall, by the beginning of 1960 the Company was able to come home and to meet together as a fraternity. Once again they could apply their energies to supporting the causes of the education of young people and the care of the elderly and infirm, as their forebears had done so notably for more than the previous six hundred years.

NOTES

1 Report from Sir William Tite to special sub-committee, Mercers' Archives, Gresham Committee minutes, 26 April 1844.

2 For a more detailed account, see Clare Willsdon, 'The Mural Decoration at the Royal Exchange', in A. Saunders (ed.), *The Royal Exchange* (1997), pp. 311–35. See also Dr Willsdon's *Mural Painting in Britain, 1840–1940* (Oxford, 2000).

3 Scrapbook, Mercers' Archives, 21 December 1904.

4 See Simon Reynolds, *A Companion to the Mosaics of St Paul's Cathedral* (Norwich, 1994), also Derek Keene et al. (eds), *The History of St Paul's Cathedral* (forthcoming, 2004), especially the chapter by Theresa Sladen.

5 GL, MS 34010/39, p. 291. See also Arnold Taylor, 'John Stow and His Monument', in *Transactions of the London and Middlesex Archaeological Society*, 25 (1974), pp. 316–21. I owe this reference to Michael Melia of Guildhall Library. Allen's *History* was in five volumes, published 1827–37; the reference to Stow's quill is in vol. III (1828), p. 68.

6 He went on to write *Latin Prose Composition* (Cambridge, 1925), *Greek Prose Composition* (Cambridge, 1927), and *Greek through Reading* (1952); Stephen Freeth, our amiable mentor, grew up with these.

7 The main history of Wolverhampton School is that by Gerald Poynton Mander, published in 1913. An excellent brief history and photographic record was compiled by Deirdre Linton in 2000.

8 GL, MS 34010/39, pp. 281, 421; MS 34010/40, p. 253.

9 GL, MS 34010/41, pp. 51, 367.

10 GL, MS 34010/41, pp. 183, 477.

11 For the later history of the archive, see p. 265.

12 Figures are taken from the Supplement to *The Taylorian*, June 1920. See also Roll of Honour, GL, MS 34100/158.

13 Pollard's VC is now part of the HAC's display of medals at Armoury House.

14 I am grateful to Raymond Lowe, churchwarden at St Jude-on-the-Hill, for telling me of the memorial.

15 GL, MS 34010/42, p. 548.

16 GL, MS 34014A/16, fols 105–08.

17 F. M. Fry and W. L. Thomas, *The Windows of Merchant Taylors' Hall* (1934).

18 Some of whom are still, happily, flourishing, and have contributed to this history.

19 For the modern period, the main history of the school is F. W. M. Draper's *Four Centuries* (1962). Much of what follows has been compiled from *The Taylorian* and from the Reports to the Court, GL, MS 34014A/14–23.

20 GL, MS 34014A/18, fols 36–40, dated 23 May 1924.

21 Ibid., fols 41–70, esp. fols 45^v, 46^v.

22 GL, MS 34014A/19, fol. 75^v. See also *Spencer Leeson. Shepherd, Teacher, Friend. A Memoir by Some of his Friends* (1958).

23 GL, MS 34014A/20, fols 11, 17.

24 GL, MS 34014A/20, fols 148–56^v. There had been other reports in between.

25 The builders were Messrs Holland and Hannen & Cubitts, of which G. R. Holland, OMT and Treasurer of the Old Boys' Football Club, was senior director.

26 The following paragraphs have been supplied by John Penton, MBE, OMT, Master of the Company 2003–04. The authors are most grateful to him.

27 Mrs E. P. Hart, *Merchant Taylors' School Register, 1561–1934*, 2 vols (1936).

28 See the detailed report to the Court in October 1940, MS 34014A/25, fols 148–59^v. In 1951, a report on the damage to the Hall was compiled by D. M. P. Liddle, Office Clerk to the Company; it is kept in the Hall.

29 Portraits of Sir Patience Ward, Sir William Pritchard, and Sir William Turner. The others were Sir John Salter (Richardson), Sir Reginald Hanson (Collier), Sir Richard Baggallay (Sant), and Sir Claudius Hunter (Beechey).

EPILOGUE

Even before the end of the War, Norman Birley was looking to the future of the school. Following the 1944 Fleming Report on Education, he set afoot the arrangements whereby each year fifteen boys attending primary schools in Middlesex and Hertfordshire were offered assisted places at Merchant Taylors' where a new form, the Third, was created to receive them. Lord Clauson, Master in 1920, told the Court:

Our predecessors made an educational ladder on which boys could climb to the university, whatever their circumstances. The ladder is still here, but a rung is missing and we must put it back.

The school profited greatly from the new intake, though the headmaster retired before it took effect. Although only fifty-five, he stood down in 1946, feeling that post-war reconstruction would need a younger man. He was succeeded by Hugh Elder who, by happy chance, was headmaster of a school founded in memory of an Old Merchant Taylor — Dean Close School at Cheltenham.[1]

There was a new openness at the Hall too. In 1962, the Company was offered a Renatus Harris organ, made in 1724 for the church of St Dionis Backchurch.[2] The instrument had suffered several removals and rebuildings, and the balcony had to be strengthened to support it, but it was still a noble acquisition. It was installed at the east end of the Hall by Noel Mander. The original case had been destroyed by enemy action, but Stephen Dykes Bower designed a new and handsome home for it. It was formally opened on 30 June 1966 with a recital by Dr (later Sir) John Dykes Bower, and a series of free public recitals was given on the delightful instrument. The Hall was enhanced further when it was realized that, in the north-west wall, a substantial portion of medieval masonry still survived. The stonework was restored and opened up into a glass-fronted alcove for the display of the Company's plate. More recently, murals by Paul Raymond and Mrs Janet Shearer have been painted to adorn the Grand and the office staircases; they represent a pageant of boats on the Thames, and a young boy looking at shipping from a high window; this one, on the Clerk's staircase, donated by Dennis Marler, has Mrs Shearer's robin redbreast as her signature in the bottom right-hand corner (Col. Pl. XXIIIA).

The Company cherishes and honours its own history and its tradition of hospitality. In 1984, Merchant Taylors and Skinners joined in a feast held at Guildhall to celebrate the 500th anniversary of the Billesden award, marking the importance of the occasion in the history of both Companies, and as a symbol of the stability of the City's government. In 1996, the Company's magnificent and voluminous archive up to 1945 was transferred to the safe keeping of Guildhall Library, where it has been lovingly catalogued by the Keeper of Manuscripts, Stephen Freeth, himself a Merchant Taylor, and where it keeps company with other records, contemporary with itself.

The Company has played its part fully in civic affairs. Since 1950, two more Merchant Taylors have served as Lord Mayor — Sir Peter Studd and Sir Brian Jenkins — and three as Sheriffs — Sir John Perring, David Brewer, and Martin Clarke, the latter two in the same year, 2002–03, which, if not unique, is very unusual.

A regular event pays proper respect to one of the most important Merchant Taylors of all — John Stow, a working tailor who loved London, and whose *Survey* was written to celebrate his birthplace. Every third year, a service is held at St Andrew Undershaft, when the Master of the Company puts a new quill pen in the stone hand of Stow's effigy, and an appropriate scholar gives a short address. Some might consider such a ceremony to be no more than a quaint affectation, but a gathering around Stow's tomb, a focus in the heart of London, is a proper celebration of amazing generations of men whose feats and achievements have been recorded in these pages — Sir Thomas White and Richard Hilles, Sir Stephen Jenyns and John Harrison, Robert Dowe, Mathias Springham, Sir William Harper, Sir William Craven and many, many others.

Their schools and charities still thrive, nourished by the support of the Company. The histories of those schools are kept alive now as subjects for senior level public examinations, essays proffered by students from Foyle & Londonderry College, Mathias Springham's old foundation, being particularly enthusiastic.[3] At Great Crosby, the original stone building, erected with John Harrison's money, still survives, in active use as the Girls' School library and computer centre, while at the Boys' School, Robert Runcie, Archbishop of Canterbury from 1980 to 1991, was one of the pupils throughout his school career; he later became an honorary freeman of the Company, like his predecessor, Donald Coggan, OMT. At Sandy Lodge, on a winter's day, the black and white of the boys' scarves remind us that these were Queen Elizabeth's own colours — black for constancy, white for purity.

The purchase in 1984 of St John's School at Northwood at last linked a preparatory school with Sandy Lodge — Dr Nairn had recommended this in 1903. St John's had been founded independently in 1920 at Pinner by Claude Wilson Norman, and had long sent boys on to Merchant Taylors' School. Sir Arthur Hockaday, a former pupil, tells us that the headmaster

was popularly known as Rhino, from his ferocious charges in the direction of any budding disorder.

He adds, however,

But I remember it as a happy place, fortunate in a staff who helped to make it so.[4]

The linking with Merchant Taylors' School has proved a successful collaboration. In 1996, the governance of both schools was changed. The whole Court of the Company, which had formed the governing body since 1561, was replaced by Merchant Taylors' Educational Trust, a smaller panel drawn from members of the Court. Both schools now benefit from more flexible meetings, and closer oversight.

In 1973, a fresh attempt was made to reconnect the Company with its own trade.[5] Robert Bright, then Vice-President of the Federation of Merchant Tailors, asked the Company to donate a handsome trophy, a sort of Victor Ludorum for the best tailor of the year. The Court agreed and invited Robert to design it. The Golden Shears competition was introduced in 1974 for excellence in tailoring, fit, and style. The models were usually the tailors themselves!

In the 1980s, in conjunction with CAPITB (Clothing and Allied Products Industry Training Board), the Golden Shears were awarded to the company with the best training record. The results were based on City & Guilds examinations.

Since three members of the trade were admitted to the livery in 1990, there has been great enthusiasm for the revised Golden Shears tailoring competition, which involves trade apprentices, students from the London College of Fashion, and other colleges with similar courses. The Company is the major sponsor and the final judging takes place at a glittering gala catwalk show in the Great Hall for the Golden, Silver, and now Bronze Shears. A trade and educational initiative to mark the millennium is the Company's continuing support for 'Practitioners in Residence' at the London College of Fashion and Central St Martins College of Art & Design.

In 1981, a catering company was set up, Merchant Taylors' Catering Ltd, so that fullest use might be made of the Hall. It has now functioned most satisfactorily for over twenty years, providing refreshments at all Company functions and for a multiplicity of others, the most important perhaps being the annual Feast for the Sons of the Clergy, first held in the Hall in 1676. A particularly glamorous occasion was the celebration, in 1999, for the award-winning film *Shakespeare in Love*. Up to 40,000 people now visit and use the Hall each year.

Just as the Merchant Taylors were the first livery company to provide an almshouse, beside the Hall, to shelter the aged, so today they give support to those who are frail. The thirty-two nineteenth-century almshouses look out across their lawn at Lee; nearby, nineteen small houses and ten bungalows, all warden-supported, bear Christopher Boone's name; a purpose-built block of sheltered housing has been called after Archbishop Coggan. At Blackheath, Dowe House, administered by a local charity, the Ranyard Memorial Charitable Trust, cares for those who require nursing, and Mulberry House has been developed for the needs of those who have become mentally infirm. The Company is believed to be the largest single private provider of sheltered housing in the London Borough of Lewisham. Treloar School and Treloar College at Alton in Hampshire provide education, therapy, care, and independent training for young people with disabilities. The Company is a significant supporter of both, and has since 1984, with the Skinners, supported a Billesden Officer whose function is to advise and help those leaving the College on how to cope better in the outside world.

Links with the Armed Services are strong. The oldest affiliation, with the Royal Fusiliers (City of London Regiment) (7th Foot), now the London Regiment, began in 1888. More recently, affiliations have been set up with the Royal Yeomanry, with HMS *Chatham*, a Type 42 frigate, and very recently with the Army Air Corps, and with HMS *Heron* (RNAS Yeovilton), the home of Naval flying.

Most fittingly, the Company celebrated the millennium with a service in St Paul's Cathedral on 21 September. Richard Chartres, Bishop of London, himself a Merchant Taylor and liveryman, was the preacher. The other impressive festivity was a concert given on 19 March 2000 at the Barbican Centre, with orchestras and choirs drawn from the pupils of six Merchant Taylors' schools — the school at Sandy Lodge was joined by Wolverhampton, the two schools at Crosby, Foyle & Londonderry College, and Wallingford. The concert opened with a fanfare commissioned from Simon Lasky OMT, continued with madrigals, and works by Purcell, Vaughan Williams, and Rachmaninov, and ended with Haydn's 'Nelson' Mass. It was a most unusual and moving occasion.

Entering the twenty-first century, the Company remains progressive and forward-looking. As recently as 2001, a Livery Committee was set up to increase the involvement of both liverymen and freemen in the affairs of the Company; since 1993, women have been eligible to join the livery. Honorary freemen are still appointed.

The 500th anniversary of the 1503 Charter, when the Company became known as *Merchant* Taylors, was celebrated with a lecture by the distinguished historian, Professor Jeremy Black of Exeter University, together with a commemorative booklet by Matthew Davies on the Charter; by an exhibition, held at the London Institute Gallery in Mayfair, of artwork drawn from the Company's schools; and by an educational seminar.

That extraordinary survival, the Hall itself, remains, cherished by the Company, providing good service after more than six centuries. The Merchant Taylors continue to develop their links with the trade, and to maintain strong ties with the City and the country.

CONCORDIA PARVAE RES CRESCUNT

NOTES

1. Francis Close was rector of Cheltenham from 1826 to 1857 when he became Dean of Carlisle. The school opened in 1885.
2. Demolished 1879. See Nicholas Plumley, *The Organs of the City of London* (Oxford, 1996), pp. 147–49.
3. Information and copies of essays gratefully received from Dr Maureen Alden, Department of Classics, The Queen's University, Belfast.
4. Nigel Pauli (ed.), *I Remember . . . Reminiscences of St John's School* (1995), typescript.
5. Information kindly supplied by Michael Skinner, Merchant Taylor.

APPENDIX ONE

MASTERS OF THE TAILORS AND LINEN-ARMOURERS OF THE CITY OF LONDON AND, FROM 1503, OF THE MERCHANT TAYLORS' COMPANY, 1300–2003

From 1398 onwards, the names of almost all the Masters of the Company are recorded in one or more of the main series of Company records. Earlier names occur in deeds, wills and other documents relating to members of the Fraternity of St John the Baptist in the fourteenth century. The first three Masters, de Ryall, Pecche and Tilneye, are referred to in some sources as 'Pilgrims', reflecting the important religious and charitable activities of the fraternity in the Middle Ages.

Note: spellings of surnames did not become standardized until around the mid-eighteenth century. Consequently, for the earlier Masters, the list below represents the most common forms found in the archives of the Company, particularly the accounts and Court minutes, and in other sources relating to these individuals, such as personal papers and the records of the City government.

1300 Henry de Ryall	1415 William Jowdrell	1446 Thomas Reymond
1351 John Pecche	1416 John Weston	1447 Richard Benton
1376 John Tilneye	1417 William Holgrave	1448 William Foster
1384 William Rule	1418 Ralph Bate	1449 John Stone
1388 John Dymock	1419 Ralph Holland	1450 Thomas Breux
1389	1420 Robert Fenescales	1451 John Gylle
1390	1421 Ralph Shocklache	1452 William Latoner
1391 Thomas Sibsay	1422 Richard Nordon	1453 William Knotte
1392 John Orewelle	1423 John de Bury	1454 John Belham
1393 John Partrich	1424 Alexander Farnell	1455 George Ashton
1394	1425 Richard Reynold	1456 John Prynce
1395	1426 John Caston	1457 John Jordan
1396	1427 John Knotte	1458 William Boylet
1397	1428 William Chapman	1459 William Langdon
1398 John Buk	1429 Philip Possell	1460 Robert Colwich
1399 Clement Kyrton	1430 John Thorne	1461 John Derby
1400 John Fauconer	1431 Geoffrey Gibbon	1462 William Person
1401 John Ballard	1432 Roger Holbech	1463 Roger Tego
1402 Robert Eland	1433 John Kyng	1464 John Fayreford
1403 Richard Lynne	1434 John Legge	1465 John Stodard
1404 Simon Lief	1435 John Pecke	1466 John Phelip
1405 Robert Queldrik	1436 Thomas Davy	1467 Thomas Burgeys
1406 John Colbroke	1437 John Arcall	1468 Walter Baron
1407 Peter Mason	1438 John Bale	1469 William Parker
1408 Thomas Sutton	1439 John Locok	1470 John Swan
1409 John Fulthorp	1440 Piers Saverey	1471 William Galle
1410 John Marchall	1441 Richard Skernyng	1472 Roger Warynge
1411 William Tropenell	1442 William Fyge	1473 Gilbert Keyes
1412 William Warren	1443 William Auntrus	1474 Richard Bristall
1413 John Cavendish	1444 John Langwith	1475 Richard Nayler
1414 Thomas Whityngham	1445 Thomas Gay	1476 Richard Warner/John Phelip

1477 Robert Middelton
1478 Richard West
1479 Roger Barlowe
1480 John Materdale
1481 Robert Duplage
1482 Hugh Pemberton
1483 John Lee
1484
1485 John Percyvale
1486 Thomas Cotton
1487 John Heed
1488 William Buk
1489 Stephen Jenyns
1490 John Spencer
1491 William Hert
1492 Walter Povey
1493 Thomas Randall
1494 James Wilford
1495 Owen Boughton
1496 Nicholas Nynes
1497 Thomas Petyt
1498 Thomas Bromefelde
1499 William Fitzwilliam
1500 John Doget
1501 John Kyrkeby
1502 Richard Smith
1503 Edmund Flower
1504
1505 Thomas Howdan
1506 Richard Cornhill
1507 William Grene
1508
1509 Thomas Speight
1510 John Skevyngton
1511 John Tresawell
1512
1513 John Breton
1514 Henry Dacres
1515 John Wright
1516 Richard Hall
1517
1518 William Wilford
1519
1520 Geoffrey Vaughan
1521 John Gonne
1522 John Nicholls
1523 Paul Withypool
1524
1525
1526 Robert Shether
1527 Hugh Acton
1528 John Benett
1529
1530 Richard Gibson
1531 Richard Houlte

1532 Henry Hubbathorne
1533
1534 William Wilford, the younger
1535 Thomas White
1536 John Skut
1537
1538
1539
1540 John Malt
1541
1542 Stephen Kirton
1543
1544 Robert Dawbeney
1545 Thomas Brooke
1546 Thomas Brooke/Richard Holte
1547 Thomas Offley
1548 Richard Wadyngton
1549 Nicholas Cosyn
1550 Robert Mellyshe
1551 Richard Botyll
1552 John Jakes
1553 William Harper
1554 Guy Wade
1555 William Clyfton
1556 George Heton
1557 Simon Lowe
1558 Edward Ley
1559 Thomas Ackworth
1560 Emmanuel Lucar
1561 Richard Hilles
1562 Richard Whethill
1563 Robert Rose
1564 John Olyff
1565 John God
1566 Thomas Browne
1567 Gerard Gore
1568 William Albany
1569 Robert Hulson
1570 William Kympton
1571 Richard Johnson
1572 William Hodgson
1573 Richard White
1574 Arthur Dawbney
1575 Edward Joans
1576 Walter Fyshe
1577 Anthony Radclyffe
1578 Robert Dowe
1579 William Phillipps
1580 Robert Hawes
1581 Richard Bourne
1582 Charles Hoskyns
1583 Richard Maye
1584 Henry Offley
1585 Thomas Wilford

1586 William Widnell
1587 John Toppe
1588 Nicholas Spencer
1589 George Sotherton
1590 Hugh Hendley
1591 William Dodworth
1592 Oliver Rowe
1593 Richard Procter
1594 John Churchman
1595 Reginald Barker
1596 Edward Kympton
1597 Nowell Sotherton
1598 Richard Venables/Henry Webb
1599 Walter Plummer
1600 Henry Palmer
1601 Thomas Aldworth
1602 Richard Gore
1603 Humfrey Corbett
1604 Jeffery Elwes
1605 Thomas Juxon
1606 John Swinnerton
1607 John Johnson
1608 Humphrey Streete
1609 John Vernon
1610 Thomas Rowe
1611 Richard Wright
1612 Andrew Osborne
1613 Richard Scales
1614 Randulph Woolley
1615 Thomas Johnson
1616 Charles Hoskyns
1617 Mathias Springham
1618 William Grenewell
1619 John Slaney
1620 Edward James
1621 Thomas Marsham
1622 Peter Towers
1623 Ralph Gore
1624 Edmund Crich
1625 Henry Polsteed
1626 Edward Warner
1627 Edward Cotton
1628 Robert Draper
1629 Francis Neave
1630 Henry Pratt
1631 George Benson
1632 Michael Griggs
1633 William Stanley
1634 Simon Bardolphe
1635 William Tulley
1636 Richard Turner
1637 Simon Wood
1638 Thomas Wetherall
1639 William Parsell

APPENDIX ONE: LIST OF MASTERS

1640 Abraham Reynardson
1641 Clement Mosse
1642 Nathaniel Owen
1643 Richard Andrewe
1644 William Gelsthorp
1645 Samuel Avery
1646 George Mellish
1647 George Nash
1648 Roger Gardiner
1649 Walter Pell
1650 John Stone
1651 Ozias Churchman
1652 Robert Gale
1653 Sackford Gouson
1654 Walter Bigg
1655 Tempest Milner
1656 John Ellis
1657 William Beeke
1658 Robert Lant
1659 William Bolton
1660 John Orlibrare
1661 William Turner
1662 Nicholas Delves
1663 Benoni Honiwood
1664 Henry Hampson
1665 Thomas Nevill
1666 Nathaniel Withers
1667 Edmund Lewin
1668 Edward Nash
1669 Allane Cliffe
1670 Henry Ashurst
1671 Patience Ward
1672 John Foster
1673 William Pritchard
1674 Robert Mallory
1675 John Acrod
1676 John White
1677 Robert Sewell
1678 Daniel Baker
1679 Humphrey Nicholson
1680 Edward Bushell
1681 Thomas Wandell
1682 George Archer
1683 Thomas Wardall
1684 Thomas Wardall/William Turner
1685 Peter Paravicini
1686 William Dodson
1687 John Wallis/William Ashurst
1688 Thomas Halton
1689 George Ayrey
1690 Edward Clarke
1691 Thomas Hatchett
1692 Robert Swann
1693 Thomas Darwyn

1694 John Smart
1695 Edward Wills
1696 Nicholas Ashton
1697 Robert Bedingfield
1698 Thomas Cuthbert
1699 James Smith
1700 John Page
1701 Joseph Greenhill
1702 Robert White
1703 Robert White
1704 Edward Fenwick
1705 Evan Evans/William Mead
1706 Samuel Ongley
1707 Jerningham Chaplin
1708 Edward le Neve
1709 John Ward
1710 Joseph Brooke
1711 Richard Edmondson
1712 John Wright
1713 Roger Attlee
1714 John Henly/Isaac Cocks
1715 Joseph Wandall
1716 Roger Mott
1717 John Forman/John Hollister
1718 Thomas Harris
1719 James Ball
1720 Thomas Pitts
1721 Benjamin Bradley
1722 John Cowper
1723 John Amy
1724 Matthias Prime
1725 John Hassell
1726 Giles Riddle
1727 William Boyfield
1728 William Gould
1729 Joseph Dawson
1730 Samuel Ashurst
1731 John Salter
1732 Richard Nash
1733 Joseph Locker
1734 William Pomeroy
1735 Samuel Tatem
1736 Richard Vickers
1737 Robert Westley
1738 Edmund Lewin
1739 Theophilus Dillingham
1740 Joseph Dandridge
1741 John Hollister
1742 Samuel Lessingham
1743 William Townsend
1744 George Streatfield
1745 John Picton
1746 William Dawson
1747 Timothy Colston
1748 Daniel Legg

1749 Henry Watts
1750 William Branson
1751 Samuel Herring
1752 James Dandridge
1753 Allen Evans
1754 Henry Cowling
1755 William Upfold
1756 Joseph Styles
1757 John Torriano
1758 Benjamin Fuller
1759 Nathaniel Nash
1760 Richard Neave
1761 Ive Whitbread
1762 Bartholomew Pomeroy
1763 Gearing Roberts
1764 Philip Glass
1765 Leaver Legg
1766 Joseph Dyer
1767 Nathaniel Martin
1768 John Sabatier
1769 James Walton
1770 Stephen Todd
1771 John Brome
1772 Thomas Plestow
1773 Joseph Kinder
1774 William Shenton
1775 John Davenport
1776 Edward George
1777 Thomas Geeve
1778 Miles Stringer
1779 David Thomas
1780 Thomas Davis
1781 Nathaniel Clarkson
1782 Joseph Leeds
1783 James Atkinson
1784 John Muggeridge
1785 William Anderson
1786 William Deane
1787 John Brome
1788 John Berney
1789 Guy Warwick
1790 Nathaniel Allen
1791 James Robson
1792 John Hopkins
1793 William White
1794 George Dance
1795 John Rogers
1796 Jonathan Eade
1797 Thomas Roberts
1798 Michael Eaton
1799 John Hounsom
1800 John Field
1801 John Reade
1802 Thomas Bourdillon
1803 Henry Pigeon

1804 John Thompson
1805 William Lloyd
1806 Samuel Dobree
1807 George Vander Neunberg
1808 John Leopard
1809 William Hayward
1810 William Thompson
1811 William Child
1812 Samuel Hutchinson
1813 John Capel Hanbury
1814 John Buswell
1815 Andrew John Nash
1816 Coles Child
1817 George Augustus Nash
1818 William Costeker
1819 Robert Harry Sparks
1820 James Jacks
1821 Edward Complin
1822 Miles Stringer
1823 John Rogers
1824 Richard Jennings
1825 Thomas Bulcock Burbidge
1826 John Dixon
1827 Richard Fisher
1828 Thomas Styan
1829 John Thompson
1830 Florance Thomas Young
1831 Richard Hotham Pigeon
1832 Matthias Attwood
1833 John Pelly Atkins
1834 William Woodbridge Nash
1835 George Buckton
1836 William Sutton
1837 John Alliston
1838 John White
1839 Robert Podmore
1840 Bonamy Dobree
1841 James Hunt
1842 John William Hartshorne
1843 Charles Morrice Hullah
1844 William Gilpin
1845 William Jackson
1846 Alfred Staines Pigeon
1847 Thomas Bless Pugh
1848 William Waugh
1849 Edward Thomas Complin
1850 William Robinson White
1851 Charles Robert Thompson
1852 Charles Rickards
1853 John Costeker
1854 Charles Jacomb
1855 Richard Boyman Boyman
1856 John Bonus
1857 Joseph Turnley
1858 William Nash
1859 Thomas Chatteris
1860 Charles Gordon
1861 John Ewart
1862 Thomas Bennett Spence
1863 Richard Baggallay
1864 John Watson Lay
1865 William Foster White
1866 George Parbury
1867 John Thompson Fletcher
1868 James Tyler
1869 Edward Masterman
1870 Henry Pigeon
1871 William Timbrell Elliott
1872 Thomas Weston Baggallay
1873 Charles Mathew Clode
1874 John Coysgarne Sim
1875 John Jackson
1876 Samuel Mason
1877 Oliver Henry Davis
1878 Edwin Nash
1879 Thomas Cundy
1880 Thomas Styan
1881 John Whately Simmonds
1882 James Fenning
1883 James Graves
1884 John Whittaker Ellis
1885 Eustace Anderson
1886 Robert Johnson
1887 John Blacket Gill
1888 George Baker
1889 Reginald Hanson
1890 John James Purnell
1891 John Frederick Beazley
1892 Richard Whittington
1893 Raymond Henry Thrupp
1894 Henry Kimber
1895 Frederick Morris Fry
1896 Edward Coysgarne Sim
1897 Wickham Noakes
1898 George William Barnard
1899 John Ewart
1900 Seth Taylor
1901 Edward Blakeway I'Anson
1902 Gabriel Prior Goldney
1903 Reginald Benson Jacomb
1904 Walter Baker Clode
1905 John Robert Heron-Maxwell
1906 Coles Child
1907 Charles Stanley Gordon Clark
1908 Alexander Howden
1909 Frank Thomas Baggallay
1910 Henry Lennox Hopkinson
1911 Frederick Morris Fry
1912 Cyril Wintle
1913 Charles Granville Kekewich
1914 Ernest Woolley
1915 Albert Charles Clauson
1916 Sydney Eggers Bates
1917 Mark John Simmonds
1918 George James Frampton
1919 Algernon Edward Gilliat
1920 Albert Charles Clauson
1921 Reginald Benson Jacomb
1922 Walter Lloyd Thomas
1923 Charles Roche Finnis
1924 Charles John Ritchie
1925 Percy Robert Laurie
1926 Arthur Lionel Fitzroy Cook
1927 Robert Reginald Johnston Turner
1928 Ernest Prescott
1929 Henry Cubitt Gooch
1930 William Graham
1931 George Aylwen
1932 Walter Durant Gibbs
1933 John Edward Kynaston Studd
1934 Bernard Inman Franklin-Adams
1935 Austin Blomfield
1936 Algernon Henry Moreing
1937 Henry Frederick Oswald Norbury
1938 Robert Theophilus Dalton Sayle
1939 Charles Reginald Jacomb
1940 Robert Reginald Johnston Turner
1941 William Malcolm Lingard Escombe
1942 Thomas Macdonald Eggar
1943 John Durnford Crosthwaite
1944 Charles Seymour Eastwood
1945 Anthony George Clifton-Brown
1946 Walter Cooper
1947 Percy Lester Reid
1948 Bernard Inman Franklin-Adams
1949 Austin Blomfield
1950 John Stanley Gordon Clark
1951 Piers Keane Kekewich
1952 Harold Gibson Howitt
1953 John Montgomerie Hopkinson
1954 Henry Edmund Sargant
1955 Kenneth Marr-Johnson
1956 John Durnford Crosthwaite
1957 William Malcolm Lingard Escombe

1958 Horace Field Parshall
1959 Irving Blanchard Gane
1960 Leslie Sydney Marler
1961 Douglas Algernon Gilliat
1962 William Lacy Addison
1963 James Edward Thomson Ritchie
1964 David Ducat
1965 Arthur Burnand
1966 Douglas Seth Taylor
1967 Christopher William Edward Collins
1968 John Oliver-Bellasis
1969 John Stanley Gordon Clark
1970 John Kenyon Vaughan-Morgan
1971 Hume Boggis-Rolfe
1972 Denys Burton Buckley
1973 Peter Malden Studd
1974 John Keswick Ulick Blake McGrath
1975 Matthew Henry Oram
1976 Hugh Edward Hunter Jones
1977 Antony Durant Gibbs
1978 Roland Stephen Langton
1979 Antony Turnbull Langdon-Down
1980 Anthony Wentworth Howitt
1981 Charles Gundry Alexander
1982 Christopher Henry Nourse
1983 Dennis Thomas Holme Nicholson
1984 Paul Austin Shaw Blomfield
1985 Francis Storer Eaton Newall
1986 Philip Michael Woolley
1987 Edward Fairfax Studd
1988 John Raymond Perring
1989 George Peter Theobald
1990 John Hill Pascoe
1991 George Peter Theobald
1992 The Earl of Stockton
1993 Edward Fairfax Studd
1994 John Raymond Perring
1995 John Michael Stannage Whitehead
1996 Peter Henry Ryan
1997 Martin Courtenay Clarke
1998 Patrick Michael Franklin-Adams
1999 Brian Garton Jenkins
2000 Geoffrey Holland
2001 David William Brewer
2002 John Ridland Owens
2003 John Howard Penton

APPENDIX TWO
LIST OF CLERKS, 1398–2003

Note: spellings of surnames did not become standardized until around the mid-eighteenth century. Consequently, for the earlier Clerks, the list below represents the most common forms found in the archives of the Company, particularly the accounts and Court minutes, and in other sources relating to these individuals, such as wills, inventories and personal papers.

Before 1398–1420	John Brynchele	1685–1709	Thomas Ange
1420–after 1445	Nicholas Hoper	1709–63	George North
Before 1453–54	Nicholas Mille	1763–1802	George Bristow
1454–56	William Bouchier	1803–06	John Davies
1456–64	Thomas Fillilode	1806–22	Richard Teasdale
1464–87	Thomas Kirton	1822–30	William Bovill
1487–92	William Duryvale	1830–45	John Bamber de Mole
1493–at least 1512	Henry Mayour	1845–70	Samuel Fisher
Before 1545–46	Roger Wylson	1870–90	Francis Grantham Faithfull
1546–71	John Huchenson	1890–1924	Edward Nash
1571–75	Nicholas Fuljambe	1924–38	Charles Roche Finnis
1575–87	Thomas Haselfoote	1938–48	Ewen Aylmer Robert Ramsay Fairfax-Lucy
February–March 1587	Barnabas Hilles		
1587–94	Richard Wright	1948–62	Evan Maitland James
1594–1610	Richard Langley	1962–80	John Maxwell Woolley
1610–24	Richard Baldock	1980–85	Antony Turnbull Langdon-Down
1624–36	Clement Mosse	1985–95	Derek Alan Wallis
1636–61	Robert Marsh	1995–	David Arthur Peck
1661–85	John Milner		

APPENDIX THREE
THE VALUE OF MONEY, 1300–2002

Historians are often asked how much particular sums of money in different periods are worth in today's terms. Such questions are of particular interest in the context of an institution, such as the Merchant Taylors' Company, that has been in existence for at least 700 years. The answer is normally arrived at by looking at the values of 'baskets' of commodities and wage rates, the most famous example being the 'Phelps Brown and Hopkins Index', compiled in 1956, which covers the period 1264–1954. Like the Retail Price Index (RPI) today, there is disagreement over what items should be put in such a basket, and how far a particular selection reflects the consumption patterns of certain groups in society, such as London merchants, or indeed institutions, such as the livery companies. The PB&H Index, for instance, draws predominantly on prices for foodstuffs, and uses wage figures for provincial building craftsmen. Despite these caveats, it is useful to have at least a general idea of the changing value of money over the centuries, so that the financial dealings of the Company and the activities of its members can be put into perspective. The figures below are derived from ten-year averages of the Phelps Brown and Hopkins Index up to 1954, and of the RPI figures from the Office of National Statistics from 1914 to the present day.

Years	Equivalent purchasing power in 2002 of £1
1300–09	£418
1350–59	£321
1400–09	£377
1450–59	£418
1500–09	£398
1550–59	£143
1600–09	£87
1650–59	£65
1700–09	£70
1750–59	£66
1800–09	£28
1850–59	£35
1900–09	£41
1950–59	£16
2002	£1

For further reading see L. Munby, *How Much is that Worth?* (British Association for Local History, 1989, reprinted 1996).

SELECT BIBLIOGRAPHY

The following key sources are recommended for further research. Further sources of specific relevance are cited in the notes.

A. MANUSCRIPT SOURCES

British Library
Additional MS 6563
Additional MS 38131
Additional MS 45131
Harleian MS 367
Royal MS 2. B. XII, XIII
Royal MS 14. C. VII

Corporation of London Records Office
Husting Rolls (wills and deeds)
Journals of the Common Council
Repertories of the Court of Aldermen

Guildhall Library, London: Manuscripts Section
1. Merchant Taylors' Company manuscripts
   MS 34003   Early ordinances, 1429–55
   MS 34004   Ordinance and memorandum book, c. 1510–c. 1600
   MS 34007   Book of oaths, 1491
   MS 34008   Court minutes, 1486–93 (2 vols)
   MS 34010   Court minutes, 1562 onwards (48 vols)
   Ms 34037   Index of freemen, 1530–1928 (4 vols)
   MS 34048   Master's accounts, 1398 onwards (44 vols)
   MS 34100   Miscellaneous papers (205 boxes)
   MS 34127   Book of benefactors' wills, compiled c. 1500 and after
   MS 34130   Book of abstracts of Company title deeds, compiled 1605–c. 1617
   MS 34214   Miscellaneous plans (42 folders)
   MS 34357   Treasury records, 1489–1503; Hall inventories, 1491 and 1512–49
   Ms 34360   Inventories of the Hall, 1609 and 1618

Further manuscripts from the Company's archive are referred to in the notes to the chapters.

2. Other manuscripts
   MS 5440   Brewers' Company, Account and memorandum book, 1414–40
   MS 5370   Scriveners' Company, 'Common Paper', 1357–1628
   MS 6842   St Martin Outwich, Churchwardens' accounts, 1508–28, 1537–46
   MS 9051/1   Register of wills enrolled in the Archdeaconry Court of London, 1393–1415
   MS 9171/1–9 Registers of wills enrolled in the Commissary Court of London (London Division), 1374–1502, 1516–21

Public Record Office (now part of The National Archives)
C1   Chancery, Early Chancery Proceedings
C66   Chancery, Patent Rolls
C131   Chancery, Extents for Debts
C143   Chancery, Inquisitions *Ad Quod Damnum*
C145   Chancery, Inquisitions Miscellaneous
C239   Chancery, Extents for Debts, Series II
E101   Exchequer, Accounts Various
E122   Exchequer, Customs Accounts
E179   Exchequer, Lay Subsidy Returns
E210   Exchequer, Ancient Deeds
E301   Exchequer, Court of Augmentations: Chantry Certificates
DL28   Duchy of Lancaster, Various Accounts
DL41   Duchy of Lancaster, Miscellanea
LR2   Land Revenue: Chantry Certificates
PROB 11 Registers of Wills proved in the Prerogative Court of Canterbury
SC8   Special Collections, Ancient Petitions

B. PRINTED SOURCES

The place of publication is London, unless otherwise stated.

Adams, R. H., *Memorial Inscriptions in St. John's College, Oxford, with an Introduction by Sir Howard Colvin*, Oxford Historical Society, new series, 35 (1996)

Allen, E. A., 'Public School Elites in Early-Victorian England: The Boys at Harrow and Merchant Taylors' Schools from 1825 to 1850', *Journal of British Studies*, vol. 21, no. 2 (1982), pp. 87–117

Archer, I. W., *The Pursuit of Stability: Social Relations in Elizabethan London* (Cambridge, 1991)

Archer, I. W., *The History of the Haberdashers' Company* (Chichester, 1991)

Archer, I. W., 'The Livery Companies and Charity in the Sixteenth and Seventeenth Centuries', in I. A. Gadd and P. Wallis (eds), *Guilds, Society & Economy in London 1450–1800* (2002), pp. 15–28

Arnold, J., *Queen Elizabeth's Wardrobe Unlock'd* (Leeds, 1988)

Baker, W., *Merchant Taylors' School Register, 1871–1900* (1907)

Beaven, A. B., *The Aldermen of the City of London*, 2 vols (1908–13)

Bird, R., *The Turbulent London of Richard II* (1949)

Bradley, S. and Pevsner, N., *The Buildings of England: The City of London*, rev. edn (1997)

Brigden, S., *London and the Reformation* (Oxford, 1989)

Bromley, J. and Child, H., *The Armorial Bearings of the Guilds of London* (1960)

Brooke, C. N. L. and Keir, G., *London 800–1216: The Shaping of a City* (1975)

Cambridge Urban History of Britain: Volume 1, 600–1540, ed. by D. M. Palliser (Cambridge, 2000), esp. chapters 9 (D. Keene) and 17 (C. M. Barron)

Cambridge Urban History of Britain: Volume 2, 1540–1840, ed. by P. Clark (Cambridge, 2000), esp. chapters 10 (J. Boulton) and 19 (L. Schwarz)

City of London Livery Companies' Commission, Volumes 1–5, Report and Appendix (1884)

Clode, C. M., *Memorials of the Guild of Merchant Taylors of the Fraternity of St. John the Baptist* (1875)

Clode, C. M., *Merchant Taylors' Hall anterior to 1666* (1886)

Clode, C. M., *The Early History of the Guild of Merchant Taylors of the Fraternity of St. John the Baptist, London, with Notices of the Lives of Some of its Eminent Members*, 2 vols (1888)

Clode, C. M., 'Sir John Yorke, Sheriff of London, Citizen, and Merchant Taylor', *Proceedings of the Society of Antiquaries of London*, 2nd series, 13 (1889–91), pp. 278–99

Clode, C. M., *London during the Great Rebellion, being a Memoir of Sir Abraham Reynardson, Knight, Sheriff, and Master of the Merchant Taylors' Company, 1640–41; Lord Mayor of London, Elected 1648, Dismissed 1649, Re-elected 1660* (1892)

Combe, W. and Pyne Plates, W. H., *History of the Colleges of Winchester, Eton and Westminster, with the Charterhouse, the Schools of St Paul's, Merchant Taylors, Harrow and Rugby, and the Free School of Christ's Hospital* (1816)

Costin, W. C., *The History of St John's College, 1598–1860*, Oxford Historical Society, 2nd series, 12 (1958)

Creaton, H. J., *Bibliography of Printed Works on London History to 1939* (1994)

Curl, J. S., *The Londonderry Plantation, 1609–1914* (Chichester, 1986), especially chapters XII (Merchant Taylors) and XVII (Clothworkers)

Davies, M., 'The Tailors of London and their Guild, c. 1300–1500' (unpublished D.Phil. thesis, University of Oxford, 1994)

Davies, M., 'Dame Thomasine Percyvale, "the Maid of Week" (d. 1512)', in *Medieval London Widows, 1300–1500*, ed. by C. M. Barron and A. F. Sutton (1994), pp. 185–207

Davies, M., 'The Tailors of London: Corporate Charity in the Late Medieval Town', in *Crown, Government and People in the Fifteenth Century*, ed. by R. E. Archer (Stroud, 1995), pp. 161–90

Davies, M., 'Artisans, Guilds and Government in London', in *Daily Life in the Late Middle Ages*, ed. by R. H. Britnell (Stroud, 1998), pp. 125–50

Davies, M. (ed.), *The Merchant Taylors' Company of London: Court Minutes, 1486–93* (Stamford, 2000)

Davies, M., 'Governors and Governed: The Practice of Power in the Merchant Taylors' Company in the Fifteenth Century', in *Guilds, Society & Economy*, ed. by Gadd and Wallis, pp. 67–83

Davies, M., *The Merchant Taylors' Company Charter of King Henry VII, 1503* (Merchant Taylors' Company pamphlet, 2003)

Davis, J., *Reforming London: The London Government Problem, 1855–1900* (Oxford, 1988)

Doolittle, I. G., *The City of London and its Livery Companies* (Dorchester, 1982)

Doolittle, I. G., *The Mercers' Company, 1579–1959*, ed. by A. Saunders (1994)

Draper, F. W. M., *Four Centuries of Merchant Taylors' School, 1561–1961* (1962)

Ellis, H. D., *A Short Description of the Ancient Silver Plate belonging to the Worshipful Company of Merchant Taylors* (1892)

Fry, F. M., *A Historical Catalogue of the Pictures, Herse-Cloths and Tapestry at Merchant Taylors' Hall, with a List of the Sculptures and Engravings* (1907, and supplement, 1928)

Fry, F. M. and Tewson, R. S., *Illustrated Catalogue of Silver Plate of the Worshipful Company of Merchant Taylors* (1929)

Fry, F. M. and Sayle, R. T. D (eds), *The Charters of the Merchant Taylors' Company* (1937)

Fry, F. M. and Thomas, W. L., *The Windows of Merchant Taylors' Hall* (1934)

Gawsworth, J. (ed.), *The Poets of Merchant Taylors' School (founded 1561): Their Best Songs and Shorter Poems* (1934)

Girtin, T., *The Golden Ram: A Narrative History of the Clothworkers' Company, 1528–1958* (1958)

Godber, J., *The Harpur Trust, 1552–1973* (Bedford, 1973)

Harrop, S., *The Merchant Taylors' School for Girls, Crosby: One Hundred Years of Achievement, 1888–1988* (Liverpool, 1988)

Hart, E. P., *Merchant Taylors' School Register, 1851–1920* (1923)

Hart, Mrs E. P., *Merchant Taylors' School Register 1561–1934. Volume 1, A–K; Volume 2, L–Z* (1936)

Herbert, W., *The History of the Twelve Great Livery Companies of London*, 2 vols (1834–37; repr. 1968)

Hills, O. C., *Richard Hilles, Citizen and Merchant Taylor, 1514–87* (1927)

Hollaender, A. E. J., and Kellaway, W. (eds), *Studies in London History Presented to P. E. Jones* (1969)

Hopkinson, H. L., *The History of the Site of Merchant Taylors' Hall* (1913)

Hopkinson, H. L., *Report on the Ancient Records in the Possession of the Guild of Merchant Taylors . . . in the City of London* (1915)
Hopkinson, H. L., *The History of Merchant Taylors' Hall* (Cambridge, 1931)
Hopkinson, H. L., *A Visit to Merchant Taylors' Hall* (1st edition 1922, 2nd edition 1934)
Linton, D., *Wolverhampton Grammar School* (Stroud, 2000)
Luft, H. M., *A History of Merchant Taylors' School, Crosby, 1620–1970* (Liverpool, 1970)
Mander, G. P., *The History of the Wolverhampton Grammar School* (Wolverhampton, 1913)
Merchant Taylors' Company, *The Charitable Foundations of the Merchant Taylors' Company* (1864)
Merchant Taylors' Company, *Antient Acquisitions of the Merchant Taylors' Company, 1331–1531* (c. 1885)
Merchant Taylors' School Archaeological Society, *Merchant Taylors' School: Its Origin, History and Present Surroundings* (Oxford, 1929)
Merritt, J. F. (ed.), *Imagining Early Modern London: Perceptions and Portrayals of the City from Stow to Strype, 1598–1720* (Cambridge, 2001)
Nichols, J. G. (ed.), *The Diary of Henry Machyn, Citizen and Merchant-Taylor of London, from AD 1550 to AD 1563*, Camden Society, XLII (1848)
Norman, P., 'Recent Discoveries of Medieval Remains in London', *Archaeologia*, 67, 2nd series, vol. 17 (1916), pp. 1–26, esp. pp. 1–7
Pearl, V., *London and the Outbreak of the Puritan Revolution: City Government and National Politics, 1625–43* (1961)
Prockter, A. and Taylor, R., *The A to Z of Elizabethan London*, London Topographical Society (1979)
Rappaport, S., *Worlds within Worlds: Structures of Life in Sixteenth-Century London* (Cambridge, 1989)
Reddaway, T. F., *The Rebuilding of London after the Great Fire* (1940)
Reddaway, T. F. and Walker, L. E. M., *The Early History of the Goldsmiths' Company, 1327–1509* (1975)
Riley, H. T. (ed.), *Memorials of London and London Life in the XIIIth, XIVth and XVth Centuries* (1868)
Robinson, C. J., *Register of Scholars admitted into Merchant Taylors' School from AD 1562 to 1874* (Lewes, 1882–83)
Royal Commission on Historical Monuments, Vol. 4: The City (1929)
Royal Commission, *The London City Livery Companies' Vindication* (1885)
Saunders, A. (ed.), *The Royal Exchange* (1997)
Sayle, R. T. D., *Lord Mayors' Pageants of the Merchant Taylors' Company in the 15th, 16th and 17th Centuries* (1931)
Sayle, R. T. D., *The Barges of the Merchant Taylors' Company* (1933)
Sayle, R. T. D., 'Annals of Merchant Taylors' School Library', *Transactions of the Bibliographical Society, The Library*, 4th series, 15 (1934–35), pp. 457–80
Sayle, R. T. D., *A Brief History of the Worshipful Company of Merchant Taylors* (1945)
Schofield, J., *The Building of London from the Conquest to the Great Fire* (revised edition, 1993)
Schofield, J., *Medieval London Houses* (Yale, 1994), esp. pp. 223–25
Second Report of the Commissioners Appointed to Inquire into the Municipal Corporations in England and Wales: London and Southwark. London Companies (1837), esp. pp. 35–51
Sharpe, R. R. (ed.), *Calendar of Wills Proved and Enrolled in the Court of Husting, London, 1258–1688*, 2 vols (1889–90)
Sharpe, R. R. (ed.), *Calendar of the Letter Books Preserved among the Archives of the Corporation of the City of London*, 11 vols (A-L) (1899–1912)
Sheppard, F. H. W., *London: A History* (Oxford, 1998)
Simmonds, M. J., *Merchant Taylors' Fellows of St John's College, Oxford* (1930)
Sleigh-Johnson, N. V., 'The Merchant Taylors' Company of London, 1580–1645' (unpublished Ph.D. thesis, London University, 1989)
Sleigh-Johnson, N. V., 'Aspects of the Tailoring Trade in the City of London in the Late Sixteenth and Earlier Seventeenth Centuries', *Costume*, 37 (2003), pp. 24–32
Spence, C., *London in the 1690s: A Social Atlas* (2000)
Stevenson, W. H. and Salter, H. E., *The Early History of St. John's College, Oxford*, Oxford Historical Society, new series, I (1939)
Stow, J., *A Survey of London, Reprinted from the Text of 1603*, ed. by C. L. Kingsford, 2 vols (Oxford, 1908)
Thomas, A. H. and Jones, P. E. (eds), *Calendar of Plea and Memoranda Rolls of the City of London, 1323–1482*, 6 vols (Cambridge, 1926–61)
Thrupp, S. L., *The Merchant Class of Medieval London (1300–1500)* (Chicago, 1948; repr. Ann Arbor, 1962)
Unwin, G., *The Gilds and Companies of London*, 4th edition (1963)
Veale, E. M., *The English Fur Trade in the Later Middle Ages* (Oxford, 1966; repr. by the London Record Society, 2003)
Veale, E. M., 'The "Great Twelve": Mistery and Fraternity in Thirteenth-Century London', *Historical Research*, 64 (1991), pp. 237–63
Weinreb, B. and Hibbert, C. (eds), *The London Encyclopaedia* (1983)
Whiteman, G. W., *Halls and Treasures of the City Companies* (1970)
Williams, G. A., *Medieval London: From Commune to Capital* (1963)
Wilson, H. B., *The History of Merchant-Taylors School, from its Foundation to the Present Time*, 2 vols (1812–14)
Winstanley, W., *The Honour of Merchan-Taylors, Wherein is Set Forth the Noble Acts . . . and Heroick Performances of Merchant-Taylors in Former Ages* (1668)
Woodhead, J. R., *The Rulers of London, 1660–1689*, London and Middlesex Archaeological Society (1965)
Wooley, T. G., 'The Arms and Badges of the Merchant Taylors Company', *Coat of Arms*, vol. 7 (1962–63), pp. 181–88

LIST OF SUBSCRIBERS

Mora Abell
David Adams
Reginald H. Adams
A. R. Alchin
Sir Charles G. Alexander
Richard Alexander
Johny Armstrong
Stephen Back
Professor Anthony C. Bailey
Mrs Christopher Bailey
Tony Baldry
Malcolm J. W. Barker
Mark Barty-King
Colin Beaumont-Edmonds
Thomas Seager Berry
J. W. Birch
Jeremy Bishops
P. A. S. Blomfield
Donald Bompas
Alderman David Brewer
Robert J. Bright
Richard Brooman
Gavin Brown
P. Anthony Bull (deceased)
Nicholas H. Carter
Roger Challis
Katherine Clark
Martin Clarke
Adrian Cole
John Collins
James Copping
W. David S. Cotton
Angus H. Cundey
Hamish Ian Dermit
Andrew Drysdale
Peter Ducat
W. James Eastwood
Duncan Eggar
Hugh J. M. Elder
Ancrum Francis Evans
Francis G. Feather
Patrick Franklin-Adams

Cdr Peter Gilbert
Roland Gillott
Andrew Gordon
Sam Gordon Clark
V. P. Grant
Arthur E. C. Green
Richard M. C. Green
Mrs Christopher Hall
J. P. Hall
William Haly
Julian Harrison
Philippa Hawks
Christopher Hilditch
James R. G. Hilditch
Nicholas J. Hoffman
Sir Geoffrey Holland
Tony Howitt
Charlotte Huskisson
Major T. F. Huskisson
W. D. A. Justice
Christopher A. Keljik
Nicholas Lines
Peter G. Magill
John Marks
Dennis Marler
Peregrine Massey
Anne Milner
Alexander D. E. Mitchell
Edward A. C. Mitchell
Giles A. S. G. Murphy
Ken Neville-Davies
D. T. H. Nicholson
James David Northcott
Dr Christopher Nourse
Hugh Oliver-Bellasis
Mrs John Oliver-Bellasis
Gavin Oram
Dr Julian Oram
Geoffrey J. Osborne
John R. Owens
Philip G. Parker

Peter Parr-Head
John Pascoe
Sally Patmore
David Peck
Sir John Perring
J. D. R. Price
Oliver Pritchard
Christopher Regan
Alan J. Reid
G. C. Royle
Piers Russell-Cobb
S. C. Rutherford
Peter H. Ryan
Elizabeth Shepherd
Dr John Sichel
C. G. Sim
Karle E. Simpson
Michael W. G. Skinner
William George Skinner
Oliver James Slack
J. South
Mrs J. South
H. A. Speare-Cole
R. M. J. Stewart
Roger James Storey
Andrew Studd
Sir Edward Studd
Ben Taylor
Nicholas Harvard Taylor
J. R. Terry
Vera Thomas
W. H. Thorning
John Townsend Green
Graham R. Walker
James Walker
Captain D. A. Wallis
P. H. Watkins
James Watson
John Whitehead
Thomas Bain Willcox
A. Willoughby
R. John Wiseman

INDEX

Notes: page references in italics indicate black-and-white figures or captions. The colour plate sections after pages 34, 114, and 210 are indexed by plate number: for instance, 'Col. Pl. XIII'. A page reference including n indicates an endnote: for instance, 107n14 refers to note 14 on page 107.

Historic counties are used in the index; where no county is given, locations are in London or Westminster. Churches and parishes in the City of London are indexed under the heading 'churches and parishes (City of London)'.

A
Abbey, Edwin A.   249, Col. Pl. V
Abbot, John   111
Abchurch Lane   99
Abernethy, John   229
Ackworth, Thomas (Master 1559)   270
Acrod, John (Master 1675)   271
Acton, Hugh (Master 1527)   56, 66, 83, 85, 96, 107n14, 270
Addison, William Lacy (Master 1962)   273
Addle Street ('Adlane')   59
Adelmare, Dr Caesar   119
Adyff, Richard   31
Agnus Dei see Lamb of God
aketons   50
 see also linen armour
Albany, William (Master 1568)   270
Albany, William (*fl.* 1607)   159
Albemarle, Dukes of *see* Monck
Alcegar, Juan de, *Libro de Geometria, Pratica, y Traca*   136
Aldenham (Herts.)   *54*
Aldermanbury   115
 St Mary Aldermanbury   116
  lectionary (Epistles and Gospels) presented by Sir Stephen Jenyns   6, 115, Col. Pls II, VIII
aldermen
 tailors as (before 1550)   71, 76, 82–83, 84, 99, 115
 see also City of London, Court of Aldermen
Aldersgate, George Inn   214
Aldgate   152, 175
 St Botolph Aldgate, Dowe monument   176, Col. Pl. XIII
Aldridge (Staffs.)   229
Aldworth, Thomas (Master 1601)   270
Alexander I, Tsar of Russia   234
Alexander, Charles Gundry (Master 1981)   273
Alexandra, Queen, as Princess of Wales   244
Aleyn, Roger   25
aliens *see* immigrants
Allen, John   162
Allen, Nathaniel (Master 1790)   271

Allen, Thomas   249
Allestry, ——   206
Alliston, John (Master 1837)   272
Allott, William   188
Alma-Tadema, Sir Lawrence   249
alms collectors (purveyors of alms), term originally used for Wardens   9–10, 11, 13, 28, 38
alms-giving *see* Merchant Taylors' Company, charitable activities
almshouses
 15th cent.
  Threadneedle Street   25, 28, 29, 36, 43, 74, 240
 16th cent.
  Threadneedle Street   63, 135, 138, 174–75, 176, Col. Pl. XI
  Tower Hill   29
 17th cent.
  Lee   215–16, 231
  Taunton   177–78
  Threadneedle Street   202, 205, 215, 231
  Tower Hill   29, 207, 215
 18th cent.
  Tower Hill   *133*, 231
 19th cent.
  Lee   231, 239–40, *239*, 266–67
  Tower Hill   231, 239
 20th cent.   250
almsmen and almswomen
 15th cent.   29, 42
 16th cent.   135, 138, 175, 176
 17th cent.   166, 201, 202, 203, 206, 215
 18th cent.   231, *231*, 232
Alport, ——   202
Alton (Hants.), Treloar School and College   267
America *see* Massachusetts Bay Company; Virginia
Amy, John (Master 1723)   271
Anderson, Eustace (Master 1885)   272
Anderson, John   129
Anderson, William (Master 1785)   271
Andrew, John   113–14

Andrewe, Richard (Master 1643)   271
Andrewes, Lancelot, Bishop of Winchester   124, *167*, 168
Ange, Thomas (Clerk 1685–1709)   218, 275
Anhalt, Prince of *see* Christian
Anne, Queen (consort of Richard III)   62
Anne of Bohemia, Queen   63, 174, 262
Anne Boleyn, Queen   62
Anne of Denmark, Queen   181
anniversaries (obits)   22, 25–26, 28, 37, 43, 86, 95
    abolition   96–99
    see also chantries
Apothecaries' Hall   203
Appletreewick (W.R. Yorks.)   174
apprenticeship   3, 53–57, 127–29, 158
    charitable assistance   56, 216
    education of apprentices   109
    enrolments (admissions)   7, 35, 36 (Table 3), 53–54, 81, 213
    feast for Tory apprentices (1682)   218
    geographical origins   54–55, 81
    girls apprenticed in dressmaking, 20th cent.   250
    indentures   53, *54*, 132
    numbers
        15th cent.   35, 36, 54, 81
        16th cent.   130
    regulation of
        15th cent.   40, 41, 53, 54, 55, 66, 81
        16th–17th cent.   128–29, 173
    shops run by apprentices   59
Apslund, Gunnar   255
Arcall, John (Master 1437)   269
Archer, George (Master 1682)   271
Archer, Robert   55, 109
Arden, Thomas   139n34
Armour, Revd Samuel Crawford   245
armour, soft *see* linen armour
armourers   14, 50
    King's armourers   13, 23, 50, 51
    see also linen-armourers
Armourers' and Brasiers' Company   50, 72, 73, 78, 138
Army Air Corps   267
Artillery Company (Guild of St George) (later Honourable Artillery Company)   183–84, 200, 218
Artillery Ground   184
Arundel, Earls of *see* Howard, Philip
Ashton, George (Master 1455)   61, 269
Ashton, Nicholas (Master 1696)   271
Ashurst, Henry (Master 1670)   271
Ashurst, Samuel (Master 1730)   271
Ashurst, Sir William (Master 1687; Lord Mayor 1693)   225, 271
Ashwell (Herts.), school   206, 216–17, *217*, 241–42
Ashworth, Revd John   203–05
Assheton, Dr William   218

Assistants *see* Courts of Assistants; Merchant Taylors' Company, Court of Assistants
Atkins, John Pelly (Master 1833)   272
Atkinson, Edward   159
Atkinson, James (Master 1783)   271
Atkinson, John   238
Atkynson, James   58–59
Attlee, Roger (Master 1713)   271
Attwood, Matthias (Master 1832)   272
Augar, Nicholas   195
Auntrus, William (Master 1443)   269
Austen, George   231
Austen, Jane   231, 234
Austin, Thomas   72
Avery, Samuel (Master 1645)   271
Avis, Joseph   208, 215, 218
Aylwen, George (Master 1931)   272
Ayrey, George (Master 1689)   271
Aystwick, John de   13, 14

B
Babington, Edward   137
Bachelors' Company (yeomen tailors)   41–43, 173–74, 221
    annual feast   41, 42, 127
    Budge Bachelors   206
    clothworkers as members   142
    contributions to loans and levies   143, 148, 171, 173
    Rich Bachelors   206
    Sixteen Men   43, 131, 173
    Stow as member   153
    Wardens Substitute   42, 43, 131, 173, 190, 221
Backhouse, Isaac   212, 216, 228
Bacon, Sir Nicholas   134
Baggallay, Frank Thomas (Master 1909)   272
Baggallay, Sir Richard (Master 1863)   263n29, 272
Baggallay, Thomas Weston (Master 1872)   272
Baker, Daniel (Master 1678)   222n9, 271
Baker, Elizabeth, wife of Robert   178
Baker, George (Master 1888)   272
Baker, Joan   100
Baker, Robert   178, 181
Baker, Revd William   243, 244, 250
Balcombe (Sussex)   117
Baldock, Richard (Clerk 1610–24)   194, 275
Bale, John (Master 1438)   65, 77, 269
Ball, Girling   257
Ball, James (Master 1719)   271
Ballard, John (Master 1401)   269
Banham, John   72
Bank of England   225, 235
Bank Hall (Lancs.)   195
Barbédienne, Ferdinand   *261*
Barber, ——   240–41
Bardolphe, Simon (Master 1634)   270

Bardwell, —— 221
barges, for civic ceremonies and royal events   79–80,
    199, 200–01, *201*, 206, 208–09, 225–27, 252
    built by Thomas Searle (1764)   225–26, *227*
Barker, Christopher   98
Barker, Reginald (Master 1595)   270
Barker, Thomas   203–05
Barlowe, Roger (Master 1479)   62, 270
Barnaby, Thomas   69n69, 113
Barnard, George William (Master 1898)   272
Barnes, Richard   169–71
Baron, Walter (Master 1468)   269
Barrett, Lieutenant John Cridlan, VC   252
Barriffe, William   183, 184
Bartholomew Fair   64, 76
Barton, John   65
Barton, William (*fl.* 1492)   38
Barton, William (*fl.* 1670)   208
Basford, Tristram   128
Bate, Ralph (Master 1418)   269
Bates, Sydney Eggers (Master 1916)   272
Batison, William   85
Baylie, Simon   202
Bayly, —— 136
Baynard's Castle   61
    see also Castle Baynard ward
Bayne, Henry   129
Beach, Thomas   250
Beadle, office of   29, 45, 88n34, 131, 132
Beal, James   246
Beamond (Beamont), Henry   159, 163
Beardall, Simon   194
Beatson, John   230
Beauchamp family (15th cent.)   20
Beauchamp, Sir John   146, 181
Beaufort, Henry, Cardinal, Bishop of Winchester   20–21
Beaumont and Fletcher
    The Knight of the Burning Pestle   168
    Love's Pilgrimage   201
Beazley, John Frederick (Master 1891)   272
Beddington (Surrey)   63
Bedford, —— 206
Bedford   118, 119
    Grammar School (later Bedford School)   118–19
Bedford, Dukes of *see* John, Duke of Bedford
Bedford, Earls of *see* Russell, Francis
Bedingfield, Anne   225
Bedingfield, Sir Robert (Master 1697; Lord Mayor 1706)
    225, 271
Beeke, William (Master 1657)   271
Belham, John (Master 1454)   52, 269
Bell, Richard   135
Bell Alley   138, 246
Bellamy, Dr James William   240–41, 243
Bellew family   166

Bellingham (Kent), playing fields   250, 253
Bellringer, John   100–01
Belsyre, Alexander   121
Benedetto da Majano   *261*
Benett, John (Master 1528)   270
Benson, George (Master 1631)   194, 270
Benton, Richard (Master 1447)   269
Berney, John (Master 1788)   271
Berry, Thomas (*fl.* 1560s)   134
Berry, Thomas (*fl.* 1605)   155
Berwick upon Tweed (Northumb.)   55
Best, Elias   212
Bethel, Slingsby   218
Bethlehem Hospital   14
Bewdley (Worcs.)   188
Bigg, Walter (Master 1654)   217, 271
Billesden, Robert (Mayor 1484)   82, 249
Billesden Award (1484)   81–82, *82*, 95, 238, 249, 265,
    Col. Pl. V
Billesden Officer   267
Birch, Messrs (caterers)   238
Birley, Norman   258, 265
Bishop, Richard   52
Bishop, Samuel   228
Bishopsgate   190, 191
    Bell Alley   138, 246
    St Helen Bishopsgate   26, *27*, 160, 243
Bishopsgate ward   175
Black, Jeremy   267
Black, Patrick   181
Black Death   49, 71
Black Prince *see* Edward the Black Prince
Blackburne, John, MP   237
Blackfriars   190
Blackfriars Bridge   243
Blackheath (Kent)   80, 199
    Dowe House   267
    Mulberry House   267
Blackwall Railway Company   231
Blackwell Hall   41, 65
Bland, Robert   206, 216–17
Bletchingdon (Oxon.)   188
Blitz (1940–41)   259–60
Blomfield, Austin (Master 1935, 1949)   261, 272
Blomfield, Paul Austin Shaw (Master 1984)   273
Blore, Edward   119
Blücher, Gebbard Leberecht von, Field Marshal   234,
    235
Blunt, Sir John   225
Board of Education   254
Bobbing (Kent)   211
Bodlowe, Nicholas   129
Body, William   137
Boggis-Rolfe, Hume (Master 1971)   273
Bognor (Sussex), convalescent homes   246, 250, 252

Bohun, Humphrey de, Earl of Hereford   20
Boitard, Louis Philippe   *233*
Bolde, John   112
Boleyn, Anne *see* Anne Boleyn, Queen
Boleyn, Geoffrey   21
Bollen, Henry   136
Bolton, Isabel   245–46
Bolton, Sir William (Master 1659; Lord Mayor 1666)
   202, 208, 271
Bonaventure, Thomasine *see* Percyvale
Bond Street   234
Bonde, William   133
Boniface IX, Pope   24
Bonus, John (Master 1856)   272
Bonyvaunt, William   64
Book of Oaths (1491)   *37*
Boone, Christopher   215–16, 231, 266
booths *see* shops, stalls and booths
botchers   52–53, 66
Botyll, Richard (Master 1551)   270
Bouchier, William (Clerk 1454–56)   275
Boughton, Owen (Master 1495)   31, 270
Bourdillon, Thomas (Master 1802)   271
Bourne, Richard (Master 1581)   270
Bourwell, John   63
Bovill, William (Clerk 1822–30)   230, 275
Bowcefelde, Henry   128
Bower, Sir John Dykes   265
Bower, Stephen Dykes   265
Bowman, John   55
Boyfield, William (Master 1727)   271
Boylet, William (Master 1458)   269
Boyman, Richard Boyman (Master 1855)   272
Boys, John du   148
Bracy, John   23
Bradenham, Thomas   27
Bradley, Benjamin (Master 1721)   271
Bradshaw, John   196
Branson, William (Master 1750)   271
brasses, monumental *see* tombs, monuments and brasses
Bread Street
   All Hallows Bread Street   177
   property of Merchant Taylors' Company   206
   stalls and shops   60, 174, 185, 188
Brecknock, David   63
Brembre, Nicholas (Mayor 1383, 1384)   72–73
Brentford (Middx)   187
Breton, John (Master 1513)   270
Brett, John   222n9
Brettar, John, alias Cooke   129
Breux, Thomas (Master 1450)   269
Brewer, David William (Master 2001)   265, 273
Brewers' Company   5, 33n13
Bridewell   136, 177
Bridge, John   205
Bridges, William   112

Bright, Robert   266
Brighton (Sussex)   260
Bristall, Richard (Master 1474)   269
Bristol   6, 52, 60, 120, 121
Bristow, George (Clerk 1763–1802)   275
Broad Street *see* Threadneedle Street
Brome, John (Master 1771)   271
Brome, John (Master 1787)   271
Bromefelde, Thomas (Master 1498)   270
Bromley, Sir Thomas   135
Brooke, Joseph (Master 1710)   271
Brooke, Thomas (Master 1545–46)   270
Browne, Sir Richard (Lord Mayor 1660)   199–200
Browne, Thomas (Master 1566)   127, 133, 270
Brownswerd, John   112–13
Brownyng, William   43
Brynchele, John (Clerk before 1398–1420)   43, 275
Brynningham, Richard   135
Buck, William   115
Buckeridge, John, Bishop of Ely   160
Buckett, Henry   128
Buckley, Denys Burton (Master 1972)   273
Buckton, George (Master 1835)   272
Budge Bachelors   206
Budge Row   99
Buk, John (Master 1398)   269
Buk, William (Master 1488)   270
Bukberd, Ralph   65
Bull, John   129, 159, 162, 163, 163n16
Bull, Laetitia, m. Robert Dowe   176
Bulley, John   152
Bullinger, Heinrich   102, 103
Burbeck, Edward   138
Burbidge, Thomas Bulcock (Master 1825)   272
Burgeys, Thomas (Master 1467)   269
Burghley, Lord *see* Cecil, William
Burley, Sir Richard de   25
Burnand, Arthur (Master 1965)   273
Burnard, Revd John   244
Burnsall (W.R. Yorks.)   174, 175, *176*
Burton, William   193
Bury, John de (Master 1423)   269
Bushell, Edward (Master 1680)   271
Buswell, John (Master 1814)   230, 272
butchers, mistery   11, 39
Butler, James, 1st Duke of Ormonde   218
Butson, James   137

C
Calais (France)   29, 78, 94, 148
   Company of the Staple   65, *95*
Calixtus III, Pope   25
Cambridge
   Caius College   211
   Emmanuel College   194
   King's College   123

Magdalene College   206
Merton Hall (later Newnham College)   245
Pembroke College   168, 194
St Catharine's College   117, 118
university   216, 250
  Craven Scholarships   175
Camden, William   154
camels, supporters of Merchant Taylors' Company arms   149, 200, 201
Campbell, Robert, *The London Tradesman*   233–34
Campbell, Revd Thomas   250
Campden Hill (Kensington, Middx), Phillimore Gardens   242
Campion, Edmund   120, 121
Cannon Street (Candlewick Street)   63, 205
Canterbury (Kent)   120
  Archbishops of   23, 170
    see also Coggan; Cranmer; Juxon, William; Laud; Parker; Runcie
  Cathedral, Black Prince's *jupon*   50, *51*
  King's School   258
CAPITB (Clothing and Allied Products Industry Training Board)   266
cappers   11, 86
Carent, Elizabeth, m. Thomas Juxon   189
Carew, Nicholas   63
Carleton, Thomas   13, 23, 50, 72
Carmynowe, Thomas   64–65
Carpenter, John   110
Carpenter, William   237
Carpenters' Company   138
Carringtone, John   134
Carter, John   194
Carter, Revd Robert   244
Carter, Thomas   194
Cartwright, Revd Robert   229
Cartwright, Thomas   203, 222n9
Carys, John   129
Case, Denis   135
Castle Baynard ward   115
  see also Baynard's Castle
Caston, John (Master 1426)   269
Catherine of Braganza, Queen   200, *201*, 225
Catholicism/recusancy
  in Reformation   98, 101, 103–07, 118
  later 16th cent.   153, 155, 157–58
  17th cent.   169–70, 188, 194, 211, 212, 218, 219
Cave, Sir Ambrose   142
Cavendish, Hugh   28
Cavendish, John (Master 1413)   269
Cecil, Robert, Earl of Salisbury   163n15, 166, 178
Cecil, William, Lord Burghley   138, 157
Central St Martins College of Art and Design   266
Chadwick, James   215
Chancery Lane *see* Public Record Office

chantries   23, 25–26, 37, 43, 72
  associated with schools   99, 109, 111–12, 113–15, 116, 118
  chantry priests acting as teachers   109
  dissolution   96–99, 112, 114–15, 118
  see also anniversaries (obits)
Chapel Royal   130, 159, 162
chaplains   23–28, 43
  see also chantries
Chaplin, Jerningham (Master 1707)   271
Chapman, William (Master 1428)   76, 269
Charing Cross   104
Charity Commissioners   246
Charles I, King   175, 181–83, *182*, 184–87, 190–91, 193, 199, 219
  death warrant and execution   191, *192*, 195, 196
  portrait at Merchant Taylors' Hall   207
Charles II, King   196, 199, 200, *200*, 211, 212, *212*, 218–19
  and Christ's Hospital   227
  portrait at Merchant Taylors' Hall   215
Charles Edward Stuart (Bonnie Prince Charlie)   232
Charlotte, Queen   237
Charterhouse   157–58
  Merchant Taylors' School at   243–44, *244–45*, 250, 251–55, *253*, 257
Charterhouse School (Charterhouse, later Godalming)   243, 254
charters *see* City of London, charters; Merchant Taylors' Company, charters
Chartres, Richard, Bishop of London   267
Chatham, HMS   267
Chatteris, Thomas (Master 1859)   272
Chaucer, Geoffrey   43, 174
Chaucer, Thomas   20
Cheapside   103, 104, 167, 174, 182, 200
  shops and booths   59, 234
Cheke, John   123
Chelsea (Middx)   146
Cheltenham (Glos.), Dean Close School   265
Cherry, Revd Thomas   235, 240
Chester, George   230
Chester, Dr Matthew   230
Chester, Sir William   143
Chester (Ches.)   112, 178
Chichele, John   77
Child, Coles (Master 1816)   272
Child, Coles (Master 1906)   272
Child, William (Master 1811)   272
Cholwell, William   114, 115
Chote, Albert   242
Christian, Prince of Anhalt   175
Christ's Hospital   105, 107, 121, 138, 175, 176, 227
churches and parishes (City of London)
  All Hallows Bread Street   177
  All Hallows Barking (by the Tower)   190

churches and parishes (City of London) (*continued*)
  St Alban Wood Street, parish   23, 59
  St Andrew Undershaft
    church   93, 116, 154, 175; Offley monument   Col. Pl. XIII; Stow monument   155–56, *156*, 249, 265–66
    parish   216
  St Antholin
    church   14, 175
    parish   174, 216
  St Bartholomew by the Exchange   99
  St Benet Fink
    church   43
    parish   13, 16, 102, 137
  St Botolph Aldgate
    church, Dowe monument   176, Col. Pl. XIII
    parish   176–77
  St Botolph without Bishopsgate, parish   246
  St Dionis Backchurch   265
  St Dunstan in the East   110
  St Dunstan in the West, Dacres brass   *83*
  St Giles Cripplegate, parish   216
  St Helen Bishopsgate   26, *27*, 160, 243
  St James Garlickhithe, parish   63
  St John Walbrook   14
  St Katherine Cree   44, 207
  St Lawrence Pountney, parish   122
  St Margaret Bridge Street   100, 102
  St Martin Outwich
    church   25–26, *26*, 28, 29, 42, 199; anniversary (obit) for Henry VII   22, 86, 95; in Great Fire   202
    parish   13, 25, Col. Pl. XI; *see also* Merchant Taylors' Hall
    rectors   20
  St Martin in the Vintry, parish   113
  St Mary Abchurch, parish   37
  St Mary Aldermanbury   116
    lectionary (Epistles and Gospels) presented by Sir Stephen Jenyns   6, 115, Col. Pls II, VIII
  St Mary Aldermary
    church   56, 240
    parish   30
  St Mary le Bow
    church   14, 110, *172*
    parish   231
  St Mary Woolnoth
    church   37, 113
    parish   29, 155
  St Michael Cornhill   152, 160, 178
  St Mildred in the Poultry, parish   206
  St Olave Silver Street   44
  St Paul's Cathedral *see* St Paul's Cathedral
  St Peter Cornhill
    church   27
    parish   13, 27, 28; *see also* Cornhill
  St Peter Westcheap   38
  St Sepulchre Newgate, Newgate Bell   176, *177*
  St Stephen Coleman Street, parish   99
  St Stephen Walbrook, parish   188
Churchman, John (*fl.* 1405)   25, 26, 29, 73–74
Churchman, John (Master 1594)   270
Churchman, Ozias (Master 1651)   193, 271
City and Guilds of London Institute   243, 250, 266
City of London
  charters   3, 7, 11, 86, 219
  churches *see* churches and parishes
  in Civil War   185–87, 188–91
  Common Council, size and composition   4, 71–72, 77, 99
  Court of Aldermen   4, 7, 38, 77
    annual elections introduced (1376)   71
    liveries worn by   64
    and mayoral elections   76, 77, 84
    see also aldermen, tailors as
  and defence of Calais   78, 94
  freemen *see* freedom of City
  funds raised from livery companies   78, 94, 142, 143, 144–45, 151
  government
    13th–15th cent.   3–5, 6–7, 50, 71–89
    see also Common Council (above); Court of Aldermen (above); Mayor (Lord Mayor), office of; Sheriff (below)
  liveries worn by City officials and representatives   63–64
  loans and grants to Crown
    14th–16th cent.   78, 94, 151
    17th cent.   183, 184, 186–87, 188, 201, 202
  and Mary I's succession   103
  Mayors *see* Mayor (Lord Mayor), office of
  members of parliament   64, 83, 185, 225
  parishes *see* churches and parishes
  population   3, 35, 71, 151
  port, customs accounts   65, 83
  reforms proposed, 19th cent.   237, 243, 246–47
  regulation of apprenticeship   53, 55
  regulation of stall-holders   60
  relations with Merchant Taylors' Company
    to 1500   71–89
    16th cent.   142–46
  Sheriff, office of   3–4, 76
  Trained Bands   146, 185, 187, 189
  and Ulster Plantation   171–73, 183, 185
  and Virginia settlement   173
  wards   4, 6, 7, 71, 72
    see also individual wards by name
  watch   80, 145–46
  and Wyatt's rebellion   103–07
  see also Guildhall; livery companies; Royal Exchange
City of London Regiment   267
City Press, The   249

Civil War   181–97, 199, 217
Clarence, Dukes of *see* George, Duke of Clarence; Thomas, Duke of Clarence
Clarendon, Earls of *see* Hyde, Edward
Clarendon Commission   243
Clark, Charles Stanley Gordon (Master 1907)   272
Clark, John Stanley Gordon (Master 1950, 1969)   272, 273
Clark, Revd Joseph   230, 244
Clarke, Edward (Master 1690)   222n6, 271
Clarke, Martin Courtenay (Master 1997)   265, 273
Clarkson, Nathaniel (Master 1781)   226, 271
Clauson, Albert Charles (Master 1915, 1920)   265, 272
clergy
 members of Fraternity of St John the Baptist   20–21, 24, 28
 see also chantries; chaplains
Clerk, John   60
Clerk, office of *see* Merchant Taylors' Company, Clerk, office of
Clerkenwell, priory of St John of Jerusalem   41, 42
Cliff, ——   128
Cliffe, Allane (Master 1669)   271
Clifton-Brown, Anthony George (Master 1945)   272
Clive, Robert, Lord   227
Clode, Charles Mathew (Master 1873)   238, 242–43, 251, *261*, 272, Col. Pl. XXI
 Early History of the Guild of Merchant Taylors (1888)   86–87
 Memorials of the Guild of Merchant Taylors (1875)   9, 242–43, 247
Clode, George   238
Clode, Walter Baker (Master 1904)   272
Clopton, Robert (Mayor 1441)   76, 77
Close, Francis, Dean of Carlisle   265
cloth finishers   65, 141–42, 177
 see also dyers; fullers; shearmen
cloth trade
 15th–16th cent.   57, 62, 63, 64–66, 74–76, 83, 86, 141, 151
 17th cent.   166
cloth yard, silver   59, *60*, 94, 221
clothing
 piccadills   178, 181
 ready-made garments   220, 238
 second-hand   52–53, 66
 uniforms, Civil War   188
 see also Great Wardrobe; linen armour; liveries; tailor's craft
Clothing and Allied Products Industry Training Board (CAPITB)   266
Clothworkers' Company
 banquet to celebrate Culloden   232
 charitable activities   107n34
 and City and Guilds of London Institute   243
 and expedition to Le Havre   148
 and Irish settlement   173, 185, 232, 242
 James I and   159, 160
 origins   39, 87
 relations with Merchant Taylors' Company   141–42, 157, 201, 220
 Rowe's charity   138
 size, 16th cent.   36
 in Wyatt's rebellion   105
Clough, Henry   82
Clyfton, William (Master 1555)   270
Cobham, Eleanor, Duchess of Gloucester   22
Cockerham, ——   138
Cocks, Isaac (Master 1714)   271
coffee houses   214, 215
Coggan, Donald, Archbishop of Canterbury   254, 266, 267
Coke, Sir Edward and Lady Elizabeth   175
Cokke, William   55
Colborn (Colbron), Henry   216
Colbroke, John (Master 1406)   269
Colchester (Essex)   65
Coleman Street   185
 school   196
Coleraine (Co. Derry)   232
Coles, John   201, 202, 216
Coles, Joyce, wife of John   216
Colet, John, Dean of St Paul's   168
College of Heralds   149
Collins, Christopher William Edward (Master 1967)   273
Cologne, John de   13, 50
Cologne, Roger de   10, 11, 13
Colson, Robert   63
Colston, Timothy (Master 1747)   271
Colwich, Robert (Master 1460)   42, 56, 81, 82–83, 269
Combe, John   *54*
Common Council *see* City of London, Common Council
companies *see* livery companies
Complin, Edward (Master 1821)   230, 272
Complin, Edward Thomas (Master 1849)   272
convalescent homes   246, 250, 252
Cony, John   51
Cook, Arthur Lionel Fitzroy (Master 1926)   272
Cooke, John, and wife (*fl.* 1564)   138
Cooke, John, alias Brettar (*fl.* 1577)   129
Cooper, Henry   128
Cooper, Robert   166
Cooper, Samuel   239
Cooper, Walter (Master 1946)   272
Copthall   139n44
Corbett, Humfrey (Master 1603)   270
Cordwainers' Company   41, 72, 73, 81
Cornhill, Richard (Master 1506)   117, 270
Cornhill
 mansion of Crepin family (?'*viell' hostiell*')   13, 14, 16, 110
 St Michael Cornhill, church   152, 160, 178

Cornhill (*continued*)
   St Peter Cornhill, church and parish   13, 27, 28
   schools   110
   White Lion Court   16
   see also Royal Exchange
coronations   61–62
   Edward IV   78
   Elizabeth I   146
   Elizabeth of York   80
   Henry VII   22, 26, 62, 64, 84
   Mary I   103
   Richard III and Anne   62, 64
'corporations'   74
   see also 'incorporation'
Costeker, John (Master 1853)   272
Costeker, William (Master 1818)   272
Costerdyne, George   173, 232
Cosyn, Nicholas (Master 1549)   97, 101–02, 270
Cottesbroke, William   77
Cotton, Edward (Master 1627)   270
Cotton, Sir Robert   154, 242
Cotton, Thomas (Master 1486)   270
Coulthirst, Robert   *145*
Courtenay family, Earls of Devon   16
Courts of Assistants   38–39
   see also Merchant Taylors' Company, Court of Assistants
Cove-Smith, Ronald   252–53
Covent Garden   181
Coventry (Warwicks.)   22, 120, 121, 193
Coverdale, Miles, Bishop of Exeter   102, *102*, 129, 137
Coverdale, William   129, 137
Cowling, Henry (Master 1754)   271
Cowper, John (Master 1722)   271
Cragge, George   128
Crane, ——   80
Crane Court   194
Cranmer, Thomas, Archbishop of Canterbury   103
Craven family   174, 175
Craven, Sir William (Lord Mayor 1610)   174–75, 215, Col. Pl. XVIII
Creek, John   41, 74
Crepin family   14
Crepin, Edmund   13, 14, 16
Crich, Edmund (Master 1624)   270
Criche, John   227
Crick (Northants.)   175
Crispe, Abigail, m. Abraham Reynardson   190
Crispe, Sir Nicholas   182, 190
Crofte, Richard   128
Cromwell, Oliver   183, 190, 191, *192*, 199, 219
Cromwell, Richard   189
Cromwell, Thomas   101–02
Crosby, Sir John   21
Crosby (Lancs.) *see* Great Crosby
Crosse, Samuel   193

Crosthwaite, John Durnford (Master 1943, 1956)   272
Crown
   charters to Merchant Taylors' Company *see* Merchant Taylors' Company, charters
   Great Wardrobe   13, 50, 52, 61–63, 146, 181
   and Reformation   96–97
   relations with Merchant Taylors' Company and City
      14th–15th cent.   13, 50–52, 62, 64, 71–89; loans and grants   78
      16th cent.   62–63, 146–49; loans and grants   94, 151
      17th cent., loans and grants   183, 184, 186–87, 188, 201, 202
   and statute of mortmain (1391)   14, 73–74, 96
   see also individual monarchs by name
Cubitt, Thomas   239
Cuckfield (Sussex)   116
   schools   116–18
Culloden, Battle of (1746)   232
Cundy, Thomas (Master 1879)   272
Customs House   156
Cuthbert, Thomas (Master 1698)   271
Cutler, Edward   137
cutters, tailors', proposed registration   250
cutting boards ('shaping boards')   59, 130, 209n5

D
Dacres, Henry (Master 1514)   83, *83*, 132, 270
Dalbeney, Robert *see* Dawbeney
Danby, Earls of *see* Osborne
Dance, George, the younger (Master 1794)   237, 271
Dandridge, James (Master 1752)   271
Dandridge, Joseph (Master 1740)   271
Dandy, Andrew   215
Darling, John   215
Darwyn, Thomas (Master 1693)   271
Daubrie, Robert   229
Davenant, Ralph   99
Davenport, John (Master 1775)   271
Davies, John (Clerk 1803–06)   275
Davis, Oliver Henry (Master 1877)   272
Davis, Thomas (Master 1780)   271
Davy, Henry   61
Davy, John   128
Davy, Thomas (Master 1436)   269
Dawbeney (Dalbeney), Robert (Master 1544)   30, 270
Dawbney, Arthur (Master 1574)   128, 270
Dawson, Joseph (Master 1729)   271
Dawson, William (Master 1746)   271
de Blank, Joost, Archbishop of Cape Town   254
de Mole, John Bamber (Clerk 1830–45)   275
Deane, William (Master 1786)   271
Dekker, Thomas   174
Delves, Nicholas (Master 1662)   201, 214, 271
Derby, John (Master 1461)   269

Derby, William de   10
Derby, Earls of   245
    see also Henry IV, King
Desmond, Sir John   135
Desmond, Earls of see Fitzmaurice
Detmar, L. G.   *207*
Devereux, Robert, 3rd Earl of Essex   166
Devon, Earls of   16
Dicke, Nicholas   136
Dillingham, Theophilus (Master 1739)   271
Dinham family (of Hartland and Nutwell, Devon)   63
Dinham family (of Lifton, Devon)   113
Dinham, John (of Lifton, Devon)   114
Dinham, Thomasine, prioress of Cornworthy   113
Disraeli, Benjamin, 1st Earl of Beaconsfield   243
Dissolution see chantries; Reformation
Ditcher, William, alias Tetforde   153
Dixon, John (Master 1826)   272
Dobree, Bonamy (Master 1840)   272
Dobree, Samuel (Master 1806)   272
Doctors' Commons, school   196
Dodson, William (Master 1686)   271
Dodworth, William (Master 1591)   128, 270
Doget, John (Master 1500)   270
Dolfyn, Walter   88n28
Donkyn, Robert   138, 246
Dorebarr, Thomas   203
Dormibee, ——   220
doublets   52, 58, 67
Dove Bros, Messrs   262
Dover (Kent)   80
Dowe, Alice, wife of Henry   175–76
Dowe, Henry   175
Dowe, Laetitia, wife of Robert   176
Dowe, Robert (Master 1578)   131, 154, 168, 175–77, 215, 270, Col. Pl. X
    monument   176, Col. Pl. XIII
Dowgate ward   115
Downe, Thomas   100, 101
Downes, Revd John   229
drama
    masque for Charles I and Henrietta Maria (1634)   183
    plays performed by Merchant Taylors' School   123, 201, 227–28
Draper, Robert (Master 1628)   194, 270
Drapers' Company   5, 64, 72, 78, 79, 82
    and City and Guilds of London Institute   243
    Drapers' Hall   84
    and education   111
    fraternity   14, 17n26
    members of Fraternity of St John the Baptist   21–22, 23
    relations with Merchant Taylors' Company   21–22, 64, 65, 74–77, 81–82, 84, 86, 87, 141
Drayton, John   51, 61

dressmaking, apprenticeships in, 20th cent.   250
Drewe, Laurence   129
Drewry, Midshipman George Leslie, VC   252
Drury Lane, theatre   227–28
du Boys, John   148
Ducane (Duncane), James   181
Ducat, David (Master 1964)   273
Duckett, Sir Lionel (Lord Mayor 1573)   148
Dudley, Ambrose, Earl of Warwick   129, 148
Dudley, Lord Guildford   103
Dudley, Robert, Earl of Leicester   157
Dugard, William   193, 195–97
Duncane, James see Ducane
Dunedin (New Zealand)   250
Dunwich (Suffolk)   225
Duplage, Robert (Master 1481)   62, 270
Durbin, Leslie   262
Durham, Bishops of see Tunstall
Durst, Alan   257
Duryvale, William (Clerk 1487–92)   *37, 44*, 275
Dutch see Netherlands
Dyer, Joseph (Master 1766)   271
dyers   60, 65, 136
Dymock, John (Master 1388)   269

E
Eade, Jonathan (Master 1796)   271
East India Company   165, 175, 190, 225, 227, 235
Eastcheap   185
Eastwood, Charles Seymour (Master 1944)   272
Eaton, Michael (Master 1798)   271
Eden, John   134–35
Edmondson, Richard (Master 1711)   271
education
    Education Act (1870)   242
    Education Act (1902)   242
    see also Cambridge; Merchant Taylors' Company, schools; Oxford; schools
Edward I, King   7, 9
Edward II, King   7
Edward III, King   13, 30, 51, 53, 174
    charter (letters patent) (1327)   *9*, 11, 50, 71, 73
Edward IV, King   61, 78, 81, 82
Edward V, King   62
Edward VI, King   97, 102–03, 112, 119, 137
Edward VII, King, as Prince of Wales   243–44
Edward the Black Prince   51
    jupon in Canterbury Cathedral   50, *51*
Edward, John   59
Edwardes, John   168
Edwards, Thomas   206, 217
Eggar, T. M. (solicitors)   260
Eggar, Thomas Macdonald (Master 1942)   272
Eikon Basilike   196
Eland, Robert (Master 1402)   269

Elbow Lane   205
Elder, Hugh   265
Eldon, Earls of *see* Scott, John
Elizabeth I, Queen   123, 130, *144*, 145, 158, 165, 166
    Queen's tailors   59, 62–63, 136, 146
    relations with Merchant Taylors' Company   129, 146–49, 151–52, 156
Elizabeth, Duchess of York (later Queen Elizabeth, the Queen Mother)   255, 262, Col. Pl. XXIV
Elizabeth, Princess, later Queen of Bohemia   175, 178, 181, 183
Elizabeth of York, Queen   80
Elliott, William Timbrell (Master 1871)   272
Ellis, John (Master 1656)   271
Ellis, Revd John Joseph   240
Ellis, John Whittaker (Master 1884)   272
Elnor, Bartholomew   194
Elwes, Jeffery (Master 1604)   270
Elwood, Thomas   202, 203
Ely, Bishops of *see* Buckeridge; Wren, Matthew
embroiderers   60, 181
    see also Carleton, Thomas
Englefield, William Alexander Devereux   260
Epping Forest (Essex)   243
equipment *see* tools and equipment
Escombe, William Malcolm Lingard ('Mac') (Master 1941, 1957)   262, 272
Escott, John   186
Essex, William   72
Essex, Earls of *see* Devereux
Estfield, Sir William   64
Eton (Bucks.)   117–18, 123
evangelicals *see* Protestantism
Evans, Allen (Master 1753)   271
Evans, Evan (Master 1705)   271
Evans, Henry   131
Evans, Pierce   129
Evelyn, John   200, 215, 222n40, 231
Evelyn, Mary   222n40
Everard, ——   201
Evesham (Worcs.)   188
'Evil May Day' (1517)   81
Ewart, John (Master 1861)   272
Ewart, John (Master 1899)   272
Ewelme (Oxon.), almshouses   29
Eworth, Hans   Col. Pl. XII
Exeter (Devon)   6, 120
    Bishops of *see* Coverdale, Miles
Exilbe, Miles   133–34
Exton, Nicholas (Mayor 1386, 1387)   73
Eyre, Simon   110–11

F
Fabyan, Robert   84
Fahey, James   *241*, Col. Pl. XIX
Fairfax, Thomas, 3rd Lord   190
Fairfax-Lucy, Ewen Aylmer Robert Ramsay (Clerk 1938–48)   260, 275
Faithfull, Francis Grantham (Clerk 1870–90)   275
Farewell, Richard   218
Farington, William   234
Farman, Patrick   *145*
Farnell, Alexander (Master 1424)   65, 269
Farringdon   244
Farthinghoe (Northants.)   111
Fastolf, Sir John   20
Fauconer, John (Master 1400)   269
Fayreford, John (Master 1464)   269
Feake, Christopher   188
feasting
    Mayor's election banquet   79, 94, 175
    see also Merchant Taylors' Hall, *events at*
Federation of Merchant Tailors   266
Fell, John   194–95
Fenchurch Street   137, 156
Fenescales, Robert (Master 1420)   64, 269
Fenning, James (Master 1882)   245, 247, 272
Fenwick, Edward (Master 1704)   271
Ferrers, Peter (Beadle)   29, 45, 88n34
Field, John (Master 1800)   271
Fifth Monarchy men   188, 200
Figge, Thomas   128–29
Fillilode, Thomas (Clerk 1456–64)   44, 275
Finch, Francis   188
Finch Lane   159, 205
Finnis, Charles Roche (Master 1923; Clerk 1924–38)   254, 272, 275
Firman, William   138
First World War   252, 254, 257, 258
Firth, Joseph Firth Bottomley   237, 246
Fisher, John, Gentleman of the Chapel Royal   130
Fisher, Captain John   241
Fisher, Richard (Master 1827)   272
Fisher, Samuel (Clerk 1845–70)   275
Fisher, Thomas   Col. Pl. XIII
fishmongers, mistery   5, 11, 39
Fishmongers' Company   72, 73, 78, 79, 249
    Fishmongers' Hall   203, 207
    pageant decoration   Col. Pl. XVII
Fitzhugh, Robert, Bishop of London   28
Fitzjames, Richard, Bishop of London   100
Fitzmaurice, Maurice, Earl of Desmond   25
FitzThedmar, Arnold   7, 8
FitzThomas, Thomas (Mayor 1261–65)   7
Fitzwilliam, William (Master 1499)   84, 87, 270
Five Members   185, 186
flax-women   178
Fleet Street   104, 113, 206
    Salisbury Court   183
Fleetwood, Robert   157

Fleetwood, William, Recorder of London   157–58
Fletcher, Hanslip   *253*
Fletcher, James   221
Fletcher, John Thompson (Master 1867)   272
Fletcher, Thomas (*fl.* 1568)   129
Fletcher, Thomas (*fl.* 1645)   190
Florence, merchants from   78, 103
Florey, James   203
Flower, Edmund (Master 1503)   22, 86, 99, 116–18, 270
Fludd, David   135
Forde, Hector   207
Fordham, Emily   246
'foreigns' *see* immigrants
Forest Gate (Essex), All Saints, Drewry memorial window   252
Forman, John (Master 1717)   271
Forte, Henry   208
Foster, Dr —— (*fl.* 1610)   170
Foster, John (Master 1672)   271
Foster, William (Master 1448)   269
Fowke, John   185
Foxe, John, *Acts and Monuments*   99, 100, *101*, *105*, 118
Foxe, Richard   121
Foy, John   168
Foyle & Londonderry College *see* Londonderry
Frampton, George James (Master 1918)   272
France
    Revolutionary and Napoleonic Wars (1793–1815)   232, 234, 238
    see also Calais; La Rochelle; Le Havre; Paris; Strasbourg
Franklin-Adams, Bernard Inman (Master 1934, 1948)   272
Franklin-Adams, Patrick Michael (Master 1998)   273
Franks, Robert Hugh   238
fraternities (guilds)   5–6, 14, 23, 28, 41, 73
    Bedford   118
    Cuckfield   116
    Grocers' Company   6, 8, 14
    Parish Clerks   22
    Pewterers' Company   42
    Skinners' Company
        Fraternity of the Assumption   42
        Fraternity of Corpus Christi   6, 11, 14, 22, 23, 82
    tailors *see* Bachelors' Company; Fraternity of St John the Baptist
    see also misteries
Fraternity of St John the Baptist   7–11, 14–16, 19–34, 37–38
    chapels and chaplains   23–28, 43
    membership   19–20, 28–30, 35, 36
        'honorary' members   19–23, 24, 28
    reincorporated as Merchant Taylors' Company (1503)   13, 85
    and statute of mortmain   14, 73–74
    see also Merchant Taylors' Company; Tailors and Linen-Armourers

Frederick, Count Palatine, later King of Bohemia   178, 181, 183
Frederick-William III, King of Prussia   234
'free sowers'   58
freedom of City
    means of obtaining   7, 11, 39, 237
        by apprenticeship   3, 36, 56, 127–28
        by patrimony   3, 129
        by redemption   3, 36, 129
    see also Merchant Taylors' Company, freemen
Freemasons   227
Freeth, Stephen   265
Friday Street   97, 166, 211
    Saracen's Head   48n44, 94, 214
Fry, Frederick Morris (Master 1895, 1911)   249, 272
Fuljambe family   132
Fuljambe, Nicholas (Clerk 1571–75)   119, 131–32, 136, 251, 275
Fuller, Benjamin (Master 1758)   271
fullers   39, 58, 60, 65
Fulthorp, John (Master 1409)   269
funerals of Merchant Taylors, 15th–16th cent.   28, 29–31
    see also hearse-cloths
furs *see* parmenters; skinners
Fyfield, manor (Oxon.)   120
Fyge, William (Master 1442)   269
Fyshe, Walter (Master 1576)   62–63, 136, 146, 148, 270

G
Gale, Robert (Master 1652)   271
Galle, Henry   63, 113
Galle, William (Master 1471)   269
gambesons   50
    see also linen armour
Gamble, Ellis   218
Gane, Irving Blanchard (Master 1959)   273
Gardiner, Roger (Master 1648)   271
Gardiner, Stephen, Bishop of Winchester   102, 104, 105
Gardner, Arthur   137
Garlickhithe   41
    St James Garlickhithe, parish   63
Garrett, George   185
Garrick, David   227–28
Gascony, trade with   66, 84
Gauden, John, Bishop of Worcester   196
Gay, Thomas (Master 1445)   63, 269
Gedney, John (Mayor 1427–28, 1447–48)   21
Geeve, Thomas (Master 1777)   271
Gelsthorp, William (Master 1644)   271
Genetas, Benedict   58
Genoa, trade with   66, 103
Gentlemen Ushers   206
George III, King   232, 237
George IV, King, as Prince Regent   234, 235
George VI, King, as Duke of York   255

George, Duke of Clarence   20, 81
George, Edward (Master 1776)   271
Gerard, *see also* Jerrard
Gerard, Gilbert   129
Germany
   schoolboys from, visit Merchant Taylors' School
     (1913)   251–52
   see also Magdeburg
Gerveys, William   38
Gheeraerts, Marcus, the Younger   Col. Pl. XVIII
Gibbon, Geoffrey (Master 1431)   269
Gibbons, Grinling   219, 231
Gibbons, William   208
Gibbs, Antony Durant (Master 1977)   273
Gibbs, Joan   166
Gibbs, Hon. Walter Durant (Master 1932)   258, 272
Gibson, John   244, 256
Gibson, Richard (Master 1530)   270
Gibsone, Francis   128
Giles, Nathaniel   159, 162, 163
Gill, John Blacket (Master 1887)   272
Gilliat, Algernon Edward (Master 1919)   272
Gilliat, Douglas Algernon (Master 1961)   273
Gilpin, William (Master 1844)   272
girdlers   11
Glass, Philip (Master 1764)   271
Gloucester   120
   Bishops of *see* Thompson, Giles
   Parliament held at, 15th cent.   51, 61
Gloucester, Dukes and Duchesses of *see* Cobham,
   Eleanor; Humfrey, Duke of Gloucester; Richard III,
   King
Goad, John   202, 207, 211, 212, *213*, 216
God, John (Master 1565)   270
God Save the King, origins   163n16
Godalming (Surrey) *see* Charterhouse School
Godfrey, Sir Edmund Berry   212
Godfrey, Thomas   55, 109
Goffage, John   242
Golden Shears tailoring competition   266
Goldney, Gabriel Prior (Master 1902)   272
Goldsmiths' Company   6, 7, 8, 11, 44, 72, 73, 77
   apprentices   109
   attendance at royal events   80
   charitable activities   28
   charters   73, 74
   in Civil War   190
   and dissolution of chantries   97
   and education   111
   fraternity of St Dunstan   6
   Goldsmiths' Hall   72
   loans to Henry VII   78
   and May Day Muster (1572)   148–49
   and mosaic decoration of St Paul's Cathedral   249
Gonne, John (Master 1521)   270
Gooch, Henry Cubitt (Master 1929)   272

Goodman, —— (16th cent.)   154
Goodman, William   Col. Pl. XI
Gordon, Charles (Master 1860)   272
Gore, Gerard (Master 1567)   137, 270
Gore, Sir John (Lord Mayor 1624)   174
Gore, Ralph (Master 1623)   194, 270
Gore, Richard (Master 1602)   270
Goswell Street   243
Gould, William (Master 1728)   271
Gourge, Stephen   115
Gouson, Sackford (Master 1653)   271
Gower, John   174
Grafton, Richard   153
Graham, William (Master 1930)   272
grammar schools *see* schools
Gravenor, ——, Quartermaster-General   190
Graves, James (Master 1883)   272
Gray, Nicholas   194
Graye, Anne, wife of Robert   177
Graye, Robert   177–78, Col. Pl. X
Gray's Inn   157
Great Crosby (Lancs.)
   chapel   195, 229, 230
   grammar school
     founded 1620   194
     17th cent.   193, 194–95, 201, 203–05, 216
     18th–19th cent.   229–30, 241–42, 244–45
     20th cent.   252, 266, 267
   school for girls (Halsall bequest)   230
   school for girls (opened 1888)   245–46, *257*, 258, 266,
     267
Great Fire (1666)   202, 260
Great Missenden (Bucks.)   158
'Great Twelve' companies   14, 87
   see also livery companies
Great Wardrobe   13, 50, 52, 61–63, 146, 181
Great Yarmouth (Norfolk)   145
Green, Revd Thomas   228
Greenhill, Joseph (Master 1701)   271
Greenwich (Kent)   80, 226
   May Day Muster (1572)   148–49
Gregory, Matthew   61
Grene, Edmund   118–19
Grene, William (Master 1507)   270
Grenewell, William (Master 1618)   270
Gresham, Sir Richard (Lord Mayor 1538)   143
Gresham, Sir Thomas   129, 142, 143
Gresham College, professors   129, 159, 168
Gresyle, Thomas   45
Greville, Sir Fulk   156
Grey, Sir George   243
Grey, Lady Jane   103
Grey, William, Bishop of London   21
Grey Friars monastery, church, Jenyns monument   96,
   116, Col. Pl. VIII

Griffith, Richard   205
Griggs, Michael (Master 1632)   270
Grindal, Edmund, Bishop of London   124, 153
Grinking, ——   175
Grocers' Company   5, 6, 39, 72–73, 78, 79, 82
    charitable activities   107n34
    claim to 'ypocrise house'   132
    contributions towards Royal Exchange   144
    fraternity of St Antholin   6, 8, 14
    Grocers' Hall   79, 94
    minute books   9
Grose-Hodge, Humfrey   254
Guild of St George *see* Artillery Company
Guilden Morden (Cambs.)   242
Guildhall
    apprentices enrolled at   53
    building works, 15th–16th cent.   78–79, 94
    freedom granted at   56
    function in City government   4
    Parliament held at (1642)   185
Guildhall Library   265
guilds *see* fraternities
Gurney, Sir Richard (Lord Mayor 1641)   184–85, 186, 187
Gwynn, Matthew   168
Gyldeford, Robert de   10
Gylle, John (Master 1451)   269

H
haberdashers   60, 151, 166
Haberdashers' Company   78, 86, 130, 190
    Haberdashers' Hall   97
Haile, Thomas   127
Hailey, Malcolm, Lord   244
Haines, Edward   220
Hakeday, Richard   20
Hale, Canon William   249
Halifax, Earls of *see* Savile
Hall, Richard (Master 1516)   270
Hall, Robert   202
Halliday, Sir Leonard (Lord Mayor 1605)   158–59
Halsall, Revd Anthony   230
Halsall, Catharine   230
Halton, Thomas (Master 1688)   271
Ham (Kent)   228
Ham House (Surrey), fire-irons   219
Hamer, Ralph   177
Hampden, John (one of Five Members)   185, 186
Hampson, Henry (Master 1664)   271
Hampstead Garden Suburb (Middx),
    St Jude-on-the-Hill, Raphael memorial   252
Hampton Court (Middx)   186, 200
Hanbury, John Capel (Master 1813)   272
Handel, George Frederick   231
Hanse merchants   103

Hanson, Sir Reginald (Master 1889)   263n29, 272
Harbour Master's Office   241
Harper, Alice, wife of Sir William   118, 119
Harper, Margaret, wife of Sir William   119, 138
Harper, Sir William (Master 1553)   93, 95, 118–19, 123, 148, 270
    house in Lombard Street   118, 119, 137
    as Lord Mayor (1561)   118, 119, 124, 142
Harpur Trust   119
Harrington, Sir James   196–97
Harris, —— (*fl.* 1660s)   206
Harris, John   104
Harris, Renatus   265
Harris, Thomas (Master 1718)   271
Harrison, *see also* Haryson
Harrison, Edmund   181
Harrison, John   194, 203, 230
Harrison, Stephen   *172*
Harrisone, Nicholas   132
Hart, Ernest Parsons   257
Hartlebury Castle (Worcs.)   188
Hartopp, Valentine   173
Hartshorne, John William (Master 1842)   272
Harvey, William   196
Haryson, *see also* Harrison
Haryson, Richard   128
Haselfoote, Thomas (Clerk 1575–87)   132, 275
Hassell, John (Master 1725)   271
Hastings (Sussex)   211
Hatchett, Thomas (Master 1691)   271
Hatherley, John (Mayor 1442)   77
hatters   86
Hatton, Sir Christopher   129
Hawes, Sir James   129
Hawes, Robert (Master 1580)   137, 270
Hawkwood, Sir John   53, 174
Hayles, Stephen   123
Hayne, William   168, 194
Hayward, Edmund   232
Hayward, William (Master 1809)   272
Hazelrigg, Sir Arthur (one of Five Members)   185, 186
Hazlitt, W. C.   241
Hearne, ——   158
hearse-cloths
    c. 1480–1500   13, 30, *30*, 31, 98, 237, 260, *Frontispiece*
    c. 1520–40   30–31, 98, 237, 260, Col. Pl. II
Heaumer, Hugh le   50
Hedon, Robert   118
Heed, John (Master 1487)   40, 270
Helston (Cornwall)   189
Hemming, John   161
Hendley, Hugh (Master 1590)   270
Henly, John (Master 1714)   271
Henrietta Maria, Queen   182, 183, 186
Henry III, King   6, 8

Henry IV, King 51, 61, *75*
  as Earl of Derby 63
Henry V, King 20, 51, 61, 79
Henry VI, King 46, 61, 76, 78
Henry VII, King 78, 79–80, 84, *85*, 86, 87, 94
  anniversary (obit) for 22, 86, 95
  and charter of Merchant Taylors' Company (1503) 13, 22, 84–87, 93, 95, Col. Pl. VI
  coronation 22, 26, 62, 64, 84
  King's tailors 56, 59, 61, 62, 63
  member of Fraternity of St John the Baptist 22
Henry VIII, King 81, 86, 93, 102, 183
Henry, Prince of Wales (son of James I) 159, 160, 162, 181
Heralds, College of 149
Hereford, Earls of *see* Bohun
heresy, in Reformation 99, 100
  see also Protestantism
Heron, HMS 267
Heron-Maxwell, John Robert (Master 1905) 272
Herring, Samuel (Master 1751) 271
Hert, William (Master 1491) 37, 270
Hervy, Walter (Mayor 1272–73) 7
Heryot, William (Mayor 1481) 79
Hessey, Revd James Augustus 243
Heton, George (Master 1556) 145, 270
Heton, William 133
Hettie, William 122
Hexham (Northumb.) 54
Heygate, Ralph 201
Heylyn, Peter 168
Hide(s), John 129, *130*
Hill, Henry 107n14
Hilles, Barnabas (Clerk 1587) 275
Hilles, Gerson 166
Hilles, Richard (Master 1561) 29, 104, 136, 137, 166, 270
  evangelicalism 98, 101–03, 106
  and Merchant Taylors' School 106, 122–23, 124
Hitchin (Herts.) 242
Hoccleve, Thomas, 'The Regement of Princes' 49
Hockaday, Sir Arthur 266
Hodgeson, Robert 157
Hodgson, William (Master 1572) 134, 270
Hogarth, William 218
  The Rake's Progress 234
Holbech, Roger (Master 1432) 269
Holborn (Middx) 119
Holborn Viaduct 243
Holden, Charles 256
Holder, Susan, wife of William 188
Holder, William 188
Holgrave, William (Master 1417) 43, 269
Holland, Geoffrey (Master 2000) 273
Holland, Ralph (Master 1419) 39, 56, 64, 74, 76–77, 81, 269

Holland, Sam 262
Holland *see* Netherlands
Holles, Denzil, later 1st Baron (one of Five Members) 185, 186
Hollister, John (Master 1717) 271
Hollister, John (Master 1741) 271
Holmes, Alexander 221
Holmes, Thomas, and wife 153
Holmes, William 231
Holsworthy (Devon) 114
Holte, *see also* Houlte
Holte, Richard (Master 1546) 138, 270
Holy Lamb *see* Lamb of God
Honiwood, Benoni (Master 1663) 271
Honourable Artillery Company *see* Artillery Company
Hooke, Robert 207, *207*, 208, 231, 259
Hope, George 238
Hope, Ralph 146
Hoper, Nicholas (Clerk 1420–after 1445) 43, 275
Hopkins, John (Master 1792) 271
Hopkinson, Henry Lennox (Master 1910) 250–51, 252, 272
Hopkinson, John Montgomerie (Master 1953) 272
Hornby, Christopher 58–59
Horsey, William 100–01
Horsley, John 166
Hoseland, manor (Sussex) 211
hosiers 52, 53
Hoskyns, Charles (Master 1582) 270
Hoskyns, Charles (Master 1616) 270
hospitals (London)
  St Anthony's Hospital (Threadneedle Street) 72
    school 110, 122
  St Bartholomew's Hospital 250, 257
  St Mary of Bethlehem, hospital 14
  St Thomas of Acon, hospital 72
  see also religious houses (London)
Houfe, E. A. S. 262
Houghton, John 178
Houlte, *see also* Holte
Houlte, Richard (Master 1531) 270
Houndsditch 176
Hounsom, John (Master 1799) 271
houpelonds, fashion for 49
hours of work, regulation 66, 67
Howard family, Dukes of Norfolk 63, 212
Howard, Charles, 11th Duke of Norfolk 235
Howard, Sir John (later 1st Duke of Norfolk) 63, 113
Howard, Philip, Earl of Arundel 157
Howard, Thomas, 8th Duke of Norfolk 227
Howdan, Thomas (Master 1505) 270
Howden, Alexander (Master 1908) 272
Howes, Edward 155
Howitt, Anthony Wentworth (Master 1980) 273
Howitt, Harold Gibson (Master 1952) 272

Hubbathorne, Sir Henry (Master 1532; Lord Mayor 1546)   142, 270
Huberstey, Robert   128–29
Huchenson, John (Clerk 1546–71)   131, 275
Huchenson, Ralph   124, *167*, 168
Hullah, Charles Morrice (Master 1843)   272
Hulson, Robert (Master 1569)   148, 174, 270
Humfrey, Duke of Gloucester   20, 22, 32, 76, 78
Humfrey, Anthony, and wife   134
Humfrey, Humfrey   128
Hundred Years' War   20, 49, 71, 77–78
Hunne, Richard   99–101, *101*
Hunt, James (Master 1841)   272
Hunter, Beatrix, m. William Craven   174
Hunter, Sir Claudius   263n29
Hurdis, ——   159
Hutchinson, Samuel (Master 1812)   272
Hyde, Edward, 1st Earl of Clarendon   183, 186, 199
Hyde Park Corner   104
Hymeson, Rowland   60

I
I'Anson, Edward (architect)   243, *244*
I'Anson, Edward Blakeway (Master 1901)   272
illuminated manuscripts
　book of privileges, ordinances, and 'goostly tresoure'   11, 19, 86, 95–96, Col. Pls III, V–VI
　lectionary (Epistles and Gospels) owned by Sir Stephen Jenyns   6, 115, Col. Pls II, VIII
immigrants ('foreigns')   7
　tailors   38, 52, 66, 81, 141, 142, 173, 220
'incorporation'   73–74, 84–87
Ingres, Jean Auguste Dominique   234
Inns of Court   182–83
　see also Gray's Inn; Middle Temple
Ireland
　grants for (1640s)   186, 188
　Merchant Taylors' Company's Irish estate (Ulster Plantation)
　　17th cent.   171–73, 183, 185, 205, 218, 231–32, Col. Pls XIV–XV
　　18th cent.   232
　　19th cent.   242, 243
　soldiers sent to (1566)   148, 152
　trade with, 15th cent.   55, 135
　see also Londonderry
Ironmongers' Company   6, 77
irons see pressing irons
Irving, Sir Henry   249
Isaacson, ——   200
Italy see Florence; Genoa; Venice

J
Jacks, James (Master 1820)   272
Jackson, John (Master 1875)   272
Jackson, William (Master 1845)   272

Jacob, Giles   137
Jacomb, Charles (Master 1854)   272
Jacomb, Charles Reginald (Master 1939)   272
Jacomb, Reginald Benson (Master 1903, 1921)   272
Jakes, John (Master 1552)   270
James I, King   155, 181, 183
　relations with Merchant Taylors' Company and City   158–59, 165–66, 171, 175
　　banquet at Merchant Taylors' Hall (1607)   20, 159–63, 171, 174, 175, 181, 215
　　triumphal procession through City (1604)   171, *172*
James II, King   219–20, *220*
　as Duke of York   211, 218–19, Col. Pl. XX
James Edward Stuart ('Old Pretender')   219
James, Edmund   190
James, Edward (Master 1620)   270
James, Evan Maitland (Clerk 1948–62)   275
Janssens, Cornelius   Col. Pl. XVIII
Jarman, Edward   203
Jasper, Stephen   56, 61
Jeans, Sir James   244
Jeffreys, George (Judge Jeffreys)   219
Jeffries, Alexander Baird   254
Jenkins, Sir Brian Garton (Lord Mayor 1991; Master 1999)   265, 273
Jenkyns, William   138
Jennings, Richard (Master 1824)   240, 272
Jenyns, Margaret, wife of Sir Stephen   115–16
Jenyns, Sir Stephen (Master 1489)   6, 38, 40, 93, 115–16, 270
　as alderman   83, 115
　arms   *117*
　lectionary (Epistles and Gospels)   6, 115, Col. Pls II, VIII
　as Mayor (1508)   79, 87, 115, 142
　as merchant   65, 83
　monument and anniversary (obit)   96, 107n14, 116, Col. Pl. VIII
　as Sheriff   79, 84
　and Wolverhampton Grammar School   115–16, 250
Jerrard, see also Gerard
Jerrard, Nicholas   193
Joans, see also Jones
Joans, Edward (Master 1575)   270
Joans, Evan   135
John, Duke of Bedford   20, 63
John the Baptist, St
　feast of Decollation (29 August)   6, 41, 42
　feast of Nativity (24 June)   6, 9, 25, 31, 36, 73
　　watch held on   145–46
　images and scenes from life   30, 31, 94, 98
　　on hearse-cloths   30, *30*, 31
　　statue after Benedetto da Majano   *261*
　　see also Lamb of God
　as patron of tailors' guilds   6
　　see also Fraternity of St John the Baptist

Johnson, John (Master 1607) 159, 270
Johnson, Richard (Master 1571) 119–20, 270
Johnson, Richard (17th cent.) 166
Johnson, Robert (Master 1886) 272
Johnson, Thomas (Master 1615) 170, 270
Jones, *see also* Joans
Jones, Hugh Edward Hunter (Master 1976) 273
Jones, Inigo 166, 181
Jones, William 146
Jonson, Ben 151, 159, 161, *161*, 162–63
Jordan, John (Master 1457) 269
Jordan, Thomas 218
Joseph, Charles 100–01
journeymen 38, 41, 58, 128, 130
Jowdrell, William (Master 1415) 269
Judde, Andrew 121
jupons 50, *51*
   see also linen armour
Jupp, Richard 232–33
Juxon, Arthur 166
Juxon, Elizabeth, wife of Thomas 189
Juxon, John (*fl.* 1626) 229
Juxon, John (*fl.* 1643) 189
Juxon, Thomas (Master 1605) 270
Juxon, Thomas (1614–72) 188–90
Juxon, William, Bishop of London, later Archbishop of Canterbury 124, 168, 189–90, 191

K
Kekewich, Charles Granville (Master 1913) 272
Kekewich, Piers Keane (Master 1951) 272
Kelly, Sir Gerald Col. Pl. XXIV
Kennington Palace (Surrey) 31
Kentish Town (Middx) 208
Kesteven, Robert de 58
Ketelwell, Henry 88n28
Keyes, Gilbert (Master 1473) 65, 269
Kidde, John 194–95
Killingholme, Robert 110
Kimber, Henry (Master 1894) 272
Kinder, Joseph (Master 1773) 271
King, Samuel 216
King's armourers 13, 23, 50, 51
King's College London 240
King's pavilioners (tent-makers) 13, 51, 61
   see also Yakesley, John de
King's skinners 61
King's/Queen's tailors (serjeant-tailors) 13, 61, 64, 181
   under Henry VII 56, 59, 61, 62, 63
   under Elizabeth I 59, 62–63, 136, 146
Kingsfeild, Christopher Col. Pl. XIII
Kingsland, Simon 173
Kirkleatham (N.R. Yorks.)
   church, Coulthirst brass *145*
   Sir William Turner's Hospital *208*, 210n15

Kirton, *see also* Kyrton
Kirton, Stephen (Master 1542) 99, 270
Kirton (Kyrton), Thomas (Clerk 1464–87) 44, 275
Kneller, Sir Godfrey 215, 219, 259
Knotte, John (Master 1427) 269
Knotte, William (Master 1453) 269
Knox *see* Noxe
Kympton, Edward (Master 1596) 270
Kympton, William (Master 1570) 137, 148, 157, 270
Kyng, John (Master 1433) 269
Kyrkeby, John (Master 1501) 270
Kyron Lane (later Skinners' Lane) 63
Kyrton, *see also* Kirton
Kyrton, Clement (Master 1399) 269

L
La Rochelle (France) 148
Lamb of God (*Agnus Dei*) motif 6, 30, *30*, 82, 94, 159
Lambarde, William 154
Lambeth (Surrey), barge builders of 208, 225, 226
Lancaster 230
Langbourn ward 84
Langdon, William (Master 1459) 269
Langdon-Down, Antony Turnbull (Master 1979; Clerk 1980–85) 273, 275
Langham, George 186
Langland, William, *Piers the Plowman* 65
Langley, Richard (Clerk 1594–1610) 155, 162, 170, 251, 275
Langryk, John 60
Langton, Roland Stephen (Master 1978) 273
Langwith, Ellen, wife of John 37, 58
Langwith, John (Master 1444) 37, 58, 269
Lansdale, —— 159
Lant, Robert (Master 1658) 271
Lasky, Simon 267
Latoner, William (Master 1452) 269
Laud, William, Archbishop of Canterbury 169, 184, *189*, 190, 195
Lauderdale, Dukes of *see* Maitland
Launceston (Cornwall) 114–15, 186
Laurie, Percy Robert (Master 1925) 272
Lavendor, Nathaniel 201
Lawrence, James Clarke 243
Lawrence, Mary 215
Lawrence Pountney Lane 201
Lay, John Watson (Master 1864) 272
Le Havre (France) 148
Le Neve, Edward (Master 1708) 271
Le Neve, Peter 212
le Waleys, Henry (Mayor 1273) 7
Leadenhall 53, 110–11, 154
Leadenhall Street 175
Leamington (Warwicks.) 252
Lee, *see also* Legh; Leigh; Ley

Lee, John (Master 1483)   63, 270
Lee, Sir Robert (Lord Mayor 1602)   142–43, 158, 162, 175
Lee (Kent)
   Boone's almshouses and school   215–16, 231, 240
     Lee Place   231
   Merchant Taylors' Company almshouses   231, 239–40, *239*, 266–67
   sheltered housing   267
Leeds, Joseph (Master 1782)   271
Leeson, Spencer, later Bishop of Peterborough   254–55, 258
Legate, Peter   134
Legett, Robert   44
Legg, Daniel (Master 1748)   271
Legg, Leaver (Master 1765)   271
Legge, John (Master 1434)   61, 269
Legh, *see also* Lee; Leigh; Ley
Legh, William   113
Leicester   120
Leicester, Earls of *see* Dudley, Robert; Montfort, Simon de
Leigh, *see also* Lee; Legh; Ley
Leigh, Cassandra   231
Leighton, Frederic, Lord   249
Lem, Joseph   203, 207, 208, 215, 216, 218
Lenthall, William   185
Leopard, John (Master 1808)   272
Lessingham, Samuel (Master 1742)   271
Levant Company   190
Lewin, Edmund (Master 1667)   203, 215, 271
Lewin, Edmund (Master 1738)   271
Lewisham (London Borough)   267
   see also Lee
Ley, *see also* Lee; Legh; Leigh
Ley, Edward (Master 1558)   270
Ley, Edward a   133
Leybourn(e), William   206, 213–14, Col. Pl. XVI
Liddle, Duncan   259
Lief, Simon (Master 1404)   269
Liège (Belgium)   56–57
Lilly, *see also* Lylly
Lilly, Henry   Col. Pl. XIV
Lime Street   25
Lime Street ward   115, 154
Limerick (Ireland)   135
Lincoln   10, 120
linen armour   *10, 11–13, 49–52, 51*
linen-armourers   8, 9, 11–13, 49–52
   see also Fraternity of St John the Baptist; Tailors and Linen-Armourers
Linkes, ——   176–77
Lipsett, Anthony   232
Lisle, Sir John   114
Lisle, Viscounts *see* Plantagenet
Lithgow, William   187

Little Minories *see* Minories
liveries   5, 9, 63–64, 80
Liverpool Ladies' College   245
livery companies
   origins   6, 35
   see also Armourers' and Brasiers' Company; Brewers' Company; Carpenters' Company; Clothworkers' Company; Cordwainers' Company; Drapers' Company; Fishmongers' Company; Goldsmiths' Company; Grocers' Company; Haberdashers' Company; Ironmongers' Company; Mercers' Company; Merchant Taylors' Company; Painter–Stainers' Company; Pewterers' Company; Plaisterers' Company; Saddlers' Company; Scriveners' Company; Skinners' Company; Stationers' Company; Tylers' Company; Vintners' Company
liverymen *see* Merchant Taylors' Company, liverymen
Lloyd, William (Master 1805)   272
Lloyde, Luys   133
loan funds   56, 120, 138, 145, 166–67, 201
   Sir Thomas White's charity for young clothiers   120, 193
Locan, Richard   55
Lock, Thomas   203
Locker, Joseph (Master 1733)   271
Lockwood and Mawson, Messrs   245
Locok, John (Master 1439)   77, 269
Lollards   99
Lombard Street
   Cardinal's Hat, school   110
   property of Merchant Taylors' Company   137, 178, 209
     mansion bequeathed by Sir John Percyvale   111, 113, 118, 119, 137–38, 143
     Pope's Head Tavern   175
London, Bishops of
   members of Fraternity of St John the Baptist   20, *21*, 24, 28
   see also Chartres; Fitzhugh; Fitzjames; Grey, William; Grindal; Juxon, William; Sandys; Stokesley; Sudbury
London, City *see* City of London
London Bridge   101, 104, 137, 138, 200
   wardens   76
London College of Fashion   266
London County Council   249
London Regiment   267
London Tavern   238
Londonderry (Co. Derry)   186, 232
   school (now Foyle & Londonderry College)   173, 266, 267
Long Wittenham, manor (Oxon.)   120
Lord, ——   228
Lord Mayor, office of *see* Mayor (Lord Mayor), office of
Lorymer, Simon   45
lottery (1567)   146–48, *146*

Love, Walter   217
Lovekyn, George   56, 59, 61, 62, 63
Lovell, Thomas   156
Lowe, Simon (Master 1557)   104, 270
Loyal London (ship)   202
Lucar, Emmanuel (Master 1560)   99, 103, 104, 123, 130, 270
Lucas, Margaret   215
Ludgate   63, 104, 137, 190
  prison   76
  shops and stalls   59–60, 65, 137
Lupo, Thomas   162
Lurtin, John   230
Lydgate, John   174
Lylly, *see also* Lilly
Lylly, Gilbert   133
Lymly, Thomas   136
Lynde, William   88n34
Lynne, John and Elizabeth   138
Lynne, Richard (Master 1403)   269
Lytillskyll, Rowland   54

M
Macclesfield (Ches.)   112–13
  Grammar School (later King's School), founded by Sir John Percyvale   99, 111–13, 123
Macdonald, Alexander   Col. Pl. XXI
mace, silver   *60*, 94
Machin, George   238
Machyn, Henry   103, 104, 142, 242
Macmillan, Alexander Daniel Alan, 2nd Earl of Stockton (Master 1992)   273
Macmillan, Harold, 1st Earl of Stockton   261
Macosquin (Co. Derry)   173
Madox, Thomas   169
Magdeburg (Germany), sack of (1631)   186, 187
Maidstone (Kent)   186, Col. Pl. XIV
Maitland, John, 1st Duke of Lauderdale   219
Mallory, Major ——   206–07
Mallory, Robert (Master 1674)   271
Malt, John (Master 1540)   62, 270
Man, Isle of   230
Manby, Thomas   185
Manby, William   183
Manchester (Lancs.)   260–61
  Bishops of *see* Warman
Mander, Noel   265
Manor of the Rose   122, 256
Mapylton, John   23
marblers   23
March, Earls of *see* Mortimer
Marchall, John (Master 1410)   269
Marchall, William   29
Margaret of Anjou, Queen   79
Markelius, Sven   255
Market Harborough (Leics.)   157

Markham, Humfrey   166
Marlborough (Wilts.)   256
Marler, Dennis   265
Marler, Leslie Sydney (Master 1960)   273
Marlour, Christopher   127
Marr-Johnson, Kenneth (Master 1955)   272
Marsh, Robert (Clerk 1636–61)   275
Marsham, Thomas (Master 1621)   270
Martin, Misses   251
Martin, Charles Trice   251
Martin, Nathaniel (Master 1767)   271
Mary I, Queen   103–06, *106*, 119, Col. Pl. XII
Mary II, Queen   220
Mary of Modena, Queen   219
Mary Queen of Scots   148
Mason, Peter (Master 1407)   27–28, 269
Mason, Samuel (Master 1876)   272
masque for Charles I and Henrietta Maria (1634)   183
Massachusetts Bay Company   185
Master, office of *see* Merchant Taylors' Company, Master, office of
Masterman, Edward (Master 1869)   272
Materdale, John (Master 1480)   31, 270
Mathews, Charles   228
Mathews, John   232
Maye, Richard (Master 1583)   270
Mayor (Lord Mayor), office of
  elections
    banquets   79, 94, 175
    liveries worn at   63
    troubles at, 14th–15th cent.   72–73, 76–77
  and Henry VII's welcome   ·80, *80*
  liveries worn by   64
  procession to Westminster (pageant, Lord Mayor's Show)
    14th–15th cent.   21–22, 79, 94, 142
    16th cent.   103, 118, 142
    17th cent.   142–43, 158–59, 174, 175, 199–200, 206, 218
  role in City government, 14th–15th cent.   3–4, 38, 40, 76, 77
  tailors as   84, 142–43, 158–59, 174, 175, 218, 225, 232, 265
    see also Bolton, Sir William; Browne, Sir Richard; Craven, Sir William; Harper, Sir William; Jenyns, Sir Stephen; Lee, Sir Robert; Percyvale, Sir John; Pritchard, Sir William; Reynardson, Sir Abraham; Rowe, Sir Thomas; Swinnerton, Sir John; Turner, Sir William; Ward, Sir Patience; White, Sir Thomas
Mayour, Henry (Clerk 1493–at least 1512)   43, 44–45, *44*, 86, 94, 95–96, 132, 275
McGrath, John Keswick Ulick Blake (Master 1974)   273
Mead, William (Master 1705)   271
Medlicott, Arthur   *130*

Meeke, Simon, son of John 129
Mellish, George (Master 1646) 271
Mellyshe, Robert (Master 1550) 270
Mercers' Company
  apprentices 57
  and Assheton's Annuity Scheme 218
  attendance at royal events 79, 80
  charter (1394) 73, 74
  and City and Guilds of London Institute 243
  in Civil War 188
  and defence of City 78
  and dissolution of chantries 97
  and education 111
    St Paul's School 122, 168
  liveries 64
  loans to Henry VII 78
  and mayoral election (1384) 72
  Mercers' Hall 65, 203, 207, 260
  minute books 9
  and mosaic decoration of St Paul's Cathedral 249
  property in St Antholin's parish 174
  relations with Merchant Taylors' Company 80, 86
  representation on Common Council 72
  and Royal Exchange 130, 144
  size and importance 5, 82
Merchant Adventurers, Society of 65
Merchant Taylors' Catering Ltd 266
Merchant Taylors' Company
  annual feast (1300–1530) 9, 31–32, 36, 73
  archives
    book of privileges, ordinances, and 'goostly tresoure' 11, 19, 86, 95–96, Col. Pls III, V–VI
    care of 202, 237, 250–51, 260, 265
    Court minute books, Book 'I' 9, 39
    Great Register 39, 40
    inventory (1512) 30, 31, 44, *45*, 94
    inventory (1609) 9, 39, 94
  arms
    1st grant of arms (1481) 6, 13, 25, 30, 51, 82, Col. Pl. V
    2nd grant of arms (1586) 143, 146, *147*, 149, 200, Col. Pl. XI
    from barge 226
    on brass *145*
    above entrance to Merchant Taylors' Hall 203
    frontispiece to Oliver and Leybourne surveys 214
    on hearse-cloth 31
    on mace 94
    on Merchant Taylors' Company properties 213
    on Offley Rosewater Dish *95*
    pageant based on (1602) 143
    in Wolverhampton church *117*
  charitable activities
    15th–16th cent. 28–31, 98–99, 138
    17th cent. 166, 215–16, 221
    19th–20th cent. 246–47, 250, 252, 266–67

    see also almshouses; almsmen and almswomen; loan funds; schools (below)
  charters
    1327 *8–9*, 11, 50, 71, 73
    1341 71, 73
    1390 36, 73
    1408 74, *75*
    1440 22, 64, 74, 76, 77
    1465 81
    1503 13, 22, 84–87, 93, 94, 95, 267, Col. Pl. VI
    1558 106, *106*
    1685 219
  Clerk, office of 29, 43–45, 131–32, 133, 194, 230, 254, 260, 275
    William Duryvale (1487–92) *37*, 44
    Henry Mayour (1493–at least 1512) 43, 44–45, *44*, 86, 94, 95–96, 132
    Nicholas Fuljambe (1571–75) 119, 131–32, 136, 251
    Richard Langley (1594–1610) 155, 162, 170, 251
    John Milner (1661–85) 202, 206, 207, 214, 215, 218, 219, 251
    Richard Teasdale (1806–22) 235, 238
  cloth yard, silver 59, *60*, 94, 221
  common seal 74, 94, Col. Pl. III
  Court of Assistants
    elects Master and Wardens 36, 127
    number of members 39, 130
    organization of meetings 39–40, 131–32
    origins 38–39
    prayer at quarterly meetings 98
    role in resolving disputes 40–41, 66–67, 133–36, 153, 166
  and education *see* Oxford, St John's College; schools (below)
  freemen
    admissions 11, 39; by apprenticeship 36, 56, 127–28; by patrimony 128; by redemption 36, 129
    freemen outside the livery *see* Bachelors' Company
    numbers 35–36, 130
  hearse-cloths
    c. 1480–1500 13, 30, *30*, 31, 98, 237, 260, *Frontispiece*
    c. 1520–40 30–31, 98, 237, 260, Col. Pl. II
  'incorporation' 73–74, 84–87
  liverymen
    admissions to livery 36, 129, 130, 163, 206
    apprentices of 54, 55, 81
    attendance at Mayoral elections 77
    members of Fraternity of St John the Baptist 28–30, 35
    misbehaviour, 15th cent. 41
    numbers: 15th cent. 36; 16th cent. 130; 19th cent. 247n10
    occupations 142, 238
    shortage of, 17th cent. 213, 217

Merchant Taylors' Company (*continued*)
  liverymen (*continued*)
    women members of livery ix, 267
  mace, silver *60*, 94
  Master, office of
    duties 29, 37–38, 39–40, 127, 130–31
    election and installation 25, 31, 32, 36
    list of Masters 269–73
    origins of office 9; first mention in charter (1390) 73; term 'pilgrim' originally used 9–10, 11, 38
    wives and widows 36–37
  motto 149
  plate 31, 94–95, *95*, 98, 116, 202, 207, 265
    see also cloth yard (above); mace (above)
  portraits 120, 178, 207, 215, 237, 259, 260, Col. Pls IX–X, XVIII, XXI
  properties, management
    16th cent. 94, 97, 131, 136–38
    17th cent. 156, 175, 178, 215, 218; destroyed in Great Fire and later rebuilt 203, 205–06, 213–15
    18th cent. 227
    19th cent. 239
    see also almshouses; Ireland, Merchant Taylors' Company's Irish estate; Lombard Street, property of Merchant Taylors' Company; Merchant Taylors' Hall; schools (below)
  relations with City
    to 1500 71–89
    16th cent. 142–46
  relations with Crown
    14th–15th cent. 13, 50–52, 62, 64, 71–89
    16th cent. 62–63, 146–49
    see also individual monarchs by name
  relations with other livery companies
    Clothworkers 141–42, 157, 201, 220
    Drapers 21–22, 64, 65, 74–77, 81–82, 84, 86, 87, 141
    Mercers 80, 86
    Skinners 82, 87, 141; *see also* Billesden Award
  schools 98, 99, 109–25, 266, 267
    see also Ashwell; Great Crosby; Lee; Londonderry; Merchant Taylors' School; Wallingford; Wolverhampton
  size, 15th–17th cent. 35–36, 130
  Wardens, office of
    duties 29, 37, 38, 39, 127, 130–31
    election and installation 25, 31, 32, 36
    'lower' and 'upper' 37
    origins of office 5, 9, 10; first mention in charter (1390) 73; term 'purveyors of alms' (alms collectors) originally used 9–10, 11, 13, 28, 38
  see also Bachelors' Company; Fraternity of St John the Baptist; Merchant Taylors' Hall; Tailors and Linen-Armourers
Merchant Taylors' Educational Trust 266
Merchant Taylors' Hall
  general
    general views *46–47*, Col. Pl. XXI
    inventory (1512) 30, 31, 44, *45*, 94
    inventory (1609) 9, 39, 94
    maps and plans *15, 204–05, 226, 228*, Col. Pls XI, XVI
  history
    establishment, 14th cent. 8, 13, 14–16
    Civil War 185, 190
    Great Fire and subsequent rebuilding 202–03, 206–07, 215
    redecoration, 19th cent. 237–38
    Second World War, bomb damage and subsequent restoration *258–59*, 259–62
    since 1960 265, 266
  events at
    annual feast (1300–1530) 9, 31–32, 36, 73
    Artillery Company exercise (1638) 183–84
    Bachelors' Company annual feast 41, 42, 127
    banquet for Duke of Wellington (1814) 234–35
    banquet for James I (1607) 20, 159–63, 171, 174, 175, 181, 215
    feast for Tory apprentices (1682) 218
    lavish dinners, 19th cent. 238, 246
    Mayor's election banquets 79, 94
    plays performed by Merchant Taylors' School 123, 201
  chapel 16, 23, 25, 31, 36, 94
  Clerk's staircase, mural by Janet Shearer 265, Col. Pl. XXIII
  Court Room *15*, 16, 259
  Dining Room *see* Parlour (below)
  Drawing Room *see* King's Chamber (below)
  foundation arches *12*, 16
  garden *15*, 136–37, 159, 183, 206
    damaged in Great Fire and later refurbished 202, 207, 215
    replaced by courtyard Col. Pl. XXIV
  Grand Staircase *15*, 215, 226, 227, 259, 262, 265
  Great Hall *15*, 16, 159, 227, Col. Pls XXI, XXIII
    armorial stained glass 252, 262, Col. Pl. XXII
    collapse of ceiling (1851) viii
    destroyed 1940 and later reconstructed 259, 262
    organ 265
    screen (1673) 207, *207*, 259
    ship(s) for pageants hung from rafters 158, 162, 175, 215
  King's Chamber (later Drawing Room) 159, 162, 215, 227, 237, 259, *259*, 262
  kitchens *15*, 16, 94, 137, 159, 206, 262
    rebuilt 15th cent. 31, 36, 42, *42*
    rebuilt after Great Fire 205, 215
  Library *15*, 259
  Little Parlour 221
  Muniment Room 237, 259, 260
  Parlour (or Dining Room) *15*, 16, 31, 41, 136, 206, 227, 237, Col. Pl. XXIV

refurbished after Great Fire   202, 203, 215
    destroyed 1940 and later reconstructed   259, 260–61
  Poor Box   259–60
  Treasury   93–94, 202
  undercroft   *14*, 16, *24*
  'ypocrise house'   132
Merchant Taylors' School
  foundation (1561)   106, 122–23
  16th cent.   121, *122*, 123–24, 132, 142, 156–57, 176
  17th cent.   166, 167–69, 182, 188, 190, 192, 195–97, 201, 207–08, 212, 216
    destruction in Great Fire and subsequent rebuilding   202, 203, 207, 208, *209*, 214–15
    Titus Oates and   211, 212, 213, *214*
  18th cent.   227–28, 230–31
  19th–20th cent.   230–31, 240–41, *241*, 242, Col. Pl. XIX
    at Charterhouse site   243–44, *244–45*, 250, 251–55, *253*, 257; playing fields   250, 253
    at Sandy Lodge site   254–58, *255*, 265, 266, 267
merchants, tailors as *see* cloth trade
Merick, William   148
Mermaid Tavern   96
Metropolitan Board of Works   243
Metternich, Prince   234
Mew, Colonel ——   205
Middelton, Robert (Master 1477)   270
Middle Temple   157, 183
Mildmay, Thomas   96
Mille, Nicholas (Clerk before 1453–54)   275
Millennium, commemoration   266, 267
Milner, John (Clerk 1661–85)   202, 206, 207, 214, 215, 218, 219, 251, 275
Milner, Tempest (Master 1655)   271
Milton, John   196
Minories   154
  Little Minories   214
Missenden, Great (Bucks.)   158
misteries   5–7, 11, 38–39
  see also fraternities (guilds); Tailors and Linen-Armourers
Moleyns, Adam   22, 76
Molyneux, Anne   230
Molyneux, Edward   118
Molyneux, Richard, 2nd Viscount   188
Moncastre, James   85
Monck, Christopher, 2nd Duke of Albemarle   218
monopolies   165, 166
Montfort, Simon de, Earl of Leicester   7
monuments *see* tombs, monuments and brasses
Moore, Colonel John   195
Moore, Nathaniel   228
Moorfields   137, 138, 215
Mora, prebendal estate   156
Mordeyne, Thomas   202

More, John   72
More, Sir Thomas   100, 110, 174
Moreing, Algernon Henry (Master 1936)   272
Morgan, William   *204–05*
Moroni, Giovanni Battista   59, Col. Pl. IV
Mortimer, Roger de, Lord Mortimer, later 2nd Earl of March   20
Mortimer, Roger de, 4th Earl of March   63
mortmain, statute of (1391)   14, 73–74, 96
Mosse, Clement (Clerk 1624–36; Master 1641)   186–87, 194, 271, 275
Mott, Roger (Master 1716)   271
Mounpeillers, Robert de   8
Muggeridge, John (Master 1784)   271
Mulcaster, Richard   123–24, *123*, 142, 168, 228, 240, 253
Munday, Anthony   142–43, 158, 175
Murray, Gilbert   244, 253
music
  at banquet for James I (1607)   159, 161–63
  at feasts and ceremonies, medieval   32, 79, 80
  at Lord Mayor's pageant (1561)   142
  masque for Charles I and Henrietta Maria (1634)   183

N
Nairn, Dr John Arbuthnot   250, 252, 253–54, 266
Napoleonic Wars *see* Revolutionary and Napoleonic Wars
Nash, Andrew John (Master 1815)   235, 272
Nash, Edward (Master 1668)   271
Nash, Edward (Clerk 1890–1924)   275
Nash, Edwin (Master 1878)   272
Nash, George (Master 1647)   193, 271
Nash, George Augustus (Master 1817)   235, 272
Nash, Nathaniel (Master 1759)   271
Nash, Richard (Master 1732)   271
Nash, William (Master 1858)   272
Nash, William Woodbridge (Master 1834)   272
National Archives *see* Public Record Office
Nayler, Richard (Master 1475)   65, 83, 269
Neave, Francis (Master 1629)   270
Neave, Richard (Master 1760)   271
Needham, Gervaise   193
Nelson, Horatio, Viscount, funeral procession   226
Netherlands   141, 153, 165, 183, 186, 255
Neunberg, George Vander (Master 1807)   272
Nevill, Colonel Thomas (Master 1665)   202, 208, 271
Neville family   20
New Exchange (Strand)   178
New River Company   215
New Zealand   250
Newall, Francis Storer Eaton (Master 1985)   273
Newbury, Battle of (1643)   189
Newgate Prison   8, 76, 82, 196
  Newgate Bell (now in St Sepulchre Newgate)   176, *177*
Newington Butts (Surrey)   196
Newton, William Godfrey   254–57

Nicholls, John (Master 1522)   116, 270
Nichols, John Gough   242
Nicholson, Dennis Thomas Holme (Master 1983)   273
Nicholson, Humphrey (Master 1679)   271
Nightingale, Elizabeth, m. Robert Baker   178
Nixon, Anthony   176
Noakes, Wickham (Master 1897)   272
Noble Street   158
Nollekens, Joseph   262
Norbury, Henry Frederick Oswald (Master 1937)   272
Norbury, Richard   72
Nordon, Richard (Master 1422)   29, 48n45, 65, 76, 79, 269
Norfolk, Dukes of see Howard family
Norman, Claude Wilson   266
Norman, John (Mayor 1453–54)   21–22, 88n41
Normansell, John   170
Norris, Daniel   203
North, George (Clerk 1709–63)   275
Northall, Henry   136
Northampton, John of (Mayor 1381, 1382)   71, 72
Northampton   120
Northern Rebellion (1569)   102, 148
Northiam (Sussex)   216
Northop (Flints.)   212
Northumberland, Earls of see Percy
Northwood (Middx)
   St John's School   266
   see also Sandy Lodge
Norwich   211
Nottingham   120
Nourse, Christopher Henry (Master 1982)   273
Nowell, Alexander, Dean of St Paul's   129
Nowell, Alice, m. Henry Dowe   175–76
Nowers, ——   206
Noxe, John   136
Nynes, Nicholas (Master 1496)   270

O
Oates, Lucy, wife of Samuel   211
Oates, Samuel   211
Oates, Titus   211–13, *214*
obits see anniversaries
officia (craft organizations)   5
Offley, Henry (Master 1584)   270
Offley, Hugh   105
Offley, Richard   131, 137, 178
Offley, Sir Thomas (Master 1547)   93, 97, 101, 103, 122, 138, 270
   contribution to expedition to Le Havre   148
   as Lord Mayor (1556)   142
   monument   Col. Pl. XIII
   and Royal Exchange   144
   as Sheriff   104–5
Offley, Thomas (Senior Warden 1574)   131
Offley, William   95, *95*
Offley Rosewater Dish   *95*
Ogard, Sir Andrew   20
Old Change   194
Oliver, John   203, 205, 206, 213–14, Col. Pl. XVI
Oliver-Bellasis, John (Master 1968)   273
Olyff, John (Master 1564)   137, 270
O'Neill, Shane   148
Onesley, Agnes   135
Ongley, Samuel (Master 1706)   271
Onley, Thomas   205
Oram, Matthew Henry (Master 1975)   273
ordinances of livery companies   76, 86, 95
Orewelle, John (Master 1392)   269
Orlibrare, John (Master 1660)   271
Ormonde, Dukes of see Butler
Osborne, Andrew (Master 1612)   159, 270
Osborne, Thomas, 1st Earl of Danby   212
Östberg, Ragnar   255
Oteswich, John de   26, *27*
Oteswich, William de   26
Oughtred, William   196
Owen, Nathaniel (Master 1642)   271
Owen, Thomas   159
Owens, John Ridland (Master 2002)   273
Owthwayte, John   129
Oxford
   apprentices   81
   Brasenose College   111, 157, 229
   Christ Church   120–21
   in Civil War   187, 192
   Corpus Christi College   121
   Gloucester College   121
   Holywell Music Room   231
   New College   113, 118, 119, 254
   Pembroke College   229
   The Queen's College   170
   St Bernard's College   120–21
   St John's College
      banners and vestments   121, Col. Pl. VII
      Canterbury Quad (1631–36)   *189*
      chapel   157
      in Civil War   192
      Craven bequest   175
      fellows   195
      foundation (1555)   106, 120–22
      library   175
      and Merchant Taylors' School   124, 169, 230–31, 243; see also scholarships (below)
      Presidents   121, 160, 168, 169, 190, 230, 241
      scholarships   63, 98, 121, 169; from Merchant Taylors' School   121, 123, 124, 166, 192, 195, 208, 258
      students and graduates   157, 191, 208, 211, 212, 228
   Somerville College   258
tailors' guild   6

Trinity College   121–22, 175, 196
university   169, 216
   Boat Club   227
   Craven Scholarships   175
   University College   227
Oxford, Earls of   64
Oxford and Cambridge Schools Examination Board   253, 254

P
Paddesley, John (Mayor 1440)   76
Page, John (Master 1700)   271
pageants
  James I's triumphal procession through City (1604)   171, *172*
  Lord Mayor's procession to Westminster (Lord Mayor's Show)
    14th–15th cent.   21–22, 79, 94, 142
    16th cent.   103, 118, 142
    17th cent.   142–43, 158–59, 174, 175, 199–200, 206, 218
painter-stainers   22, 25, 31
Painter-Stainers' Company   130, 260
painters, mistery   11
palls *see* hearse-cloths
Palmer, Henry (Master 1600)   270
Palmer, Roundell, 1st Earl of Selborne   246
Palmer, Thomas   128
Pampilon, John   29
Paravicini, Peter (Master 1685)   219, 271
Parbury, George (Master 1866)   272
Paris
  Lycée Condorcet   253
  tailors from   61
Parish Clerks, fraternity   22
parishes (City of London) *see* churches and parishes
Park, John   134
Parker, John   174
Parker, Matthew, Archbishop of Canterbury   98, 153, 154
Parker, Robert   174
Parker, Thomas   42, 63
Parker, William (Master 1469)   269
Parker, William (*fl.* 1673)   211
Parkes, Joseph   237
parmenters   8
Parratt, William   232
Parsell, William (Master 1639)   270
Parshall, Horace Field (Master 1958)   273
Partrich, John (Master 1393)   52, 269
Pascoe, John Hill (Master 1990)   273
Passeware, William   23
Paston, John   63
patrimony, admission to freedom by   3, 129

patron saints
  of fraternities   6
  see also John the Baptist, St
pattern books   49
Pault, William   61
pavilion motif
  in arms of Merchant Taylors' Company   13, 51, 82
  on hearse-cloths   30, *30*
pavilioners *see* tent-makers
Pawley, George   207
Peacock, ———   242
Peale, Nicholas   133
Pecche, John (Master 1351)   10, 11, 269
Peck, David Arthur (Clerk 1995–)   275
Pecke, John (Master 1435)   269
Pelham, Thomas   118
Pell, Walter (Master 1649)   207, 271
Peltry   8
Pemberton, Hugh (Master 1482)   26, 33n7, 40, 62, 83, 94, 270
  as general merchant   65, 66, 83
Pemberton, Katherine, wife of Hugh   26
Pennington, Abigail, wife of Isaac   187
Pennington, Isaac (Lord Mayor 1642)   185, 186, 187, 191
Penton, John Howard (Master 2003)   273
Pepys, John   209n5
Pepys, Samuel   200, 202, 208
Percy family (15th cent.)   20
Percy, Henry, Earl of Northumberland   31
Percyvale, Sir John (Master 1485)   29, 40, 83, 84, 94, 111
  anniversary (obit)   96
  chantry   37
  as general merchant   66, 84
  Lombard Street mansion   111, 113, 118, 119, 137–38, 143
  and Macclesfield Grammar School   99, 111–13
  as Master (1485)   22, 83, 270
  as Mayor (1498)   71, 79, 84, 94, 142
  plate given/bequeathed by   31, 94
Percyvale, Thomasine, née Bonaventure, wife of Sir John   37, 58, 63, 84, 94, 112, 113
  and school at Week St Mary   99, 113–15
Perring, Sir John Raymond (Master 1988, 1994)   265, 273
Person, William (Master 1462)   269
Peryn, John   *167*
Peterborough, Bishops of *see* Leeson
Petingale, William, and wife   135
Peto, Henry   239
Petyt, Thomas (Master 1497)   59, 65, 270
Pewterers' Company, Fraternity of St Michael   42
Phelip, John (Master 1466, 1476)   269
Phellipps, William   128
Philip II, King of Spain   103–04, 106, *106*
Philipps, John   129

Phillipps, William (Master 1579)   270
Phillips, —— (fl. 1680)   214
Phillips, J. R.   246
Phillpotts, James Surtees   119
Physick, Edward   235, 262
piccadills   178, 181
Piccadilly   178, 212, 234
Picton, John (Master 1745)   271
Pigeon, Alfred Staines (Master 1846)   272
Pigeon, Henry (Master 1803)   271
Pigeon, Henry (Master 1870)   272
Pigeon, Richard Hotham (Master 1831)   272
pilgrim, term originally used for Master   9–10, 11, 38
Pinner (Middx), St John's School   266
Pitt, William, the Younger   262
Pitts, Thomas (Master 1720)   271
Place, Francis   237
plague
   14th–15th cent.   55
     Black Death   49, 71
   16th cent.   151, 158, 160, 174
   17th cent.   171, 182, 195, 201–02
Plaisterers' Company   138
Plantagenet, Arthur, Viscount Lisle, and Lady Lisle   62
plate   31, 94–95, *95*, 98, 116, 202, 207, 265
   see also cloth yard; mace
Platoff, Matvei Ivanovich, Count   234, 235
Plestow, Thomas (Master 1772)   271
Pleyman, Morrys   129
Plomer, ——, and wife   134
Plumer, Sir Walter (fl. 1660s)   206
Plummer, Walter (Master 1599)   *129*, 270
Plymley, John   228–29
Plymley, John, the younger   229
Plymouth (Devon)   190
Podmore, Robert (Master 1839)   272
Pole, William and Alice de la   29
Pollard, 2nd Lieutenant Alfred Oliver, VC   252
Polsteed, Henry (Master 1625)   270
Pomeroy, Bartholomew (Master 1762)   271
Pomeroy, William (Master 1734)   271
poor, support for *see* almshouses; almsmen and almswomen; Merchant Taylors' Company, charitable activities
Pope's Head Alley   206, 215
Pope's Head Tavern   175
Popish Plot (1678)   212
Portuguese Ambassador, and Charterhouse   157–58
Possell, Philip (Master 1429)   269
Poultry   59, 215
Pountney, Sir John *see* Pulteney
Povey, Walter (Master 1492)   25, 33n7, 38, 40, 56, 270
   and cloth trade   62, 65
Powell, David   134
Poynings, Sir Adrian   148

Pratt, Henry (Master 1630)   270
Pratt, Thomas   134
Preistley, Anne, m. Robert Graye   177
Prescott, Ernest (Master 1928)   254, 272
pressing irons   59, 130, 136
Price, Roger   166–67
Pride, Colonel Thomas   190, 211
priests
   clergy members of Fraternity of St John the Baptist   20–21, 24, 28
   see also chantries; chaplains
Prime, Matthias (Master 1724)   271
Prince Regent *see* George IV, King
Pritchard, Sir William (Master 1673; Lord Mayor 1682)   218, 219, 271
   portrait   215, 263n29
Proby, Peter   222n9
Procter, Richard (Master 1593)   270
Protestantism
   in Reformation   98, 99–103, 104, 106–07, 165
     Wyatt's rebellion   104–07
   17th cent.   165, 171, 184
   see also Puritans
Prynce, John (Master 1456)   95, 269
Public Record Office (now The National Archives)   251, 260
Pugh, Thomas Bless (Master 1847)   272
Pugin, Augustus   Col. Pl. XIX
Pulteney (Pountney), Sir John (Mayor 1330, 1333, 1336)   122
Puritans, 17th cent.   185, 191, 193, 194–95
Purnell, John James (Master 1890)   272
purveyors of alms *see* alms collectors
Pye, Thomas   115
Pym, John (one of Five Members)   185, 186

Q
Queen Street   239
Queen's tailors *see* King's/Queen's tailors
Queldrik, Robert (Master 1405)   269

R
Raby, ——   169
Radcliffe, Thomas, 3rd Earl of Sussex   129, 131
Radclyffe, Anthony (Master 1577)   270
Ramsay, Allan   237
Randall, Thomas (Master 1493)   65, 270
Randoll, Robert   *14*
Ranyard Memorial Charitable Trust   267
Raphael, Edward   252
Ratcliffe, wharf at   137
Rauf, Walter   61
Raven, Thomas   173
Ravens, Ralph   *167*
Rawlett, Daniel   193, 194
Raymond, *see also* Reymond

Raymond, Paul   265
Reade, John (Master 1801)   271
Reading (Berks.)   119, 120, 121, 141, 169
recusancy *see* Catholicism/recusancy
redemption, admission to freedom by   3, 36, 129
Reformation   93–108, 165, 184
   see also chantries, dissolution
Reid, Percy Lester (Master 1947)   272
Reignoldes, Harry   134
religious houses (London)   19
   Clerkenwell, priory of St John of Jerusalem   41, 42
   Grey Friars, church, Jenyns monument   96, 116, Col. Pl. VIII
   see also hospitals (London)
Relyk, William   110
Renter, office of   45
Report on London (1837)   237
Restoration (1660)   199
Revolutionary and Napoleonic Wars (1793–1815)   232, 234, 238
Reymond, *see also* Raymond
Reymond, Thomas (Master 1446)   269
Reynardson, Abigail, wife of Abraham   190
Reynardson, Sir Abraham (Master 1640; Lord Mayor 1648)   190–92, 199, 215, 225, 232, 271, Col. Pl. XVIII
Reynardson, Anne, m. Sir Robert Bedingfield   225
Reynardson, Eleanor, wife of Abraham   190, 191
Reynold, Richard (Master 1425)   269
Rich Bachelors   206
Richard I, King   3
Richard II, King   36, 61, 63, 71–73
Richard III, King   61, 62, 64
   as Duke of Gloucester   20, 81
Richards, John   162
Richardson, Sir Albert   261–62
Richardson, William   232
Richmond, Sir William Blake   249
Rickards, Charles (Master 1852)   272
Riddle, Giles (Master 1726)   271
Ridge, Richard   136
Rise, John   161
Ritchie, Charles John (Master 1924)   272
Ritchie, James Edward Thomson (Master 1963)   273
Roberson, Revd J.   241
Robert of Gloucester, *Chronicle*   163n4
Roberts, Gearing (Master 1763)   271
Roberts, Richard   226
Roberts, Thomas (Master 1797)   271
Robertson, Dr William   229
Robins, Mary, m. Robert Smith   157
Robson, James (Master 1791)   271
Roe, John   232
Roedean School (Sussex)   253
Rogers, John (Master 1795)   271
Rogers, John (Master 1823)   272
Rolls, Michael   205, 219, 222n6

Rood Lane   137
Roos, Beatrice de, wife of Thomas, Lord Roos   25
Rose, —— (18th cent.)   228
Rose, Robert (Master 1563)   130, 270
Rosemary Lane, almshouses *see* Tower Hill
Rossi, Henry   238
Rossi, John Charles Felix   238
Rowe, Mary, wife of Sir Thomas   142, 143
Rowe, Oliver (Master 1592)   270
Rowe, Colonel Owen   191
Rowe, Sir Thomas (Lord Mayor 1568)   99, 138, 142, 143, 144–45, 148, 215
Rowe, Thomas (Master 1610)   270
rowers (clothworkers)   141–42
   see also Clothworkers' Company
Royal Academy   249
Royal Commission into Livery Companies (1880s)   246–47
Royal Commission on Public Schools (1864)   250
Royal Exchange   130, 142, 143–44, *172*, 203, 234, 249
   Joint Grand Gresham Committee   188, 249
   murals   249, Col. Pl. V
   statue of James II   219
Royal Fusiliers (City of London Regiment) (7th Foot), now London Regiment   267
Royal Yeomanry   267
Rucker family   162
Rule, William (Master 1384)   72, 269
Runcie, Robert, Archbishop of Canterbury   266
Rupert, Prince   187
Rushock, manor (Worcs.)   116, 169, 188, 193, 228, 229
Russell, Charles   254
Russell, Francis, 4th Earl of Bedford   181
Russell, William   99
Ryall, Henry de (Master 1300)   9, 174, 269
Ryan, Peter Henry (Master 1996)   273
Ryckemour, Thomas   136
Ryton (Salop.)   175

S
Sabatier, John (Master 1768)   271
saddlers, fraternity   14
Saddlers' Company   41, 72, 73, 77
Saffron Walden (Essex)   118
St Albans (Herts.), Bishops of   258
St Anthony's Hospital (Threadneedle Street)   72
   school   110, 122
St Bartholomew's Fair   64, 76
St Bartholomew's Hospital   250, 257
St Davids (Pembs.), Bishops of   20
St George's Fields   148
St Giles in the Fields, parish   217
St James's Square, Norfolk House   234
St John, John   52
St John's, Clerkenwell *see* Clerkenwell, priory of St John of Jerusalem

St Martin in the Fields, church   178
St Martin le Grand, college   14, 110
St Mary Axe, schoolhouse   207
St Mary of Bethlehem, hospital   14
St Paul's Cathedral
   before Great Fire   24, 72, 80, 166–67, *172*
      chapel of St John the Baptist   13, 23–25, 31, 72;
         table of grants and privileges   19, 24–25
      in Civil War   187, 190
      Deans of *see* Colet; Nowell
      Lollards' Tower   100, *101*
      prebendal estate of Mora   156
      schools   109–10
      trial of Richard Hunne   100
   after Great Fire
      farewell service for Merchant Taylors' School (1933)   257
      Millennium service   267
      monuments to Napoleonic war heroes   238
      mosaic decoration   249
      rebuilding under Wren   203, *204*, 213
      scholarship for choirboy   250
St Paul's Churchyard   156, 167, 174, 200
St Paul's School   122, 168
St Peter's Hill, Doctors' Commons, school   196
St Swithin's Lane   194
St Thomas of Acon, hospital   72
saints, fraternities dedicated to   6
   see also John the Baptist, St
Sale, ——   235
Salisbury (Wilts.)   6, 120
Salisbury, Earls of *see* Cecil
Salisbury Court   183
Sallust, motto of Merchant Taylors' Company from   149
Salter, Sir John (Master 1731; Lord Mayor 1739)   225, 263n29, 271
Sanderson, Lancelot   230
Sandforth, John   132
Sandwich (Kent)   65
Sandy Lodge (Middx), Merchant Taylors' School   254–58, *255*, 265, 266, 267
Sandys, Edwin, Bishop of London   148
Saracen's Head *see* Friday Street
Sargant, Henry Edmund (Master 1954)   272
Saumaise, Claude de   196
Savage, John   79
Savage, Thomas, Archbishop of York   111, 112
Saverey, Piers (Master 1440)   269
Savile, George, Earl of Halifax   218
Saye, William   186
Sayle, Robert Theophilus Dalton (Master 1938)   252, 272
Scales, Richard (Master 1613)   *130*, 159, 270
schools   98, 99, 109–25, 157, 175, 266, 267
   see also Ashwell; Great Crosby; Lee; Londonderry; Merchant Taylors' School; Wallingford; Wolverhampton

Schorter, John   67
scissors and shears
   as emblem of tailors' craft   30, *30*, 31, 58, 59
   part of tailors' equipment   58–59, 60, 130
Scotland
   apprentices from   55
   Charles I and   184, 188, 190
Scott, Elizabeth   256
Scott, Sir Giles Gilbert   254, 256
Scott, John, 1st Earl of Eldon, portrait   237
scriveners   43, 44, 45
Scriveners' Company   44
seal of Merchant Taylors' Company   74, 94, Col. Pl. III
'searches' of tailors' premises   32, 38, 52, 57–58, 64, 67
   Bachelors' Company demands right to search (1688)   221
   increased rights to search under 1440 charter   76, 77
   rivalry with Clothworkers   141–42, 201, 220
   rivalry with Drapers   64, 76, 77
Searle, Thomas   225, 227
second-hand clothing industry   52–53, 66
Second World War   258–60
Sedlescombe (Sussex)   211
Seething Lane   208
Sefton (Lancs.)   230
   see also Great Crosby
Selborne, Earls of *see* Palmer
Selby, Richard   135
Selden, John   196
selds   59–60
Sellindge (Kent)   170–71
serjeant-tailors *see* King's/Queen's tailors
sermons, in memory of benefactors   98, 99
Sevenoak, William   110
Sevenoaks (Kent)   110
Severne, Thomas   Col. Pl. XX
Seward, John   110
Sewell, Robert (Master 1677)   271
sewing machine, introduction of   238
Sewragh, Luke   77
Seymour, Edward, Duke of Somerset (Protector Somerset)   97, 115
Shaa, Sir John   111
Shackleton, Miss M. H.   246
Shadbolt, ——   206
Shads Key   206
'shaping boards' *see* cutting boards
Sharpe, *see also* Sherpe
Sharpe, Revd Lancelot   240
Shavelock, Roger   65
shear-grinders   141
Shearer, Janet   265, Col. Pl. XXIII
shearers   141–42
   see also Clothworkers' Company; shearmen
Shearman, Montague   244

shearmen   39, 58, 60, 65, 84
   see also shearers
shears see scissors and shears
Shenton, William (Master 1774)   271
Shepherd, George   Col. Pl. XXI
Shepherd's Alley   206
Sheppard, Matthew   188–89
Sherborne Lane   205
Sheriff, office of   3–4, 76
Sherpe, see also Sharpe
Sherpe, John   67
Sheryngton, Walter   22
Shether, Robert (Master 1526)   117, 270
Ship Tavern   169
ships
   carried in pageants/hung in Merchant Taylors' Hall,
      16th cent.   143, 158, 162, 175, 215
   HMS *Chatham* and *Heron*   267
   Loyal London (King's ship)   202
   see also barges
Shirley, James   168, 182
Shocklache, Ralph (Master 1421)   269
Shoe Lane   137
shop-boards   59, 136
shops, stalls and booths, tailors'
   medieval   56–57, 58, 59–60, 65, 67
   16th cent.   174, 185, 188
      in Royal Exchange   130
   18th cent.   *229, 233,* 234, Col. Pl. XVII
Short, John   207
Shorter see Schorter
Shorthose, ——   203
Shottesham, Thomas, and wife   130–31
shrievalty see Sheriff, office of
Sibsay, Thomas (Master 1391)   269
Sictor, John   186
Sidney, Sir Philip   174
silk trade   58, 66, 177, 185
Sim, Edward Coysgarne (Master 1896)   272
Sim, John Coysgarne (Master 1874)   272
Simmonds, John Whately (Master 1881)   272
Simmonds, Mark John (Master 1917)   272
Simond, Robert   67
Simpson see Symsone
Simpson, manor (Devon)   114
Singleton, William   134
Sir John Cass Foundation   250
'sixes and sevens', origin of   82, 87
Sixteen Men (Bachelors' Company)   43, 131, 173
Skelton, John, *Magnificence*   93
Skernyng, Richard (Master 1441)   39, 269
Skevyngton, John (Master 1510)   85, 270
skinners   8, 60, 63, 82
   King's skinner   61

Skinners' Company   11, 72, 73, 77, 79, 81, 249, 267
   apprentices   54
   charter (1393)   73
   Fraternity of the Assumption   42
   Fraternity of Corpus Christi   6, 11, 14, 22, 23, 82
   relations with Merchant Taylors' Company   82, 87, 141
   see also Billesden Award
Skinners' Lane   63
Skippon, Philip   187
Skrimshaw, Jane   231, *231*
Skut, John (Master 1536)   62, 270
Slaney, John (Master 1619)   270
Slyfelde, Walter   128
Smallwood, Revd Dr George   199, 201
Smart, John (Master 1694)   271
Smith, Albert   241
Smith, Charles Fox   238
Smith, Cynthia   258
Smith, Edmund   124, 168
Smith, James (Master 1699)   271
Smith, Mary, wife of Robert   157
Smith, Richard (Master 1502)   85, 270
Smith, Robert   157
Smith, William (17th cent., usher)   193, 211, 212
Smith, William (18th cent., builder)   229
Smithfield   100
   meat market   243, 244
   Pie Corner   138
   see also St Bartholomew's Fair
Smythe, Anne   133
Smythe, John   129
Snowdon, John   55–56
Soame, Thomas   183
Society of Antiquaries   154
Society of Merchant Adventurers   65
soft armour see linen armour
Somerset, Robert   23
Somerset, Dukes of see Seymour
song schools   109, 110
Soper Lane   8
Sotheby's   262
Sotherne, ——   159
Sotherton, George (Master 1589)   270
Sotherton, Nowell (Master 1597)   *128*, 159, 270
South African War   257
South Sea Bubble   225
Southampton (Hants.)   59, 254
Southwark Bridge   239
Southwark (Surrey)   65, 81, 104, 129, 133
Spain, trade with   66, 84
Sparks, Robert Harry (Master 1819)   272
Spear, Francis   262
Speed family   156–57
Speed, John   156–57, *160,* 217

Speight, Thomas (Master 1509)   270
Spekyngton, Thomas   45
Spence, Thomas (Warden, *fl.* 1670s)   207
Spence, Thomas Bennett (Master 1862)   272
Spencer, John (Master 1490)   270
Spencer, Nicholas (Master 1588)   142, 148, 270
Spencer, Robert, 2nd Earl of Sunderland   218
Spenser, Edmund   124, 171
Spenser, John   *167*
Spicer, William   117–18
Springham, Mathias (Master 1617)   *131–32*, 159–60, 173, 232, 270
Stacey, F. A.   250
Stacy, Margery   135
Stacye, John   129
Stad, Captain John   214–15
Stadler, J.   Col. Pl. XIX
Stafford family   20
stalls *see* shops, stalls and booths
standard measures   59
   silver cloth yard   59, *60*, 94, 221
Standysh, ——   138
Stanley family, Earls of Derby   245
Stanley, William (Master 1633)   270
Staple, William   168, 195
Staple, Company of the (Calais)   65, *95*
Staplegrove (Som.)   178
Stationers' Company   196
Stempford, John   133
Stevens, John   195, 196
Steventon, John   205, 214
Stockport (Ches.)   111
Stockton, Earls of *see* Macmillan
Stodard, John (Master 1465)   269
Stokesley, John, Bishop of London   102
Stone, John (Master 1449)   269
Stone, John (Master 1650)   193, 271
Stone, Nicholas   156
Stonehouse, wharf at   137
Stoop, Dirck   *201*
Storr, Francis   193
Stourbridge (Worcs.)   188
Stow, Elizabeth, wife of John   153, 155–56
Stow, John   8, 142, 143, 145–46, 152–56, *152*, 162, 265–66
   Annales of England, The   153, 154
   on Hawkwood   53
   begging licence   155, *155*
   Chronicle of Robert of Gloucester   163n4
   monument   155–56, *156*, 249, 265–66
   Survey of London, A   143, 154–55, *154*
     on almshouses   29
     on liveries   64
     on origins of Merchant Taylors' Company   8–10
Stow, Thomas (brother of John), and wife   153
Stow, Thomas (father of John)   152
Stradbroke (Suffolk)   175

Strand, New Exchange   178
Strange, ——   206
strangers *see* immigrants
Strasbourg (France)   98, 102
Stratford-le-Bow (Essex)   118
Streatfield, George (Master 1744)   271
Streatham (Surrey)   216
Streete, Humphrey (Master 1608)   270
Streeter, Robert   231
Stringer, Anthony   143
Stringer, Miles (Master 1778)   271
Stringer, Miles (Master 1822)   272
Strode, William (one of Five Members)   185, 186
Strype, John   *226*
Stuart, Dr William   231
Studd, Edward Fairfax (Master 1987, 1993)   273
Studd, John Edward Kynaston (Master 1933)   272
Studd, Sir Peter Malden (Lord Mayor 1970; Master 1973)   265, 273
Styan, Thomas (Master 1828)   272
Styan, Thomas (Master 1880)   272
Styles, Joseph (Master 1756)   271
Suckley (Suckliffe), Agnes   138
Suckley, Henry   134, 138, 148
Sudbury, Simon, Bishop of London   20, 23
Suffolk Lane
   Manor of the Rose   122, 256
   see also Merchant Taylors' School
sugar bakers and refiners   166, 188, 189
sumptuary legislation   49, 67
sun, device of Fraternity of St John the Baptist/Tailors' Company   30, 31, 82, 94
Sunderland, Earls of *see* Spencer
Sussex, Earls of *see* Radcliffe
Sutcliffe, T. W.   261
Sutton, John   112
Sutton, Sir Richard   111, 112
Sutton, Thomas (Master 1408)   269
Sutton, Thomas (*fl.* 1572)   133
Sutton, Thomas (*fl.* 1575)   138
Sutton, William (Master 1836)   272
Swallowe, ——   137
Swan, John (Master 1470)   31, 37, 83, 269
Swan, Rose, wife of John   37
Swann, Robert (Master 1692)   271
Sweden, architectural influence   255–56
Swinnerton, Sir John (Master 1606; Lord Mayor 1612)   142, 159, 160, 162, 163, 174, 270
Swoytell, George   128
Symsone, Daniel   135–36

T

Tacuinum Sanitatis of Liège, drawings of tailors' workshops   *56–57*

tailor's craft
    medieval 49–69
    16th cent. 130, 135–36
    17th cent. 181, 220–21
    18th cent. 233–34
    19th cent. 238
    20th cent. 250, 266
    see also clothing
Tailors' Hall see Merchant Taylors' Hall
Tailors and Linen-Armourers 8–13, 22
    craft 49–69
    government 35–48
    list of Clerks 275
    list of Masters 269–70
    relations with City and Crown 71–89
    and Tailors' Hall 14–16
    see also Fraternity of St John the Baptist; Merchant Taylors' Company
tallow-chandlers 23, 152, 167
Tannar, Daniel 166
tapestries 94, 98, 237
Tarbock, Jane 202
Tatem, Samuel (Master 1735) 271
Tatham, John 199, 200
Taunton (Som.)
    almshouses 177–78
    church 178, Col. Pl. X
tawyers 8
Tayllour, John 142
Taylor, —— (fl. 1666) 202
Taylor, Douglas Seth (Master 1966) 273
Taylor, Seth (Master 1900) 272
Taylor, Thomas 135
Taylorian, The 252
Teasdale, Richard (Clerk 1806–22) 235, 238, 275
Tego, Roger (Master 1463) 63, 269
Temple, Jennings 250
Tenante, Stephen 128
tent-makers (pavilioners) 13, 30, 49–52, 61, 174
Terence, Eunuchus 227
Tetford, William (fl. 1492) 45
Tetforde, William, alias Ditcher (fl. 1568) 153
Thames, river
    civic and royal ceremonies 79–80, 199, 200, 201
    Nelson's funeral procession 226
Thames Street 131, 137, 205, 239
Thane, John 237
    British Autography 144, 166, 182, 212, 214, 220
Theobald, George Peter (Master 1989, 1991) 273
Thirty Years War 165, 183
Thomas, Duke of Clarence 64
Thomas, —— (widow, fl. 1573) 134
Thomas, David (Master 1779) 271
Thomas, John 242
Thomas, Thomas 128

Thomas, Walter Lloyd (Master 1922) 272
Thompson, see also Tompson
Thompson, Charles Robert (Master 1851) 272
Thompson, Giles, Bishop of Gloucester 124, 167
Thompson, John (Master 1804) 272
Thompson, John (Master 1829) 272
Thompson, William (Master 1810) 272
Thorne, John (Master 1430) 269
Thornton, —— 158
Thoroughgood, —— 206
Thorpe Salvin (W.R. Yorks.) 132
Threadneedle Street (formerly Broad Street)
    almshouses
        15th cent. 25, 28, 29, 36, 43, 74, 240
        16th cent. 63, 135, 138, 174–75, 176, Col. Pl. XI
        17th cent. 202, 205, 215, 231
        see also almsmen and almswomen
    Banca Commerciale Italiana 260
    property leased by Merchant Taylors' Company 137, 205
    see also Merchant Taylors' Hall; Royal Exchange; St Anthony's Hospital
Three Cranes Wharf 104, 136, 137, 166, 186, 199, 206
    land compulsorily purchased for Southwark Bridge 239
Throckmorton, Sir Nicholas 104–05
Thrupp, Raymond Henry (Master 1893) 272
Tilneye, John (Master 1376) 52, 269
Tite, Sir William 249
Tobbyn, William 135
Todd, Stephen (Master 1770) 271
tombs, monuments and brasses
    Grey Friars monastery, Jenyns monument 96, 116, Col. Pl. VIII
    Kirkleatham, Coulthirst brass 145
    St Andrew Undershaft
        Offley monument Col. Pl. XIII
        Stow monument 155–56, 156, 249, 265–66
    St Botolph Aldgate, Dowe monument 176, Col. Pl. XIII
    St Dunstan in the West, Dacres brass 83
    Westminster Abbey, Henry VII monument 85
Tomkins, —— 176–77
Tompson, see also Thompson
Tompson, Laurence 135
Toms, William 26
Tonbridge (Kent) 121
Tonge, Dr Israel 212
tools and equipment 58–59, 130, 136
    see also scissors and shears
Toppe, John (Master 1587) 134–35, 270
Torriano, George 222n9
Torriano, John (Master 1757) 271
Torrigiano, Pietro 85
Totenham, John de 10

Tottenham Green (Middx) 190, 199
Tower Hill, almshouses 29, *133*, 207, 215, 231, 239
Tower of London 104, 192, 197
Tower Street 97
Towers, Peter (Master 1622) 270
Townley, Revd James 227–28
Townsend, William (Master 1743) 271
Towton, Battle of (1461) 63
Trafalgar, Battle of (1805) 226
Trained Bands 146, 185, 187
   Green Regiment of the City Trained Bands 189
Trappys, Stephen 28, 42, 65
Tresawell, John (Master 1511) 270
Triminges, Dorothy 201
Trinity Lane 137, 205
Trollope, Anthony, *The Warden* 246
Trolop, —— 154
Tropenell, William (Master 1411) 61, 64, 74, 269
Troutbeck, Revd Wilfred 230
Tulley, William (Master 1635) 270
Tunstall, Cuthbert, Bishop of Durham 100
Turner, Richard (Master 1636) 270
Turner, Robert Reginald Johnston (Master 1927, 1940) 259, 272
Turner, Sir William (Master 1661, 1684; Lord Mayor 1668) *145*, 206–07, 208, *208*, 210n15, 219, 222n6, 271
   portrait 215, 263n29
Turnley, Joseph (Master 1857) 272
Twiste, Philip 129
Twyford, Nicholas 72
Tyler, James (Master 1868) 272
Tylers' Company 138
Tysdall, Richard 135

U
Ulster Plantation *see* Ireland
uniforms, Civil War 188
University College London 240
Unwin, George 74
Upfold, William (Master 1755) 271
Usk, Thomas 72

V
Van Dyck, Sir Anthony 181, *182*
Vane, Richard a 135–36
Vaughan, Geoffrey (Master 1520) 270
Vaughan-Morgan, John Kenyon (Master 1970) 273
Veale, Richard 166
Venables, Richard (Master 1598) *128–29*, 270
Venice, trade with 66, 78
Venn, John 183, 184, 185, 186, 187–88, 191, 192, *192*, 232
   wife of 185, 188, 192
Venner, Thomas 200
Vernam, Thomas 128
Vernon, John (Master 1609) 159, 178, 215, 270, Col. Pl. X

Vickers, Richard (Master 1736) 271
Victoria Cross, awarded to former pupils of Merchant Taylors' School 252
Vintners' Company 6, 7, 72, 79
Vintry, street and ward 84, 94
Virginia, colonization 157, 165, 173
voting slips *128–32*

W
Wade, Guy (Master 1554) 270
Wadlok, Robert 58
Wadyngton, Richard (Master 1548) 270
Walbrook 166
   St John Walbrook, church 14
   St Stephen Walbrook, parish 188
Wales
   tailors from 134, 135
   trade with 55
Waleys, Henry le (Mayor 1273, 1281, 1298) 7
Wall, Ralph 173
Waller, Sir William 188
Wallingford (Oxon.), school 217, 267
Wallington, Nehemiah 185
Wallis, Derek Alan (Clerk 1985–95) 275
Wallis, John (Master 1687) 271
Walsingham, Sir Francis 129, 134
Walton, James (Master 1769) 271
Wandall, Joseph (Master 1715) 271
Wandell, Thomas (Master 1681) 271
War Damage Commission 260, 262
war memorials
   First World War 252, 257
   South African War 257
Ward, Sir John (Master 1709; Lord Mayor 1718) 225, 271
Ward, Sir Patience (Master 1671; Lord Mayor 1680) 201, 208, 218, 271
   portrait 215, 263n29
Wardall, Thomas (Master 1683–84) 219, 271
Warden, Thomas 135
Wardens, office of *see* Merchant Taylors' Company, Wardens
Wardens Substitute (Bachelors' Company) 42, 43, 131, 173, 190, 221
Wardrobe *see* Great Wardrobe
wards 4, 6, 7, 71, 72
   see also individual wards by name
Waring, Gerard 229–30
Waring, Revd John 229
Warman, Guy, Bishop of Manchester 257
Warner, Edward (Master 1626) 270
Warner, Richard (Master 1476) 269
Warren, William (Master 1412) 269
wars *see* Civil War; First World War; Hundred Years' War; Revolutionary and Napoleonic Wars; Second World War; South African War; Thirty Years War

Warwick, Guy (Master 1789)　271
Warwick　120
Warwick, Earls of see Dudley, Ambrose
Warynge, Roger (Master 1472)　269
Waterman, Sir George　215
Waters, Robert　203
Watkins, Dame Honora　205
Watling Street　97, 104, 174
Watney, Dr —— 260
Watt, Sir James (Lord Mayor 1607)　159, 160
Watts, Henry (Master 1749)　271
Waugh, William (Master 1848)　272
Webb, Henry (Master 1598)　*129*, 270
Webster, John　174
Webster, Samuel　245
Wedgwood china　232
Week St Mary (Cornwall), school founded by Thomasine Percyvale　99, 113–15, *114*
Wellesley, Arthur, 1st Duke of Wellington　234–35, 237
　bust　*235*, 262
Wendesley, —— 129
West, Richard (Master 1478)　270
West, Robert　*26*
Westley, Sir Robert (Master 1737; Lord Mayor 1743)　225, 271
Westmelle (Westmill), Giles de　10, 11
Westminster
　Abbey　21, 103, 142
　　monument of Henry VII　*85*
　Henry VII at　79, 80
　Mayor's procession to (pageant, Lord Mayor's Show)
　　14th–15th cent.　21–22, 79, 94, 142
　　16th cent.　103, 118, 142
　　17th cent.　142–43, 158–59, 174, 175, 199–200, 206, 218
Weston, John (Master 1416)　269
Wetherall, Thomas (Master 1638)　270
Whaddon, William　25
Wharton, Thomas　218
Whethill, Richard (Master 1562)　127, 270
Whinney, H. D. C.　261
Whitbeck (Cumb.)　134
Whitbread, Ive (Master 1761)　271
White, Joan, wife of Sir Thomas　122
White, John (Master 1676)　271
White, John (Master 1838)　272
White, Ralph　127
White, Richard (Master 1573)　137, 270
White, Robert (Master 1702–03)　271
White, Sir Thomas (Master 1535)　66, 93, 97, 119, 136, 139n44, 160, 270
　apprenticed to Hugh Acton　56, 66
　bequest of plate　95, 116
　charitable activities　106–07, 119–20, 123, 169, 193
　　foundation of St John's College, Oxford　106, 120–22, Col. Pl. VII
　contribution to expedition to Le Havre　148
　as Lord Mayor (1553)　98, 101, 103–07, 119, 142
　portraits　120, 237, Col. Pl. IX
　portrayed in pageant (1624)　174
　statue at Merchant Taylors' School　257
　and Wyatt's rebellion　103, 106–07
White, William (Mayor 1489)　84
White, William (Master 1793)　271
White, William Foster (Master 1865)　243, 272
White, William Robinson (Master 1850)　272
White Lion Court see Cornhill
Whitehall　146, 151, 185, 199, 200, *201*, 226
　Banqueting House　165–66, 183, 191
Whitehand, see also Whithande
Whitehand, Robert (fl. 1713)　*133*
Whitehead, John Michael Stannage (Master 1995)　273
Whitelocke (Whitlocke), Sir Bulstrode　168, *168*, 183, 191
Whithande, see also Whitehand
Whithande, Robert (fl. 16th cent.)　128
Whiting, —— 203, 207
Whitmore, Elizabeth, m. Sir William Craven　175
Whittington, Richard (Dick), (Mayor 1397, 1406, 1419)　21, 28, 29, 53
Whittington, Richard (Master 1892)　272
Whityngham, Thomas (Master 1414)　41, 269
Wick near Pershore (Worcs.)　188
Widnell, William (Master 1586)　270
Wilding and Kent, Messrs (Grafton House, 164 New Bond Street)　234
Wilford, see also Wylford
Wilford, James (Master 1494)　65, 83, 94, 99, 132, 270
　annual sermon in memory of　98, 99
　will, provision for upkeep of roads in Surrey and Sussex　201, 216
Wilford, Nicholas　176
Wilford, Thomas (Master 1585)　137, 148, 270
Wilford, William (Master 1518)　270
Wilford, William, the younger (Master 1534)　270
Wilkinson, Henry　124
Wilkinson, Robert　*47*
Willesden (Middx), playing fields　250
William III, King (William of Orange)　219–20
Williams, Revd Henry　250
Williams, Lewis ap　135
Willis, Francis　121, 124
Wills, Edward (Master 1695)　271
Wilmslow (Ches.), school　112
Wilson, see also Wylson
Wilson, —— (almsman, 16th cent.)　138
Wilson, —— (lessee, fl. 1681)　215
Wilson, Revd Harry Bristow　228, 240
Wilson, William　170, 193
Winchecombe, Simon　14, 50
Winchecombe, Thomas　31

Winchester (Hants.)   113–14, 254, 258
   Bishops of   166
      see also Andrewes; Beaufort; Gardiner
   St Cross   246
Windsor (Berks.)
   Deans of   168, 188
   Windsor Castle   187–88, 191
Wintle, Cyril (Master 1912)   272
Withers, Nathaniel (Master 1666)   202, 208, 271
Withypool, Paul (Master 1523)   93, 270
Woburn Abbey (Beds.)   238
Wodecok, William   73
Wolle, Robert   134
Wolsey, Thomas, Cardinal, Archbishop of York   87, 100
Wolton, James   129
Wolverhampton (Staffs.)
   Grammar School
      16th cent.   112, 115–16
      17th cent.   112, 169–71, 188, 192–94, 201, 203, 212, 216, 228
      18th cent.   228–29
      19th–20th cent.   250, *251*, 252, 267
   St Peter's church, gallery   *117*, 170
Wolverstone, Edmund   173
women
   almswomen
      15th cent.   29
      16th cent.   135, 175, 176
      17th cent.   166, 201, 203, 215
      18th cent.   231, *231*, 232
   in Civil War   187
   dressmaking, apprenticeships for girls, 20th cent.   250
   education
      girls' schools   123, 230, 245–46, 258, 266, 267
      schools founded by women   113
   flax-women   178
   members of livery   ix, 267
   silkwomen   58
   tailors   *56*, 58
   wives of Masters, title of 'Mistress'   36–37
   wives of tailors, involved in disputes   134, 153
Wood, Simon (Master 1637)   270
Wood Street   13, 72
Woodcock see Wodecok
Woodwarde, Thomas   129
wool, export trade   65, 141, 165
Wooller, John   159
Woolley, Ernest (Master 1914)   272
Woolley, John Maxwell (Clerk 1962–80)   275
Woolley, Philip Michael (Master 1986)   273
Woolley, Randulph (Randle) (Master 1614)   159, 170, 215, 270
Worcester   120, 188
   Bishops of see Gauden
working hours, regulation   66, 67
Worston, Robert, son of John   *54*
Worthington, Sir Hubert   260–61
Wren, Christopher, Dean of Windsor   168, 188
Wren, Sir Christopher   168, 188, 203, 207, 208, 213, 231
Wren, Matthew, Bishop of Ely   124, 168
Wren, Susan, m. William Holder   188
Wright, John (Master 1515)   270
Wright, John (Master 1712)   271
Wright, Richard (Clerk 1587–94; Master 1611)   159, 170, 270, 275
Wrighte, Alice   134
Wriothesley, Sir Thomas   Col. Pl. VIII
Wriothesley, Thomas, 1st Lord   190
Wyatt, Sir Thomas   103–07, *105*
Wycliffe, John   99, 100, 101
Wylford, see also Wilford
Wylford, Thomas   133
Wylson, see also Wilson
Wylson, Roger (Clerk before 1545–46)   275
Wynge, John   45
Wynne, Eleanor, m. Abraham Reynardson   190, 191

Y

Yakesley, John de   13, 14, 30, 51, 174
yard-sticks ('tailor's yard')   59
   see also cloth yard
Yarmouth (Norfolk)   145
yeomen (freemen outside the livery) see Bachelors' Company
Yeovilton (Som.), RNAS   267
Yomans, Francis   131, 132, 139n89, 165
Yonge, see also Young
Yonge, William   137
York   6, 120
   Archbishops of see Savage; Wolsey
York, Dukes of see George VI; James II
Young, see also Yonge
Young, Florance Thomas (Master 1830)   272
Young, John   21
Young, Robert   195
Young, Walter   104
Younge, Elizabeth   133